Information, Power, and Democracy

The link between liberty and knowledge is neither static nor simple. Until recently, the mutual support between knowledge, science, democracy, and emancipation was presupposed. Recently, however, the close relationship between democracy and knowledge has been viewed with skepticism. The growing societal reliance on specialized knowledge often appears to actually undermine democracy. Is it that we do not know enough, or that we know too much? What are the implications for the freedom of societies and their citizens? Does knowledge help or heed them in unraveling the complexity of new challenges?

This book systematically explores the shifting dynamics of knowledge production and the implications for the conditions and practices of freedom. It considers the growth of knowledge about knowledge and the impact of an evolving media. It argues for a revised understanding of the societal role of knowledge and presents the concept of "knowledge societies" as a major resource for liberty.

NICO STEHR is Karl Mannheim Professor of Cultural Studies at the Zeppelin University, Friedrichshafen, Germany, and Founding Director of the European Centre for Sustainability Research at his university. His recent publications include: *Who Owns Knowledge: Knowledge and the Law* with Bernd Weiler (2008), *Knowledge and Democracy* (2008), *Society: Critical Concepts in Sociology* with Reiner Grundmann (2008), *Climate and Society* with Hans von Storch (2010), and *Experts: The Knowledge and Power of Expertise* (2011) and *The Power of Scientific Knowledge: From Research to Public Policy* (2012), both with Reiner Grundmann.

Information, Power, and Democracy
Liberty Is a Daughter of Knowledge

Nico Stehr

Zeppelin University

CAMBRIDGE
UNIVERSITY PRESS

CAMBRIDGE
UNIVERSITY PRESS

University Printing House, Cambridge CB2 8BS, United Kingdom

Cambridge University Press is part of the University of Cambridge.

It furthers the University's mission by disseminating knowledge in the pursuit of education, learning and research at the highest international levels of excellence.

www.cambridge.org
Information on this title: www.cambridge.org/9781107120754

© Nico Stehr 2016

This publication is in copyright. Subject to statutory exception
and to the provisions of relevant collective licensing agreements,
no reproduction of any part may take place without the written
permission of Cambridge University Press.

First published 2016

A catalogue record for this publication is available from the British Library

Library of Congress Cataloging-in-Publication Data
Stehr, Nico author.
Information, power, and democracy : liberty is a daughter of knowledge / Nico Stehr, Zeppelin University.
pages cm
Includes bibliographical references and index.
ISBN 978-1-107-12075-4 (Hardback : alk. paper) – ISBN 978-1-107-54381-2 (pbk. : alk. paper)   1. Liberty.   2. Power (Social sciences)
3. Democracy.   4. Knowledge.   I. Title.
JC585.S72 2016
320.01'1–dc23   2015023752

ISBN 978-1-107-12075-4 Hardback

Cambridge University Press has no responsibility for the persistence or accuracy of URLs for external or third-party internet websites referred to in this publication, and does not guarantee that any content on such websites is, or will remain, accurate or appropriate.

Contents

List of figures	page viii
List of tables	ix

Introduction	1
The genealogy of the relation between knowledge and liberties	2
Knowledge enhances democracy	3
The tension between knowledge and freedom	5
Competing accounts of democratization	8
Should knowledge be the operative factor?	9
Knowledgeability	10
The sociohistorical context of modern democracies	12

1 Coming to terms	14
Knowledge: a capacity for action?	17
Transforming knowledge into processes and (processed) things	28
Which knowledge is meant, and why?	33
Information and knowledge	37
Why should knowledge or information be a political asset?	49
Democracy: who rules?	52
Liberty: which liberty is meant?	62
Freedom *from* and freedom *for*	63
Political liberty	67
Economic freedom	68
Social or civil liberties	69
The problem of power	70

Excursus: How much knowledge does democracy need, and how expensive should it be?	76

2 Accounts of the conditions for the possibility and the resilience of liberty	82
Knowledge and liberties	86
The role of formal education (schooling)	89
The social phenomenon of knowledgeability as a form of soft power	97
Knowledgeability as a bundle of competencies	101
Civil society organizations	108
Political culture	113

v

	The role of the "media"	115
	The nation-state and democracy	122
	Intergovernmental networks	125
3	**The economic order ensures (defeats) liberty**	**129**
	The role of prosperity	135
	Affluence as a basis for democracy	144
	Economic growth and democratic society	150
	Inequality and democracy	152
	Economic well-being and knowledge	159
4	**Scientia est libertas**	**162**
	The origins and the vision of science	168
	Science as a model for democracy	169
	The ethos of science and democracy	171
	Are (scientific) knowledge and democracy compatible?	176
	The Vienna Circle	179
	John Dewey: science and democracy	183
	Lippmann, Dewey, and democratic governance	188
	What forms of knowledge enhance democracies?	191
	Excursus: An inconvenient democracy: knowledge and climate change	192
5	**The knowledge of the powerful**	**204**
	Herrschaft kraft Wissen	209
	The iron law of oligarchy	215
	The inescapable bond of science and power	219
	The new knowledge classes	227
	The meaning producers	227
	The informational producers	233
	The creative class	237
	The global class	240
6	**The knowledge of the weak**	**243**
	Political action in knowledge societies	248
	Governing knowledge societies	255
	Political knowledge	270
	Measuring political knowledge	276
	The new public sphere	280
	Soft power and democracy	284
	Democracy and knowledge	294
	Scientific knowledge and common sense	297
	The gap between common sense and scientific knowledge	303
	What can be done?	307
	Modern society and the stratification of knowledge	310
	The new risks of knowledge	311
	The fragility of expertise	315
	Knowledge as a weapon of the "weak"	320

Reconciling democracy and knowledge as property 329
Enabling knowledge? 331
A realistic appraisal 333

Knowledge and democracy: summary and conclusions 336

Bibliography 339
Index 393

Figures

1 Media freedom and political knowledge *page* 120
2 Perception of income differences as too large in relation to the Gini coefficient of different countries 157

Tables

1 Survey questions designed to measure political knowledge *page* 276
2 Overview of rejected EU referendums, 1972–2008 281

Introduction

> The advancement and diffusion of knowledge is the only guardian of true liberty. James Madison (1825:492)[1]

> The more that deliberation and reflection and a critical spirit play a considerable part in the course of public affairs, the more democratic the nation. Emile Durkheim ([1950] 1992:89)

The relations between *information/knowledge* and *liberties* (and therefore democracies) in modern, highly complex, and bureaucratic societies, and their change in the course of more recent history, present us with a multitude of fascinating issues that deserve to be explored more systematically.[2] After all, the relations between liberty and knowledge are not forever fixed. Knowledge or, better, *knowledgeability*,[3] may serve the resistance of the allegedly weak in society, rather than – as is more often feared – cementing the authority and power of the powerful. This study is about the citizen's exercise of power in the modern era, aside from the power put into effect at the ballot box.

An initial synopsis of the knowledge-guiding interests of my study is best given in the form of a range of broad questions and issues. The main questions I will ask, and issues I will investigate, concern (1) the genealogy of the relation between knowledge and liberties; (2) whether

---

[1] See *Three Letters and Other Writings of James Madison* (J. P. Lippincott & Co., 1865 [reprinting letter to George Thomson (June 30, 1825)]:492).
[2] The subtitle of my inquiry constitutes a liberal adoption of Friedrich Schiller's emphatic assertion, in the spirit of his age, that "art is a daughter of liberty." Schiller's metaphor may be found in his second letter written to the Duke of Holstein-Augustenburg, first printed in the *Horen* in 1795 under the title "Ueber die ästhetische Erziehung des Menschen." However, Schiller is not the first to have expressed a sentiment analogous to similar convictions. In a letter to François d'Ivernois written in 1795, Thomas Jefferson identified freedom as "the first-born daughter of science" (The Marquis de Condorcet, [1796] 1996). expresses with conviction a similar "indissoluble" linkage between not only "the progress of knowledge and that of liberty," but also "virtue and the respect for the natural rights of man."
[3] I will explicate in detail the term "knowledgeability" in a subsequent section of the introduction.

knowledge indeed enhances democracy; (3) the tensions between knowledge and freedom; (4) competing accounts of the process of democratization; (5) whether knowledge should be the operative factor or (6) whether this should rather be knowledgeability; and (7) the sociohistorical context of modern democracies.

The genealogy of the relation between knowledge and liberties

An inquiry into the connections between knowledge and democracy must, of course, critically assess the meaning of the central terms of the inquiry. Neither democracy nor knowledge should be viewed in a transcendental sense. Rather, knowledge and democracy refer to historical phenomena, not found objects. Democracy and knowledge are essentially contested terms. Sensitivity to the various meanings of the core terms of the inquiry is an important form of enlightenment. But one should not dismiss the theoretical and practical utility of these terms out of hand as a result of their essential contestedness. At the same time, it is important to move beyond documenting and describing the contested nature of the terms, and to commit oneself to a particular usage. Otherwise, one will remain a prisoner of the mere exegesis of the multitude of ways in which democracy and knowledge have come to be understood. A permanent reflection *within* one's communication on the *preconditions* of communication leads to a dead end (cf. Luhmann, 2002a:291).

It is perhaps immediately understood that in any comparative investigation of traditional and modern life-worlds, as well as in the case of my own analysis, reference has to be made to *specific forms of knowledge* and *specific manifestations of democracy*. More to the point, the typical forms of knowledge found in medieval times, the natural law-absolutistic world of the seventeenth and eighteenth centuries, or the closed colonial world of the nineteenth century in which the "truth" was predetermined, are all antagonistically opposed to democracy. A society that is not open, or at least not prepared to be open, to social change is unable or unwilling to tolerate forms of knowledge that are preliminary, uncertain, contested, and critical (cf. Plessner, [1924] 1985:7–9).

At one time, and in some contexts, the connection between (scientific) knowledge, democracy, and emancipation were self-evident; for example, scientific movements were closely tied to democratic movements. Images of democracy were largely based on a theory of universal competence and a natural human disposition to democracy, despite the voices of a few critics.

My interest in this study, therefore, centers on the interrelation of democratic political institutions or, more generally, democratic society and knowledge. Is it the case, as Max Weber ([1906] 1994:69) noted, that the "genesis of modern 'freedom' presupposed certain unique, never-to-be-repeated historical constellations," among them most prominently "the conquest of life by science"? Does the knowledge of individuals, especially in the sense of knowledgeability, enhance their liberty? Can we speak of a *knowledge-boundedness* of democratic institutions? In what ways do knowledge – perhaps also the media delivering and representing knowledge (information) in society[4] – and liberty strengthen each other? Does modern science in particular fortify democracy, and democracy science in return? Or, on the other hand, is it perhaps the case that knowledge and democracy conflict with each other in the course of their respective development? Do enhanced knowledge and information impede democracy? Are we confronted with a union of knowledge and power due to the indispensability of expert advice, and might this conflation signal the "death of democracy" (cf. Lakoff, 1971)? Does a "technocratization" of knowledge lead to a concentration of political power, especially in the hands of the executive branch of government, and, in its wake, political apathy and a withdrawal of broader segments of society from political participation (Eisenstadt, 1999:90)?

Knowledge enhances democracy

That democracy – if only within the scientific community, itself presumed to be "free from corrupting intrusions and distractions," as Michael Polanyi ([1962] 2000:15) describes it – strengthens the creation of knowledge is perhaps the least controversial, but by no means uncontested, assertion.[5] That knowledge strengthens liberty is less obvious,

---

[4] My specific case in point could be the ongoing debate about the changing world of publishing, including the function of publishing houses. Stephen Carter (2009), for instance, is concerned about the likely disappearance of the traditional book. Books, he notes, "are essential to democracy. Not literacy, although literacy is important. Not reading, although reading is wonderful. But books themselves, the actual physical volumes on the shelves of libraries and stores and homes, send a message through their very existence. In a world in which most things seem ephemeral, books imply permanence: that there exist ideas and thoughts of sufficient weight that they are worth preserving in a physical form that is expensive to produce and takes up space. And a book, once out there, cannot be recalled. The author who changes his mind cannot just take down the page" (available at www.thedailybeast.com/blogs-and-stories/2009-03-17/wheres-the-bailout-for-publishing/p/).

[5] In Michael Polanyi's ([1962] 2000) description of the sociopolitical organization of the "Republic of Science," where he praises the virtue of freedom in science, there are strong

4 Introduction

even to those who are convinced that it should do so.[6] In the course of the development of knowledge, emancipation *through* knowledge may be obscured. The growing reliance on specialized knowledge in policymaking detracts from the capacity of many to intervene in decisions arrived at and executed within political institutions.

Is it perhaps possible to demonstrate that the improved collective educational chances and abilities of citizens (democratization of education) enhance their effective political participation opportunities (politicization)? Is it more specifically the growing scientific literacy and affinity to science and technology of the population at large that foster the emergence of democratic institutions and attitudes, as John Dewey ([1938] 1955) maintained in the 1930s; and/or is it mainly a democratic environment that supports an undogmatic scientific practice, as Robert K. Merton ([1938] 1973) emphasizes in the 1940s in the face of the contemporary onslaught of vicious totalitarian political regimes, perhaps echoing earlier convictions as forcefully expressed by David Hume?[7] Or are we perhaps dealing with *reciprocal* interchanges between the scientific community and the political order of society?[8] Is knowledge a

---

authoritarian and elitist tendencies as a normative prescription and social basis for creativity and progress in the scientific community. In Polanyi's republic, leading scientists or "masters lord over the rest ('apprentices') on the basis of an 'extraterritorial' exemption from the general democracy of the wider society" (Jarvie, 2001:346).

[6] In "The Republic of Science," Polanyi ([1962] 2000:14) also stresses what has become for him a self-evident historical process: "For at least three hundred years the progress of science has increasingly controlled the outlook of man on the universe, and has profoundly modified (for better or worse) the accepted meaning of human existence. Its theoretic and philosophic influence was pervasive." Philip Kitcher (2010b:858) describes the basic vision of John Stuart Mill's philosophy in terms that suggest a close affinity between knowledge and freedom: "I interpret Mill as proposing that the ability to determine our own central values and to pursue them is the most fundamental form of freedom. Gaining knowledge is important for the realization of this freedom, and freedom of discussion is important for the role it plays in enabling people to gain relevant forms of knowledge."

[7] The philosopher David Hume ([1777] 1985:118) leaves no doubt as to the nature of the "causal" linkage that must obtain between knowledge and democracy: "it is impossible for the arts and the sciences to arise, at first, among peoples unless that people enjoy the blessing of a free government ... An unlimited despotism ... effectively puts a stop to all improvements, and keeps men from attaining ... knowledge." Daniel Lerner (1959:23) advances a negative case in the context of speculating about the future of *social science* in the world: "During the past generation, [the social sciences] have come under very heavy attack from the new despotisms of the twentieth century. As part of their counteroffensive against libertarian foundations of modern democracy, the Fascist, Nazi, and Communist regimes have officially outlawed and intellectually deformed the social sciences as we have known them."

[8] I will also make reference to the issue of the democratization of knowledge generating processes (e.g., Neurath, [1945] 1996:255; Feyerabend, [1974] 2006) and the scientification of politics (e.g., Mannheim, [1929] 1936; Bell, 1960), as well as the

democratizer, or are uninformed individuals actually a boost for democracy (cf. Couzin et al., 2011)? Though fervent laments about the broad ignorance, mediocrity, and manipulation of the voter have continued to be common ever since the introduction of universal suffrage, never before have so many people been informed about the affairs of the state as today (cf. Aron, [1965] 1984:115–116).[9]

One author who has explicitly addressed these issues, and offers initial conclusions that are anything but ambivalent, is Robert Kuhn (2003):

> The usual rationale for spending public monies on scientific projects large and small is that they have the potential to make our lives longer, healthier, safer, happier, more productive, and more pleasant. That science, even "pure" science can strengthen democracy and promote participation in the political process, both in the United States and throughout the world, is hardly ever mentioned. It should be. Scientific literacy energizes democracy ... and this is an important ancillary benefit of the promotion of science.

The tension between knowledge and freedom

The issue of the compatibility or incommensurability of liberty and equality, as has often been stressed, is one of the central themes of the theory of liberalism (see, for example, John Rawls [1971] or Ronald Dworkin [2002]). More recently, but not only under contemporary circumstances, the close linkage between democracy and knowledge has been viewed with skepticism, and science has been accused of being dominating and oppressive. Is it therefore possible, on the other hand, reasoning in analogy to the argument of Max Horkheimer[10] – who

---

assessment of its consequences and the scientification of the self-understanding of modern citizens and their world-views (Thorpe, 2009).

[9] Otto Neurath ([1945] 1996), in a previously unpublished manuscript that carries the title "Visual Education: Humanization Versus Popularization," defines knowledge as a more or less connected set of empirical statements and arguments. The transmission of knowledge is therefore the transfer of assertions and arguments. Inasmuch as the transfer of knowledge becomes more common and general, one is able to speak of a democratization of knowledge. Neurath adds that insofar as everyone participates directly or indirectly in common decisions, a general circulation of knowledge is decisive for a "smooth" functioning of democracy.

[10] For example, in the critique by Karl Marx of the Gotha Program of the German Workers Party. Analogous observations about the incompatibility of equality and liberty can be found in the works of John Stuart Mill and Alexis de Tocqueville, as well as in their respective reflections about each other. Cf. de Tocqueville, who offers the following observations about Canada in his book *The Old Regime and the Revolution* (Mill, [1856] 1998:280–281): "In Canada, at least as long as Canada remained French, equality was joined with absolute government"; and Mills' review of de Tocqueville's *Democracy in America* in the *London Review* (1835). Isaiah Berlin (1949/1950:378), in contrast,

opposed Karl Marx in this regard – that justice and freedom do *not* support each other, and that democracy and knowledge actually do not assist each other?

The assertion about a lack of convergence between democratic governance and knowledge applies with particular force to contemporary social theorists of the 1960s and 1970s. Dominant social theoreticians in this era were convinced that a kind of ironclad linkage of power and knowledge existed. The monopolization of knowledge by those in power accounts for their ability to maintain power and oppress the powerless.[11] Are advances in knowledge, especially rapidly growing and changing knowledge that are based as it were on the increasing specialization of scientific practice, barriers to democracy?

Holding issues of globalization and internationalization of political and economic processes at bay, can the widely cited "crisis of democracy" perhaps be traced to the growing gap between highly specialized knowledge and everyday knowledge of the life-world, as the former is increasingly used as a political resource, while the capacity of the ordinary citizen to engage in highly specialized political discourse is continually eroded? Scientific knowledge is no longer a mainly public, but a private, good; and the unequal distribution of and access to scientific and technical knowledge is indeed seen as a major impediment to the possibility of citizen participation in contemporary governance processes. Is the process of depoliticization – that is, the increasingly skeptical view of many groups of democratic governance in modern societies – perhaps the consequence of a growing reliance on specialized knowledge in modern societies?

The threat to democracy that issues from an uneven distribution of knowledge in modern societies – a gap that in the course of the unrelenting growth of knowledge may have become even more pronounced, thus producing knowledge gaps, information overload, and governance by experts – has in the eyes of many observers radically displaced earlier, optimistic Enlightenment views regarding the resilience and even the

---

describes the New Deal era of President Roosevelt in the United States as "this great liberal enterprise," and as the "most constructive compromise between individual liberty and economic security which our own time has witnessed" (compare also the discussion on the relation between well-being, *agency*, and liberty in the *Dewey Lectures* delivered by Amartya Sen [1985:177–181]).

[11] Tony Judt (2005:479) substantiates the conclusion of prominent social theorists in these decades: The power of the powerful is no longer based on the premise of a once dominant control of natural resources and human capital, but on a monopoly of knowledge. This applies to knowledge about the natural world; knowledge about public life and the life-world; knowledge about subjective identities; and knowledge about the very production of knowledge.

possibility of a democracy based on a general circulation of knowledge in society.[12] Numerous authors, from Max Weber to Robert Michels and from Joseph Schumpeter to Martin Lipset, have explicated these and other threats to representative democracy. Given the unstoppable advance of bureaucracy in modern societies, Max Weber ([1918] 1994:159), for example, feared a kind of *pacifism of social impotence* of the citizenry, for in the face of a "growing indispensability and hence increasing power of state officialdom ... how can there be any guarantee that forces exist which can impose limits on the enormous, crushing power of this constantly growing stratum of society and control it effectively? How is democracy even in this restricted sense to be *at all possible?*" Political processes that rely to an increasing extent on the input of highly specialized, scientific knowledge, as Gianfranco Poggi (1982:358) implies, discourage "citizens from entertaining and expressing opinions on political matters based only on their natural competence for moral judgment." Is the apparently growing distrust of and withdrawal from active (traditional) political participation (e.g., electoral turnout, public engagement in political parties and unions [cf. Putnam, 2002:404–416]) of many segments of the population in many democracies an outcome of a delegitimation of critical, participant citizenship[13] or an indication of new, indirect forms of democratic participation (e.g., Rosanvallon, [2006] 2008)? Contemporary scientists discern additional threats to democracy related to the complexity of global problems such as poverty, resource depletion, food production, or climate change. In this context, reference is at times made to an *ineffective democracy,* powerless to cope with urgent global harms.[14]

But even if a contraction of the democracy-enhancing social role of scientific knowledge cannot be attributed to the growing societal reliance on specialized knowledge, it could be the changing "character" of knowledge – in the sense of a changed understanding of the major virtues and consequences of knowledge – that transforms its role in supporting liberties. The societal consequences of modern science and

---

[12] There is good reason to be skeptical toward the idea that either the notion or the realities of the knowledge gap or the information overload, however defined, are genuinely new. One has only to refer to the convergence of societal diagnoses proposed, at the dawn of the last century, by Georg Simmel, Sigmund Freud, and Walter Benjamin, among others, of a cultural age displaying severe overstimulation, discontinuities, and overload.

[13] An extensive discussion of the genesis of the term "citizen" may be found in Dahrendorf (1974).

[14] The late climatologist Stephen H. Schneider (2009), in his book *Science as a Contact Sport*, frames the question in a different way: "Can democracy survive complexity?" Compare with the excursus on "an inconvenient democracy" in this study.

technology (biotechnology, genetics, machine-based medicine, nanotechnology) are now often seen as the authors of some of the major problems faced by society and its institutions.

Competing accounts of democratization

The emergence of, transition to and decline of democratic institutions, governance, and societies always appear to be a matter of historical uniqueness, with exceptional and distinctive forces and circumstances at work. In the minds of actors directly engaged in these processes, as well as those of outside observers, these appear to be an idiosyncratic combination of distinctive trends, rare events, and exceptional opportunities. Is it the case, as Max Weber ([1906] 1994:69) noted, that the "genesis of modern 'freedom' presupposed certain unique, never-to-be-repeated historical constellations," among them most prominently "the conquest of life by science"? It would therefore seem to be a very difficult, if not an intangible, prospect to arrive at a generalization about the conditions that facilitate or hinder sustainable democratic rule, or even make it possible.[15] But scholars have tried; and they have reached a number of worthwhile general conclusions that facilitate our understanding of the conditions for the possibility of democracy and the persistent challenges it faces (cf. Gleditsch and Ward, 2008).

The contention that liberty is a daughter of knowledge appears to find its strongest competitors, not only intellectually but also politically, in the thesis that either the market process itself is a facilitator of freedom or, more specifically, that certain market outcomes are the *catalyst* of liberty and democracy. Both John Maynard Keynes and Joseph Schumpeter, to name but two outstanding minds from the field of economics from the past century, have commented on the affinity between capitalism and liberty. For John Maynard Keynes, as far as vital human activities are concerned, capitalism is not the ultimate goal, nor is it an end in itself:

[15] Among the phenomena that are frequently given consideration, or are even ascribed a significant role, in processes of democratization are certain personal attributes, as for instance the moral values of the primary actors (e.g., Somer, 2011). In this analysis, I will forego the examination of individual, i.e., psychological characteristics of the relevant actors, since these phenomena lie outside my frame of reference – which should not be taken to mean that they do not contribute to democratic movements and to the maintenance of democracies. My interest also does not apply to the much more questionable thesis that the immutable terrain and its unique geographical features are responsible for the political regime found in a particular location: it is not only how we see the terrain, but it is its actual physical characteristics that affect us. Geographical determinism, including climate determinism, has largely fallen into disrepute within science, yet there are also, at present, attempts to revive it (e.g., Kaplan, 2012).

Capitalism for Keynes, as expressed, for example, in his essay, "Economic possibilities for our grandchildren" (1930), "was necessary for freedom, but the activities of a capitalist society were not themselves an essential part of what freedom was all about" (Backhouse and Bateman, 2009:663). In a much stronger sense than Keynes, Joseph Schumpeter (1942:297) maintains in his *Capitalism, Socialism and Democracy* that "modern democracy is a by-product of the capitalist process." More recently, Schumpeter's elementary thesis finds support from another eminent economist: Mancur Olson. As Olson (2000:132) stresses, "it is no accident that the countries that have reached the highest level of economic development and have enjoyed good economic performance across generations are all stable democracies." However, the assertion that capitalism is a foundation of liberty is obviously not without its detractors, most prominently among Marxists and Socialists, but also among liberal theorists; for example, Max Weber ([1906] 1980), who sees a capitalist economic order and democracy in essential opposition. To put it in a less oppositional manner: for the critics of the elective affinity of liberty and capitalism, the intersection of capitalism and democracy is small.

I will make reference to and critically examine various theoretical approaches that emphasize other nationally endogenous (e.g., the role of formal education, values, institutions, media) and nationally exogenous processes of contagion, dissemination, and imitation seen to be conducive in democratization processes.

Should knowledge be the operative factor?

I would like to characterize knowledge as a generalized *capacity to act* on the world, as a model *for* reality, or as the ability to set something in motion. Defining knowledge as a capacity to act – in contrast to mere behavior, that is, habitual action – suspends judgment about what it may accomplish or about the exact practical role of knowledge in social relations;[16] that is, especially, about the ways in which we get from knowledge as a method of acting on the world to action itself, and about what social structures may assist or defeat such efforts.

The capacity *to get things done*, that is, the ability *to do* something in order to affect reality (in an effort to reach certain goals as well as the

---

[16] As Giorgio Agamben (2014:482) notes in a discussion of the power (faculty) to act: "The term *faculty* expresses ... the way in which a certain activity is separated from itself and is assigned to a subject, the way in which a living being 'has' his or her vital practice. Whatever faculty (for example, feeling) ... comes to be distinguished from feeling in the act can be referred to as the subject's own."

ability to intervene in a context that may change in another direction entirely) is not symmetrical with the capacity to act (knowledge). The capacity to get things done depends on the *circumstances of action*. The specific circumstances of action that favor the ability to get things done depend on the *control* actors exercise over the circumstances of action (*Gestaltungsspielraum*).[17] Knowledge may be present, but for lack of the capacity to transform (e.g., to govern) this knowledge, it cannot be employed. On the other hand, actors and organizations may have the necessary authority, power, or material resources to impact reality, yet nonetheless lack the capacity to act. It will be my contention that one of the most forceful capacities to act is *knowledgeability* – knowledgeability here defined as "a bundle of competencies."

Knowledgeability

The importance of the knowledge of civil society for democratic forms of government has, of course, been examined in past inquiries and studies. However, these works fall short, not necessarily because they relate to other historical periods and societal conditions, but rather because the central analytical concepts and assumptions of an analysis of democracy and knowledge are liberally *conflated*. This applies with particular force to the interchangeability of the terms *information* and *knowledge*, and *knowledge* and *knowledgeablity*. I will try to show that – taking a cue from Ludwig Wittegenstein's suggestion that philosophical (sociological) problems become more transparent if we formulate them as issues that pertain to the meaning of concepts – the separation between knowledge and information is profitable; and, more importantly, that an extension of the notion of knowledge in the sense of knowledgeability is of greater theoretical and practical value.

Knowledgeability represents a broad and heterogeneous *bundle of competencies* – not in the sense of strictly psychological dispositions (as

---

[17] Claus Offe's (2013:77) definition of the *state* resonates with the emphasis placed here on the capacity to get things done as the necessary step to implement knowledge as a capacity to act: "In order for the state to '*be*' a state, it is not sufficient that its organs (the police, the military, the courts, the prisons) are capable to effectively neutralize rival pretenders to coercive power. In addition, it must be capable to '*do*' something, namely 'govern'. Being able to govern means to perform collectively binding decisions effectively designed and implemented to protect and promote, through an ongoing production of policies, societal conditions and processes (such as law and order, economic growth, property relations, the ultimate authority of the will of God or the ruling party, particular notions of social justice and social progress etc.) that rulers deem worth protecting and promoting."

argued by Lane 1953)[18] that have enabling capacities, and therefore noticeable effects, on the *process* of collective participation and inequality formation in modern societies, as well as on individual well-being. In the realm of politics and political participation, the competencies that make up knowledgeability, for example, the ability to have opinions of one's own (cf.Hirschmann, 1989), enhance and promote the interest in and the capability to reason about political affairs; to arrive at political decisions independently; to influence other actors; and, last but not least, to increase the social pressure on major institutions (church, government, business, education) to expand and to fulfill their accountability to the citizens.[19]

Both the growth of the self-organizing capacity of small groups of actors and the *loss* of the once considerable strength and influence of large social institutions are, as I will emphasize, part of the societal transformations that have to be taken into account.[20] Aside from the very notions of knowledge and democracy, the questions these changes pose are: Is democratic governance a daughter of knowledge? Is the knowledgeability of citizens[21] one of the most effective, even if *indirect*, pathways to the sustenance and future of democratic forms of governance? On the other hand, are uneven and low levels of public knowledge a burden on democracy? What forms of democratic governance are realistically possible under contemporary conditions and constraints faced by modern societies? Has democracy simply become an outdated political vision in the complex, fragile, and uncertain universe in which we live?

What counts, in terms of the impact of knowledgeability on the nature of the political regime, is above all the extent to which citizens can effectively *curtail* the power of the powerful. In order to have such an impact and be effectively represented in political decisions, what counts is not only *actual participation*, in the sense of being *present* in political contexts. It is in this sense that Hanna Pitkin (1967:144) defines "representation," noting that "representation means the making present of

---

[18] I am referring to Robert Lane's (1953:653–656) typology of political identities, which he developed in analogy to David Riesman's distinction between "inner-directed" and "outer-directed" individuals.

[19] Daniel Bell (1973:44) points out that any new regime or social system generates a strong sense of social rejection among those who feel excluded or threatened. Among the primary social tensions and new social differences in postindustrial societies would be especially the "conflict generated by a meritocracy principle which is central to the allocation of position in the knowledge society."

[20] I have examined the issue of how it is ever more difficult to govern, plan, and organize a well-ordered, consistent, and unified modern society in *The Fragility of Modern Societies: Knowledge and Risk in the Information Age* (Stehr, 2001), not void of frequent surprises.

[21] For a discussion of the genealogy of the idea of "citizen," see Dahrendorf (1974).

something that is nevertheless not literally present." Second, the impact of knowledgeability enhances the capacity of citizens to govern themselves. The ability to govern oneself at the collective level enhances social organizations of self-government, and therefore also the conditions for democracy.

The sociohistorical context of modern democracies

An answer to the basic question of the interrelation between democracy and knowledge requires both a theory of society and an understanding of sociopolitical conditions in contemporary societies. A theory of modern society is a necessary requirement as a foundation and reference point, because neither do democratic institutions come in only one form; nor are sociopolitical phenomena static; nor is knowledge, its societal importance and degree of freedom in society, fixed.

Among the widely accepted assumptions about the nature of modern societies is not only that we live in a society in which the volume of available knowledge is unprecedented but also that we live in a society in which one needs *much more knowledge* in order to live and make a living. Indeed, there can be little doubt that the collective volume of knowledge has increased immeasurably in the course of human history. Similarly, the *kind* of knowledge now available differs significantly from past knowledge (e.g., Elias, 1971).

The existence of humans in prehistorical or simple societies was precarious and fragile. The enlarged reservoir of knowledge in modern societies has undoubtedly changed some of the basic existential conditions of its members, as compared to simple societies and the precarious nature of their lives. The growing collective and individual volume of knowledge, characteristic of modern societies, has also introduced new existential problems – for example, in the relations between societies and their natural environment – which demand political action. At the same time, sociologists representing various social theories collectively describe a massive setback in terms of the degree of freedom the population is allowed in modern societies: "In western societies, there is a progressive decline in the political freedom of citizens to influence the development of their society and, by extension, their personal lives" (Blokland, 2011:1).

Although the question of democracy and knowledge is not a widely discussed issue in the scientific community or in society at large at the present time, this does not necessarily signal that the issue is settled. Practical political conflicts, as for example the persistent and exemplary dispute between the state of New York and the city of New York over the question, "How expensive should knowledge be?", indicate that the topic is a viable theme for social research. Then there are, as indicated, growing concerns about an "inconvenient democracy." Climate scientists, public intellectuals, and members of the media ask whether humankind, and democratic institutions in particular, are able to respond in an adequate and timely manner to the threats posed by climate change. I will make reference to both of these disputes in detail.

The *dynamics* of modern forms of knowledge production and the unrelenting transformation of the conditions and practice of freedom assure that the linkages between liberty and knowledge undergo and are subject to changes.[22] Moreover, both the social order of knowledge, especially the rapid enlargement of scientific knowledge, and democracy itself persistently face novel challenges and problems in contemporary society. It is time for a reconsideration of both democratic governance and the role of knowledgeable actors – a reexamination that is aware of and sensitive to the dynamic, changing nature of modern society and the relations between knowledge and democracy.

Our understanding of the interrelations of knowledge and social conditions, as well as the nature of societal change, is far from extensive. As Thomas Luckmann (1982:259–260) was able to emphasize a couple of decades ago, "we do not know with any degree of certainty to what extent historical transformations of knowledge and the social distribution of knowledge are consequences and to what extent causes of general social change." This statement is as accurate today as it was then. With the following reflections, I hope to offer a small contribution to reducing the deficit in this regard.

I am grateful to colleagues who have commented on the manuscript or portions of the text in progress: Heribert Adam, Marian Adolf, Hella Beister, Sven Eliaeson, Ronald M. Glassman, Reiner Grundmann, Ragnvald Kalleberg, Jacquelyne Luce, Paul Malone, Alexander Ruser, Scott McNall, and Hermann Strasser.

In different sections of my study, I refer to and utilize earlier texts – this applies in particular to the discussion of the term *knowledge*, the difference between knowledge and information, the risks of knowledge, and the governability of modern societies – which I developed in response to different substantive issues, but which are linked to the present analysis for theoretical and empirical reasons. These references to earlier reflections have always been reexamined in light of new ideas, and have been changed and extended as a result.

---

[22] As Friedrich Hayek (1960:366) observes in stating his own preference for the term *liberty* rather than *freedom*, a widely accepted distinction between the two concepts does not exist. Hence I will use the terms interchangeably.

1 Coming to terms

> A greater degree of civil freedom appears advantageous to the freedom of the mind of the people, and yet it places inescapable limitations upon it; a lower degree of civil freedom, on the contrary, provides the mind with room for each man to extend himself in full capacity. Immanuel Kant ([1784] 1986:269)

There are hardly any other words in any language that are as frequently employed as are *democracy* and *knowledge*. For this reason alone, both terms are embedded in systematic ambiguity (Merton, 1957a:497). Nor are there many words that consistently meet with such partiality and approval as *democracy* and *knowledge*. Put more formally, the terms *democracy* and *knowledge* typically perform the speech-act of commending what they describe (cf. Sartori, 1968). Given the strong aura that these terms carry, it is impossible to avoid the conclusion that all political ideologies use *democracy* and *knowledge* to legitimate, rather than to enlighten (Saward, 1993:63–64).

At the same time, there are few other *social* phenomena that are generally more significant for modern societies than knowledge and democracy. Even political regimes that are authoritarian systems prefer to claim that they constitute democracies; even states that are considered liberal democracies have their "dark side."[1] A study employing objective criteria concludes that in the last century, there is not only an unambiguous trend toward democratization of modern societies, but at present, more than half of all states are democracies (Mansfield and Pevehouse, 2006; Sorensen, 2010:441). Although democratic sentiments are not necessarily a robust determinant of democratization (cf. Teorell and Hadenius, 2006; Berg-Schlosser, 2003),[2] as the World Values Survey demonstrates (Inglehart, 2003), a clear majority of the global population endorses democracy.

---

[1] Michael Mann (1999:23) has noted and documented that "liberal democracies *have* committed massive cleansing, sometimes amounting to genocide – in colonial contexts where large social groups were defined as lying outside of the 'people'."

[2] A response to Teorell and Hadenius' conclusion about the efficacy of values in democratization can be found in Welzel and Inglehart (2006).

By the same token, the socioeconomic (and military) importance of *scientific and technical* knowledge has grown in production processes, and is regarded as both the motor of societal change and the source of the problems faced by society in general and the political system in particular. At least at the collective level of societies, the dissemination of democracy around the world coincides with the immense growth of knowledge *and* knowledgeability, as well as with a historically unprecedented increase in the *general* standard of living within many societies; notwithstanding, of course, the fact that many households have not emancipated themselves from the constraints of basic survival, and that poor educational achievements are far from eradicated.

The favorable appeal that surrounds the abstract terms *knowledge* and *democracy*, and the general disapproval that surrounds their absence – for example, in the sense of "we know very little" or "totalitarian regime" – is virtually without competition when it comes to the usage of concepts that characterize *societal* conditions other than merely psychological or individual dispositions such as love, luck, dignity (see Ober, 2012), or health. By the same token, and as Immanuel Kant already observes, there are very complex relations (circles) between both liberty and knowledge, and deficits of knowledge and democracy.

Both the term *knowledge* and the concept of *democracy* are ambivalent and essentially contested terms.[3] It is also not possible to refer to robust empirical indicators that unambiguously signify what characterizes knowledge-based *or* democratic societies. But the contestedness of the terms and the lack of firm empirical referents cannot mean that efforts to utilize these terms for an analysis of their potential interrelationships should be relinquished. On the contrary, it is necessary to carefully define the usage of these terms in the context of this inquiry, precisely *because* there is a lack of agreement regarding their meaning and regarding how they should be employed in a study that examines their linkages in modern society. However, such an examination cannot content itself with an endless genealogy and exegesis of and lament about the contestedness of the terms *democracy* and *knowledge*. After all, we have not only to get on with the purpose of the study, but an

---

[3] Dalton, Shin, and Jou (2007) present an analysis of the public understanding of democracy throughout the world, based on a range of empirical studies. In these studies the reference to freedom and civil liberties as the essential characteristics of democracy is the most common answer of the respondents. According to Dalton, Shin, and Jou (2007:147), these findings permit the conclusion that the idea of democracy is not merely a Western concept, understood only by affluent and well-educated citizens. Instead, the findings suggest that democracy "embodies human values and that most people understand these principles" (also Sen, 2003).

exegesis without end would also only confirm, as it were, the ambivalence and disputed meaning of these concepts.

The term of *democracy* resonates closely with another abstract and controversial concept, namely *freedom*.[4] Freedom and democracy are *relational* terms. Neither freedom nor democracy has ever been completely realized. That is why democracy can never mean the complete absence of forms of authority and power (the power of humans over humans), or absolute liberty. Nor can *democracy* refer to the participation of all in every political decision (cf. Luhmann, [1986] 1987:126–127), or the existence of democratic rule merely on the basis of professing democratic ideals (cf. Brecht, 1946:199).

Liberty and democracy refer to (usually asymmetric) social *relations* among individuals and social conditions rather than to individual conditions, attributes, and feelings. If democracy and freedom designate individual states – for example, a person is said to be free and capable of expressing her opinions – then the state of freedom of such an individual derives from preexisting social conditions that allow for the possibility of being free; for example, being free from a miserable marriage through divorce, given the existence of a specific legal set of framework.

It is less obvious, perhaps, to make the case that *knowledge* is also a relational concept. That *knowledge* is a relational concept is less evident because of the widespread association of the term with such robust attributes as *truthful, reliable, observer independent, fully warranted,* or *objective* and *valid for everyone*. Knowing is a relation not only to things and facts, but also to rules, laws, and programs. Some sort of participation is therefore constitutive for knowing: knowing things, rules, programs, and facts is "appropriating" them in some sense, including them within our field of orientation and competence. The intellectual appropriation of things can be made independently or objectively. That is, symbolic representation of the content of knowledge eliminates the necessity of coming into direct contact with the things themselves. One can, in other words, acquire knowledge from books. The social significance of language, writing, printing, data storage, and so forth is that they represent knowledge symbolically, or provide the possibility of objectified knowledge. Put somewhat differently, the possibility of the social exchange and circulation of knowledge are dependent upon media of different sorts (bytes, paper, diagrams, charts). Whether the storage media represent other than neutral means of storing knowledge is

---

[4] At this point, I want to bracket out any reference to the fundamental concern that democracy and freedom of the individual may be at odds, as is recognized and discussed by John Stuart Mill and Alexis de Tocqueville, for example.

controversial (cf. McLuhan, 1964; Edwards et al. 2011:1401). The most recent claim in this respect, of course, would be to suggest that the Internet not only shapes what counts as knowledge but also transforms knowledge itself (see Weinberger, 2011); or, somewhat earlier, the assertion by Jean-François Lyotard ([1979] 1984:4) that the hegemony of computers determines what will be accepted as knowledge claims.

Thus, most of what we today call knowledge and learning is not direct knowledge of facts, rules, and things, but rather *objectified* knowledge. Objectified knowledge is the highly differentiated stock of intellectually appropriated nature and society that may also be seen to constitute the cultural resource of a society. Knowing, then, is *grosso modo participation* in the cultural resources of society. However, such participation is of course subject to stratification; for example, due to a differential access to the Internet and, thus, to the ability to take advantage of the information available. The life chances, lifestyle, and social influence of individuals depend on their access to the stock of knowledge and information at hand.

Freedom and knowledge, although widely seen as referring to virtuous or "good" things, are ambivalent notions. They are not only "incompletely descriptive" (cf. Cranston, 1971:18), but are also *essentially contested concepts* (cf. Gallie, 1995–1956).[5] If we are told that someone is knowledgeable or that someone is free, we are not able to tell much about the person or group except in the most general, and therefore less than intelligible, sense. Thus, some further light needs to be shed on the terms of freedom (democracy) and knowledge. I will first turn to the definition of knowledge.

Knowledge: a capacity for action?

I would like to characterize knowledge[6] not as *something that is so* but as a generalized *capacity to act* on the world, as a model *for* reality, or as the

---

[5] Walter B. Gallie (1955–1956:168–169) notes that "we find groups of people disagreeing about the proper use of the concepts, e.g., of art, of democracy, of the Christian tradition. When we examine the different uses of these terms and the characteristic arguments in which they figure we soon see that there is no one clearly definable general use of any of them which can be set up as the correct or standard use." But even after these incongruities among or different functions of terms have been pointed out, terminological disputes do not end. Although disputes centered on these concepts are "not resolvable by argument of any kind, [they] are nevertheless sustained by perfectly respectable arguments and evidence. This is what I mean by saying that there are concepts which are essentially contested, concepts the proper use of which inevitably involves endless disputes about their proper uses on the part of their users."

[6] My discussion of the concept of knowledge at this point is indebted to a number of earlier efforts. First, I have discussed the various facets of the concept of knowledge in some

ability to set something in motion (Stehr, 1994).[7] The capacity to act, the ability to put something into motion, extends to the capacity to generate "symbolic action." For example, symbolic action may involve the ability to formulate a hypothesis, carry out a ritual, find a new metaphor for an established term,[8] assess "facts," organize the literature on a topic or defend a thesis against "new facts." The capacity to act, in other words, refers not merely to the possibility of accomplishing something in terms of a material and physical performance such as, for example, to make fire, to drive a car, to sell a share or to defend oneself against an attacking person. Capacities to act also refer to *intellectual* abilities, such as may be found in the detailed description of the bundle of skills that I call *knowledgeability*.[9]

As far as I can see, *energy* as the "capacity to do work" would be a second major capacity for action (White, 1995).[10] Here, a brief reference

---

detail in my study *Knowledge Societies* (Stehr, 1994). In the meantime, I have taken up this issue again and again for different reasons. In all cases, I have extended the discussion of the concepts of knowledge and information by adding new aspects. This also happens to be the case at this point. However, I have never abandoned the basic definition of knowledge as a capacity for action. Although my inquiry into the social nature of knowledge does not aim to locate the *scientific meaning* of scientific knowledge, as does Hans Reichenbach (1951) in his *The Rise of Scientific Philosophy*, I am in agreement with his stipulation that "he who inquires into the nature of knowledge should keep his eyes open and be willing to accept any result that cogent reasoning brings to light; it does not matter if the result contradicts his conception of what knowledge should be." The definition of knowledge as the capacity to act is of course in sharp contrast to knowledge as "authenticated knowledge" (e.g., Dretske, 1981) or knowledge as "justified belief" (e.g., Huber, 1991; Nanoka, 1994).

[7] The German term that best describes knowledge as a generalized capacity to act would be *Handlungsvermögen*. The verb *vermögen* signals "to be able to do," while the noun *Vermögen*, in this context, is best translated as "capacity" (rather than "fortune" or "wealth"). Georg Simmel ([1907] 1989:276), in his discussion of money as a generalized code, uses the concept *Vermögen* to describe the fact that money is more than merely a medium of exchange; his definition of money thus transcends a merely functional understanding of its social capacities.

[8] I refer in this context, for example, to Donald Schon's ([1963] 1967) reflections in *Displacement of Concepts* or, more specifically, to Andrew Haldane's ([2009] 2013) proposal that to understand the paradigm of economics, one should view the financial crisis at the beginning of this century through the prism of the life sciences, especially epidemiology and ecology.

[9] This is most likely the reason why Norbert Elias (1984:252) defines knowledge as "the social meaning of human-made symbols, such as words or figures, in its *capacity as means of orientation*" (my emphasis).

[10] Nor should one neglect the important role of energy as a lever for the development of sustainable democratic governance in regions of the world that lack access to affordable energy sources. As our 2013 *Hartwell Paper on Innovation* (Prins et al., 2013) stresses, for example: "Most of those people alive today who are left without electricity live in South Asia and Sub-Saharan Africa and are among the poorest in the world. The role of stable, safe, and affordable energy in bringing economic growth and development to such populations is well known and well documented; and there is no doubt that access to

to the socio-historical variability of energy and knowledge as capacities to act might be helpful: In the nineteenth and twentieth centuries, fossil fuels have been the most important capacities that made possible the dominant forms of economic activity in particular, and social action in general. As a consequence, the social institutions and the organizations that controlled the production, distribution, and use of fossil fuels – and this included, last but not least, the labor movement during this historical time period – constituted the major power centers of industrial society. It follows that the "carbon democracy," as described by Timothy Mitchell (2009), belongs to an ever-increasing degree to the past. The carbon democracy is being replaced by the "knowledge democracy." The societal significance of energy, in terms of a capacity to act, is displaced by knowledge as that very capacity.

Without question, *language* (cf. Hayek, [1988] 1991:106–110; Koselleck, 1989:211) and *power* (Giddens, 1984:15) should also be counted among the transformative capacities to act (or, even more generally, the totality of the *material and immaterial conditions of action* are a part of our capacities to act. Knowledge is not merely an abstract phenomenon, a way of interpreting the world or making sense of oneself. Knowledge put to work as *know-how* (cf. Zelenyi, 1989; Ackoff, 1989)[11] co-creates, sustains, and changes existential conditions.[12] Knowledge is not only passive knowledge – as the first step toward action and changes of reality, it is also capable of legitimating, defending and sustaining social conditions or to organize resistance against the forces of reality.[13]

---

electricity, and modern energy more generally, is a prerequisite for economic and political empowerment."

[11] The notion of knowledge as know-how indicates that knowledge as a cultural resource – although at times embedded in material objects – constitutes, as DiMaggio (1997:267; Swidler, 1986) generally defines culture, a "tool-kit" as opposed to those who would argue "that people experience culture as highly integrated, that cultural meanings are strongly thematized, that culture is binding, and that cultural information acquired through experience is more powerful than that acquired through other means."

[12] As a result, the societal legitimacy of any support for scientific research, but also the legitimacy of scientific knowledge itself in society, is mostly a function of the *use value* of science. In the forefront of most discussions in society about science is the utility of the knowledge generated by science, and therefore the capacity of science to construct or alter the conditions of the life-world (cf. Tenbruck, 1969:63).

[13] The thesis that knowledge is a model of reality that will enlighten and alter reality is also related to Albert Borgmann's (1999:1) definition of information, more precisely, to his concept of the "recipe" as a "model of *information for reality.*" However, power is not connected to knowledge "as such" or to knowledge alone in much the same way as technology as such does not constitute power. Only in connection with human action and action under certain conditions can knowledge change or influence reality. Only then can one usefully speak of knowledge as power. For Niklas Luhmann (2002b:97–98), this definition of knowledge as a capacity for action is not an alien conception of knowledge; in his observations on the educational system of society

It should be stressed also, and this is of considerable importance in the context of this analysis, that it is much more difficult to *protect knowledge* from others than to *restrict* them from gaining access to capital or weapons (see Elias, 1984:252–252).

Moreover, knowledge is an anthropological constant. Although knowledge does not always attain the same societal significance throughout history, it is of course of importance in all societies and in all social relations, not only in modern knowledge societies.[14] The *temporal* dimension of knowledge is future-oriented. In terms of the *practical* interrelation of knowledge and action, for instance, C. P. Snow's uncritical, optimistic observation of the 1950s ([1959] 1964:11) is doubtlessly accurate: scientists "have the future in their bones."

Defining knowledge as a capacity to act implies, for heuristic purposes, silence about the *sources* of knowledge, the ways in which it is *generated*, its *validity*, and its *social distribution*; and temporarily, knowledge suspends judgment about what it may accomplish, or its exact practical role in social relations – that is, especially, about the ways in which we get from knowledge as a way of acting on the world to action itself, and what social structures may assist or defeat such efforts. With my attempt, for heuristic reasons only, to suspend the relation between knowledge and social action I want to avoid attributing an immediately performative (knowledge equals control) or immediately persuasive efficacy to forms of knowing (cf. Kahan et al., 2012) and thus privileging knowledge, or ignoring the limits of the power of knowledge, imposed by society (Stehr, 1991; Prewitt, 2010; Sarewitz, 2010).

In addition, based on the definition of knowledge as a capacity for action, it can be concluded that the search for new knowledge, or efforts to discard existing knowledge, is based not so much on the desire to operate a "transformation of the unknown into the familiar" (Luhmann,

---

("the educational system produces knowledge"), for example, he emphasizes that based on knowledge one is able to open up opportunities – or, based on a lack of knowledge, "obstruct opportunities" - that may give one's life a particular direction. The specificity of Luhmann's (1990:714) conception of knowledge is even more precisely expressed in his description of the work of modern science: "Science cannot be understood any longer as the representation of the world as it is, and science therefore must also give up on the claim to be able to teach others about the world. Science provides an exploration of possible complex constructions that can be attributed to the world and act as a form, that is, produce a difference."

[14] For anthropologists, for example, knowledge has become a central problematic in their work on cross-cultural encounters and their study of empire building. Using the knowledge perspective, their studies of colonial societies theorize colonialism as a "conquest of knowledge" (e.g., Cohn, 1996), and as one foundation for constituting modern forms of knowledge (Ballantyne, 2011).

1990:148), but rather on the desire to expand the volume of existing possibilities for action.

In principle, however, knowledge may indeed be assimilated to liberty, insofar as knowledge constitutes the principal capacity for action for individuals and small groups of actors.[15] Despite the initial silence in our definition of the term *knowledge* – about the practices of knowledge production, for example – the traditions we will rely on to reflect on and represent reality are, as will be emphasized more closely, linked to the ways in which social reality is constituted, acted upon, or governed.

My understanding of knowledge therefore implies, or does not *a priori* exclude, that it may function as a powerful force for allegedly weak individuals and groups who generate and organize resistance against existing or planned measures of social control by large social institutions, such as the state, companies, science, political parties, and so forth. Resistance against the powers-that-be may, for example, amount to "passive resistance, tactical withdrawal, or clever circumvention of rules" (Rosanvallon, [2006] 2008:121), the development of alternative policy goals, the refusal to obey authority, the organization of protests (cf. Lipsky, 1968), and so forth. The ability to mistrust, and hence to resist, is enhanced by knowledgeability.

My definition of the term knowledge is first and foremost indebted to Francis Bacon's famous observation that knowledge is power[16] (a somewhat misleading, but common, translation of Bacon's Latin phrase: *scientia est potentia*).[17] Bacon suggests that knowledge derives its utility from its capacity to set something in motion; modern examples for this include new communicative devices, new forms of power, new regulatory regimes, new chemical substances, new political organizations, new financial instruments, or new illnesses, among others. One concrete

---

[15] The mere reference to knowledge as a potential capacity that enhances liberty does not impress skeptics, nor allay their concerns about the actual role of knowledge in the affairs of society and the possibility of freedom in human affairs. After all, as has been widely asserted, knowledge may enhance repression, thus raising, for example, the difficult question of the relations between power and knowledge.

[16] An analysis of the various implications of Bacon's metaphor "scientia est potentia" can be found in Garcia (2000). Among the important implications that Bacon derives from his metaphor is the assertion that individuals provided with experimental skills and practical knowledge are those most entitled to hold executive office, rather than the aristocracy of blood.

[17] Etymologically, however, power refers to ability, and "to make a difference" would be among the most basic definitions of the concept of "ability." In that sense, and therefore not in the sense in which the concept of power is usually used in discussions about power in social relations, namely as power exercised to accomplish something or as power over someone, the basic definition of power as an ability resonates with the notion of knowledge as a capacity (compare Dyrberg, 1997:88–99).

22   Coming to terms

example of knowledge as a capacity for action comes from Claude Shannon (1948): In 1948, Shannon published a small paper entitled "The Mathematical Theory of Communication."[18] In this paper he explained how words, sounds and images could be converted into blips and sent electronically. Shannon foretold the digital revolution in communications. Knowledge as a symbolic "system" enables people to act on the world.

My conception of knowledge as a capacity to act thereby opens space for the idea of *agency* in knowledge-dependent processes (Sen, 1985:203–204; Barth, 2002:3). Knowledge structures reality. Knowledge is a model for reality.[19] Knowledge is future sensitive. The added value of knowledge, therefore, should be seen as a capacity to illuminate and potentially to transform reality.[20] It is in this sense that knowledge is facilitative, and possibly transformative in getting things done.[21] Putting

---

[18] As Freeman Dyson explains in a review in the *New York Review of Books* (March 10, 2011): "In 1945 Shannon wrote a paper, 'A Mathematical Theory of Cryptography,' which was stamped SECRET and never saw the light of day. He published in 1948 an expurgated version of the 1945 paper with the title 'A Mathematical Theory of Communication.' The 1948 version appeared in the *Bell System Technical Journal*, the house journal of the Bell Telephone Laboratories, and became an instant classic. It is the founding document for the modern science of information. After Shannon, the technology of information raced ahead, with electronic computers, digital cameras, the Internet, and the World Wide Web."

[19] Compare Ian Hacking's (1983:146) notion of modern natural science that "has since the seventeenth century been the adventure of the interlocking of representing and intervening." This conception resonates with our broader conception of knowledge as a capacity to act. Hacking (1983:146) adds that we consider as real "what we can use to intervene in the world to affect something else, or what the world can use to affects us."

[20] The idea that knowledge is a model for reality that illuminates, discloses and transforms but also displaces reality, resonates with Albert Borgmann's (1999:1) conception of the "recipe" (or plans, scores, and constitutions) as a "model of *information for reality*." It would be misleading to suggest that that there is an immediate connection between knowledge as such or knowledge on its own power. Only in connection with human conduct and under certain conditions of action will knowledge be put to work and thereby become capable of influencing and changing reality. It is only under these circumstances – knowledge as a capacity to act put to work – that it is meaningful to refer to knowledge as power. Niklas Luhmann (2002c:97) is not averse to such a conception of knowledge and power. In his observations about the educational system of society ("education produces knowledge"), for example, he notes that it is on the basis of knowledge that one gains new options that in turn influence the direction of one's life. The special character of knowledge, as defined by Luhmann ([1992] 1994:20), can also be deduced from his observation of the work of modern science accomplishes: "Science can no longer comprehend itself as a representation of the world as it is, and must therefore retract its claim of instructing others about the world. It achieves an exploration of possible constructions that can be inscribed in the world and, in so doing, function as forms, that is, produce a difference."

[21] As will be noted, the definition of knowledge as a capacity for action would extend to the definition of knowledge developed by Lupia and McCubbins (1998:6) in their study of knowing and democratic decision making. They define knowledge as "the ability to

knowledge to work or into practice is in many instances a political act and, in any case, a *social* occurrence (also Dewey, 1929:131–132; Gehlen, [1940] 1993:341–355; Krohn, 1981; 1988:87–89).[22]

The term *potentia* – that is, *capacity* – is employed by Francis Bacon to describe the power of knowing. Knowledge is *becoming*.[23] More specifically, Bacon asserts at the outset of his *Novum Organum* (I, Aph. 3) that "human knowledge and human power meet in one; for where the cause is not known the effect cannot be produced. Nature to be commanded must be obeyed; and that which in contemplation is the cause is in operation the rule." The success of human action can be gaged from changes that have taken place in social reality (Krohn, 1981; 1988:87–89),[24] and last but not least, knowledge acquires *distinction* because of its apparent ability to transform reality. As a result, (most of) the reality we confront, and increasingly so, arises from and embodies knowledge.[25] On the other hand, of course, knowledge ages and depreciates over time.

Science is not merely, as it was once widely thought, the solution to the mysteries and miseries of the world; it is, rather, the becoming of a world.

predict the consequences of actions." Such a definition of knowledge is of course outcome neutral.

[22] The pragmatic philosophy of science aims, as is well known, in the same future-oriented direction; John Dewey (1929:132), for example, stresses that "the business of thought is not to conform to or reproduce the characters already possessed by objects but to judge them as potentialities of what they become through an indicated operation."

[23] That knowledge is *becoming* is reflected in a fundamental change in metaphysics from an ontology that stresses being to an ontology of becoming.

[24] The conception of knowledge advanced here resonates with Ludwig von Mises' (1922:14) *sociological* definition of *property*; von Mises suggests that as a sociological category, "property represents the capacity to determine the use of economic goods." The ownership of knowledge, and thus the power to dispose of knowledge, is as a rule not exclusive. This exclusivity, however, is required by jurisprudence in the definition of property or of the institution of ownership. Formal law, as is well known, recognizes owners and proprietors; in particular, it recognizes individuals who ought to possess, but do not possess. In the eyes of the legal system, property is indivisible. It is also of no importance what concrete material or immaterial "things" are at issue. Likewise, the sociological significance of knowledge lies primarily in the actual ability to dispose of knowledge as capacity for action.

[25] It is relevant here to refer to the social role of the knowledge generated by the natural sciences and the humanities, the social, and cultural sciences. For Niklas Luhmann ([1981] 1987:55), for example, the social role of natural science occurs via the effect such knowledge has on *action* and, through action, on *experience*. For the humanities, exactly the opposite is the case: the influence of cultural knowledge is via experience (experiencing), and *only* via experiencing, on action (for an account of the difference between action and experience in Luhmann's work, see Luhmann, 1979). Whether or not one follows Luhmann's distinction and the reasons he adduces to justify the difference between acting and experiencing, the idea that knowledge represents a capacity for action is implicit in Luhmann's difference.

Knowledge not only arises from a specific context, but also creates that context.[26] The idea that knowledge is a capacity for action that transforms, or even creates, reality is perhaps almost self-evident in the case of social science knowledge,[27] but less persuasive, given the prevailing conception of the distinctive attributes of scientific knowledge in the case of the natural sciences. In the case of contemporary biology, however, one is prepared to acknowledge that biological knowledge extends to the fabrication of new living systems. Biology does not simply study nature; biology transforms and produces novel natural realities.[28] Biology and biotechnology are closely linked.[29]

---

[26] As Duncan Kennedy (2010:88) stresses in a discussion of Bruno Latour's political epistemology, scientists are "seen as skilled practitioners rather than figures with privileged access to impersonal, objective, transcendent truths or laws." Scientists generate know-how, or capacities to act.

[27] In the case of the humanities and the social sciences, an example would be the idea of a thought experiment that has to be translated into action, the political economy as it were would be embedded in the economic order (Callon, 1998) or the economic model realized in the world of financial markets. Donald MacKenzie (2006) illustrates one such case in his analysis of the Black-Scholes model, which has influenced the trading of warrants. The model described by the American economists Carmen Reinhart and Kenneth Rogoff in a paper published in 2010, "Growth in a time of debt," illustrates that the policy-affecting ideas do not necessarily have to be "true" to change reality. Their assertion that economic growth goes into reverse gear as soon as the total debt of a country reaches more than 90 percent of its gross domestic product has been found to be likely based on a calculation error. As Paul Krugman ("The excel depression", *New York Times*, 18 April 2013) pointed out in a comment, "the paper came out just after Greece went into crisis and played right into the desire of many officials to 'pivot' from stimulus to austerity. As a result, the paper instantly became famous; it was, and is, surely the most influential economic analysis of recent years." The relevant sociopolitical circumstances of action at the time of the publication of the Reinhart/Rogoff paper favored the implementation of the model. Thus, the practical power of the model and its ideas were quite independent of the "truth" of the model. Hayley Stevenson and John Dryzek (2012:192) interpret the concepts of reflexive modernization or reflexive traditionalization as the ability to recognize alternative modes of discourse: "Reflexive modernisation and reflexive traditionalisation alike mean space opens up for the configuration of discourses to be itself influenced by reflective choices of competent agents, simply as the result of enhanced awareness of alternative discourses. To the extent this capacity becomes dispersed and inclusive, there is potentially good news for democracy."

[28] The observation that modern humans are increasingly "acting into nature" can be found in Hannah Arendt's (1961:59) discussion of the technological world in which we live: "The world we have come to live in, however, is much more determined by man acting into nature, creating natural processes and directing them into the human artifice and the realm of human affairs."

[29] The conception of knowledge as a generalized capacity to act, as a model for reality and, if enacted, as reality, constitutes a kind of reversal of the Heisenberg principle. The Heisenberg principle – or rather, in this instance, using a nontechnical language, the observer effect – refers to the fact that the phenomenon under observation is altered through the act of observing (which makes for the phenomenon observed to be unobservable). In the case of defining knowledge as a capacity to act, the phenomenon

Knowledge, as a generalized capacity for action, acquires an "active" role (that is, it is put to work) in the course of social action only under certain circumstances, namely where social action does not follow purely stereotypical (effortless) patterns (Max Weber), or is strictly regulated in some other fashion.[30] Knowledge assumes significance under conditions where social action, for whatever reason, is based on a certain degree of freedom (*Gestaltungsspielraum*) that allows for and necessitates mental efforts and exertion.[31] The circumstances of action I have in mind may also be described as the capacity of actors to alter or stabilize a specific reality. However, the capacity *to get things done*, to alter and affect reality, as well as the ability to intervene in a context that otherwise would change, is not symmetrical with the capacity to act (knowledge). Knowledge and control should not be conflated (cf. Tenbruck, [1972] 1977:222).[32] As I have already stressed, the ability to do something is dependent on the control over the conditions of action. Most observers would say that the control of the conditions of action depends on power.[33]

is potentially altered in such a way that in the end it resembles the abstract image one has of the phenomenon (cf. Scott, 1998:14, note 6). In the case of the emerging modern forest science of the nineteenth century, for example, this meant "to create, through careful seeding, planting, and cutting, a forest that was easier for state foresters to count, manipulate, measure, and assess," turning the "real, diverse, and chaotic old-growth forest into a new, more uniform forest that closely resembled the administrative grid of its techniques" (Scott, 1998:15).

[30] Based on the basic idea that knowledge constitutes a capacity for action, distinctive categories or forms of knowledge can, of course, be developed depending on the enabling function that knowledge may be seen to fulfill. I believe that Francois Lyotard's ([1979] 1984:6) attempt to differentiate "payment knowledge" and "investment knowledge," in analogy to the categorical distinction between expenditures for consumption and expenditures for investment, constitutes an example of such a functional differentiation between more or less distinctive forms of knowledge.

[31] Niklas Luhmann's ([1992] 1998:67) observations about the conditions for the possibility of decision making perhaps allow for an even broader use of knowledge. Decision making "is possible only if and insofar as what will happen is uncertain." Assuming or depending on whether one assumes that the future is most uncertain, the deployment of knowledge in decisions to be made may extend to many more social contexts, even to those that are otherwise characterized by nothing but routine attributes and habitual conduct.

[32] Friedrich Tenbruck ([1972] 1977:223) offers the following sober observation about the linkages between knowledge, control, and foresight: "Foresight and control is highly fragile in reality, it can be shown that a persistent progress of knowledge neither leads necessarily to an improvement of foresight nor to an improvement of control."

[33] Indeed, the definition of knowledge as a capacity to act encourages the observer to differentiate between social phenomena and processes of knowledge and power. Barry Barnes (1988:58) in his discussion of the *Nature of Power* assimilates knowledge and power much more closely; power is an aspect of the distribution of knowledge; he even offers the observation that "social power *is* the capacity for action in a society." Additional power is never equally distributed throughout society: "Social power is *possessed* by those with discretion in the direction of social action [...] to gain power is

26   Coming to terms

The control exercised may obviously vary from limited and broad to insignificant. Knowledge may be present but, lacking the capacity to transform this knowledge, it cannot be employed. On the other hand, actors and organizations may have the necessary authority, power, or material resources to change reality, yet lack the capacity to act.

Karl Mannheim ([1929] 1936) defines, in much the same sense, the range of social conduct in general, and therefore the contexts in which knowledge plays a role, as restricted to those spheres of social life that *have not been routinized* and regulated completely, in which routine rule following is not the rule.[34] For, as he observes, "conduct, in the sense in which we use it, does not begin until we reach the area where rationalization has not yet penetrated, and where we are forced to make decisions in situations which have as yet not been subjected to regulation" (Mannheim, [1929] 1936:102).[35] Concretely:

The action of a petty official who disposes of a file of documents in the prescribed manner or of a judge who finds that a case falls under the provisions of a certain paragraph in the law and disposes of it accordingly, or finally of a factory worker who produces a screw by following the prescribed technique, would not fallunder our definition of "conduct." Nor for that matter would the action of a technician

[34] to gain such discretion." In this sense, the notion of the *Gestaltungsspielraum* of actors is close to Barnes' conception of discretion. However, I would maintain that knowledge and discretion are not quite the same. *Gestaltungsspielraum* refers to the ability of actors to get things done because they control relevant circumstances of action. In order to get things done, one needs the power to command specific resources of action. Thus, the *deployment* of knowledge in particular social contexts cannot be detached from the *relations of power* in that context.

See also Karl W. Deutsch's (1961) notion of social mobilization, or Emile Durkheim's ([1950] 1991:125–126) observations about routine, immovable societal conditions in contrast with societal conditions in which the malleability of society becomes increasingly more comprehensive. Durkheim ([1950] 1992:89) concludes from the divergence between routine and governance that "a people is more democratic the greater the role of reason, reflection and critical spirit is evident in the regulation of its public affairs." From an "interactionist" perspective, organizations or any other social structures constitute "negotiated orders" (Strauss et al., 1964). However, this cannot mean that any and every aspect of the social reality of an organization is continuously available or accessible to every member for negotiation. Only particular, limited aspects of the organizational structure are available for disposition, and only with respect to these contingent features of social action members of the organization can mobilize knowledge in order to design and plan social conduct with a view to realize collective practical tasks (cf. also George H. Mead's [1964:555] concept of "reflexive action").

[35] Similar conceptions may be found in Friedrich Hayek's 1945 essay on the "Use of knowledge in society," which is in fact a treatise in praise of decentralization, the importance of knowledge of local circumstances for action, and the price system as an agency that communicates information and constitutes the answer to the question of how to coordinate forms of local knowledge. Hayek ([1945] 1948:82) emphasizes that "as long as things continue as before, or at least as they were expected to, there arise no new problems requiring a decision, no need to form a new plan."

Knowledge: a capacity for action? 27

who, in achieving a given end, combined certain general laws of nature. All these modes of behavior would be considered as merely "reproductive" because they are executed in a rational framework, according to a definite prescription entailing no personal decision whatsoever.

For Mannheim, the question of the relation of theory to practice is, then, restricted precisely to situations that offer a measure of discretion in social conduct, and which have not been reduced to a corset of strictly ordered and predictable patterns of social action. It cannot be ruled out, however, that even under these circumstances, where situations are repeated with routine regularity, elements of "irrationality" (that is, openness) remain.[36] The ability to deploy new knowledge is just as crucial as is the process of finding knowledge.

But under what other circumstances is the search for open conditions of action triggered at all; and on what basis is a particular course of action chosen and legitimized? The search for open attributes of action, and therefore considerations to put knowledge to work or to consume knowledge, can be triggered by a variety of events and conditions. Among the main triggers are disappointed expectations, as well as hope, resistance encountered (Luhmann, 2002a:99), the necessity to justify oneself, or doubt experienced. Disappointed expectations, hope, doubt, or resistance are major incentives to explore opportunities to mobilize and use knowledge to create a new sense of balance in terms of a stabilization of expectations. Aside from disappointed expectations, a large set of circumstances that trigger the search for and selection of knowledge as capacity of action are socio-structural changes. In other words, "when things go on happening in the same way, habit will suffice for conduct; but when circumstances are changing continually, habit, on the contrary, must not be in sovereign control. Reflection alone makes possible the discovery of new and effectual practices, for it is only by reflection that the future can be anticipated" (Durkheim, [1950] 1992:90).[37] The

---

[36] A study by an economist (Howitt, [1996] 1998) who raises various conceptual issues in an attempt to quantify and measure knowledge in order to incorporate knowledge into economic theory resembles, at least in part, the definition of knowledge as a capacity for action: "I define knowledge in terms of potentially observable behavior, as the ability of an individual or group of individuals to undertake, or to instruct or otherwise induce others to undertake procedures resulting in predictable transformations of material objects" (Howitt, [1996] 1998:99). Aside from the somewhat cumbersome nature of the definition, its restriction to the manipulation of *material objects* is a drawback, as is the essentially black box of "procedures" and "observable behavior." Finally, Howitt appears, at least at the conceptual level, to conflate knowledge with action.

[37] Relevant in this theoretical context is also Boltanski and Thévenot's (1999:359–361) term *moments critique* (critical moments): "People, involved in ordinary relationships, who are doing things together – let us say, in politics, work, unionism,- and who have to

choice of courses of action is obviously a complex matter, ranging from imposed to habitual to accidental or carefully chosen options. If the choice of a course of action is neither accidental nor imposed, deliberations about the legitimacy of courses of action are based, for example, on patterns of world views, ideas, social imageries (Taylor, 2004), or moral convictions.

Transforming knowledge into processes and (processed) things

The definition of knowledge as a capacity for action has a number of advantages. For example, it implies that knowledge for action always has multi-faceted implications and consequences. The term *capacity* for action signals, as I have already implied, that knowledge may be left unused; it may be employed for irrational ends; it may be unable to be mobilized to change reality; or general opposition and resistance to novel capacities of action may be considered a virtue in some social circles. Different world views, ideas, social imageries, and cultural and moral convictions lead to various efforts to suppress capacities to act that actually exist. The economist and sociologist Werner Sombart (1934:266), under the heading of the "taming of technology," calls for the creation by the state of a Cultural Affairs Commission, whose mandate it will be to decide whether "an invention should be discarded, passed on to a museum or whether it should be realized in practice." Such efforts at controlling knowledge include legal regulations imposed by the state or actions by civil society organizations.[38] What is at stake involves what should be called "knowledge politics" (cf. Stehr, 2005).

The thesis that knowledge (including technical knowledge) is, in the absence of friction, inevitably pushed to its limit and that it is autonomously realized and implemented almost without regard for its consequences (as argued, for instance, by C. P. Snow [cf. Sibley, 1973]), represents a fatalistic view that is not uncommon among observers of major technological developments, for example. Even if the realization of knowledge claims is not seen to have quasi-automatic practical qualities, the inevitable and rapid translation of knowledge into practice might be seen to follow from the widely shared conviction, as expressed by Werner

---

coordinate their actions, realize that something is going wrong; that they cannot get along any more; that something has to change."

[38] David Edgerton (2011) sums up the "meaningful" resistance to innovative capacities to act under the heading "In praise of Luddism."

Sombart (1934:262), for example, that "we are now used to it that everything we are capable to do and execute, will in fact be done and executed."

However, the notion that science and technology inherently and inevitably force their own realization in practice fails to give proper recognition, by assuming such automaticity in the realization of technical and scientific knowledge, to the context of its implementation (also Heilbroner, [1967] 1994). Any conception of the immediate practical efficacy of scientific and technological knowledge (for example, in the sense that "there is nothing as practical as a good theory") overestimates the "built-in" or inherent practicality of knowledge claims fabricated in science. Suffice to say at this point that the implementation of knowledge as a capacity for action relies upon existing frameworks and conditions of social action (Grundmann and Stehr, 2012).[39]

It would be equally misleading to conclude that the conception of knowledge as a capacity for action, and not as something – using the most traditional contrasting imagery – that we know to be true, supports a reversal of the metaphor "knowledge is power" into "power equals knowledge." Indeed, the implementation of knowledge requires more than knowing how to put something into motion. Getting things done can at times be quite difficult. As T. S. Eliot perceptively notes in his poem *The Hollow Men* (1925): "Between the idea / And the reality / Between the motion / And the act / Falls the Shadow." The realization of capacities for action, on the one hand, and the power – or, rather, control – over some of the circumstances of action, on the other hand, are allies. The relation is not symmetric. Knowledge does not always lead to power. Power does not lead to knowledge, nor does power always rely on knowledge (cf. Touraine, 2001). Nonetheless, an important but open and contested question is how knowledge production and the circulation of knowledge are coproduced by power structures.

The sheer incapacity of a person or a group of persons to translate knowledge into action does not necessarily mean that the person or group lacks *political liberty*, either with reference to a specific situation

---

[39] A plausible example for the linkage – that is, the potential distance between knowledge and action – is provided by a study carried out by Stephanie Snow (2012:1). Snow examined the implementation of a new understanding of strokes as an emergency condition that lead to medical procedures adopted within a short period of time in hospitals in England and other countries. Snow summarizes the findings of her study: "The challenges of implementation stemmed from organisational and professional barriers rather than scientific or technological difficulties. Stroke's historical status as a non-treatable illness was a barrier to the adoption of acute treatments. Building new pathways for stroke patients by developing protocols for paramedics and emergency room staff originated as a local solution to a local problem but were taken up widely."

or in a more general sense. If a person is unable to build a house, for example, he or she is likely to be too poor or to lack the necessary resources to realize the goal, but not because he or she is deprived of political liberty. However, if we assume or are proponents of the theory that the missing material resources are solely the result of constraints imposed by other actors – for instance, the state – then the incapacity to realize one's goal is of course the consequence of an absence of political liberties (see also Berlin, [1958] 1969:122–123).

If one refers to "society as a laboratory," as Wolfgang Krohn and Johannes Weyer (1989:349; 1994) do, in order to capture the idea that research processes and the risks associated with them – for example, in the case of nuclear technology, the planting of genetically modified seeds or the use of chemicals with certain undesirable side effects – are transferred outside the established (closed-system) boundaries of science into society, they also alert us to the necessity that the replication of laboratory effects outside the laboratory require as a basic precondition the ability to control the social conditions under which the effect was produced or observable in the first instance. It is only then that the initial observation of an effect can be replicated. This also means that every "realization" of knowledge, not only of major experiments, requires the ability to control the circumstances of social action. Put differently, the "application" of scientific knowledge in society demands an adjustment to the existing conditions of action, or a transformation of social conditions according to the standards set by science (Krohn and Weyer, 1989:354).[40]

In the sense of our definition of knowledge, *scientific and technical* knowledge clearly represent "capacities for action or capacities to intervene." But this does not mean that scientific knowledge should be seen as a resource that is incontestable; that it is not subject to interpretation; that it travels without serious impediments (in the sense, for example, that knowledge travels even more effortlessly than money and spreads instantly)[41]; that it can be reproduced at will; or that it is accessible to

---

[40] A similar inference is drawn by Hans Radder (1986:675) who refers to successful technological production, or the closure of technical systems that require that both material *and* social conditions be satisfied: "The creation and maintenance of particular social conditions (for example, a bureaucratic and centralist administration in the case of nuclear energy) is necessary in order to be able to guarantee the permanent technological success of a project." The control of a closed system outside of the laboratory (or, for that matter, the realization of a thought experiment) requires social power, that is, connecting "experimental or technological success and macro-social factors" (Radder, 1986:664).

[41] As Peter Drucker, for example, speculates in his description of the "next society" (*Economist*, November 1, 2001). Moreover, in this essay Drucker tends to conflate information and knowledge; this conflation is quite common (e.g., Barth, 2002;

all – nor that scientific and technical knowledge primarily conveys unique and generally effective capacities for action.

What counts in modern societies – especially in the sense of gaining advantages in societies that operate according to the logic of economic growth and are dependent on the growing wealth of significant segments of the population – is access to and command of the marginal additions to knowledge, rather than the generally available stock of knowledge, as the motor of incremental modernization seen as an extension process (cf. Kerr, 1963:vii; Stehr, 2001).[42] Although scientific and technical knowledge acquires a most significant role as the source of additional capacities for action in modern societies, the science system is by no means the only source of novel knowledge (cf. Casas-Cortés, Osterwell, and Powell, 2008).

The sociological definition of knowledge as a capacity for action has the benefit of viewing knowledge as a phenomenon that is embedded in social relations, as an agency-related matter and not as a static phenomenon with context-free or context-freeing attributes such as truthfulness, empirical conformity, or objectivity.[43] The sociological, rather than the classical, conception of knowledge[44] also alerts us to the great variation of stocks of knowledge within and among societies, between adults and children, for example; or between advanced and traditional societies. In addition, the notion of knowledge as a capacity for acting on the world makes if evident that knowledge should be distinguished from the much broader concept of "culture" (cf. Barth, 2002:1–2). In order to set something in motion, assisted by knowledge as a capacity for action, we are often able to rely on one of multiple but different capacities for action in order to transform reality (reach a certain goal) in a desired manner. For instance, we are capable of using both knowledge and energy as

---

Kitcher, 2006). Indeed, it is a Sisyphean task to advance opposing arguments for the virtue of differentiating between knowledge and information (cf. Stehr and Adolf, forthcoming).

[42] It is worth noting that Peter Drucker (1969:269) sees the economic benefits of knowledge in "knowledge economy" extend, and to an equal degree, to all forms of knowledge. What counts, he adds, is the applicability of knowledge, not whether it is "old or new." What is relevant in the social system of the knowledge economy is "the imagination and skill of whoever applies it, rather than the sophistication or newness of the information." My assertion, in contrast, would be that it is meaningful to distinguish between the stock of knowledge at hand and the incremental additions to knowledge, or novel capacities for action. The fabrication process, transaction costs, implementation, and return of each form of knowledge are not identical.

[43] Compare the emergence of the notion of "socializing cognition" within the field of cognition science (Böckler et al., 2010).

[44] Following the "classical" definition of knowledge, knowledge is "justified true belief, true opinion combined with reason" (Hilpinen, 1970:109).

capacities for action in order to build different vehicles for the purpose of transporting us to specific destinations.

As I have emphasized, the notion of knowledge as a capacity for action alerts us to be careful about designating knowledge as power, especially the power exercised by the powerful, or about asserting that power equals knowledge. However, the plain designation of knowledge as a capacity for action leaves the linkage between knowledge and governance unexamined. The linkage between knowledge and governance – where the command of knowledge could mean, for instance, the power to *boost* the capacity to govern; or it could just as well mean the ability to *restrain* those who govern from imposing their will on the governed – could be a matter of particular forms of knowledge. Knowledge could refer, for example, to the command of specialized forms of knowledge, such as technical know-how, rather than commonsense knowledge.

First, I will therefore refer to various attempts to classify and distinguish different forms of knowledge. Knowledge could also mean, second, the command (or lack) of different degrees of political knowledge or information as a prerequisite for an "enlightened" participation in the affairs of society. Indeed, social research, especially survey research, into the volume of political knowledge among voters, for example, has a long tradition of supporting the verdict that under most circumstances, the volume of political knowledge of voters is limited. But in this context, as I will try to show, the differentiation between knowledge and information is significant. Third, within the context of a theory of democracy that stresses the strong presence of particular social norms and values as the foundation of democratic governance, knowledge could denote the virtues of ways of producing knowledge embedded in specific moral relations. The scientific community is often cited as just such a social institution that practices and confers these values. Fourth, and most relevant to the core issue under consideration, would be the idea that a "close relative" of knowledge is crucial for a better understanding of the interface between democracy and knowledge. The "close relative" of knowledge I have in mind is knowledgeability. Knowledge and knowledgeability are not identical, nor are knowledge and information. A concise definition of knowledgeability would be the extent to which individuals and collectivities are in charge of their lives, are able to self-organize their lives and are – of particular importance in this inquiry – capable of developing/asserting/being open to new and persuasive ideas. Ideas are statements that recommend themselves as calls for action; for example, "the advance of knowledge is a desirable undertaking." A more detailed explication of the term knowledgeability, and the specific competencies that represent knowledgeability, can be found in the next part of the study. The idea that science is the harbinger of liberty that exemplifies democratic values is examined in a separate section.

In the next section of this chapter, I will pursue in greater detail the issue of what knowledge may be meant when I refer to the basic theme of my inquiry: is liberty a daughter of knowledge? It is indeed knowledge, defined as a capacity for action; but more precisely, it is knowledgeability. And it is in this sense that my inquiry differs fundamentally from the standard literature on the theme of the relation between democracy and knowledge. In the standard literature, the main topic involves consideration of the *political knowledge* of citizens, voters, members of political parties and movements in democratic societies. More accurately, reference to often-lacking political knowledge actually refers to the volume and the kind of *political information* that actors command.

By conflating knowledge and information as assets of citizens and treating them as a foundation for democratic governance and meaningful participation in democratic decision making, or by merely stressing the importance of information, information infrastructure and information resources as crucial attributes for the possibility of democracy, observers tend to reduce the significance of such resources to the question of access and provision of knowledge and/or information (e.g., Webster, 1999:375). Hence, my argument will be that it is important not only to clearly differentiate between knowledge and information, but also to stress the role of knowledgeability for democracy.

Which knowledge is meant, and why?

> Some time during the Age of the Empire [1875–1914] the links had snapped between the finding of scientists and the reality based on, or imaginable by sense experience; and so did the links between science and the sort of logic based on, or imaginable by common sense. Eric Hobsbawm ([1994] 1996:534)

Although the difference between commonsense knowledge (in the sense of knowledge generally available) and specialized knowledge is older, Eric Hobsbawm's dating of the origins of the break between what may be part of ordinary sense experience and what is *not* accessible to regular sense experience, as well as what is imaginable by the logic governing common sense and science, vividly reminds us that our categories of knowledge are sociohistorical constructs.[45]

---

[45] For a discussion of the historical origins of the category of common sense, see Rosenfeld (2008).

The number of well-explicated general definitions of knowledge, forms of knowledge and the complex linkages to other cognitive activities, such as "understanding," has been fairly limited, at least within the field of sociology.[46] In the case of definitions of distinct categories of knowledge, we really have not moved much beyond Max Scheler's proposal, first advanced in the 1920s, of different forms of knowledge. In one of the early contributions to the tradition of the sociology of knowledge, Scheler distinguishes knowledge of salvation (*Heils-* or *Erlösungswissen*), cultural knowledge (*Wesens-* or *Bildungswissen*) and knowledge of domination (*Herrschafts-* or *Leistungswissen*), based on the idea that "each type of knowledge develops its own language and style of expression" (Scheler, [1926] 1992:209). Moreover, each form of knowledge is linked to specific roles: practical knowledge is associated with the scientist and the engineer, cultural knowledge is related to the sage, and knowledge of salvation to the saint. In the great civilizations, one or the other knowledge type tends to predominate.

For Scheler, knowledge serves a becoming; more precisely, the becoming of a different reality. Depending on what kind of becoming knowledge serves, Scheler distinguishes cultural knowledge, which enables the individual to enlarge and clarify his identity, from knowledge of salvation, a form of metaphysical knowledge "by which the nucleus" of a person "seeks to partake in ultimate being and the very *source* of all things," and knowledge of domination or control, which "in a practical way, serves the transformation of the world" (Scheler, [1926] 1992:42).

From a contemporary perspective, especially a philosophy of science perspective, it is remarkable that Scheler refers to knowledge of salvation, which transcends the domain of the life-world. The willingness to affix the label of knowledge to metaphysical assertions is in the following centuries replaced within the philosophy of science – especially in the positivistic traditions – by an insistence on a strong differentiation of metaphysical claims from scientific knowledge. It is only with the development of the modern sociology of knowledge that the robust dichotomy between these forms of knowledge is no longer taken for granted; and as a result, one might speak of a belated rehabilitation of Scheler's category of knowledge of salvation (cf. Stehr and Meja, 2005).

Scheler ([1926] 1960:207), for example, asserts essentially the same fateful development. Of the three ideal types of knowledge that he

---

[46] One example of the complex relation between knowledge and other cognitive activities, given such a definition, might be sufficient: Hannah Arendt (1953:380) maintains that there is a symmetric relation between knowledge and understanding; that is, there is no knowledge without understanding and no understanding without knowledge.

identifies, only the last type of knowledge – the ability to control and produce effects – has been ever more exclusively cultivated in the Occident for the purpose of "changing the world," while knowledge of culture and knowledge of salvation have been successively relegated to the background (cf. also Scheler, [1925] 1958:43).

What is even more commonly found, as has been indicated, are dichotomous distinctions between forms of knowledge, most prominently the demarcation between scientific and everyday, or commonsense, knowledge (Berger and Luckmann, 1966). Most often, this distinction is based on epistemological considerations. Knowledge produced through scientific research is of superior quality; it has distinctive patterns of justifications; it is closer to or conforms with reality; it lacks irrational qualities; it is more "truthful" than everyday knowledge; and, last but not least, it is practically much more efficient in everyday life, as the success of technology, based on scientific knowledge, conclusively demonstrates.

As Russell Hardin (2003:4) is therefore able to stress:

Ordinary knowledge is almost entirely grounded in hearsay from a supposedly credible or even authoritative source, although commonly the credentials of the source are not compelling, and perhaps even more commonly we can no longer remember the source or its quality. Nevertheless, we will typically not double-check what our newspaper or encyclopedia or even our memory says; we will stop our inquiry sooner rather than later.

In the meantime, the dichotomy between everyday and scientific knowledge has itself become taken for granted; as a result, nonscientific knowledge is at best a residual category. As a consequence, the social sciences have hardly dealt systematically with the peculiarities and status of everyday knowledge;[47] especially as the assumption prevails, at least in the context of classical sociological theories of society,[48] that traditional and conventional forms of knowledge will sooner or later be completely displaced by scientific forms of knowledge even in everyday life.

The point of departure of such a widely held view among social scientists – past and, to a lesser extent, present – is, as Peter Weingart (1983:228) perceptively points out, that our primary means of action orientation are replaced "in more and more spheres of life, by the production and application of systematic knowledge"; and that this process of replacement occurs as different aspects of life successively

---

[47] Steven Lukes (2007), however, has recently made an interesting effort to examine the issue of apparently irrational beliefs in everyday life.
[48] The exceptions among classical social theories would include the theory of society developed by Vilfredo Pareto, or Sigmund Freud's psychoanalysis.

become the object of scientific scrutiny. Concretely, the displacement in dominant forms of knowledge implies that on the basis of scientific knowledge, "different frames of reference and modes of attribution are established for social action and/or existing orientations are proven to be irrational or erroneous with respect to accepted purposes." The result, according to Weingart, is that "reflective reasoning, in light of competing components of systematic knowledge, takes the place of the internalization—on which its taken for granted status depends in the first place—of norms and values."

A slightly different dichotomy between (highly specialized) knowledge and everyday, nonrational knowledge is also frequently advanced, since specialized knowledge claims are often equated with scientific knowledge. As a result, this dichotomy, too, reduces itself to the asymmetrically expressed differentiation between scientific and other forms of knowledge encountered in society, which despite their longevity and practical utility come to be seen as tenuous ideas and opinions. Overall, our prevailing views about what is knowledge are driven by epistemological positions that rely on a strict separation between scientific and nonrational knowledge. Social scientists have interpreted demarcations of this kind as a strong hint that there exists a sensible division of labor between epistemology and specific fields of scientific activity. Indeed, the taboo against a sociological analysis of the content of scientific knowledge was largely respected until a few years ago.

It is unavoidable, especially in the context of the relation between knowledge and democracy, to take up the contentious question of the relation/difference between knowledge and information. In my view, the basic difference between knowledge and information first of all pertains to the available volume of information and knowledge in modern societies: Information is plentiful and inexpensive, although by no means without significant restrictions on access (Galison, 2004). Knowledge is scarce and expensive – in ways that need to be and will be specified.[49] In addition, and more importantly, the difference between knowledge and information refers, secondly, to the kind of "work" that information and knowledge are capable of accomplishing in society; for example, in the case of information such work extends to the ability of information to represent a calculus capable of making otherwise quite different products appear commensurate.

---

[49] Peter H. Lyman, Hal R. Varian, et al. (2003), "How much information?," www.sims.berkeley.edu/how-much-info-2003 (accessed December 24, 2011). See also Rowley, 2007 on the so-called "Knowledge hierarchy" ranging from data through information and knowledge to wisdom.

Information and knowledge

Before attempting to further differentiate between knowledge and information and explore their relations – without wanting to argue that the two phenomena stand in full isolation from each other – the initial dilemma that has to be addressed explicitly is whether it is sensible or even possible to distinguish between them, especially in light of the fact that in contemporary analysis they are often employed as virtual equivalents in scientific and everyday discourse (e.g., Stewart, 1997; Faulkner, 1994:426; Gossner, 2010).

However, I would like to present some considerations in favor of the need to distinguish between information and knowledge, and the benefits of doing so. Given that, among other factors, the semantics of information and knowledge have changed over time, it would be misleading to argue that today there is only one solitary distinction between information and knowledge. It is equally important to stress from the outset that knowledge and information have attributes in common. Their most important common attribute is that neither information nor knowledge is self-evident and free of context. Nor should it be forgotten that both information and knowledge usually are communicated to represent true claims and often are understood as such. However, I would like to suggest that a breakdown of the unity of knowledge and information is of value.

It is my contention – obviously focusing less on the symbolic infrastructures or media in which knowledge and information may be embedded – that the substance of information primarily concerns the properties of products or outcomes,[50] while the stuff of knowledge refers to the qualities of processes, operations or inputs.[51] As a result, knowledge is not only embedded in texts, unless one imagines the world as being a world of texts, but is also materialized in (processed) things, infrastructures, and ways of living (see Hörning, 2001:190), as is energy.

---

[50] I do not want to suggest that information, given my definition, carries no meaning; the price of a product or a certificate attached to it exemplifies information, and information about the product also carries meaning; for example, the price may reflect the social desirability of a product and the certificate the moral status of a product (as in the sense that a more expensive variety may signal its environmental quality). By the same token, the information conveyed by social statistics is not necessarily (only) a reflection of social reality, but rather an explication of its problems; they refer to what could be, and in this sense they confer meaning to options for action to be taken.
[51] Along the same lines, another tempting difference between information and knowledge would be to refer to information as information of bodies and knowledge as knowledge of minds, or the difference between signals (knowledge) and noises (data, information). In our world, the volume of noises (big data) grows exponentially while our knowledge increases at a much slower pace (cf. Silver, 2012).

38 Coming to terms

But before I attempt to explicate in more detail the distinction between information and knowledge as a distinction between attributes of product and process, a discussion of the various other ways of linking the two concepts is in order.

Many dictionaries and scholarly treatises simply define information as a certain kind of knowledge,[52] or refer to the apparent ease with which knowledge is converted into information.[53] A similar symmetry between information and knowledge is evident if one defines information as "knowledge reduced and converted into messages that can be easily communicated among decision agents" (Dasgupta and David, 1994:493). Another way of emphasizing the essential symmetry of information and knowledge is to suggest, from a more historical perspective, that the wide circulation of knowledge converts knowledge into information ("knowledge becomes information when it becomes an object of consensus and gets banalized as 'common knowledge'" [Hecht and Edwards, in Edwards, 2011:1422]).

In yet other definitions of information and knowledge, information is simply conceptualized as a subspecies, an element or the raw material of a number of knowledge forms. For example, knowledge becomes "actionable information" (Jashapara, 2007); information is codified knowledge as well as indirect knowledge (see Borgmann, 1999:49); knowledge is defined as the cumulative stock of information (Burton-Jones, 1999:5); or "information is always only information in the light of certain knowledge" (Abel, 2009:17).[54] Similarly, knowledge in general is

---

[52] At this point, one general and one specific example for the widespread conflation of information and knowledge may suffice: "Information evolved as a category of knowledge ... by comparison with knowledge it has been usually more detached from the theoretical context in which it was produced ... Information is characteristically more restricted to the technical practical surface of knowledge ... Information is often but thin knowledge" (Ezrahi, 2004:257). In the literature dealing with political knowledge, one also frequently encounters statements that join information and knowledge as essentially identical phenomena, and this often despite the explicit rejection of such an identity by the authors: Elo and Rapeli (2011:134) underline that "one of the most crucial weaknesses of scholarly work on political knowledge and its interplay with media has been the insufficient distinction between knowledge and information," only to insist that "contrary to knowledge, *information* refers to an attractively packed, purified, maximally reduced and concentrated piece of knowledge." I will refer to and document the conflation of political information and political knowledge in much of the literature in later sections of the study.

[53] Cases in point are discussions that concern the instrumentalization of knowledge; that is to say, knowledge that is converted into or reduced to information (cf. Malik, 2005:30).

[54] Another notable merging of information and knowledge occurs in the context of normative disputes about withholding or suppressing information for national security purposes. In discussions about keeping information secret, an argument known as the "mosaic" theory is developed. The mosaic theory holds that "seemingly insignificant

Information and knowledge 39

seen to extend to "tacit knowledge" (cf. Polanyi, 1967:204–206) and to other categories of knowledge (Dosi, 1996:84).[55]

But is there such a phenomenon as "tacit" information? The outcome of many efforts to define knowledge and information appears always to remain the same: knowledge and information become indistinguishable (see Wikström and Normann, 1994:100–111).[56] The extent to which the terms *information* and *knowledge* have been made indistinguishable by such a widespread indiscriminate usage raises, last but not least, the problem of the futility of any alternative effort that aims not at conflating, but at distinguishing their meanings and referents (cf. Malik, 2005). It is self-evident that knowledge loses much of its privileged position if it is conflated with information.

In spite of the apparent appeal of conflating information and knowledge, efforts are launched from time to time to differentiate between information and knowledge. Starbuck (1992:716), for example, suggests that knowledge refers to a stock of expertise and not to a flow of information.[57] Thus, knowledge relates to information in the way that capital or assets connect to income. Kenneth Boulding (1965:103–104) warns that we should not regard knowledge as a mere accumulation of

---

information may become significant when combined with other information" (Jaffer, 2010:873). In the end, the argument goes, combining many bits and pieces of innocuous information allows for insights into how the whole operates.

[55] In his monograph *Economics of Knowledge*, Dominiqie Forey (2006:4) opts for a definition of information that resonates with Dosi's definition of information: "Information ... takes the shape of structured and formatted data that remain passive and inert until used by those with the knowledge needed to interpret and process them." Information is subordinate to knowledge. The reproduction of information in turn is based on the straightforward economic principle of a doubling.

[56] One of many examples that could be quoted in support of my observation about the frequent conflation of information and knowledge in – not only – the social science literature: Frank Webster (1999:374), in an essay on "knowledgeability and democracy in an information age," observes that "in a healthy democracy, so runs the argument, if citizens are to play a full part in the political process, then they must have made available to them the knowledge that allows for effective engagement." In the same paragraph he adds: "It follows logically that appropriate information is a mainstay of the democratic process." Essentially the same usage of concepts may be found in the following observation by Webster (1999:375), "while I would not dissent from the view that what might be called 'social information' is a prerequisite of democracy, I am reluctant to endorse the argument that more knowledge, in itself, is a positive development." A frequently noted dictum from 1822 in a letter to W. T. Barry by the fourth United States President, James Madison, does exactly the same, treating knowledge and information as interchangeable.

[57] Insofar as knowledge acquires a superior intellectual reputation, it is easy to understand that – as Brown and Duguid ([2000] 2002:119) note – "people are increasingly eager that their perfectly respectable cache of information be given the cachet of knowledge." One of the consequences of such efforts is that the regions of overlap or mixture between knowledge and information are strengthened.

information. Knowledge, in contrast to information, has a structure: sometimes it is a loose network, sometimes a quite complex set of systemic interrelations. Fritz Machlup (1983:644) refers to the possibility that one may acquire new knowledge without receiving new information. Summing up the distinction between knowledge and information, Machlup prefers to claim "information in the sense of telling and being told is always different from knowledge in the sense of knowing. The former is a process, the latter a state. Information in the sense of that which is being told *may* be the same as knowledge in the sense of that which is known, but *need* not be the same." The act of delivering (information) is one side of the coin, the "object" that is being delivered (knowledge) the other (also Machlup, 1984:63–65).[58]

Brown and Duguid ([2000] 2002:119–120) stress that knowledge, in contrast to information, has at least three distinctive attributes. First, knowledge usually entails a knower; second, knowledge is harder to detach than information; and third, knowledge requires a greater effort of assimilation: "knowledge is something we digest rather than merely hold." But only rarely, in definitions designed to differentiate between information and knowledge, does one find any reference to practical usefulness or correctness as salient characteristics of knowledge and information.

If there is another side to the ledger, it is the *unease* with the practice of liberally conflating information and knowledge both in everyday life and in scholarly reflections, and reducing or extending them to an all-inclusive "mental material," as viewed by many. It is true, of course, that in public places such as airports, shopping centers, or train stations, one rarely finds a counter or booth marked "knowledge" rather than "information." It is likely, however, that prevailing practices of conflating knowledge and information – for example, in legal (cf. Easterbrook, 1982) and economic discourse – will prove to be more persuasive than efforts designed to distinguish between them. After all, who is able to clearly distinguish between the information and the knowledge society?[59]

---

[58] In his classic study, *The Production and Distribution of Knowledge in the United States*, in which Fritz Machlup (1962:15) attempts to empirically measure the size of the knowledge and information-based economy, he calls for a close bond of information and knowledge: "Linguistically, the difference between knowledge and information lies chiefly in the verb form: to *inform* is an activity by which knowledge is conveyed; to know may be the result of having been informed. 'Information' as the act of informing is designed to produce a state of knowing in someone's mind. 'Information' as that which is being communicated becomes identical with 'knowledge' in the sense of that which is known."

[59] My effort to find a sociologically adequate difference between information and knowledge is oriented as well as developed in distinction to an observation by Warren Weaver (1949:4) in his seminal essay "Recent contributions to the mathematical theory

An equally formidable barrier to any new or renewed attempt to sociologically separate knowledge and information (and/or to point to their commonalities) is the almost insurmountable mountain of competing conceptions of knowledge and/or information embedded in and indebted to multiple epistemological perspectives or pragmatic purposes. Knowledge and information may be distinguished based on economic considerations or other social points of reference: the different ways in which they are produced, stored, diffused, consulted, and applied; their typical carriers and the distinct social consequences they may be seen to have in society. I will refer to some relevant conceptions of knowledge *and* information, thereby recognizing the tremendous difficulties faced by efforts to sustain and codify differences between knowledge and information.

One of the more traditional and, in many languages, entrenched distinctions among knowledge forms is the opposition – as explicated by William F. James – between *knowledge of acquaintance* and *knowledge-about* (in theory). Though these terms appear to be somewhat clumsy in English, they signify an asymmetrical dichotomy that is present in many languages: as indicated, for example, by the terms *connaître* and *savoir*, *kennen* and *wissen*, or *noscere* and *scire*. And as William F. James (1890:221) observes, with respect to this opposition of these forms of knowing:

I am acquainted with many people and things, which I know very little about, accept their presence in the places where I have met them. I know the color blue when I see it, and the flavor of a pear when I taste it; I know an inch when I move my finger through it; a second in time, when I feel it pass; an effort of attention when I make it; a difference between two things when I notice it; but *about* the inner nature of these facts or what makes them what they are, I can say nothing at all.

For Alfred Schutz (1975:120), in a summary definition of the Jamesian difference between these forms of knowledge, knowledge-about "refers to that comparatively very small sector of which everyone of us has

of communication": "*Information* must not be confused with meaning." Ikujiro Nanoka's (1994:16) example of a telephone bill is relevant in this case: "A telephone bill, is not calculated on the basis of the content of a conversation but according to the duration of time and the distance involved." However, I do not follow Weaver's (1949:4) syntactic definition or his assertion that "information is defined as the *logarithm* of the numbers of choices. The 'bits' communicated are distinguished by what is transported which are either the capacity to set something in motion or as something that conveys attributes of processes and products." Information in a semantic sense can convey a particular view, which in turn is not necessarily identical to the interpretation of the information by the reader or listener, for example the observation that a certain price of goods is outrageous.

thorough, clear, distinct, and consistent knowledge, not only as to the what and how, but also as to the understanding of the why, regarding a sector of which he is a 'competent expert.'" In contrast, knowledge of acquaintance "merely concerns the what and leaves the how unquestioned" (Schutz, 1975:12).

The differences between knowledge of acquaintance and knowledge-about described by William James resonate in turn with Gilbert Ryle's (1945/46; [1949] 2002:27) distinction between *knowing-that* and *knowing-how*. Knowing-that encompasses the knowledge that one is able to articulate, while knowing-how includes in addition what is best described as tacit knowledge; and therefore the volume of the latter is more extensive than that of the former type of knowledge (e.g., Ryle, [1949] 2002:41). The distinction by James and Ryle also suggests a possible difference between information and knowledge, whereby information becomes less penetrating and consequential, and a more superficial and fleeting cognizance of the attributes of a process or the instructions about an object.[60] Knowledge of acquaintance or knowledge of attributes (World Bank, 1999:1) – for example, the quality of a product, the diligence of a worker or the profitability of a company – refer to the presence or absence of information among market participants about relevant economic "data." In this sense, economic discourse has always made reference to the importance of information, but also to incomplete information and its function in pricing mechanisms or market transparency, for instance. The attributes of information in this sense indicate that information plays an instrumental role in social conduct.

But the distinction between knowledge and information, even in its most elementary sense, is not only an asymmetrical dichotomy but also a difference that is supposed to have its dynamic, and even progressive, elements.[61] For what might be called knowledge-about becomes

---

[60] However, Gilbert Ryle ([1949] 2000:56) stresses that knowing-that does not necessarily entail or typically result in knowing-how. But in order to take on board the distinction between knowing-that and knowing-how as the basis of the distinction between information and knowledge, it would be helpful *not* to start the process with a reference to knowledge in general, and therefore try to make the case that the difference between knowing-that and knowing-how is a distinction between *forms of knowledge*; thereby insisting, of course, that information is a form of knowledge.

[61] Debra Amidon (1997:17), who promotes the notion of knowledge management in a knowledge economy, claims that "*knowledge* is information with meaning" and "*information* is data with context." The concepts, in addition, "when applied to any community, ... refer to the sum total of experience and learning that reside within an individual, group, enterprise, or nation." Similarly, in a recent essay that attempts to describe "successful knowledge management projects," one finds the following definition: "knowledge is information combined with experience, context, interpretation, and reflection" (Davenport, DeLong, and Beers, 1998:43). I doubt that

Information and knowledge 43

acquaintance-with as knowledge develops, matures, or becomes more explicit and articulate. James (1890:221) indicates as much when he observes that the two kinds of knowledge are, "as the human mind practically exerts them, relative terms." As a result, the distinction, as later interpretations of James show as well (e.g., Park, 1940), comes closer to the dichotomy between scientific knowledge in the sense of formal, analytic, rational, and systematic knowledge, and "information."

Given the general attention paid to Daniel Bell's (1979) theory of postindustrial society, and the extent to which, for Bell, knowledge is constitutive of such a society, it is worth giving some thought to his definitions of information and knowledge, articulated within the context of his theory of modern society. First, Bell refers to what is an anthropological constant, namely that knowledge has been necessary for the existence of any human society. In other words, knowledge is a basic provision for social relations and social order.

What is therefore new and distinctive about the postindustrial society "is the change in the character of knowledge itself. What has now become decisive for the organization of decisions and the control of change is the centrality of theoretical knowledge – the primacy of the theory over empiricism, and the codification of knowledge into abstract systems of symbols that can be utilized to illuminate many different and varied circumstances. Every modern society now lives by innovation and growth and by seeking to anticipate the future and plan ahead" (Bell, 1968:155–156). However, the distinction between forms of knowledge that have run their course because they "informed" industrial society and theoretical knowledge constitutive of postindustrial society does not necessarily affect Bell's general differentiation between information and knowledge, to which I will now turn.

By information, Bell (1969:168) suggests, "I mean data processing in the broadest sense; the storage, retrieval, and processing of data becomes the essential resource for all economic and social exchanges (in postindustrial society)." Bell's conception of information is indistinguishable from the technical conception of communication, in which the meaning, exchange, and transfer of a piece of information are independent of the carriers (source and receiver) of information. By knowledge, in contrast, he means "an organized set of statements of fact or ideas, presenting a reasoned judgment or an experimental result, which is transmitted to others through some communication medium in some systematic form"

such highly ambivalent notions will take us much beyond treating information and knowledge as black boxes, or the dilemma of conflating information and knowledge.

44   Coming to terms

(Bell, 1979:168).[62] It would appear that the technical conception of communication applies to knowledge as well, although Bell makes implicit reference to the distinct epistemological status (or value) of knowledge and information, which results in a hierarchical and asymmetrical gradient between knowledge and information. As a result, information is easily dubbed "mere" information, while knowledge is methodically generated, sorted and judged. Nonetheless, the dichotomy has strong disembodied strains. That is, there is no reference to the contingent character of information and knowledge, or to the need to interactively render knowledge and information intelligible and negotiate whether it is valuable or appropriate. At least implicitly, the concepts depict innovation and the fabrication of incremental knowledge as a fairly smooth, straightforward, and well-behaved process.

Given Bell's scientific and technological conception of the communication and acquisition of knowledge and information, the strong assumption is that both knowledge and information travel virtually unimpeded. In addition, the linkages, if any, that may exist between information and knowledge remain ambivalent. At best, it would seem that Bell's conception of knowledge and information contains the claim that information is the handmaiden of knowledge. Moreover, this notion tends to be overly confident about the (uncontested?) authority, trustworthiness, and power of information and knowledge. According to Bell, knowledge is primarily abstract, disembodied, formal, individual – and aspires to be universal (or knowledge in space). It seems to me that Bell's interpretation raises more questions than it answers.[63]

A different perspective, offered by an economist, conflates the notion of information with what Bell considers to be the very characteristics that distinguish information from knowledge. Information, it is suggested, "entails well-stated and codified propositions about 'states of the world' (for example, 'it is raining'), properties of nature (for example, 'A causes B') or explicit algorithms on how to do things" (Dosi, 1996:84); knowledge, on the other hand, includes cognitive categories, codes of interpretation of information, tacit skills and problem-solving skills, and

---

[62] Bell (1973: 175), in addition, offers an "operational" definition of knowledge when he indicates that knowledge "is that which is objectively known, an intellectual property, attached to a name or group of names and certified by copyright or some other form of social recognition."

[63] A perhaps somewhat underdeveloped critique of Bell's definition of the term *information* may be found in a recent publication by Schiller (1997:106–109). Schiller emphasizes the positivistic usage of the concept of information by Bell. The positivistic usage implies, first and foremost, that Bell decides to eliminate any reference to social or cultural contexts within which information is generated or deployed.

search heuristics that can be reduced to explicit algorithms. On the basis of this dichotomy, information comes close to or is even identical with what many conceptualize as codified knowledge; while knowledge, in this case, is close to the notion of tacit knowledge; and tacit knowledge becomes the key to interpreting knowledge (cf. Dosi, 1996:82–86).[64]

Tacit knowledge represents, if one follows Polanyi's (1967:204–206) classic definition, knowledge elements that are defined only fleetingly, are passed primarily orally, are characterized by a high degree of dependence on person and context and therefore cannot be explicitly taught or appear in textbooks and curricula. Knowledge and information are at least implicitly almost always inseparably welded together (e.g., Wikström and Normann, 1994:10–11; Malik, 2005) or are defined as a bridge between information and knowledge (e.g., Luhmann, 2002b:99). In any case, the conceptual fusion of knowledge and information is an unmistakable sign that knowledge has lost its privileged position. At the same time the close equation of knowledge and information eliminates or suppresses a number of interesting (interdisciplinary) questions (see also Fuller, 2002:16–20). I would like to highlight some of these topics that favor a separation of information and knowledge in some detail below.

Nonetheless, a discussion of the interrelation between knowledge and information provides an opportunity to summarily recapitulate some of the comments we have made about the role of knowledge in social affairs. Knowledge, as we have defined it, constitutes a capacity for action. Knowledge is a model for reality. Knowledge enables an actor, in conjunction with control over the contingent circumstances of action, to set something in motion and to structure reality. Knowledge allows an actor or actors to generate a product or some other outcome. Knowledge is ambivalent, open, and hardly blind to the specific meaning that knowledge claims contain. But knowledge is only a necessary, and not a sufficient, capacity for action. As indicated, in order to set something into motion or generate a product, the circumstances within which such action is contemplated must be subject to the control of the actor. Knowledge that pertains to moving a heavy object from one place to the next is insufficient to accomplish the movement. In order to accomplish the transfer, one needs control over some medium of transportation that can be used for moving heavy objects, for example. The value that resides in knowledge, however, is relational in the sense that it is linked to

---

[64] The terms "tacit knowledge" or "local knowledge" find increasing usage in the social sciences, but their definition is essentially contested (compare the extensive documentation of the different usages of the terms *tacit* or *local knowledge* in science studies by Cambrosio and Keating, 1998).

its capacity to set something into motion. Yet knowledge always requires some kind of attendant interpretive skills and a command of the situational circumstances. In other words, knowledge – its acquisition (see Carley, 1986), dissemination and realization – requires an active actor, a knower who "has a particular history, social location and point of view" (Oyama, 2000:147). Knowledge involves appropriation and transaction, rather than mere consumption or assimilation. It demands that something be done within a context that is relevant beyond being the situation within which the activity happens to take place. Knowledge is conduct. Knowing, in other words, is (cognitive and collective) doing and the active accomplishment of multiple actors.[65]

In contrast, the function of information, as we would see it, is both more restricted and more general. Information is something actors have and get. It can be reduced to "taking something in." Information can be condensed into quantifiable forms. It is therefore possible and sensible to conclude that someone has more information than someone else. It is much more difficult and contentious to conclude that one person commands more knowledge than another person.

In its compacted form, information can migrate more easily. Information does require sophisticated cognitive skills but places fewer intellectual demands on potential users. Information is immediately productive, but not necessarily politically neutral (Burke, 2000:116–148). This applies, for example, to maps, timetables, legal records, charts, bibliographies, censuses, questionnaires, directories, and so forth. In many instances, there is no need to be the master over the conditions of its implementation, as is the case for knowledge as capacity for action. Information is more general. Information is not as scarce as knowledge. It is much more self-sufficient. Information travels and is transmitted with fewer context-sensitive restrictions. Information is detachable. Information can be detached from meaning. It tends to be more discrete than knowledge. In addition, the access to and the benefits of information are not only (or not as immediately) restricted to the actor or actors who come into possession of information. Information is not as situated as is knowledge.[66]

---

[65] It is mainly for this reason that Blackler (1995:1022) suggests that knowledge is "embrained" (dependent on conceptual skills and cognitive abilities), "encultured" (dependent on processes of achieving mutual understanding), "embedded" (dependent on systematic routines), "embodied" (dependent on action), and "encoded" (dependent on signs and symbols) – that is, located in brains, dialogue, and symbols. Needless to say, such a conception of knowledge makes it a most complex phenomenon, one that is not sufficiently characterized by pointing to a couple of constitutive attributes.

[66] If I am not mistaken, the description of the resource that information typically conveys and that is explicated here resonates with Gregory Bateson's (1972:482) definition of

Information, in comparison to knowledge, can have a very high depreciation rate over time. The information that share X is a good buy rapidly loses its value. The information about the value of purchasing the share quickly depreciates, and does so not only as a result of its wide communication and the possibility that many will follow the advice. In other words, information may quickly reach its marginal utility. If, however, one wants to ensure that information depreciates quickly, one should act, and encourage others to act, according to the information.

The use of knowledge can also be quite restricted and limited in its use-value, however, because knowledge alone does not allow an actor to set something into motion, though information may be a step in the acquisition of knowledge. The acquisition of knowledge is more problematic. In general, a simple and quite straightforward model of communication is appropriate for the purposes of tracing the "diffusion" or transfer of information. Whether it is even possible to speak of a transfer of knowledge is doubtful. The "transfer" of knowledge is part of a learning and discovery process that is not necessarily confined to individual learning.[67] Knowledge is not a reliable "commodity." It tends to be fragile and demanding, and has built-in insecurities and uncertainties.

---

information as "news of a difference." Elsewhere, Bateson (1972:381) indicates that information is that which "*excludes* certain alternatives." That is, according to classical information theory, as Bruner (1990:4) also stresses, "a message is informative if it reduces certain alternatives." Preexisting codes allow for the reduction of possible alternative choices. However, by defining information as pertaining to "any difference which makes a difference in some later event," Bateson moves the idea of information, it seems to me, closer to the notion of knowledge as a capacity for action, especially if one adds the questions of what difference information makes, or about what and for whom information makes a difference. Niklas Luhmann's (1997:198) central conceptual platform (see Bechmann and Stehr, 2001) allows him to follow Bateson's definition of information as a difference that makes a difference, inasmuch as the "news" – which could be an increase in the population or a change in climatic conditions – alerts a system and thereby triggers new system conditions. But as Luhmann ([1984] 1995:67) therefore also stresses, "a piece of information that is repeated is no longer information.... The information is not lost, although it disappears as an event. It has changed the state of the system and has thereby left behind a structural effect; the system then reacts to and with these changed structures."

[67] In a study of the diffusion of business computer technology, Attewell (1992:6) emphasizes that "implementing a complex new technology requires both individual and organizational learning. Individual learning involves the distillation of an individual's experiences regarding a technology into understandings that may be viewed as personal skills and knowledge. Organizational learning is built out of this individual learning of members of an organization, but it is distinctive. The organization learns only insofar as individual insights and skills become embodied in organizational routines, practices, and beliefs that outlast the presence of the originating individual."

48   Coming to terms

Good examples of information are price advertising and other market information, such as the availability of products (*signaling* function).[68] Such information is easy to get, is often robust and easy to hold, and can certainly be useful. In the context of the modern economy, it is very general and widely available, but the consequences of having such information as such are minimal. From the point of view of a consumer, price information combined with knowledge about the workings of the marketplace may constitute a capacity to effectuate some savings. But information about prices does not enable us to generate insights into the advantages or disadvantages of the different economic regimes within which such prices are generated. A comparative analysis of distinct economic systems and the benefits they may have for different groups of actors requires special economic knowledge.

Not unlike language, information has attributes, especially on the supply side, ensuring that it constitutes – certainly to a greater extent than is the case for knowledge – a public good. It is not enabling, in the sense of allowing an actor to generate a product. Information merely reflects the attributes of products from which it is and can be abstracted. Knowledge refers to and specifies attributes of process or input, while information refers to attributes of product or output (state). As Charles Lindblom (1995:686) explains with respect to the attributes of commodities and services and the decisions consumers make about commodities and services, in many instances in the marketplace, "how and where the refrigerator was made, whether the work force was well treated, whether the process produced harmful wastes, and the like, you have no control over and little knowledge of." The consumer is typically informed about the price of the fridge, the energy efficiency, the life expectancy, the warranty, the colors, the volume it may hold, the size, and so on. None of the information provided enables you to find out about the process of building the refrigerator, let alone the ability to construct it yourself.

---

[68] Albert Borgmann (1999:1–2), in his delineation of information and types of information, also emphasizes the signaling function of information; in addition, he differentiates between "natural" or immediate, "cultural," and "technological" information. The acquisition, the nature of the embeddedness in specific contexts (for example, technical or cultural artifacts such as maps of the transmission), and the transmission of the information all play a role in assigning information to a particular category. For the time being, these types of information, which emerged in different historical periods, continue to coexist in modern society. However, Borgmann (1999:2) is skeptical that the coexistence will last: "Today the three kinds of information are layered over one another in one place, grind against each other in a second place, and are heaved and folded up in a third. But clearly technological information is the most prominent layer of the contemporary cultural landscape, and increasingly it is more of a flood than a layer, a deluge that threatens to erode, suspend, and dissolve its predecessors."

Why should knowledge or information be a political asset?

Among the core issues of my inquiry into the linkage between knowledgeability and liberty is of course the question of why knowledge (not information) should be considered – or, in fact, is – a political asset for and in democracies. In order to advance my argument, I will first list some of the major theoretical and empirical observations that suggest a close linkage between knowledge per se and the kind of political regime that is possible under conditions of an often differential access to and command of knowledge. For heuristic purposes, the focus will be on assertions that see the widespread grasp of (rational) knowledge, intellectual skills, and the level of formal education generally by the citizens of a state as a crucial asset when it comes to the very possibility of democracy and its survival over time.

The idea is that knowledge is constitutive for specific value commitments that are conducive to the workings of a democratic society; knowledge strengthens the rejection of political beliefs that would question the virtue of democratic ideals; knowledge supports the capacity to engage in rational dialogue and reduces doubts that one is able to participate meaningfully in political discourse; knowledge enhances the comprehension of some of the salient attributes of democratic regimes, for example, the existence and the legitimacy of social cleavages; knowledge allows for the proper evaluation of policy alternatives, and provides enabling intellectual skills for the assessment of competing political goals. In an even more general sense, and as noted in Philip Kitcher's (2006:1205) reflections about the association between democracy and knowledge, advances in knowledge should go hand in hand with advances in the development of the political institutions of societies. Although Kitcher stipulates such a nexus, he quickly points out that the political realities do not favor it.

One of the foremost theoreticians of democracy, Robert A. Dahl, refers in this context to the analogous need for an enlightened understanding on the part of citizens concerning the nature of political matters as a core requisite and attribute of democracy. With the term *enlightened understanding*, Dahl (1994:30–31; also Dahl, 1977:11) wants to stress that democracy cannot simply be justified by summing up the unarticulated, uninformed opinions of a majority of citizens, which should then be translated into political action: "It is foolish and historically false to suppose that enlightenment has nothing to do with democracy.... . Because advocates of democracy have invariably recognized this, they have also placed a great stress on the means to an informed and enlightened citizenry, such as education, discussion, and public deliberation." The call for an enlightened understanding of political issues and decisions by the citizens implies that governments ought to be evaluated according to the opportunities they furnish for the acquisition of knowledge – and for state-offered alternative learning opportunities offered by the state – and their capacity to ensure that the required enlightened understanding is in fact achieved (cf. Dahl, 1977:12).

The criterion of enlightened understanding is not only, as Dahl (1977:18) accepts, one of the most difficult to put into practice, but also the most resistant – among the three criteria he enumerates as constitutive for a procedural democracy[69] – when it comes to defining it with any precision. The problem, of course, is to determine what exactly constitutes an enlightened understanding; how access to such knowledge can be gained; how comprehensive it should be; how difficult it is to acquire; and which resources and efforts the state, or for that matter the citizens, are required to mobilize. These important questions remain unanswered.[70] Dahl (1977:18) offers an idea about the limits to which such a demand can be pushed: "It would be profoundly unrealistic today to expect citizens, even highly educated ones, to have enough technical knowledge" to enter, for example, into the technical economic discourse about the trade-offs between inflation and unemployment. One general, and possibly the most important answer to these difficult questions, is that they are the unplanned and unanticipated consequences of the transformation of modern societies into knowledge societies.

Seymour Martin Lipset (1959:79) counts the collective educational accomplishments of a society among the most important requisites of democratic states. The association between educational level and democracy is not without remarkable deviant cases, as the cases of National Socialism in Germany and Fascism in Italy or the appeal of authoritarianism to parts of the intelligentsia demonstrate. Detractors of the role and influence of schooling on democratic beliefs might argue that the actual educational practices found in many schools are more effective in limiting sentiments for liberty and experiences of liberty: regimentation, discipline, the suppression of creativity and curiosity, to name but a few traits of regimes of schooling, are hardly promising foundations for sentiments and experiences of liberty.[71]

---

[69] Aside from the criterion of enlightened understanding, the doctrine of procedural democracy, in relation to its citizens, rests on the criteria "political equality" and "effective participation." It is easy to surmise that the three criteria are closely intertwined.

[70] See my subsequent excursus on "How much knowledge do we need, and how expensive should knowledge be?"

[71] Seymour Martin Lipset (1959:70) suggests that the "statistical preponderance of evidence supporting the relationship of a variable such as education to democracy

If we follow Lipset's considerations, it is not so much the volume of knowledge or information that citizens command that impacts the relation between democracy and knowledge, but rather the importance of democracy-enhancing individual and collectively shared value-orientations or, as Robert Dahl (1977:1) argues, "the ways in which we think about ourselves as a people," that support the existence and the stability of democracy. Of course, as Lipset, (1959:79) also notes, value-orientations and educational achievement are connected:

> Education presumably broadens men's outlook, enables them to understand the need for norms of tolerance, restrains them from adhering to extremist and monistic doctrines, and increases their capacity to make rational electoral choices.

Harold D. Lasswell (1966:36) suggests that particular patterns of value distribution (as objects of human desire) are characteristic of a free society; a democratic society hinges on the proper distribution in society of the interrelated values of power (in the sense of the ability to participate in political decisions), respect (the ability to freely express oneself), and knowledge (factual knowledge of the potentialities of human beings):

> Where the dignity of man is fully taken into account, power is shared, respect is shared, knowledge is shared. A society in which such values are widely shared is a free society.... Wherever power is shared it is easier to maintain a sharing of respect and knowledge.

The case for the desirability of an equal distribution of knowledge as a foundation for realizing democratic governance is made by Lasswell (1966:45) as follows: "If democratic forms of power are to be full-blooded with reality, the overwhelming mass of mankind must be provided with enough intellectual skills to make proper evaluation of policy goals and alternatives."[72]

Aside from assertions about the general virtue of knowledge for democracy, we find a large number of empirical studies assessing the political knowledge of the population. The data that have accumulated are

---

indicates that the existence of deviant cases (such as Germany, which succumbed to dictatorship in spite of an advanced educational system) cannot be the sole basis for rejecting the hypothesis." The deviant case of Germany, however, also signals that a higher educational level of the population can be associated with indoctrination into undemocratic convictions.

[72] The practical realization of the widely shared value of possessing power, respect and knowledge is conditioned by sets of other social factors that may either enhance or retard their social distribution. Most recently, Wilkinson and Pickett (2009) have examined the empirical association between the overall distribution of income in a society and various other individual attributes, such as health.

abundant. The search for ways of measuring and assessing the role of political knowledge is based on assumptions similar to those that see an overall benefit for democracies populated by well-informed citizens. But how well-informed is well-informed (see Schutz, 1946)? I will address this issue at greater length in a later in chapter 6 discussing what is called the "political knowledge" of voters and citizens in contemporary societies. What should already be stressed is that political knowledge is most often defined as "factual information about politics that is stored in long-term memory" (Carpini and Keeter, 1996:10).[73]

Michael Delli Carpini and Scott Keeter (1996:272) have reviewed the extensive data about what Americans know about politics. Their conclusion is that political knowledge in the sense just defined makes a difference. Citizens who are better informed are "more likely to participate in politics, more likely to have meaningful, stable attitudes on issues, better able to link their interests with their attitudes, more likely to choose candidates who are consistent with their own attitudes, and more likely to support democratic norms." Nonetheless, we need to ask not the normative question, "Who should rule?" but rather the empirical question, "Who actually rules in democratic societies?"[74]

Democracy: who rules?

After severe setbacks during the first decades of the last century – in 1941 there were only eleven democracies left in the world (cf. Keane, 2009:xxiii) – it is during the latter part of the twentieth century that democracy has become a dominant belief and reality throughout much of the world.[75] Although democracy commands wide respect around the globe as the most desirable form of political rule, democracy is neither universally practiced nor everywhere accepted. Democratic governance

[73] See in addition the research undertaken in 1994 by Schuman and Corning (2000) in which they attempted to ascertain the "knowledge" (actually information) of their Russian respondents about various historical events during the past six decades in Russia and the Soviet Union.
[74] Karl Popper ([1960] 1968:25) calls questions such as "Who should rule?" questions that are authoritarian in spirit. Such a question provokes an authoritarian answer, such as "the best" or "the wisest." In the question, "Who should rule?," "should" ought to be replaced – in the spirit of critical rationalism – by a "completely different question such as 'How can we organize our political institutions so that bad or incompetent rulers ... cannot do too much damage'."
[75] Compare the results of the *World Values Survey* about the extent to which democracy is supported worldwide. The survey data indicate that "in country after country throughout the world, a clear majority of the population endorses democracy" (Inglehart, 2003:51). *Gallup* survey results also indicate that democracy is the political regime most preferred by citizens around the world (Gallup-International, 2005).

has now "achieved the status of being taken to be generally right. The ball is very much in the court of those who want to rubbish democracy to provide justification for that rejection" (Sen, 1999:5). In short, the coexistence of liberties and democratic governance – especially in its populist conception – is a close one, even though democracies have abused individual freedoms and rights.[76] However, in many democratic countries, the general affirmation of democratic principles and ideals goes hand in hand with a sense of widespread disenchantment regarding the actual accomplishments of representative democracy (cf. Norris, 2011a:236–246).[77]

Moreover, contemporary economic, political, cultural, technical and social developments, and crises mean that new and different forms of democracy,[78] as compared to the past, are bound to emerge in the future. One of the most salient challenges to contemporary forms of democracy, as I will point out below, is posed by global problems, but also by global promises and the need for future forms of global governance. That regional or national actors are increasingly powerless to address and deal with problems and opportunities that know no boundaries is widely taken for granted. But whether democratic global governance (without the disenfranchisement of social actors; cf. Fisher and Green, 2004) is possible, as is fervently hoped in many quarters, remains an as yet completely

---

[76] Indeed, some measure of freedom is the essential element of democracy. As a result, and as Samuel Huntington (1984:194) expects, the "long term effect of the operation of democratic politics is probably to broaden and deepen individual liberty." Frank H. Knight (1938:318) stresses, in a discussion of the general meaning of democracy, that "the notion of free government represents a paradox, a seeming contradiction. For coercion, the antithesis of freedom, is the essence of government."

[77] In its annual global survey of political conditions, *Freedom House* has noted that democracy since 2000 has not gained much ground around the world but peaked around the same year. In 63 percent of the countries that were independent in 2000, voters could change their government by election (Bitros and Karayiannis, 2013:127). Whether such statistics warrant the conclusion, as Joshua Kurlantzick (2013:6) argues, that "democratic meltdowns... have become depressingly common" is a contested assertion. Perhaps a more considerate conclusion could be that democracies are changing; after all, why should democratic regimes be immune to sociopolitical and socioeconomic transformations?

[78] In the context of postwar discussions of "political development" as a form of modernization (cf. Deutsch, 1961; Huntington, 1965), democratization is but one attribute of political development in addition, for example, to "rationalization," "national integration," and "mobilization or participation." As Samuel P. Huntington (1965:388) has stressed, along with other prominent political theorists of the day (see Almond and Verba, 1963), the culture of political participation "distinguishes modern politics from traditional politics." These observations and sentiments are in strong contrast, of course, to the concerns expressed and witnessed in subsequent decades in modern societies, and not only by political theorists, about the gradual but persistent decline in (formal) political participation.

unanswered question. How will global forms of governance be able to develop, for example, and persist in a manner commensurate not only with the imagination but also with the commitment of their citizens (Anderson, 1991)? Among the other serious challenges faced and the pressures experienced by democracy in nation-states is the great – and recognized – increase in sociocultural, ethnic, and religious diversity, social differentiation and pluralization (see Bohman, 1999a) within society, and the close linkages of such diversity across the narrow boundaries of nation-states (cf. Glazer, 2010; Stepan, Linz, and Yadow, 2010).

Not surprisingly, with the spread of democracy across the world in the last decades, the voices that criticize democracy for various reasons, both from the left and from the right wings of the spectrum of political convictions, have risen as well; in the eyes of some critics, for example, democracy has become *inconvenient*, because democratic regimes in general and nation-state-based democracies in particular appear to be lackluster and ineffective in responding in a timely manner to urgent global crises, such as climate change (e.g., Shearman and Smith, 2007), migration, infectious diseases, terrorism, or the financial crisis.[79] The fundamental political concern is, as it were, globalization without global governance.[80]

In addition, the conclusion that we are living, at least in Western democratic societies, in "postdemocratic conditions" can be encountered more frequently as the main diagnosis of the political nature of modern societies (e.g., Jörke, 2005). The term *postdemocracy* is generally intended to capture the shrinking process of the political power of citizens in modern societies, while the diagnoses of a growing political passivity and powerlessness refers to very different engines of relevant national or international societal developments, including, for example, "consumerism" (Wolin, 2001); the power of the media and public opinion research; global capitalism (Crouch, 2004); or the decline in

---

[79] See my more detailed excursus "An inconvenient democracy" at a later point in this book. The criticism meant here is distinct from the critique issued by the spokespersons of authoritarian regimes; the critique of democratic institutions, on the contrary, is a "carefully argued, social-scientific, and respectable critique of democracy that has been developed largely by Western scholars" (Gilley, 2009:113).
[80] While the majority of observers would concur that we do not, but may yet, need some form of global governance, there are individuals and groups convinced that powerful but secretive forms of global governance already exist (e.g., www.google.se/search?q=global+round+table+club+of+rome&ie=utf-8&oe=utf-8&aq=t&rls=org.mozilla:en-US:official&client=firefox-a, accessed September 20, 2011). However, an examination of whether globalization depoliticizes or contributes to the repoliticization of segments of the public, especially where democratic societies exist, is not part of this inquiry (but see Arce and Kim, 2011).

sovereignty of the nation-state (Hobsbawm, 1996:271–274; Held, 1991:885–887; Dahrendorf, 2002:11).

One of the additional salient themes of recent criticisms of democracy, preferred by the more conservative critics, refers not only to deficiencies of democratic institutions and governance, but also to the lack of capabilities and know-how of ordinary citizens and voters – repeating earlier concerns (e.g., Lippmann, [1922] 1997) about the feasibility of democracy under such conditions, namely the lack of civic competence (Dahl, 1992) – or, more disparagingly, the political ignorance and irrationality of many citizens of democratic states (e.g., Posner, 2003:16; Caplan, 2007; Somin, 2009) as well as their glaring deficit of relevant cognitive skills and knowledge and, therefore, of the ability to participate effectively in political decision-making processes.[81]

Existing democratic regimes take on a wide range of practices and trajectories in the course of history and are quite heterogeneous. Normative accounts and ideals of democracy that try to answer the questions of who rules, what liberties are protected, and what entitlements are respected are equally varied. On these grounds alone, it is not possible to arrive at a consensual definition of democracy (cf. Whitehead, 2011; Markoff, 2011). Democracy is a complex institutional undertaking of balancing forces and ordering expectations, with a view to reaching collectively binding decisions that set incentives, constraints and sanctions for preferred patterns of social conduct. Following Charles Tilly (2007:7), four types of definitions of democracy can be distinguished.[82] The definitions tend to emphasize constitutional (legal norms of the

---

[81] There are numerous contemporary observations in the scientific literature and in the media that deplore the lack of cognitive skills and knowledge among the citizens of modern societies; for example, the energy researcher Vlacav Smil (quoted in an interview with Robert Bryce in the *Energy Tribune* in 2007; see www.robertbryce.com/smil) insists: "There has never been such a depth of scientific illiteracy and basic innumeracy as we see today. Without any physical, chemical, and biological fundamentals, and with equally poor understanding of basic economic forces, it is no wonder that people will believe anything." Other scientists have on occasion used much harsher words to dismiss the public as partners in a conversation about scientific and technological issues (see Mooney, 2010:2). See also the survey results published under the headline "Public praises scientists; scientists fault public, media" and mentioned in a subsequent footnote http://people-press.org/report/528/. I will discuss this and similar assertions, as well as the impact of the lack of knowledge and cognitive skills of society's ordinary members, at greater length in a subsequent part of the study.

[82] In addition to institutional attributes, some conceptions of democracy focus on desirable psychological or personality traits of citizens. Daniel Lerner (1958:59), for example, stresses the importance of empathy, denoting "the general capacity to see oneself in the other fellow's situation, whether favourably or unfavourably." In a later section, the idea of specific psychological attributes as conducive to democratic governance, as enumerated by Bernard Berelson (1952), will be discussed in greater detail.

regime); substantive (conditions of life and politics promoted); procedural (governmental practices); or process-oriented (a minimum set of processes in place) attributes of democratic regimes. The most common definition of democracy in the scientific literature focuses on the institutions and procedures of democratic governance, thus considering institutions and procedures to be a means to an end for the sake of liberty (Popper, [1963] 2012:240).

I will discuss various meanings of the term of democracy, its origins and current realities, responding to the question of who rules or who governs – keeping in mind that it is very difficult to negotiate the traps of what is an essentially contested notion – before I describe what is a realistic conception of the possibility of broad democratic participation and contestation in contemporary society (cf. Huntington, 1984:195).[83] A *realistic* conception of broad democratic participation, and therefore the possibilities of taming and constraining the domination of the most powerful decision makers – for example, through periodic elections – is indebted to the view that our theories should be swayed by the realities of modern society. Among such realistic considerations would be that the "causes" for the transition to and sustainability of democracy do not follow ahistorical patterns, but are themselves subject to secular changes. A standard requirement, however, is that democracies do not exclude *a priori* collectivities that are permanent residents of a country from political participation, for example, those who are not property owners, or those who are women, slaves, poor people, and so forth (cf. Dahl, 1998:37–38).

Until the French Revolution, the notion of democracy was a term found mainly in scholarly discourse. The concept of democracy, then, gradually extends its reach beyond scholarly discourse and acquires a more general meaning, for example, in historical reflections about the past, or as a notion that is applied to problematize contemporary sociopolitical conditions (see Palmer, 1953; Maier, 1971; Williams, 1988). In

---

[83] Compare, for example, the vigorous debate in the late 1960s and 1970s among political philosophers, sociologists, and political scientists about the very idea of democracy: advocates of a purely descriptive and neutral empirical theory of democracy (e.g., Dahl, 1961) found themselves to be the target of extensive criticisms, despite their self-understanding as politically neutral proponents of an essentially ideological and conservative perspective of democracy (e.g., Bay, 1965). In his examination of the debate, Skinner (1973) concludes that, given the arguments put forward by both sides, neither the critics nor the criticized have been able to substantiate their charges or perspectives. As Skinner (1973:303–304) sums up his assessment, the application of the term *democracy* by Dahl and other empirical theorists to the type of political system represented by the contemporary United States has a politically conservative bias; at the same time, the perspectives of the empirical theorists of democracy also represent an argument against those who have sought to question the democratic character of the values and practices enumerated by these theorists.

the modern era, the typical formula for democracy, especially as it finds expression in the constitution of a country that aspires to be democratic, emphatically demands that "all the political power is derived from the people."[84] This formula signifies the sovereignty of the people, who are both the subject and the holders of the constitution-making authority. Under these constitutional terms, liberty and political equality are a universal right,[85] at least for those empowered by constitutional norms to act as free citizens (Leibholz, 1938). Citizens have the right to be consulted on state policies and personnel. In principle, the consultation offered to the state is binding (cf. Tilly, 1999:415).

The various discussions concerning the norm of equality of citizens are evidence of the fact that most definitions of democracy focus on the obligations of the collectivity – in particular, the state – vis-à-vis the general public. The supply of quantitative information generated by state agencies about sociodemographic and socioeconomic "facts" – for example, unemployment figures, population changes, crime rates, divorce statistics, foreign trade statistics, number of new cars, GDP figures, and so forth – are now part of the obligations the state is expected to fulfill for its citizens (see Webster, 1999:374–375).

However, one can also point to obligations of the populace toward the state or the collectivity of citizens. Citizens can be held responsible for actions of the authorities of the state, as is demonstrated, for example, by the discussions about a "collective responsibility or guilt" of Germans for the crimes of the Nazi regime.[86] However, in only a few exceptional circumstances democratic participation is exercised in the form of a *direct* democracy. A competitive party system tends to be a conspicuous attribute of most modern democratic regimes.

---

[84] Hence the emphasis in Sheldin S. Wolin's (1994:11) conception of democracy on the political potentialities of ordinary citizens and their "possibilities for becoming political beings through the self-discovery of common concerns and of modes of action for realizing them."

[85] Although not to the exclusion of the other norm, constitutional theories of democracy tend to stress the norm of equality, while communitarian theories of democracy emphasize social integration (cf. Eisenstadt, 1999:11).

[86] After the revolution in Bavaria of 1918, Otto Neurath (1919:1), who was in charge of an office for economic planning of the revolutionary government, made a strong plea for civic responsibility by pointing out: "[W]ith one blow the revolution has made every adult inhabitant of German territory into a member of a consistently implemented democracy. This means nothing less than that every man and every woman is co-responsible for what happens [there]. The social order has become, instead of our fate, our own deed, our sin. Everybody eligible to vote influences which forces and which principles will come into play. More than ever, it is incumbent on each individual to learn about the essential characteristics of our social order and other possible orders of life."

In defining a general working conception of democracy for my inquiry, I cannot refer to the multitude of often unique social, political, or economic problems to which the founding of a specific democratic society originally was expected to respond and attempt to solve, although there is hardly any doubt that these historical conditions democratic society was expected to deal with continue to impose their imprint on specific countries to this day (cf. Ankersmit, 2002). The emergence of democratic society, either under peaceful conditions or through the voluntary surrender of autocratic rule or by violent overthrow of an established regime, also has a lasting impact on the nature of democratic society in specific countries and their neighbors. As the history (Dahl, 1994:25–27) and different normative concepts of democracy tell us, democracy can take on many forms, ranging from radical egalitarian to parliamentary democracy, from plebiscitary to representative types (cf. Leibholz, 1938:96–100), and many forms in between.

It would be far too simple a setting for an examination of the relations between democratic regimes and knowledge, of course, if such an inquiry concentrated on the historical emergence of the notion of democracy, perhaps asking in addition about the conditions and the individuals who made such reflections possible in the first place – although there can be no doubt that early reflections about democracy constitute an exemplary case of enabling, or practical knowledge, which ultimately triggered fundamental political reforms.

What is needed for a broader set of questions about the practical relations between knowledge and liberty is a general conception of what constitutes an existing democratic society, and therefore a society in which the ideals of earlier scholarly discourse on democracy have been put into practice in different ways. From a historical perspective, therefore, my inquiry extends to the last 100 years, give or take a few decades, and to many of the so-called developed countries. For some countries, it was the nineteenth century in which voting rights were transferred for the first time to certain segments of society. In other countries of the developed world the franchise, especially to all portions of society, was not granted until the twentieth century. The franchise granted first to small segments of the population and later to larger and larger groups assures that in a formal sense, at least, "citizens" begin to exercise a degree "of collective control over government decisions, whether directly by an assembly, indirectly through elected representatives" (Dahl, 1999:915), or by other means.[87]

---

[87] The process of enfranchising continues to this day. In Austria, for example, in 2007 the political franchise was granted to 16-year-olds (see also Touraine, 2001:120).

In practice, (electoral) representation takes on various institutional forms and constitutes an emerging property of the political system.[88] In the context of democratic theory, representation is usually seen as the best available substitute for more inclusive forms of democracy. The practical complexities of representation between actors and agents are a well-established issue in democratic regimes (e.g., Pitkin, 1967; Urbanati and Warren, 2008:389–391). However, the virtue of democracy is not merely a matter of representation. In addition, more recent societal and global transformations indicate, as Urbanati and Warren (2008:390) note, that "the landscape of democratic representation is ... clouded by the growing complexity of issues, which increasingly strains the powers of representative agents, and thus their capacities to stand for and act on the interests of those they represent." I will take up the matter of the growing complexity of political issues, and the chances of political participation and consultation of larger segments of society concerning complex social, political, and economic questions that are in need of democratic decision making, in much greater detail at a later point in this study. For advocates of strong forms of democracy or "mass-sovereignty," "representation is incompatible with freedom because it delegates and thus alienates political will at the cost of genuine self-government and autonomy" (Barber, 1984:145).

More recently, in addition to and often in competition with formally regulated and sanctioned representation, which I would like to designate as forms of *political* democratization, new, informal, nonelectoral, and, in terms of time, limited forms of representation emerge in democratic society (cf. Urbinati and Warren, 2008:402–408), which I would like to label forms of political *participation*.[89] Active political participation constitutes forms of societal democratization. Participation is not necessarily the opposite of representation. As David Plotke (1997:19) emphasizes, "the opposite of representation is not participation. The opposite of representation is exclusion. And the opposite of participation is abstention." Whether representation, as defined here, and participation, based typically on nonelectoral representation, are strictly dichotomous forms of political governance or constitute a continuum of political actions, is a

---

[88] For an analysis of the properties of the political community that make the emergence of genuine representation (the kind of relationship between political bodies such as assemblies or councils of citizens) more likely, see Prewitt and Eulau (1969).
[89] An analogous idea stems from Anthony Giddens (1999), who argues for the necessity of a "deepening of democracy itself," which he calls "democratising democracy." Democratizing democracy can take on many forms; however, it mainly means an "effective devolution of power."

contested matter (cf. Urbinati, 2000:759).[90] My contention is that these are not only different forms of realizing political influence, but also, compared to different democratic regimes of the past, of different significance. The importance of influencing policy directions linked to representation declines in modern societies, while pressures brought to bear on policies by way of forms of participation increase.[91]

In the postwar years, a small group of economists – Kenneth Arrow, Mancur Olson, and Anthony Downs – independently of each other advanced three fundamental theoretical claims against the consistency of arguments that relied on the requirement of broad political participation as an essential attribute of democracy. I will focus on Kenneth Arrow's formal *impossibility theorem*. Arrow starts with the observation that in capitalist democracies, there are essentially two ways of exercising social choice. Voting typically involves political decisions, while choices in the marketplace involve economic decisions. Voting and markets facilitate collective choice, just as dictatorship and convention would limit it.

The question Arrow ([1951] 1963:2) poses is this: "Is it formally possible to construct a procedure for passing from a set of known individual tastes to a pattern of social decision-making, the procedure in question being required to satisfy certain natural conditions." Disregarding the difference between the collective choice mechanisms of market and voting, and employing stringent assumptions, such as the "rationality" of all actors, *all* individual preferences – not only those of a particular actor – and their order must be reflected in the collective outcome, and in such a manner that choices are not imposed, Arrow examines ways of aggregating individual preferences. He concludes that a voting mechanism cannot simultaneously comply with all of the conditions of or assumptions made about all possible preference orders.

---

[90] Max Weber ([1917] 1994:121–122), for example, points out that political democratization does not necessarily imply or lead to societal democratization; he refers to the United States as his historical example for such a development: "The absence of barriers in America's political 'democracy' ... has not prevented the gradual growth of an estate of 'aristocrats' alongside the crude plutocracy of property (as people here believe), and the slow, but generally overlooked growth of this 'aristocracy' is just as important for the history of American culture."

[91] Contemporary developments in digital technology, for example, not only enable citizens to gain access to information and knowledge about political affairs more easily than in the past, but in principle also enable them to get involved in and influence policy decisions. For example, Coglianese (2003:1) discusses public participation in "administrative rulemaking processes." In the United States, government agencies and their unelected officials "create thousands of regulations that affect nearly every aspect of social and economic life." Whether such an involvement occurs and is effective remains open.

The huge literature following Arrow's discussion of public choice includes reformulations that extend, weaken, or replace the initial conditions and derive implications from these revisions. In this respect, Arrow's framework has been an instrument for generalizing voting theory and critically evaluating and broadening social choice theory.

The answer to the question "Who rules?" under the terms of a democratic constitution is therefore straightforward: the constitution empowers all the people. The answer to the question "Who governs?" is less clear-cut and highly dependent on the circumstances of the case at hand. The authority to make relevant decisions and to govern may be delegated, of course, especially in the case of large-scale communities (cf. Dahl, 2005).

One of the fundamental normative and formal principles of a democratic society is political equality (the unity of citizens in a community) and equality of protection from arbitrary action by the state. Such a principle excludes any social differentiation of citizens on the basis of property, gender, or education, but may include discrimination on the basis of territorial residence or specific psychological and legal attributes. Actual participation (and protection) varies along such demographic lines as age, class, ethnic, and religious membership, relevant issues at hand, common interests, and the capacity of groups to mobilize resources to become involved in democratic decision-making processes. The outcome of participatory democratic processes will almost always be a fluctuation of minorities and majorities. The minority accepts the legitimacy of decisions carried by the majority. The minority has given its consent *a priori*.

In practice, and of particular relevance to our inquiry, the constitutional principle of equality tolerates a considerable measure of *inequality* in terms of being either well-informed, poorly informed or not informed at all as a participant in political decision-making processes. In other words, despite the announced rejection of inequality (and the enforceable right to dismantle inequalities), there will be a considerable asymmetry in the influence exercised in democracies. Though all citizens have the right to be consulted on state policy and personnel, actual interest and participation in such decisions will be quite skewed. The actual influence, the potential, and the ability to be heard through various forms of participation of citizens, groups of citizens, social movements, or civil society organizations will be highly stratified. Those who "know" enjoy authority (Luhmann, 1990:149). In principle, however, the possibility of political participation is an intrinsic virtue of democracy, and "to be prevented from participation in the political life of the community is a major deprivation" (Sen, 1999:9).

Liberty: which liberty is meant?

> Conceptions of freedom directly derive from views of what constitutes a self, person, man. Isaiah Berlin ([1958] 1969:135)

The analysis of the concept of "freedom" (openness; choice; independence), or the lack of constraining power and the societal conditions that support liberty, is relatively underdeveloped in comparison to the categories and the analysis of the negation of freedom, be it through social control, power, or domination. However, it could be argued that any analysis of power is at the same time an analysis of liberty. A study of freedom is always also a study of the conditions that constrain freedom. This is especially true if one understands the concepts of freedom and its negation to be dichotomous. Whether one really gains access to the term and condition of freedom on the basis of such a dichotomous understanding of liberty will be examined in the discussion that follows. First, I will discuss the concept of liberty in general and distinguish between liberty *from* and liberty *for* and stress the need for a sociological concept of liberty; a concept of liberty, as many classical sociologists already have stressed (e.g., Georg Simmel), that is embedded in social relations.[92]

As will become evident, most discussions of the concept of freedom do not incorporate any reference to knowledge: "Freedom is defined by things that surround the *individual* – rights, resources, and options – but seems to be independent of anything in the individual himself or herself" (Ringen, 2008:25; emphasis added). Second, I will ask which *kind* of freedom is meant, and distinguish between political, economic, and social or civil liberties.

When it comes to conceptions about how much freedom from constraints is reasonable, permissible, or in fact possible, one invariably encounters different answers to these questions, as noted by Isaiah Berlin; distinctive conceptions of the nature of self and the dangers of "manipulation" of self – as recent history and present political circumstances in a significant number of societies only too clearly demonstrate. As indicated, any conception of freedom *from* includes references to constraints on the exercise of choice, perhaps even as a condition for the possibility of freedom *from*. Take for example, Edmund Burke's (1955:180) observation, in his *Reflections on the Revolution in France*, that

---

[92] Georg Simmel ([1908] 1992:98–99) emphasizes in *Soziologie* that liberty is not a solipsistic phenomenon but a social accomplishment and therefore not restricted to the singularity of an individual or an attribute that forever sticks to the person.

"the restraints on men as well as their liberties, are to be reckoned among their rights." Therefore, and however successful democratic governance may turn out to be in protecting the liberties of persons and organizations, democracy cannot be expected to succeed in abolishing power and authority (Luhmann, [1986] 1987:126–127). Persistent social asymmetries, the constraints of everyday life, and the unequal distribution of many socially relevant resources and attributes ensure that power cannot simply be eliminated from the life-world. Aside from the practical difficulties in eliminating differences, one of the virtues of liberal democratic societies is their tolerance of social differences. Power and authority can be restrained but remain a fact of life in democratic societies.

Freedom *from* and freedom *for*

Since the concepts of freedom or liberty – given that there is no broadly accepted distinction between the two terms, I will employ them interchangeably (Berlin, [1958] 1969:121) – are hardly clear-cut terms that allow us to refer back, with precision, to specific (individual or corporate) liberties, let alone the capacity to exercise any particular choices, it is necessary to specify which freedoms are meant. Inasmuch as the term *liberty* refers to the core of the concept and practice of democracy, and since the concept of liberty is contentious, we can reasonably infer that there are a multitude of conditions that are experienced as democratic settings having attributes that enable choice. It is less contentious to suggest that whatever liberties or freedoms are emphasized, none of them can ever be expected to be realized in a manner that fully transcends the presence of the social phenomena of power and authority.

First of all, we might generally distinguish between liberty *from*, in the sense of the absence of interference from others, and liberty *for*, in the sense of the possession of the "freedom to act" (Sen, 1994:125). The distinction between liberty *for* and liberty *from* is of course very broad and lacks specificity.[93] The notion of liberty *for* resonates closely with the

---

[93] Amartya Sen (1994:125), for example, notes that the notions of liberty *for* and liberty *from* are silent about what a person is permitted or able to *achieve*: The freedom to achieve "relates to what a person is free to have – on the basis of her own actions and those of others." Sen (1994:125) refers to the example of being hungry and nonhungry: "The so-called 'right not to be hungry' would relate to the freedom to achieve – the achievement in this case is being non-hungry – and this freedom can come about either through the person's earnings being high enough to buy an adequate amount of food, or his being given a certain amount of food or an adequate minimum income through a system of social security, permitting him to achieve the state of being non-hungry (if he so chooses)." The capability to achieve, or the "opportunity aspect of freedom" (Sen, 1993a:522), refers to the actual ability (liberty) of a person or a group to realize a

classical liberal ideals of freedom of speech, contract, and association; while the notion of liberty as liberty *from* emphasizes symbolic and material constraints under the control of other actors, which could be imposed on persons, but which should be restrained in the interest of a defense of liberty. Perhaps the best-known passage and lesson from John Stuart Mill's classic *On Liberty* ([1869] 1999:13) concerns the limits of (collective or individual) liberty for, and what later scholars have dubbed the "harm principle":

> The object of this Essay [on liberty] is to assert one very simple principle, as entitled to govern absolutely the dealings of society with the individual in the way of compulsion and control, whether the means used be physical force in the form of legal penalties, or the moral coercion of public opinion. That principle is, that the sole end for which mankind is warranted, individually or collectively, in interfering with the liberty of action of any of their number, is self-protection. That the only purpose for which power can be rightfully exercised over any member of a civilized community, against his will is to prevent harm to others. His own good, either physical or moral, is not a sufficient warrant.

Mill's principle continues to be invoked in contemporary debates about restrictions on the liberty of individuals; for example, in debates about restrictions on smoking in public places. While the limits imposed on the liberty of individuals as formulated by Mill appear to be straightforward, the exact definition of harm is always a wicked problem (cf. Reeves, 2007:265–268).

The notion of liberty from sensitizes us to the range of conditions and external impediments that can *restrain* our liberty of action, while the idea of liberty for alerts the observer to the varied ways in which one might be able to *exercise* one's liberty unobstructed by others.[94] Under conditions of liberty from, we are free from arbitrary external factors that could limit our freedom.[95] In the case of liberty for, we are independent to exercise

---

particular goal; while the "process aspect of freedom" (Sen, 1993a:523–524) is concerned with the lack of interference from others and the autonomy to make choices (irrespective of their realization).

[94] The distinction between liberty *from* and liberty *for* resonates with Isaiah Berlin's ([1958] 1969:121–122) conception of positive, self-directive liberty, which involves answers to the questions "what, or who, is the source of control or interference that can determine someone to do, or be, this rather than that?" and his notion of negative liberty: "What is the area within which the subject – a person or group of persons – is or should be left to do or be what he is able to do or be, without interference by other persons."

[95] Bernhard Barber's reservations regarding championing liberties for are based on the assumption that such a stance one-sidedly favors the market, thereby creating a tension, for example, between the consumer as a private chooser and the citizen as a public chooser. Barber (2008:74–75) explains, "citizens cannot be understood as mere consumers because individual desire is not the same thing as common ground; public goods are something more than a collection of private wants."

our liberty, even in the face of efforts of other actors to constrain our conduct.[96] In the case of both instances of liberty, however, the rulers or the government, as John Stuart Mill ([1869] 1993) describes it, "were conceived ... as in a necessarily antagonistic position to the people whom they ruled."

When the neoliberal economist Milton Friedman (1962) offers the following observation about the role of government in human affairs, namely that every act of government intervention limits the arena of individual freedom directly and threatens the preservation of freedom indirectly, he refers to liberty as the freedom *from* state intervention. Similarly, when Friedrich Hayek (1960:11; also Friedman, 1962:15) indicates that he is concerned in his plea for a *Constitution of Liberty* with "conditions of men in which coercion of some by others is reduced as much as possible in society" and defines such a state of affairs "as a state of liberty or freedom," his notion of freedom refers to liberty *from* coercion.

Economists tend to embrace both definitions of liberty. The emphasis among economists is on individual or personal freedom, although their definition also makes evident that liberty is a social relationship. In this sense, "'freedom' refers solely to a relation of men to other men, and the only infringement on it is coercion by men" (Hayek, 1960:12; Oppenheim, 1960:118) and not, as might also be the case, to environmental conditions such as the climate. Climatic conditions are seen as conditions of action beyond the control of all actors. Liberty from means to have freedom, to whatever degree, from the intervention of others, including the capacity of others to control the conditions of actions within which one is able to execute one's own intentions. Of course, liberty *from* constraints in the formal sense of the term does not mean that such a person in fact has the capacity to engage in a certain conduct.[97]

When Hannah Arendt argues, in distinctive contrast to Milton Friedman and Friedrich Hayek, that "political freedom, generally speaking, means the right 'to be a participant in government,' or it means nothing,"

---

[96] In an often quoted definition of liberalism, C. B. Macpherson (1962:3) defines liberty as the ability to exercise one's individual capacities, thereby linking freedom, innovation, and social relations: The "individual is free inasmuch as he is the proprietor of his person and capacities ... freedom is a function of possession. Society becomes a lot of free equal individuals related to each other as proprietors of their own capacities and of what they have acquired by that exercise"; see also Geuss (2002) on the contemporary discontents with liberalism.

[97] As Raymond Aron ([1964] 1984:123) emphasizes, "To be *free* to do something and *capable* of doing something are two *toto genere* different concepts. Incapability thus becomes deprivation of freedom only when it results from the intervention of other individuals."

she clearly defines liberty not as formal freedom, but rather as the capacity to take part in the deliberations of government, and therefore as liberty *for* (even more generally, "liberty *to do* something" or "liberty *to be* something"). The loss of the capacity for political action is the defeat of liberty *for*. The idea that liberty represents liberty *for* something can be further specified by suggesting that it could mean the freedom of *action* or the freedom of *thought*.

At least a number of difficult issues remain unresolved. Doubts as to whether it is indeed possible to differentiate liberties for and liberties from are justified. Is it not the case that freedom from and freedom for say much the same thing?

The contested general conceptions of liberties do not necessarily assist in conclusions about *which* liberties and *what* freedoms should be present, and to which extent, in society to deserve the label of democracy. The differentiation between liberty for and liberty from tells us little about their relationship and how much private liberty we have to give up in order to enable sufficient public authority. Where and how do we draw the line? That a line must be drawn is clear, and that such a line is context-sensitive is also evident. As Isaiah Berlin ([1958] 1969:124) therefore asks: "What is freedom to those who cannot make use of it? Without adequate conditions for the use of freedom, what is the value of freedom?" These sentiments are echoed, as it were, by Friedrich Hayek's (1960:12–13) critique of the conditions that constitute freedom *for*, when he insists that it is more important to have the capacity to carry out one's intentions and plans than to have the ability to follow many courses of action, although the latter is by no means insignificant attribute of individual liberty.[98]

The type of freedom that is of particular interest in my context is "social freedom" (see Oppenheim, 1960). Part of this concept of freedom is the freedom of certain actors to influence the scope of action of other actors. Next, I will turn to the question of what liberties count. I will begin with political liberties.

---

[98] Hayek (1960:61) formulates the principle of freedom from coercion as follows: "Whether he is free or not does not depend on the range of choice but on whether he can expect to shape his course of action in accordance with his present intentions, or whether somebody else has power to manipulate the conditions as to make him act according to that person's will rather than his own. Freedom thus presupposes, that the individual has some assured private sphere, that there is some set of circumstances in his environment with which others cannot interfere." Hayek's observations resonate closely with Isaiah Berlin's ([1955] 2002:111) differentiation of forms of liberty in the world of antiquity and forms of political freedom in the modern world. In the world of antiquity, the central issue was "who will govern?". In the modern world, the core question becomes "how broad is the power of government?". In the modern world, the differentiation between the private and the public sphere becomes relevant.

Political liberty

In the case of conceptions of political liberty, it may be useful to distinguish, in analogy to the difference between liberty for and liberty from, between ways in which citizens relate to the political system and ways in which the political world relates to individual and collective actors. A political system may impose stricter or more lenient expectations and responsibilities on citizens – for example, whether or not voting is mandatory – or the actors may enjoy limited or complete freedom in forming political opinions and exercising such views within the political world. The institutional relevance of political liberties extends to the impact that collective political liberties have on other institutions in society; for example, the function of collective freedoms for the stability of economic policies in a society (cf. Ali and Isse, 2004).

Along these two axes of self-possessed or restrained liberty within the political system, one is bound to encounter many formations of political freedoms, ranging from highly liberated, knowledgeable, and informed citizens free of any significant dependence on the opinions and authority of other actors or associations of individuals, to individual citizens whose liberty is at best limited to abstaining from participating in any formal political exercise. A significant attribute of the kind of political liberty citizens may exercise would refer not only to the capacity of individuals to freely choose the kind of political role they desire, but also extend to their ability to move freely between multiple political roles, and the legitimacy granted by the political system permitting such switches between alternative roles.[99]

Otto Neurath, a prominent member of the Vienna Circle (cf. Popper, 1973), to whom I will refer in more detail later in this study, advances a rather helpful conception of the nature of political liberties. In the context of discussing the conflict that exists between state planning and liberty, Neurath notes that the essential difference between an authoritarian and a democratic regime rests on the kind of loyalty expected of its citizens, and on how steadfast such loyalty is expected to be, including of course loyalties to particular world views. The foundations of authoritarian governance rest on the "tendency for one, and only one loyalty to 'devour' all the others ... various loyalties are not permitted to grow up

---

[99] John Stuart Mill ([1873] 2009:259) considered the core message of his essay *On Liberty* to be the description of the essence of (his) liberalism, namely the multitude of conflicting individual roles and opinions in society: "the importance, to man and society, of a large variety in types and character, and of giving full freedom to human nature to expand itself in innumerable and conflicting directions."

side by side" (Neurath, [1942] 1973:429), and therefore on the prohibition on changing one's world views based on one's own reasons. The ability to join a variety of associations, organizations, and clubs, or express political sympathies with multiple associations, or with what are described more recently as *civil society* organizations, constitutes the institutional basis for political freedom:

> The "freedom" of a democratic country might be described by the fact that each member is permitted to have more than one loyalty, e.g., to his family, to his local community, to his profession, to his political party, to his church, to his lodge, to an international movement and to his county. One expects, in a democratic country, that a citizen knows how to handle these various loyalties and to assemble them in one way or another. (Neurath, [1942] 1973:429)

Raymond Aron ([1965] 1984) defines political liberty more narrowly as the equal ability to take part in and influence the "fate of the collectivity," represented by persons chosen in an election. Aron attempts to move beyond a mere abstract conception of political liberty by inquiring about the status of liberty in a "technical world" (a world then still divided by the Cold War). Aron asks whether political liberty in industrial societies, in the sense of meaningful political participation not only in the context of work but also in the realm of leisure, is in fact fictitious, especially in light of the immense power exercised over the individual worker by the rationalization of work and his status as a captive of market forces over which only the hidden persuaders have control. And since Aron also notes a widespread trend toward the manipulation of public opinion with the help of the mass media, he also wonders whether it is still possible for really independent political views to emerge. The exact answer to what Aron himself describes as a pessimistic assessment of the state of political liberty depends on the constitutional realities of each country.

Aron ([1965] 1984:101–104) observes, for example, that political liberties are best protected in the United States, in contrast to European democracies (where parliamentary procedure and control has deteriorated to ritualistic conduct), because the influence of the public and the control of the government by representative agents are best assured in the United States. Nonetheless, Aron warns that political liberties are in decline; but they have not vanished. The existence of political parties, labor unions, and consumer associations forms one of the significant barriers against the disappearance of political liberties.

Economic freedom

Among the concrete freedoms proclaimed by the *Atlantic Charter* in 1941 are two freedoms that are not incorporated in traditional liberal concepts of liberties: *freedom from want* and *freedom from fear*.[100] I will concentrate on the former, the freedom from want, as a norm that belongs to the general category of economic freedoms. A number of observers argue, for example, that the democratic principles of equality and unimpeded political participation are meaningless if citizens lack the necessary existential resources for engaging in politics and participating politically. That is why one tends to encounter in this context the view that any interest in democratic governance in impoverished societies merely represents hope and concern for an improvement of the material conditions. It is undoubtedly the case that Western democracies are also, as a rule, prosperous societies; as a result, one should not be surprised to find that in many parts of the world, democracy is closely conflated with affluence, equality, and security.

While the standard of living for most people did not change for centuries, and poverty and hunger were a standard condition of everyday life, today commodities and services that were once luxuries are widely affordable necessities. We are living, surely from an economic (capital) and educational (capital) point of view, in a historically unprecedented time. In the developed world, capabilities, in the sense of affluence and educational levels, are by no means uniform and equally distributed, yet they are widespread, and much more so than at any other time in history. Nonetheless, prosperity remains stratified, and in some societies severe material inequities exist; similarly, neither the memory nor the presence of hunger has vanished, and poverty has not been eliminated. Efforts to ensure that all individuals enjoy the material resources sufficient for self-realization should be seen as an extension of the classical liberal concept of freedom (cf. Aron, 1985:194).

Social or civil liberties

Aside from political and economic liberty, there is a broad field of liberties or choices on the basis of options, as the capabilities approach emphasizes (Sen, 1985, 1999) – perhaps even more important to many individuals and groups than the independence to exercise political and economic action free of constraints from the state, major societal

---

[100] The Atlantic Charter was conceived by British Prime Minister Winston Churchill and U.S. President Franklin D. Roosevelt as the blueprint for the postwar world, issued in August 1941. Many of the postwar treaties – for example, the GATT treaty – and the independence of previous colonial nations benefited from the charter. One might as well place close to all the forms of freedom identified in 1941 – and therefore not only with respect to the economic sphere – the idea of the liberty of choice. Perhaps the freedom of choice is a kind of meta-liberty.

institutions, and fellow citizens – namely the freedom to express oneself in ways that suit one's idiosyncratic desires and preferences. Although expansive, next to political and economic liberty and the importance usually attached to them not only in theory but also in practical affairs, the category of "social" or "civil freedom" at first glance appears to represent merely a residual category of liberties.

The concept of civil or social liberties may be found in John Stewart Mill's ([1869] 1999:1) classical treatise *On Liberty*. He makes the point in his very first sentence that the subject of his essay "is not the so-called Liberty of the Will, so unfortunately opposed to the misnamed doctrine of Philosophical Necessity; but Civil, or Social Liberty: the nature and limits of the power which can be legitimately exercised by society over the individual." Given the wide range of possible social and civil liberties, Mill's own discourse focuses on the liberty of thought, including the "liberty of the press." In general, as Mill explains ([1869] 1999:13): "The only freedom which deserves the name, is that of pursuing our own good in our own way, so long as we do not attempt to deprive others of theirs, or impede their efforts to obtain it." Of course, the powers of society over the individual in modern society are considerable.

Irrevocably intertwined with the question of freedom and democracy is, as we have seen, the question of power. I will therefore turn to the "problem of power." I will attempt to offer a counterintuitive notion of the social phenomenon of power in modern societies.

The problem of power

The dominant view of power as the manifestation of a specific social relationship between actors or groups almost always sees power in all its historical forms as the power of the powerful. It is the power that negates the body, represses, governs, suppresses, and so forth. In the course of history, in the eighteenth century for example, power in the form of new technologies may take on a more "concrete and precise character" and its grasp of a "multiple and differentiated reality" (Foucault, [1977] 2000:125) becomes more efficient.[101] The entire existence of individuals and groups is under the control of powerful individuals and institutions. By definition, in the long run, power is always the power of those who

---

[101] As Michel Foucault ([1973] 2000:86) explains, this is the subjugation of the body for the purpose of transforming it into labor power; that is, for "the control authorities that appeared from the nineteenth century onward, the body acquired a completely different signification; it was no longer something to be tortured but something to be molded, reformed, corrected, something that must acquire aptitudes, receive a certain number of qualities, become qualified as a body capable of working."

rule. How can it possibly be otherwise? But do concrete social, political, or economic contexts always exhibit power in such a categorical manner? Are the powerless always without power?

According to the prevailing conception of power, power signifies a deep hierarchical asymmetry among social actors and groups. Power generates dichotomous relations and penetrates most social contexts. Social actors either have power, or are subjected to power. The resources, assuming that one is able to define resources independently of power that may be mobilized to exercise power, and independently of the kind of resources that may serve in such a function, invariably seem to flow to those who are already powerful. Power generally constrains, and both those who are able to constrain and those who are constrained are virtually always distinct and locked into distinct social categories. These considerations tend to be assimilated to the view that power is a zero-sum phenomenon, which is to say "that there is a fixed 'quantity' of power in any relational system and hence any gain of power on the part of *A* must by definition occur by diminishing the power at the disposal of other units" (Parsons, 1963:233). Only under exceptional, revolutionary circumstances, a complete reversal in power relations is possible (cf. Tilly, 2007). Since revolutions are exceptional events in history, the role of power in social relations determines what really happens in society.

This traditional understanding of power is well represented by the classical definition of power by Max Weber, who views power as the opportunity for an individual in a social relationship to achieve his or her own will, even against the resistance of others. Power tends to be theorized from the perspective of the powerful. What is power able to accomplish? Power realizes constraints on behalf of the powerful. Only in a marginal sense can it be said that those who are constrained figure into the prevailing equation of power; except, of course, in the sense that power is deployed and exercised at their expense. Most often, therefore, *power over others* is the primary point of reference for prevailing definitions of social power. For example, Michel Foucault ([1973] 2000:85) refers in this sense to the "power to extract knowledge from individuals and to extract a knowledge *about* those individuals," and then to organize such knowledge for the gain of those powerful enough to extract it in the first instance. The role of the powerless represents a general incapacity that is an inalienable attribute of their very existence, and the powerless tend in the long run to be confined to that very status. The human will of the subordinates becomes hostage to the fortunes of the knowledge of the powerful, and therefore suffers a fate not unlike those individuals who, in the context of climate determinism, are prisoners of the fortunes of climate, "too passive and powerless to respond proactively, or even reactively" (Hulme, 2011:250) to environmental conditions.

Talcott Parsons' (1957:139) critique of the prevailing conception of power is therefore illuminating (cf. Allen, 2003:38–44). In a review of C. Wright Mills' (1956a) *The Power Elite*, Parsons criticizes Mills' "zero-sum" concept of power, which is used not as a "facility for the performance of function in and on behalf of the society as a system, but is interpreted exclusively as a facility for getting what one group, the holders of power, wants by preventing another group, the 'outs' from getting what it wants."[102] Mills is interested only in "*who* has power and what *sectoral* interests he is serving with his power, not in how power comes to be generated or in what communal rather than sectoral interests are served" (Parsons, 1957:140). For Parsons, power is not only an intrinsically effective deterrent; in conflating his conception of power with that of "authority" as conceptualized by Max Weber, power also becomes a "generalized medium of mobilizing resources for effective collective action, and for the fulfillment of commitments made by collectivities to ... their constituents; it too [not unlike money] must be both symbolically generalized and *legitimized*" (Parsons, 1963:243; my emphasis).

If one conceives of power as a generalized capacity for social action, then such "secondary," collective rather than merely distributive effects of the use of power come into view as part of the potential impact of power. But this is not all. At the same time, in conformity with this perspective of power, the actual role of power in social relations is no longer as exaggerated as is the case for the traditional conception of power, and it therefore does not under all circumstances become the sole, constraining cement that holds society together.

The distribution of power is not a zero-sum game, since power can expand in association with the enlargement of the resources that serve as media of power; it also may be distributed to different degrees in concrete situations; access to resources that may confer power are not forever (that is, in the long run) limited to the powerful; and the

---

[102] In a later essay on the notion of power, Talcott Parsons (1963:251) refers to the breakdown of the zero-sum doctrine in the case of money (through credit creation), and argues that money may serve as a model in the case of power to lever the same doctrine in this case as well. In a complex series of arguments, Parsons (1963:254) points, for example, to equivalents to the role of credit creation in the political system: "In the case of democratic electoral systems, political support should be conceived as a generalized grant of power which, if it leads to electoral success, puts the leadership in a position analogous to that of the banker." Political power in this sense is not fixed, but rather created; and it grows, but it also leads to new risks and uncertainties.

movement of power in a swing-like motion between groups becomes possible. Concrete social, political, or economic circumstances may therefore be characterized, also not permanently, by a distribution of power that does not display categorical features of an either- or phenomenon, but may rather exhibit such characteristics of power to different degrees across the collective of actors (see Oppenheimer, 1960).

These changes have to be seen in connection with the structural transformations of contemporary society. Appropriating Adolph Lowe's (1971:563) astute insights, it is a change from social realities in which "things" simply "happen" (at least from the point of view of most people) to a social world in which more and more things are "made" to happen. Advanced society may be described as a *knowledge society* because of the incursion of all its spheres by scientific and technical knowledge and the intensified application of knowledge to knowledge (Drucker, 1993:65).[103] Therefore, what is new in knowledge societies and what makes for their peculiar character is the societal weight and significance that knowledge assumes. Knowledge is not only highly esteemed; it also commends and recommends itself independently of how it is put to work. Knowledge is present in all social institutions. It is not confined, as a code, to a special social system for its production and use; it is everywhere. All social action and communication requires knowledge (see Luhmann, 1990:147).

The modern world, including nature, is increasingly the product of knowledge as a capacity to act. The change from industrial to knowledge society is one of degree, as is the case for most historical changes. In knowledge societies, the individual's capability of doing and being whatever she/he desires is considerably enhanced. As a result, the dependence of humans on humans grows significantly. The detachment of many actors from the influence of major social institutions and system-overarching social collectivities such as labor unions, political parties, civic groups, and educational institutions of course lessens these collectivities' influence on the individual, and they no longer constitute the almost "fate-like" social contexts in which identities and worldviews were shaped and reshaped.

The societal changes within the emerging frame of knowledge societies that I have in mind, and therefore the change in the social distribution of

---

[103] Peter Drucker (1993:69) elaborates his idea as follows: "Where there is effective management, that is, *application of knowledge to knowledge*, we can always obtain the other resources. The fact that knowledge has become the resource, rather than *a* resource, is what makes our society 'postcapitalist.' It changes, and fundamentally so, the structure of society. It creates new social dynamics. It creates new economic dynamics. It creates new politics" (emphasis added).

power, can also be described in the following way: in the case of large and influential social institutions, but also in the case of individuals and small social groups the balance of autonomy (power; openness; emancipation) versus conditionality (powerlessness; alienation) is shifting. The sum total of conditionality and autonomy is not constant. Both autonomy and conditionality of social action are capable of growing; they may also decline. In knowledge societies, in contrast to the classical vision of the exercise of power of large institutions, which presupposes a "strong" state or church, the degree of both the perceived and the real autonomy of individuals and small social groups increases, while the extent of conditionality of social action shrinks. In the case of large social collectivities such as the state, large corporations, science, the church, and so forth, the extent to which their conduct is conditioned may decline as well – for example, they may become less dependent on natural conditions – but their autonomy or ability to impose their will on society does not increase in proportion. In an era of a distinct multiplication of decision makers, the large institutions of modern societies are no longer as strong as they once were, and they are incapable of taking charge of a dispersed society with many detached islands of authority and power.

Conditionality and autonomy or openness of social action is not only a function of the social distribution of knowledge, but also of the political conditions in society. Thus, the fundamental question that this study addresses concerns the interrelation of knowledge and democracy. Following Niklas Luhmann's ([1986] 1987:126) comment that the unique attribute of democracy is its openness toward the choice of future possibilities, the societal balance of conditionality versus autonomy (openness) of social action at any given time is a function of a dual constraint, namely the nature of the political order of a society and the availability of knowledge.

One of the most interesting practical collisions and conflicts of democracy and knowledge in this context – and one that I will treat in more detail in the following *Excursus* – is a political and legal conflict, lasting for many years, between the Government of the State of New York and the City of New York. This controversy, which was finally settled by New York courts, was about nothing less than the question of how much knowledge future citizens and voters of the City of New York need to have, as called for in the constitution of the State, in order to become competent participants in democratically organized political processes and in civic duties such as serving as jurors. The answer to the demands of the constitution is also a response to the question of how many resources the state must deploy in order to reasonably meet the constitutional expectations. And this – at least implicitly – means nothing less than offering an answer to the question of the costs the public is asked to shoulder in order to impart such knowledge in the public education system. The legal battle finally ended on November 20, 2006, with a ruling by the highest court of the State of New York, the Court of Appeals. The court convicted the State of New York and enjoined it to provide the City of New York with an additional $1.93 billion each year for the urban New York public school system.

Excursus: How much knowledge does democracy need, and how expensive should it be?

> The democratic citizen is expected to be *well informed* about political affairs. He is supposed to know what the issues are, what their history is, *what the relevant facts are*, what alternatives are proposed, what the party stands for, what the likely consequences are (emphasis added).
> Berelson, Lazarsfeld, and McPhee (1954:308)

By the demanding standards Bernard Berelson and his colleagues formulated in their classic study of the formation of voter opinion, most voters in most countries, not only in the decade of the 1950s but also today, fall short of their stringent expectations. But the commonsense view of the kinds of intellectual qualities democratic citizens should have, as well as the preeminent opinion among professional observers in particular, is often that citizens in democratic societies should be knowledgeable and well informed.[1] This applies with particular force to political information or knowledge. Political information is the key currency or code that governs democratic politics and citizenship (e.g., Lakoff, 1971:12; Delli Carpini and Keeter, 1996:8). Information, ideally objective information, is the source of political preferences. The idea that resilient democracies depend on informed citizens is by no means a new insight; nor is the expectation that the state and the political system have to shoulder the responsibility for providing the foundations for adequate citizenship.[2]

---

[1] Notable dissent from what is otherwise the dominant view among professional observers may be found in Popkin (1991), who advances the unorthodox view that citizens need not be informed in order to render good political judgments. And as I will note later, at least Berelson (1952) himself, in a single-authored paper, is quite prepared to accept lower standards of the volume of political information among voters.

[2] Kuklinski et al. (2000:791) are of the opinion that those in the best position to offer relevant information, namely "elected officials and members of the media, lack the incentive to do so. Politicians want their preferred policies to prevail . . . [while the media seeks] to gain and maintain its viewers' interest. Rather than present general facts and place them in context, it reports specific events and personal situations, and the more vivid, the better."

Not only the founding fathers of the American democracy, but also the classical observer of the American revolution, Alexis de Tocqueville (e.g. [1835–40] 2000:291), offer extensive observations regarding the question "how much knowledge do citizens require, and what knowledge do they need?" as well as "can adequate knowledge guarantee the persistence of democratic regimes?" During this period in history, at the dawn of mass democracies, the response to the latter question was mostly in the affirmative. Thomas Jefferson, for example, is explicit in his expectation and demand: In a letter to Colonel Edward Carrington (Koch and Peden, 1944:411–412) written on January 17, 1787, he emphasizes:

The basis of our government being the opinion of the people, the very first object should be to keep that right; and were it left to me to decide whether we should have a government without newspapers or newspapers without a government, I should not hesitate a moment to prefer the latter. But I should mean that every man should receive those papers and *be capable of reading them* (my emphasis).

More than a century later, a similar response to the relation between education and democracy had become almost conventional wisdom. John Dewey (1916), for example, views broad and even high levels of educational attainment as a precondition for democracy, while Seymour Martin Lipset (1959:80), in the postwar era, concludes in a cross-national empirical study on the same set of questions that "high" levels of educational achievement are a necessary condition for the existence and stability of democratic society. Even more recent empirical work tends to support the same conclusion (e.g., Barro, 1999; Przeworski et al., 2000). Seymour Martin Lipset (1959:79) has summarized the results of a number of comparable empirical studies at the end of the 1950s, and concludes "the most important single factor differentiating those giving democratic responses from others has been education. The higher one's education, the more likely one is to believe in democratic values and support democratic practices." An examination of the role and experience of science advising and the formation of science policy in the United States in the late 1950s (last but not least in the wake of the launching of Sputnik, the first manmade satellite, by the Soviets in the fall of 1957) emphatically concludes that "a democratic nation can only cope with the scientific revolution if thoughtful citizens know what it truly entails" (Dupré and Lakoff, 1962:181).

However, it is also John Dewey (1916:108–110) who warns against treating education as a *black box*. An authoritarian personality, an elevated deference to the state and a high level of formal education are – as the case of Germany demonstrates – compatible. Dewey ([1916] 2005:57) notes that in the case of the German educational system, "the educational process was taken to be one of disciplinary training rather than of personal development ... only in and through an absorption of the aims and meaning of the organized institutions does he attain true personality." In other words, the philosophy of education and the aims of the educational system "required subordination of individuals to the superior interests of the state." The realization of the subservient personality as the primary goal of the educational policy, not only in imperial Germany but for decades to come, demanded the "thoroughgoing 'disciplinary' subordination to existing institutions." Dewey's observations are a useful reminder that a high formal level of education in a society does not necessarily lead to support for democratic values and conduct. The association between formal educational achievement and democracy is a complex relationship that requires careful attention to the nature of the actual education system. I will examine the Lipset thesis of the linkage between educational accomplishment and democracy in a subsequent part of the study in much greater detail. But first I would like to pursue the question of how much knowledge and information the citizen of modern societies needs to acquire, and the related issue of the volume of resources the state has to invest to accomplish such an outcome. There can be little doubt that these questions are highly complex and contentious, as the long-lasting conflict between the State of New York and the City of New York over educational finances readily demonstrates.[3]

For over a decade, the State of New York and the City of New York were entangled in a legal battle over the question of whether the State of New York provided fair and sufficient financial means for the gigantic

---

[3] A comparable and equally drawn-out legal dispute between the State of New Jersey and plaintiffs who argued that the state provided inadequate funding to some school districts in order to ensure the "provision of educational services sufficient to enable pupils to master the Core Curriculum Content Standards" was settled by the Supreme Court of New Jersey on May 24, 2011 in favor of the plaintiffs. The court enjoined the State of New Jersey to increase state education aid by $500 million in the coming school year, distributed among thirty-one school districts in historically poor cities. The Court concluded that the State failed to meet its constitutional burden to make sure that a "thorough and efficient education" was provided. The New Jersey constitution indeed charges the State with the fundamental responsibility to educate schoolchildren: "The Legislature shall provide for the maintenance and support of a thorough and efficient system of free public schools for the instruction of all the children in the State between the ages of five and eighteen years" (N.J. Const. art. VIII, § 4, 1). The fundamental right to an adequate education extends to all children in the State. The court relied in its decision on Special Master's Opinion/Recommendations to the Supreme Court, submitted by Judge Peter E. Doyne (source www.judiciary.state.nj.us/opinions/index.htm and Winnie Hu and Richard Pérez-Peña, "Court orders New Jersey to increase aid to schools," *New York Times*, May 25, 2011).

public school system of the City of New York.[4] The legal dispute ran its course parallel to the so-called "educational standards movement," which has been fighting for the continual improvement of the expectations and standards attached to a high school diploma. In a number of American states – for example, in Kentucky – courts have indeed prescribed much higher, clearly defined standards.

At first glance, this is apparently one of those everyday rhetorical disputes between different political jurisdictions over contested questions of revenue sharing between various political levels – a familiar occurrence in any democratic society. The State of New York provides approximately half of the school budget for the City of New York. One of the most recent judgments in this legal action, however, has made reference to a fundamental philosophical or constitutional problem: Which skills, information, and proficiencies should the modern state be *minimally* obligated to communicate successfully to students in its schools, and how expensive must an education system be that guarantees standards of this type? The developments in the New York dispute make it evident that this conflict over how to answer the question under debate is ultimately based on a problem that must be decided within the political system.

The constitution of the State of New York stipulates that the State is obligated to guarantee "the maintenance and support of a system of free common schools wherein all the children of this state may be educated." The interpretation of this constitutional norm as an obligation for the state to make possible a "sound, basic" education was concretized by the Court of Appeals of the State of New York, in a judgment of 1995. This court further ruled that the public school system must be in a position to guarantee that students "function productively as civic participants capable of voting and serving on a jury." In a later judgment in 2001, a judge of the Constitutional Court of the State of New York ruled that as jurors, citizens are required to answer complex questions: Jurors "must determine questions of fact concerning DNA evidence, statistical analysis and convoluted financial fraud, to name only three topics." The State successfully appealed this judgment.

In June 2002, however, the Appellate Division of the State Supreme Court of New York defined a restrictive interpretation of this constitutional norm: On the basis of relevant constitutional standards, the State

---

[4] I rely on the accounts of the conflict between the state of New York and the city of New York found in the *New York Times*, especially the article dated June 30, 2002 ("Johnny can read, not well enough to vote?"); and subsequent coverage in the same newspaper, especially "School financing case argued before State's highest court," *New York Times*, October 11, 2006 (also Scherer, 2004–2005).

is not obliged to finance more than a *minimal* education. More concretely, after eight or nine years, students should be able to read political parties' campaign literature; serve the courts as jurors; and fulfill the requirements of an employment that makes minor demands on them. The high school diploma should only ensure that the student had acquired the ability "to get a job, and support oneself, and thereby not be a charge on the public fiscus."

The court's decision was variously received: In some quarters, this minimal educational requirement was understood as a kind of capitulation on the part of the State. In others, the judges were praised for their wise decision, since (more) money was not necessarily an adequate solution to the educational dilemma – other factors also influenced students' opportunities of acquiring cultural capital. The court emphasized that its task had been only to determine the citizen's minimum rights to education as laid out in the constitution; indeed, the schools of the City of New York guarantee this minimum demand. A claim for compensatory education, for instance, is therefore untenable. And to the extent that the citizens disagree with these minimum goals, they will have to replace the responsible politicians by electoral means. The plaintiff, The Campaign for Fiscal Equity, filed an appeal.

Could this ruling by one of the highest courts of the State of New York be an arbitral verdict that reflects the spirit of the industrial, and not that of the knowledge society, namely to be able to find one's way to the voting booth and function as a juror? Indeed, as the court formulated in its opinion of 2001, jurors must nowadays be well acquainted with complex statistical analyses, DNA-based evidence, or convoluted financial transactions.

The legal dispute finally ended (with no possibility of appeal) on November 20, 2006 with a verdict by the highest court of the State of New York, the Court of Appeals, in which the State of New York was ordered to provide an additional 1.93 billion dollars annually for the city school system. This sum is considerably less than the 4.7 billion dollars that a lower court had rules to be appropriate. The final judgment was based on the recommendation of a commission appointed by New York State Governor Pataki in 2004. In a dissenting opinion from that of the majority of the court, one of the two judges in the minority states that "a sound basic education will cost approximately $5 billion in additional annual expenditure. I remain hopeful that, despite the court's ruling today, the policymakers will continue to strive to make schools not merely adequate, but excellent, and to implement a statewide solution." The four judges responsible for the majority judgment of the court were all appointees of Governor Pataki.

The following sections will be dedicated to the analysis of the "endogenous" and "exogenous" societal preconditions of democracy.[5] One has to be cognizant of the fact that many paths lead to democratic governance. Some of these efforts have obviously failed and have left little trace; but the losing efforts "have at every moment affected the final outcome, sometimes by retarding and sometimes by speeding up its development" (Ferdinand Braudel, qtd. in Lazarsfeld, 1957:53). The focus of the next section will be on nonmaterial factors. The subsequent section of the analysis will, then, deal with the significance of economic patterns, wealth, and inequality for the emergence and stability of democracy, and the possibility of democratic backsliding.

---

[5] In her comparative study of the democratization process, Barbara Wejnert (2005) distinguishes between internal features of a country, among which she mainly counts socioeconomic factors, and external diffusion processes. A comparison of the influence of both of these features leads her (Wejnert, 2005:73) to conclude "the diffusion predictors of spatial proximity and networks were robust predictors of democratic growth in both the world and across all regions."

2 Accounts of the conditions for the possibility and the resilience of liberty

Man can know: thus he can be free.
Karl Popper ([1960] 1968:6)

Liberties evolve on the basis of particular social forces; the survival of liberties may depend on other social forces, if not the same forces. But in some countries, even the highest virtues may not ensure that democratic institutions endure. In any case, there is quite a large and vibrant collection of competing hypotheses referring to distinctive requisites and conditions that make the development, intensification, and persistence of democratic political systems possible. Social theories and ideas[1] developed to account for the origins, the legitimacy, the stabilization, the distribution across the globe, and the sustainability of democracies are of considerable value, not only within social science disciplines, but also especially as ideas (for example, "democracy is a desirable form of governance") in the world of politics, since they always include practical advice on how to advance the process of democratization.

I will enumerate and discuss only a few, if the most central, of these rival theses.[2] Among the societal processes that are seen to be most likely responsible for the emergence and enforcement of democratic regimes

---

[1] A further noteworthy discussion of the concept of "ideas" – in contrast to knowledge and information – may be found in the context of describing the range of competencies that make for the social phenomenon of knowledgeability. In the present context, ideas refer to statements that have the potential of making it more or less directly onto the political agenda, encouraging political action of a specific kind found in the statement (cf. Stanley Fish, "Ideas and theories: the political difference," *New York Times*, May 2, 2011).

[2] I will refrain from taking up the essentially contested notion that geographic, climatic, or other natural conditions, however much transformed or deployed by social forces, are more suitable for democratic governance. One of the specific geographical forces that has been discussed for a considerable time is the dependence of democratic governance, in historical times, on rainfed agriculture. Karl August Wittvogel in his *Oriental Despotism* (1967) famously took up the idea already discussed by Adam Smith, John Stuart Mill, and Karl Marx about the association between autocracy and large-scale irrigation. More recent investigations by Bentzen, Kaarsen, and Wingender (2012), based on different data sets and statistical methods, find support for Wittvogel's assertion that otherwise remains a highly contested observation (e.g., Mann, 1986).

are references, often rather ambivalently formulated, to socioeconomic and sociopolitical imperatives or values[3]; that is, to factors and forces internal or external to the political system (see Rustow, 1970) which enforce a definite path on history. Francis Fukuyama, for example, explains his famous and controversial thesis of the end of competing ideologies toward the end of the twentieth century in the wake of the so-called "third-wave" of democratization (Huntington, 1991; Shin, 1994) by stressing that "there are fundamental economic and political imperatives pushing history in one direction, towards greater democracy" (see also Fukuyama, 2014).[4] But as the official justification for the Iraq war in 2003 demonstrates, United States government officials have indeed expected to see democracy emerge from the barrels of guns, perhaps mimicking Mao Zedongs's famous aphorism that political power at least "grows out of the barrel of a gun."[5]

Even a brief summary of attributes and processes inherent and external to the political system, such as the importance of a peaceful societal order (Olson, 2000:119), the knowledgeability of the members of society, the role of education (Oelkers, 2000; Botero, Ponce, and Shleifer, 2012), the moral budget of society (Alvey, 2001),[6] the function of the media, and political culture, as well as attributes specific to each nation-state or transnational network makes it clear that the totality of these factors, in one way or another, may play a role in democratic processes. The same is true for the interaction of social processes, such as the relation between the education and the knowledge of the population. In any case, given the complexity of relevant factors, it is difficult to formulate predictions about the political future of individual nations (see also Huntington, 1984:215–218).[7]

---

[3] One example of the values or ideals that are considered significant in processes of democratization is the complex of subjective, emancipative values emphasized by Welzel, Inglehart, and Klingemann ([2001] 2003:341]), for instance, as part of a more comprehensive "syndrome" of factors that collectively facilitate social progress. Widely prioritized values such as "preferences for freedom," for example, doubtless have social effects, but they do not "determine," as Welzel and Inglehart (2005:82) also stress, "all forms of collective action, above all not the strategic actions of elites."
[4] Quoted in Michael Grove, "Why I fear today's brave world," *The Times*, May 16, 2003.
[5] See Benjamin Ginsberg, "Why violence works," *The Chronicle of Higher Education*, August 12, 2013 (http://chronicle.com/article/Why-Violence-Works/140951/).
[6] In an empirically based study Botero, Ponce, and Shleifer (2012:17–18) conclude that that there is – independently of the particular form of government – a universal positive correlation between the collective level of education of a nation and the quality of its governance. The authors speculate that the volume of complaints addressed to the state by members of society is responsible for the relationship in question: "We argued that educated citizens complain more, and that these complaints lead to better conduct by officials fearful of being punished, and therefore to a higher quality government."
[7] More than a quarter of a century ago, Samuel Huntington (1984:116) was bold enough to discuss the chances of democratization in the Islamic countries of the Middle East. His

The emphasis in many of the "classical" studies of the development of political regimes has been on sweeping, long-term domestic patterns of democratization, for example, national patterns of class relations and the impact of domestic characteristics of society on the emergence of democratic regimes (cf. Capoccia and Ziblatt, 2010). More recent work, in contrast, has attended to short-term moments of regime transformation, the impact of cultural factors, "iconic events" such as the fall of the Berlin Wall, the role of the media, world views, and values found in religion and ethnic membership, for example; and last but not least, the importance of transnational processes, for instance, the role of intergovernmental networks and global trends. The volume and range of studies that have focused on the role of cultural conditions for the emergence and the resilience of democratic governance are rather small. Studies that have examined the importance of cultural phenomena and processes for the nature of economic conduct are much more numerous and insightful (cf. Fernández, 2010).

In the context of the Iraq war, but not only in the case of this particular conflict, many observers have been convinced that there is a close linkage between religious convictions – or even more generally, certain cultural dispositions – and the possibility of democratic institutions. The provocative assertions by Samuel P. Huntington (1993) of a deep and unbridgeable antagonism between distinctive civilizational regions of the world is animated by his strong conviction that cultural differences, rather than ideological and economic factors, have a causal impact on the nature of the political regimes in societies (also Norris and Inglehart, 2002): "The great divisions among humankind and the dominating source of conflict will be cultural" (Huntington, 1993:22). I will specifically consider the question of the relevance of cultural dimensions and the importance of the political culture for the emergence and endurance of democratic regimes in the next sections of this chapter.

It is evident that there are different historical paths to democracy. Just compare the fate of democracy in such countries as India, Germany, Hungary, Portugal, or Chile in the last century; or more recently, the political experience of some of the formerly autocratic or authoritarian societies in the Arab world.[8] For this reason alone, the number of

---

expectations were reserved: "Among the Islamic countries, particularly in the Middle East, the prospects for democratic development seem low.... The Islamic revival ... would seem to reduce even further the likelihood of democratic development.... In addition, many of the Islamic states are very poor.... Those that are rich ... are controlled by the state."

[8] The varied historical experiences of transitions to democracy have led to efforts to find classificatory typologies of transformative processes to liberty; Huntington (1991), for

essentially competing theoretical accounts of social and cultural conditions that allow for the possibility of liberty and assure the persistence of freedom in society is large. These multiple approaches cannot simply be ignored in the context of my inquiry. Nor can the notion that history necessarily aims at transitions toward democracy be easily overlooked. In the case of a teleological view, the outcome of history is predetermined, or the result of a process largely governed by a form of *Eigengesetzlichkeit* or inherent regulation that assures that democracy will prevail; while economic, cultural, and psychological or "environmental" factors contribute marginally, if at all, to such an outcome.

The major explanation among the contenders for the conditions that give rise to freedom – aside from a teleological conception of history that I reject – refers to the performance of the economy of a country. I will discuss the economic thesis at some length in Chapter 3. Although reference to economic conditions and other societal conditions, such as education, literacy, or economic policies, are often conflated in discussions of the circumstances that give rise to and sustain liberties, in this chapter only accounts that make explicit reference to processes other than economic conditions will be presented and discussed.

The social, legal, psychological, and cultural features that are seen as playing a prominent role in accounts of the historical emergence of liberty for large segments of the population in modernizing societies are not easy to separate, since they are often discussed in conjunction with each other. The difficulties associated with a clear-cut separation make immediate sense, since the factors adduced are often connected either in location or in time, and stand in relations of mutual influence. On the other hand, modern differentiation theories of modern society would stress the autonomy of major social institutions, at least in the case of developed societies, and therefore often argue for the preeminence of a particular social institution (law, education, science, religion) as a condition for the rise of democracy.[9] The stress on economic conditions and

example, distinguishes between transformations (imposed from above), interventions (externally imposed), replacements (revolutions), and transplacements (negotiated transitions).

[9] A number of examples in the history of different societies indicate that democratic institutions and the rule of law (*Rechtsstaat*) do not necessarily coexist in practice. There are examples of nations with democratic institutions but rudimentary independent legal institutions, and societies that enjoy the rule of law in the absence of democratic processes. This contradictory diagnosis also applies to the factor "religion." The classics of the social science theory (Marx, Weber, and Durkheim) attribute a central social function to religion as a motor in the course of the development of modern societies. In contemporary theories of democracy, as Robert Barro (1999:175) emphasizes, "the theory of the interplay between religion and political structure" is

processes can be justified, and not only in theory, with respect to the key role of the economy for the nature of the existential conditions that prevail in a society and the frequent claim that we are witnessing an "economization" of all spheres of life in modern societies: The educational or health institutions of a society, but also its economic system (see Stehr, 2007) or the knowledge culture therefore fall under the strict imperative of economic thought and displace institution-specific goals.

Knowledge and liberties

Aside from the persistent and still unbroken belief in societal progress, for example, of constitutional arrangements within societies,[10] liberal thinkers of the nineteenth century in particular were convinced that the widespread dissemination of knowledge constituted an emancipatory force. Thus, the liberal English philosopher John Stuart Mill (1806–1873), in *The Spirit of the Age* – published in 1831 after his return to England from France, where he had encountered and taken in the philosophy of history in the political thinking of the St. Simonians and the early Comte – affirms his conviction that progress is possible in society as the result of the intellectual accomplishments of his own age. But progress and the improvement of social conditions are not, Mill argues, the outcome of an "increase in wisdom" or of the collective accomplishments of science. They are rather linked to the general diffusion of knowledge throughout society:

Men may not reason better, concerning the great questions in which human nature is interested, but they reason more. Large subjects are discussed more,

---

hardly ever present. The significant influence of religious affiliation or the dominant religion in a modern society probably operates primarily in response to or in conjunction with other social and cultural characteristics and processes (see also Michel, 1992). An empirical investigation (Vlas and Gherghina, 2012; see also Woodberry, 2012) with reference to data from the *European Value Survey* (from 1999) confirmed the conclusion that the immediate correlation between religion and democratic attitude is not clear-cut.

[10] As Eric Hobsbawm notes in an interview with the Indian magazine *Outlook India* (www.outlookindia.com/full.asp?fodname=20041227&fname=Hobsbawm+%28F%29&sid=1), in the nineteenth century, in the world of political practice, the conviction of civilizational progress meant "growing constitutionality, and in international relations, greater civility in arrangements between states. A good example of the former was the gradual disarming of the civilian population and the limitation of coercive power to the state and its agents. Another is the aversion to torture to extract information. All states, even imperialist powers, believed that there had to be a different, and a better way to obtain information. Trial and punishment had to be operated in a different way. Let me remember how strong this tradition was. There was a time when the US did not want to have a secret service. It was born of the now quaint sounding belief that gentlemen did not read each other's letters."

and longer, and by more minds. Discussion has penetrated deeper into society; and if greater numbers than before have attained the higher degrees of intelligence, fewer grovel in that state of abject stupidity, which can only co-exist with utter apathy and sluggishness (Mill [1831] 1997:8).

John Stuart Mill was a great admirer of the classic study of American society by Alexis de Tocqueville; as a matter of fact, Mill wrote a review of *Democracy in America* (1835–1840) that was published at almost the same time as his *The Spirit of the Age*. But there are decisive differences between Mill and de Tocqueville in their judgment of democracy, especially concerning the role that the knowledge held by citizens has for and in democratic regimes. De Tocqueville closes his observations about American society by observing that the educational attainment of its citizens is an influential force in maintaining democracy in America. While Mill has considerable confidence in the independent capacity of enlightenment, education and knowledge, and intellectual skills as the *necessary* condition for the strength of democratic regimes, de Tocqueville sees knowledge as the *sufficient* condition for democracy. From Mill's assumption it follows that intellectuals and scientists play a significant political role in democracies; in the case of de Tocqueville, it is the ordinary citizen and his or her immediate political practice that strengthens democratic political systems. According to de Tocqueville, what strengthens democracy above all is the individual citizen's immediate experience of the collective decision-making practice in the political system.

Mill's observations in the mid-nineteenth century, a period he regarded as an age of profound moral and political transition, and in particular his expectation that such beneficial consequences for society as increased individual choice for a greater number of people (and hence their emancipation from "custom") will be the result of a broader diffusion of knowledge and education, but not necessarily of scientific knowledge in the narrow sense of the term, resonates with the idea of modern society as a knowledge society; in particular, with the prevailing distribution of power in knowledge societies, the regime of inequality, and the role of the major institutions that largely controlled the social conditions not only in Mill's century, but also well into the twentieth century.

The perhaps uncritical trust advocated by liberal thinkers of the nineteenth century, such as John Stuart Mill or Alexis de Tocqueville, in the broader societal dispersion of knowledge as the basis for social and political progress, has been subjected to considerable stress in subsequent decades, and has of course met with severe objections. Among the notable skeptics is Friedrich Hayek (1960:326), for example, who emphasizes that "in their rationalist liberalism they [Mill, de Tocqueville] often presented the case for general education as though the dispersion of knowledge would solve all major problems and as though it were necessary only to convey to the masses that little extra knowledge which the educated already possessed in order that this 'conquest of ignorance' should initiate a new era ... Knowledge and ignorance are very relative concepts, and there is little evidence that the difference in knowledge which at any one time exists between the more and the less educated of a society can have such a decisive influence on its character." Hayek doubts that the principle of obligatory education in the hands of a single authority is a good thing, and argues in favor of the greatest possible variety of educational opportunities.

The undifferentiated view that education, once in place – and the more education, the better – will generate a strong inclination to favor democratic governance and support democratic institutions, however, remains a widely shared perspective. In the following sections I would like to critically explore this notion and the empirical evidence that has been amassed, and extend the basic thesis further to include particularly strong individual and collective resources that strengthen democracy. The basic thesis I will present employs a voluntaristic model of participation. This model suggests that unforced political interest and participation are best served by knowledgeability, the competence to take part in democratic decision-making processes, and the capacity to tolerate competing perspectives; that is, the ability to have an open mind.

The typical empirical indicators used to measure the knowledge of civil society are, in the case of modern societies, the degree of formal schooling; and in societies that are modernizing, the degree of literacy of the population. I will begin with a discussion of formal schooling and its linkage to democratic sentiments and support for democratic institutions and participation.

However, one needs to recognize that reflections about the role played by the formal education of large segments of the population in the formation and resilience of democratic governance is a phenomenon of the late twentieth century. As long as access to education in general, and higher education in particular, was highly stratified, social theoreticians were inclined to discuss the inhibiting role of education with respect to efforts to install democratic principles in social organizations such as political parties or government. Robert Michels ([1915] 1949:92) is only one among a number of social scientists and leaders of the working class movement in the nineteenth and early twentieth centuries to speak disparagingly of the "incompetence of the masses" and to believe that the authority of their leaders will inevitably, in the long run, be "destructive to the very principle of democracy." The principle source of power that negates efforts to establish democratic governance is the "indispensability" of the leaders of the working class movement and their political organization. The specific source of power, however, is the educational advantages enjoyed by the leaders.[11] Michels does not merely refer to the degree of formal education of the leaders but also to their accumulated experience gained in practical political settings. It is only after some of the hurdles to a broad dissemination of education were dismantled that reflections about the role of formal education in establishing and sustaining democracy could become credible hypotheses.[12]

The "knowledge explosion" of the twentieth century is part of a functional democratization, the growing diffusion of social power. Although the expansion and democratization of knowledge, as Norbert Elias (1984:253) notes, is still in its infancy, "the rise of educational standards reached so far, has been enough to increase very noticeably the power potential of a country's population." It is the observation about the general expansion and societal diffusion of education that has driven the analysis of the nature of its association with the democratization process.

The role of formal education (schooling)

> The faster the enlightenment of the population, the more frequent the overthrow of the government.
> Samuel Huntington (1968:47)

Formal educational attainment or years of education often serve, especially in empirical studies (most often based on cross-sectional data)

---

[11] For some reason, Michels' crucial observation about the advantageous role of education (specifically of *Bildung*, which is not identical with but exceeds that which tends to be understood as education) for the leadership of working-class organizations is missing from the English translation of his study *Political Parties*. In the original, Michels ([1915] 1970:81) explicitly emphasizes that the workers themselves are creating their new masters, "whose higher education is in the arsenal of their accumulated means of authority the most potent weapon." Michels ([1915] 1949:93) adds "the incompetence of the masses is almost universal throughout the domains of political life, and this constitutes the most solid foundation of the power of the leaders ... Since the rank and file are incapable of looking after their own interests, it is necessary that they should have experts to attend to their affairs."

[12] *Union Democracy*, the classical empirical research study of the U.S. International Typographical Union by Seymour Martin Lipset, Martin Trow, and James Coleman ([1956] 1962:464), published half a century after Robert Michels' analysis, confirms and explicates the "iron law of oligarchy." The study by Lipset and his colleagues shows that "where an effective and organized opposition [within the union] does exist, it does so only because the incumbent administration does not hold a monopoly over the resources of politics." *Union Democracy* demonstrates in "what ways the nature of printing as occupation and industry tends to make more widely available than is true for most private organizations the resources of democratic politics."

carried out in modern societies, as a *proxy* for the volume of knowledge, the cognitive abilities, or the information a person is assumed to command. Exactly what kind of symmetry exists between knowledge/information, cognitive capacities, and educational attainment, let alone the extent of the political activity of individuals, is far from self-evident, requires scrutiny, and has been a somewhat neglected theoretical issue (cf. Oelkers, 2000:5; Bauer, 2003). However, a common perspective, backed by considerable empirical evidence, holds that high levels of schooling, college and university education, and their rapid expansion go hand in hand with an enlargement of the collective enlightenment of the population, the cultivation of political interest (Wolfinger and Rosenstone, 1980), and political participation (e.g., Hillygus, 2005; Mayer, 2011; skeptic: Kam and Palmer, 2008, 2011). Not only are the enabling consequences of education – that is, active political participation – an important precondition for democracy and a major force in how democratization processes evolve, but they also play an important role in maintaining the political stability of democratic countries and engender general life satisfaction (cf. Pacheco and Lange, 2010).

Robert Putnam (1995b:68) therefore has good reason to elevate formal education to the status of "the best individual-level predictor of political participation." In a narrower sense, civic education programs are expected to confer democratic citizenship values to their participants (e.g., Finkel, 2003). Over the past decades there has been an abundance of such programs, supported by international organizations and private donors. How effective such efforts are in promoting democratic values is difficult to establish (cf. Finkel and Smith, 2011).[13] The common view is that education, including civic education programs, fosters a "culture of democracy" (see Chong and Gradstein, 2009); and as a result, the returns from education justify the extensive involvement of the state in providing for public schools and universities, as well as the many public policies directed toward the education of its population.

But as Robert Dahl (1992:50) notes in a much more skeptical tone, the capacity to comprehend political issues based on the average level of

---

[13] The findings of an empirical study by Finkel and Smith (2011:432–434) of the nationwide *Kenyan National Education Programme*, which between 2001–2002 reached some 15 percent of the population of Kenya with more than 50,000 activities coordinated by non-governmental organizations, make evident that "the potential impact of adult civic education on strengthening democratic political culture in transition societies is far beyond what has previously been estimated." The educational programs described are likely to be incapable of compensating for democracy deficits of another sort; nor should one expect such programs to be capable of simply eliminating existing ethnic and religious prejudices.

education may not have kept pace with the increased complexity of policy issues and politics in modern democratic states, even though the average educational attainment has significantly risen in many countries.

One of the best-known studies of this kind, and a highly influential general assertion about the promotion of democracy by formal educational attainment, may be found in Seymour Martin Lipset's (1959:79–80) study of the social requisites of democracy:

> Education presumably broadens men's outlooks, enables them to understand the need for norms of tolerance, restrains them from adhering to extremist and monistic doctrines, and increases their capacity to make rational electoral choices ... If we cannot say that a high level of education is a sufficient condition for democracy, the available evidence does suggest that it comes close to being a necessary condition.

Recent large comparative studies – for example, by Robert Barro (1999), Adam Przeworski and his colleagues (2000), or Edward Glaeser and his colleagues (2004) – confirm the view that the *average years of schooling* of a population and the presence of democratic institutions in a country are positively related. These studies are based on cross-sectional correlations, omitting the influence of country-fixed attributes, and could therefore suffer from a potential omitted variable bias; hence, as Acemoglu and colleagues (2006:44) emphasize, "existing inferences may be potentially driven by omitted factors influencing both education and democracy in the long run."

A close link between education and democracy would also mean that changes in democracy should be observed as being a result of collective changes in the level of education in a society. For example, a country should become more "democratic" as its citizens become more educated. But this is not the case: "Countries that become more educated show no greater tendency to become more democratic" (Acemoglu et al., 2006:44). The exact nature of the omitted factors that influence both education and democracy remain unexamined, at least in the study by Acemoglu and his colleagues. Omitted factors could refer to collective attributes and time-sensitive factors, such as the level of economic development of a country; the level of economic compensation for years of education; or the shape of the distribution of years of schooling among the population as a whole; but also to country-fixed effects, that is, attributes of a society that are time-invariant, such as the early density of indigenous populations; or to environmental factors, such as the climate of a region. Acemoglu and colleagues (2006:47) indicate that their findings lead them to the conclusion that "there is no empirical relationship between education and democracy once country-fixed effects are included, and therefore they cast considerable doubt on the causal effect of education on democracy."

Amparo Castelló-Climent (2008) challenges, or better, adds important theoretical insights and extensive empirical results to the discussion of the relation between democracy and education. She employs a different statistical technique to enquire into the relation between education and democracy that enable her to control for country-specific factors; in addition, she incorporates a measure of the societal *distribution of education* into her analysis. The measure of the distribution of years of education is, of course, sensitive to the possibility that the measure of the collective educational attainment in a country is confined to or represents the educational achievement of a minority elite. Following a suggestion initially expressed by Bourguignon and Verdier (2000), Castelló-Climent (2008:180) finds, for her sample of 104 countries for the period between 1965–2000, that a more equal distribution of education (as measured by the share of education attained by at least 60 percent of individuals in the country) is a better predictor of democracy (using the *Freedom House Political Rights Index*)[14] than is an increase in the average years of formal schooling of the population aged twenty-five and over.

These findings regarding the significance of the distribution of education persist after controlling for omitted variables (per capita income, investment share of GDP, urbanization rate, population size, health indicators, the gap between male and female schooling, the Gini coefficient, ethnolinguistic fractionalization, percentage of Muslims in the country) that impact on both education and democracy. None of the controls change the main finding reported by Castelló-Climent (2008:186). In addition, the author controls for country-fixed effects (represented by geography, for example) and endowments, concluding that the findings are not changed. Thus, these findings are in concert with Lipset's views

---

[14] The *Freedom House Political Rights Index* (cf.www.freedomhouse.org) is based on a checklist of twenty-five questions concerning political rights and civil liberties in a country. Freedom House annually assigns every recognized country in the world scores on political rights and civil liberties. The accumulated responses are aggregated into a single score from 1 to 7, indicating greater liberties the closer the score comes to 1. The political rights questions contain three sub-categories: electoral process, political pluralism and participation, and the functioning of government. The civil liberties questions include four subcategories: freedom of expression and belief, association and organization rights, rule of law, and personal autonomy and individual rights. An alternative measure is the so-called POLITY score (Marshall and Jaggers, 2005), to which I will refer in the discussion of the role of transnational networks as a motor of democratization (see also Högström, 2013). For arguments for a new approach to measure democratic regimes, see Coppedge et al. (2011:248) who "touch briefly on six key issues of conceptualization and measurement: definition, precision, coverage and sources, coding, aggregation, and validity and reliability tests."

about the impact of formal education on the political governance of a society and its prevailing political attitudes and social values.

Another empirical study of recent date, which can also be considered support for the Lipset thesis, examines the positive influence of education on the political participation and civic engagement of the public. First, however, Thomas Dee (2003:2; also Milligan, Moretti, and Oreopoulos, 2003) emphasizes that this correlation may be spurious because it is quite possible that individuals "who grew up in cohesive families and communities that stressed civic responsibility may also be more likely to remain in school. The plausible existence of such unobservables implies that conventionally estimated correlations might spuriously overstate the true civic returns to education." Second, the empirical data of its own study make it clear that education has a statistically significant influence on voting behavior and selected values (support for freedom of speech). Even more important is another result of Dee's study (2003:24). The author "assessed whether increases in educational attainment have causal effects on civic outcomes by exploiting possibly exogenous sources of variation in schooling that should otherwise be unrelated to civic outcomes in adulthood (i.e., the geographic availability of two-year colleges as a teen and exposure to child labor laws as a teen). The results suggested that educational attainment, both at the post-secondary and the secondary levels, has large and independent effects on most measures of civic engagement and attitudes."

Recent political upheavals and revolutions in some countries of the Middle East have shown that the path toward democratic governance and human dignity is a long one. At the same time, the recent events in the Middle East triggered a renewed interest in the role of changing patterns of formal education, and with it emerging expectations about the personal and collective future of the population of these countries, including that of women, and their possible impact on the popular uprising not only in Arab countries, but also on prodemocracy protests in other societies (cf. Glasius and Pleyers, 2013). Robert Barro and Lee Jong Wha (2010) have documented in what way the rapid increase in schooling in these countries affected the political upheavals: "Egypt and Tunisia, for instance, all registered large gains in total years of schooling among the population aged 15 and above, respectively rising from 2.6 to 7.1 years and from 3.2 to 7.3 years between 1980 and 2010. Out of the top 20 countries in the world as ranked by increases in general schooling during this period, there were eight Arab League countries" (Campante and Chor, 2011; also Drucker 1968:1248). By the same token, the participation of women – not only well-educated women – appears to have been a significant part of the move toward a democratic polity in these countries.

The significant and rapid increase in the schooling of large cohorts of the younger population as well as their access to global information streams raises the question to what extent these skills, and their allied expectations about adequate economic rewards, are translated into gainful employment – or into political activities, should a country fail to provide satisfactory financial compensation and jobs that require the skills gained. Campante and Chor's (2011) study offers a compelling answer to the question of the impact of schooling on political activities in societies with a low-skilled economy, but a rapid increase in the skill levels of significant portions of their population: the economies of the Middle East are, as yet, typically not skill-intensive economies. The Arab world for the most part lags behind other world regions in building knowledge-based economies. Thus, it would appear that "an interaction between individual skills and the dearth of economic opportunities that reward those skills lies at the heart of the political turmoil that has shaken the Arab world" (Campante and Chor, 2011:2). The evidence presented by Campante and Chor (2011b:20) shows that "individuals whose income underperforms what would have been predicted given their level of schooling are more inclined to use their human capital in political activities such as demonstrations, strikes, and occupation of buildings." What matters in premodern and modernizing societies, as a number of historians and sociologists have hypothesized (e.g., Stone, 1969; Lerner, 1958), is not so much the increase in formal education among the population, which begins to exert an influence only later, but rather the degree of literacy.

Christopher Hill (1967:124), in a review of Peter Laslett's *The World We Have Lost* (1965), doubts that political participation and direct participation in the revolutionary political changes in a nation were historically reserved exclusively for the reading and literate members of society: "The French, Russian, and Chinese Revolutions, like the English, are inconceivable without the political actions of illiterate masses, however much lead the literate may have given them." To clarify this question, I will respond to an empirical study by John Markoff (1986), who investigated the connection with the literacy rate of the population in France at the time of the French Revolution.

First, however, I would like to make reference to Daniel Lerner's (1958) three-phase model of democratization or modernization processes, in which the degree of literacy plays a significant role as a motor of social change. Lerner (1958:60) argues that the development of participatory societies occurs in three phases:

Urbanization comes first ... Within this urban context develop both of the attributes which distinguish the next two phases – literacy and media growth. There is a close reciprocal relationship between these, for the literate develop the media which in turn spreads literacy. But, literacy performs the key function in the second phase. The capacity to read, at first acquired by relatively few people, equips them to perform the varied tasks required in the modernizing society ... Out of this interaction develop those institutions of participation (e.g., voting) which we find in all advanced modern societies.

The literacy rate of the population, according to the three-phase model, is quite unequivocally a decisive impetus for the democratization of a society. Since Lerner formulated this thesis in the mid-1950s, however, it has become clear that in many developing countries, at least in the short and middle term, literacy is not developing the required thrust. This should not be taken to mean that there may not be an increasingly close relation between literacy and democracy in the future. Whether the literacy factor will then have the force anticipated by Lerner, however, cannot be predicted. In any case, more recent cultural, economic, or transnationally induced social developments will have a comparably great influence on democratization.

There are a number of hypotheses that address the question why the literacy rate of a population should influence their political attitudes and political action. This includes, for example, the thesis that in societies in which the work of cultural transmission relies on the oral tradition rather than written narratives and history, politics have a different face. Politically relevant legitimations of the past can be used much more easily in written cultures as a critical contrast in current conflicts. It is easier to see that things could be different. Resistance and opposition can be easily legitimated and objectified. In written cultures, the ability to come into contact with critical political thinking is greater since the dissemination of these ideas is easier to accomplish. Finally, the political mobilization is easier to organize in societies with written cultures and their media. Markoff (1986:326) emphasizes that literacy "greatly increases [the possibility] to send multiple parties the same message; to send messages that do not degrade with distance or the passage of time; to receive responses to one's queries and criticisms of one's proposals that are thoughtfully addressed to the central matters at hand because one's queries and proposals have been scrutinized at leisure and in detail." Markoff's empirical study of the French Revolution is an attempt to test the thesis of the importance of literacy for organized political action in the context of the major political revolutions. Markoff's concrete, empirical question is: What is the relationship between the geography of the revolt and the geography of the literacy level in France in 1789? The data of the geographical distribution of reading and writing skills in France reported from department to department showed significant differences, with rates of 5–91 percent. Markoff's (1986:332) study demonstrates first of all that "there are no consistent signs that literacy, by increasing the capacity for coordinated activity, indiscriminately made mobilization for all purposes easier ... There are also no apparent signs of the kind of free-floating alienation, resentment, or dissatisfaction that is sometimes believed to characterize the thought processes induced by literacy."

However, Markoff is not yet convinced that the different literacy levels of the French population remained completely without political consequences. The general willingness not to rebel against the prevailing political conditions may very well go hand in hand with different political strategies in counties with varying levels of literacy, that is, the reading and writing skills "may still have been significant in shaping the forms that contentiousness assumed and the targets against which that mobilization was directed" (Markoff, 1986:333).

Based on these considerations, Markov arrives at a new hypothesis with respect to the counties in which there was a political mobilization: Was the reading and writing ability in these cases of importance? Markoff's (1986:334) data show that

at the highest level of literacy there is a dramatic jump in the likelihood that a *bailliage* experienced attacks on the lord, the church, or the state; that there is a consistent and considerable decrease in occurrences of the Great Fear (i.e., this was a widespread rural panic in which peasant communities sought arms and leadership to defend themselves against nonexistent attacks from bandits or townsfolk or aristocrats or foreign armies) as literacy climbs; and that, although there is considerable variation, there is no consistent relationship between literacy and subsistence action.

Markoff sums up the results of his study results as follows: "[I]f any regions may be said to have produced social movements that pressed for change in critical social institutions instead of for an immediate stopgap in a crisis, it was those in the most literate areas of rural France." The reading and writing abilities of different regions of France during the French Revolution had an impact not so much on the general political action but on the forms of this political action (Markoff, 1986:342).

Despite the intense analytical and empirical efforts, it should be noted that the expected relationship between education, especially in terms of the formal degree of education, and democratization or barriers to democracy remains an ambivalent and contested thesis. In particular, given the large number of intervening factors, such as a person's age, family affiliation, or social origin, the possible causal relationship between cognitive abilities and education is controversial (cf. Carlsson, Dahl, and Rooth, 2012). This ambivalent conclusion also applies to the potential connection between knowledgeability, cognitive processes, and democratization.

The social phenomenon of knowledgeability as a form of soft power

> Once works of the intellect had become sources of force and wealth, each development of science, each new piece of knowledge, each new idea had to be considered as a seed of power put within reach of the people.
> de Tocqueville ([1835–40] 2000:5)

> Wissensfunktion und politische Funktion lassen sich letztlich nicht trennen.[15]
> Niklas Luhmann (1990:149)

The term "knowledgeability" is not a common expression found in social science discourse; nor is the concept, as a result, an essentially contested notion (following the usage of this idea as explicated by Gallie, 1955–1956). Nonetheless, a few discussions in social science that make reference to knowledgeability may be found. Before I will advance my own specification of the term, and without wanting to become too entangled in extensive terminological debates, I would first like to briefly deal with the concept of "knowledgeability" as deployed by Anthony Giddens (1984:21–22), for example, in the context of his structuration theory. His knowledge-guiding interest is "to try to show how we might develop a view of social analysis which recognises the knowledgeability of social actors, but at the same time acknowledges the bounds of that knowledgeability, and thereby allows you to use some of these insights in a context which doesn't sacrifice institutional study" (in Mullan, 1997:81).

Giddens' term *knowledgeability* refers to practical knowledge (practical consciousness), and thus knowledge as a "normal" or everyday point of reference of social action shared by many – although in a tacit, or not immediately apparent or accessible, sense (Giddens, 1984:xxiii; see also Berger and Luckmann, 1966).[16] Knowledge, so defined, is a condition for social action. Using Pierre Bourdieu's terms, common sense or practical knowledge almost always corresponds to the nonreflexive *sens pratique*. Practical knowledge refers to an immediate competence in making sense of the world. However, it is a competence that is, as it were, oblivious to itself (Bourdieu, [1980] 1990:19). It does not contain

---

[15] "In the final analysis, the function of knowledge and the political function cannot be separated."

[16] Friedrich von Hayek (1945:523) also refers (in his essay "The use of knowledge in society") to "problems" and that it is important to stress "that economic problems arise always and only in consequence of change." Social change leads to a mobilization of knowledge for as "long as things continue as before, or at least as they were expected to, there arise no new problems requiring a decision, no need to form a new plan."

the knowledge of the practices it generates. The practical mode of relating to the social world is, as Bourdieu ([1980]: 1990:19) also describes it, a relation of "learned ignorance" (*docta ignorantia*).[17]

Giddens' usage of the term *knowledgeability* appeals principally to these universalistic, ahistorical attributes of practical knowledge found in all societies at all times, and not to the questions taken up in this study: what is the role and importance of knowledgeability as a core attribute of agency for democracy; how and why does knowledge increase; how is knowledgeability distributed in modern societies; how do the knowledge-based experts and professions mediate knowledge and political action; does highly specialized knowledge endanger democracy; what are the (possibly) changing relations of influence between sociostructural characteristics of societies and knowledgeability; how does knowledge give rise to authority, solidarity, or economic growth; and what influence does knowledge have on governance, and therefore the power structures of societies? And finally, to what extent may knowledgeability serve as a barrier, and not as facilitator, to the concentration of societal power? Could knowledge or knowledgeability be a weapon of the weak in society – a weapon enhanced by the establishment of local information and knowledge infrastructures, for example those that are no longer controlled only by the powerful in a community?

Anthony Giddens' interest centers on the community of knowledge shared among actors against the backdrop of the unintended consequences of their action (Giddens, 1981:28); my interest focuses on the knowledge that, even if only temporarily, is not at hand and must again and again be obtained by actors. Giddens presents an ontological thesis; I am basically concerned with the fact that actors do not content themselves with knowing, but rather want to know more than their fellow-actors, and thus with the problem that knowledge in social contexts is an excluding, stratifying, or distributive phenomenon of social action.

My definition of *knowledgeability* and its social distribution as both an individual and a corporate attribute of social conduct – which therefore

---

[17] John Dewey ([1916] 2005:) offers essentially the same perspective on commonsense knowledge when he writes: "Habits reduce themselves to routine ways of acting, or degenerate into ways of action to which we are enslaved just in the degree in which intelligence is disconnected from them. Routine habits are unthinking habits: bad habits are habits so severed from reason that they are opposed to the conclusions of conscious deliberation and decision. As we have seen, the acquiring of habits is due to an original plasticity of our natures: to our ability to vary responses till we find an appropriate and efficient way of acting. Routine habits, and habits that possess us instead of our possessing them, are habits which put an end to plasticity."

may well be a most significant attribute in sociohistorical processes that account for the emergence and endurance of "regions" of liberties – refers *neither* to what is typically called common sense, nonreflexive, or ordinary knowledge; *nor* to specialized scientific-technical knowledge as representing the core of knowledgeablity and agency.

At the same time, the concept of knowledgeability, as I use it in this study to refer to a bundle of competencies embedded within social contexts, stands in a more or less – perhaps rather less – close relationship to such concepts as cleverness, wisdom, or judgment. These latter concepts, as far as I can see, refer primarily to individuals' intellectual capabilities that are additionally valued in a collective due to their rarity but which, like the concept of knowledgeability, are also aimed at producing practical achievements.

Knowledgeability should not be conflated with knowledge, and especially not with its frequent proxy in empirical studies: years of formal schooling as a measure of the degree of learning of a person. After all, measures of years of formal schooling hide the immense variety of educational and vocational accomplishments in very different institutions of learning. This is especially the case for societies with a highly differentiated and stratified "supply" of educational opportunities.

Knowledgeability is closer to what is at times defined as *reflexive* or *theoretical* knowledge; thus, common sense and theoretical knowledge refer to different domains of the substance and the social distribution of knowledge in society. Knowledgeability does not refer to individual, isolated cognitive agents. Reference is always to communities of cognitive actors. Knowledgeability should be conceptualized as a bundle of social competencies that drive the process of political and economic participation, for example, and that are related to specific dispositions, as I will enumerate. Knowledgeability should be seen, for instance, as the ability of actors and groups of actors to move items of concern onto a particular (political) agenda; to develop and practice new forms of political attentiveness (social attentiveness, see Rosanvallon, [2006] 2008:40); as bottom-up innovation (cf. von Hippel, 2006)[18]; and as the foundation stones of patterns of social inequality that both generate and maintain social prestige and status in modern societies.

---

[18] "Democratized" innovation processes, for example, refer to the capacity of users of products and services – both firms and individuals – to innovate, independently of their degree of formal education, for themselves, rather than rely on manufacturing-centric innovation (von Hippel, 2006:1).

Of particular interest – though I cannot analyze this issue in detail at this point[19] – are of course the social conditions that promote or hinder the societal mobilization of knowledgeability (e.g., so-called "critical moments" of social action [Boltanski and Thévenot, 1999] in contrast to the far more typical conditions of action that are largely unproblematic and routine [see Luckmann, 1982]) as well as the places in society where knowledgeability tends to be acquired (cf. Sörlin, 2002). Recently, for example, frequent reference has been made not only to the importance of the Internet as an engine of knowledgeability, but also to the dangers posed by influential Internet companies using software codes to systematically "personalize," and thereby control and limit, individual Internet access.[20]

As I have indicated, knowledgeability should not be conflated with years of formal education, although there is bound to be a significant association between years of schooling and knowledgeability, for example in terms of the conviction of having control over events, which is likely to be associated with higher levels of formal education (cf. Schieman and Plickert, 2008) and occupation status. An emphasis on years of schooling and/or tertiary education often makes the misleading implicit reference to isolated agents and accomplishments, devoid of any social embeddedness. As the enumeration of specific knowledgeability traits listed below shows, knowledgeability is a collective achievement and always has collective references (cf. Fuerstein, 2008:78), for example in the specific sense of the network of reference groups of an individual actor (see Grofman and Norrander, 1990). However, the attribute of knowledgeability of an actor, or a group of actors, may well extend to persons with little, if any, formal education. Aside from highly speculative assertions about the difference between level of education and knowledgeability, reference to educational attainment is the best general indicator for the role education may play in nurturing and sustaining democracy (cf. Dewey, [1916] 2005).

These abstract observations about the growing role of knowledge in modern societies, especially about the mobilization of knowledge by growing segments of the population, are not yet linked to observations about the acquisition and inheritance of these resources from generation to generation. However, if one follows Bourdieu's assertions about the acquisition of the social resource of knowledge, one would expect that knowledge, as

---

[19] However, I refer to my discussion of "open" conditions of action that prompt demands for knowledge, in the first instance.
[20] See Eli Pariser, "When the Internet thinks it knows you," *New York Times*, May 22, 2011.

part of the more general resource of cultural capital, should primarily be found among selective strata of society who are able to take advantage of the capital controlled by their families (cf. Bourdieu, [1979] 1984).

This is certainly true of a more or less large sector of the total population; but it does not explain how further strata of the population (the supposedly weak strata) may acquire the attributes of knowledgeability despite a deficit of inherited cultural capital. Access to and facility with these attributes apparently is not only a function of inherited, traditional capabilities, but is codetermined by the fundamental openness of knowledgeability. At the same time, Bourdieu's findings leave open the question of why and how the extent of available knowledge in society, and thus the resource of knowledgeability, grows (cf. Goldthorpe, 2007). After all, one of the unique attributes of knowledge, in comparison to other societal resources, is that it lacks restrictive zero-sum qualities; rather, it is much more difficult to control or limit access to this resource as compared to others.

Knowledgeability as a bundle of competencies

> The way the modern state and economy are organised ensures that a privileged position is permanently given to *socialised training* and thereby to 'education' (*Bildung*) ... this being one of the most powerful factors in status groups (*ständisch*) differentiation in modern society.
>
> Max Weber ([1917] 1994:103–104)

As I have already had occasion to stress in the context of inquiring into the interdependence of prosperity and democracy, nothing in the history of the industrialized countries of Western Europe and North America resembles the experience of the years between 1950 and 1985. By the end of this period, the perpetual possibility of serious economic hardship, which in earlier periods had threatened the well-being of up to three-quarters of the population, now affected only one fifth. Although real poverty still existed in even the richest countries, the material standard of living for most people improved almost without interruption, and quite rapidly, for thirty-five years. In addition, during the same period access to higher education doubled or tripled in many countries. This unprecedented prosperity and the growing access especially to higher education mark this period as unique. Many individuals and families are better off than ever before in the history of humankind. Many people – not all, of course – have more choices, including those concerning education.

The focus on knowledgeability not only points to a new foundation of political interest and participation but also puts the spotlight on more effective pressures from citizens demanding the accountability of institutional arrangements.[21] Exactly what mental and social resources of action allow for the possibility of new forms of participation? And how broadly do these resources need to be distributed in society in order to extend participation to non-elite strata of a population? More concretely, how does knowledgeability function as a resource in struggles for power or dominance in political representations?

Knowledgeability, formulated in a less abstract fashion than in the previous section, represents a broad and heterogeneous *bundle of competencies*; not, however, in the sense of strictly psychological dispositions (cf. Lane, 1953)[22] that have enabling capacities, and therefore noticeable effects on the *process* of collective participation and inequality formation in modern societies, as well as on individual well-being. In this respect, the knowledge ability approach has a certain affinity with that of Amartya Sen (e.g., 1984, 2002) and Martha Nussbaum (e.g., 2000) who in distinctive ways but also jointly developed (Nussbaum and Sen, 1993) the capabilities approach, that is, humans seen as self-determined beings who arrange their lives in cooperation and reciprocity with others on the basis of certain skills. The practice of the human capabilities identified by Nussbaum and Sen in order to achieve certain goals constitute human life: "The central capabilities are not just instrumental to further pursuits: they are held to have value in themselves, in making the life that includes them fully human" (Nussbaum, 2000:74).[23] In the realm of politics and political participation, the competencies that make up knowledgeability enhance and promote the interest in political affairs and the ability to reason about them, to arrive at political decisions independently and to influence other actors.

In this sense, knowledgeability possesses qualities that are unlike earlier, more singular and often ascriptive mechanisms of political participation and social inequality, for example. Unpacking the bundle of competencies means enumerating some of the important specific capacities conferred by knowledge, capacities that are mobilized variously in accordance with the demands of specific social contexts. The concrete

---

[21] Daniel Bell (1973:44) remarks that any new social system generates hostility among those who feel left out or threatened by it. Among the primary cleavages and sources of tension in the "emerging post-industrial society is the conflict generated by a meritocracy principle which is central to the allocation of position in the knowledge society."

[22] My reference is to Robert Lane's (1953) typology of political character, in analogy to David Riesman's inner-directed and outer-directed individuals.

[23] Amartya Sen (1992:5) enumerates a number of distinctive goals whose realization depends on the abilities of a person: "The functionings included can vary from the most elementary one, such as being well-nourished, avoiding escapable morbidity and premature mortality, etc., to quite complex and sophisticated achievements, such as having self-respect, being able to take part in the life of the community, and so on."

distribution, the substitutive possibilities and multiple interdependencies among competencies result in an ever less "coherent" and transparent, at times even invisible, system of inequality in modern knowledge societies. Both political participation and social patterns of inequality and well-being become a heterogeneous and context-dependent figuration, instead of a generalized asset. I will list below the most important social and cognitive competencies and capabilities that drive not only sociopolitical participation but also inequality and well-being in modern society.

The capacity to exploit discretion. Since the social rules and legal norms and regulations that govern ordinary and extraordinary social conduct are never constituted and enforced in ways that do not allow for discretionary interpretation and execution, the (for example, financial) competence to mobilize discretion refers to the capacity of individuals to gain comparative advantages – for example, in such areas as taxation, investment, consumption, schooling, and income (cf. Ambuehl, Bernheim, and Lusardi, 2014). For instance, tax authorities are now confronting the problem of the "disappearing taxpayer." It is anticipated that tax revenues will fall worldwide because companies can move to avoid levies and because electronic commerce is virtually impossible to tax (cf. *The Economist,* May 31, 1997).

The facility to organize protection. The capacity to put protective devices and measures in place is a matter of specialized competence, enabling actors to mobilize access to differential knowledge in order to ensure, for example, that assets and entitlements are protected against structural or inordinate depreciation (see Klapper, Lusardi, and Panos, 2012; Lusardi, 2013).[24] The symbolic or material opportunity costs of the failure to organize protection and diagnose opportunities of course can be considerable.

The authority to speak (cf. Bourdieu, 1975; Lyotard, [1979] 1984) and effectively participate in various settings of society, which extends, for example, to the ability, the self-confidence, and self-esteem to introduce items onto the agenda or to challenge the discourse of experts (see Feyerabend, 1978:96–97). One of the conditions for democratic control is the capacity, if one happens to be in the opposition, to place items on the political program of the day. The authority to speak/participate

---

[24] Annamaria Lusardi (2013) has shown in a large-scale empirical study of the borrowing patterns of American consumers that "it it is not only the shocks inflicted by the financial crisis or the structure of the financial system but that the level of financial literacy also plays a role in explaining why so many individuals have made use of high-cost borrowing methods."

extends to the ability to formulate alternative political goals or to empower nonexperts to judge experts' points of view. The ability to raise one's voice is based on differential knowledge and information, which under contemporary circumstances is a function also of media literacy (cf. Mihailidis and Thenenin, 2013) and produces a parallel social division in opposition to those not authorized to participate. The authority to speak in order to dissent applies, for instance, to many features and situations[25] in everyday life, but also extends to the ability of lay audiences or persons to enter a discursive field or habitat of expertise as "speakers and confront the alleged truth of the discourse that justifies those practices" (Larson, 1990:37). By the same token, the inability to mobilize information and master knowledge is increasingly interpreted as a sign of personal failure and could be quite independent of the modes of exclusion/inclusion closely associated with differential (formal) education.

The faculty to engage (possibly conflicting) multiple viewpoints.[26] The ability to hear, to tolerate, to improvise, to consider rival points of view, or to expand or bring them closer together through networking – for example, in the field of political discourse, investing, health, or collective action, but also many other perspectives in mundane life, everyday or extraordinary – is a distinct cognitive asset in arriving at one's standpoint, defending it, and persuading others of the value of a perspective or decision. The faculty to engage, articulate, and perhaps even integrate multiple viewpoints ("integrative complexity" [cf. Tetlock, 2002]) extends to the ability to aggregate and collate what amounts to "dispersed knowledge" (Hayek, 1945:519) in society.[27] In other words, one of the intellectual conditions for the possibility of effectively deploying this trait of knowledgeability is familiarity with multiple fields of

---

[25] Sprague and Rudd (1988) have examined the nature and the extent of organizational dissent in high-technology industry.

[26] C. W. Mills' (1959:7) conception of *sociological imagination* represents almost exactly the capacity to engage different points of view: "The sociological imagination is the capacity to shift from one perspective to another – from the political to the psychological; from examination of a single family to comparative assessment of the national budgets of the world; from the theological school to the military establishment; from consideration of an oil industry to studies of contemporary poetry. It is the capacity to range from the most impersonal and remote transformations to the most intimate features of the human self – and to see the relations between the two."

[27] Friedrich Hayek's (1945:519) classic formulation of dispersed knowledge refers to the discrete knowledge distributed among *economic* actors in the marketplace only: "The peculiar character of the problem of a rational economic order is determined precisely by the fact that the knowledge of the circumstances of which we must make use never exists in concentrated or integrated form but solely as the dispersed bits of incomplete and frequently contradictory knowledge, which all the separate individuals possess."

knowledge.[28] In the field of political activities, the ability "to coordinate many discrete bodies of knowledge, diversely distributed across the political community" (Fuerstein, 2008:78), rather than the full-fledged command of any specific, for example, disciplinary body of knowledge, represents a salient attribute of knowledgeability. Last but not least, the capacity to engage multiple viewpoints in a democracy extends to the ability to tolerate conflicting ideas or simply display an open mind.[29]

The ability to mobilize defiance and organize resistance constitutes another crucial component of the stratifying mode of knowledge (cf. Essed, 1991). To challenge the practices of experts, the state, or corporations and insist on accountability constitutes an important asset of knowledge as a capacity to contribute to participatory capabilities. A case in point would be the development and extension of moral markets (Stehr, 2008), the ability to generate political attentiveness as a way of surveilling the powerful or the activities of social movements targeting corporate, educational, and other institutions and demanding transparency and accountability (Walker, Martin, and McCarthy, 2008). In the same sense, the ability to evade surveillance by the state or in the marketplace, to formulate discourses of resistance and obtain spaces of self-regulated autonomy, acquires considerable significance, and is based on the capacity to mobilize tools that are typically seen as exclusively scrutiny enhancing instruments.

The capacity of avoidance, resilience, and exclusion is a further stratifying trait that can be enlisted in accordance with different knowledge bases. Such strategies ensure that some of the risks of modern society are distributed differentially; for example, in the areas of safety concerns, psychological resilience, exposure to conflict or violence, health risks (cf. Meghir et al., 2013), or environmental degradation. The capacity of avoidance extends to the ability to tolerate risks, build up resilience and security against potential dangers as well as endure failure. By the same token, the tremendous growth of the "informal economy" in most advanced societies – that is, of the most varied forms of economic transactions that, irrespective of their legality, are beyond the control of

[28] See Robert Twigger, "Master of many trades," *Aeon*, November 2013, www.aeonmagazine.com/world-views/anyone-can-learn-to-be-a-polymath/ (accessed November 30, 2013). Cf. also Adolf, Mast and Stehr, 2013.
[29] The ability to tolerate conflicting points of view has considerable affinity to John Rawls' (1997:766) notion of public reason: In a democratic society "citizens realize that they cannot reach agreement or even approach mutual understanding on the basis of their irreconcilable comprehensive doctrines. In view of this, they need to consider what kinds of reasons they may reasonably give to one another when fundamental political questions are at stake. I propose that in public reason comprehensive doctrines of truth or right be replaced by an idea of the politically reasonable addressed to citizens as citizens."

the state and the legal system – may be seen as one of the major socio-economic consequences of the rise of knowledgeability as a stratifying principle that affects the material basis of well-being.

The ability to generate new and persuasive ideas or opinions,[30] for example, on the basis of the capacity to apply knowledge to knowledge that may find its place on the basis of unforced persuasion – for example, on the political agenda of the day.[31] Since neither knowledge, as the capacity to act, nor information describing features of a person or a thing contain specific references to what to do, let alone the circumstances and commitments that would allow for them to be set in motion, ideas have the unique ability to recommend and mobilize action by virtue of the diagnosis of a state of affairs contained in the statement of ideas. Ideas ("the basis of social inequality is unjust") contain kernels of a call for action. As is the case for all of the parts of the bundle of competencies I have enumerated, the benefits for the individual or collectivity that come with opinions and ideas can of course have their direct or indirect downside; they do not only confer status and satisfaction and bring about social and political change.[32]

The range of social competencies generally amounts to stratified facilities for *mastering the quality of one's life*; that is, the capacity to take initiatives and responsibility, for example, for one's health (life expectancy),[33] financial well-being, personal life, aspirations, one's community,

---

[30] Joseph Nye (1990) designates the ability to generate new and persuasive ideas that may make it onto the political agenda of the day as a form of soft power. The notion of soft power nicely captures the varied attributes of knowledgeability.

[31] The ability to generate new and persuasive ideas as one of the competences that make for knowledgeability has a "soft" affinity to cognitive characteristics of the economic function of the "creative class," as described by Richard Florida in his *The Rise of the Creative Class* (2002). Aside from the "super-creative core" of the creative class made up of occupations such as scientists, university professors, poets, and architects, there is a diverse group of professionals who "engage in creative problem-solving, drawing on complex bodies of knowledge to solve specific problems"; what the group of professionals "are required to do regularly is think on their own" (Florida, 2002:69).

[32] In the context of discussing ways of measuring the quality of life that transcend the conventional economic indicator of the GNP, Albert Hirschman (1989) asks whether "having an opinion" is a good that should be incorporated into a measure of the quality of life of a country. Hirschman (1989:77) offers the following assessment employing the language of economics: "The forming and acquiring of opinions yields considerable utility to the individual. At the same time, if carried beyond some point, the process has dangerous side effects – it is hazardous for the functioning and stability of the democratic order. Under present cultural values these side effects do not enter the individual calculus – they are like external diseconomies.

[33] In a comprehensive U.S. panel study of the *associations* between several individual and family traits of children aged between fourteen and fifteen and adult health at age forty-one, especially the effect of adolescent cognitive and noncognitive factors, Koestner and Callison (2011:63) conclude that "cognitive ability and self-esteem have significant,

career, or long-term security; to keep multiple viewpoints and trade-offs in mind simultaneously; to insist on accountability; to detect "loopholes"; to locate and gain assistance for mastering these tasks; and, finally, to make a difference in what is collectively considered in need of repair/ change. They represent the generalized effects of a differential access to and reflexive awareness of relevant knowledge bases.[34] The abilities to decide, to mobilize defiance, to exploit discretion, to develop ways of coping, to organize protection, and to develop new ideas are a significant part of such strategies, and therefore of the conviction (internal efficacy*)* that one is in charge, and not merely the victim of fortuitous circumstances, or subject to the constraints others impose.[35] The growing knowledgeability of actors in modern societies, or the enhanced bundle of competencies, represents the foundation of the ability of *self-organization* of small groups of actors in different social roles; for instance, as consumers, tourists, workers, students, or politically active citizens. The bundle of competencies that represents knowledgeability strengthens the capacity of individuals to engage in independent political reasoning and, as the case may be, influence the political opinions of others (external efficacy). Hence, knowledgeability represents the capacities of individuals and groups to generate and follow through their own ideas and plans – but by no means under conditions that are completely free from "manipulation" by other individuals (Stigler, 1978:214). Knowledge is present in all social institutions. It is not confined, as emphasized, to a

direct associations with adult health." An earlier British analysis found that cognitive skills had associations with later health at an even larger magnitude than the U.S. study (cf. Carneiro et al., 2007). Cognitive ability was measured using the score on the *Armed Forces Qualification Tests* (AFQT) test. The test measures word knowledge, paragraph comprehension, arithmetical reasoning, and mathematics knowledge. Koestner and Callison (2011:64) also asked whether "adolescent cognitive and noncognitive factors are potential explanations of gender and racial disparities in health. Overall, we found little evidence that these factors can explain much of the differences in health we observe between men and women and black and white persons." The authors did find differences that accounted only for a small portion of the standard deviation difference between black and white persons.

[34] In the United States, the social location of many of these activities can be found in what Peter Drucker (1989:187) calls the "third" sector of nonprofit, nongovernmental, "human change" institutions (or the "civil society sector," as Salamon and Anheier [1997] have called it). The third sector is actually the "country's largest employer, though neither its workforce nor the output it produces show up in the statistics. One out of every two adult Americans – a total of 90 million people – are estimated to work as volunteers in the third sector" (Drucker, 1989:197).

[35] In an essay discussing the social and cognitive foundations of invention and innovation (Adolf, Mast, and Stehr, 2013), we have attempted to demonstrate the theoretical usefulness of the bundle of competencies that make up knowledgeability for a sociological theory of innovation; in other words, a theory of innovation that transcends the more common economic theory of innovation.

special (sub-) social system for its production and use (cf. Luhmann, 1990:147). Knowledgeability, by the same token, is not only found in a particular social system of society but can be mobilized in any social system. Since it cannot only be mobilized in the political system, though the function of knowledgeability within the political system is at the center of the present inquiry, knowledgeability is system transcendent and may be operative in all social systems. Like knowledge, knowledgeability is everywhere; of course, it is everywhere to different degrees. However, knowledgeability is not everywhere is social science theory and in the analysis of the foundations of democracy and its sustainability. Despite my own, foregoing emphasis on the essential role of knowledgeability rather than merely information or knowledge in societal and political life, in the following discussion and interpretation of the condition supportive for the emergence of liberty and the resilience of democratic governance, the emphasis shifts and critically follows the *standard interpretation* of the role of knowledge and especially information in democratic affairs.

Civil society organizations

The general argument for the importance of civil society organizations, to be found in the public domain and located somewhere between (political) governance and the family, and independent of state power for the promotion of democratization and democracy in modern societies, together with the social force of the interrelated notion of social capital, is taken almost for granted.[36] Sociologists and political scientists saw civil society as something almost like a panacea against the community of the society-busting developments; that is, on the one hand, against the growing individualism and, on the other hand, the allegedly amplifying power of the state.[37]

Writing in the 1830s, for example, Alexis de Tocqueville saw the multitude of voluntary associations in America as a barrier against the otherwise atomizing, centrifugal effects of democracy. Similarly, Emile Durkheim ([1930] 1947:28), in *The Division of Labor*, assigns considerable weight

---

[36] In contrast to the prevailing social science perspective about the constructive role of civil society organizations as the motor of and a stabilizing factor in democratization processes, Guillermo O'Donnell and Philippe Schmitter (1986) are convinced that certain cultural and normative ideas but also civil society organizations are not the impetus but at best the product of democratic governance (also Schmitter, 2010a:18).

[37] Cf. Gertrude Himmelfarb's essay "Civil society reconsidered," *The Weekly Standard*, Band 17, Nr. 30 (April 23, 2012).

to intermediary or secondary associations as a bulwark for a functioning democracy and social cohesion.[38]

In short, there is a long-standing agreement in the social science literature, especially among those who advance a radical theory of democracy (see Cohen and Arato, 1992:19), employing Ernest Gellner's (1994) succinct formulation: "no civil society, no democracy." Civil society, as Pierre Rosanvallon (2006:193) notes, "indeed has a 'politics,' but a discreet and silent one, the result of a multitude of deliberations in low voices and discreet choices that are never tallied." The absence of civil society organizations is therefore seen as a formidable hurdle to the very development of democratic conditions, while the decline in civic engagements in democratic societies is seen as a danger to democratic governance. Political transformations in a number of Latin American Countries, South Korea, the Philippines, or Poland in the last few decades of the twentieth century have underscored the importance of voluntary associations for the emergence of democratic societies (cf. Wnuk-Lipinski, 2007:683–690).[39]

Opposing this finding, there is a radically different diagnosis of the development of relations between citizens and public affairs in the developed societies in recent decades. This diagnosis asserts a significant weakening of civil society organizations and a retreat into the individual shell of the citizen and the family. Eric Hobsbawm (1996:272) affirms such a transition, and sketches the development in question and some of its origins in the eighties and nineties of the last century in a fashion otherwise typical of this conclusion regarding the decline of the state of modern civil society:

There can be little doubt that the links between citizens and public affairs are in the process of attenuation, at least in states with democratic politics, for various reasons. The decline in ideological mass parties, politically mobilizing electoral 'machines' or other organizations for mass civic activity (such as labour unions) is one of them; another is the spread of the values of consumer individualism, in an

---

[38] Seymour M. Lipset (1959:84–85) specifies some of the constructive political functions of intermediary organizations and institutions that make civil society an effective force in and for democratic societies: "They are a source of countervailing power, inhibiting the state or any single major source of private power from dominating all political resources; they are a source of new opinions; they can be the means of communicating ideas, particularly opposition ideas, to a large section of citizenry; they serve to train men in skills of politics; and they help increase the level of interest and participation in politics" (see also Skocpol, 2004; Bailer, Bodenstein, and Heinrich, 2012:302–303).
[39] Samuel Huntington (1991) refers to this historical period in the late twentieth century as representing "a third wave of democratization" that received an enormous boost from the end of the Cold War.

age when the satisfactions of rising material consumption are both widely available and constantly advertised.

In contrast, present-day manifestations of growing civic engagement, at least in some societies – for example, among the so-called post-9/11 cohort in the United States (Sander and Putnam, 2010) – supported by specific political events and social transformations and by the enhanced technical capacities to stay connected, represent perhaps a further evolution in the political role played by civil society organizations. The voices of new generations, as it were, have become noticeably louder.

The actual role civil society organizations are expected to perform varies depending on the conception of democracy. As Shmuel Eisenstadt (1999:11) notes, the "constitutional conception of democracy tended on the whole to emphasize the autonomy of civil society as against the state, while the participatory, and especially the communitarian conceptions of democracy could often imply a tendency to conflate the state and civil society." Nonetheless, there is of course, in contemporary societies in particular, a broad variety of civil society organizations and associations – some large, some small, some influential, others weak – and still other civil society organizations with only a short life and a single issue on their agenda.

The term civil society tends to be associated or even conflated with the concept of *social capital*. Social capital (Coleman, 1988; for a critical view of the term, see Smith and Kulynych, 2002) is seen to be vital for the functioning and the stability of democratic societies (e.g., Putnam, 1993; Fukuyama, 2001:7). Social capital represents the capacity of self-organization, that is, the ability to form voluntary civil society organizations, patterns of social interaction, and networks that are autonomous from the state and governed by generalized norms of reciprocity. By definition, this includes the possibility of negative externalities undermining democratic procedures, since membership in civic organizations tends to be stratified, for example, or as a result of excessive rent-seeking on behalf of interest groups. Thus, who exactly benefits from civil society organizations is a relevant issue (cf. Putnam and Goss, 2002:9),[40] as is the indication that not all civil society organizations are supportive of democratic governance. Reference to a decline of collective social capital in a society implies, of course, that "some of the fundamental social and cultural preconditions for effective democracy may have been eroded." In recent decades, this is the "result of a gradual but widespread process

---

[40] Social capital is not only unequally distributed but also "accumulated most among those who need it least. Social capital may conceivably be even less equitably distributed than financial and human capital" (Putnam, 2000:415).

of civic disengagement [at least in the United States]" (Putnam and Goss, 2002:3). The question this raises is: What is the political implication of the loss of collective social capital?

The range of civil society organizations can perhaps best be described as including, on the one hand, formal associations such as labor unions, religious organizations and political parties; and, on the other hand, much less formally organized civic activities such as protests, petition signing, demonstrations, ad-hoc organizations for a single, dedicated purpose (getting a measure on the ballot; organizing a plebiscite) and boycotts of a product or corporation. The appeal of the less formal civic organizations is the ease with which one enters or leaves the activity, while formal civil society organizations are subject to oligarchic tendencies, which means that they tend to be ruled by a small elite and take on many bureaucratic attributes.[41]

Since it is widely accepted that civil society formations represent a strong foundation for the evolution and endurance of democracy, the thesis tends to carry strong normative connotations representing, as it were, speech-acts that commend themselves (cf. Broman, 2002:5). In order to avoid prejudging the case, the relation between civil society formation and democracy should be treated as an open issue, thus allowing one to arrive at a more distanced perspective without prejudging the nature of the relationship. This also requires that civil society organizations are not treated as a black box. Attention has to focus on the type of civic association, and the possibility that not all organizations are naturally democratic. Nonetheless, of course, members of civil society organizations may be strongly committed to the idea that their activities are a motor for democracy. But why and how will the presence of vital civil society organizations enable (in a nonviolent manner), enhance, and consolidate democracy? What kind of civil society organizations serve – and to what extent – to mediate successfully between institutional frames of democracy and the participation of ordinary citizens in democratic processes? Equally relevant is the question of what political, economic or cultural processes tend to curb social, and hence political, participation. One must assume that the limits to individual and collective civic participation are not only the result of individual traits, such as the educational attainment of a person, but also the outcome of systemic attributes of relevant social contexts, such as the ethnic heterogeneity of communities, the structure of social inequality or the extent to which the economy of

---

[41] See Chapter 5 in this study for a more detailed description of Robert Michel's *Iron Law of Oligarchy*.

a community is locally controlled or governed by outside corporations (cf. Blanchard and Matthews, 2006).

It is important to note initially that the reference to civil society associations stresses the role of ordinary citizens, of those who are governed, rather than legal frames, "rational" market relations, abstract ideals or institutional settings in the emergence and continued existence of democratic society. The empirical evidence over the past thirty-five years for sixty-seven countries (see Karatnycky and Ackerman, 2005) suggests that the likelihood of a transition from an authoritarian regime to liberal democracy is "over four times higher for transitions supported by strong and nonviolent civic coalitions than for those unsupported by any civic organizations at all (Shin, 2007:267).

The development of civil society organizations that enable democracy presumably occurs prior to the struggle for democracy, since civil society is seen as one of the motors of democratization, or the transition from an authoritarian political regime to democratic governance. Various key social features, such as the existence of free channels of communication or public spaces not controlled by the state, must be in place for politically effective voluntary associations to emerge in what otherwise are hostile political conditions. The reasons for the failure of civil society organizations to surface are also linked to conditions that existed prior to any struggle for democracy. The literature in each instance assigns special importance to the political culture of a society.

The concept of political culture will be discussed in more detail in the next chapter suffice to say that the attitude held toward the virtue of democracy itself is a core attribute of the political culture of a society. Without the manifest or latent support (practical or normative) for democracy among ordinary citizens, the chances for a democratic regime to emerge and be sustained over time are slim. Once legitimacy (trust) and efficacy are extended to the political regime, its survival is obviously not assured, but it is also far from uncertain. Latent support for democracy may only extend to soft democratic convictions that are not translated into political action, while manifest support would include practical action, participation, and involvement in the political affairs of a community or society (see Klingemann, 1999).

Much of the discussion of the role of civil society organizations has focused on their affirmative contributions (see van der Meer and van Ingen, 2009), such as the democratic socialization of the membership, engaging in the political process, translating personal troubles into public concerns, or on the protection associations offer, rather than on any oppositional role – or the route of "exiting" (Hirschman, 1970) – of these associations for democracy. Thus, the role of civil society and its organizations as places of resistance to the policies and political platforms of established political actors is somewhat underexposed. As Seymour Martin Lipset (1959:84) observes, intermediary organizations can be a source of "countervailing power, inhibiting the state or any single major source of private power from dominating all political resources; they are a source of new opinions; they can be the means of communicating ideas, particularly opposition ideas, to a large section of citizenry; they serve to train men in the skills of politics; and they can help increase the level of interest and participation in politics." Hence the issue of the growth of the self-organizing capacity of civil society; and so the political purposes that are served by the enlargement of the ability of civil society to engage in political activities (and perhaps to withdraw from politics) become an important issue (Lipset, 1959:84–85).

Political culture

As we have seen, one of the important theoretical perspectives that attempt to account for the dissemination, functioning, and endurance of democratic institutions, expectations, and conduct emphasizes the significance of the diffusion of cultural attributes[42] in the process of the spread of democratic regimes across the world (cf. Meyer et al., 1997), as well as the possibility that traditional cultural preferences – especially authoritarian values as found, for example, in the Confucian tradition – may block democratization. However, whether this actually applies to Asian countries with a Confucian tradition is a contested matter (see Dalton and Ong, 2005). With a view toward the examination, in the next chapter of the importance of economic factors on democracy formation and democratic stability, it can almost be taken for granted that cultural processes form at least a kind of bridge between the political and the economic systems of society, if not an independent influence on political transitions and democratic governance. Every political regime is indeed embedded in a set of purposes and meanings, such as efficacy, tolerance, cooperation, and trust; we may therefore refer to subjective political attitudes, political world views and values, ideologies, transcendental beliefs, peculiar national convictions or, even more generally, the

---

[42] The diffusion of cultural influences may be seen as evidence for the possibility of both a soft and, in terms of time, a longer form of the effective spread of democratic preferences and ideas of what a state should look like. In contrast, the active intervention of intergovernmental organizations may be seen as a form of deliberate, forceful attempts to transform a society within a short duration into a different political and economic regime (see also the section on intergovernmental networks and their influence of the dissemination of democratic patterns of governance and political models).

sociocultural ethos (civic virtues) found in a society in their impact on the kind of political system instituted in that country, as well as to the repercussions of the "political culture" on the political regime of a society. As the list of dispersed attributes of political culture already indicates, empirical research and theorizing on political culture is equally diverse and lacks analytical precision. In this section, I will only highlight some of the features of the varied theories and research on political culture, and focus on the issue of the homogeneity of the culture of a society.

The political culture of a society is not necessarily identical, as Gabriel Almond (1956:396) stresses, with the culture of a society, nor is it synonymous with the political system. No doubt there are attributes of the substance of political cultures that either support democratic constitutions or demonstrate affinities with authoritarian regimes. In the first case, this applies to societies where there is a high degree of trust among the citizens, for example. In the second case, this applies to societies in which hierarchical social relations prevail (see also Lipset, 1959:89 and Huntington, 1984:209). For example, several Commonwealth countries may have a common political culture but different kinds of political regimes, while a set of Western European countries may have similar political systems but different political cultures. Nonetheless, the convergence between political culture and institutional settings is an issue that determines the consolidation of democratic practices in the long run.

Aside from the nature of the political culture, there is first of all the contentious question of the significance of the *homogeneity* of the political culture in its impact on the political regime of a society. The United States, rather than France or England, is seen to have developed a homogeneous culture, at least until the 1950s. Lipset (1959:89) describes the common American political culture as one anchored in the veneration of the Founding Fathers, their principles, and other popular American presidents. In his essay *On Liberty*, John Stuart Mill ([1859] 2010:235) insists that representative democracy is only possible in a society that is largely culturally homogeneous: For example, free institutions are next to impossible to establish and sustain in a country made up of different nationalities. Among a people without "fellow-feeling, especially if they read and speak different languages, the united public opinion, necessary to the working of representative government, cannot exist." Even though a number of prominent political scientists (Dahl, 1971; Lijphart, 1977) and – not only in recent years – populist political parties in a number of modern, democratic societies have repeated Mill's assertion, there is no empirical evidence to support the linkage between cultural homogeneity and democracy. One of the most recent extensive and comparative empirical studies, which investigated the relationship between social homogeneity and democratic practices in 166 states (Fish and Brooks, 2004), arrives at the conclusion that the degree of ethnic, linguistic, or religious diversity has no noticeable effect on the democracy of a country.

When it comes to analyzing the substance of the political culture, approaches and results vary widely. They range from Lipset's (1959:89) assertion of the importance of a common "secular political culture," especially nationwide rituals and holidays that serve to maintain the legitimacy of democratic practices, to the idea that it is the commitment to democratic values that is the pivotal ingredient of the democratic ethos.

A further significant thesis about the forces that affect democratic regimes concerns the role of the media. For example, is representative democracy in fact a media democracy? I will turn to this issue next. However, I will differentiate between the role of the media prior to the Internet and the impact of the Internet on democracy. The broadcast society relies on communication options *before* the invention and the widespread dissemination of the Internet or an inquiry-based communication option (at least from Google's point of view). In retrospect, broadcast society's communication options are often employed as a benchmark against which to assess the societal role of the Internet. Not infrequently, such assessments are nostalgic evaluations of an age that has been lost forever (e.g., Sunstein, 2001). Moreover, in the context of contrasting the media of different periods, and therefore as a means of differentiating periods, the assertion that the media of the broadcast society are stable, linear, and authoritative, whereas the media of the Internet age are dynamic, interactive, and fragile in nature, is contentious (see Edwards et al., 2011), being itself embedded in specific historical contexts, transporting different premises and carrying out different discursive work.

The role of the "media"

> A newspaper is not only able to suggest a common plan to men; it provides them with the means of carrying out in common the plans that they have thought of for themselves.
> de Tocqueville ([1835–40] 2000:518)

> We are so submerged in the pictures created by the mass media that we no longer really see them, much less the objects they supposedly represent. The truth is, as the media are now organized, they expropriate our vision.
> C. W. Mills (1956b:333)

As Alexis de Tocqueville already suggests, there can be little doubt that the paths of communication and the institutions in which communication media are embedded (film studios, television stations and corporations, universities, the state, and legal norms) have an impact on the political dynamics of the social system. This is the case for verbal communication as well as communication that later employs paper and then promotes paperless communication. The most radical idea in this context would be the assertion, as stressed by C. W. Mills, that the means of communication are not separate from us; if they do not structure consciousness, then they at least co-structure it. Each communication option creates new mental habits and patterns of thought. One of the most widely accepted hypotheses is that the media are a fundamental pillar of democracy, just as well-informed citizens play an active role in democratic processes. Media content should therefore ensure that well-informed citizens in fact exist. However, whether the influence of the so-called mass media on the structure of consciousness is immediate and unmediated, that is, whether the impact is not filtered by social interaction and does not take time, is an essentially contested appraisal (see Graber, 2003). If you link the special role that the means of communication are seen to play in their impact on individual consciousness to the actual development of political realities, you invariably encounter the work of Harold Innis and his classic study *Empire and Communication* from 1950. Innis undertakes the comprehensive task, in the sense of the *longue durée* of human history, of combining historical changes in the tendencies to aggregation and disaggregation of empires, with their forms of communication and their influence on the consciousness of the actors as a condition for the possibility of certain political and organizational structures. Innis' magic triangle of media, consciousness, and political system distinguishes between the *time-binding* and the *space-binding* role of media for civilizational development:

Media that emphasize time are those that are durable in character, such as parchment, clay and stone. The heavy materials are suited to the development of architecture and sculpture. Media that emphasize space are apt to be less durable and light in character, such as papyrus and paper. The latter are suited to wide areas in administration and trade. (Innis, [1950] 2007:26)

Communication options that "emphasize time favour decentralization and hierarchical types of institutions, while those that emphasize space favour centralization and systems of government less hierarchical in character." Large political regimes survive, according to Innis, by finding "compromises" between communication options.

Novel technical means of communication change the horizon of perception of actors. Once horizons are altered, often involuntarily, the context of action changes; for example, the range of perception, the patterns of contact among actors, or the relevance of traditional value orientations. Tony Ballantyne (2011:256) sums up the social changes in indigenous communities in New Zealand following the introduction of new means of communication by the colonizer as follows: "There were new opportunities for trade and travel, there were new plants, animals, and commodities to buy and sell, and new ideas and experiences to evaluate and process." The process of extension as the dominant pattern of social change (see Stehr, 1994:29–32) of the *Kai Tabu* communities in New Zealand not only changed their traditional world but also allowed for the preservation of traditional knowledge and social structures. Using Harold Innis' ([1950] 2007:26) terminology, the new communication option represented by the introduction of paper had both time-binding and space-binding functions.

The power of new media at that time, dominated by those who could handle them, that is, read and write, transformed and repressed, but never completely eliminated, the importance and value of indigenous culture (Ballantyne, 2011:259). Given these observations about the role of media in colonial societies, are there parallels to the role of the media in modern societies, particularly in their influence on the politics of these societies? Whatever may be the answer to this question, what changed in any case is democracy. And therefore the answer, in terms of Harold Innis' primary assumption, initially has to be that the meaning of democracy changes as a result of the change of the dominant media. Democracy and the forms of communication are not transcendental social phenomena.

The tangled and contradictory findings on this issue are that the new media, as was the case for the so-called mass media of the last century (radio, television), are seen to be responsible for the trivialization of political contexts; the loss of importance of modern, professional journalism; and the withdrawal of citizens from the political stage. Moreover, the new media permit politicians to seek direct access to voters, with the likely outcome that politics is increasingly defined by susceptibility to populist promises and attitudes of demagoguery. The changing patterns of media consumption from analog to digital media, for example, or from newspapers to television and the Internet are supposed to go hand in hand with the decline of the volume of social capital in society (see Putnam, 1996:14). Increased television viewing, according to Putnam, leads to a decline in civic engagement: on the one hand because the time factor plays a role, and on the other hand because of the repulsive image of the external world portrayed by television.

Not all media have the same effects or the same impact in all societies (see Starr, 2004). As the Nazi era shows, mass media flourish not only in free societies, but also in authoritarian societies. Robert Putnam is convinced that different media have significantly different effects; for example, when newspaper reading and television viewing is compared. A number of empirical studies in countries with a high proportion of commercial television stations show that the newspaper-reading individuals are politically better informed than those who watch TV more often (Norris, 1996:478). But in this case as well, the types of newspaper found in different countries are not identical.

My incomplete list of the negative consequences the new media may have for the political realities of a society makes evident that these assessments are strongly influenced by judgments indebted to the perspective of cultural criticism. This applies to Putnam as well as to Adorno and Horkheimer (1947), with their diagnosis of the power of cultural industry (*Kulturindustrie*) in modern societies, the theoreticians of postmodernism (e.g., Baudrillard, 1988), or the earlier diagnosticians of the social consequences of the "mass media." Fears associated with the emergence of mass society (Mills, 1956a:320–322; Kornhauser, 1959)[43] were no doubt substantiated and accelerated by the novelty, potential power, and early ubiquity of mass communication and mass media.[44] And with these changes, a subtle but significant shift occurs in the analysis of the workings of modern society. Concerns about manifest exploitation, intimidation, force, and coercion give way to discussions about the psychological effects of mass persuasion as well the idea that "the maximum effectiveness of the mass media of communication operate toward the maintenance of the going social and cultural structure rather than toward its change" (Lazarsfeld and Merton, [1948] 1957:473).[45] The almost

---

[43] William Kornhauser (1959:121) stresses "aristocratic and democratic critics [see Kornhauser, 1959:25–38] alike believe that mass society is *vulnerable to totalitarianism*." Kornhauser (1959:128) concurs with the critics, suggesting that "major social discontinuities in social process produce mass movements by destroying pre-established intermediate relations and by preventing the formation of new associations aligned with the social order." In a critique of the theory of mass society published in 1956, Daniel Bell (1956:75) was able to observe that the theory of mass society has been, aside from Marxism for several decades, the most influential social theory in the contemporary Western world. The theory of mass society was central to the pessimistic critique of bourgeois society.

[44] The term has fallen into disrepute or refers, at best, to an era of communication transmission that has been displaced by newer technologies that place greater control in the hands of the user (e.g., Chaffee and Metzger, 2001:369).

[45] Lazarsfeld and Merton ([1948] 1957:472), in taking up the themes of the mass society perspective, end up offering a differentiated treatment of the power of the mass media. Their examination of the preconditions in which the mass media may be able to achieve their "maximum propaganda effect" (when they operate in a situation of virtual "psychological monopoly," or when the objective is one of canalizing rather than modifying basic attitudes, or when they operate in conjunction with face-to-face

magical belief in the enormous cognitive persuasiveness and power of the mass media over popular culture, in deteriorating esthetic tastes and the diminution of critical faculties,[46] to some degree resonates with similar present-day concerns now directed toward the massive forces of cultural globalization.

Media studies have often embraced the idea of the commercialization and commodification confronted by the public. Narratives that include complaints about the dumbing down of the public and the general decline of public communication are common (see McNair, 2000:201).

The opposing diagnosis of the role of the media in contemporary societies speaks about the growing chances of citizens' political participation based on access to the media, as well as the political struggle to keep the flow of media-provided information free from the immediate or mediated control of the state,[47] for example, by means of efforts to put pressure on private media outlets, to block access to particular content pages, or to shut down the Internet completely. The diagnosis that the media foster democratic norms and processes is based on the idea that the free media support expectations of greater political participation and enlarge the political knowledge of citizens; that barriers against efforts to control what users may "consume" are enhanced; and that communication becomes more and more a matter of a conversation among equals. The modern media contribute to the development of a political mass market (cf. Bösch and Frei, 2006), a mass market that eases the transition from dictatorship to democracy. Put in even more positive terms, some observers are convinced that the assemblage of communication options is able to heal existing democracy deficits for which the media may be co-responsible, by building bridges between politics and an alienated public disappointed with political realities (e.g., Coleman, 1999; Coleman and Blumler, 2009). The losses or deficits usually enumerated in this context, and already identified and listed by Putnam (2000), are a loss of social capital and trust in politicians and politics, as well as a growing sense of powerlessness and ignorance of voters, and the decline of what at one time was a rather tight coupling of citizens to the political parties of the center, which dominated politics in the postwar decades in many countries.

---

contacts) leads them to cautiously conclude that these social prerequisites "are rarely satisfied conjointly in propaganda for social objectives."

[46] For a contrasting contemporary view, see Riesman ([1950] 1961:290–292), who stresses the liberating and competence-enhancing role of the movies of the day, for example.

[47] The *New York Times* (June 12, 2011; "U.S. underwrites Internet detour around censors") reports efforts supported by the U.S. State Department to develop a shadow Internet and mobile phone system, designed to support dissidents in repressive countries in gaining access to the Internet and cell phone system that is shut off in such countries.

120 Accounts of the possibility and resilience of liberty

Media freedom and political knowledge

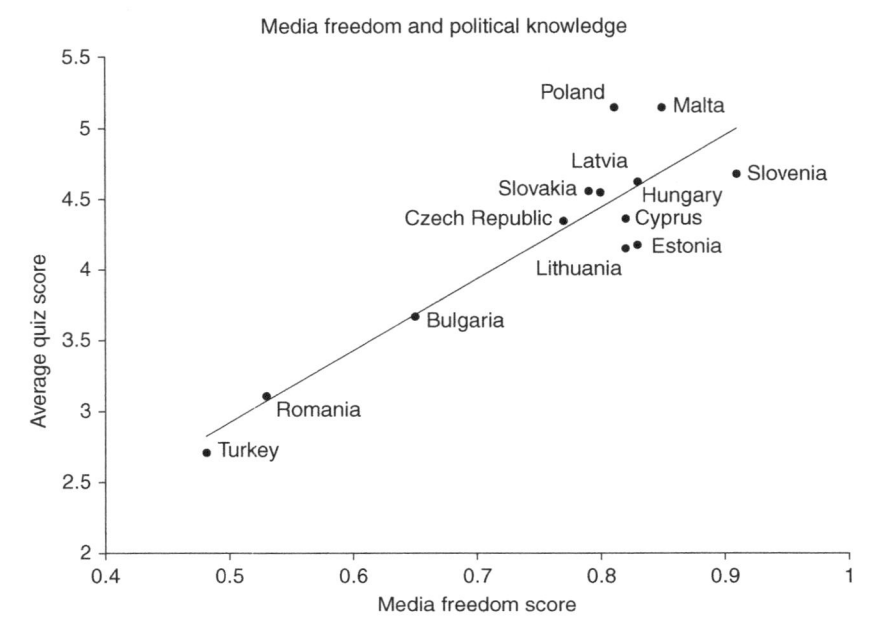

[Scatter plot showing Average quiz score (y-axis, 2 to 5.5) versus Media freedom score (x-axis, 0.4 to 1) with data points for: Turkey, Romania, Bulgaria, Lithuania, Czech Republic, Slovakia, Latvia, Hungary, Cyprus, Estonia, Poland, Malta, Slovenia, with a fitted regression line.]

Figure 1 Media freedom and political knowledge
Source: Leeson (2008:158)

In a large empirical study based on information dating from the year 2004, Peter Leeson examined the interrelation between *media freedom* from government control[48] and citizens' political knowledge,[49] political participation, and voter turnout (see Figure 1). Leeson (2008:155) found

---

[48] Leeson's (2008:159) key independent variable, "media freedom," is based on scores in a report by *Freedom House* (2004) for the year 2003.

[49] The dependent variable "political knowledge" (better defined as political information) is based on survey responses of the Candidate Countries Eurobarometer (2004) survey of Central and Eastern Europeans (as well as Turks). In October and November 2003, "this survey quizzed more than 12,000 citizens on nine basic political facts of the European Union (EU) in the following EU candidate countries: Bulgaria, Cyprus, the Czech Republic, Estonia, Hungary, Latvia, Lithuania, Malta, Poland, Romania, Slovakia, Slovenia, and Turkey" (Leeson, 2008:157). The index of political information is based on the responses of the interviewees to the following true/false questions: "1) The EU is made of 15 states (True); 2) The European Community was created after World War I (False); 3) The European flag is bright blue with yellow stars (True); 4) There are 15 stars on the European flag (False); 5) Headquarters of the EU are in Brussels, Strasbourg, and Luxembourg (True); 6) Members of the European Parliament are directly elected by the citizens of the EU (True); 7) There is a President of the EU directly elected by all the citizens (False); 8) The EU has its own anthem (True); 9) There are no borders between the EU (True)" (Leeson, 2008:157).

that "where government owns a larger share of media outlets and infrastructure, regulates the media industry more, and does more to control the content of news, citizens are more *politically ignorant and apathetic*" (emphasis added).

With respect to political information, in a regression analysis involving and restricted to the EU Candidate countries (including Turkey), Leeson controls for the influence of both individual attributes such as income, age, and education of the respondents to the Eurobarometer survey and institutional characteristics of the countries, including percapita GDP and public expenditures on education. After controlling for these intervening variables, the observed significant relation between media liberty and political information remains a strong one. This also applies to measures of political participation. Nonetheless, as one might expect, individual income, education and age are all positively related to the results of the administered political information test. A single cross-sectional analysis is insufficient to establish causality.

The essentially contested conclusions about the use of different media and their impact mean that it is not difficult to find studies that come to opposite findings. One finds authors who diagnose political passivity brought about by the media, while others come to the opposite conclusion: the media are seen as mobilizers. Uslaner (1998), for example, cannot find any link between television viewing and the loss of social capital; but the opposite "causality" might be equally plausible. Individuals who show a lack of interest in out-of-house social contacts consume a lot of television (Norris, 1996).[50] Nor is there a close relation between the perception of the imaginary world of television and the perception of the real world. Yet it is possible that the new world of the new media supports more frequent and intensive contacts among individuals. However, the increased number of contacts may not involve face-to-face contacts anymore.

A cross-national empirical study (Curran et al., 2009) of the news content in Denmark and Finland (with different public broadcasting regimes), Great Britain (private as well as public broadcasters), and the United States (almost exclusively commercial broadcasters) indicates that public broadcasters offer a more comprehensive news program than commercial stations, and that the viewing of news strengthens and helps to reduce differences in the volume of information among viewers. Whether the function of the media last mentioned is perhaps accidental

---

[50] Pippa Norris (1996:479), in her critique of Putnam's (1995a) perspective, adds that "America is ... high as a generation of joiners, with a dense network of civic associations."

(for example, one waits for the program one is really interested in while the newscast is still running) remains an open matter. Insofar as television stations aim to reach a national audience, it does not come as a surprise that international news appears to have lower priority. The fact is that U.S. commercial television stations, not surprisingly, show few reports about international events.

The nation-state and democracy

Much of my discussion of the conditions for and the endurance of liberty has focused on traditional societal attributes and features such as the culture, the educational system, or the nature of the media system of a society. I have reason to call these attributes of societies that either enhance or block the emergence of democracy and freedoms *traditional* societal processes, because they typically tend to conceive of democracy as an attribute of the nation-state and, in the end, "imprison democracy through state territorialisation" (Conolly 1991:476). The traditional, nation-specific attributes represent an entirely appropriate focus of the analysis for a given historical time and place.

However, the concept of country or nation has lost a good part of its political and economic meaning. Once these nation-specific features of society lose their centrality and weight as foundations for the transformation of society, new attributes are added. Hence a generalization that might emerge from these discussions concerns the very importance of the nation-state for democracy. If such a conclusion is warranted, then a decline in the sovereignty of the nation-state, for example, could also spell a weakening of nation-based, country-specific processes and, therefore, national democratic institutions. The motor of the contemporary decline of the sovereign nation-state is, of course, mainly provided by transnational entities untamed by the nation-state, as well as by political, economic, and environmental globalization trends. If one adds to these trends the development of information technology, the Internet and the extension of financial markets beyond the boundaries of countries, the pertinent question becomes whether democracy is possible within and beyond the boundaries of the nation-state or whether it is in fact enhanced by the same transformations.

The traditional unit of (macro-) social scientific analyses tends to be society, in the sense of the nation-state. In sociological discourse, society becomes indistinguishable, for all intents and purposes, from the nation-state; while in political discourse, the state is the uncontested center toward which all reflection converges. For example, the organization of the state is the pivotal problem in political theory. The focus of most theoretical efforts in economic discourse has similarly been the nation-state.[51] Any germane social transformations in such a context primarily occur as the result of mechanisms that are part of and built into the structure of a given society. Nonetheless, the conflation of modern society with the nation-state is an ideological and epistemological legacy of the nineteenth century origins of social science discourse. There may well have been and perhaps still are reasons for the conflation of the boundaries of the political, economic, and social system with those of the nation-state. For example, the formation of social science discourse itself coincides with the constitution of the identity of the modern nation-state and violent struggles among independent nation-states defending their own government, civil society, economy, armed forces, and culture. Indeed, it was and typically still is the nation-state that assumes ultimate authority over its citizens. Today, it is inadequate to retain the restrictive framework and image of the territorial state.

The major institutions of modern society – the market economy, the state, education, religion, science, and everyday life, but also the ecology of a society – are all profoundly affected by a progressive "globalization" of human affairs, or by circumstances in which "disembedded institutions, linking local practices with globalised social relations, organize major aspects of day-to-day life" (Giddens, 1990:79). The expanding and boundary-crossing flows of individuals, communication, commodities, images, crime, money, diseases, and knowledge, as well as both nation-unspecific problems and opportunities challenge borders, render states less significant, change identities, and reposition spaces; but they do not dispose of them altogether.

As Eric Hobsbawm (1996:272; see also Grundman and Stehr, 2011), for example, points out,

[a] major reason for the crisis of the social-democratic and Keynesian policies which dominated Western capitalism in the third quarter of the century is precisely that the power of states to set levels of employment, wages and welfare expenditures on their territory has been undermined by exposure to international competition from economies producing more cheaply or more efficiently.

The eclipse of time of transit and distance as barriers to economic activities and communication, environmental changes that recognize no boundaries, the global connectedness of the electronic media, the

---

[51] In German, social science, political economy became *Nationalökonomie*. For a discussion of the traditional centrality of the nation-state and its sovereignty within political theory, especially theories and critiques of liberal democracy (see Held, 1991; Magnusson, 1996:29–48).

progressive internationality of the scientific community, of financial networks, the growing transnational cultural activities, and the dynamics of multinational corporate activity and political institutions all represent persuasive evidence for reorienting the focus of the analysis of these bases of democracy away from society and the unit of the nation-state toward groups of national societies, networks of transnational political and economic power, and divisions not only within the world but also in the global society. To question the adequacy of such an emphasis does not necessarily imply that the notions of "global society" and of a global economic and cultural unity or even human uniformity are uncritically embraced. Nor does a shift in the primary theoretical referent toward a transnational focus inherently imply a definitive response to the question of whether the project of modernity continues to unfold, albeit under new circumstances and at a new level, or alternatively signals the emergence of an entirely new historical epoch.

However, to claim that the nation-state is no longer the sole and dominant focus is to acknowledge the existence of systemic relations and trends that divide as well as unite, and that reduce the range of the sovereignty, power, and autonomy of the nation-state in extremely important respects. Local, regional, and national identities and social action are now intermeshed with various cultural and economic forces that reside at a distance and transcend national boundaries. What is at issue are not absolute similarities in development, but relational convergences and the assimilation of foreign worlds into local contexts. For example, will national differences in interest rates and their movements relative to each other tend to converge in all nation-states? And how do economic actors cope with or construct adjustments through local practices to fluctuations induced elsewhere?

Present-day social science discourse recognizes these new realities, although it typically remains entangled in perspectives that deny the need to reassess the notion of society as a nation-state. Paradoxically, both the dissolution and the decentering of the nation-state encourage forces that once again make local and regional identities both plausible and more viable. In other words, globalization does not merely refer to processes that originate elsewhere and affect everyone in the same passive fashion. Globalization must be understood as an active response by specific communities to developments that may not be locally controlled but nevertheless have adaptive local repercussions. The disembedding of forces must be combined with a "reembedding" of activities that result in the "reappropriation or recasting of disembedded social relations so as to pin them down (however partially and transitory) to local conditions of time and place" (Giddens, 1990:79–80).

Intergovernmental networks

> There are no examples of effective democratic institutions beyond the nation state.   Ralf Dahrendorf (2000:1067)

As we have seen, the large majority of analyses of democratization processes emphasize – in agreement with Ralf Dahrendorf[52] – domestic factors focusing exclusively on processes within states. In opposition to Ralf Dahrendorf's observation about the limits of democracy defined by the boundaries of the nation state, one of the more recent hypotheses about the global dissemination of democratically governed states refers to the enabling, and perhaps even active, role of the large number of transnational and intergovernmental organizations that have sprung up since World War II (Torfason and Ingram, 2010).

Referring to the example of state secrecy and the extent to which the state may counter domestic democratic pressures against secretive behavior by the state agencies by virtue of the state's monopoly on designing classification schemes and controlling political symbols of allegiance, danger, and security, William Connolly (1991:479) suggests that cross-national, nonstate democratic movements and associations may transcend the walls of the state and lead to "global channels through which to publicize state practices of secrecy and manipulation, helping to delegitimize them in several states simultaneously." Nonstate, international associations "might help to invigorate democratic energies within states, [and] exert external pressures upon the secret practices of the states," as well as on the political allegiances, identifications, and energies of its citizens (Connolly, 1991:479). The outcome is the distinct possibility not that disloyalty to the nation-state is the only political imperative, but that loyalties and legitimacies extend transnational alliances.[53]

---

[52] To quote but two scholarly expressions supporting these sentiments: Hedley Bull (1977:252) remarks that "there is not the slightest evidence that sovereign states in this century will agree to subordinate themselves to a world government founded upon consent"; and Robert Keohane (2006:77) stresses that the chance for democratic accountability in world politics "would be utopian in the sense of illusory – impossible of realization under realistically foreseeable conditions."

[53] Discussing "globalizing democracy," Benjamin Barber (2000:16) agrees that a global polity is missing although it is necessary to, for example, temper the excesses of the global markets. He adds the provocative thesis that "we have globalized our economic vices ... but not our civic virtues" (Barber, 2000:17) However, Barber's observation is erroneous since the presence of many of the economic vices he enumerates such as crime, drugs, hate, and terror are vices that have been present in many societies even without the current globalization process as their motor. Robert O. Keohane (2006:79) is slightly more optimistic about the possibility of global governance and offers, in spite of continuing power asymmetries in world politics, a *"pluralistic accountability* system"; that is, an accountability system that curtails abuses of power.

Not only the number of transnational state organizations (IGOs) and the number of their members but also the number of international nonstate organizations that are, in turn, connected to the IGO's in many ways have significantly risen since the end of the World War II (e.g., Beckfield, 2003). Torfason and Ingram emphasize, in contrast to cultural processes or the use of force, the influence of *normative* attributes anchored within the social structures of transnational networks. Their inquiry focuses on the structure of networks of voluntary memberships in transnational associations, as for example the World Bank or the International Monetary Fund. By now, more than 300 international state organizations exist. Further examples for such transnational state organizations would be the European Central Bank, the International Court at The Hague, the International Atomic Energy Agency, or the International Panel on Climate Change.

On the basis of this information, the central hypothesis of Torfason and Ingram (2010:356) is that "this network has been fundamental to the diffusion of democracy, such that states that come into contact with more democratic states in the IGO network are themselves more likely to democratize." The influence of these transnational networks on democratization, administratively weak though they may be, is communicated by way of the dominant normative orientations present within these networks and not, for instance, via power relationships within the networks, as for example due to the unequal potential strengths of individual member states. As a result, the authors speak of the strength of weak transnational networks.

Which of the available normative orientations in these networks play a role in this context, and what factors are in turn responsible for the dominance of these values? Concerning the influence of international nonstate organizations, Torfason and Ingram (2010:356) concur with Boli and Thomas' (1997) observation that "IGOs promote 'world citizenship,' an individualistic, egalitarian construct that justifies democratic governance and delegitimizes autocracy." Similar patterns of values are represented by international state organizations, and they apply in particular not necessarily to the influence of the organization as such, but rather to the influence exerted bilaterally among individual members.

The authors of the network study, however, do not investigate the sources of the democratic values that are disseminated via the structures of the network, nor do they concern themselves with the individual persons who carry out the processes of diffusion of international norms. Rather, they emphasize both the significance of the legitimacy of the *Western* concept of democracy in global society and the privileged position of Western societies in these transnational organizations.

Katerina Linos' (2011) analysis is also concerned with the diffusion of international political norms. However, she chooses to emphasize the key role played by national political elites, and their electoral incentives or political capacity to "import" foreign policy models and international organization recommendations by attempting to either realize or block them domestically. The theoretical perspective advanced by Linos focuses on the citizens' generally limited information about international developments and the bias toward policies enacted in large and proximate countries. The empirical information for the United States utilized by Linos indicates that the voters' opinions have a significant impact on the readiness of politicians to mimic foreign policies and policy models. More precisely, as Linos (2011:692) stresses, "domestic leaders may only be able to promote international models domestically to the extent that domestic publics shift their views."

The trend toward democracy observable in the past few decades certainly cannot be attributed to the influence of transnational organizations alone; and yet, as Torfason and Ingram (2010:359) stress, the "channels of contact offered through IGOs provided important support for this process and hastened it. IGOs provide interpretation and interaction venues for elites, while also supporting a shared identity among the populace of member states; this increases the likelihood of change consistent with shared norms and decreases the likelihood of inconsistent change."

Two hypotheses are being empirically tested here: (1) The influence of any state upon the status of democracy in another member state is dependent upon the degree to which both states are interconnected (in how many organizations do both countries participate?) within the network of international organizations; and (2) in terms of promoting democracy, the influence of networks of international organizations made up of democratic states is greater than that of less democratic states.[54]

A further important approach to the analysis of democratization processes that also emphasizes external, international factors is based on the observation that there tends to be a cluster in time and space in terms of both the global diffusion of democracies and the transition to democratic regimes. One group of authors (Gleditsch and Ward, 2008:263) infer

---

[54] The operationalization of the dependent variable on the level of democracy and autocracy in 187 states follows the POLITY IV project of Marshall and Jaggers (2005); it is based on a number of indicators that are, then, combined into a single score: for example, the presence of specific institutions linked to the competitiveness and openness of executive recruitment and political participation in general.

from their observation that there must be "diffusion mechanisms" that have a significant impact on national political institutions and transition processes. Gleditsch and Ward (2008:264; also Boix and Stokes, 2003) point to the importance of external factors affecting changes in the balance of power between ruling elites and opposition groups, as well as changes in the preference and assessment of particular forms of governance among contending political groups. The concrete mechanisms of diffusion are coercion, competition, learning, and various forms of social emulation. Policy choices and political models of other countries, for example, may influence the political opinions of citizens who consider such proposals or ideas as credible policy options. Politicians may in turn interpret shifts in public opinion espousing foreign models – for example, in the field of family policies – as an incentive to recommend the very models nationally. According to such a diffusion scenario, one should expect, as Katerina Linos (2011:692) suggests, to "see more substantial diffusion in policy areas that are salient to the electorate, as compared to policy fields and countries where elites are shielded from public scrutiny and able to impose their preferred policies." Although democratization processes are as a rule set in motion as the result of different processes and by a wide range of political actors, the general conclusion of the authors of the study on the diffusion of democratic policies and political preferences is that "external factors are generally better indicators of the prospect for transition than domestic country attributes" (Gleditsch and Ward, 2008:264), and that exclusively domestic attributes are not the sole factors enhancing the prospects of democracy.

Political freedom supporting societal developments in the modern world almost always includes a strong reference to economic activities as one key or the keys of social evolution in general. However, the successes and the risks associated with the development of competitive markets, as Amartya Sen (1993a:519) for example has pointed out, are far more commonly associated with the consequences for individual (material) well-being and are less often examined in their impact on the degrees of individual freedom. Moreover, at present the concern that the flourishing commerce, growing trade, and expanding industry are adversaries of freedom, though an issue that had been discussed extensively in pre-industrial times and during the beginning of the industrial period, is hardly a central theme of the discussions about the opportunities and the levers of freedom in modernity.

3 The economic order ensures (defeats) liberty

> Poverty is the cause of the defects of democracy. That is the reason why measures should be taken to ensure a permanent level of prosperity ... Where democracies have no middle class, and the poor are greatly superior in number, trouble ensues, and they are speedily ruined.
>
> Aristotle, *Politics*, p. 35

The contention that liberty is a daughter of knowledge appears to find its strongest intellectual, but also political, competitors in the thesis that either the market process itself is a facilitator of freedom or, more specifically, that certain market outcomes are the catalyst of liberty and democracy. Both John Maynard Keynes and Joseph Schumpeter, to name but two outstanding minds from the field of economics from the past century, have commented on the affinity between capitalism and liberty. For John Maynard Keynes, as far as vital human activities are concerned, capitalism is not the ultimate goal or an end in itself: capitalism for Keynes, as expressed for example in his essay "Economic possibilities for our grandchildren" (1930), "was necessary for freedom, but the activities of a capitalist society were not themselves an essential part of what freedom was all about" (Backhouse and Bateman, 2009:663). In a much stronger sense than Keynes, Joseph Schumpeter (1942:297), in his *Capitalism, Socialism and Democracy*, maintains that "modern democracy is a by-product of the capitalist process." More recently, Schumpeter's elementary thesis finds support from another eminent economist: Mancur Olson. As Olson (2000:132) stresses, "it is no accident that the countries that have reached the highest level of economic development and have enjoyed good economic performance across generations are all stable democracies." However, the assertion that capitalism is a foundation of liberty is obviously not without its detractors, most prominently Marxists and Socialists, but also liberal theorists such as Max Weber ([1906] 1980), for example, who see a capitalist economic order and democracy in essential opposition. But put in a less oppositional manner:

in the view of the critics of the elective affinity of liberty and capitalism, the intersection of capitalism and democracy is in fact small.

Insofar as the market process argument is concerned, it is not only far less frequently and intensively advanced than is the market outcome argument as a vehicle in the promotion of liberty in society. It also appeals to what can only amount to an ideal market condition, namely free and unencumbered competition that is expected to radiate into society at large. The result of perfect competition, as the economist Frank H. Knight (1960:29) notes, "is ideal cooperation, though the wish to benefit others is excluded from individualistic motivation, as well as that of obstructing their activities." It is generally recognized that so-called market failures exist in abundance, of course, and thereby lessen the charm of the argument of free competition as the motor for freedom in society at large.

General statements about the affinity of economic prosperity and democracy are not only often voiced by social scientists, but they are also a salient part of the policy goals of transnational organizations (e.g., World Bank, United Nations; cf. Newman and Rich, 2004) and individual nations who devote growing resources to the strengthening of the democratic governance of countries that receive their assistance. And yet such statements leave us in the dark not only about their abstract nature but also about these important questions: at what point in the development of society does the capitalist process brings about a democratic regime, and exactly what social positions in modern society are of particular political importance as a guarantor of freedom? Are these positions – as some might argue in the case of industrial society – perhaps those of the owners of the means of production? Or are we talking about the citizens as politically active subjects? Since the significance of consumption in contrast to the production sector is growing in modern societies, we might be able to observe that a displacement of the societal importance of roles is taking place. The political significance of the role of the citizen might be displaced by the political significance of the role of the consumer, since consumer decisions in the marketplace resonate so strongly in the political system (see Sagoff, [1988] 2008:47–52; Stehr, 2008).

More generally, with respect to the basic thesis that the capitalist economic order is a motor of political liberties: how can individual freedom be exercised effectively if, as one might presume, economically underprivileged individuals and groups are denied any economic power? Both the idea that liberty is a daughter of knowledge and the idea that democracy is closely connected to advances in the material well-being of a society have their roots in the optimistic Enlightenment tradition. As it happens, the argument goes, wealthy countries tend to be democratic societies.[1] As Benjamin Friedman (2008:50–52) surmises, the linkage

between rising living standards and either social attitudes or political institutions is not limited to low-income countries, or to the mere establishment of new electoral institutions. In America, for example, eras in which economic expansion has delivered ongoing material benefits to the majority of the country's population have mostly corresponded to eras when opportunities and freedoms have broadened, political institutions have become more democratic, and the treatment of society's unfortunates has become more generous ... Conversely, many of the horrifying antidemocratic phenomena that so marred Europe's twentieth-century history ensued in a setting of pervasive economic stagnation or decline.

Although there are numerous assertions in the literature and in the world of politics that "the level of national income is the most important factor explaining inter-country variations in the degree of democracy" (Borooah and Paldam, 2007), there is an automatic linkage neither between the developmental pattern of material wealth, economic growth, and the societal distribution of wealth or income and democracy, nor between the growth of knowledge and liberties. If such a habitual association in the case of either knowledge or prosperity would obtain, then the growth of liberties should have taken place much earlier in history, and reversals to autocracies should rarely have been possible. But political decay, as Samuel P. Huntington (1965:393; 1968:86; Tilly, 2003b) reminds us, or de-democratization, cannot be ignored; political developments – as ample examples from history demonstrate – are in principle reversible processes, and require theories of political decay.[2]

---

[1] Robert Fogel (2008:95), in an essay that attempts to forecast the relation of capitalism and democracy in 2040, notes that "richer countries that were the chief bastions of liberal democracy during the second half of the twentieth century – the EU15, the United States, and Japan – will decline in relative importance by 2040. In 2000, these groups represented 51 percent of global GDP, but by 2040 their combined share is projected to decline to 21 percent. Most worrisome is the projected decline in the EU15 from 21 percent to just 5 percent of the global share of GDP. Given Western Europe's role during the past several centuries as the cradle of liberal democracy – exporting it to the New World, Oceania, and other continents – who will take up the slack during the next generation?" Fogel's answer is Asia.

[2] Huntington (1968:86) criticizes the then dominant models of modernization and development because they are "only partially relevant to many of the countries to which they are applied. Equally relevant would be models of corrupt and denigrating societies highlighting the decay of political organizations and the increasing dominance of disruptive social forces." See also Guillermo O'Donnell's (1973) model of authoritarian rule and economic advance from the early seventies of the last century, a period when such issues acquired particular attention given that a number of autocratic regimes sprang up in Latin America and in Africa.

In the long run, though, economic prosperity (achieved by commercial society) and (representative) democracy, especially in the sense of economic liberties, may well be more compatible (see Dunn, 2008; Feng, 1999:410), as casual observations during the Cold War era, for instance, would seem to confirm. In the case of the latter thesis, which is the most widely discussed assertion about the linkage between the social organization of economic conduct and democracy, it is argued that economic well-being, if not persistent economic growth, and possibly the legitimacy of patterns of collective income and wealth inequalities, as accomplished by a largely autonomous economic system in modern societies, is a (necessary or even sufficient) condition for the possibility and sustainability of democratic society; or, seen from a more static and singular factor view, that the presence of democratic institutions such as access to and ownership of private property guarantees freedom.[3] The major issue is therefore whether a rising standard of living represents more than an improvement in the material well-being of individuals and groups, in that it also enhances the (cognitive) capabilities of the members of society, shapes their political beliefs and behavior (cf. Inglehart and Welzel, 2010)[4] and, in the end, the nature and the prevalence of moral convictions in society (cf. Stehr, Henning, and Weiler, 2006; Friedman, 2006).

However, as some observers have noted (e.g., Barro, 1999:S182; also Robinson, 2006:504), we do not have a well-developed theory that accounts for the possible affinity between prosperity and democracy, or political system and economic returns. Such a theory remains to be developed. Whether such a theory stresses contingent, perhaps even fortuitous, factors and choices (e.g., O'Donnell and Schmitter, 1986), or is best constructed with reference to power alignments and networks or to still other processes, such as the role of key elites, the form of government (Knutsen, 2011) or the regime history of a country (Gerring, Kingstone, and Lange, 2011), remains to be seen.

What is evident, however, is that prevailing analyses and empirical approaches fail to take agency into consideration, especially the differential cognitive capacities of individuals and collectivities (knowledge) and

---

[3] A limitation of the observation about the influence of the social organization of economic affairs (the economy) on democratic governance (the political system) must be that the genealogy of earlier forms of democracy cannot have been the result of market processes because markets, just as the networks in the modern sense, date from the mid-nineteenth century (cf. Polanyi, 1947:113).
[4] Inglehart and Welzel's (2010:553) theory of modernization stipulates "rising levels of existential security are conducive to a shift from traditional values, and from survival values to self-expression values." The modification in values toward a preference for liberties, for example, is seen to be robust and linked to civil society, gender equality, and democratization.

the societal conditions that enable an extension of such capabilities; that is, commitments to ideas such as justice, security, freedom, health, world views, and happiness, as well as the quality of governance, and how all these might interact with economic conditions.[5] Moreover, the knowledge-guiding interest of inquiries into the relation of the nature and the fruits of the economic system and democracy, more recently, are mainly those executed by economists, using conventional statistics of prosperity. In addition, the interplay between long-term and short-term macrosocietal processes such as institutional transformations, and microsocial processes such as world views of individual actors or their desire for political freedom, affect both the emergence of democracies and their continuance is rather complicated and hardly well understood. For example, economic development, especially faster economic growth than in otherwise similar countries (as argued by Minier, 1998), may support the emergence of democratic governance but could also provide stability for authoritarian regimes. Using a large survey conducted in 2006 by the World Bank and the European Bank for Reconstruction in twenty-eight post-transition countries, Grosjean and Senik (2011:365) "find a positive and significant effect of democracy on support for a market economy, but no effect of market liberalization on support for democracy." In general it can be said, as Max Weber (e.g., [1904] 1952:443) had already emphasized, that the transition to novel societal conditions and, of course, democratic governance is not a single, dedicated process. The impact of economic development is therefore both conditional and contextual.

In my analysis of the linkages between economic development and democracy, I would like to distinguish between the *prosperity* and the *affluence* of a society. Prosperity refers to the measures of the distribution of attributes (income, property, assets) considered to represent wealth; while affluence refers to the concentration of these attributes. As a result, depending on the research-guiding interest, different statistical measures apply.

The difference between prosperity and affluence is one of different historical periods. Affluence precedes prosperity, though prosperity is often accompanied by affluence. Societies became prosperous in the post-war era; that is, nothing in the history of the industrialized countries in Western Europe and North America resembles their experiences

---

[5] Exactly such a reference to the theoretical and empirical deficits of accounts of democratic transitions may be found in Stephen Haggard's and Robert Kaufmann's (1997:265) critique of existing theories of regime transitions: it is impossible "to formulate a theory of democratic transition that does not ... address the factors that shape actors' preferences and capabilities in the first place and the conditions under which they might change over time."

between 1950 and the present. The economic boom differed in its timing from country to country, but as Alan Milward (1992:21; see also Judt, 2005:324–353) has stated succinctly:

> By the end of this period the perpetual possibility of serious economic hardship which had earlier always hovered over the lives of three-quarters of the population now menaced only about one fifth of it. Although absolute poverty still existed in even the richest countries, the material standard of living for most people improved almost without interruption and often very rapidly for thirty-five years. Above all else, these are the marks of the uniqueness of the experience.

The emancipation from economic vulnerability and subjugation, which Marx and Engels had not foreseen, but which Keynes ([1930] 1935) anticipated in the midst of the global slump in the late 1920s, and which does not occur to the same extent and at a similar pace in all industrialized countries, provides not only for the material foundation of new forms of inequality (see Stehr, 1999), but also for morally coded markets.

What is at issue is the *kind* of economic development; economic development that both survives serious economic crises and sustains democratic governance. Economic prosperity, in the sense of the economic well-being of many households achieved in some countries prior to World War II, and today in many developing nations, is not sufficient for sustainable democratic governance. The prosperity of many households and its societal consequences much more likely represent conditions that foster democracy.

What is new about the development toward a much greater degree of general prosperity is not that prosperous households are able to afford a luxurious lifestyle. What is new is that a large proportion – as a matter of fact, the majority of households in the developed world – have enough funds to live a lifestyle that only a few decades ago was restricted to the wealthiest strata of the population in these societies. And as Paul Bellow, executive director for market and industry analysis at General Motors, notes, as quoted in the *New York Times*,[6] "the level of material comfort in this country [the USA] is numbing; you can make a case that the upper half lives as well as the upper 5 percent did 50 years ago." Even the average household is wealthy by comparative historical standards. But John Maynard Keynes, in his prediction in the early 1930s of social life and economic conditions a century later, did not attend to the questions of distribution among the global population or the concentration of societal wealth (Stiglitz, 2008:41–42). Today, as larger portions of

---

[6] Janny Scott and David Leonhart, "Class in America: shadowy lines that still divide," *New York Times*, May 15, 2005.

income go to capital owners and the highly skilled members of the labor force, economic inequality persists and has become even more pronounced in some countries in recent decades.

Within the scientific community, attention to and research into the linkage between not merely prosperity but also affluence and democracy can perhaps best be dated to Seymour Martin Lipset's classic 1959 empirical inquiry into some of the social requisites of democracy, especially the importance of economic development for democratic governance. Lipset (1959:75) postulated that the "more well-to-do a nation [is], the greater the chances that it will sustain democracy." The data Lipset (1959:76–79; see also Crain and Rosenthal, 1967) deploys in order to test his hypothesis are postwar statistics. But Lipset's approach stimulated a host of subsequent inquiries into the relation between economic development and democracy down to this day. It this context, it is not only economic development that counts but also, as I have emphasized, the historically unique increase in the wealth of nations and individual households in subsequent decades in the developed world. Hence, in an examination of the significance of collective prosperity or the wealth of households of a country, Jenny Miner (1998:241) refers to a more than two-centuries-old omission, and asks whether it is not time to overcome this omission: "*prospérité* has not yet been added to the *liberté, égalité, fraternité* associated with democratic activists. Should it be?"

The role of prosperity

When it comes to a definition of prosperity (and also of affluence) economists typically focus on easily quantifiable indicators; first and foremost, of course, on one conventional statistic: the gross domestic product (GDP). The advantage is that we are dealing with a single figure that can be related to a variety of other easily available numbers, such as the size of the population or the number of households. As economists would also maintain, the GDP statistic is a form of enabling information that can quickly be translated into policy measures.[7]

The major assumption is, as it were, that the growth of the GDP reflects an enhancement of the wealth of a nation and its inhabitants. The conviction that a country and its citizens are better off as the national GDP grows is by no means a belief current only among economists. It is a widely shared sentiment among the public, the media and in politics; so too, however, is the increasing critique of the GDP statistic as an

---

[7] Cf. "The rise and fall of the G.D.P.," *New York Times*, May 10, 2010.

adequate and accurate measure of the prosperity of a society. Aside from a narrow, material conception of prosperity, enhanced by the use of statistical information both readily available for a large number of countries and adequate for longitudinal comparisons, the GDP numbers are not designed to differentiate among the *sources* (let alone the *consequences*) of prosperity.

It is possible that there could be an association between the source of a nation's wealth and its prevailing political regime. For example, it is widely assumed that natural resource wealth, especially that from petroleum, natural gas, and minerals, as first suggested by Mahdavy (1970), is a curse for democracy (Ross, 2001; Robinson, Torvik, and Verdier, 2006; Aslaksen, 2010; Ramsey, 2011). More recently, however, attention has shifted to the possibility that resource reliance may in fact be a political blessing. Stephen Haber and Victor Menaldo (2011:26), on the basis of a longitudinal analysis of the relation between resource dependence and regime type, reach the conclusion that oil and mineral reliance does not promote dictatorship over the long run; if anything, the opposite is true. However, the main focus of most empirical studies is on the possibility that resource wealth enhances authoritarian governance.

Kevin K. Tsui (2010:111), for example, presents findings from a worldwide data set of the distribution of oil reserves and oil discoveries, suggesting "that oil wealth [total oil-initially-in-place] is causally related to long-term democratic development" in a *negative* way. The negative relation exists across the board "rather than disproportionally affecting large oil producers from the Arab world" (Tsui, 2010:90). The explanation, according to Tsui (2010:90), is that oil-rich autocratic leaders are in opposition to democratic development because "they will have more to give up from losing power when they are overthrown by either the population ... or other non-democratic challengers."[8] By the same token, as the wealth generated from oil declines – for example, as a result of lower oil prices – the impetus for democratic development in autocratic societies increases. In this special instance, it is quite evident that prosperity does not depend on democracy.

Once economists, the media, politicians, and the public turn their attention to a society's quality of life, they begin to follow the critique

---

[8] An alternative account of the persistence of autocratic political regimes in resource-rich countries is offered by Bearce and Laks Hutnik (2011), who suggest that the resource curse actually amounts to an immigration curse. Transition to democracy in resource-rich autocratic regimes is hampered by large-scale immigration. Immigration into such countries makes democracy less likely, because it "facilitates redistributive concessions to appease the population within an autocratic regime" (Bearce and Laks Hutnik, 2011:689).

of the conventional measure of a country's well-being (cf. Kennedy, 1968; Hirschman, 1989). The GDP as a gauge of the wealth and the well-being of nations has been challenged for a variety of reasons (cf. Stiglitz, 2005).[9] There is, first, the general critique that prosperity and progress should not be based on a single economic measure; or, at least, the GDP measure should be extended and improved (an example would be the *Human Development Index or HDI*).[10] Second, the critique often refers to the argument that the transition to a sustainable economy and society requires new measures of well-being. In addition, it is wise to remember that the prosperity and growth measured by conventional indicators cannot be extended indefinitely into the future or should not and will not necessarily be valid anymore for all groups in society (cf. Skidelsky and Skidelsky, 2012).

Alternatively, more inclusive measures designed to "dethrone" the GDP statistic are being developed.[11] The measures that are being constructed, such as the *Canadian Well-Being Index*[12] or the *State of the USA*,[13] refer to areas such as health, education, employment, and the environment of a country. The State of the USA measure aims ultimately to include some 300 indicators on issues that range from crime measures to energy, infrastructure, and housing statistics, as well as economic data. The most recent effort is that of the *Commission on the Measurement of Economic Performance and Social Progress* (the Stiglitz-Sen-Fitopussi Commission)[14] established by President Sarkozy of France. The Commission

---

[9] Simon Kuznets (1973:257), the inventor of so-called national accounts, self-critically notes, at least for the case of developed economies: "It seems fairly clear that a number of analytical and measurement problems remain in the theory and in the evaluation of economic growth in the developed countries themselves; and that one may look forward to major changes in some aspects of the analysis, in national economic accounting, and in the stock of empirical findings, which will occupy economists in the developed countries in the years ahead."

[10] The Human Development Index includes, along with additional indicators, education and health data (cf. http://hdr.undp.org/en/statistics/). A further extension of the HDI can be found in Ranis, Stewart, and Samman (2006) (also Ringen, 2010).

[11] Otto Neurath ([1937] 2004) advanced one of the first salient criticisms of the conventional statistic of the wealth of nations in a contribution to the journal *Zeitschrift für Sozialforschung*. Neurath's proposal dealt with what he called *Lebenslagen* (conditions of life) as a way of measuring the contribution of the whole set of social institutions of a society to the wealth of nations. Neurath argues for the use of a very broad conception of *Lebenslage* indicators, extending to the totality of living conditions, for example to nonmonetary social systems. Neurath ([1937] 2004:514–515) suggests that the definition of the conditions of life should not only include reference to "food, housing, clothing, theatre, sickness, occupational fatigue and leisure time" but also to measures of the "subjective feelings" of the pleasures and pains experienced by individuals.

[12] www.ciw.ca/en/Home.aspx (accessed June 16, 2013).

[13] www.stateoftheusa.org/ (accessed June 16, 2013).

[14] www.stiglitz-sen-fitoussi.fr/en/index.htm (accessed July 24, 2013).

concluded that a new measure of the quality of life requires data beyond the measures of the conventional GDP-based information on at least six additional indicators: health, education, environment, employment, interpersonal connectedness, and political engagement. Even more difficult is the development of much more subjective but quantitative measures of well-being, such as feelings of happiness, that could in turn be related to political convictions, participation, willingness to engage in contentious policy debates, and support for democratic governance.

The difficulties associated with any of these proposals are easy to enumerate. How can one achieve any agreement on what specific indicators should be incorporated into a new measure of the wealth of a nation? How can a standardized methodology be developed? How can potential users be persuaded to switch statistical measures? The critique that statistical measures are mere statistical constructs will not be easily silenced.

The general conviction that not wealth but, rather, the very existence of markets, smooths the progress of freedom is based on a conjecture that can easily be dismissed as representing an unrealistic assumption: "Claims that markets facilitate freedom rest on the assumption that every buyer and every seller can turn to alternatives" (Lindblom, 2001:188). But as we all know only too well, alternatives are often quite restricted both for suppliers and consumers, and in many cases are entirely absent. Coercion, intimidation, compulsion, inequality, indifference, and moral considerations are only a few of the often-present conditions that constrain the market conduct of sellers and buyers. Moreover, the assumed spillover effect from the market process to the political system is far from self-evident. These effects often remain obscure. The relationship between economic institutions – with the economic freedom *from* or freedom *for* they might permit – and political as well as social and civil liberties is not necessarily a symmetric one. Economic liberties do not assure political and civil or social freedoms, and political and civil liberties do not always go hand in hand with economic liberties (cf. Kennedy, 2010).

As far as the observations about economic outcomes are concerned, we have to distinguish between at least three distinct assertions about the association of economic and democratic conditions. There is, first of all, the view that the origins of democracy are linked to material developments; and, second, as the motto from Aristotle already indicates, the decline of an already established democratic regime may be hastened by a significant economic downturn, large-scale poverty, or the development of a significant gap between rich and poor. A specification of the general thesis about the linkage between prosperity and democracy suggests, in addition, that the nature of the economic system that achieves prosperity is relevant, that is, mainly in the form of "capitalist" development.

Since the focus of my inquiry is on factors that either enhance democracy or contribute to its demise it is, of course, not on the opposite (causal) linkage, namely on whether democracy in general, or other political, legal, or institutional processes embedded in democratic regimes, may (directly or in a mediated way [Baum and Lake, 2003; Narayan et al., 2011; Reenock, Staton, and Radean, 2013]) encourage or slow *economic development* (cf. Sirowy and Inkeles, 1990; Huntington, 1987; Feng, 1997; Jacobson and de Soysa, 2006; Doucouliagos and Ulubasoglu, 2008; Norris, 2011b:8–11 and 14–19); for example, reference may be made to the so-called "Lee hypothesis" (named after its advocacy by the former president of Singapore, Lee Kuan Yew), claiming that economic development is best guaranteed by nondemocratic systems; or to the idea that natural environmental settings – for example, climatic conditions – may be an essential barrier to or, as the case may be, an advantage for economic development (cf. Sen, 1999:5–6; Sachs et al., 2004; Dell et al., 2012).[15]

In a series of empirical studies, the economist Robert Barro (1996, 1999, 2000; Sirowy and Inkeles, 1990; Przeworski and Limongi, 1993) has examined the favorable impact of macrosocietal attributes on economic growth; for instance, the maintenance of the rule of law, free markets, a significant degree of autonomy of the economy from state intervention, and the presence of a significant volume of human capital. By the same token, additional economic growth *retarding* attributes of democracy have been identified; for example, the tendency to redistribute income (including land reforms) in favor of the rich, and the significant role of vested-interest lobby groups in regimes with representative legislatures (cf. Barro, 1996:1; Helliwell, 1994:244). In general, however, the exact conditional influence, for example, of different types of democracy, democratic processes and institutions, or widely held democratic attitudes among the citizens of a country on economic development is an essentially contested issue (cf. Barro, 1999). More recently, Torsten Persson and Guido Tabellini (2006, 2007), using increasingly sophisticated empirical procedures, and Boix's (2011) longer-term panel data

---

[15] The studies by the economic historians Joel Mokyr (1990) and David Landes (1998) present evidence that economic prosperity is the result of the adoption of market institutions, limited government intervention, and the protection of property rights. Feng (1997:398–399) suggests that "democracy is likely to have a significant *indirect* effect on growth through its impact on political stability ... Regular government change is likely to have a positive effect on growth, as it tends to represent political and economic adjustments in response to demands to the society, including economic stimuli."

find that the transition to democracy of a society is positively correlated with economic growth[16] and income; and, conversely, the abandonment of democracy leads to a decline in economic development.[17]

On the other side of the ledger, we find Amartya Sen's (1983) remarkable discovery of the fact that famines have never occurred in any independent and democratic country. Sen's thesis also refers to the impact of democracy on economic conditions; but Sen (1999:8) arrives at an even broader observation that stresses "the positive role of political and civil rights [as it] applies to the prevention of economic and social disasters in general" (also Miljkovic and Rimal, 2008).

While Aristotle represents one of the earliest and strongest supporters of the view that there is an unalienable linkage between economic conditions and the sustainability of democracy, Max Weber ([1906] 1994:68), discussing the state of constitutional democracy in Russia at the turn of the twentieth century – although these writings are perhaps not at the peak of his scholarship[18] – is equally adamant but extremely pessimistic when he writes,[19] "the outlook for the chances of 'democracy' and 'individualism' would be very poor indeed if we had to rely for their development on the effects produced by the 'laws' of *material* interests." For Weber, at least in this essay, the price for economic security and well-being of the "masses" actually is their loss of liberty; the masses would enter into a modern version of "*housing for the new serfdom.*" Weber ([1904] 1994:69) leaves no room for interpretation when he sternly

---

[16] The sequences of societal changes also matter; that is, countries that liberalize their economy before extending political rights do better economically (cf. Persson and Tabellini, 2006).

[17] Torsten Persson and Guido Tabellini (2007:3) sum up their findings as follows: "Our empirical findings suggest that empirically relevant heterogeneities are indeed present across countries, meaning that the flexibility allowed by semi-parametric methods is important. We show that transitions from autocracy to democracy are associated with an average growth acceleration of about 1 percentage point, producing a gain in per capita income of about 13 percent by the end of the sample period. This 1 percent growth effect is imprecisely estimated, but larger than most of the estimates in the literature using straight difference-in-difference methods.... The effect of transitions in the opposite direction is even larger: a relapse from democracy to autocracy slows down growth by almost 2 percentage points on average, which implies an income fall of about 45 percent at the end of the sample. These effects are much larger than those commonly found in the literature."

[18] For a different judgment of Weber's scholarly accomplishments regarding Russian affairs a century ago, see Pipes (1955).

[19] In the context of the same analysis, Max Weber stresses that the spread of Western culture and the capitalist economy to Russia would not "guarantee that Russia would also acquire the liberties which had accompanied their emergence in European history... European liberty had been born in unique, perhaps unrepeatable circumstances, at a time when both the intellectual and the material conditions for it were exceptionally propitious" (Pipes, 1955:383; also Weber, ([1904] 1994:43).

stresses that it is absurd to see any elective affinity between the success of developed capitalism and liberty: "If the *only* things that mattered were 'material' conditions and the constellation of interest directly or indirectly 'created' by them, any sober observer would be bound to conclude that all *economic* auguries point in the direction of a growing *loss* of freedom" (see also Marshall, 1950:34). How is liberty under the conditions of developed capitalism even possible; how can freedom possibly survive at all under the rule of capitalism? The fundamental tension, it can be argued with Weber, "posed by democracy and citizenship rights is that they can infringe on the prerogatives and operations of capitalism" (Jacobs, 2010:24); on the other hand, strong actors may deploy extensive economic liberties to suppress the liberties of the weak. Weber's iron conclusion does not answer the question of *which* social changes or historical events are responsible for the emergence and the sustainability of democratic political systems. But Weber is not speechless.

He enumerates a number of historically unique social conditions that much later will also play a part in Seymour Martin Lipset's (1950, [1960] 1963) inquiries into the conditions that favor democracy and the genesis of modern liberty; chief among them "certain unique, never-to-be repeated historical constellations" (Weber, [1906] 1994:69; also Bunce, 2001). He then proceeds to the most important reasons: expansion overseas and the peculiar structure of the early "capitalist" epoch in Western Europe[20]; the advances of science and the conquest of life by science in the (Hegelian) sense, the "coming-to-self of Mind"[21]; and finally, "the specific 'ethical' character and 'cultural values' of modern man have been molded by certain ideal notions of value which grew out of a particular set of religious ideas rooted in a concrete historical epoch, in conjunction with numerous other, equally specific, political constellations and the material preconditions" (Weber, [1906] 1990:70). The enumeration of cultural conditions as requisites for democracy reiterate Weber's rejection of the idea that economic well-being played a crucial historical role in the emergence of democratic regimes.

---

[20] Max Weber refers to Werner Sombart's *Der moderne Kapitalismus* as an important scholarly source for some of the important early features of capitalism. Modern capitalism as a really existing form of the economy and society is of course a multiple dwelling, in which many families of capitalism reside, from the state-directed capitalism of China to the free market of the United States or Singapore.

[21] Weber ([1906] 1994:70) elaborates and extends this point as follows: "But the work of ordering our outward lives rationally has now been done, at least 'in principle,' and doubtless after countless 'values' have been destroyed. The universal effect produced by the conditions of commercial life today is to make our outward lives uniform by 'standardising' production. Today science (*Wissenschaft*) as such no longer creates a 'universal personality'."

Max Weber's pessimistic views are unusual because the much more frequent (political) assertion – especially today – would be to argue that economic prosperity assures, perhaps more or less automatically, not only the persistence of democratic political conditions but also the emergence and perseverance of social trust and legitimacy in democratic institutions, and therefore accounts for a considerable measure of the liberty of individuals. And as Peter Drucker (1939:35) notes, such a declaration of (or at least the hope for) a strong link between economic advance and freedoms may be found in the political programs of both capitalist and socialist parties: "Capitalism as a social order and as a creed is the expression of the belief in economic progress as leading toward the freedom and equality of the individual in the free and equal society. Marxism expects this society to result from the abolition of private profit."

More recently, Milton Friedman (1962:10; also 1958:168), the vigorous proponent of free market capitalism, more cautiously asserts that democracy depends not so much on economic prosperity; rather, free markets and private enterprise in particular are the necessary, but not the sufficient, conditions for political liberty and democracy, a form of economic organization Friedman labels "competitive capitalism." But capitalism "must be accompanied by a set of values and by political institutions favourable to freedom" (Friedman, 1958:168). After all, Friedman adds, there are prominent historical examples ranging from Fascist Italy and Spain to Japan before World War II, where private enterprise and totalitarian political regimes existed side-by-side. On the other hand, few, if any, historical examples of societies come to mind confirming that political liberty is not also associated with "something comparable to a free market to organize the bulk of economic activity" (Friedman, 1962:9). Yet free markets may not always be sufficient to prevent the abolition of political and other liberties, as well as the emergence of serious strains on democracy (see Reich, 2007).[22] And, as

---

[22] As far as I can see, there are no historical examples where democratic political systems have attempted to *eliminate* the market system. Charles Lindblom (2001:230) is convinced that the answer to the question of why a democratic regime has never attempted to abandon the market system completely points to widely shared world views; that is, "a remarkably high degree of conformity in thought endorsing or accepting the market system ... The historical connection rests on a state of mind, not on the mechanics of market system and democracy." The uniformity of world views among the masses is the consequence of successful efforts by nongovernmental elites to influence the convictions of the masses: "Any society not governed by either a landed aristocracy, where a market system has not yet been established, or by a revolutionary elite, where a market system has been abolished, will be governed by a diffuse elite whose privileges and power depend on the rules and customs of the market system."

Charles Lindblom (2001:236) cautiously suggests, "the market system holds democracy down to a low level ... obstructing a more genuine yet feasible democracy."

The economic mechanism that is primarily responsible for a contraction of democratic conditions and opportunities is the inequality in income and wealth generated and sustained by the market system. In addition, the influence – often obstructive – of large corporations on the democratic political life of a country represents another important barrier to genuine political equality. The obstruction of democracy arises when corporations are granted rights and powers as legally fictitious individual citizens; for example, civil rights granted to individual citizens allowing the corporation to go to court as an injured person (Lindblom, 2001:240).

Thus, as Milton Friedman (1962:8) also stresses, it would be a delusion to assume that a fundamental division exists between the social institutions of politics and the economy: "Economic arrangements play a dual role in the promotion of a free society. On the one hand, freedom in economic arrangements is itself a component of freedom broadly understood, so economic freedom is an end in itself. In the second place, economic freedom is also an indispensable means toward the achievement of political freedom."[23]

The assertion that prosperity, or more narrowly, rising per-capita incomes and improving living standards resulting from economic growth, not only bring about visible improvements in the existential conditions of individuals but also shape the "character" of society, especially the "moral character of a people" (Friedman, 2005:4), as well as the social and political nature of society, is a thesis that of course resonates with the view that persistent gains in prosperity may be supportive of democratic conditions. Friedman (2005:4) more generally, and optimistically, expects that economic growth, in the sense of "a higher standard of living for the clear majority of citizens – more often than not fosters greater opportunity, tolerance of diversity, social mobility, commitment to fairness, and dedication to democracy." Even though the impacts on society listed by Friedman may have many reasons, as Friedman (2005:9; also Stiglitz, 2005) concedes, the "effect of economic growth and stagnation is an important and often central part of the story." But as we have seen, any generalization that prosperity depends on democracy is unwarranted.

---

[23] The social mechanism Friedman (1962:15) has in mind and that assures that the economy does not operate as a basis for power is a system of checks and balances; more specifically, "by removing the organization of economic activity from the control of political authority, the market eliminates this source of coercive power."

In the following sections of this chapter, the question that will be discussed in greater detail concerns the empirical relation between economic affluence, economic growth, the distribution of income and wealth, and democratic society. Less attention will be focused on the impact of democracy on economic growth, a question that also has received considerable thought, especially in light of the presence of large contemporary societies that have achieved significant economic growth and wealth, at least for the time being, without a wholesale shift of the political system to democratic rules and procedures.[24]

Affluence as a basis for democracy

> Commerce is a cure for the most destructive prejudices; for it is almost a general rule that wherever we find agreeable manners, there commerce flourishes; and that wherever there is commerce, there we meet with agreeable manners.
>
> Montesquieu, *The Spirit of the Laws* ([1748] 2007:316)

In a widely cited essay about the American "national character" published in the early 1950s, the historian David Potter ([1954] 1958:112) examines the relationship between high standards of living, or relative affluence, and democracy. He offers the sober and straightforward assessment that a democratic society blossoms in nations that are materially well off (cf. also Lippmann, [1922] 1997:197). Hence, one is able to assert, democracy depends on affluence.

The hypothesis that democracies endure in prosperous societies is confirmed as an empirical regularity, as related by Adam Pzreworski (2004:9):

> No democracy ever, including the period before World War II, fell in a country with a per capita income higher than that of Argentina in 1975, $6,055. This is a startling fact, given that since 1946 alone forty-seven democracies collapsed in poorer countries. In contrast, thirty-five democracies spent 1046 years in wealthier countries and not one died. Affluent democracies survived wars, riots, scandals, economic and governmental crises, hell or high water.

---

[24] Lyle Shannon's (1958:381) extensive empirical analysis of the correlation between a wide range of socioeconomic factors (such as available resources, per-capita livestock, per-capita production and consumption of noncommercial fuels, etc.) and dichotomized forms of governance (self-governance vs. non–self governance) indicates that "self-government is found at every level of development." Matthew Baum and David Lake (2003:345), in a recent study using a set of time-series cross-section statistical investigations, conclude what earlier studies did not find, namely that there is an effect of democracy on economic growth; however, it "is subtle, indirect, and contingent on levels of development."

The explanation why this should be the case would make plausible reference to a number of societal consequences that are all conducive to democracy in one way or another, and depend on the availability of significant economic resources that can be invested by individuals or the state in raising levels of literacy and education, and that enable broader-based access to knowledge and information. As Samuel Huntington (1984:199; see also Acemoglu and Robinson, 2000 and Acemoglu and Robinson, 2012:364–367) points out, there are a number of additional sociopolitical consequences that do go hand-in-hand with economic affluence in a country and encourage democracy: a moderation of political conflicts and social cleavages as a result of the presence of inclusive institutions, especially if the degree of inequality is softened or hidden due to a persistent increase in the affluence of a nation. In addition, as the complexity of a society and its economy increases, it is more and more difficult to rule such a social system in an authoritarian manner.

The experience of the global financial crisis in September 2008 would appear to support the conclusion about the persistence of democratic governance in wealthy nations (cf. Diamond, 2011). After all, none of the Western market economies hit hardest by the worst financial crisis since the Great Depression experienced a dramatic political revolution. Established, well-institutionalized democracies have a better chance of survival. However, the financial crisis did have political repercussions even in wealthy nations, as will be discussed at a later stage.

As we have already seen in the previous part, the survival of democratic regimes is related to the years of schooling of the population of a country. Education and income are correlated. The effect of material well-being appears to have a stronger influence than education (see Przeworski, 2004). By the same token, it would follow that a democratic regime is not suitable for nations that have a low standard of living, and whose inhabitants suffer from material deprivation.[25] Potter's assertion culminates in the thesis that "economic abundance is conducive to political democracy." Potter's conclusion is not without its detractors in the literature. Sociohistorical studies that display an affinity to Max Weber's analysis of prerevolutionary Russia – for example, Barrington Moore's *The Social Origin of Dictatorship and Democracy* (1966) – arrive at the conclusion that the possibility of the emergence of democracy is not necessarily tied to the global spread of the capitalist economic order.

---

[25] The behavioral economist Sendhil Mullainathan and the social psychologist Eldar Shafir (2013) have examined the influence of "scarcity" and, at least by implication, "abundance" on cognitive processes (and indirectly the propensity to support democratic governance).

The path to "capitalist" democracy depends on historical conditions that are not necessarily repeated.

In the late 1950s, in a seminal work in the cross-national quantitative research approach, Seymour Martin Lipset (1959) examined the societal requisites for democracy anew, employing a sociological and behavioral, rather than a political, philosophy viewpoint. Inspired by the then-dominant modernization theory, his focus is on social fundamentals that are external to the political system; for example, values, economic well-being, social mobility, social institutions or country-specific historical events. Lipset posits that one ought to be able to identify a number of actually existing conditions in a number of countries conducive to the support for democracy and its sustainability. His efforts concentrate on two social requisites, one mainly "material" (affluence) and the other "cultural": *economic development* and *legitimacy*. In his more comprehensive study of the social basis of politics, *Political Man* ([1960] 1963:64), Lipset adds *effectiveness*, or the actual performance of the political system, as an additional foundation stone for the persistence of democratic governance. By the same token, once the political system fails to deliver on all three fronts – intrinsic legitimacy, actual performance, and economic development – the stability of democratic governance is seriously jeopardized.

Lipset is careful to label his comparative analysis of political systems as an illustrative case in support of plausible theoretical interpretations. A cross-sectional correlational analysis and its results cannot claim to have found the *causal* sequences among the individual and collective variables that form part of his analysis. Economic development – and not merely capitalist economic development – is introduced by Lipset as "the economic development complex" (comprising industrialization, wealth, urbanization, and education). The hypothesis Lipset (1959:75) investigates is that "the more well-to-do a nation, the greater the chances that it will *sustain* democracy" (emphasis added). The various components of the economic development complex are highly correlated. Legitimacy is defined in its traditional sense as the general assent to authority,[26] and refers to the degree to which social institutions are valued as such and considered to be right and proper. Lipset does not expect, even on theoretical grounds, to find a high correlation between structural factors such as income, education, religion, and democracy, since the political system does operate autonomously.[27] As the case of

---

[26] See Max Weber (1946:78).
[27] The thesis of the relative independence of the political system is supported by the fact that we find today a larger number of poor countries in the world that are nonetheless democratically governed (cf. Vanhanen, 2003).

the history of Germany in the last century shows, a set of unique historical factors may drive the establishment of political forms contrary to favorable structural settings. Germany is an example "of a nation in which the structural changes – growing industrialization, urbanization, wealth, and education – all favoured the establishment of a democratic system, but in which a series of adverse historical events prevented democracy from securing legitimacy" (Lipset, 1959:72). *Novel, country-specific historical circumstances* may therefore account for both the rise of democracy and its failure to be established in a society. As we will see, Lipset's approach, which focuses on the then-popular modernization theory, has more recently been revived in the context of much larger and more sophisticated empirical analyses of the relation between prosperity/affluence and democracy.

The empirical test and the extensive theoretical narrative that Lipset offers are based on comparisons of affluent Western European and English-speaking countries and Latin American nations. In the case of the former set of nations, he distinguishes between "stable democracies" and "democracies and dictatorships" since World War I. In the case of the Latin American nations, Lipset differentiates between "democracies and unstable dictatorships" and "stable dictatorships."

For the purpose of testing his hypothesis, Lipset constructs indices of wealth, industrialization, education, and urbanization for each category of countries, compiled from census figures for each nation. The main indices of wealth, for example, are aggregates of per-capita income, number of persons per motor vehicle and per physician, and the number of radios, telephones, and newspapers per thousand persons. In all cases – wealth, industrialization, urbanization, and education – Lipset finds a significant correlation between these indicators and democratic regimes in both regions of the world considered in his study. For example, groupings of countries with the lowest per-capita income tend to fall into the category "less democratic" while those with the highest per capita fall into the category "more democratic."

In addition, Lipset turns to the question of the legitimacy and effectiveness of the political system, as well as the mechanisms that reduce the intensity of social cleavages in society, as requisites of democracy. Conditions which "serve to moderate the intensity of partisan battle ... are among the key requisites for a democratic political system ... the character and content of the major cleavages affecting the political stability of a society are largely determined by historical factors" (Lipset, 1959:91–92). However, in affluent Western societies three main divisions stand out: (1) religious issues; (2) universal rights; and (3) distributive justice, whereby cross-cutting bases of cleavages and the resolution of legal and socioeconomic divisions (see Marshall, 1950) are best for the vitality of democracy.

Legitimacy that may be unequal in strength by social strata and effectiveness of the actual performance of the political system – for example, in the sense of a sustainable and steady increase in the overall wealth of a society – are elements of the political system itself.[28] Effectiveness and legitimacy tend to be linked. But even the stability of strongly legitimate political systems is threatened if a breakdown of their effectiveness occurs repeatedly, or over a longer period. Knowledge about the strength of the legitimacy of a nation's political regime, however, allows for a reasonable hypothesis about the stability of its political institutions.

His inquiry culminates in what has become known as the *Lipset thesis*: economic affluence is supportive of democracy (also Shannon, 1958). Lipset (1959:75) suggests that this thesis is actually an intellectual conception that can be traced from Aristotle down to the present age. Many observers have repeatedly advanced the view that "only in a wealthy society in which relatively few citizens lived in real poverty could a situation exist in which the mass of the population could intelligently participate in politics and could develop the self-restraint necessary to avoid succumbing to the appeals of irresponsible demagogues." Yet Lipset (1959:103) is quick to qualify his own thesis by observing that his conclusion does not justify the optimistic hope that "an increase in wealth, in the size of the middle class, in education and other related factors will necessarily mean the spread of democracy or the stabilizing of democracy."

As the quote from Lipset makes clear, there is at least one other significant element that is decisive in addition to the absence of widespread poverty, the containment of social cleavages, and the effectiveness and legitimacy of the political regime; namely, certain cognitive facilities that enhance political participation and enable "entry" into the often highly contested political activities in democracies. After all, in order to "intelligently participate in politics," as Lipset indicates, affluence alone is neither an immediate nor a sufficient asset. That is why many similar empirical inquiries that follow Lipset's theoretical perspective and empirical design promptly add the intervening dimension of educational achievement or any other indication of the "intelligence," literacy or cognitive capacity of individuals to the attribute of prosperity or affluence as an engine of sustainable democracies.

---

[28] For Lipset (1959:89), following Gabriel Almond's (1956:396) conception of the symbolic attributes of political legitimacy, a major test of legitimacy "is the extent to which given nations have developed a common 'secular political culture,' national rituals and holidays which serve to maintain the legitimacy of various democratic practices."

A recent large-scale panel study of 100 countries covering the period from 1960 to 1995 by Robert Barro (1999:S160), for example, confirms Lipset's findings. Barro finds that improvements in (various measures of) the standard of living (per capita GDP) and educational attainment predict increases in the subjective propensity to democracy. By the same token, Barro (1999:S160) notes, democracies that emerge without prior economic development tend to not last, confirming the general indication that democracies rest on wealth/affluence. Barro employs a narrow definition of democracy focusing on the role of elections – that is, the political right to take part in general elections. Evelyn Huber, Dietrich Rueschemeyer, and John D. Stephens (1993:74–75; summarizing Rueschemeyer, Stephens and Stephens, 1992), using a case-study method, also confirm the basic Lipset thesis, although their underlying explanatory apparatus differs: "*Capitalist* development is related to democracy because it shifts the balance of class power, because it weakens the power of the landlord class and strengthens subordinate classes." In addition, "the working and the middle class – unlike the subordinate classes in history – gain an unprecedented capacity for self-organization due to such developments as urbanization, factory production, and new forms of communication and transportation." The relationship between democracy (especially universal [male] suffrage) and (this time they use the neutral term) level of development is not unilinear or automatic. If one factor figures most prominently in their account, it is the balance of class power and historically uniquely constructed class interests. It is not the mere increase in prosperity or per-capita income that favors a democratic regime; what is more important and crucial for democracy, according to Huber, Rueschemeyer, and Stephens (1993:85), are class and sociostructural changes, caused by industrialization and urbanization.

An even more recent comprehensive empirical analysis of the relation of a country's higher per-capita "income" and democracy by Daron Acemoglu and colleagues (Acemoglu et al., 2008:836) that is theoretically closely related to Lipset's work, since both rely on the modernization theory, concludes that the conventional thesis in the political economy literature concerning a "causal" effect of income per capita on democracy *cannot* be supported.[29]

---

[29] The conclusions of Acemoglu et al. are contested: Che and colleagues (2012), for example, argue that the results of Acemoglu et al. (2008) may be an artifact of their methodological approach. In a study employing a different methodological procedure (system-GMM) but based on the statistics Acemoglu and colleagues used, these authors reach the conclusion that there is indeed a positive correlation between income levels and democracy processes.

Although income and democracy are positively correlated, there is no evidence of a causal impact during the postwar era or even during the entire last century. Instead, and as Lipset had already stressed, it would appear that unique, country-specific historical conditions "in development paths are responsible for much of the statistical association between long-run economic and political changes" (Acemoglu et al., 2008:836). A probability-sample survey of the new Chinese middle class drawn from the urban population of three cities carried out by Chen and Lu (2011:707), which measures support for democracy as a positive attitude "toward a set of democratic norms and institutions," finds that attitudinal support for democracy is weak. As a matter of fact, and assuming that the reported findings are valid and reflect more than political desirable responses, "most members of this new middle class are in favor of individual rights ... [but] they shun political liberties – such as the freedom to demonstrate and to form organizations – and are not interested in democratic institutions, such as fully competitive election of leaders without restriction ... nor enthusiastic about participating in government affairs and politics" (Chen and Lu, 2011:715–716).

These findings also lend support to the observation and complication of the relation between modernization and economic well-being as a country-specific phenomenon, dependent on processes that may affect not only the economic but also the political development of a society. However, a longer historical perspective – beyond a century – might show that the interaction between general affluence and democracy is stronger than the often-reported mere statistical association.

Economic growth and democratic society

Although it is not altogether self-evident to distinguish between the contributions that material prosperity or economic growth may make to the emergence and persistence of democratic regimes, the question of the role and the experience of persistent improvements in material conditions should be considered a distinctive issue (and asset) in the context of the relations between affluence and democracy. A concise definition of what economists typically mean by the term *economic* growth is provided by Simon Kuznets (1973:247): "A country's economic growth may be defined as a long-term rise in the capacity to supply increasingly diverse economic goods to its population, this growing capacity based on advancing technology and the institutional and ideological adjustments that it demands."

The thesis at the base of this definition would be that economic growth might have a positive significance for the legitimacy and popularity of a country's government. This formulation already makes it clear that the influence of economic growth can prop up both autocratic and democratic governments, just as the reverse may be true: that a period of economic stagnation or recession might put into question the legitimacy and public support of the political regime. In short, do the form, pace, and longevity of economic growth have a systematic influence on a society's political makeup? The relevant international comparative theoretical standpoints and empirical research results are ambiguous; the findings are to some extent contradictory. The majority of previously undertaken analyses of the correlations between economic development and democracy were carried out during the 1950s and 1960s of the last century, when great importance was attributed to the question of "modernization," particularly in developing societies. The relation between democracy and forms of economic development in established democracies must therefore be considered as a separate, specialized problem.

It is obvious that, although they were generally advocates of democracy (cf. Sirowy and Inkeles, 1990:127), political scientists either took as the premise of their analyses a *conflict of objectives*: democracy is a luxury that an economically developing society cannot afford, and/or growth is a prerequisite for democracy (and thus an authoritarian regime can function in the meantime); or were convinced of the fundamental *convergence* of democracy and economic order. The grounds for one position or the other are easily enumerated: on the one hand, it was argued, political instability has dysfunctional consequences for the economic welfare of a society (this is the case even when there are ostensibly democratic institutions in place)[30] – a position that can easily be applied to modern national economies. The particular economic challenges of a developing society – for example, with respect to the necessity of financing investments or weathering a slump in consumer spending – cannot be met, or so the argument goes, without (centrally coordinated) coercive state measures (cf. Kuznets, 1955).

On the other hand, those authors who speak of a fundamental convergence of economic development and democratic institutions in developing societies come to the conclusion that the processes necessitating centralization under authoritarian control, as described by the conflict perspective, simply do no such thing. The authors who represent the

---

[30] Sirowy and Inkeles (1990:129) explain their assertion as follows: "The electoral politics that are inherent in democracy may well act to distort the economy and incapacitate the government as officials shift their allegiances among policies based on short-run political expediency, rather than focusing exclusively on policies oriented toward national development in the long-run."

convergence thesis regarding democracy and economic growth refer rather to the dysfunctional consequences of centralized control, such as the tendency to corruption and the squandering of resources, and to the importance of economic and political pluralism for the development of the economic system (e.g., Goodin, 1979). Finally, Sirowy and Inkeles (1990) point out that there is a viewpoint critical of both the conflict and the convergence argument. The skeptic viewpoint assumes that there is hardly any significant influence of democratic institutions on a society's economic growth. This is also true of the influence of economic growth on a country's democratic political conditions.

It is likely that different historical circumstances and settings in different regions and countries of the world, and distinctive trajectories and dependencies of economic development, contribute to a diversity of linkages between patterns of economic development, democratization, and democratic governance. In any case, what makes any analysis difficult, especially in the sense of generating typical patterns, is that relevant relations need not be linear; rather, they show patterns of delay, have divergent paths and different critical junctures, respond to distant processes, or have sudden impacts (cf. Treisman, 2011). Findings from empirical studies carried out to date therefore lack a clear-cut pattern. Different theoretical perspectives, methods, indicators, independent variables, modes of analysis, timings, and sizes, among other dissimilarities, make comparison difficult. The conflict perspective (e.g., O'Donnell, 1978), the convergence thesis (e.g. Diebolt et al., 2013), and the skeptical point of view all find empirical support (e.g., Marsh, 1988).[31]

Inequality and democracy

In fact, it was precisely the *inequality* of the distribution of wealth and of capital which made possible those vast accumulations of fixed wealth

---

[31] A detailed meta-analysis has been carried out by Sirowy and Inkeles (1990:150-151): "The studies examined are divided nearly equally with respect to whether a negative relationship or no relationship was found between democracy and economic growth ... much empirical work remains to be done." A quarter century later, the same empirically based conclusions appear to be valid: "The impact of economic growth on the survival of democracy is hard to determine. Empirical patterns show that democracy is more fragile in countries where per capita income stagnates or declines. But the direction of causality is not clear: do democracies die because they perform poorly or do they perform poorly because they are about to die?" (Przeworski, 2004:10). Przeworski, Alvarez, Cheibub, and Limongi (2000:11) note that the survival of democratic governance improves in the wake of an observed positive economic performance of a nation over a period of three or more consecutive years. The deaths of democracies, on the other hand, "follow a clear pattern: They are more likely when a country experiences an economic crisis, and in most cases they are accompanied by one."

and capital improvements which distinguished that age from all others. Herein lay, in fact, the main justification of the Capitalist System.

John Maynard Keynes ([1919] 2009:17)

It is not only in John Maynard Keynes' ([1919] 2009) treatment of *The Economic Consequences of the Peace* but also prominently in his *General Theory of Employment, Interest and Money* (e.g., 1936:342–343) that we find repeated references by the author to the "social and psychological *justification* for significant inequalities of incomes and wealth" (emphasis added). It is perhaps self-evident that market outcomes do not automatically ensure fair distributional patterns of income and wealth.

However, wider ranging discussions of patterns of economic inequality not only extend to normative considerations that might justify existing social structures of inequality, but such discussions are concerned also with the function of economic inequality for political life in democracies. Thus, they address such questions as the possible impact of inequality on participation in a regime and its political legitimacy; the degree of inequality that democratic societies are capable of tolerating; and whether democracies are actually able to reduce economic inequalities. But first I will describe ways of statistically capturing economic inequalities.

Social scientists interested in the societal distribution of wealth and incomes have spent disproportionate energy on examining the *concentration* of wealth in societies and displayed considerably less interest in changes in the average level of economic well-being over time. Special statistical measures of dispersion, such as the Gini coefficient or the Lorenz curve, have been deployed to reduce the empirical pattern of inequality to a single figure. The Gini coefficient, for example, can range from 0 to 1. A low figure represents a more equal distribution of household income; a high figure a significant concentration of prosperity. Countries with low Gini coefficient are the Scandinavian societies, for instance: In Sweden, the Gini coefficient as a measure of income inequality stood at 0.25 in 2005 and at 0.41 for Portugal in the same year.[32] In Europe, at least, the Gini coefficients have remained almost constant between 1995 and 2005. Significantly higher concentrations of income may be found in African and Latin American countries. In the United States, the coefficient in 2007 stood at 0.45.[33]

---

[32] See www.eurofound.europa.eu/areas/qualityoflife/eurlife/index.php?template=3& radioindic=158&idDomain=3 (accessed June 30, 2012).
[33] See www.nationmaster.com/graph/eco_dis_of_fam_inc_gin_ind-distribution-family-income-gini-index (accessed August 15, 2013).

Although measures of concentration of wealth or family income of course fail to reflect general increases or declines in the average standard of living of households in a society over a certain period of time, they may be strongly related to the possibility, legitimacy, participatory patterns, and stability of democratic governance – in the sense that the *absence* of extreme inequalities in household income generally fosters democracy (cf. Huntington, 1984; Solt, 2008), while deep cleavages of economic inequality might suppress political engagement, especially among the poorer strata of society (Dahl, 2006:85–86; Tilly, 2003b). Changing forms of inequality in modern societies and their intrusion into the political process will not change the threat to democracy of unequal social categories; as Charles Tilly (2003a:36) maintains, "they do so by providing beneficiaries of inequality with incentives and means to subvert or opt out of equal rights, equal obligations, equal consultation, and equal protection."

But it is also entirely probable that persistent improvements in the standard of living outweigh, across the board, the *status quo*, or even increase, of the concentration of economic inequality in a society; that is, the magnitude of the decline in the real cost of living may outweigh the rise in overall economic disparity (cf. Federal Reserve Bank of Dallas, 1998). The expectation was, at least until two or three decades ago, that the industrial society and, even more generally, the modernization process is bound to produce a system of social inequality which in the end will be less hierarchical, more standardized and leveled; will reflect individual abilities more closely; will be more open and, therefore, much less rigid than the inequality found in the initial phases of industrialization with its often impenetrable class boundaries (e.g., Schelsky, 1955:218–242; Dahrendorf, [1957] 1959:274; 1967:68; Goldthorpe, 1966:650). These convictions of the ultimate fairness of the market outcomes of industrial society gave rise, for many years, to a broad lack of interest among social scientists in questions of social inequality. However, the lack of attention to issues of inequality cannot be attributed to a triumph of equality in industrial society.[34]

---

[34] John K. Galbraith (1957:85) was of the opinion that the lack of interest in the phenomena of social inequality at the time can be attributed, on the one hand, to the fact that the degree of inequality in capitalist societies, contrary to Marxist expectations, did not increase; and, on the other hand, to the fact that the societal influence of the wealthy, at least in the United States, was less pronounced. Today, however, not only the Occupy Wall Street movement but also some economists focus on inequality, the 99 percent versus the 1 percent. The economist Robert H. Frank (2007), for example, published a plea for a policy focus on social inequality rather than economic growth (also Noah, 2012). Nonetheless, the issue of inequality has, at least in the United States, gained little if any political grip (cf. Nichols Lemann, "Evening the odds," *The New*

As indicated, however, consistently growing and stable results of the productive process, the elasticity of prosperity (vertical mobility, diversification of wealth, cf. Boix, 2003; Freeman and Quinn, 2012), and improvements in the overall standard of living conditions in virtually all households would appear to have compensated for the lack of any significant redistribution of social rewards and costs (cf. Galbraith, 1957:95; also Gellner, 1983:22), at least in some countries,[35] and are likely to account for both the widespread comfort and content of the day, even in the face of growing inequality in society, and the decline in the propensity to take part in formal political activities (cf. Leijonhufvud, 2008). In other countries, for example in the United States, massive inequalities have been "naturalized," linked to the idea of individual merit and the outcome of inherited talent (cf. Rasanvallon, [2011] 2013:105). The gradual sense of progress captured in observations about the postwar era, however, does not necessarily signify that major social conflicts generated by structures of social inequality (entitlements, poverty, unemployment, increased upward flow of money) have withered away and disappeared altogether, even in autocratic societies.

By the same token, inadequate economic returns, especially for the educational achievements of younger cohorts of society, and rising gradients of socioeconomic inequality may trigger political activity and resistance against the ruling "class" (see Campante and Chor, 2012). As Seymour Lipset (1959:31) in his seminal paper on economic development and political legitimacy asserts: "Democracy is related to the state of economic development. The more well-to-do a nation, the greater the chances that it will sustain democracy" (see also Friedman, 2010). In the modern world, constant improvements in economic effectiveness that "lasts over a number of generations, may give legitimacy to a political system; in the modern world, such effectiveness mainly means constant economic development" (Lipset, 1959:91; also Przeworski, 1991:32).

Yorker, April 23, 2012). As Peter Thiel notes in an interview in the *American Prospect* (March/April 2012 issue): "In the history of the modern world, inequality has only been ended through communist revolution, war or deflationary economic collapse."

[35] Branko Milanovic (2012) has examined changes in global rather than within country patterns of inequality. The rise of the Chinese and Indian economies in the last two decades has slightly decreased global inequality, offsetting the rise of inequality within developed nations. However, "global inequality is much greater than inequality within any individual country" (Milanovic, 2012:9). Most of the variation in global inequality is a matter of location. Hence, Milanovic (2012:27) concludes, "migration is likely to become one of the key problems—or solutions, depending on one's viewpoint—of the 21st century ... [because] either poor countries will become richer, or poor people will move to rich countries."

But in this respect, too, the optimism of the heroic days of the late fifties and early sixties has given way to a more differentiated picture, in particular to the realization that the expected modification or even decline in economic inequality has not been achieved; although a noticeable leveling in some respects has taken place, for example, in the areas of life expectancy, health care, and certain provisions of social security. However, changes in the power structure or relations of authority in industrial society are much too difficult to discern, as are the difficulties of agreeing on simple measures of the degree of concentration of household incomes. Yet it is wise to conclude with Georg Simmel ([1907] 1978:440) that while the widespread "rise in the level of knowledge as a whole" in modern societies is indeed remarkable, and its effects on the social inequality regime in societies is profound, it does not follow that the structures of inequality, as a result, will be significantly flattened, or are about to disappear.

The widening gap of income distribution in many of the most prosperous countries of the world in the wake of the economic development of the past two decades, and the political ramifications this may have in the long run, are receiving increasing attention among social scientists in the last few years. The evidence of growing and new forms of social exclusion accumulates.[36] The robustness and steep gradients of the new forms of inequality are remarkable; the inequalities influence not only the political behavior (cf. Lupu and Pontesson, 2011)[37] but threaten to become a burden on democracy.[38]

However, the following chart shows that the relationship between perceived income differences in a larger number of countries with significantly different income levels (as measured by the recent Gini coefficient for each country) is either compatible with the perception of income differentials that are too large in countries with a relatively low Gini

---

[36] One of the more remarkable divisions emerging most recently is the unequal use of mobile airwaves. Arieso, a company in England that tracks the usage of mobile devices, found that in 2009 the top 3 percent of heavy users generated 40 percent of the network traffic. Only a couple of years later, the same category of users commands 70 percent of the traffic (as quoted in "Top 1% of mobile users consume half of world's bandwidth, and gap is growing," *New York Times*, January 5, 2012).

[37] In their empirical analysis of the political consequences of the structure of social inequality in developed democracies, Noam Lupu and Jonas Pontusson (2011:312) conclude that "government policy tends to become more redistributive as earnings in the upper half of the distribution are more dispersed and less distributive as earnings in the lower half are more dispersed."

[38] The economist and *New York Times* columnist Paul Krugman ("Oligarchy, American style," *New York Times*, November 4, 2011) suspects that "we have a society in which money is increasingly concentrated in the hands of a few people, and in which that concentration of income and wealth threatens to make us a democracy in name only."

Inequality and democracy 157

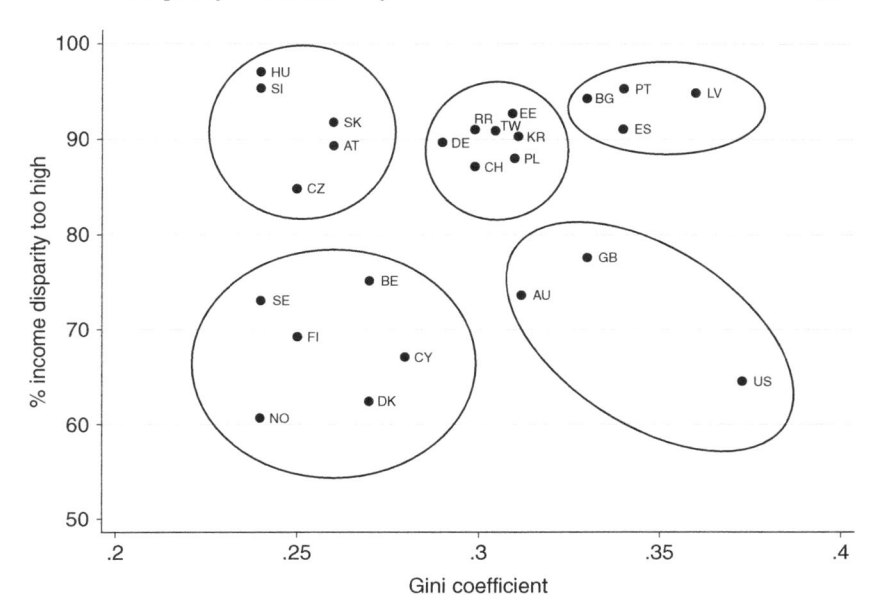

Figure 2 Perception of income differences as too large in relation to the Gini coefficient of different countries
Source: ISSP 2009/2010; Gini-Index: Social Indicators Monitor (SIMon); USA, AU: LIS-Database

coefficient (for example in the case of Hungary, Austria, Slovakia) or with opinions that a high concentration of income levels (USA, Australia, UK) is tolerable in countries with a high Gini coefficient.

Income inequality has been rapidly increasing in recent years in many of the OECD countries and beyond. For example, in 2008 in Great Britain, the top 10 percent had incomes twelve times higher than the bottom 10 percent, which is up from eight times greater twenty-five years ago. Income inequality is rising even in Scandinavian countries, as well as in Germany, and is rising exceptionally in countries such as India, China, and Brazil.[39] The question of what doctrines, including moral conceptions and social conditions, permit the perpetuation of these new structures of unequal economic rewards remains unanswered for the time being but could prove to represent a serious challenge to established democratic regimes.

---

[39] See www.guardian.co.uk/society/2011/dec/05/income-inequality-growing-faster-uk (accessed July 31, 2013)

The notion of the truly disadvantaged (Wilson, 1987), or underclass, which encloses multiple generations of individuals, attempts to capture the phenomenon of the irreversibility of social class membership and the lack of any prospect for social mobility. Although the term underclass is inadequate in terms of traditional class theory – since the truly disadvantaged do not form a class-in-itself with the prospect of becoming a class-for-itself, and the underclass is far from organizing itself – it is still a concept that conveys the ironclad social position of individuals and families who find themselves at the bottom rung of the ladder of inequality. The apparently permanent status of large segments of society as truly disadvantaged is reflected in the inability of members of these segments to obtain a job even as the economies are expanding. The responsibility for such hardened patterns of inequality is often seen to be linked to the competitive nature of economic globalization (e.g., Dahrendorf, 1996:238). The most recent empirical studies (e.g., Stewart, 2011), however, assign the responsibility for this trend to the economic and tax-related advantages enjoyed by the *finance sector*.[40]

Frederick Solt (2008) has undertaken an empirical analysis of the impact of economic inequality on political engagements (political interest, frequency of political discussion, and electoral participation) in a diverse sample of rich and upper middle–income democracies, using cross-national survey data for twenty-two countries mainly based on information gathered by the *World Value Survey*, the *Eurobarometer*, and the *European Election Survey*. The Gini coefficient for household income inequalities serves as the measure of national economic inequality. In addition, a large number of control variables are employed. The overall findings suggest that collective inequality reduces the political engagements of the nonaffluent strata (also Soss, 1999) and thereby potentially enhances the political power of the affluent segments of society. Among the implications of Solt's (2008:58) findings are:

Declining political interest, discussion of politics, and participation in elections among poorer citizens with rising inequality attest to the increased ability of relatively wealthy individuals to make politics meaningless for those with lower incomes in such circumstances. The results of this study indicate that democracy is more likely to fulfill its promise of providing political equality among all citizens when economic resources are distributed more equally.

But how exactly collective patterns of inequality are translated into different patterns of political engagement remains a black box.

[40] See www.guardian.co.uk/society/2011/dec/05/income-inequality-growing-faster-uk (accessed July 31, 2013). See also OECD, *Divided We Stand: Why Inequality Keeps Rising* (OECD, 2011).

Nonetheless, such empirical findings and prospects of robust patterns of economic inequality in modern societies already seem to incorporate the answer to questions about the impact of democracy on inequality. Robert Anderson (2012:12) points out that a comprehensive support for democracy is not observable in all affluent societies. One of the possible causes for the differences in the degree of support for democracy may be the form of economic inequality found in these societies: "Countries with high levels of income inequality tend to have lower levels of support for democracy than countries with low levels of income inequality."[41]

Does democracy reduce economic inequality? A number of empirical studies have tried to find an answer. Beginning with the 1996 World Bank publication by Deininger and Squire (1996), the answers remain inconclusive. The World Bank study, using the simple dichotomy of democratic versus nondemocratic countries (also used in subsequent analyses), found that democracy means less inequality. More recently, Timmons (2010) used an updated and revised data set for a larger set of countries, but over a longer period of time. Timmons' (2010:742) findings are unambiguous. He "finds nothing indicating a systematic relationship between democracy/civil liberties and lower economic inequalities." The findings remain the same when limited to the countries used in the World Bank study. The results of the study by Timmons suggest that neither the simple dichotomy democratic/nondemocratic nor the way inequality has been operationalized may be valid indicators to capture the impact of democracy on inequality. The gradient of inequality and its changes over time may be less significant than the impact of democracy on the general standard of living.

Economic well-being and knowledge

The theoretical presumption supported by robust empirical findings shows that information, knowledge, and knowledgeability enhance the economic well-being of individuals and collectivities. It is widely taken for granted that economic well-being increasingly depends on the societal level of knowledge and information. In the context of the emerging knowledge-based economy (cf. Stehr, 2002), the association between knowledge and economic success/growth at both the individual and the collective level should become even more evident than has been the case in the past (see Weede and Kämpf, 2002).

---

[41] Anderson (2012:4) employs data from the 2001 *World Values Survey* for a total of 35 countries.

As modern economies add a new factor of production – knowledge – to the traditional factors of production of industrial societies – land, labor, and capital – the latter factors of production are declining in importance while the economic significance of knowledge and information increases. The obvious conclusion drawn by the OECD, among many other observers of the modern economy, would therefore be that the "most effective modern economies will be those that produce the most information and knowledge – and make that information and knowledge easily accessible to the greatest number of individuals and enterprises" (Schleicher, 2006:4). And as the same author argues, robust evidence shows that "countries and continents that invest heavily in education and skills benefit economically and socially from that choice. For every euro invested in attaining high-skilled qualifications, tax payers get even more money back through economic growth" (Schleicher, 2006:4).

While empirical findings regarding the economic importance of investing in education in the modern economy would appear to be conclusive, the evidence that points to an increase in individual and collective capacities of knowledge, information, and educational attainment as a result of economic well-being is less conclusive. As a matter of fact, such questions are rarely systematically posed because of the widely taken-for-granted assumption that considerable levels of prosperity are one of the main engines of the growth of knowledge in society. From a more distanced perspective concerning the link between economic well-being and the growth of knowledge, there is the matter of different time scales: knowledge once acquired is, at least under many circumstances, an economic resource that does depreciate, perhaps as fast as economic well-being is capable of reversing the fortunes of a declining societal volume of knowledge and information.

Summing up, the evidence based on many efforts both theoretical and empirical and launched over more than a century ultimately remains less than stellar that democracy enhances the economic well-being of societies, or that the widely accepted thesis of the benefits of the political nature of society for the economic system can be substantiated. This is not to say that the thesis may not carry considerable weight over longer historical periods, or that it does not have substantial ideological appeal. Moreover, since the developmental paths of societies vary significantly, such labels as *industrial* or *postindustrial* society hide and brush over historical specificities. In the center of the doubts about and the hopes for democracy, to be discussed in the following section in the next chapter, is the role of the scientific community.

While the thesis that liberty is a daughter of knowledge appears to stand in a seemingly inexorable conflict with the claim that it is actually the type and the benefits achieved by the economic conditions of a society that is the real catalyst of freedom, it is the possible affinity of the social organization of science and its fundamental normative ideas that are much more likely to be seen as supportive of democratic processes. In the following chapter, I will therefore analyze not only the idea of the exemplary political function of the social organization of science but also the presumption that scientific knowledge has inherent antiauthoritarian features (see, e.g., Elias, 1984:262; Schmitt, 1984:125). What is still missing from such a general assertion about the political archetype of scientific knowledge is the ability to respond to the critical question: What form of scientific knowledge exactly fits the bill, since scientific knowledge is not homogeneous?

4 Scientia est libertas

> [It] is intensely desirable and under certain conditions practicable that all human beings become scientific in their attitudes ... It is desirable because this attitude forms the sole ultimate alternative to prejudice, dogma, authority, and coercive force exercised in behalf of some special interest.
> John Dewey ([1938] 1955:38)

> [T]he social sciences tend, not to restrict personal liberty, but rather to expand the domain of free choice by clarifying the rational alternatives.
> Daniel Lerner (1959:31)

If one imagines in a thought experiment that science could or should serve as the model for democratic governance, two basic possibilities open up that may serve such a societal function of the scientific community. On the one hand, and as John Dewey anticipates, the hope would be that the fruits of science might be a motor for advancing democratization based on the persuasive and exemplary forms of the rational *knowledge* science generates[1] and its successive, broad dissemination throughout society.[2] Similarly, Daniel Lerner assigns to the (social) sciences an

---

[1] In a debate about the social role of science entitled "Science is not your enemy," Steven Pinker (2013) makes the contemporary case for the (immediate) practical benefits of scientific knowledge for democratic governance, namely by limiting or ending unending political debates about the benefits of specific policy goals. In an age of big data, Pinker maintains, "the analysis of large, open-access data sets of numbers or text – signals can be extracted from the noise and debates in history and political science resolved more objectively." At best, we can, on the basis of such data, arrive at definitive answers to previously unresolvable questions such as "do peacekeeping forces really keep peace" or "do terrorist organizations get what they want?" Thus, "the application of science to politics not only enriches our stock of ideas, but also offers the means to ascertain which of them are likely to be correct."

[2] Since actual scientific forms of knowledge are not of one piece, one needs to exactly specify, in the context of this hypothesis, what attributes scientific knowledge must have in order to render the "work" of promoting democratic political conditions possible. John McGinnis (2006:51), for example, anticipates a golden age of social scientific empiricism in the near future. He expects that knowledge as expertise in the form of empiricism should find strong resonance in democratic societies, since such knowledge represents a much more "democratic expertise" in comparison to other forms of knowledge because it

"emancipatory" role in society. Social science knowledge is seen to broaden, not restrict, the field of free choice open to the members of society. More specifically, the social sciences offer views of the range of possible courses of action by clarifying available rational alternatives in an objective manner.

On the other hand, the alternative perspective stresses the exemplary nature of the scientific community as a democratic organization that serves as a model for societal governance – based also on the idea that science and democracy share specific epistemological commitments (see Dahrendorf, [1963] 1968:254–255). Robert K. Merton's ethos of science, which I will explicate in this section, refers to exactly this nexus between morality and the benefits of scientific work that offers itself as an ideal for the choice of the desired form of governance.

In the first case, and in the end, society's citizens literally become model scientists and carriers of scientific knowledge that throughout society has managed to displace all other, inferior – that is, traditional and everyday forms – of knowledge. But there is also a possible downside: The prospect of the excessive dependence of society and politics on scientific knowledge can seriously undermine the liberty of individuals and their ability to participate in democratic governance and effectively control the conduct of the state apparatus. I will take up this point and the associated fears for democracy through governance by expertise at greater length in a subsequent section of my study. In general, the first assumption is that science affects the *thinking* of society's members and thereby enhances democratic forms of life.

In any event, a critical distance and ambivalence toward the societal impact of science, scientific knowledge and, not to be left out, technical developments, is one of the constants of reflexive observations about science in different intellectual traditions (e.g., in Marxism, anarchism, and feminism, see Horkheimer, [1932] 1982; Croissant and Restivo, 1995:67–80).

Within the context of the second perspective, the prospects for a democratization of society through science could rest, for example, on the manifest ability of all members of the scientific community to contribute to the collective enterprise of advancing knowledge. On the

---

is "replicable, transparent, and shareable" (compare Max Weber's related arguments of more than a century ago in favor of the "virtues" of empirical social research; see Stehr, 1989). In addition, McGinnis argues, the knowledge generated by empiricists today is disciplined in the form of blogs and information markets. But as long as there is no preexisting consensus about how reality is to be studied, one must assume that contrary to the hopes of McGinnis, "independent" research will continue to lead to contested empirical findings.

negative ledger of such an idea, there is perhaps not only the extensive bureaucratization of modern science that could restrict the individual participation and that of small groups of citizens not only in the governance of science but by analogy in society as well, but the fact that science is a highly stratified and differentiated social organization. The highly competitive and unequal nature of the scientific community of course reflects the unequal achievements of scientists but also their unequal status, since one can hardly speak of an equal and equally important participation of all the members of the scientific community. Science has both democratic and democracy-adverse social traits (cf. Salomon, 2000).

Last but not least, there is the more ambivalent and modest expression about the virtues of science in general, conflating the contribution of scientific knowledge and its organizing principles. In his autobiographical account *From Immigrant to Inventor*, the Serbian-American physicist and inventor Michael Pupin ([1922] 2007:273), for instance, claims a most decisive role for science in a resilient democracy: "Only science can make the world safe for democracy."

In any event, the common expectation of both models is that science determines the conduct and the thought of society's members. Furthermore, the nature of the influence of science on society cannot be easily separated from the influence of society on science. That is why I will present and discuss, in the following sections of this chapter, positions that emphasize the importance of scientific knowledge for the democratization of society as well as those approaches that rely more on the impact of democratic practices and sanctioned behaviors in the scientific community.

John Dewey's theory of the exemplary relationship of behaviors and values in the scientific community is a good example of the often close linkage of behavior and attitudes in observations of the societal significance of the social organization and social norms prevalent in the scientific community. Dewey was not only convinced that commonsense attitudes ought to become "scientific" and thereby transcend typical attributes of ordinary thinking, namely prejudice and dogma, and support reasoned deliberation in society, but also he believed that the social organization of science could resolve one of the fundamental dilemmas of modern societies, namely find a proper balance for a social conduct that enhances authority, on the one hand, and restricts liberty, on the other hand. It is in science that Dewey ([1936] 1939:359) recognizes a practical solution to the conflictual relation between authority and freedom: "in spite of science's dependence for its development upon free initiative, invention, and enterprise of individual inquirers, the authority of science issues from and is based upon collective activity, cooperatively organized." The stress between forces pulling into the direction of collectivities (authority) and individuality (liberty) has been successfully mended in the scientific community. Hence Dewey's ([1936] 1939:360) suggestion that the "operation of cooperative intelligence as displayed in science is a working model of the union of freedom and authority" in society at large, overcoming, for instance, the excessive egoistic individualism praised and practiced in the economic system. Extending the solution of the relation between liberty and authority (or stability and change) from the limited field of science to the larger realm of human relations can only be advantageous to society and help to solve the general dilemma of the linkage between freedom and collectivity. Despite Dewey's favorable diagnosis of the social organization of the scientific community, the latter undoubtedly continues to this day to contain strong elements of egalitarian (e.g., obliteration by incorporation, cf. Merton, 1995:408–410]) and elitist norms and conduct (e.g., the Matthew effect, cf. Merton, [1968]).

Nonetheless, the assumption that the self-governing scientific community exemplifies democratic norms and that the ledge democratically generated in science, including social scientific knowledge and the knowledge produced in the humanities, directly as well as indirectly fosters and protects democratic society is, indeed, a widely held conviction in "past and present deliberations about science and democracy both in science and in the major social institutions of modern society."[3] Another relevant and well-known belief that is also already in evidence in the eighteenth and nineteenth century is the notion that we should promote a scientification of society. Scientific knowledge represents a resource for the progressive improvement of society. The improvement of society occurs not only through the material innovations science and technology generate. Science also brings about moral and political improvements of social life and represents the most promising way of dealing with the problems and troubles of society. As many observers would note, both those social institutions in society that aim to accomplish practical goals such as the political system, and the world of art, literature, and the media have taken on the spirit and the ways of thought of the natural

---

[3] Sanford Lakoff (1966:12) nicely sums up the point of view about the normative convergence of science and democratic society : "The essence of the democratic idea is the belief that, to the extent possible, each individual and society collectively must be free to make well-informed choices. Insofar as scientific norms prescribe openness and the freedom to challenge given truths, they are eminently compatible with the essential norms of democracy."

sciences, in particular (Brooks, 1965:69).[4] In other words, the influence of the sciences on the life-world is not restricted to the utilitarian function of scientific knowledge but extends to the growing displacement of traditional views by scientific perspectives.

Freely constructed and widely available knowledge and information, reason, and enlightenment are often seen to constitute one of the most important and most effective barriers against some of the impassionate and ideological attractions of nondemocratic rule, arbitrary political power, and excessive promises. Scientific perspectives are seen to heal serious and unresolved societal and economic problems such as high levels of youth unemployment, severe social and cultural cleavages, broad-based withdrawal from political participation, or distrust in the political leadership of the day. The Age of Enlightenment more than any other age advocated and defended these convictions about the symmetry of knowledge and democracy. Indeed, many of the practical projects and policies of the Enlightenment Age, "like a universal language, demonstrative encyclopedias, museums of science, public instruction and the like, were meant to enhance the role of knowledge and information in building up, and managing, the political world without relying on hierarchical authorities" (Ezrahi, 2004:265), were – in contrast to previous historical periods – apprehended as characteristic of the world view of the Enlightenment.

The issue whether such a broad assertion is mainly a feature found in laudatory addresses celebrating the role of science and technology in modern society or, in fact, reflects the realities of both the workings of the scientific community today and the nature of its impact on the life of modern society, represents a complicated set of questions that will be investigated in this chapter.

At this point, I will deliberately exclude from consideration the opposite assertion, namely that democratic societal structures have an effect on the development, dissemination, and growth of knowledge. That the rise of the sciences – in the nineteenth century, for example – was assisted by the flourishing democratic ideas and early political institutions of the time is probably not in doubt. Conversely, the question of the importance of democracy for science always takes center stage in critical

---

[4] Harvey Brooks (1965:82) illustrates his observations about the broad-based cultural influence of the physical and the biological sciences on society as follows: "The most frequent case is that in which a scientific concept has served as a metaphor for the description of social and political behavior. This has occurred, for example, in the case of the concepts of relativity, uncertainty, and energy. In other cases, such as evolution and psychoanalysis, the concept has entered even more deeply into our cultural attitudes."

reflections as soon as democracy is jeopardized, most recently by the totalitarian regimes of Nazism, fascism, and communism, which treated the scientific enterprise and its territory as part of its ideological and material domain.

Part of the set of issues to be examined is also the more pessimistic assertion that scientific knowledge is not generated in a cooperative, critical manner and that the scientific community tends to be as oligarchic as any other large social institution. If Robert Michels had not chosen to investigate the democratic practices of the German Social Democratic Party in his seminal study of oligarchic tendencies in an organization that aspires to and fights for democratic goals, which I will discuss in greater detail in the next section of this chapter, his attention might instead have focused on the scientific community, and the results might very well have been similar.

But then it could be argued that the production of scientific knowledge results in, and perhaps even requires, social hierarchies that reflect, for example, major differences among scholars in achievement or differential access to the infrastructure of research and to social and cultural capital (cf. Merton, 1968, 1988). Is, therefore, the hope of the Enlightenment philosophers, of natural scientists in the nineteenth century and of the Pragmatists in the following century, to mention but some groups, that science will encourage or even induce exemplary democratic practices outside of the scientific community an illusion, perhaps merely a false hope, since science is ruled by experts and experts tend to be aligned in an oligarchic manner? Or is it the case that scientists have been successful in practicing liberal democratic norms within the scientific community while "its relations with the outside grew more and more hierarchical and mystical; they became relations of domination" (Böhme, 1992:53)? Yet, in the course of the history of Western science, as Roy MacCleod (1997:369) stresses, "the rhetorical alliance [of science] with the forces of reason, moderation, liberalism, and individual freedom" was strong. However, the alliance between science and democratic values soon found its severe critics.

In the context of this section, I will concentrate on both the internal social relations of science and on how the social organization of the scientific community radiates out onto the political relations and institutions of society as an exemplary model of democratic governance. I will also take up the issue of the ways in which scientific knowledge as it penetrates the way of thinking throughout society is seen to enhance democracy. The frequent assertion about the ways in which scientific knowledge might actually limit democratic governance is discussed at length in a separate section of the study.

The origins and the vision of science

> The great movement of liberation which started in the Renaissance ... was inspired throughout by an unparalleled epistemo-logical optimism: by a most optimistic view of man's power to discern truth and acquire knowledge.
> Karl Popper ([1960] 1968: 5)

Although Karl Popper ([1960] 1968:8) is convinced that the philosophical optimism of the age of the Renaissance as well as later theories of science (Francis Bacon and René Descartes) are coresponsible for one of the unique spiritual and moral revolutions in human history, he does not subscribe to the thesis, at least in this abbreviated sense, that "men can know: thus he can be free." For Popper ([1960] 1968:29), who considered himself to be a political liberal and who admired the unique human capacity to think, the "pessimistic" insight that humans are essentially ignorant was as an even greater human capacity. We should indeed continually strive to know, though what we learn in this effort is that we do not know very much: "This state of learned ignorance might be a help in many of our troubles. It might well be well for all of us to remember that, while differing widely in the various little bits we know, in our infinite ignorance we are all equal."

If the scientific community indeed constitutes the kind of social institution, pattern of social conduct, set of social norms, and orientations that represents liberty at its best, and if by virtue of such an exemplary appeal it is indeed destined to be adopted by the cultural systems of its surrounding social institutions (politics, religion, education, morality), then the success of the scientific community in exporting its values did not begin immediately with the rise of the New Science in seventeenth century England or France.

As a matter of fact, the social functions of science in the seventeenth century were marginal and science was isolated from some of the major social institutions such as the schools or the universities of the time. The incipient scientific community did not achieve cultural legitimacy by displacing competing values but "by guaranteeing nonintervention in the prevailing institutions and ideologies" (Daele, 1977:30–31) of the dominant political and cultural institutions of the absolutist societies of the day.[5] Gernot Böhme (1992:53) supports this analysis when he observes that we "have to face the fact that science soon after its beginnings has divorced itself from the general democratic and emancipatory

---

[5] The only intellectual context "from which institutionalized science did not dissociate itself were the 'useful arts'" (or technology) (Daele, 1977:31).

movements ... science as a social structure put to work the ideals of liberal democracy largely within its own house – but the relations with the outside grew more and more hierarchical and mystical; they became relations of domination."

But the lack of success in exporting the values of science promptly and directly into society does not mean that the vision of science, its values, and orientations that began to be institutionalized in the early scientific community does not resonate with the assertion that was subsequently so strongly defended, namely that *scientia est libertas*. What was the vision of science that the founders of modern science tried to realize?

Science as a model for democracy

The idea that the social organization of scientific community, the methods of science in general, and the ways in which knowledge is generated are exemplary for the political community of society if not for society at large is, as indicated, a well-known assertion found in many writings and addresses of scholars.

An even stronger vision of the societal role of the scientific community would assert that science may not only illuminate but even control the path of history and, if so, would do it in a "desirable" manner. Similarly, the idea that the kind of social organization science ideally represents resembles that of a free, competitive market system is a contention that stresses the elective affinity between the effective functioning of science and the principles of market society, elevating science to the status of a model society.

In this sense and in a somewhat simplified analogy, Michael Polanyi ([1962] 2000), for example, observes that the desirable "Republic of Science" resembles that model of a free society where independent scholars join in modes of voluntary cooperation and competition.[6] Since the coordination of economic conduct is only a special case of the general, higher principle of a coordination of social conduct on the basis of reciprocal adaptation, the social coordination of the scientists' activities in the scientific community is based on the same principle, the reciprocal adaptation of research results that, initially, were generated independently. And as long as the self-organized coordination (including the evaluation process of the findings) of scientific activities functions

---

[6] Michael Polanyi's own construction of the Republic of Science is, however, based – in addition to the extraterritorial status of science – on the paradoxical exemption from the very principles of liberty and democracy he otherwise promotes (for a critique of Polanyi's contradictory position, see Jarvie, 2001).

efficiently, we can expect the process of scientific progress to operate efficiently as well, in analogy to the workings of the "invisible hand" (Polanyi, [1962] 2000:3). At the same time, the epistemological and social norms of science – for example, efforts to assure intellectual transparency, the capacity to transcend the ascriptive attributes (for example, social and economic backgrounds) of those who advance knowledge claims, problem-solving conduct based on solidary behavior, and organized skepticism towards authorities – can be designated as values that should at least codetermine social conduct in democracies in general. Insofar as one extends the existential conditions of a republic of science to or into society at large, a "free society" (a society of inventors or discoverers), doing without collective guidelines, will assure the uninhibited aspiration to achieve individual excellence in order to realize a "broad spectrum of truth."

Even more fundamentally, a question needs to be asked: Is science following democratic principles, and can it therefore be a role model for the political system of modern societies, and is science itself open to democratic control? The responses to this question are not consensual. Optimistic assessments of the exemplary societal importance of science generally date back to a time where the practice of doing science contrasted sharply with today's practices. What characterizes these visions about the exemplary nature of the activities of the scientific community with regard to society is of course its historical origins and context. These statements date from an era where science was an enterprise quite different from the present age. In the last few decades, the size of the scientific community has, of course, grown enormously. But even more important is the role of science and technology as motors of economic growth.

In a postwar discussion of the relation between freedom and planning, the philosopher of science Charles Morris (1948:154) is convinced that the methods of science "will themselves be methods by which the open society improves and corrects its existing institutions." Daniel Greenberg (2001:331), in contrast, in a study of contemporary science and society, quotes the Nobel Prize–winning chemist Kary Mullis as noting that "probably the most important scientific development of the twentieth century is that economics replaced curiosity as the driving force behind research." It is not only that research in many scientific fields is very costly and that such research in academic settings would not be possible without state or corporate sponsorship. With respect to the second part of the question, one bitter response is that of Daniel Greenberg (2001:207) who concludes that the "unfortunate, non-democratic truth is that science in the United States, and other nations, too, prospers in a state of disengagement from public understanding of the substance of science, the relative priorities among fields of science, and the peculiarities of science politics." The consequences of science and technology may be open to public view, but not the scientific community.

The ethos of science and democracy

The ethos of science,[7] or the "standardized social sentiments toward science" as conceptualized by Robert Merton ([1942] 1973:267–278), was published at a time when many scientists and intellectuals felt, for obvious reasons and for a certain time, that science was threatened by totalitarian political regimes both from the left and from the right wings of the political spectrum (Boas, 1938; cf. Turner, 2007). The autonomy of science was further put in doubt by nation-specific cultural wars (cf. Hollinger, 1995:443–444; [1983] 1996).

Merton ([1942] 1973:267) is quite explicit: "Incipient and actual attacks upon the integrity of science have led *scientists to recognize their dependence on particular types of social structure*." The conflicts in question have also prompted, as Merton ([1942] 1973:268) argues, a clarification and reaffirmation of the ethos of science. Although the pursuit of science is not confined to democratic societies, it is perhaps easy to see that science flourishes more productively once it has achieved a degree of autonomy and is immune to political attacks and jealousies (cf. Merton, [1938] 1973:254–258). But the issue I would also like to explore is how the institutional imperatives Merton identifies as the ethos of science enhance political democracy, for example, in terms of social imperatives that support "innovation-promoting and learning-based contexts of democratic institutions and culture" (Ober, 2010:38).

Merton ([1942] 1973:268–269) describes the ethos of science representing the "cultural structure of science" as that

affectively toned complex of values and norms which is *held to be binding* on the man of science. The norms are expressed in the form of prescriptions, proscriptions, preferences, and permissions. They are legitimized in terms of institutional values. These imperatives, transmitted by precept and example and reinforced by sanctions are in *varying degrees internalized by the scientist*.... Although the ethos of science has not been codified, it can be inferred from the moral consensus of scientists as *expressed in use and wont*, in countless writings on the scientific spirit and *in moral indignation directed toward contraventions of the ethos*" (italics added).

---

[7] This discussion partly draws on my paper (Stehr, 1978) on the Mertonian norms of science.

Merton specifies four basic moral imperatives that provide a foundation for the social relations of science and the professional identity of individual scientists and, therefore, constitute important elements of the sociocultural structure of science. These include:

1. *Universalism* prescribes that knowledge claims in science should be evaluated and accepted or rejected according to impersonal cognitive criteria rather than the "personal or social attributes of their protagonist" (Merton, [1942] 1973:270) and that careers and opportunities in science should be based on achievement and competence only. (The choice of words is perhaps significant; the expression "should be" suggests that the prescription is a target but not necessarily a consistent scientific practice.)
2. *Communism* refers to the interrelated "communal" (public) character of scientific knowledge claims; to the corresponding limited "rights" of the originator(s) to recognition and esteem, resulting in the distinctive and anomalous character of intellectual property in science; and to the imperative not to withhold knowledge claims-an imperative reinforced by the "incentive of recognition, which is, of course, contingent upon publication" (Merton, [1942] 1973:274).
3. *Disinterestedness*, the moral imperative at the institutional level of science, is largely self-explanatory; it points to a distinctive structure of control exercised over the individual motives of scientists.
4. *Organized Skepticism* is "both a methodological and an institutional mandate" (Merton, [1942] 1973:277). Knowledge claims should not be accepted without (socially organized) scrutiny but should be warranted with reference to the technical norms of science.

In addition, Merton ([1942] 1973:269–270) refers to certain technical (or methodological) norms, certified knowledge (the institutional goal of science), and institutional values as further elements of the culture of science. Certain other norms – for instance, "individualism," "rationality" (Barber, 1952:86–90; Barnes and Dolby, 1970:9), "objectivity," and "generalization" – and various other formulations have been suggested as part of the ethos of science; these norms were intended to be largely compatible with the original formulation advanced by Merton.

Another norm mentioned by Merton ([1957] 1973:294) is the "emphasis upon originality on the institutional plane" in the scientific community; originality, as emphasized in the context of the same essay, counterbalances humility, thereby creating a potential normative conflict ([1957] 1973:303, 305; see also Merton, 1976). It has often been observed, therefore, that science as a social institution is, like any other societal institution, characterized by potentially incompatible normative demands (norms and counternorms).[8] As long as potentially conflicting norms are not "compartmentalized" (Deutscher, 1972), they may generate "ambivalence"; for example, ambivalence toward claims of priority, particularly in the context of multiple independent discoveries. Finally, Merton emphasizes that there have been comparatively few empirical instances of deviant responses to particular norms of science (Merton, [1957] 1973:321), and stresses that his theory of social structure and anomie also applies to the institution of science (Merton, [1957] 1973:308, note 51).

The four basic moral imperatives of science are more than mere moral principles. They are linked in distinct ways to the cognitive development of science. For, as Merton ([1942] 1973:270) notes: "The mores of science possess a methodological rationale but they are binding, not only because they are procedurally efficient, but because they are believed right and good. They are moral as well as technical prescriptions." Niklas Luhmann (1969, 1970), too, writing from a functional-structural perspective, has described the functional necessity for social mechanisms to operate as cognitive mechanisms in science. Thus, a definite correlation between moral imperatives and the advancement of scientific knowledge is implied. For instance, "objectivity precludes particularism. The circumstance that scientifically verified formulations refer in that specific sense to objective sequences and correlations militates against all efforts to impose particularistic criteria of validity" (Merton, [1942] 1973:270). In other words, the norms do not merely regulate the behavior or the social relations of members of the scientific community; they also enhance, in distinct ways, the institutional goal of science, which is the continuing extension of certified knowledge claims.

Much of the discussion of the Mertonian formulation of the ethos of science revolves around the question of whether these norms are in fact adhered to in the scientific community. Merton's critics express doubt that the norms he identified govern the behavior of scientists and that, therefore, they are beside the point. However, followers of Merton's description of the ethos of science are convinced that the ethos continues to have utility in efforts to understand how science works. As a matter of fact, Ragnvald Kalleberg (2007) is of the opinion that Merton's early analysis of the ethos of science has recently gained in significance as a result of the growing commercialization of scientific research that tends to undercut basic norms such as impartiality.

---

[8] A discussion of the sociostructural antecedents and consequences of norms and counternorms in social organizations may be found in Merton (1976).

Given Merton's (1942) carefully crafted "scientific" explication[9] of the ethos of science in his 1942 essay,[10] then explicitly entitled "A Note on Science and Democracy," the specific sociohistorical and intellectual context with which these ideas resonated and to which they responded may account for the frequently decontextualized discussions of the ethos of science in subsequent decades. Merton's essay in the middle of World War II and after almost a decade of the Nazi regime, as well as authoritarian political regimes elsewhere, expressed the then-widespread conviction that science and democracy were mutually supportive and that science was threatened by totalitarian regimes.

The contribution of science to society and, therefore, the elective affinity of science and democracy is due to the closeness between the ethos of science and the moral foundations of democracy. The norm of universalism, for example, is deeply embedded in the impersonal character of the scientific community; moreover, "expediency and morality coincide" (Merton, [1942] 1973:272).

As Merton (1968:588) stresses with respect to the norm of universalism, "the ethos of the social institution of science is taken to include universalistic criteria of scientific validity and scientific worth, thus involving values easily integrated with the values of a free society in which it is men's capacities and achievements which matter, not their ascribed status or origins." Thus, "the *ethos of democracy* includes universalism as a dominant guiding principle. Democratization is tantamount to the progressive elimination of restraints upon the exercise and development of socially valued capacities. Impersonal criteria of accomplishment and not fixation of status characterize the open democratic society" (Merton, [1942] 1973:273; emphasis added). In a negative sense, "the challenging skepticism of science interferes with the imposition of a new set of values which demand an unquestioning acquiescence" (Merton, [1938] 1973:257).

The *institutional* autonomy of science under attack and in reverse in totalitarian regimes symbolizes the loss of an essential attribute of democracy, namely liberty, brought about by the interference of an all-powerful institution, the state: "With a shift from the previous structure

---

[9] The reference to "scientific" is meant to signal that Merton's essay refrains from incorporating any explicit reference to the time and place of the essay and to historical or biographical circumstances that might have prompted the author to engage with the topic and to approach the theme in a particular fashion (cf. Stehr and Meja, 1998).

[10] The essay was published in the initial volume of the then-new *Journal of Legal and Political Sociology*, edited by an émigré from France, George Gurvitch. Later versions carried the explicit title "The ethos of science" (e.g., Merton, [1942] 1996). The essay was changed slightly during its various reprints.

where limited loci of power are vested in the several fields of human activity to a structure where there is one centralized locus of authority over all phases of behavior," (Merton, [1938] 1973:259) the exemplary sentiments of science are now opposed by an external, all-powerful authority. Hence, in a liberal society, "integration derives primarily from the body of cultural norms toward which human activity is oriented. In a dictatorial structure, integration is effected primarily by formal organization and centralization of social control" (Merton [1938] 1973:265). The result is the decommissioning of functional differentiation.

Even though Merton is quite explicit about the elective affinity between the ethos of democracy and the ethos of science, he does not offer an elaborated perspective on the linkages between the moral foundations of science and governance. Merton appears to assert that morality commends itself on the basis of morality. The linkage between the ethos of science and democracy thereby becomes a speech-act that commends itself. Merton concentrates on elaborating the nature of the ethos of science and stops short of developing a theoretical perspective that examines the fragility and the tensions of the relation between the norms of science and political practice generally, and how individuals and groups might benefit in their struggle from the elective affinity of scientific practices and political agency.

The discussion of an "inconvenient democracy" in the following *excursus*, although confined to the role of climate science in policy making and the democratic process, makes evident how tensions between the desire to reach certain goals (e.g., environmental goals) come into tension and conflict with democratic processes if the achievement of the desired outcome becomes paramount and is defended, for example, in the name of framing the issue as "objectively" settled, thereby disguising the defense of a certain outcome and the means of reaching the goals as an uncontested matter preempted by science (that is, as a form of political technology).

There can be little doubt that the mitigation of or adaptation to climate change is what the planners Horst Rittel and Melvin Webber (1973) called, in a seminal paper, "wicked problems." What makes problems wicked problems, as Prins and colleagues (2010) have explained in their Hartwell Paper I,

is the impossibility of giving it a definitive formulation: the information needed to understand the problem is dependent upon one's idea for solving it. Furthermore, wicked problems lack a stopping rule: we cannot know whether we have a sufficient understanding to stop searching for more understanding. There is no end to causal chains in interacting open systems of which the climate is the world's prime example. So, every wicked problem can be considered as a symptom of another problem.

One exogenous indicator of wicked problems is the disenchantment and frustration of those who have recognized the issue in question as a major social problem – and can in some cases look back on a thirty-year effort to alert the public and politics – yet find the response by society and politics to be lacking in resolve and urgency and who therefore step up the rhetoric by demanding nothing short of a "war" on the problem. This can in fact be observed as one peruses some of the titles of recent book publications on climate change, for example: *Storms of My Grandchildren: The Truth about Climate Change Catastrophe and Our Last Chance* (Hansen, 2010) or *Science is a Contact Sport: Inside the Battle to Save Earth's Climate* (Schneider, 2009).

Are (scientific) knowledge and democracy compatible?

> As a scientist I cannot but be a democrat, for the realization of the demands resulting from the laws of nature, from the nature of man, is only possible within a democratic state. Rudolf Virchow ([1848] 1907)

In a letter to his parents during the age of the German Revolution of 1848–1849, Rudolf Virchow, the influential physician, anthropologist, biologist, and politician, affirms his deep conviction about a close if not essential linkage between scientific knowledge and democracy. Virchow's beliefs still echo the convictions of the philosophers of the Enlightenment and their faith that knowledge is emancipatory and furthers freedom and autonomy in society. In that age, the idea that the advance of knowledge equals progress was taken for granted. But since the proposition that knowledge equals freedom and more knowledge equals more freedom has fallen into disrepute in our age, it is well worth briefly mentioning that it did not find strong support until the era of the philosopher Francis Bacon (1561–1626) who, of course, did much to expedite its acceptance and promotion in society. Bacon was fully cognizant of the fact that the identification of advances in science and advances in society could not be taken for granted but had yet to be established, especially among the ruling classes. In much of antiquity the idea of progress was completely absent, and in the Middle Ages human progress was not expected to arrive with or derive from the secular sciences.

If one wants to date or to point to perhaps crucial historical events that represent the beginnings of the decline of a society-wide, broad-based confidence in science, one has to refer to what is called the *nuclear age*, and the atom bomb of 1945 in particular, but also to the development of (and resistance to) nuclear power and the initial public nuclear protests in the 1950s.[11]

The political discussion about the "moral" status of nuclear science prompted John Dewey ([1927] 1954:231) in his afterword to *The Public and Its Problems*, written in July 1946, to point out that though "aspects of the *moral* problem of the status of physical science have been with us for a long time ... the consequences of the physical sciences ... failed to obtain the kind of observation that would bring the conduct and state of science into a specifically *political* field. The use of these sciences to increase the destructiveness of war was brought to such a sensationally obvious focus with the splitting of the atom that the political issue is now with us."

In past decades, as attacks on science such as, for example, the early public controversy in the 1920s and the subsequent disputes in the United States surrounding legislative efforts to forbid the teaching of "evolution," prompted a vigorous defense of science as a bulwark against such "reactionary enterprises." For the proponents of evolution theory, scientific knowledge ought to be rallied to actively influence public opinion, thereby discouraging the persistent and widespread prevalence of "traditional errors" among the public. The *Association for the Advancement of Science*, for example, must assume responsibility for the unintelligent who unfortunately carry political influence: "Scientific knowledge in its broadest sense [must be made] an integral part of education from the beginning to the end" (Robinson, 1923:vii). Though the contested issue of the teaching of evolution in public schools continues to surface today, partly shored up by a few scientists, support for a curriculum that is more inclusive also comes from selected members of the scientific community who are not necessarily committed to a single cause such as "intelligent design" but are in favor of open, unimpeded inquiry. Below, I will briefly refer to a prominent philosopher who supported such a stance, namely Paul Feyerabend. What makes these disputes relevant to considerations about the relation between democracy and scientific knowledge claims is the one frequent feature of these debates, namely the reference to a suppression of ideas, the lack of tolerance for views that contest dominant notions, or the claim that such public contests have no relation to democracy and its values.

---

[11] As Robert K. Merton 1952 stresses in his introduction to Bernard Barber's book *Science and the Social Order* (1952), "the explosion over Hiroshima and other experimental atomic explosions, have had the incidental consequence of awakening a dormant public concern with science. Many people who had simply taken science for granted, except when they occasionally marvelled at the Wonders of Science, have become alarmed and dismayed by these demonstrations of human destructiveness."

Insofar as one of the essential and therefore timeless features of a well-functioning democracy is the presence of an adequate pluralism of conflicting, broad-based doctrines (Rawls, 1997:765–766) and the dominant epistemic norms of knowledge production in science tend to favor an emergent consensus and not the liberal coexistence of ideas, one is forced to ask about the compatibility of scientific knowledge that aspires to be consensual and conducive to democracy. However, the tensions between scientific knowledge and democratic societies cannot be reduced to the formal difference between the norms of science and the democratic norms that allow for a plurality of ideas. Among the sources of conflict between scientific knowledge and democracy are the societal consequences of particular scientific ideas and technical capacities that collide with established values or pose risks associated with the introduction of new technical artifacts and the diffusion of new sets of meaning apprehended by various social groups.

Yet another fundamental source of conflict comes into view if one considers contemporary science, following Paul Feyerabend (e.g., [1974] 2006:365), as the home of an ideology: "Science is just one of many ideologies that propel society and it should be treated as such." Science was, for a time, especially during the seventeenth and eighteenth centuries, at the forefront of an intellectual war of liberation against authoritarianism and superstition. Today, however, Feyerabend ([1974] 2006:360) argues, science has deteriorated into an ideology fraught with sanctified, oppressive truths that are immune to criticism, and with practices of indoctrination: "Science has now become as oppressive as the ideologies it had once to fight." The practice of modern science inhibits the freedom of thought and therefore comes into conflict with what is an essential attribute of democracy, namely the peaceful coexistence of sets of ideas. In society, there are ideological pressures that drive out all forms of knowledge except those that originate from science. The lesson to be learned, according to Feyerabend, from the particular authority science enjoys in society is the necessity of a separation between science and the state in the interest of the defense of democracy and liberty, especially in the field of public education.

On the other hand, there is the opposite view that sees scientific knowledge as a force that, due to the deliberative processes that promote solidarity across conflicts of interest, allows for consent among the members of a society, helps to improve political decisions, and tends to ease societal tensions. What comes into mind in this context is the role of scientific knowledge as an allegedly rational decision guidance. Thus, scientific knowledge will lead to good decisions.

Another compatible and constructive alliance between science-based knowledge and democracy is conceivable if certain societal consequences, such as, for example, prosperity, health, security, education, and so forth, are counted among the indirect benefits, or even the proper functions, of science.

But I will first turn to the "epistemic attitudes" (cf. Uebel, 2004:47) of the Vienna Circle, a group of scholars that was active during the post–World War I era, and their manifesto in favor of a scientific world-conception (*Wissenschaftliche Weltauffassung*). The scientific world-conception proposed by the Vienna Circle is based on a different image or conception of knowledge. What they advance is an image of knowledge that is opposed to metaphysics and supposed to be of practical efficacy in the struggle for a democratic society.

The Vienna Circle

In the 1920s of the last century, the question of the utopia of a new and, more specifically, free and equitable society is once more posed. The Vienna Circle's remarkable rationale and design for such a utopia stands out among its competing blueprints. The reflections of the Vienna Circle represent, in the tradition of the Enlightenment, and as highlighted by Elisabeth Nemeth (1994:114), ways in which science itself becomes the site of utopia. The Circle, not all of whose members were professional philosophers – far from it – not only expected a scientification of knowledge but also a scientification of the world. Scientific knowledge informs but does not determine life.

In my brief exposition of the Vienna Circle, I will stress this particular philosophical and political position rather than the vision of a systematic unity of science advocated by some of its members. I also will try to abstain from what often amounts to a caricature of the philosophical and political positions of the members of the Circle in some of the more recent critical accounts, where they are seen as conservative proponents of the status quo, with a deep positivistic commitment and a technocratic conception of governance (e.g., Marcuse, 1964; Habermas, 1968). The philosophical and political perspectives advocated by the Vienna Circle were hardly homogenous (cf. O'Neill, 1999; Ibarra, Andoni and Mormann, 2003); instead, the members of the Circle generated a number of distinctive positions within the philosophy of science, as well as political arguments. I will focus primarily on Otto Neurath's views. Neurath is a follower of the Enlightenment philosophy and a reformer for whom the societal context of science is of enormous importance. The recurrent theme that can be found throughout his diverse works is the idea of a conception of knowledge as an instrument of emancipation (see Cartwright et al., 1996:89–95).

I also plan to deemphasize what the Circle may be best known for both in its early and its later stages, namely its antimetaphysical stance. According to the Vienna Circle members, metaphysical propositions are hypotheses which, although claiming to be about matters of fact, refer to domains beyond possible experience; as a result, metaphysical propositions are not amenable to treatment by the logico-empirical methods practiced in various scientific disciplines and fail to generate knowledge.[12]

The manifesto of the Vienna Circle, *Wissenschaftliche Weltauffassung* [The scientific world-conception] (*Verein Ernst Mach*, [1929] 1981),[13] published in 1929 by the members of the Circle and in all likelihood written by Otto Neurath,[14] but also Hans Hahn and Rudolf Carnap (cf. Neurath, 1930/1931),[15] supports its position concerning the interrelation between science and society in an exemplary fashion. In order to first clarify the concept of *wissenschaftliche Weltauffassung*, reference may be made to an essay published in 1930/1931 in the inaugural volume of the newly founded journal *Erkenntnis* entitled *Wege der wissenschaftlichen Weltauffassung* ["Ways of the Scientific World-Conception"]. In this essay, Otto Neurath (1930/1931:107) spells out exactly why this notion rather than the popular notion of the scientific Welt*anschauung* (worldview) is the appropriate label for the Vienna Circle project: "If one refers to scientific Welt'*auffassung*' as opposed to philosophical Welt'*anschauung*', the concept 'world' refers not to a completed whole, but the daily growing field of science." Neurath – closely allied to the then-current sociology of knowledge – stresses that the move toward thinking within the scientific world-conception is linked to concrete social changes, that

---

[12] Within philosophy, metaphysical systems in this sense include, for example, the works of Hegel, Bergson, or Heidegger.
[13] An English translation of the Manifesto may be found in Neurath (1973).
[14] In his memories of Otto Neurath whom he first met in Vienna after the end of World War I, Karl Popper (1973:54) refers to the probably crucial role of Neurath in the formation of the Vienna Circle: "I have little doubt that it was Otto Neurath who, in the hope of a philosophical reform of politics, attempted to give the circle of men around Schlick and Hahn a more definite shape: and thus it may have been he, perhaps more than anybody else, who was instrumental in turning it into the 'Vienna Circle'."
[15] Otto Neurath, Hans Hahn, and Rudolf Carnap would later be labeled the "left-wing" of the Vienna Circle not only because they expressed a political preference for the Viennese socialists but also on the basis of their formulation of a "scientific world-conception" that was closely allied to specific sociopolitical goals (cf. Nemeth, 1994:116; Reisch, 2005). After the failure of the Viennese workers' uprising in February 1934, the "Ernst Mach Society" (*Verein Ernst Mach*) was outlawed by the Vienna police because of its affinity to the socialist party.

is, "Our thinking is a tool, it depends on social and historical conditions" (Neurath, 1930/1931:123). A little later, Otto Neurath ([1931] 1983:58) radicalizes his statement and emphasizes that the so-called "Vienna Circle of *wissenschaftliche Weltauffassung*" should be named, less misleadingly, the "Vienna Circle of physicalism."[16] The latter label is more appropriate, since the term "'world' is a terminus that is missing from the scientific language and *Weltauffassung* is often confused with *Weltanschauung*."

The 1929 Manifesto of the Vienna Circle stresses two matters: On the one hand, societal transformations impact on intellectual changes (Neurath, 1930/1931:124)[17] and, on the other hand, the intellectual tools of metaphysics are alien to the practice of science and constitute a form of knowledge that is ineffective in practice. The intellectual tools of science become instruments of a rational reorganisation of society, a renewal of the economic system, and a reform of education (Verein Ernst Mach, [1929] 1981:304).

By its empirical and positivistic orientation, the scientific practice of the Vienna Circle is linked, according to its own understanding, not only to the spirit of its age (and, in this case, post-World War Vienna, also known as Red Vienna; see Gruber, 1991) but also to the spirit of a new age (Verein Ernst Mach, [1929] 1981:314). Logical, objective empiricism and political visions are not contradictory. On the contrary, the unity of empirical-logical science is a means of integrative socio-political conduct.

The nature of the developments so confidently sketched by the Vienna Circle, and the convergence of sociopolitical world views and scientific value views they imply is, more precisely, the result of the persisting

---

[16] Ernest Nagel (1936b:41) offers a useful summary of the "physicalism" perspective of the Vienna Circle. The Circle, first of all, rejects the differentiation of the sciences into natural sciences and the humanities and, hence, asserts "the subject-matter for all empirical inquiry is the world of spatio temporal events. It recognizes that events and objects may be of different degrees of complexity, but claims that apart from differences in special techniques required to explore their structures a common logical method is applicable in every department of knowledge. Hence it maintains that every proposition in the *Geisteswissenschaften* [humanities], which is significant in the sense specified by the theory of meaning already sketched, is translatable into the universal language of physics. There is therefore only one kind of knowledge, only one science (though it may be departmentalized for reasons of convenience), and only one kind of general subject-matter-spatio temporal events and objects differently related to one another."

[17] Otto Neurath is even more explicit in his own writings in his rejection of the idea that the practice of science is a kind of extraterritorial domain in relation to society at large (e.g., Neurath, 1931; 1944:46–47; Uebel, 2000) and that there is, therefore, such a phenomenon as presuppositionless knowledge.

development of the modern production process, which is more and more technology intensive and leaves less and less space for metaphysical ideas (Verein Ernst Mach, [1929] 1981:314). The affinity between science and society is also associated with the disappointment shown by the broad masses at approaches that proclaimed and favored traditional metaphysical and theological teachings. As a result, the masses in many countries are more self-conscious than ever before, refuse to accept these metaphysical teachings and, in concert with their socialist affinities, now lean toward a down-to-earth empirical perspective (Verein Ernst Mach, [1929] 1981:314–315).[18]

The Vienna Circle is therefore quite optimistic, despite anticipated conflicts and political difficulties, that their image of knowledge and their form of "rational" scientific knowledge as a planning or rationalizing tool is capable of realizing the mutually dependent and reinforcing potential of broad social transformations and liberty that will, in the long term, generally prevail in practice, initial concrete evidence being already at hand: "We see how the spirit of the scientific world view increasingly shapes and permeates the personal and public life, education, architecture, the design of economic and social life according to rational principles. The scientific world view serves life and life absorbs it" (Ernst Mach Society, [1929] 1981:315).[19]

For the Vienna Circle, a distinctive harmony between science and societal change will, then, form an inextricable partnership, as it were, on the path to and the design of the future. On this track toward the future, a down-to-earth science is a partner and a guarantor of liberty. At least this is the message Ernest Nagel (1936a:9) brings along on his return from a journey to the centers of European analytical philosophy. He gives an account of the lectures and seminars of Moritz Schlick he had attended at the University of Vienna. In the context of one of these teaching functions Nagel realizes what the extrascientific motives of and the reasons for the considerable public resonance enjoyed by the Vienna Circle happen to be: "Analytical philosophy *is* ethically neutral *formally*; its professors to *not* indoctrinate their students with dogmas as to life, religion, race, or society. But analytical philosophy is the exercise of

---

[18] In 1918, the philosopher of science Hans Reichenbach, one of the early and consistent proponents of a scientific philosophy, notes with conviction: "The whole movement of scientific philosophy is a crusade. Is it not clear that only by ending the dogmatism of irresponsible claims to know moral truth, that only by clarity and integrity in epistemology, people can attain tolerance and get along with one another?" (quoted in Uebel, 2004:62).

[19] Peter Galison (1990), for example, has examined the intellectual affinity of the Vienna Circle and the Bauhaus movement of Dessau.

intelligence in a special field, and if the way of intelligence becomes part of the habitual nature of man, no doctrines and no institutions are safe from critical reappraisals."[20]

John Dewey: science and democracy

> The genuine problem is the *relation* between authority and freedom.
> John Dewey ([1936] 1939:344)

The pragmatist's social philosophy, especially as articulated by John Dewey – born in 1859 – is of interest in my context of analysis because of two major premises of his philosophical stance: first, for Dewey, the nature and the origins of knowledge (e.g., 1938:149) are contextual (Kaufmann, 1959; Mirowski, 2004); knowledge is actively driven and cultivated by *in situ* experiences, and doubt is constitutive for knowledge: to "set up a problem that does not grow out of an actual situation is to start on a course of dead work." Dewey also consistently displays an interest in the social dimensions of science. And, second, he assigns an explicit, emancipatory role to knowledge in society as a problem-solving undertaking without subscribing to a linear, unreflective instrumentalist model of scientific knowledge. Science and democracy are freely assimilated to each other. Science is not a self-contained republic to itself but an institution that should serve the community. For example, in his *Democracy and Education*, John Dewey ([1916] 2005:134) argues that "genuinely scientific theory falls within practice as the agency of its expansion and its direction to new possibilities"; it follows that the "ultimate end and test of all inquiry is the transformation of a problematic situation" (Dewey, 1938:491).[21]

---

[20] As Ernest Nagel (1936a:9) further reports, "the content of the lectures (by Moritz Schlick), though elementary, was on a high level; it was concerned with expounding the theory of meaning as the mode of verifying propositions. It occurred to me that although I was in a city foundering economically, at a time when social reaction was in the saddle, the views presented so persuasively from the *Katheder* were a potent intellectual explosive. I wondered how much longer such doctrines would be tolerated in Vienna."

[21] John Dewey (1938:500) affirms some of the attributes of knowledge as a capacity to act when he observes that social "conditions are never completely fixed," which "means that they are in process – that, in any case they are moving toward the production of a state of affairs which is going to be different in *some* respect." And the initial purpose of the "operations of observation" is, therefore, "to differentiate conditions into obstructive factors and positive resources" with the aim to "indicate the intervening activities which will give the movement (and hence its consequences) a different form from what is would take if it were left to itself."

In doing so, the pragmatists consistently set themselves apart from a view of science that conceives of generating scientific knowledge as a process operating in strict isolation from the affairs of everyday life or merely in the interest of a small segment of society.[22] In the eyes of pragmatism, the virtue of social science is its close affinity to the problems of the day. The importance of the social sciences for practical affairs can be considerable; and the social sciences thereby deliberately take moral and political responsibilities on board. The social sciences are supposed to aid human communities in improving their capacities for collective action; science, given such ambitions, "marks the emancipation of mind from devotion to customary purposes and makes possible the systematic pursuit of new ends. It is the agency of progress in action ... This projection of new possibilities leads to search for new means of execution, and progress takes place; while the discovery of objects not already used leads to suggestion of new ends" (Dewey, [1916] 2005:231).

John Dewey (1859–1962), along with Charles Sanders Pierce and William James, is considered the core representative of American pragmatism. However, Dewey himself is not convinced that the term pragmatism does justice to his conception of the nature and the purposes of scientific inquiry. He prefers to avoid the contested attributes of the concept of pragmatism (see Kallen, 1934) and stresses instead that not only his own central knowledge-guiding interest but that of all cognitive operations concerns the function of consequences in inquiry as a necessary test of the validity of propositions constructed in science. In pragmatism all perception is shaped by and all cognitive activity is considered in light of their functionality for action. And it is, therefore, in this sense that Dewey acknowledges that his own philosophical position may be called "pragmatic."

John Dewey (1938:492) is, as he makes clear in his *Logic* (1938), which in turn is an extension of his *Studies in Logical Theory* published four decades earlier, a firm opponent of the idea that "scientific inquiry is genuinely scientific only if it deliberately and systematically abstains from all concern with matters of social practice." This thesis applies with equal force to both the natural and the social sciences. The logic of social inquiry begins and ends with its "intrinsic reference to practice" (Dewey, 1938:510). Although the separation of theory and practice in the social sciences as well as in their conception of the practical role of the social sciences among "persons directly occupied with management of practical

---

[22] As a result, Dewey (1984:107) stresses the importance, for him, of the question "what science can do in making a different sort of world and society. Such a science would be the opposite pole to science conceived merely as a means to special industrial ends."

affairs" (Dewey, 1938:493) is still a matter of widespread acceptance, Dewey of course argues that this assumption needs to be overcome to effectively employ the social sciences as a reconstructive and transformative social force.

In the world of practical affairs, the diminished role of the social sciences is underwritten by the conviction among actors in the world of practical affairs that the "problems which exist are already definite in their main features." The consequence of this assumption therefore is that the "work of analytic discrimination, which is necessary to convert a problematic situation into a set of conditions forming a definite problem, is largely foregone" (Dewey, 1938:493).

The result is that there will be a disjuncture between the adequacy of the methods brought to bear on the problem and a clear conception of the nature of the problem delivered by science. The likely outcome is a worsening of the situation in the world of practical affairs. The physical sciences have already overcome the backwardness of the social sciences in this respect and have succeeded in achieving a constructive convergence of problem definition and the methods brought to bear in efforts to find practical solutions. Proper social inquiry as scientific inquiry needs to accomplish the "determination of an indeterminate situation" (Dewey, 1938:iii).

This does not imply, however, that the social sciences can and must slavishly imitate the physical sciences or, worse yet, replicate a misconception of the natural sciences. Such a fruitless procedure only results in "useless" findings.[23] Social facts are always connected to human purposes and consequences (cf. Dewey, 1931:276).

What can be done to convert a commonsense construction of problems into definite problems? For Dewey this step requires first of all that the perception and interpretation of a situation be stripped of its moral attributes. However, this does not mean that social inquiry is free of "judgments of evaluation." The meaning of the latter assertion is that the analysis of practical situations involves the consideration of alternative possible ends: "Social inquiry, in order to satisfy the conditions of scientific method, must judge certain objective consequences to be the end which is *worth* attaining under the given conditions" (Dewey, 1938:503).

---

[23] However, Max Horkheimer (1947:46–49), in his monograph *Eclipse of Reason*, argues that John Dewey's "worship of the natural sciences" means that he is a captive of the methods and the philosophy of the natural sciences, which makes it impossible for him to take a critical stance; Dewey's own position is much less scientistic than Horkheimer's interpretation would suggest. In a 1929 essay on the "quest for certainty," Dewey (1929:200) says that his convictions would be misinterpreted "if it were taken to mean that science is the only valid kind of knowledge" (see also Biesta, 2007:472–473).

Representative of Dewey's ([1916] 2005:192) conception of science is his definition of the scientific and societal function of philosophy:

Philosophy [in contrast to the positivistic conception of science] thus has a double task: that of criticizing existing aims with respect to the existing state of science, pointing out values which have become obsolete with the command of new resources, showing what values are merely sentimental because there are no means for their realization; and also that of interpreting the results of specialized science in their bearing on future social endeavor.

In an even more general sense, Dewey (1941:55) is hopeful that science "must have something to say about what we do, and not merely about how we may do it most easily and economically."

I also need to refer to and briefly consider some of the chief criticism that has been leveled against the pragmatic approach to knowledge and action. First among the prominent objections is the charge of mere instrumentalism as a result of treating mental activity mainly in terms of its functionality and stressing the instrumental character of knowledge. Dewey's vigorous argument in favor of coupling science and action not only carries forward the optimistic commitment of his age to reformism and societal progress but also led to the charge that his position represents a strong argument in favor of excessive social engineering (cf. Rogers, 2007). But the idea that knowledge plays a vigorous role in action and constitutes an active element of "communication and participation" among humans is actually an attractive attribute of Dewey's theory of action; as a result, knowledge represents the capacity to overcome blockages, obstructions, and dogmatism and enables the critical analysis of alternative courses of action. John Dewey (1984:105) views the way science is integrated into contemporary society as flawed but argues that this can be overcome and is not intrinsic to science: "The concept that natural science somehow sets a limit to freedom, subjecting man to fixed necessities, is not an intrinsic product of science ... [but] a reflex of the social conditions under which science is applied so as to reach only a pecuniary function."

A second criticism extends to the close linkage between action and knowledge in terms of the present and therefore the neglect of traditions, the past, eternal values, and history generally. However, by stressing the importance of novel problems for action, the pragmatic attitude actually assumes a skeptic stance and a distance toward habitual, routine conduct and emphasizes the constructive role of ideas in action. In this instance, but also in other points, the epistemic attitude of the Vienna Circle and John Dewey's pragmatism converge. The manifesto of the Vienna Circle emphasized the emancipatory power of scientific knowledge, stressing that "the logical clarification of specific scientific concepts, statements and methods liberates one from inhibiting prejudice" (Verein Ernst Mach [1929] 1981:316).

A third objection extends to the willingness of pragmatists to treat social and natural processes as jointly embedded in social action, or as phenomena that are not a priori in an antagonistic relation. In light of the renewed, contemporary discussion about the relation of nature and society, this criticism is perhaps not as significant as it was once thought to be.

John Dewey, in a self-exemplifying manner and consistent with his social philosophy, saw himself not only as a public intellectual who got involved in the political and social affairs of his time but also reflected on such intervention. Both positions are of interest here; we will concentrate on Dewey's reflections about the relations between scientific inquiry, the power of knowledge, and the public role of scientists.

In Dewey's ([1927] 1954) discussion of *The Public and Its Problems*, he refers to the inordinate and historically unprecedented increase in the volume of knowledge and the extent to which, at the same time, the volume of errors and half-truths that circulate in society has simultaneously increased, perhaps even more significantly than the scientific knowledge that circulates in society. The access to "scientific" knowledge by the public, however, is severely limited due to the large "apparatus" one is required to command, for example, in terms of the special language necessary to comprehend the knowledge claims and the intellectual advances made in science. As Dewey ([1927] 1954:163) emphasizes, "science ... is a highly specialized language, more difficult to learn than any natural language. It is an artificial language, not in the sense of being factitious, but in that of being a work of intricate art, devoted to a particular purpose and nor capable of being acquired nor understood in the way in which the mother tongue is learned." Scientific knowledge that revolutionized the existential conditions in society thereby becomes a mystery and an inaccessible, dark form of discourse for most people, turning them into speechless actors. The labor needed to acquire the apparatus for accessing scientific knowledge by far exceeds the resources needed to command any other "means" of human action. As a result, the power of knowledge in modern societies is faced by most of its citizens with utter helplessness. The majority of the people are unable to intervene into the workings of science, are unable to comprehend science, and are passively exposed to its consequences; most citizens are therefore unable to utilize the fruits of science, let alone control them (Dewey, [1927] 1954:141). What may be done to overcome such an asymmetry in the power relations between science and the life-world?

One of the possible reactions to this dilemma is the response Walter Lippmann furnished at the time.

Lippmann, Dewey, and democratic governance

In 1922, the prominent American journalist Walter Lippmann (1889–1974), who generally agrees with John Dewey's diagnosis of the poor contemporary conditions of democratic governance in the United States, published his influential treatise *Public Opinion*; a book reprinted many times without revisions since the original edition. In *Public Opinion*, Lippmann ([1922] 1992) attempts to justify the idea of an elite democracy, echoing earlier observations and demands in this regard.[24] Lippmann's own main thesis concerns the limited reflective capacity of the average citizen. The widespread cognitive deficits of the public are exacerbated and made more vulnerable by the complex conditions of modern society. The average citizen does not know what is politically going on, cannot reflect about it accurately and, as a result, is unable to act knowledgeably. Thus, the "masses" can at best assume a basically passive role in democratic governance. The crisis of democracy stems not from a lack of democracy but from a permissive surplus of democratic participation by largely uninformed citizens. The solution is governance by elites.

But how are the deficient views of the world held by the masses of voters generated in the first place? Walter Lippmann's ([1922] 1992:54–55) response is an almost up-to-date account of the foundations of cognitive experiences and decisions, even though it is not free from assumptions about inherited, passive thoughtways: "For the most part we do not first see, and then define, we define first and then see ... we pick

---

[24] Observations found in Machiavelli's *Discorsi*, for example, represent one of the many forerunners of such an idea. Nonetheless, it is worth citing Walter Lippmann's ([1922] 1992:193) views from his *Public Opinion* treatise in some detail: "In the absence of institutions and education by which the environment is so successfully reported that the realities of public life stand out sharply against self-centered opinion, the common interests very largely elude public opinion entirely, and can be managed only by a specialized class whose personal interests reach beyond the locality. This class is irresponsible, for it acts upon information that is not common property, in situations that the public at large does not conceive, and it can be held to account only on the accomplished fact." One of the salient *recent* criticisms of democracy – repeating earlier concerns (now often backed by quantitative information; e.g., Converse [1964] 2006) by Lippmann about the feasibility of democracy – refers to the lack of civic competence or, more disparagingly, the political ignorance of many citizens of democratic states (Hardin, 2006; Gilley, 2009:117–120; Somin, 2009). The legal scholar (7:16), for instance, suggests that the average citizen is "basically ignorant" about political affairs, and democracy should never aspire to be anything but a means of rotating elites.

out what our culture has already defined for us, and we tend to perceive that which we have picked out in the form stereotyped for us by our culture." John Dewey agrees that habitual beliefs and conduct are detrimental to democratic governance. However, it is the nature of the existing political process, and not nature as such, that enhances passivity; a submissiveness of the masses is not inevitable. Dewey is convinced that it is possible to encourage reflective intelligence based on a dissemination of the scientific spirit throughout society (cf. Grube, 2010).

The function of journalism is to operate as a kind of transmission belt between politics and the public. In an elite democracy, it is the task of journalists to offer the information and the knowledge produced by the technical and the political elite to the public in ways that make them comprehensible to their readers and listeners. If certain views are not those of the elite, then the media are co-responsible for generating public consent (manufacture of consent). As a result, the media play a decisive role in the control of public opinion. As can easily be gathered, Lippmann was not convinced that democracy would effectively function if a large measure of power would rest in the hands of the general public.[25]

John Dewey responds to the challenge by Lippmann in his book *The Public and Its Problems*. He offers an alternative conception of how to overcome the dilemma of the growing cleavage between scientific knowledge in society and the apparent deficit of the majority of its members to comprehend such knowledge.[26] Dewey's response represents an important cultural critique of the decade of the 1920s in the United States; it is a critique free of illusions: the main condition for a democratic public is a form of knowledge and insight that does not yet exist.[27] A dominance of elites or the governance of experts does not characterize the form of

---

[25] In an experimental study, Dennis Chong and James Druckman (2007) test the power of elites to frame public opinion. The experimenters conclude that "framing effects depended more on individual evaluations of the quality of frames than on the frequency with which they were received" and that competition among frames offers, as does motivation, "protections against arbitrary framing effects" (Chong and Druckman, 2007:651–652). Alternative frames tend to stimulate and induce reflections on the merit of competing interpretations; similarly, a strong motivation to acquire political information and reflect about politics influence the framing effects of elites.

[26] The diagnosis of and concern about a growing gap between a rapidly expanding volume of modern scientific knowledge and the capacity of the average citizen to comprehend such knowledge, or about antirationalist views of larger segments of the population, continues to be part of a number of analyses of the culture of contemporary American society (e.g., Jacoby, 2008).

[27] One of the main preconditions mentioned by Dewey ([1927] 1994:166) is the "freedom of social inquiry and of justification of its conclusions"; and the communication "of the results of social inquiry is the same thing as the formation of public opinion" (Dewey, [1927] 1994:177).

democracy Dewey has in mind. On the contrary, he advocates the popularization of scientific knowledge, public participation, and a widespread open discussion of political decisions (e.g., Dewey, [1927] 1954:178–179; see also Benson, Harkavy, and Puckett, 2007), but a "genuine public policy cannot be generated unless it be informed by knowledge, and this knowledge does not exist except when there is systematic, thorough, and well-equipped search and record" (Dewey, [1927] 1954:178–179).[28] In contrast, a class of experts, Dewey ([1927] 1954:207) stresses, "is inevitably so removed from common interests as to become a class with private interests and private knowledge, which in social matters is not knowledge at all" (cf. Westhoff, 1995). Dewey rejects the view that experts or intellectuals, for that matter, are disinterested observers and actors outside the "class structure."

Walter Lippmann situates his thesis about the necessity of a democratic regime governed by an elite and the need to manufacture consent with the aid of the media on a similarly basic premise. He is convinced that individual actors are incapable of sufficiently articulating and defending their interests. John Dewey, however, is convinced that it is possible to realize the idea of a democratic public; a democratic public requires the effective communication of knowledge to the public. The public is in principle open and willing to be receptive to such communication.

The realization of a democratic public requires, as Dewey ([1927] 1954: 208–209) stresses, an "improvement of the methods and conditions of debate, discussion, and persuasion. That is *the* problem of the public." The improvement of public discourse depends, as Dewey also repeatedly emphasizes, "upon freeing and perfecting the processes of inquiry and of dissemination of their conclusions. Inquiry indeed is a work that devolves upon experts. But their expertness is not shown on framing and executing policies, but in discovering and making known the facts upon which former depend." The intellectual division of labor between science and the public does not vanish. Scientists "are technical experts in the sense that scientific investigators and artists manifest expertise. It is not necessary that the many should have the knowledge and skill to carry on the needed investigations; what is required is that they have the ability to judge of the bearing of the knowledge supplied by others upon common concerns" (Dewey [1927] 1954:208–209).

---

[28] Dewey ([1927] 1994:142) is committed to the idea that the impetus for the transformation of entrenched social institutions and traditional conduct will most likely come from science: "Science marks the emancipation of the mind from devotion to customary purposes and makes possible the systematic pursuit of new ends."

What forms of knowledge enhance democracies?

Science "was the dream of a secular culture in which the rationality of science would produce the rationality of the world ... Humans who see reality only through the lens of scientific knowledge, not taking serious any scientifically not demonstrable idea would be self-conscious individual, whose creator, science imagined, it would be."

Friedrich Tenbruck ([1977] 1996:190)

The assertion that scientific knowledge somehow enhances democratic regimes may be further specified by the claim that certain types of knowledge provide sustenance to democratic governance. For example, John O. McGinnis (2006:51), who anticipates an golden age of social science empiricism just around the corner, advances the case for expertise in the form empiricism as a form of knowledge that resonates most closely with democratic governance, since empiricism is a more "democratic expertise" than other types of knowledge. It is a more democratic expertise because it is "replicable, transparent, and shareable." In addition, knowledge generated by empiricists is disciplined by information inputs of blogs and information markets. Unfortunately, McGinnis tends to exaggerate the incontrovertible nature of empiricism when he, for example, attributes to empiricism the possibility for such expertise to have built-in consensual features which, through independent efforts, lead to "replicable, transparent, and shareable" knowledge emerging, for instance, from any inspection of the "facts." Unless there is a kind of preexisting consensus about what it takes to inspect reality and how to go about doing so, the independent observations tend to lead to contested results.

The disparity emerging from an inspection of the facts within the scientific community, or even society at large, might, of course, be at least partly healed by a common perspective that assures a degree of consensus in selecting and interpreting reality. But in science, no such common perspective is in sight, nor can we expect to find, across societies, such commonalities representing the evolution of "global knowledge."[29]

---

[29] Among the conditions for the possibility of "global knowledge" formation are primary school curricula that despite profound differences in the political economy of nations are very similar throughout the world while "national characteristics are only weakly related to curricular emphases. Only the expectation of sharply increased similarity over time receives limited support; change is modest, though most countries include all the standard subjects in the curriculum" (Benavot et al., 1991:97; Meyer, Kamens, and Benavot, 1992). Whether such standardization in the basic structure of primary school curricula can indeed form the bases for "global knowledge" regimes and therefore the kind of consensual movement toward empiricism remains an open question.

Excursus: An inconvenient democracy: knowledge and climate change

[M]y own experience and everyday knowledge illustrate that comfort and ignorance are the biggest flaws of human character. This is a potentially deadly mix.   Hans Joachim Schellnhuber (2010)[1]

The martial celebration of a decisionism that bursts the limits of the boredom of deliberation came to be seen ... as the royal road to the will's restoration.   Pierre Rosanvallon (2006:191–192)

In an article published in the summer 2012,[2] in the face of a robust set of extreme weather events (e.g., droughts, floods, and heat) on different continents of the world and the latest findings in climate science, though not shared in detail by all scientists that deal with the questions of the causes and consequences of climate change, the economist Jeffrey D. Sachs (2012)[3] calls for much-needed political consequences:

The evidence is solid and accumulating rapidly. Humanity is putting itself at increasing peril through human-induced climate change. As a global community, we will need to move rapidly and resolutely in the coming quarter-century from an economy based on fossil fuels to one based on new, cutting-edge, low-carbon energy technologies. The global public is *ready to hear* that message and *to act upon it*. Yet politicians everywhere *are timid*, especially because oil and coal companies are so politically powerful. Human well-being, even survival, will depend *on scientific evidence and technological know-how* triumphing over shortsighted greed, political timidity, and the continuing stream of anti-scientific corporate propaganda (my emphasis).

---

[1] The climate scientist Hans Joachim Schellnhuber in an interview with *Der Spiegel* (Issue 12, March 21, 2010, p. 29) in response to the question why the messages of science do not reach society.

[2] This excursus on the doubts expressed by some climate scientists and other observers of climate policies was originally written jointly with Hans von Storch. I have added extensive materials and context to the original essay. A much-shortened version was published in *Society* (Stehr, 2012a).

[3] Jeffrey D. Sachs, "Our summer of climate truth," *Project Syndicate* (July 27, 2012): www.project-syndicate.org/print/our-summer-of-climate-truth.

The dispute about climate change, its repercussions for the world, alternative conceptions of (historical and moral) responsibility and effective ways of responding is of course a profound and at times controversial sociopolitical issue. The political controversies linked to the nature of and the responses to climate change are deeply embedded in contradictory political world views; for example, the clash between conservative and liberal positions that advocate the withdrawal of the state from many of the affairs of society and those who see the solution to the thorny issues of climate change in a response in terms of more and deeper interventions of the state into the market and social behavior generally.

Throughout modern history, there are assertions about the withering away of politics and the substitution of the reign of power of men over men by the authority of scientific knowledge. Without identifying himself with the position in question, the economist Frank H. Knight (1949:271) refers to a naïve positivistic conception of the relation between scientific knowledge and societal problems that is repeated many times in the context under discussion: "Science has demonstrated its capacity to solve problems, and we need only understand that those of the *social order* are of the same kind" (emphasis added).

With the emergence of urgent global environmental problems a new, or a recall of an old, vision of the role of scientific knowledge in political governance is becoming evident. The grand vision of the new political role of scientific knowledge is, in turn, embedded in a broad disenchantment with the practical efficacy of democracy, the conviction that the public is unable to comprehend the nature of the problems faced by humankind, but also a misconception about the societal role of knowledge and, in particular, scientific knowledge.[4] The philosopher Philip Kitcher identifies himself with this position vis-à-vis democracy and the challenges presented to humankind by the forces of climate change. Kitcher (2011a:243) laments that "the failure to treat issues of climate change with the seriousness they deserve stems from many forms of ignorance and many causes." But a primary cause for Kitcher (2011a:243) is, and "this is an enormous tragedy, a huge failure of

---

[4] In a recent opinion piece in the *Seattle Times* (March 26, 2010) under the headline "Beyond Climate Change: Reframing the Dialogue over Environmental Issues," the atmospheric scientist John M. Wallace of the University of Washington suggests, in the spirit of this disenchantment, that "given the limited understanding of the intricacies of climate science, the human tendency to be more concerned with current issues than with what the climate will be like in 100 years from now, and the growing inequities in per capita fossil fuel consumption between countries like the United States an those like India, an enlightened energy policy on the basis of concerns about global warming is a tough sell."

worldwide democracy."[5] In short, it is not a lack of good ideas or technical feasibility that is the problem, the predicament stems from failures that can be ascribed to the political system (cf. Zakaria, 2013).

As a result, convictions expressed about the fundamental deficiency of democratic governance stand in essential contradiction to another form of alarm and strong doubt expressed about threats to democracy posed by experts, the very experts – one might assume – who warn humankind and policy-makers about the immense dangers to modern societies by global warming. Who is able to engage the authority of experts, and how? However, for Kitcher (2011:248), the greatest stumbling block to enacting policies that begin to cope with the impact of climate change is not that experts or scientists assume power in society, it is the erosion of scientific authority. The erosion of scientific authority minimizes the chances for scientists-cum-experts to lead society out of its impasse (cf. also Keller, 2011).

The historian Eric Hobsbawm ([2007] 2008:118–119), for example, is not convinced that political systems that make use of general elections (electoral democracy) necessarily contribute to guarantee the effective freedom of the press or to ensure the rights of citizens and an independent judiciary. Hobsbawm's skepticism toward democracy, however well intentioned, extends to doubts about the effectiveness of democratic states[6] in solving complex global problems such as global warming. He thereby joins a growing chorus of critical voices – within the scientific community and the media – that are certain that democratic societies are unable to effectively and timely attack global environmental problems.[7]

---

[5] For a critical analysis of Kitcher's position, see Brown (2004, 2013).
[6] The general secretary of the *Friends of Europe*, Gilles Merrit, speaking on the occasion of the "Green Week" conference organized annually by the European Commission, emphasized that "our problems are linked to two issues we are most proud of: democracy and free markets." What he had in mind first and foremost were solutions to environmental issues (cf. www.euractiv.com/en/sustainability/guilt-card-green-taxes-hailed-force-sustainable-consumption-news-494868).
[7] Without wanting to pass judgment, one may also note how history repeats itself, since the current skeptical voices from within the scientific community and the media remind one of a similar kind of disbelief in the 1970s, when the main contentious issue of the day was the question of the limits to growth and the survival of mankind; or, as Robert Heilbroner (1974:124) writes, resolutions "of the crises thrust upon us by the social and natural environments can only be found through political action." Scientists warned about the essential slowness, limited capacity, lack of legitimacy, and inflexibility of democratic political institutions and expressed their preference for authoritarian solutions (e.g., Heilbroner, 1974:123–148 and Hardin, 1977). Robert Heilbroner (1974:134) stresses, with considerable reluctance and candor, that the "passage through the gantlet [of the crises] ahead may be possible only under governments capable of rallying obedience far more effectively than would be possible in a democratic setting." Some forty years later, Dennis Meadows (2011), co-author of the *Limits to Growth*, reiterates his strong suspicion

At least implicitly these observers claim, for example, that if those who disagree or are voiceless were more enlightened – that is, were taking on board the "objective" framing of options – they would pursue the same course of action. As Isaiah Berlin ([1958] 1969:134) stresses, such a state of affairs "renders it easy for me to conceive of myself as coercing others for their own sake, in their, not my, interest. I am then claiming that I know what they truly need better than they know it themselves. I am and all others who share my convictions are at liberty to suppress the liberties of those who are not what they should be."

There also is a parallel justification of "the power of superior (objective) knowledge" and the legitimacy of decisions supported by and derived from such knowledge. Part of such a justification is, for example, a specific understanding of the function of the institution of the state. Emile Durkheim ([1950] 1992:92) refers to this convergence of political legitimacy and knowledge when he remarks:

> If the State does no more than receive individual ideas and volitions to find out which are more widespread and 'in the majority', as it is called, it can bring no contribution truly its own to the life of society ... The role of the State, in fact, is not to express and sum up the unreflective thoughts of the mass of the people but to superimpose on this unreflective thought a more considered thought, which therefore cannot be other than different.

Contemporary considerations in the 1920s and 1930s about science and the adequacy and capacity of democratic governance to cope with the rapid advance of scientific knowledge, the accumulation of urgent societal problems and the rapid rise of the complexity of the world, for example, as a result of the growing size of the population, resonate with today's discussions about the global environmental problems and the capacity of democracy to adequately respond. Some scientists, not only Marxists, were prepared to accept and even urge a stronger regulation of society in the face of massive social and economic problems and, hence, to sacrifice some democratic rights. Franz Boas (1939:1), for example, in defending science against the onslaught of totalitarianism concedes that some forms of individual liberty have to be surrendered but liberty within science has to be defended:

> The restrictions which we accept as unavoidable consequences of the inventive genius of mankind and the size of our population do not extend to the domain of thought. Even if we wanted to we could not maintain absolute individualism in social and economic life, but it is the goal to which we strive in intellectual and

concerning the barrier, due to the "slowness" and the "short-sightedness of governance," to needed action and solutions in the face of growing threats to our civilization.

spiritual life. It took us a long time to free thought from the restraints of imposed dogma. This freedom has not by any means been achieved completely. The thoughts of many are unconsciously or consciously so restrained, and attempts at the forcible repression of thought that run counter to accepted tenets of belief are still too frequent. A bigoted majority may be as dangerous to free thought as the heavy hand of a dictator. For this reason we demand fullest freedom of expression, so that our youth may be prepared for an intelligent use of the privileges and duties of citizenship.

The awkwardness of Boas's position Kuznets evident once we refer to an earlier manifesto in which Boas (1938:4) still emphasized a kind of zero-sum game in the defense of liberty: "Any attack on freedom of thought in one sphere, even as nonpolitical a sphere as theoretical physics, is in effect an attack on democracy itself." For other scientists at the time, for example John Bernal (1939), the need to regulate and restrict liberty had to be applied to both science and society.

Activist climate scientists, politicians, and many other observers agree that the 2009 Copenhagen climate summit and the subsequent Cancun, Durban, and Warsaw conferences in December 2010, November 2011, and 2013 were failures. In their aftermath, a couple of issues addressing the status of democratic governance in modern societies are intensively debated. The first issue concerns the role of climate science knowledge in political deliberations about climate policy. Can science tell us what to do? The strong desire to reach specific policy outcomes, spelled out by the scientific community, leads scientists to at least sympathize with the suspension of democratic processes.

The second, and more implicit, issue concerns the relationship between democracy and time. Are democracy and societal institutions that are governed by principles of liberty such as the marketplace capable of dealing with harms and risks to society that are located in the future? Political theory has been noticeably silent on this theme. However, we can glean some insights into these questions via the work of the renowned American economist and political scientist Charles E. Lindblom, who examined the complex interrelations between knowledge, markets, and democracy. These interrelations are just as relevant today, not just because of the serious effects of the recent financial and economic crisis.

As is well known, the supposed virtues of an unrestrained free market can easily be questioned. Many thoughtful and informed observers are skeptical toward unrestrained markets or are self-consciously opposed to the concept of a liberal market. For example, a couple of years ago the widely accepted solution to financial crises was, in their eyes, a fencing-in of the market by the state and society. Policy makers and climate scientists, for example in the *Fourth Carbon Budget: Reducing Emissions through the 2020s* (December 2010) by the official UK *Committee on Climate Change*, while offering advice on how to reach ambiguous targets in emissions reduction during the coming years and decades, also express their doubt about the capacity of an "unrestrained" market to reach such goals and, therefore, advocate a return to elements of "central planning" as interpreted by at least one major newspaper in the UK.[8] With respect to the electricity market of the future in the UK, the report states that

> Current market arrangements are highly unlikely to deliver required investments in low-carbon generation. Tendering of long-term contracts (e.g., Low-Carbon Contracts for Differences or Power Purchase Agreements) would reduce risks which energy companies are not well placed to manage (i.e. carbon price, gas price and volume risk), and would provide confidence that required investments will be forthcoming at least cost to the consumer. Other mechanisms (e.g., reliance on a carbon price alone or extension of the current Renewables Obligation) would not ensure the required investment, and would involve unnecessarily high costs and electricity prices. Given the need to decarbonise the power sector and the long lead-times for low-carbon investments, reform of the current market arrangements to include a system of tendered long-term contracts is an urgent priority.

Much less common, however, as Lindblom also stresses, if not taboo, is an open and explicit expression of doubt about the virtues of democracy, with the obvious exception of certain leaders of decidedly undemocratic nations. In particular, it has traditionally been the case that scientists have rarely raised serious misgivings in public about democracy as a political system.

But the times are changing. Within the broad field of climatology and climate policy, growing concerns about the virtues of democracy and a mounting appeal to exceptional circumstances can be discerned. The expressed impatience with democracy goes hand-in-hand with the closure of the function the IPCC (Intergovernmental Panel on Climate Change) is seen to serve. Increasingly, IPCC no longer considers itself a scientific organization with the mandate to offer alternative policy options for political discussion and decision but as a body demanding that options for political action identified and championed by it are actually realized (cf. Pielke, 2007).

The underlying hope is, of course, that an appeal to extraordinary circumstances, that is, a threat to the very existence of humankind "alone might be able to give capacity and palpable energy back to a failing or hampered [political] will" (Rosanvallon, 2006:191). It is not just the

---

[8] Michael McCarthy, "Central planning is the only way to hit CO_2 targets," *The Independent*, December 7, 2010.

deep divide between knowledge and action that is at issue, but an inconvenient democracy that is identified as the culprit that holds back action on climate change.[9] As Mike Hulme (2009) has noted, it can be frustrating to learn that citizens have minds of their own, that climate politics is understood to represent a political field, and that science is no longer seen to the public as nothing but a meritorious discursive field.

Leading climate scientists insist that humanity is definitely at a crossroads. A continuation of present economic and political trends will lead to disaster if not to a collapse of human civilization. To create a globally sustainable way of life, we immediately need, in the words of the German climate scientist Hans Joachim Schellnhuber, a "great transformation." What that statement exactly means is vague. Part, if not at the core, of the required great transformation is, in the eyes of some climate scientists as well as other scientists who are part of the great debate about climate change, a new political regime and new forms of governance as expressed, for example, by the Australian scholars David Shearman and Joseph Wayne Smith (2007) in their book *The Climate Change Challenge and the Failure of Democracy*: "We need an authoritarian form of government in order to implement the scientific consensus on greenhouse gas emissions." Clearly, therefore, as Shearman and Smith (2007:4) conclude, "humanity will have to trade its liberty to live as it wishes in favor of a system where survival is paramount." Mark Beeson (2010:289) agrees with Shearman and Smith's political conclusion and adds that "forms of 'good' authoritarianism, in which environmentally unsustainable forms of behavior are simply forbidden, may become not only justifiable, but essential for the survival of humanity in anything approaching a civilised form." The conclusion can only be that present political conditions in China, especially the strong state, attain global significance.

The well-known climate researcher James Hansen resignedly and frustratedly as well as vaguely adds that "the democratic process does not work."[10] In *The Vanishing Face of Gaia*, James Lovelock (2009)

---

[9] A leading U.S.-based environmental blog (*Grist*; January 21, 2011) notes for example: "Is a nation ruled somewhat autocratically by engineers and scientists better equipped to confront the 21st century than a nation that has always been suspicious of intellectuals, a nation increasingly ruled by the checkbooks of lobbyists and the entrenched industries they represent? It would be horrible, if it were true, and this is the unconquerable nut of the problem the U.S. now faces: if we can't get it together to transition to a sustainable resource base, what hope is there for the co-occurrence of both democracy and lasting material civilization?" (www.grist.org/article/2011-01-21-is-chinas-quasi-dictatorship-better-prepared-for-the-21st-centur)

[10] Although the framing is new, there is nothing new, as David Runciman (2013a) has documented, "about this outburst of disgust with the workings of democracy. Nor is it distinctly American. Europeans (with the possible exception of [contemporary]

emphasizes that we need to abandon democracy in order to meet the challenges of climate change head on. We are in a state of war.[11] In order to pull the world out of its state of lethargy, the equivalent of a "nothing but blood, toil, tears, and sweat" global-warming speech is urgently needed. Why is such a radical political change at any price deemed essential, and how is it feasible?

On the one hand, various national and global climate policies seem unable to reach their own modest goals, such as those of the expiring Kyoto agreement. On the other hand, given the steady accumulation of more and more robust findings about the causes and consequences of human-induced climate change, it would seem to be evident that the accomplishments of political action witnessed to date are incompatible with the goals set forth by climate policy advocates, especially with respect to the regional or global mitigation of greenhouse gases. It is important to also stress that the described diagnosis of the flaws of the failing but dominant political approach concentrates, to the quasi-exclusion of other forms and conditions of action, on the effect that governance ought to achieve, namely a reduction of greenhouse gas emissions. By focusing on the effects or goals of political action (what government should do) rather than its conditions (what government can do), the contentious issue of climate change is reduced from a sociopolitical to a technical issue (cf. Radder, 1986). The result of these considerations is the depoliticization of climate change (and the politicization of climate science). By concentrating on the effects that require mitigation efforts, the impression prevails that the remedies are primarily subject to technological regulations and adjustments.

These factors – including the reduction of a sociopolitical to a technical issue – have led some prominent voices in the community of climate scientists and the science of climate policy to adopt a now clearly discernable skeptical attitude toward democracy. Democracy, an emerging argument holds, is a political system that is both inappropriate and ineffective to meet the challenges posed by the consequences of climate change in politics and society, particularly in the area of the necessary

---

Germans) are just as disenchanted with their elected politicians. Lamenting the failings of democracy is a permanent feature of democratic life, one that persists through governmental crises and successes alike."

[11] In an interview with the *Guardian's* Leo Hickman (March 29, 2010), James Lovelock argues that one of the main obstructions to meaningful action combating climate change are political regimes that are democratic since "even the best democracies agree that when a major war approaches, democracy must be put on hold for the time being. I have a feeling that climate change may be an issue as severe as a war. It may be necessary to put democracy on hold for a while."

emission reductions. Democratically organized societies are too cumbersome to avoid climate change; they neither act in a timely fashion nor are they responsive in the necessary comprehensive manner. The "big decisions" in the case of climate change that have to be taken require a strong state. The endless debate should end. We have to act – that is the most important message. And that is why democracy becomes an *inconvenient* democracy in the eyes of these observers. In another historical context, decades ago, Friedrich Hayek (1960:25) pointed to the paradoxical development that follows scientific advances: it tends to strengthen the view that we should "aim at more *deliberate and comprehensive control of all human activities*". Hayek (1960:25) pessimistically adds: "It is for this reason that those intoxicated by the advance of knowledge so often become the enemies of freedom."

The growing doubts about the functionality of democracy and the suspicion that human motives and world-views are unyielding[12] go hand in hand with a further escalation of warnings about the apocalyptic consequences of global warming for humanity. In a 2009 report, the so-called *Global Humanitarian Forum* warns against 300,000 heat death losses a year and damages of 125 billion USD. That these figures, when used to justify comprehensive global policy action, are nothing but political arithmetic, is often overlooked. However, it is not only an inconvenient democracy that leads civilization down an escalating path toward a "stone age existence" (Lovelock, 2006:4) for the whole planet. According to some observers, it is the iron grip of the forces of climate that is supposed to eliminate – within a few years or decades – human freedom and agency, anyway, and therefore extinguish the social foundations of democracy. Combining both observations leads to the paradoxical conclusion that it is only through the elimination of democracy that democracy can be saved.

Without wanting to follow into the footsteps of the radical skeptics and alarmists: the emerging trend of emphatic criticism of democratic governance cannot simply be ignored or considered as marginal voices to be neglected. In order to understand the dissatisfaction with democracy among some scholars and experts, we must understand the underlying dynamics.

---

[12] Jedediah Purdy's (2009:1137) remarks, in this context, about the "nature" of human beliefs and world views are closer to the mark: "Such pessimistic arguments have in common that their cogency depends on taking 'human nature'-people's characteristic motives-as a permanent fact, at least for practical purposes. When those arguments have failed, it has been partly because 'human nature' has changed, not randomly, but as democratic politics has drawn people's motives in a relatively egalitarian direction."

First, we are informed that the robustness of the consensus in the science community about human-caused climate change has in recent years not only increased in strength but that a number of recent studies point to far more dramatic and long-lasting consequences of global warming than previously thought. In such a circumstance, how is it possible, many scientists ask, that such evidence does not motivate political action in societies around the world? Why is the consensus in climate science not a "mobilizing narrative" (Hulme, 2009:325)?

Second, the still-dominant approach to climate policy shows little evidence of practical success. One result of the recent global recession may well be an unintended reduction of the increase of CO_2 emissions. The worldwide reaction to the economic crisis, however, shows very clearly that governments do not conceive of a reduction in the growth of the wealth of their populations as a useful mechanism toward a reduction of emissions. On the contrary, everything is set in motion worldwide to foster a resumption of economic growth. Jump-starting the economy means emissions will raise again.

Third, the discussion of options for future climate policies support the impression that the same failed climate policies must remain in place and are the only correct approach; these policies simply have to become more effective and "rational." It follows that international negotiations must lead to an agreement on concrete but much broader emission reduction targets. Only a super-Kyoto can still help us. But how the noble goals of a comprehensive emission reduction can be practically and politically enforced remains in the fog of general declarations of intent and only sharpens the political skepticism of scientists.

Fourth, in the architecture of the reasoning of the impatient critics of democracy, one notes an inappropriate fusion of nature and society. The uncertainties that the science of natural processes (climate) claims to have eliminated is simply transferred to the domain of societal processes. Consensus on facts, it is argued, should motivate a consensus on politics. The constitutive uncertainties of social, political, and economic processes are treated as minor obstacles that need to be delimited as soon as possible – of course by a top-down approach.

Fifth, the discourse of the impatient scientists privileges hegemonic players such as world powers, states, transnational organizations, and multinational corporations. Participatory strategies and imagination are only rarely in evidence. Likewise, global mitigation has precedence over local adaptation. "Global" knowledge triumphs over "local" knowledge. It not only is hopeless by implication, one could argue, to count on the public; not only is "the science of climate change too complicated for democratic publics to understand" (Runciman, 2013b:313–314) but the concerns and hopes of the public are relentlessly focused on the present or the immediate future.

Finally, the sum of these considerations leads to the conclusion that democracy itself is inappropriate, that the slow procedures for the implementation and management of specific, policy-relevant (that is, in other words, immediately performative) scientific knowledge result in massive, unknown dangers. The democratic system designed to balance divergent interest has failed in the face of these threats. According to the *New York Times* columnist Paul Krugman, all of this is about nothing less than a betrayal of the planet and, for his colleague Thomas Friedman, evidence that the authoritarian state of China presents a model to be admired and perhaps copied.[13]

The growing impatience of prominent climate researchers and the perhaps still implicit argument for large-scale social planning constitutes an implicit embrace of now popular social theories.[14] We especially think, in this context, of Jared Diamond's (2005) theories about the fate of human societies. Diamond argues that only those societies have a chance of survival that practice sustainable lifestyles. Climate researchers have evidently been impressed by Jared Diamond's deterministic social theory. However, they have drawn the wrong conclusion, namely that only authoritarian political states guided by scientists (or experts) make effective and correct decisions in the climate issue. History teaches us that the opposite is the case. Therefore, today's China cannot serve as a model. Climate policy must be compatible with democracy, otherwise the threat to civilization will be much bigger than just that of changes in our physical environment (cf. Baber and Barlett, 2005; Dryzek and Stevenson, 2011). In short, the alternative to the abolition of democratic governance as the effective response to the societal threats that are likely to come with climate change is more democracy and the worldwide empowerment and enhancement of the knowledgeability of individuals,

---

[13] But not only influential commentators reach this conclusion: the central question pertaining to political governance that emerges from discussions of environmental degradation and global warming, as Mark Beeson (2010:289) stresses, is "whether democracy can be sustained in the region [of Southeast Asia] – or anywhere else for that matter – given the unprecedented and unforgiving nature of the challenges we collectively face. . . . In such circumstances, forms of 'good' authoritarianism, in which environmentally unsustainable forms of behavior are simply forbidden, may become not only justifiable, but essential for the survival of humanity in anything approaching a civilised form." Beeson (2010:289) answers his own question by suggesting that in China "an authoritarian regime has arguably done more to mitigate environmental problems than any other government on earth."

[14] In some ways, that is, the dispute about the role of democracy in the face of massive societal problems resonates with the vigorous and contentious debate among scientists about the virtues of economic planning during World War II (e.g., Hayek, 1941).

groups, and movements that work on environmental issues.[15] The existence of "treacherous" policy problems (that is, "wicked problems"- policy issues such as climate change that refer to open, complex, and insufficiently researched systems) and societal complexity as such are not a contradiction to democratic governance and the possibility of democratic participation. The latter may well be more difficult. But the difficulties and ailments of democracy do not justify arguing for its abolition.

It is hardly imaginable that social and cultural scientists today would follow the counsel offered more than a century ago by the German Protestant theologian and liberal politician Friedrich Naumann (1909:626–627): "Perhaps it is not entirely incorrect, to commence the discussion of the political forces with a reflection on the *power of non-political people* ... These people are governed, they are forced to pay taxes, they will be punished if they ride on the sidewalk or if they do not have their children vaccinated, but that they are a political power, is even beyond their own imagination" (my emphasis). Indeed, such an observation cannot be found in the reflections of the vast majority of contemporary social and cultural scientists. Their opposition to Naumann's topic will be taken up later in my study.

---

[15] Obviously, I am not the first one to make this claim and draw such a pointed conclusion; John Dewey ([1927] 1994:146), for example, perceptively notes "the cure for ailments of democracy is more democracy."

5 The knowledge of the powerful

Grave doubts and reservations about the viability of democratic governance – that is, the ability to reach political decisions with the assistance of institutional arrangements that assure the participation of the largest number of citizens including a reasonably general distribution of information – have been raised by social scientists from multiple vantage points. In Chapter 4, I spelled out some of the hopes for and concerns about democracy linked to the societal role of the institution of the scientific community. The philosophers of the Vienna Circle and John Dewey occupy the more optimistic part of the spectrum of views about the contribution of science to democratic governance; Walter Lippmann and some scientists from the contemporary climate science community, for example, represent the more pessimistic tendency and, as they likely see it, the realistic observers with respect to the political ideal of democracy as a means of governance for modern societies facing highly difficult and unsolved, if not unsolvable, complex problems. I will now turn to the role that scientific knowledge may have once it is disseminated to society and to the particular patterns of dissemination that tend to be established in society. The preeminent view of the pattern of the social distribution of knowledge generated by the scientific community in modern societies tends to stress its asymmetric structure and, therefore, the highly stratified access to the use of such knowledge for political purposes, a view that, of course, amounts to the assertion that knowledge primarily flows to the powerful.

Thus, the question of a significant concentration of knowledge in modern societies will be at the center of my inquiry, in the following chapter, into the varied themes of the societal role of scientific knowledge. More specifically, my focus will be on the advancement of knowledge and its burdens, as some of the orthodox answers to queries about the societal circulation of knowledge would suggest. The answer to the question of the political consequences of the typical social distribution of (specialized) knowledge in modern societies rests almost exclusively on the premise that specialized knowledge, in terms of power-enhancing knowledge, is not only distributed in a highly unbalanced manner but is also controlled and effectively deployed by the elites of society. In opposition to the now conventional thesis about what amounts to an almost iron law of the societal distribution of knowledge and its socioeconomic and sociopolitical consequences, I will discuss my doubts about the empirical and theoretical adequacy of the conventional perspective in the subsequent section. There, I intend to focus on a much less frequently examined possibility, namely that knowledge may serve as a powerful "weapon" for the weak of a society, that is, for ordinary citizens who are able to mobilize knowledge for the advancement of their purposes and interests.

But first, I will propose an exposition of the conventional thesis. The view that there is a strong symmetry or distinct convergence of knowledge and social, economic, and political power rests on a number of assumptions. Depending on the theoretical perspective, we encounter for example the thesis that political, economic, and social dominance is operative by virtue of its privileged control of knowledge; for example, the idea that there is an emerging global class whose power is a function of their privileged access to productive political, economic, or cultural knowledge that can, if necessary, be commanded through their ability to mobilize relevant experts who are the carriers of such knowledge. Moreover, in as much as the legitimacy of authority (and power), productivity and superior means of violence in modern societies may be seen to, today, rest on knowledge and not on property, assertions referring to the power of knowledge in contemporary society also tend to claim that there is a symbiosis between knowledge and social, political, and economic power.

In general, however, there is no agreement among those observers who diagnose a trend toward a concentration of knowledge in the hands of small social strata about its likely societal consequences for contemporary societies. Depending on the standards against which such trends are pitted, the concentration of knowledge in society is seen as either beneficial for the welfare of all citizens or in violation of fundamental democratic rights, for example. Similarly, observers are in disagreement about the reasons for the concentration of knowledge in what, then, are seen as the "leaders" in different institutions in society.

I will first make brief reference to three perspectives that resonate with the general idea that modern – including contemporary (if not future) – society produces new structures of inequality that are closely tied to the selective control of scientific and technical knowledge as well as to cultural and human capital. Later in this chapter, I will discuss four specific notions of the idea of the emergence of new classes in contemporary society: the meaning producers, the informational producers, the creative class, and the global class, each of which benefits from the privileged access of its members to new bodies of knowledge in their societies.

Heinz Eulau (1973:170), for example, refers in the early seventies to a skill revolution (but not "skill elites") as one of the outstanding characteristics of industrial and technological society. What is new is the extraordinary specialization and proliferation of occupations that demand highly developed skills. According to Eulau, the skill revolution cuts across "class boundaries," affecting both the middle and the working classes. Daniel Bell (1971:5) who also, and at about the same time, refers to technological and scientific developments as the driving force of societal and political change and to political decision-making that "will have an increasingly technical character" does not agree. He predicts the emergence of a new leadership that does not involve "businessmen or corporations" anymore but "research corporations, the industrial laboratories, the experimental stations, and the universities" (Bell, 1967:27). For Bell, the working class is shrinking and the "class of knowledge workers is becoming predominant in society" (Bell, 1967:4).[1]

As we have seen, Eulau (1973:1721) is less convinced that we will witness the emergence of a skill elite; since the skill revolution is not the only major societal trend, "tendencies contrary to the skill revolution evoked in response to social malfunctioning may attenuate or dissipate the concentration of power in the hands of those who have the new skills and specialized knowledge." As the political result of the skill revolution, Eulau (1973:189) cautiously anticipates that some kind of "deliberative governance" in policy making and the delivery of human services may become a pervasive feature of governance in a future society.[2]

Alvin Gouldner (1978:159) identifies a knowledge-based modern social class that he calls the *New Class*: "The New Class is elitist and self-seeking and uses its special knowledge to advance its own interests and power, and control its own work situation ... The power of the New Class is growing ... The power of this morally ambiguous New Class is on the ascendant and it holds a mortgage on at least *one* historical future." Gouldner's (1978:163; also 1979) delineation of the New Class also assumes that their power and influence derives from their exclusive command of technical knowledge. Because of its command of the

---

[1] The list of observers who for similar reasons expected the emergence of a political power elite based on knowledge and the loss of power by owners, workers, and consumers could easily be extended (cf. Young, 1961; Galbraith, 1967).

[2] A political scientist who refers to the growing influence of experts as a positive transformation in contemporary society is Robert Lane (1996) who in the same essay also advances the notion of a "knowledgeable society."

"technical knowledge of the forces of production and means of administration, the New Class already has considerable de facto control over the mode of production and hence considerable leverage with which to pursue its interests." The contending classes pursue a contest for control over the machinery of production and administration, and "this is partly a contest between the class which has legal ownership of the mode of production and the class whose technical knowledge increasingly gives it effective possession of the mode of production."[3]

In the subsequent chapter, in contrast, I will address questions that concern the *distribution* of knowledge; the chapter will focus on the politics in knowledge societies and address the likelihood of meaningful participation in the political realm of far larger segments of society and the extent to which such opportunities are dependent on actors' knowledgeability.

In general, it would be entirely accurate to say that the typical theoretical interest in the relation between knowledge and power has focused not on the possible dilution of power through knowledge but on the extent to which knowledge tends to be a resource that almost naturally flows to the already powerful in society and hence functions as "power over" others (see Parsons, 1963). The working assumption of the subsequent chapter is *not*, however, that the societal distribution of knowledge must inevitably be characterized by a sharp asymmetry in the access to and possession of knowledge and that its usage is mainly mobilized for the purpose of maintaining whatever social, political and economic advantages the "ownership" of knowledge of the privileged may engender.

But in the current chapter this is precisely the premise of the analysis of what amounts to an almost iron law of the societal distribution of knowledge and therefore the close kinship of knowledge and power in society. Knowledge is viewed as the handmaiden of the power of the powerful and as tending to serve in a most straightforward manner to defend, recreate, or improve initial advantages. It follows, of course, that under these circumstances knowledge and democracy are not compatible – as has been argued over the decades by many observers and has prominently found its specific attribution in the so-called "iron law of oligarchy" and in versions of class theory designed to give impetus and credibility to such perspectives.

---

[3] The observations by Daniel Bell and Alvin Gouldner date from the late 1960s and early 1970s. In the meantime, a number of critiques of the idea of a *class* of knowledge workers and similar notions have appeared. In general, the assertion that these strata in fact represent a social class in the technical sense of the term has been questioned (e.g., Stehr and Adolf, 2009; Marks and Baldry, 2009) or has prompted calls for empirical studies (e.g., Darr and Warhurst, 2008).

The so-called (political) *knowledge gap* hypothesis, which as a rule includes the liberal conflation of the notions of information and knowledge (e.g., Jeffres, Neuendorf, and Atkin, 2012:59),[4] is as good an example as any of the observation that proceeds from the assumption that the social circulation of knowledge tends to be highly stratified and that any hopes as well as efforts to "equalize" the distribution of knowledge by employing a variety of media including the Internet, for example, tend to fail, if not to increase the initial inequality in the command of political knowledge and information. The original formulation of the knowledge gap hypothesis is by Phillip Tichenor and his Minnesota colleagues (1970; see also Tichenor, Donohoe and Olson, 1980). Based on data from news diffusion studies, time trends, a newspaper strike, and a field experiment, as well as a reinterpretation of the findings of these studies, the authors conclude that "increasing the flow of news on a topic leads to greater acquisition of knowledge about that topic among the more highly educated segments of society" (Tichenor et al., 1970:159).

A better understanding of what exactly produces these results requires a reference to the contingent conditions that are associated with the access to and acquisition of information/knowledge. Communication choices, access, attention, and usage of contents are obviously shaped by a host of social and political factors. With respect to the reasons for the knowledge gap, interpretations – whether referring to situation-specific forces such as motivational interests (cf. Genova and Greenberg, 1979), the specific social context, or transsituational factors such as educational background, gender, and age – vary considerably (cf. Ettema and Kline, 1977; Holbrook, 2002). Still, all observers agree that the knowledge and information gap is real and difficult to overcome. In the meantime, the knowledge gap thesis has been enlarged and extended to differences in the command of knowledge capital among nations and regions of the world. In analogy to the within-society differences, doubt tends to be expressed that between-society information gaps can be overcome in the future. On the contrary, the likely persistence of the gap is stressed, arguing that "the knowledge gap will likely widen the disparities between rich and poor, imprisoning many developing countries in relative poverty" (Persaud, 2001:108).

---

[4] The idea of an "information overload" brought about in the modern era by the Internet has considerable elective affinity, at least in some respects, to what then becomes its twin concept, namely the knowledge gap thesis, since reference to an information overload amounts to a concern that the "wealth" of available information will make us, not unlike the lack of knowledge, as it were, incapable of finding our ways; we are forced to submit to powers outside ourselves in order to be able to act.

However, as we have seen, on the surface if not in the center of concerns about the functioning of democratic governance there is the expectation that large numbers of citizens should participate, which under the best of circumstances could result in governance by laypersons. In an essay in the *New York Times* (January 2, 2000) about the large proportion of eligible American nonvoters, we find the observation that more than half of the children in the United States live in households where neither parent votes. The year 2000 also saw the first presidential election in the United States since 1924 where a majority did not vote.

Herrschaft kraft Wissen

One of the most famous, significant, and consequential analyses of the authority of (instrumental as well as one-dimensional) knowledge and technical expertise is, of course, Max Weber's theory of bureaucracy or, more generally, his theory of the intrinsically rationalizing instruments of modern political power, where he argues that

> bureaucratic administration means fundamentally the exercise of control on the basis of knowledge (*'Herrschaft kraft Wissen'*). This is the feature of it which makes it specifically rational. This consists on the one hand in technical knowledge which, by itself, is sufficient to ensure its position of extraordinary power. But in addition to this, bureaucratic organizations, or the holders of power who make use of them, have the tendency to increase their power still further out of experience in the service. For they acquire through the conduct of office a special knowledge of facts and have available a store of documentary material peculiar to themselves (Weber [1922] 1964:339).

Weber unquestioningly stresses, in this context, the supreme efficiency and soulless power of specialized expert knowledge. His theory resonates with an idealized, thoroughly old-Prussian conception of – and perhaps personal experience with – the alleged efficacy of the military and civil service apparatus (cf. Spittler, 1980; Niethammer, [1989] 1992). Since the "master" the bureaucracy serves (whether it is the "people" or a parliament) "always finds himself vis-à-vis the trained official, in the position of a dilettante facing the expert" (Weber, [1922] 1978:991), it is difficult to imagine how to counter the authority of the expert bureaucracy.

But experience much more generally tends to show, as Weber ([1922] 1964: 339) suggests in the context of his delineation of basic sociological categories in *Economy and Society*, that the bureaucratic organization is "capable of attaining the highest degree of efficiency and is in this sense formally the most rational known means of carrying out imperative control over human beings. It is superior to any other form in precision, in stability, in the stringency of its discipline, and in its reliability. It thus makes possible a particularly high degree of calculability of results for the heads of the organization and for those acting in relation to it."

The primary source of the "superiority of bureaucratic administration lies in the role of technical knowledge which, through the development of modern technology and business methods in the production of goods, has become completely indispensable." Therefore, Weber ([1922] 1964:337–338) argues, "it makes no difference whether the economic system is organized on a capitalistic or a socialistic basis." Bureaucracy constitutes a form of "domination based on knowledge." It is capable of attaining levels of efficiency, reliability, precision, or modes of rational control not only the administrative apparatus of the state but no other form of modern legitimate authority is able to attain. According to Weber ([1922] 1978:225), there is only one institution that is superior to bureaucracy in the command of technical knowledge, namely the "capitalist entrepreneur, within his own sphere of interest. He is the only type who has been able to maintain at least relative immunity from subjection to the control of rational bureaucratic knowledge." The advantages enjoyed by capitalist enterprises in terms of specialized knowledge with respect to their sphere of interest is the result of a kind of Darwinian selection that occurs in the marketplace: "Errors in official statistics do not have direct economic consequences for the responsible official, but miscalculations in a capitalist enterprise are paid for by losses, perhaps by its existence" (Weber, [1922] 1978:994).

The authority of the administrative apparatus is based on technical knowledge and derives from impersonal legal norms[5] and continuous procedurally correct work carried out by officials in offices with clearly circumscribed spheres of competence. Thus, there is a convergence or even symbiosis of legal norms, sanctions, and knowledge; the effective application of general, standardized legal norms requires the use of general, abstract knowledge. Domination by legal norms routinizes and strengthens domination by technical knowledge. It should be noted, however, that the close convergence of legal rules and the notion of knowledge as an objective, technical, and impersonal discourse, as described by Weber, is a legacy, and mainly representative, of the nineteenth century. In its classical vision, the primary object of knowledge within the state bureaucratic organization in particular is "the legal

---

[5] The "belief in the 'legality' of patterns of normative rules and the right of those elevated to authority under such rules to issue commands" constitutes the foundation of legal authority (Weber, [1922] 1964:328).

system, particularly those parts of it establishing the governmental and administrative apparatus, controlling its activities, and regulating its relations to private individuals. Law was seen as the speech itself of the state" (Poggi, 1982:356).

Rational bureaucratic knowledge thrives in a soulless, passive social environment that has been "dehumanized." Bureaucracy provides the sentiments demanded by the external apparatus of modern culture most effectively and develops its characteristic features especially well: "the more it is 'dehumanized,' the more completely it succeeds in eliminating from official business love, hatred, and all purely personal, irrational, and emotional elements which escape calculation" (cf. Weber, [1992] 1964:340). This is appraised as its special virtue by capitalism. The more complicated and specialized modern culture becomes, the more its external supporting apparatus demands the personally detached and strictly objective *expert*, in lieu of the lord of older social structures who was "moved by personal sympathy and favour, by grace and gratitude" (Weber, [1922] 1978:975). Modern bureaucracy succeeds in rationalizing the irrational; it tends to operate at its best when it manages to avoid conflicts between formal and substantive rationality, for example, by usurping the goal-setting function of the politician. It is therefore decisive for Weber ([1922] 1978:979) that, despite the realm of relatively unregulated conduct even in highly rational settings (for example, in the legal system), that "in principle a system of rationally debatable 'reasons' stands behind every act of bureaucratic administration, namely, either subsumption under norms, or a weighing of ends and means." In short, modern bureaucracy exemplifies purposive-rational action in all its elements.

The formal theory (or ideal type) of bureaucracy depicted by Weber is at the core of his account of modernization. Bureaucracy offers the most apparent and visible contrast to traditional society and its systems of administration.[6] The "degree of advance towards a bureaucratic ... officialdom provides the decisive yardstick for the modernization of the state" (Weber, [1922] 1978:320). Moreover, bureaucracy is for Weber something akin to a natural-historical category. And compared to other "social supports of the modern social order" it stands out "owing to its much greater inescapability" (Weber, [1922] 1978:834). The merciless passivity of the individual demanded by the modern system of rule, the fatalism, and the triumph of bureaucratization – based on a division of labor – of all forms of life in the modern world will later be summed up by

---

[6] For a discussion of the development of the concept of "rational organization," see Karl Mannheim (1935:28–30).

Adorno and Horkheimer in the term "the managed world," exactly because of its incomparably rational form.[7]

Ultimately, the rationality of technical specialization in the context of bureaucratic organization conceals the model of the machine, and thus the danger of the probably unbreakable domination of reason based on pure functionalism:

> An inanimate machine is mind objectified. Only this provides it with the power to force men into service and to dominate their everyday working life so completely as is actually the case in the factory. Objectified intelligence is also that animated machine, the bureaucratic organization, with its specialization of trained skills, its division of jurisdiction, its rules and hierarchical relations of authority. Together with the inanimate machine it is busy fabricating the shell of bondage which men will perhaps be forced to inhabit some day, as powerless as the fellahs of ancient Egypt (Weber, [1922] 1978:1402).

Aside from the legally sanctioned rights in the constitution of modern states and therefore the formal limits to the domination of the state bureaucratic apparatus, the only means of resistance to the state bureaucracy freely available to its citizens is the creation of organizations that are bound to be subject to the same process of domination. But echoing Robert Michels' ([1915] 1958) study of political parties, Weber ([1922] 1964:338) cautions: "When those subject to bureaucratic control seek to escape the influence of the existing bureaucratic apparatus, this is normally possible only by creating an organization of their own which is equally subject to the process of bureaucratization."[8]

In *Economy and Society*, Weber delineates "legal authority with a bureaucratic apparatus" or the superiority of technical knowledge; but elsewhere in his political writings he explores the "dysfunctions" and imperfections of bureaucracies, the limits of bureaucratic conduct and its institutional linkages (e.g., the linkages to social class and its aspirations in specific historical contexts). Legal authority becomes subject to

---

[7] Whether there is a contradiction of interests in Weber's work in terms of knowledge – on the one hand they are directed toward an analysis of the realization of individual freedoms and the institutionalization of pluralistic domination in advanced western societies, and on the other hand they emphasize (and under certain circumstances evaluate positively) the process of increasing the rationalization or even technologization of contexts for action and, thus, the passivity of the individual in modern societies – is not under discussion here (but see Alexander, 1987).

[8] Max Weber surely had difficulties imagining social organizations that are created and dominated not from top to bottom but from bottom to top, as is perhaps the case for the Internet. However, we will have to wait and see whether regulation, and therefore the alleged inevitability of bureaucratic organizational architecture, will also invade and permeate the Internet at some future point. Attempts to regulate access to contents will surely be made in different social and national contexts. Whether they can be effective is another matter altogether.

routinization, "trained incapacities," and antinomies; conflicts can arise (Merton, 1939:560–568) and the costs of subordination, as well as inertia, can mount. Bureaucracies not only accumulate knowledge, but also attempt to protect this knowledge from access by "outsiders" (cf. Weber, [1922] 1968:990–993) and strive to almost completely avoid public discussion of their techniques, while political leaders are increasingly "dilettantes." The experts can only be controlled and kept at bay by other experts (Weber, [1922] 1968:994). Who controls the administrative apparatus? According to Weber ([1922] 1964:338), such control is only to a certain degree possible for the nonspecialist; in general, the "trained permanent official is more likely to get his way in the long run than his nominal superior, the Cabinet minister, who is not a specialist."

But the ability of the state to effectively implement its action, and the relative superiority of rational bureaucratic knowledge, are limited, as Weber knew. The only group that can escape the control of rational bureaucratic knowledge is represented, as indicated, by the capitalist entrepreneur. Only he is able to maintain relative immunity from legal authority. It is interesting to examine why Weber ([1922] 1968:994) thinks that the capitalist is more or less beyond the reach of state bureaucracy. According to Weber, the ability of the state to intervene in economic affairs is relatively ineffective because of the capitalist entrepreneur's superior knowledge of the facts and the corporation's ability to shield pertinent information from outsiders even more effectively than civil servants can.

The convergence of relevant forms of knowledge and legal norms that is at the heart of Weber's conception of bureaucracy is progressively undermined in the twentieth century and beyond as a result of the extension of the scope of the functions and the scale of ambitions of the modern state. Knowledge still counts. But the monopoly-like role of juridical discourse, and therefore the nature of the cognitive basis of state domination, are increasingly replaced and challenged by the relevance of other forms of knowledge, especially scientific knowledge. Diverse forms of knowledge from scientific disciplines other than legal discourse become more and more relevant and are summoned and shaped by the state with its enlarged managerial responsibilities. Social knowledge other than juridical knowledge becomes a constitutive aspect of bureaucratic organizations and the basis for policy decisions in order to administer the social problems now assigned or appropriated by the state.

The increase in the reliance of bureaucratic organizations on other than legal forms of knowledge has a multitude of positive and negative, anticipated and unanticipated consequences for the state in its efforts to impose its will on the conduct of other social institutions and individuals. Among the negative consequences there is, as Poggi (1982:358) points out, a downgrade of common sense that "assigns the citizenry the role of passive, uncomprehending spectators (and perhaps beneficiaries) even of state activities which affect them quite closely." I will attempt to show that the opening up of bureaucratic organizations to other forms of knowledge has the opposite effect, namely a noticeable loss in the ability of legal authority to "get things done." As a result, it is justified to speak of a loss of knowledge-based authority and power of state institutions. Such a conclusion is already warranted if the assumption of the growing relevance and availability of multiple forms of knowledge is extended to ordinary citizens, as well. Why should the knowledgeability of citizens be a static attribute?

Another question is whether, once bureaucratization and "rationalization" in large-scale organizations have reached a state of "maturity" (assuming that such organizations ever achieve a notable measure of rationality), further structural changes in organizations or authority relations will still primarily be driven by spontaneous market forces and efficiency considerations. Empirical research on modern organizations indicates that these corporate actors are far from being models of efficiency and rationality. Moreover, organizational change is not always driven, and even increasingly less so, by efficiency considerations; nor does this necessarily result in gains in effectiveness and rationality (cf. DiMaggio and Powell, 1983).

Organizational styles and success are less and less based on bureaucratic models. A decline in centralization, homogeneity, and reliance on hierarchy is increasingly typical of the organizational spectrum found in modern societies. The number of organizational patterns increases, and the "life expectancy" during which certain organizational structures serve as examples decreases. On the basis of extensive field research carried out in the 1980s, Kanter (1991; also Barzeley, 1992) concludes that although the magnitude of the trend is not entirely clear, large corporations have moved into a postbureaucratic phase. The adoption of nonbureaucratic and nonhierarchical organizational models can be traced back as far as to aerospace projects in World War II, but has clearly accelerated. The waning and delegitimation of bureaucracy in corporations is a response to rapidly changing organizational environments, characterized by greater contingencies and uncertainties that require not risk-aversion, uniformity, order, and repetition but creativity, flexibility, detachment, and performance. For the employees of these corporations, postbureaucratic organizational strategies hold out the promise, as Kanter (1991:75) also stresses, of greater satisfaction and rewards; but "more of those benefits are contingent on what the individual – and the team – does and not on what the corporation automatically provides."

The large and varied group of workers laboring to disseminate knowledge in modern society, however, is not only employed by the state. Many workers are self-employed. The classes of civil servants and professionals display considerable kinship, not only from a theoretical point of view, but also from a comparative historical perspective. They can therefore be discussed in conjunction. For example, despite important differences in their historical careers, the German bourgeoisie and the Anglo-American middle classes had many commonalities because both "rose to prominence largely on the strength of those qualities that are shared by the models of profession and bureaucracy" (Gipsen, 1988:563).

Although the German-Italian sociologist Robert Michels was not the first to observe a tendency toward oligarchical structures in larger associations, earlier views on the same trajectory toward the domination of a small clique in such organizations, for example Karl Marx and Friedrich Engels, were more optimistic that any concentration of power in the hands of a few leaders was bound to vanish as socialist associations and their membership, for example, "matured." Michels was less expectant as to whether what has since become known as "the iron law of oligarchy" could be overcome and displaced by the more democratic forms of internal governance of large voluntary associations.

The iron law of oligarchy

Robert Michels ([1915] 1949:93), in his classic study of the "really existing" undemocratic tendencies in large, formal organizations, especially in organizations that publicly aspire to and fight for democratic goals, refers to an almost "natural" state of incompetence and immaturity found in the mass of people in modern democracies. And since the rank and file are incapable "of looking after their own interests, it is necessary that they should have experts to attend to their affairs." Seldom is the rank and file willing to shake off the authority of the expert leaders and dismiss them from control.[9] Party politics, for example, becomes the

---

[9] Whether the disillusioned conclusion Michels ([1915] 1949:95) draws in light of the social tendencies he observes, namely that "social democracy is not democracy, but a party fighting to attain democracy," represents an inevitable fate of large scale, formal organizations generally, and therefore constitutes a kind of iron law of oligarchy, is contestable, though many observers are prepared to concede that Robert Michels has discovered one of the few law-like regularities found to date by social scientists (cf. Lipset, Trow, and Coleman, [1956] 1962; Baccaro, 2001).

business of the full-time, professional politician; a condition that describes present-day politics in many democratic countries equally well.

Michels ([1915] 1970:86–87) further argues that among the complex social tendencies that act as a barrier against the realization of democracy is organizations. Insofar as organizations form a strong structure they engender differentiations. Aside from the size of a social organization, be it a democratic state, a political party or a labor union, it is the nature of the tasks an organization is expected to fulfill that generates extensive structures around the division of labor within the organization. Division of labor generates specialists. Specialists enjoy authority. Expertise dominates and, as Michels ([1911] 1949:401) formulates succinctly: "Who says organization says oligarchy."

Although the function of the "leaders" of the organization is formally subjected to control by those led, "this control is condemned, as the organization grows, to a pseudo-existence. . . . The sphere of democratic control is restricted to ever smaller circles." The emerging differentiations are of a hierarchical nature and stem from "technical needs" as well as practical circumstances. Michels ([1915] 1970:75) observes that even "the radical tendency in the social democratic party ... does not object to this regression. Democracy is nothing but a form, they say. And form must not dominate content."

Leadership positions in growing organizations are filled on the basis of competence, which results in a considerable gradient, in terms of formal instruction, between the ordinary members of the organization and its leaders. In proletarian political parties, the "deserters of the bourgeoisie become the leaders of the proletariat, not in spite of, but because of, that superiority of formal instruction which they have acquired in the camp of the enemy and have brought with them thence." These steep differences in competence and experience do not only count within the party organization, they also count in other political contexts such as, for example, in parliament. The outcome is that the elites become indispensable. Technical competence implies authority and oligarchies within oligarchies are formed. The negation of democratic principles is complete. On the basis of these observations, as indicated, Michels ([1911] 1949:55) reaches the conclusion that social democracy is not democracy but a party fighting to attain democracy. The meta-conclusion for Michels ([1915] 1970:96), and therefore for the relationship between knowledge and democracy as practiced by the organizations he observed, is that democracy ends up becoming a form of governance of the best, and that means an aristocracy.

Robert Michels' *Political Parties* is a case study inquiry into the nature of the Social Democratic Party at the beginning of the last century. This would justify the question whether Michels, with the iron law of oligarchy, had indeed discovered a timeless, general "sociological law."[10]

One of the foremost answers to the limits of the generalizability of Michels' iron law of oligarchy comes from a study by Seymour Martin Lipset, Martin Trow, and James S. Coleman ([1956] 1962). In their now equally classic study *Union Democracy*, in which Lipset and his colleagues examine, inspired by Robert Michels, democratic processes in an American labor union in the postwar era, the International Typographical Union (ITU), Lipset, Trow, and Coleman conclude that the democratic control by ordinary members of the union leadership is possible in principle.[11] According to Lipset, Trow, and Coleman, the fact that is responsible for their finding and, therefore, for a possible revision of Michels' iron law is that the ITU typically has had two competing parties. However, Lipset and his colleagues consider their effort a deviant case study that does not topple Michels' *general* theory but clarifies and amplifies the iron law of oligarchy.[12]

---

[10] For example, what is Michels' concept of democracy against which he charts the observed tendencies toward oligarchy in the German Social Democratic Party? Philip Cook (1971:785) stresses that Michels' view is that of a radical syndicalist, "not of democracy as an institutional form or as decision-making process, but 'democracy,' the syndicalist egalitarian social and political ideal" (also Scaff, 1981). Whatever falls short of direct participation or "the principle of mass-sovereignty" (Michels, ([1915]: 1970:93) of all of the members in organizational decision-making processes constitutes a violation of such an ideal of a democratic regime; which means that, for Michels, democracy is a principle and not a process that may be more or less approximated in practical political life.

[11] By the same token, Robert Alford (1985:295) suggests that Athens in the late fifth and early fourth centuries BC represents another case that mitigates Michels' iron law: "Athens success is related to its practice of universal male citizen participation in the administration of the city." Similarly, the optimistic discussion in the 1960s and 1970s of the possibility of industrial democracy within the confines of modern-day factories sought to reconcile either capitalist ownership of the means of production with democracy or state ownership of the means of production and democratic governance in state-owned factories.

[12] As Lipset (1959:70) emphasizes later, although their research effort discovered "the clearest exception to Robert Michels' 'iron law of oligarchy'," the study was not intended to be a report on the ITU as such but was "the best means available to test and amplify Michels' 'law'." The outcome of the examination of the deviant case therefore was to illuminate rather than to falsify the general theory put forward by Michels. Several prominent contemporary scholars have seconded Michels' now more than a century old observations, arguing that large modern political party organizations have not made much headway toward intraparty democratic governance (e.g., Allern and Pedersen, 2007). Modern political parties are often controlled by political professionals (see Katz and Muir, 1995). In contrast, Karl Loxbo (2013:549) who studied the development of intraparty democracy in the Swedish Social Democratic Party between the 1950s and 1990s concludes that "leaders ... lost some of their previous ability to control, while activists seemed to count for more than they did in the heyday of the mass party ... these results suggest that an equally plausible

Lack of information, passivity, and lack of interest of rank-and-file members in the affairs of an organization is in the interests of the powerful and supports their capacity to perpetuate power advantages. As Lipset and his colleagues ([1956] 1962:402) therefore emphasize, "the less the members know or desire to know about policy, the more secure the leaders are. The single-party organization in a trade union consequently acts to dampen participation, while in the ITU, membership interest and activities are the lifeblood of the party."

In the context of interpretations of the extraordinary asymmetry and highly stratified nature of the social distribution of knowledge, the thesis of the emergence of modern society as a knowledge society, as it were, is in danger of acquiring a peculiar elitist taint since the proportion of those who feel secure in their own ability to competently command knowledge resources, or who anticipate that they will benefit from the features of the emergent society, must be small and cannot possibly extend to the "masses" of citizens. Everywhere, it seems, the already powerful have understood the effective utility of knowledge advantages and the exclusive use of technical innovations.

However, the powerful, or interpretations that stress the "naturally" stratified consequences of serious deficits and astonishing surpluses in access to knowledge, have usually also overestimated both the security and the permanence of their knowledge advantage. Major societal institutions that assumed that their power base was secure now discover that their authority and influence has in fact been seriously eroded.

A further concern about the acceleration of knowledge advances and its impact on social relations, aside from the apprehension that there is a tendency to a concentration of knowledge and a lack of equality in the distribution of its socioeconomic benefits, is captured in the phrase that knowledge is somehow "frightening." For example, a few years ago, the so-called millennium bug was a reason, for many, for alarm and a sense of unease that "society is growing dependent on a lattice of technology that is now so far-reaching, interconnected, and complex that no one completely understands it, not even the priesthood that writes its digital code."[13] Michel Crozier ([1979] 1982:126) alludes to similar psychological reasons why people may be scared and dismayed by knowledge advances: "Knowledge implies the risk of change. It confronts people without concern for their wants or what they believe are

assumption is that party leaders are losing, rather than gaining, control over internal policy-making and agendas."

[13] The quotation may be found in "Computers and Year 2000: A Race for Security (and Against Time)," *New York Times*, December 27, 1998.

their needs. It throws the established intellectual and social world into turmoil." But does it do so universally?

The claim that knowledge advances pose a risk to established patterns of social stability and may threaten traditional belief systems is obviously associated with the conviction and expectation that scientific-technical knowledge is highly subversive of the status quo and most effective in dislodging such traditions. This claim is a corollary of the thesis that knowledge naturally flows to the powerful, that it has *conserving* consequences when examined from the point of the view of the powerful, and a *destabilizing* impact on those without power. The ways in which knowledge becomes an intimidating and frightening force are as a result attributed to its ability to negate traditional forms of knowledge and to enlarge and strengthen the grip on power of the already influential social groups. It follows that knowledge is not only seen as distributed in a highly stratified manner but also as presenting a zero-sum phenomenon that virtually displaces and eliminates the conventional knowledge mainly found and relied on in nonprivileged segments of society. In the final analysis, knowledge and knowledge advances affirm the centralization of cognitive authority in the hands of a few.[14]

The premise manifest in these observations, namely that the supposed societal monopolization of knowledge proceeds just as easily as that of capital or of the instruments of violence, will be questioned in principle in the following sections of this chapter. The thesis I therefore want to explicate is that it is much more difficult to withhold knowledge from others (see also Elias, 1984:251–252). But first it will be necessary to spell out the opposite but often stated hypothesis – based on different theoretical traditions – that there is symmetry between power and knowledge.

The inescapable bond of science and power

> The ownership of knowledge confers authority. This person can teach the others. The individual who claims authority, must therefore base it on knowledge. The knowledge function and political function cannot be separated, in the final analysis. Niklas Luhmann (1990:149)

---

[14] Crozier ([1979] 1982:128) describes some of the emerging convictions and relations – which he does not see as unique to our age, however, and which he goes on to reject – as follows: "The fact is that we do not seem to control anything anymore. Experts are everywhere, imposing limits, making people recognize their limitations, determining the right options. All important decisions are made by different technicians, who have no consideration for what people are going through. Some people think that eventually computers will be able to make all decisions without us."

By the same token, Michel Foucault's (e.g., [1975] 1977:32) major work is designed to display the complicity of knowledge in disciplining and repressing people. Knowledge and power are like Siamese twins: "Power produces knowledge; ... power and knowledge directly imply one another; ... there is no power relation without the correlative constitution of a field of knowledge, nor any knowledge that does not presuppose and constitute at the same time power relations."[15] But does the fact that knowledge and political authority are inseparable always benefit only a particular social stratum, namely the stratum of the powerful?

In spite of his critical reflections and the critical stance Michel Foucault assumes toward the powerful segments of society, he takes for granted, in his genealogy and archeology of social problems and topics such as madness, clinical medicine, the penal system, and sexuality, which blend the problems of power and knowledge, that each of the disciplinary sciences associated with these organized activities is "successfully" implicated in modern society's attempt to control and shape its citizens ("governmentality").[16]

What on the surface had been primarily a political and legal matter becomes invested with newly fabricated dimensions of scientific knowledge. Practical or political knowledge, like power, is a context-specific phenomenon. One needs to examine the sociopolitical practices in which knowledge is embedded. Foucault ([1969] 1972:194; also Foucault, [1975] 1977:305) thus describes his "knowledge-guiding interests" as follows:

Instead of analyzing this knowledge – which is always possible – in the direction of the episteme that it can give rise to, one would analyze it in the direction of behavior, struggles, conflicts, decisions, and tactics. One would thus reveal a body of political knowledge that is not some kind of secondary theorizing about practice, nor the application of theory ... It is inscribed from the outset,

---

[15] Nor is it sensible to expect, according to Foucault, that the conflation of power and knowledge can somehow be disentangled one day: "Knowledge and power are each an integral part of the other, and there is no point in dreaming of a time when knowledge will cease to be dependent on power ... It is not possible for power to be exercised without knowledge, it is impossible for knowledge not to engender power" (Foucault, 1977:15). The question Foucault's statement leaves open is of course who is exercising power, only the already powerful?

[16] Nikolas Rose and Peter Miller (1992:175) sum up Foucault's thesis of governmentality as follows: "Government is the historically constituted matrix within which are articulated all those dreams, schemes, strategies and maneuvers of authorities that seek to shape the beliefs and conduct of others in desired directions by acting upon their will, their circumstances or their environment ... Knowledge is ... central to these activities of government and to the very formation of its objects, for government is a domain of cognition, calculation, experimentation and evaluation."

in the field of different practices in which it finds its specificity, its functions, and its networks of dependencies.

Practical knowledge embedded in various discursive activities within different institutional settings is successively described by Foucault as a "political anatomy, a political economy, a discursive formation, a discursive disposition, and a political technology. Repressions and prohibitions, exclusions and rejections, techniques and methods bring individuals under surveillance" (Lemert and Gillan, 1982:60).

However, the power joined to knowledge and exercised by the modern state as "the political form of centralised and centralising power" (Foucault, 1981:227) in labeling, masking, censoring, segregating, prohibiting, normalizing, surveying, and oppressing (e.g., Foucault, [1975] 1977:304) its subjects by the powerful state is not total, but not quite enabling either. The conditions for the possibility of recalcitrance shown by the subject are not completely displaced; as a result, there are limits to the power exercised by state agencies (cf. Foucault, 1980:119). Although overly efficient, the knowledge/power axis, according to Foucault, is more complex and leaves room for enabling results among those that are oppressed. However, resistance as a *reaction* to the seemingly well-functioning social controls remains a blind spot in Michel Foucault's approach.[17]

The primary impression is that of the overwhelming power of knowledge embedded in the discursive practices of the state. Such a conception of the omnipotence of the state resonates strongly with much of the historical literature on empire that portrays the "overwhelming power of the early modern state in its relationship with subject people, be they members of lower social classes, bureaucrats, and administrators, or indigenous populations" (Edwards et al., 2011:1399). This impression cannot be set aside. Emphasizing, as Foucault does, the efficacy of knowledge attached to power and the extent to which it works by forcing

---

[17] Compare the conventional approach, however, with the work of David Collinson (1994:26), who has examined questions about the options, strategies, and forms of resistance (as a form of power) of subordinates in organizations (and not the issues of consensus, ignorance, or helplessness): "Why and how does resistance emerge? What discourse and practices constitute resistance? What resources and strategies are available to Those Who Resist? How do we evaluate whether resistance is effective or ineffective? What are the consequences of resistance?" Collinson (1994:49) emphasizes how knowledge and information as resources of resistance for subordinates are acquired and mobilized under certain organizational conditions for action: "Employees resist despite their insecure and subordinate organizational position and despite their never having full information and knowledge of future consequences." Further studies on the question of resistance in work organizations can be found in the anthology of Jermier, Knight and North (1994).

its imprints on subjects and society, it is difficult, if not impossible, to allow or account for the possibility of societal discontinuities. Power is enabling, if only because it has unanticipated consequences, but its agency for those who are subject to power appears to pale against the background of its productivity in stabilizing social figurations.

But Alain Touraine ([1992] 1995:168), in the face of this conception of the overwhelming power of normalization, asks with good reason: "Why reduce social life to the mechanism of normalization? Why not accept that cultural orientations and social power are always intertwined, and that knowledge, economic activity and ethical conceptions therefore all bear the mark of power, but also the mark of opposition to power?" (also Megill, 1985:140-252).[18]

In 1966, Michel Foucault published a book that was to become a philosophical bestseller in France, *Les mots et les choses* (translated as *The Order of Things* in 1970). In this book he examined biology, economics, and medicine, noting a fundamental transformation of each of them towards the end of the eighteenth century:

A monetary reform, a banking custom, a commercial practice can be rationalized, developed, maintained or dissolved each according to its appropriate form; they are always founded upon a certain knowledge: a dark knowledge that does not appear in itself in a discourse, but the necessities of which are precisely the same for abstract theories and speculations without any seeming connection to reality." (quoted in Paras, 2006:23)

This "dark knowledge" that informed all discourses he was to call *épistémè*, something that was unique to a historical period. During the eighteenth century the dominating *épistémè* was a tabular representation of reality. Anything that existed could be represented in tables. However, there is no trace of the subject who assembles these tables, a practice Kant was to ridicule as 'tabular reason' (*tabellarischer Verstand*). Foucault's conclusion was that there was no place for "man" in such an *épistémè*. Only with the advent of the modern discourse "man" moved to the center of the discourse. The implication was, for Foucault anyway, that with the end of the modern discourse man will again disappear "like a face in the sand at the edge of the sea," as he famously put it in the last sentence of *The Order of Things*.

---

[18] A very different critique of Foucault's position is put forward by Goldman (1999:34–37) who proceeds from an epistemological definition of knowledge that contrasts it against ignorance and error. Goldman maintains that the appeals to truth by political or social power used as instruments of domination or repression in many instances highlight abuses of scientific knowledge. Most of these appeals "were false, inaccurate, and even fraudulent" (Goldman, 1999:34). Moreover, truth claims can at times be used for "lethal purposes" and, at other times, for "progressive" ones.

In his next book, *The Archaeology of Knowledge*, Foucault develops a programmatic statement about the analysis of what he calls *discursive formations*: "Whenever one can describe, between a number of statements, such a system of dispersion, whenever, between objects, types of statement, concepts, or thematic choices, one can define a regularity... we will say... that we are dealing with a discursive formation" (Foucault 1972:41). Here he outlines his understanding of how knowledge and power, and discourses and objects in society relate to each other. Drawing on the example of madness he asks what it is that makes a discourse unified. He rejects the idea that there are objects out there that could be described more or less accurately through scientific language, as there cannot be "madness itself, [with] its secret content, its silent, self-enclosed truth." Rather, "mental illness was constituted by all that was said in all the statements that named it" (Foucault 1972:35). One cannot, therefore, speak of a discourse "concerning madness." The same logic applies to specific instances of madness such as neurosis or melancholia, so that it does not make sense either to speak of a "discourse concerning neurosis," or a "discourse on melancholia" as these objects come into being only through the discursive activities around the objects – the objects are in turn constituted by the discourse. Again, like in the above statement about human subjects, it is discourse that gives rise to something called objects.

Consequently Foucault rejects the idea that there could be a "prediscursive subjectivity," or experienced subjectivity that is "murmuring beneath the surface" and then taken up by scientific observation and research. Very much in agreement with the structuralists who were dominant in France at the time, Foucault asserts, "before all human existence, all human thought, there must already be a knowledge, a system, that we are rediscovering" (quoted in Paras, 2006:29). For him, the history of knowledge was "the unfolding of an anonymous process: a process of the formation and transformation of bodies of *statements* according to isolable rules" (Paras, 2006:34–35).[19]

---

[19] Eric Paras' reading of Foucault is based on Foucault's lectures at the *Collège de France* during the early 1980s. There he traces the development of Foucault's thinking in the context of his intellectual and social relations. The early dispute with Sartre, the events of 1968 and French leftwing politics, the Iranian revolution, the closeness to Deleuze, the long stays in San Francisco, and the rise of the *nouveaux philosophes* all had an important, even direct impact on his thinking. Foucault would go so far as to admit that his oeuvre lacked consistency, the only consistency being provided by his *biography* (see Paras 2006:146). Paras argues that each decisive conceptual turn in Foucault's work was provoked by the inadequacy of his theoretical framework vis-à-vis the political climate that surrounded his intellectual activities (Paras, 2006:11).

Foucault points out that this choice of terminology is for heuristic reasons, convenience, and to demarcate against the connotations of other established terms, such as science, ideology, theory, or domain of objectivity. One of the crucial tasks is to map the surface of the emergence of an object of discourse. It should be noted that it is not an object that is stable and therefore gives rise to a stable or unified discourse. It is the discursive practice that constitutes the object. Such a mapping will "show where these individual differences ... will be accorded the status of disease, alienation, anomaly, dementia, neurosis or psychosis ..." (Foucault 1972:45). He continues: "These surfaces of emergence are not the same for different societies, at different periods, and in different forms of discourse."[20] There are two more elements that are necessary for a discursive formation: specialized institutions (Foucault calls them "authorities of delimitation") and what he calls grids of specification (for example, the body, soul, or life history).

In the early 1970s Foucault took on board several political and theoretical concerns of some of his Neomarxist friends and colleagues. The resulting orientation was described as a move from *archeology* to *genealogy*. Here he fully engages with the problem of power on a theoretical level. In a discussion with his inspirator and interlocutor Deleuze, he told him: "We still don't know what power is.... And Marx and Freud are perhaps insufficient to help us to know this deeply enigmatic thing, at once visible and invisible, present and hidden, invested everywhere, that is called power. The theory of the State and the traditional analysis of the State apparatus do not, undoubtedly, exhaust the field of exercise of power's functioning" (quoted in Paras 2006:64).[21]

Discourses are linked to power and depend on knowledge. Foucault tried to escape a traditional conceptualization that interpreted power either in terms of violence or in terms of persuasion and ideology: "Now, power is not caught in this dilemma: either to be exercised by imposing itself by violence, or to hide itself, and to get itself accepted by holding the chatty discourse of ideology. In fact, every point of exercise of power is at the same time a site of transformation: not of ideology, but of knowledge. And on the other hand, every established knowledge permits and assures the exercise of power" (quoted in Paras 2006:113). What we see here is a concept of both power and knowledge that acknowledges

---

[20] There is an interesting parallel to Neurath's program of physicalism in sociology. Social scientists should investigate (and only investigate) events in space and time, look at statements that describe and classify them and look for consistency between statements.

[21] By the late 1970s Foucault's sympathy for Neomarxist analysis had vanished, largely after he aligned himself with the *Nouveaux philosophes* who had forcefully attacked the Marxist legacy in Stalinist Russia.

their generative potential (for good or bad). Foucault says that it does not make sense to see power as separate from or opposed to knowledge. Knowledge enables power to be exercised and power transforms knowledge. There is no basis for a distinction between knowledge and ideology; there is no true knowledge behind the veil of ideology.

One of Foucault's central theses was that modern industrial society emerged with the emergence of the social and human sciences. These provided the knowledge base for disciplining the workforce into a system that depended on their collaboration. The prison and the hospital, surveillance, and madness were the crucial places and issues to analyze. The books, entitled *Birth of the Clinic* (*Naissance de la clinique*) and *Discipline and Punish* (*Surveillir et punir: Naissance de la prison*), are programmatic. The term discipline is understood in a double sense: on the one hand, it is the practice of disciplining workers and citizens; on the other hand it is the discipline-based knowledge that enables power holders to discipline workers, which means that it does not make sense to separate knowledge and power. Both are fused; one cannot be exercised without the other. There is no truth that speaks to power but knowledge that has been created by the powerful to serve their purposes. Admittedly, this is a slight overstatement not necessarily borne out by Foucault's texts (although he made statements to this effect in comments and interviews). Foucault preferred to speak of the simultaneous emergence of concepts and practices, or discourses. Nevertheless, the constellation he describes by the knowledge/power nexus has strong functionalist overtones, something he would later abandon.

Eventually Foucault was to replace the concept of power/knowledge with the concept of government, a move that, according to some observers, was connected to a more general reorientation toward recognizing subjectivity (Paras, 2006). Using the power/knowledge terminology during the early 1970s, Foucault was led to an "extremist denunciation of power ... hence the question of government – a term Foucault gradually substituted for what he began to see as the more ambiguous word, 'power'" (Pasquino 1993:79, qtd. in Dean 2001:325). Thus he came to see power as a creative force that enables subjects to act upon each other in flexible relationships. He reserves the term *domination* for the repressive, unidirectional, and rigid form of power. Domination leads to a limitation of possible action since the margin of liberty is extremely limited. What Foucault then called domination is akin to what Weber and others had called power.

In an interview with Paul Rabinow, we find a description by Foucault of his own work. He says that to a certain extent he tries to analyze the relations among science, politics, and ethics or, more precisely, "how these processes may have interfered with one another in the formation of a scientific domain, a political structure, a moral practice" (Foucault 1984:386). He gives the example of psychiatry: "I have tried to see how the formation of psychiatry as a science, the limitation of its field, and the definition of its object implicated a political structure and a moral practice: in the twofold sense that they were presupposed by the progressive organization of psychiatry as a science and that they were also changed by this development. Psychiatry as we know it could not have existed without a whole interplay of political structures and without a set of ethical attitudes" (Foucault 1984:386–387). He then goes on to explain that he followed the same methodological principle in his studies on madness, delinquency, and sexuality, that is, "the establishment of a certain objectivity, the development of a politics and a government of the self, and the elaboration of an ethics and a practice in regard to oneself." He calls these three dimensions "fundamental elements of any experience" – namely (1) a game of truth, (2) relations of power, and (3) forms of relation to oneself and to others. Foucault makes the point that prevailing accounts were emphasizing only one dimension while the other two were screened out. With psychiatry, the organization of knowledge took center stage, crime was seen as a problem for political intervention, and sexuality was designed above all as an ethical problem. "Each time I have tried," Foucault says, "to show how the two other elements were present, what roles they played, and how each one was affected by the transformations in the other two" (Foucault 1994:387–388).[22]

A further transformation in Foucault's interpretation of the relation between knowledge and power occurs in his later work, specifically in his 1977 lectures at the *Collège de France*, and under the influence of the work of the *nouveaux philosophes* and his observations about the revolution in Iran. Michel Foucault's reflections now center on the subject and the changing forms of subjectivity in modern societies (see Foucault, 1982:211–212). The self-determining subject that has gained in significance also for him as a person now influences his professional point of view and thus allows him to let go of the strict symbiosis of power and knowledge (see Paras, 2006:105–116). Having in mind this radical change in his late theoretical approach, the statement that in modern societies liberty is a daughter of knowledge is no longer a utopian idea for Foucault.

---

[22] Elsewhere Michel Foucault admits that all three elements of any experience were present only in *Madness and Civilization*, and even there in a "somewhat confused fashion." Truth was prominent in *The Birth of the Clinic* and *The Order of Things* while power was studied in *Discipline and Punish* and ethics in *The History of Sexuality* (Foucault 1984:352).

The new knowledge classes

Under the general and ambivalent heading of the knowledge *class*, various more or less recent conceptions may be jointly discussed that share the idea that either the producers or the suppliers of knowledge form a social class based on their collective ability to control the production and supply of knowledge.[23] The power base of the new social class is not a socioeconomic one but can be attributed to the individual competence and creativity of their members. The knowledge monopoly achieved may result in socioeconomic and political advantages. Cleavages and conflicts between the new knowledge classes and the rest of society develop. But what is decisive for the role of the knowledge classes is their capacity to control the production and supply of knowledge.

Unlike the discussion about the role of experts in modern society, the discourse on knowledge classes does not tend to be (natural) science- and technology-centered, since the knowledge classes also include knowledge producers from the social sciences and the humanities, as aptly exemplified by Helmut Schelsky's discussion of the "meaning producers" as a new class.

The idea that such a class not based on either capital or labor evolves in modern society has been discussed under various headings. I will confine my discussion of the new concentration of knowledge to four examples of the knowledge class: (1) the meaning producers, (2) the informational producers, (3) the creative class, and finally, (4) the global class, a term more recently suggested by Ralf Dahrendorf and reserved for new forms of social inequality in contemporary societies.

The meaning producers

Helmut Schelsky's work belongs to the genre of *Zeitkritik*, that is, of a critical analysis and, typically, condemnation of certain political and social trends. Paradoxically, but also characteristically, such treatises are not intended solely for the specialist (although the substance of

---

[23] The concept of knowledge class is ultimately only a subset of the idea of a *new class*. Daniel Bell ([1979] 1980) has critically examined the origin and the various approaches of the theory postulating the emergence of a new class, as far as the latter was seen to be forming in the decades before the end of the seventies and the beginning of the eighties of the last century. Bell ([1979] 1980:164) concludes that his own diagnosis of a transformation of capitalism does not owe anything to the influence of a new class, but rather to a number of major societal changes in the postwar period, such as the growing importance of state power or the increasingly dominant hedonistic culture: "In seeking to map the course of social change, one should not mistake the froth [the new classes] for the deeper currents that carry it along."

Zeitkritik often amounts to an intellectual infighting among specialists). On the contrary, an appeal is made to public discourse at large, and many arguments resonate with traditions of general political and intellectual interest.

Schelsky argues that in all advanced industrial societies, we are witnessing the emergence and consolidation of a new collectivity of educated individuals who deal in information, knowledge, and meaning; in contrast to Alfred Weber or to Karl Mannheim's conception of socially unattached intellectuals, Schelsky's modern intellectuals, who monopolize new means of power and control, begin to form a distinct social class as the result of antagonistic social relations with all those who are merely in the business of producing socially necessary commodities. It is in the interests of the new class to mystify such antagonism and prevent it from being widely interpreted as a form of class struggle; at the same time, there is a corresponding interest in maintaining the fiction that the old class struggle continues.

The ideological confrontations conveniently hide fundamental secular societal transformations, in particular the emergence of a class of meaning-producers and legitimators who attempt to gain power by controlling the consciousness of others. *A new caste of priests* (the class of *Sinn-und Heilsvermittler*; see also Lapp, 1965:3; Roszak, 1972:263) is evolving in industrial societies, and with it new forms of authority relations and modes of organization and governance, but most importantly a new message or doctrine of secular salvation. To borrow a phrase from Stephen Engelmann (2011:168): "In the guise of serving the people they [the new class] in fact govern them."

Because of the effect on the deep structure of thought the new class is said to command and impart, the notion of ideology, we are told, is much too superficial to capture the nature of these developments. As a matter of fact, only a vocabulary that makes explicit reference to the otherworldly dimension (the impact on the soul, for example) and to historical precedents of these social formations can at all hope to be adequate. In other words, what in effect is occurring according to Schelsky is the spread of a new "secular" religiosity. Thus, any sociological analysis of these phenomena will have to reckon with the metaphysical dimension of these intellectual and social transformations of modern society. From a social evolutionary perspective, these changes represent a step backwards in history because the accomplishments of the age of Enlightenment are definitely threatened by the new "intellectual clergy."

These arguments offered by Schelsky are based on an extension and combination of Max Weber's theory of authority and power relations and his sociology of religion (as well as on certain assumptions about the nature of human nature adapted from Helmut Plessner's and Arnold Gehlen's philosophical anthropology). Schelsky maintains that there is a strict parallel between authority/power ultimately derived from the threat of physical coercion and authority/power based on intellectual means, namely the creation and control of meaning (*telos*) for individual or collective self-conceptions. This kind of influence over others is but another manifestation of control and engenders its own peculiar forms of organization and legitimation. But *Machtausübung durch Sinngebung* is by no means a phenomenon peculiar to the historical epoch of the dark ages. In its most recent historical manifestation it takes on the form of a secular "doctrine of salvation" (*Heilslehre*) authored by the new class of meaning producers in contemporary society.

The new secular religion now has reached its second- or third-century *post Marxum natum* and is about to produce, as was the case in conventional religion and theology, its own organizational structure. But what exactly is the substance of the new social religion, why is there such a strict parallel to religious doctrines, and what is its promise for the disciples?[24] The promises of secular salvation essentially consist of future "heavenly" (societal) conditions in this world; that is, of the total abolition of fear and suffering, violence and blows of fate, humiliation and insult, poverty and illness, and power and exploitation (socialism). At the same time, the message contains an incentive to turn away from present realities (thus, the others do the work). The realization of this set of promises also is identical with the ultimate fulfillment of *individual* self-realization (emancipation).

Who is part of the new class of secular priests?[25] They are what Schelsky calls the *Reflexionselite*. However, he maintains that most of the conventional sociological means of differentiating social groups (e.g., social classes or social strata, societal functions performed) including the notion of intellectuals are categorizations that are largely useless for identifying the elite in question because they all neglect or are unable

---

[24] Schelsky's (1975:76) promise for the social scientists is that "one of the most exciting intellectual and social developments of the coming decades, perhaps the coming century, will be how these doctrines of salvation and their needs for power will attempt to become dominant in advanced industrial society, how they will, in a cancerous manner, attempt to subvert and to destroy the existing rational institutions of modern society."

[25] For the purpose of this brief account of the new knowledge class as the class of meaning producers, I will not deal with Schelsky's lengthy and polemical attempt to theoretically and empirically justify his idea that we are indeed witnessing the emergence of a new *class* made up of meaning producers and legitimators; moreover, a class that it also engaged in a class struggle with those employed in the production of commodities in industrial society. Suffice to say that Schelsky argues that all of the essential characteristics of the traditional conception of class apply to the social formation of the *Reflexionselite*.

to take into account the social religiosity as an essential element of the struggle for spiritual domination among contending groups. The groups in question are, instead, best defined as *Besinnungs- oder Bekenntnisgruppen* (groups with distinctive creeds or convictions). Members of these groups typically also fulfill important social functions (especially in the domains of secondary socialization and of information, thus assuring considerable social influence) in their capacity as teachers, engineers, social scientists, authors, journalists, broadcasters, priests, and so forth, but subordinate these functions to their particular world-views in an attempt to gain wider control. The groups must be differentiated with respect to the ideas they hold.

There are four main sociostructural reasons for the very possibility of domination by these groups: (1) the increased complexity of all social relations in modern society (requiring new means for the reduction of complexity – Niklas Luhmann – for example those based on motivational considerations); (2) the transformation of (higher) education that no longer combines a moral and a scientific discourse and therefore produces a "normative" vacuum; (3) the elimination of the separation of the private and the public spheres of social life (work and politics); and (4) the genesis and distribution of "information" of particular significance to modern society that positions typically occupied by members of the new class involve. These developments in turn correspond to social changes that increase the receptivity for the new doctrines of salvation. Finally, the main organized opposition and competing world-views are likely to be found in science and technology, the existing political leadership, and the established churches.

The last part of Schelsky's treatise, entitled "Anti-Sociology," deals with his thesis that the intellectual and social origins of the disposition to preach are linked to the nature of the education of the new *Reflexionselite*, in particular the extent to which education today is governed by the canons of "abstract science." However, the main villain in all of this is sociology. We are told that the emphasis on a *sociological perspective* (e.g., its "dissolution of the person") as such is a fertile ground for the emerging secular religion and the said ambition of the new class of meaning producers to achieve power. And to the extent that sociology becomes the key science of the modern era (since in all types of societies "inner-directed" individuals give way to "outer-directed" men), as Schelsky is firmly convinced will be the case, the social and intellectual developments he has outlined become more consequential. An analysis of the core of the ideas advanced by sociologists and of the occupations that have embraced these ideas (e.g., theologians, educators, journalists) provides an insight into the main intellectual sources and the substance of the neo-theological doctrines. The question Schelsky wants to pursue most of all is the extent to which such sociological "indoctrination" will transform the views of the incumbents of professions who perform increasingly important functions in contemporary society into what Schelsky calls the "possibility" to gain control over most other members of society.

The question already signals its answer, but it also indicates that Schelsky's book is indeed a unique analysis of the practical consequences of sociological knowledge in modern society. According to Schelsky, these effects on the conscience collective are enormous and will only lessen as sociology itself is reduced, which Schelsky hopes it will be, to the status of an esoteric scientific discipline engaged in nothing more serious than the development of pure (formal) theory.

The central importance of sociology derives from the intellectual influence it has had on all other scientific disciplines and activities which aim at an understanding of meaningful social actions, relations and objects. Even the natural sciences, especially when they are applied, do not seem to be able to escape the influence of the sociological perspective. But why is it that theologians, students or art and literature, historians, journalists, writers, educators and so forth are in fact engaging in sociology? The answer simply is that a discipline which reflects the spirit of an age, the prevailing self-conception of an epoch, its dreams and hopes necessarily comes to represent *Herrschaftswissen*.[26] Also, such knowledge generated by an interest in domination gives rise to new forms of authority, now exercised by the class of meaning producers and mediators. The emerging new forms of domination, according to Schelsky, will ultimately affect all aspects of everyday life in modern society. The new forms of domination are instruction, care and control, and planning (*Belehrung, Betreuung, Beplanung*), which can be expected to gradually replace the traditional forms of power, namely political and economic subjugation and exploitation. In short, those who used to educate now dominate.

Does the domination of the sociological perspective indeed mean that sociologists exercise authority? Can one really assume that intellectual influence alone can be translated into power? Schelsky seems to think so, or at least fears that this will happen. How would such domination be legitimized? Perhaps it is thought to be self-legitimating.

---

[26] The term *Herrschaftswissen*, first introduced, as far as I can see, to social science and explicated in some detail by Max Scheler ([1925] 1960:60–69), has an affinity to the notion of knowledge generated by what Jürgen Habermas ([1968] 1971:308) has called the technical cognitive interest.

It is quickly evident that Schelsky's provocative analysis is weakest at and on this very point. One senses that Schelsky would have liked to have the evidence to convict for conspiracy. But then he points out that the practical outcomes of sociological reasoning he describes are often unintended, unanticipated, and unplanned. And as Schelsky admits, the new classes of meaning producers still lack class-consciousness. Nonetheless, the consequences of sociology, in particular its neo-theological perspective, are constitutive of the sociological orientation itself. Schelsky also indicates that the various social developments which bring about the elimination of the independence of the person as a person may well be irreversible. The very predominance of sociology under these circumstances prevents any serious examination of intellectual alternatives, although Schelsky's own polemic would indicate that there still is a measure of autonomy. Sociology today is what theology was in the medieval age or what philosophy was in the eighteenth century. But Schelsky is far from merely advancing a modern version of Comte's law of the three stages. Of course, he is denouncing sociology and issues a strong warning about the excessive influence of sociological knowledge on modern consciousness. Sociology, Schelsky feels, is often directly responsible for the very discovery and intensification of social conflict. Last but not least, sociological knowledge incorporates practical means of orientation, general enlightenment, and a vocabulary for the comprehension of life and therefore has had a most eminent impact on the nature of modern society. As a result, sociology finds itself in a paradoxical position, demystifying the authority of traditional authority but failing to question its own.

Schelsky's pessimistic assessment of sociology's effect on everyday life and on the individual, in particular, is closely linked to his description and evaluation of the historiography of social relations and to what he considers a deplorable reversal in society to a kind of latter-day organic solidarity. The debate with Schelsky therefore should primarily be on this level. It should be concerned with the ethics and the politics of developments characteristic of contemporary society and with his conservative stance on the nature of evolving social relations in this society that, Schelsky feels, eradicate many of the achievements of bourgeois culture. In other words, Schelsky appears to both draw on and distance himself from the theorists of the postindustrial society. For he stresses, with Rudolf Bahro, Radovan Richta and Daniel Bell, the growing importance of knowledge and assumes, as they do, that power is shifting into the hands of the educated. Yet, against postindustrial theorists and perhaps postmodernist theorizing, he champions a rather traditional theory of society that has to be defended against the onslaught of the new class of knowledgeables. Public policies may indeed and more often than not fail; but the language of the sociological imagination succeeds in practice.

The informational producers

In a series of imaginative and empirically grounded studies, Manual Castells (1996) suggests that modern society from the 1980s onwards constitutes a new form of society, a network society, and that the unity in the diversity of global restructuring has to be seen in the massive deployment of information and communication technologies in all spheres of modern social life.[27] The innovations in the field of communication and information technologies therefore represent, not unlike the eighteenth century industrial revolution, a major historical event and a fundamental change in the material as well as the social structure and culture of society. Echoing what has been generally stated in its most uncompromising form by Marx, the transformation of the "material culture" of modern society on the basis of the information revolution since the decade of the 1980s amounts to a historically new formation of capitalism (cf. Castells and Henderson, 1987).[28] But Castells also emphasizes that the reshaping of advanced capitalism cannot be reduced to a manifestation of mere capitalist interests.

According to Castells, the new society or network society in which the state continues to occupy a decisive function[29] is the result of a new technological paradigm and therefore a dynamic process that is propelled

---

[27] Employing Castells (2009:24) own definition, "a network society is a society whose social structure is made around networks activated by microelectronic-based, digitally processed information and communication technologies."
[28] In contrast to much of the discussion of the contentious idea that we are entering or already living in a postmodern era, for example, Castells reflections on modern societies as network societies have the distinctive merit to incorporate a discussion of the (material) conditions for the possibility of the transformation of industrial society into a network society. On the material foundation of postmodernity and its neglect in theories of postmodernity, see Stehr, 1997. Castells (2000:381) defines the new social structure of the information age as the network society because it is made up of "networks of production, power, and experience, which construct a culture of virtuality in the global flows that transcend time and space."
[29] According to Castells (1996:13) observations, the state apparatus continues to play an active and significant role in the emerging network society because it mediates in definitive ways between technological developments and societal changes: "The role of the state, by either stalling, unleashing, or leading technological innovation, is a decisive factor in the overall process, as it expresses and organizes the social and cultural forces that dominate a given space and time." The application and use of the new technologies, as Castells and Henderson (1987:5) emphasize elsewhere, "are basically shaped" by capitalist policies and, therefore, by a restricted economic logic that is dramatically enhanced in turn by the "power of the new technological means" at its disposal.

by information processing, or informationism. Given Castells' description of the network society with its essential dependence on the operation of communication technologies, one question that arises is in what way, if at all, his term of network society differs from that of the more frequently used concept of modern society as an information society.

The difference to which Castells himself points and which, in his self-assessment, constitutes a progressive conceptual step in our analytical understanding of modern society as well as a theoretical model of the information society can be explicated in analogy to the distinction between "industry" and "industrial" and refers to distinct conceptions of information and informational. At first glance, such a differentiation would not appear to yield much in the way of differences. According to Castells (1996:21) the difference between information (society) and informational (society) refers to distinct ways of viewing and knowing. The concept of information or, as he also calls it, the "communication of knowledge" implies nothing more or less than the assertion that information is of importance in all possible social formations or represents an anthropological constant found in all human societies. In contrast to information, "the term informational indicates the attribute of a specific form of social organization in which information generation, processing, and transmission become the fundamental sources of productivity and power, because of new technological conditions emerging in this historical period." Information becomes an immediately productive force (cf. Stehr, 1994: 99–104). It is of course in this organizational context that the concept of informational producers becomes relevant.

Castells therefore locates the term information on the same logical level as knowledge; both are only on the surface attached to social action while the concept informational refers to the probability that social conduct is affected in its inner constitution by information and that the social organization of social action is transformed on the basis of the utilization of information.

The close alliance of Castells' theory of society with the development of information and communication technologies as well as his conscious conflation of knowledge and information[30] make it rather difficult to

---

[30] Castells (1996:17) emphasizes for example why he cannot detect any persuasive reasons for disagreeing with the reductionist definition of (theoretical) knowledge advocated by Daniel Bell (1973:175) in his theory of postindustrial society. "Information technology" is defined by Castells (1996:30) in a manner that resonates in important respects with the term scientific work ("I also include in the realm of information technologies genetic engineering"; perhaps one might add climate science, cognitive science, econometric modeling, and impact assessment as further examples) and therefore with scientific fields that are reminiscent of Bell's conception of theoretical knowledge.

detect any decisive and robust differences between the notions of information and network society.[31] After all, for most observers, the information revolution is understood as a technical one, in the first instance. The gadgets change but not the sociocognitive frames, immediately productive knowledge, the language of entitlements, and scientific regimes.[32]

Castells' brief discussion of the stratum of informational producers occurs in the context of changing social class relationships in the network society. The new system of class relations in the network society is characterized, first, in terms of income and social status by "*a tendency to increased social inequality*" (Castells, 2000:375; Friedman, 2008:53–55). Second, processes of social exclusion not only affect disadvantaged groups but growing numbers of individuals and groups who struggle after having fallen down the ladder of social inequality. Third, if information and knowledge are the main sources of innovation, then "the new producers of informational capitalism are those knowledge generators and information processors whose contribution is most valuable to the firm, the region and the national economy" (Castells, 2000:376). The production, processing, and transmission of information is embedded in organizational contexts. Thus, the informational producer "includes a very large group of managers, professionals, and technicians, who form a 'collective worker'" (Castells, 2000:376). According to Castells, in OECD countries, the informational producers account for about one-third of the work force. The rest of the labor force is employed in jobs in which they are potentially replaceable by machines. The informational producers do not need the underclass of workers.

Castells does not indicate if or how the informational producers translate their economic influence into political power. Nor is there any

---

[31] The same deliberate ambivalence applies to Daniel Bell's definition of a post-industrial society and the idea of an information society while, at the same time, there is a strong definitional affinity to Castells' concept of the network society. The post-industrial society is, as Bell (1976:46) stresses, "basically an information society. Exchange of various kinds of data processing, record keeping, market research and so forth is the foundation for most economic exchanges ... Data transmission systems are the transforming resources of the society, just as in an industrial society created energy – electricity, oil, nuclear power – is the transforming element."

[32] Although Castells is not an explicit proponent of technological determinism, it is almost unavoidable to discover a number of ideas in his study that tend to resonate with the model of technological determinism, stressing the context-insensitive consequences of technical products rather than the social processes of innovation and deployment. It is self-evident that technology plays a crucial role in the modern life-world and in the course of economic "progress." However, technology also needs to be examined not from a "disembodied" perspective but with the help of a conception that is cognizant of the social conditions within which it emerges and is employed.

indication in Castells' analysis that the informational producers display a preference for democratic political norms and engage in organized political action to establish and sustain democratic principles in the political realm. In analogy to the transmission of energy, Castells stresses the transmission of information and power but not the transformation of power in network societies: "The power of flows takes precedence over the flows of power" (Castells, 1996:469).[33] It would appear that informational producers are prepared to serve any political master.

Who appropriates the value or the surplus added by the informational producers? In comparison to industrial society, nothing changes in network societies. The employers who hire the informational producers appropriate the surplus although the process of appropriation is more complicated than it is in industrial society. The appropriation is more complex because the informational producers are not organized, employment relations tend to be individualized, at times informational producers are self-employed, and the remuneration depends on the development of fragile financial markets. It follows that the relations between employers and informational producers does not resemble class contradiction, and the informational producers cannot be seen to constitute a class-in-itself or even for-itself. The fundamental social conflicts of the network society are those between informational producers and the underclass of workers.

True enough, the modern economy has been fundamentally retailored by the spread of computers and digital technology. With the advent of information technology modern society has become a network society. Castells suggests that the term network society is a more adequate description of modern society than is the talk of information society because the concept of network society highlights major organizational changes that go along with the technological transformation in the economy and society. It seems to me that the difference between the more established although now declining idea of modern society as an information society is not as large as Castells thinks. Both the ideas of network society and information society rest on premises that resonate with technological determinism.[34]

---

[33] By "flows" Castells (1996:412) means the "purposeful, repetitive, programmable sequences of exchange and interaction between physically disjointed positions held by social actors in the economic, political, and symbolic structures of society."

[34] For an affirmative and differentiated discussion of technological determinism within the context of large-scale transformations of the socioeconomic order of society – and beyond, see Heilbroner ([1967] 1974, 1994). For Heilbroner ([1967] 1994:65), "technological determinism is ... peculiarly a problem of a certain historical epoch – specifically that of high capitalism and low socialism – in which forces of technical change

The perspective of technological determinism can be countered by the following observations: First, in a number of developed economies, highly skilled labor appears on the scene before the dissemination of the modern information technologies. Second, the increasing importance of highly skilled labor is not a reaction to demand for such labor but, rather, the outcome of an autonomous (i.e., societally driven) supply shift. And, third, information technology actually helps entrepreneurs and managers to catch up with and reverse the rising labor costs implied by this supply shift. Therefore, the productivity paradox can help us to understand that we are not faced with a technology-driven transition from industrial to informational society or something of that kind, but rather with a societally driven transition from an industrial to a knowledge society (cf. Stehr, 2000, 2012). In this sense, then, we have entered a new modernity. The particular strength of Castells' analysis of modern society extends to observations about the nature of the new modernity rather than its antecedents.

The creative class

The claim that a new class is emerging has been repeatedly made after the end of World War II. Among the more recent theoretical perspectives that ascribe considerable social influence and authority to a particular social stratum is the idea that we are witnessing the emergence of a "creative class" and therefore a new social class in modern societies. The source of this straightforward yet elusive assertion about the emergence of a new creative social class is Richard Florida's (2002) *The Rise of the Creative Class*. Florida weaves biographical accounts and professional arguments, moving freely from I and we to they, into a chatty mosaic of the lifestyle preferences of a well-educated generation that prefers to stay right where they received their higher education.

In more or less strict analogy to prior societal formations, feudalism and industrial society, the members of the creative class, "purveyors of creativity," are the dominant social class in a distinctive phase of capitalist development. The activities of the creative class in contemporary society represent the basis for the possibility of economic growth, which indicates that Florida's idea of a creative class is first and foremost an economic notion based on the kinds of work different occupations typically carry out or are expected to perform. As his empirical indicator of the

have been unleashed, but when the agencies for the control or guidance of technology are still rudimentary." For an analysis of the function of technological determinism in historical discourse, see Misa (1988).

size and the growth of the creative class, Florida employs the occupational classifications of the *US Bureau of Labor Statistics* (which, by the way, were already used with similar intentions by Fritz Machlup [1962], in his study of the transformation of the labor market, to calculate the size of knowledge-based occupations). On the basis of this approach that makes it difficult to generate international comparative analyses (Lorenz and Lundvall, 2011:271–273), Florida (2002:75) estimates that the creative class increased from 10 percent of the workforce in 1900 to 30 percent in 1999.

According to Florida's (2002:x) description, he was engaged in a locational analysis of economic growth and concluded that "economic growth was occurring in places that were tolerant, diverse and open to creativity – because there were places where creative people of *all* types wanted to live." Location still counts but not in the sense in which location was important in the past, when accessibility to natural resources or transportation opportunities mattered. Now, location is important for attracting and holding on to talented, creative members of the labor force.

The economic revolution that allowed for the emergence of the creative class is what many observers from economics to sociology and from Daniel Bell to Peter Drucker have variously described as the knowledge-based economy, as it is now most commonly designated. The term knowledge-based economy signals that knowledge becomes an intangible core factor of the production equation alongside the more traditional factors of production such as land, labor, and capital. The transformation toward a knowledge-based economy is driven by significant changes in the nature of the labor force. The "owners" of the new factor of production, knowledge, constitute a stratum of considerable economic and presumably much more elusive political influence. Florida's uneven account of the creative class follows much the same path. Thus, his designation of membership categories of the creative class follows and incorporates previous accounts of the labor force that now also includes "knowledge workers," "symbolic analysts," "experts," and "professional and technical workers." In addition to previous descriptions of the kind of labor these strata typically perform, Florida (2002:68) proposes such characteristics of the creative class as the ways in which these individuals and their families organize and live their lives, including of course their worldviews and identities. The upshot of these reflections on the nature of the modern economy is of course that the *supply* of creative talent rather than investment in brick and mortar, plants, and equipment counts when it comes to identifying the source of economic growth and the success of regions and communities.

The creative class 239

The many comments the notion of the creative class has attracted have exclusively focused, following the intention of Florida, on the economic and practical political implications of the hypothesis. The general as well as practical appraisal of Florida's thesis about the creative class then rests, first, on defining who are its members.[35] Second, any assessment of the presence or the absence of members of the creative class in fostering regional economic advantages hinges of course on a more precise specification of the exact (causal) *connection* between the supply and the presence of creative class member and economic growth: "Does a vibrant cultural scene *cause* local prosperity ... or is it the *consequence* of local prosperity" (Polèse, 2011)?[36] Third, what accounts for the perhaps growing supply of members of the creative class?[37] None of these questions has really been satisfactorily answered. The definition of the membership is essentially ambiguous. The causal linkages between some of the empirical indicators of the social environment such as community tolerance that are seen as conducive in attracting or retaining members of the creative class in specific communities and economic growth are ambivalent.[38] The analysis of the dynamics of the changing pool of the creative class remains to be carried out (cf. Drucker, [1968] 1992, 1993; Stehr, 2000).

Since the discussion about the creative class has primarily focused on its economic role in modern society and secondarily on their impact on

---

[35] According to Richard Florida (2003:8) the creative class whose function it is to "create meaningful new forms" is stratified and contains two main clusters of occupations, the "super-creative core," including scientists and engineers, and "creative professionals" who work in a wide range of "knowledge-based occupations." Upward mobility is possible. The membership of the creative class is biased toward the top of the societal inequality rank order. Florida (2003:8) estimates that the creative class "now includes some 38.9 million Americans, about 30 percent of the entire U.S. workforce – up from just 10 percent at the turn of the twentieth century and less than 20 percent as recently as 1980." The empirical proxy for the creative class is not – as is the case for human capital – educational attainment but occupation, which in addition to the level of schooling captures an individual's "accumulated experience, creativity, intelligence, innovativeness and entrepreneurial capabilities" (Florida, Mellander and Stolarick, 2008:616). The creative class depends on an underclass of service workers trapped in low-end jobs, the working or service class that is poorly paid because these jobs do not require creative skills (Florida, 2002:322).

[36] www.city-journal.org/2011/21_4_urban-development.html (accessed December 23, 2011).

[37] It would appear that Richard Florida (e.g., 2002:70) favors a *demand type* of explanation for the growth in volume of the creative class; he notes, for example, that "as the creative content of other lines of work increases – as the relevant body of knowledge becomes more complex, and people are more valued for their ingenuity in applying it – some now in the Working Class or Service Class may move into the Creative Class and even into the Super-Creative Core."

[38] See Sands and Reese (2008); Hoyman and Faricy (2008); Pratt (2008).

everyday life in the communities and regions where its members may be concentrated, the present political role of the creative class remains in the dark. The political Florida (2002:68) concedes that the creative class is not a class-for-itself, that is, they do not (as yet) consider themselves as "a unique social grouping" with a distinct class consciousness aware of common interests. But are they even a class-in-itself? As Florida (2002:315) notes, "a little more class awareness would be a healthy thing." Thus, much of the political role of the creative class is confined to an uncertain future. The creative class is the natural and only possible stratum of leaders of the twenty-first century.

However, Florida (2002:316) is hopeful that the creative class can live up to that destiny. It has the capacity to generate *"new* forms of civic involvement appropriate to our times." The promise of collective politics at some future juncture would appear to represent a fragile prediction in light of some of the essential attributes of the creative class, first and foremost its rejection of and objection to the organizational age. The members of the creative class strive for individuality, loose ties, anonymity, diversity, openness, and authenticity and not to commonalities, let alone conformity. Preferences of this kind would not appear to make for a fertile ground for political influence and action.

The global class

The origins of the emergence of the global class, as Ralf Dahrendorf (2000) describes it using the term in the classical sense of the concept of social class, are to be found among the profound social, political, and economic consequences of the end of the Cold War in the late decades of the twentieth century. It is not that these events or the bipolar world they displaced represent the forces that allowed for the emergence of the new global class, but the end of the Cold War permitted them to evolve manifestly and more rapidly. The processes Dahrendorf has in mind are of course usually described as the globalization process. In conjunction with Dahrendorf's reputation as a conflict theorist, he stresses the contradictions and antagonisms of the economic and social forces brought about by globalization.

The decisive new forces are informational assets and the technologies (computerization, digitization, miniaturization, satellite communication, Internet, and fiber optics) that in principle assure worldwide access to these assets. The proper designation of the society that is evolving therefore is that of an information society. Equally real is the control exerted by those who form the power elite of the information society. New forces create new interests. The globalization process brings about the new global class with its unique class-specific consciousness,[39] its optimistic outlook and message of hope. Although the dominance and victory of the global class is not assured, neoliberal economic policies with their distinct emphasis on deregulation define and promote the interests of the global class. The emphasis on personality traits extends especially to creativity, flexibility, initiative, education, and innovation.

The power of global classes due to the control exerted by them over the resources of the information society is immense. The global class "has turned us into hostages, and the more 'advanced' countries are, the less resistance they meet." Our society is a slave to the global class. Although the ruling class is not omnipotent, they have definitely set the tone in many areas of the world community since 1989 (Dahrendorf, 2000:1039). With the rise of the global class and the dominance the class exerts in the knowledge economy, there will be a momentous change in the amount of socially necessary labor (see also Stehr, 2002). Dahrendorf (2000:1064) calls it the age of capital without work. The work society (*Arbeitsgesellschaft*) disappears. New forms of inequality are central to emerging forms of social conflict in a society that runs out of work.

In Chapter 6, I want to explore the thesis that knowledge as a capacity for action plays an important part in political resistance rather than having a primary function in suppressing political opposition or in cementing and perpetuating entrenched social, political, and economic hierarchies that are seen to rest on a liberal convergence of knowledge and power. The union of knowledge and power as discussed, for example, in social classlike relations of meaning producers, the creative class, or the global class, implies that knowledge in whatever form functions as a major hurdle to democratic governance. In light of the various assertions about the concentration of knowledge resources in modern society, the answer to the question posed at the beginning of my inquiry can therefore only be that knowledge impedes democracy. The opposite thesis is at the heart of the following section. Hence, the focus will shift to the power of civil society's common sense, the everyday knowledge or knowledgeability of ordinary citizens. However, before turning to the question of knowledge as a "weapon" of the weak of society, I will give a brief summary of some of the reasons for the power of knowledge as described in this chapter. What, then, accounts for Max Weber's firm observations about knowledge-based authority, or Robert Michels' iron law of oligarchy, or Michel Foucault's views on the symbiosis of power and knowledge?

---

[39] Rosabeth Moss Kanter (1995) refers in her study of the emergence and attributes of the *World Class* to the consciousness of a new cosmopolitan stratum rich in concepts, competence, and contacts.

There are two relevant issues I would like to take up in response to this question. First, why is it that knowledge is appropriated by the politically powerful, but not by the weak, and why is this knowledge powerful and very effective, even though it really only represents, as defined by me, the capacity to act? The answer to the first question is relatively simple. It needs power to monopolize knowledge and effectively deploy knowledge. The transaction costs for the acquisition of knowledge, let alone the resources needed to deploy knowledge, are simply too high to reach for vulnerable populations, enabling them to afford the fruits of knowledge.

The second answer to the question of the conditions that make for the power of knowledge refers to a related line of argument that points out that the special social significance of scientific findings is a function of the unique reliability, objectivity, reality, and conformity of the incontrovertible knowledge claims articulated in the scientific community. In short, it is about the *scientificity* (*Wissenschaftlichkeit*) of scientific knowledge. The thesis of the special characteristics of scientific knowledge has, in the meantime, been greatly demystified. The differences between everyday knowledge and scientific discoveries are not as dramatic, and scientific findings are often essentially contested assertions, their development and interpretation is influenced by nonscientific or political judgments. I am thinking, for example, of climate determinism as a more or less common belief in everyday life that is by no means absent from climate research (see the most recent article in *Nature* on civil conflicts and global climate change). In short, scientific knowledge is fragile, and this fragility may be described, from the perspective of democratic governance, as one of the virtues of scientific knowledge claims.

In any case, it is evident that whatever conditions are responsible for the power of knowledge, different social constraints affect the dissemination of knowledge in society and impede or enhance the role that knowledge plays in a democracy. One of the barriers I would like to talk about next is addressed in the following question: Is it possible to reconcile democracy and expertise? Concern about the gap between expertise and democratic governance in the political sphere is of course rooted in the premise that the citizens' right to democratic governance should not be restricted, and the expert should not have more influence than the layman. The question of the authority/power of expertise, presumably derived from the objectivity of experts' knowledge, should incorporate the question whether it is possible to directly infer instructions for political action from scientific statements.

6 The knowledge of the weak

> The state ... derives no inconsiderable advantage from [the] instruction [of the inferior ranks of the people]. The more they are instructed the less liable they are to the delusions of enthusiasm and superstition, which, among ignorant nations, frequently occasion the most dreadful disorders ... They are more disposed to examine, and more capable of seeing through, the interested complaints of faction and sedition, and they are, upon that account, less apt to be misled into any wanton or unnecessary opposition to the measures of government.
> Adam Smith [1776] 2000)[1]

> Die Lethargie dem Staat gegenüber ist keine Naturqualität, sondern wird zergehen, sobald dem Volk vor Augen steht, daß es wirklich selber der Staat ist und daß dieser kein spezialistisches Ressort der Politik bildet, das Fachleute für den Rest der Menschheit verwalten sollen.
> Theodor W. Adorno ([1951] 1986:292)

The practice of democracy requires, following the ideal conception of democracy, the "development" and the presence of an "intelligent" public capable of raising, engaging in, comprehending and deciding on political issues. What exactly does such an ideal and such a practice mean? Does it mean, as George H. Mead (1923:244–245) stipulates, that the "advance in the practice and theory of democracy depends upon the successful translation of public policy into the immediate problems of the citizens"? Or does the ideal of democratic governance call for the participation of the possibly largest number of enlightened individuals in the political affairs of a society?

If one follows, on the other hand, the prevailing view of attributes of the practice of democracy, and some observers would surely assert that such a claim is a realistic perspective, one tends to encounter a liberal mix of four arguments: (1) Not only is knowledge power but the powerful are knowledgeable; (2) the public is ignorant; (3) the exercise of power is

---

[1] See also the essay by James Alvey (2001) on the moral theory of Adam Smith and the plea by Smith for the development of a curriculum on ethics in business.

cemented through the control of relevant scientific findings by the powerful; and (4) the effective political participation of citizens is therefore seriously damaged. These arguments are not easily separated. In sharp contrast to the widespread thesis of the disenfranchisement of citizens in many societies, we observe the opening of political decisions toward a broader social participation through the development of relevant legislation – for example, on regulatory issues of any kind, testing, or construction activities at many levels within legitimate political processes (see Jasanoff, 2003:397–398). Keeping these emergent and growing developments in mind, I immediately confess, as I will explain in detail, that I do not share the discouraging thesis about the inevitable political enslavement of the individual in modern societies.

Expectations about the prerequisites for effective political participation in a democratic society and the desired rate of participation clash, of course, sharply with actual observations of forms of "mass apathy" of citizens between elections and robust empirical findings indicating that most citizens in democracies are poorly informed about politics and fail to care or be concerned about their lack of political information (Converse, [1964] 2006). One of the first observers of such a state of practical political affairs was the British academic and politician Lord Bryce (1901:331–334) who, in 1901, examined the case of America. Many empirical inquiries and voting statistics since then and especially after Word War II document the secular decline in voter participation. The decline in many OECD countries has been a steady one, and in some instances the trend has accelerated. In the early 1950s, Morris Rosenberg (1951:506) characterizes the fact that from a fifth to a third of the eligible voters in the United States abstain from voting in most elections and devote little if any time and energy to efforts to influence the politics of their country as a case of "truly monumental apathy" (also Rosenberg, 1954–1955).

Economists have a ready-made explanation for the dynamics of democratic markets (cf. Wittman, 1989) and the state of contemporary political participation. A "rational citizen" model of political participation in democratic markets (*homo politicus*) is of course a considerable abstraction from the politics as really practiced. Nonetheless the rational-citizen approach has some appeal for theorists who attempt to fashion the nature of political conduct in analogy to standard economic reasoning, ultimately in pursuit of an economic theory of democracy. The abstract rational citizen, as Anthony Downs (1957:7–8) for example has argued, is a person who "approaches every situation with one eye on the gains to be had, the other eye on costs, a delicate ability to balance them, and a strong desire to follow wherever rationality leads him." A central issue within the model of rational political conduct is the question of obtaining knowledge and information for the narrow purposes of the decision on how to vote and how to influence policy making in the periods between elections[2]; simply phrased: Decision making requires information and the acquisition of information involves transaction costs. It is therefore not entirely surprising, as one would infer from the rational-citizen approach, that both in theory and in fact the widely observed lack of information among voters is based on these assumptions.

The main costs involved in acquiring information in the context of Downs' model would be the time invested to assimilate data and to weigh alternatives as well as to gain access to other resources needed to gather and assess relevant information. The cost of accessing and employing information in any complex society is stratified, for example, by education or income. The efficiency with which information is used is also dependent on status. The information obtained and evaluated begins with and is governed by selection criteria, rules that determine what information is useful and what information is not. As Downs (1957:212) recognizes, although voters in modern democracies defer to "specialized agencies that gather, interpret, and transmit such information," the individual still needs to mobilize his or her own selection rules. Presumably, in an effort to apply and extends Downs' approach to the observed secular decline in participation rates at least at the ballot box in many democratic societies, one would have to point to the rapid increase in formal schooling of the population in these societies as the root cause for the persistent rise in abstaining from formal political participation and the decline in political trust toward democratic institutions in modern societies?

What information is it rational to acquire? The common assumption is that political information "is valuable because it helps citizens make the best possible decisions" (Downs, 1957:258). Selection rules are rational according to Downs' economic model of political decision making "if application of them provides him with information that is useful for making decisions which help bring about the social state he most prefers" (Downs, 1957:213). Downs also asks how much information it is rational to acquire. Following the rule of marginal cost-return logic, the "information-seeker continues to invest resources in procuring data until the marginal return from information equals its marginal costs" (Downs, 1957:215). In general, Downs' (1957:259) model leads him to conclude that "it is irrational to be politically well-informed because the low returns from data simply to do not justify their cost in time and other

---

[2] For the purpose of his analysis, Downs (1957:208) treats knowledge and information (data) as interchangeable terms, as is widely customary within economics.

scarce resources." The end result of Downs' rational model of political conduct and the utility of information for individual citizens is that "true political equality is impossible even in democracies as long as (1) uncertainty exists, (2) there is a division of labor, and (3) men act rationally" (Downs, 1957:259).

What fundamental criticism can be leveled at the model of rational political behavior? Immediately obvious would be a reference to and a critique of the assumptions of the rational approach to political conduct that describe a certain social status of the *homo politicus*. The voter who is behaving rationally is not unlike the rationally acting consumer: she is a social being that is largely isolated (and therefore more easily subject to manipulation by advertising) or, to give the critique a positive twist, she is an independent actor who primarily follows her own world view.[3]

However, as the majority of empirical studies of political conduct in democratic societies show – starting with the classical inquiry *Personal Influence* by Elihu Katz and Paul Lazarsfeld (1955) – the model of rational political conduct completely bypasses the decisive importance of social networks (*social context*) or the function of core value orientations[4] but also of other communication options (cf. Richey, 2008) or the timing of political messages (cf. Chong and Druckman, 2010). Individuals are not merely passive recipients of "stimuli" that originate from their environment. Varied social networks of actors count as their immediate, influential political environment. Political judgment formation is codetermined by the presence of such social networks. Some social networks might even enhance the political judgment of citizens (Kuklinski et al., 2001:411–412). But much of our preference formation and decision making is not active and carefully calculating; instead, it tends to be habitual, repetitive, and coupled to "history."

Downs (1957:7) accepts the critique that the image of the rational voter in the context of his own thought experiment is an "abstraction from the real fullness of the human personality"; the individual political actor is anything but a "calculating-machine." She is not a robot since

---

[3] For a more extensive critique of the assumptions of the rational economic actor in general and the rational consumer in particular, see Stehr (2008).

[4] Voters (or consumers, tourists, students, etc.) do not decide in a one-dimensional manner. For example, as Kuklinski and colleagues (1982:629) point out in a study examining the attitudes and the voting behavior of the American public toward the nuclear industry: "People do not decide as compartmentally as the preceding analysis implies. Arriving at the polling booth to vote on a nuclear energy initiative, they do not bring with them cost-benefit calculations, cues from reference groups, or core values; they bring them all. The unanswered question is how important is one decision making mode vis-à-vis the others. The call is for a model that simultaneously enters all potential influences on citizens' policy choices."

the future remains uncertain and unknown in the ideal model of rational opinion formation and political decision making. Nonetheless, even the diminutive self critique by Downs of his image of the rational voter indicates that his abstract individual appears to be a rather isolated human being with inherent limitations to any sophisticated political participation.

Another relevant consideration within the context of the debate about the function of declining political participation rates would be the idea that low political skills/information of individual citizens, political apathy, and a low turnout of voters in many democracies are a valuable, political stability-generating factor. Some contemporary theories of democracy that focus on the operation of the democratic system as a whole (e.g., Pateman, 1970:7; Sartori, 1962) refer to the functionality of the political apathy of the majority of the population in democratic societies and therefore tend to argue that actual participation rates are adequate in order to guarantee the stability of democracies. Such assessments of the political consequences of low interest and low participation move their normative views close to the observations of Walter Lippmann in the 1920s. Lippmann was convinced that the effectiveness and stability of the political system should take precedence and that expertise and elites are a much more likely guarantee of political stability than the participation of the great majority of voters who are uninformed in any case.

Theoretical (that is, mathematical) and experimental research carried out by an ecologist and an evolutionary biologist (Couzin et al., 2011) also focuses on the role and the influence of uninformed actors on collective decision-making processes and raises the question whether the inordinate influence of a self-interested and opinionated minority can be lessened by increasing the proportion of uninformed participants in the decision body, thus achieving a "democratic consensus" that best reflects the range of preferences, however weak they may in fact be.

The experiments reported by Couzin and his colleagues pertain to fish known as golden shiners (*Notemigonus crysoleuca*), but the authors suggest that their results may extend "to self-organized decisions among human agents" (Couzin et al., 2011:1580). The reported results of the fish experiment indicate that "uninformed individuals ... inhibit the influence of a strongly opinionated minority, returning the control to the numerical majority" (Couzin et al., 2011:1579). Hence, "uninformed individuals (defined as those who lack a preference or are uninformed about the features on which collective decision is being made) play a central role in achieving democratic consensus" (Couzin et al., 2011:1578). As the experimenter adds, with uninformed agents, the collective decision more and more resembles or regresses to that of the majority (of uninformed subjects). The decision of individuals is governed by conformity with the (behavioral) preferences of agents that are in the majority.[5] Whether the theoretical and empirical results allow for an extension to the decisions made by humans is doubtful, if only because the experimental conditions are rarely as transparent in social contexts as they appear to have been in the experimental design at hand. Moreover, it is not too farfetched to assume that the appeal of such normative assessments and experimental results of the political functions of uninformed actors and minorities proposed by political theory refer to a society that has perhaps existed in the past but does not reflect the realities of contemporary society.

It therefore is important for any consideration of the role of knowledgeability, knowledge, and information in democracy to move from the microsocial front to macrosocial attributes of modern political life. As the *excursus* on the dispute between the state of New York and the City of New York about the financing of public education illustrated, the question of how much knowledge democracy needs and how expensive it should be is not only a matter of individual choices and costs but a matter of the function of major social institutions in society. Hence, I will discuss the role of political action in modern knowledge societies. Knowledge societies provide the macrosocial frame for the nature and the possibility of political action in contemporary societies.

Political action in knowledge societies

> The democratization of the will of the state generally lacks the appropriate democratization of the knowledge from which to act.
>
> Otto Neurath ([1908] 1998:120)

On an abstract,[6] ahistorical level, the assertion that knowledge enhances democracy and liberties sounds promising and convincing yet it collides, on the one hand, with really existing political conditions in modern societies as reflected in the institutional development of modern politics and, on the other hand, the contention that the elective affinity of knowledge and freedom fails to take the dynamics of the production of knowledge into consideration. I will begin with the present. More precisely, I will first refer to diagnoses of the nature of democratic societies

---

[5] The results and the interpretation of the results of the experiments carried out by Couzin and his colleagues resemble, to some extent at least, the so-called theory of spiral silence by Elisabeth Noelle-Neuman ([1968] 1984). The theory postulates the readiness of many individuals to follow or join the views of the apprehended majority of views on a given public issue.

[6] I have discussed the governability of modern knowledge societies in previous publications, for example, in *The Fragility of Modern Societies* (Stehr, 2001).

that represent the prevailing view among professional observers of the development of democracies in much of the postwar era. Next, I will make reference to the dynamics of knowledge production in modern societies and the question of its importance in public affairs as well as the role of the public in political decision making in light of the growing significance of highly specialized knowledge claims in political action.

The conditional vulnerability of the privileged groups is evident not only in the counter mobilization of citizens but also in the decisions of business and others to commit or recommit substantial organizational and financial resources to shaping debate in Washington after a series of defeats. Put another way, the constraints on the power and dominance of business motivated their decision to expand their investment in influencing public sentiment and policy after the 1960s (Jacobs, 2010:249).

More specifically, in this section of Chapter 6, I plan to examine how the transformation of modern societies into knowledge societies has a fundamental impact on the nature of their political system. But I do not merely want to reiterate the assertions made several decades ago, especially by political scientists, about the declining governability of modern society as a result of increasing demands on state institutions and the general expansion of the functions of the state. This is the well-known problem of corporatism. Observers at the same time generally expressed regret about the loss of power of the state and set out to search for compensatory mechanisms to make up for the power deficit in order to enhance what government can do. However, the search for such mechanisms to reassert state authority is no longer typical. Instead, the loss of state efficiency and competence is today typically seen as linked to the decline in the autonomy of the nation-state. In particular, this decline is said to result from an economization of society, that is, a displacement of politics by the market (see Habermas, 1998), new transnational political (e.g., ecological and financial) issues, the new regulatory environment for state action and, last but not least, by various features and consequences of the globalization processes. One of the outcomes of the influence of the sum of these forces may also be, as Phillipp Genschel and Bernard Zagl (2008:430) observe, that "political authority today in the Western worlds is also exercised by non-state actors." This observation about the role of the state does not change the persistent centrality of the power of the state (Genschel and Zagl, 2008:430–413) as the manager of societal authority relations, its ability to decide, organize, and legitimize.

Hence, some of the most recent debates about the governability of contemporary societies share with their predecessors a distinctive state-centered perspective and an emphasis of what government should do.

The disempowerment of the state, however, is now seen as a hopeful sign. For example, it offers a much-needed response to the international linkage of political problems, and an impulse for the practice of transnational political functions. Moreover, a more comprehensive discussion of the dynamic relation of the state to its citizens, which would exceed the scope of this study, needs to be mindful of the emergence of specific sociocultural traditions and experiences in different societies that continue to affect the ways in which individuals relate to government and the state to its citizens.

The absence of what Theodor Adorno ([1951] 1986:291) has called state fetishism in the Anglo-Saxon world and the persistent presence of the remnants of the *Obrigkeitsstaat* – the feeling that the state apparatus is something different from themselves – in German-speaking countries is a case in point for culturally specific social forces. The presence of a sphere of officialdom, the alienation of many individuals from the state combined with their ready acceptance of its authority are not characteristic of attitudes and conduct toward the state in every society. Distinct experiences and traditions concerning the societal role of the state evidently affect governance and the speed with which the state responds to fundamental social changes and demands issued by civil society and based on social movements for more participatory politics (see Hisschemöller, 2005) as well as the resistance against systemic economic and political trends in modern societies (e.g., Roberts, 2008).

I will try to show, referring also to a number of recent attempts to theorize governability in modern society – without prominently invoking the transfer of competence beyond the borders of the nation-state or the irrelevance of the national boundaries in light of the global linkage of economic, ecological, and cultural processes – that there are major societal developments that are systematically underrepresented in discussions of the governance of modern society.[7] These developments are connected to and codetermined by the general extension of the capacities and capabilities, in the sense of knowledgeability, of individual citizens. The extension of knowledgeability heightens the political consciousness of citizens, increases their ability to pass political judgments, and enhances their expectation and proclivity to participate in political decision making by demanding more effectiveness, transparency, and

---

[7] A discussion of the newly prominent but imprecise or contested term "governance" may be found in Rhodes (1996) who distinguishes among at least six current usages of the term. The focus here is on the practical effectiveness of government or the activity of governing in an effort to tackle political problems of the day, whatever form it may take in practice.

accountability from those who govern at different levels of governance, which in turn "extends" the nature of the modern political community.

Another line of argument concerning the decline in the autonomy of the nation-state is Niklas Luhmann's more recent disparaging thesis about the difficulties of steering complex societies composed, as it were, of increasingly differentiated autopoietic social systems. Closed and self-referential communicative institutions such as the economy, law, science, and religion have inherent difficulties in intervening in each other's affairs (e.g., Luhmann, 1987:135). Luhmann's approach fails to concede that actual and perceived state intervention is now a routine matter. More fundamentally, any inquiry into governability must address the efficacy of state intervention as judged against the political objectives of government itself. The government's efficiency will be assessed in terms of its ability to competently execute specific policies, for example in attempts to come to grips with the financial crisis, reduce unemployment, enhance economic growth, combat anthropogenic climate change, increase social solidarity and the integration of minorities, police knowledge, reduce violent crime, and so on. Such a perspective does not necessarily ask whether intervention and government performance works well as judged in relation to an efficient allocation of market resources (cf. Wittmann, 1995), as economists assert for the workings of the economic market.[8] Judgments of the efficacy of government performance instead should be linked to apprehended advances made in relation to specific policy issues such as mobility, resource efficiency, the reduction of corruption, accountability, transparency, or educational goals. Perceived effectiveness of government performance in democratic regimes likely is a reason for the degree of popular support for democracy (see Magalhães, 2013).

Finally, I do not want to investigate in any detail the national political effects of powerlessness as suggested by the rather common as well as ambivalent observation about the growing complexity not only of societies but the world, nor the thesis that many problems indeed are overlapping, wicked problems (cf. Rittel and Webber, 1973). The observation that the

---

[8] My analysis at this point therefore follows a more functional rather than normative conception of democratic government. The normative perspective emphasizes rights, and participation as a means of ensuring democratic rights. The functional construction stresses the possibility of a peaceful, competitive change of "elites." Competition does not take place for the sake of competition but is seen as a mechanism that optimizes the allocation of scarce political competence and the legitimacy of political decisions (cf. Eder, 1995). Although I emphasize outcomes or the lack thereof, I do not mean to advocate a purely instrumentalist approach. Outcomes after all are also a matter of interpretation, symbols and process.

political problem of governance is affected by the growing complexity of the world dates back to the 1970s. The outlook appeared to be pessimistic: is it even possible, it was asked, to design social institutions that "will be able to govern a world of incredibly growing complexity" (Skolnikoff, 1976:77), let alone imagine that it might be possible, under these conditions, for the public to have any chance whatsoever of constraining and controlling the activities of large societal institutions (Fung and Wright, 2001)?

What I want to explore instead in more detail is that modern society as a knowledge society tends to produce and enable many more, and much more knowledgeable, actors to enter the political system than ever before. In this context, the question of the form any such participation may take is also of great importance (cf. Salisbury, 1975). For example, is public opinion polling a meaningful and effective proxy for more immediate and direct political participation?[9]

The chances of the state or other large social institutions of effecting and maintaining social closure (Weber, [1921] 1978:314–343), that is, their ability to control or even monopolize and deny access to resources on the basis of social attributes such as gender, class, generation, ethnic, or national origin declines in a significant way.[10] People's ability to make choices, demand accountability, and resist decisions made for them by major social institutions – that is, their ability to "govern" the course of their life and therefore become more involved in political affairs – is not necessarily the intentional outcome of a democratic political system's desire to enhance actual political involvement and active citizenship given their commitment to the right of citizens to take part in the governance of society. Although such legal prerequisites and individual capacities are necessary for an efficient or "rational" functioning of economic markets, I do not claim that an efficient political market is on horizon as well, even as the role of the state is being redefined in many countries. Legal frames are, of course, one of the foundation stones for legitimate political participation and intervention.

---

[9] For an early and thoroughgoing critique of polling and the notion of public opinion based on polling, see Blumer (1948). Public opinion polling fails to grasp the social character and the power relations of society. Similarly, Bourdieu ([1973] 1993) criticizes the naive assumptions of public opinion polling and the resulting distortions, especially the very creation of public opinion with the help of polling.

[10] A directly opposing view, as for example developed by Mettler (2007) and Mettler and Soss (2004), emphasizes the importance and priority of state policy for the political attitudes of citizens in modern societies: "Government programs and rules make up a basic and persistent presence in the lives of modern citizens. Policy analysts routinely examine the social and economic consequences of such programs, yet their political effects continue to be widely ignored" (Mettler and Soss, 2004:64).

On the contrary, as a result of new resources now commanded by many individual and collective actors, politics is becoming more fragile and the mutual linkage between power and resistance become much more evident (see Barnett and Duvall, 2005:22; Adler and Bernstein, 2005:296). The basis for social solidarity in modern society needs to be closely examined. In particular, one needs to ask whether knowledge, as a constitutive principle of modern society, can offer, possibly along with the foundations for sustainable economic growth, the basis for social solidarity or, rather, contributes to the breakdown of solidarity and of the institutional arrangements that in turn sustain such solidarity.

The growing number of individuals who command and utilize their knowledgeability in political contexts[11] does not imply that these developments signal a fundamental conflict or clash between different logics of societal development, for example, one driven by strictly "material" conditions and the other by what might be called "sociocognitive" or symbolic forces. The developments I want to describe occur in knowledge societies with social structures in which a shift of priorities from the substructure to the superstructure processes of society can be observed.

Until quite recently, social scientists – as has been demonstrated for the social science debate about the genesis and dominance of the technical state (Stehr, 1994:203–221) – were preoccupied with chronicling the immense and allegedly inevitable growth of certain functions of the state, for example, in health care, education, science and technology policies, and redistributive programs. This chronicle included an attendant focus on the centralization of power in society, the expanding economic role of governments, the enlarged role of governments as employers, and the immeasurably grown function of public welfare. These developments, equally evident in societies with very different political regimes and leaderships, were seen as a result of specific sociostructural necessities of modern society, for example of the growing complexity of economic systems and the increasing differentiation of societies more generally.

The transformations observed and analyzed by social scientists made reference to the fact that modern governments controlled half or even

---

[11] In my view, one empirical manifestation of this process is the manifest and robust growth in the share of the votes, at least in European elections, in favor of nontraditional political parties that did not even exist twenty years ago. A more pessimistic interpretation of the same trends could be that the decline in the voting share of traditional political parties both on the left and on the right wings of the spectrum signals confusion, irritation, and frailty of political commitments among the voting public (see Dahrendorf, "New labour and old liberty-comments on the third way," *Neue Zürcher Zeitung*, July 14, 1999, p. 7).

more of the national product. The large state control of economic resources profoundly affected the context within which modern politics occurred and societies were governed.[12] The fascination with social, economic, and cultural forces that appeared to rationalize, concentrate, consolidate, and centralize led to such perceptions of the structure of the technical state as those sketched by Herbert Marcuse and Helmut Schelsky. The singular focus on the technical state deflected attention from structures and processes that sustain cleavages, conflicts, diversity, loss of power, traditional norms, and plurality. In addition, as the enumeration of some of the topics already indicates, the dominant social science discourse with its focus upon the governing of modern societies was to a remarkable extent oriented to factors and forces that favored concentration and, in addition, was preoccupied with economic transformations and their impact on political developments. As Herbert Marcuse (1964:48) feared, the "decline of freedom and opposition is not a matter of moral and intellectual deterioration or corruption. It is rather an objective societal process insofar as the production and distribution of an increasing quantity of goods and services make compliance a rational technologic attitude."

Any discussion of the modern political system, political participation, political representation (see Burns, 1999), public trust in politicians and government, civic engagement as well as political realities and ideas, especially within the framework of knowledge societies, must, in contrast to the focus on the institutional structures of governance, be cognizant of the profound transformation of the modern economy: The widespread and unprecedented affluence generated by the modern economy has produced a general decline in the fortune of purely economic concerns. The transformation of modern economy has also been manifest in the substantial growth of work as a knowledge-based activity, especially among the politically active social strata. Political participation, and this includes a deliberate choice to abstain from participation as well as a redefinition of participation, is more effective if it is grounded in knowledge.

Many observers of present-day politics have recognized the importance of such changes and consequently focus their analysis on, for example, the proliferation of "new" social movements, the extension of the public sphere or the influence of "new" political ideas and not merely material interests, on policy formation and government action. Innovative ideas in the form of new "world-views" and the growing ability of

---

[12] Whether the proportion of the national product is itself a valid indicator of the state's role in intervention and redistribution remains in considerable doubt.

knowledgeable social strata to shape the agenda of political struggles in terms of their own, as well as collective, emerging interests may be seen to increasingly structure politics in modern societies (cf. Weir, 1992). The challenge of emerging social movements is not a "revolutionary attack against the system, but a call for democracies to change and adapt" (Dalton, Kuechler, and Bürklin, 1990:3).

At one level, new social movements and capital reflect the emergence of novel problems and commitments such as "postmaterial" values (see Inglehart, 1997a:52–54). Prominent new sites of political struggle of course are the natural environment, new issues of inequality, consumption patterns, or novel risks linked to enhanced capacities to act discovered by science and technology. The task new social movements typically set for themselves is to demand a more open, accountable, and transparent political process. At another level, cognitive skills and the ability to effectively intervene in the political process of large societies are an important dimension of voluntary political mobilization and activity.

My discussion of the politics and the "governability" of knowledge societies will initially concentrate on what are the increasingly traditional and perhaps even obsolete criteria of efficacy as practiced by the nation-state. The question of the internationalization, and even "globalization," of politics will be taken up in the subsequent section. Politicians continue to assert their firm grasp of the realities of the world and to claim that the most consequential changes are as always the result of political interventions. It is exactly this confident assertion that needs to be examined.

Governing knowledge societies

> One aspect of [the] new world political culture is discernable: it will be a political culture of participation.　　　Almond and Verba (1963:14)

The governability and immobility (or the temporary inability to govern) of modern democracies is, in the eyes of those who point toward this condition and describe it, always also a moral crisis. My interest in the discussion of the problem at hand, however, does not originate in any way from concerns over the collapse of the political authority of the modern state or from the search for alleged scapegoats to be held responsible for the dangers connected with the collapse of social support for the democratic state. Also my focus does not extend to therapies of these alleged conditions, particularly if they are in turn connected with fundamental doubts about the constitution of the liberal state, especially the "absolute" guarantee of freedom and equal rights that – considering the broader political difficulties of the state – are described as undermining the healing, instrumental, responsible, and disciplined citizens.

The following perhaps somewhat ambivalent warning by Wilhelm Hennis (1977:16) – issued well before the matter of the serious consequences of global warming for human civilization (e.g., Dryzek, Norgaard, and Schlosberg, [2011] 2013) was widely discussed[13] – is in some ways representative of views that may be interpreted as a justification for a dismantling of constitutional rights in an attempt to improve the capacity of the state to impose its will:

> Since all conduct, even existence itself, is based on our opinions, it is self-evident how difficult governing is or can be in communities based on absolute freedom and equality of all opinions ... It is self-evident that the vast challenges now or soon faced by humanity and individual political systems can only be met with an unusual degree of *discipline, energy and moral stringency*" (emphasis added).

In the end, systemic attributes of the liberal state, for example the expansion of its social expenditures as well as other problems it confronted, are held responsible for the crisis of democratic government of the industrialized world and its practical impotence. Thus, "what Marxists erroneously ascribe to the capitalist economy is in reality [seen as] a result of the democratic political process" (Huntington, 1975:73). The conservative German historian Ernst Nolte (1993) shares such a diagnosis and calls it a merely realistic appraisal of modern liberal politics. As Claus Offe ([1979] 1984:81), voicing his strong opposition to such views, stresses: "In the conservative world-view the crisis of governability is a disturbance in the face of which the false path of political modernization must be abandoned and nonpolitical principles of order, such as family, property, achievement, and science, must again be given their due." A return to the past, especially to the early modern or even premodern world that derived its coherence from an adherence to centralized, hierarchical, and patriarchal religious sanctions, is of course an absurd demand.[14]

---

[13] Dryzek, Norgaard, and Schlosberg's ([2011] 2013:3) observation that "climate change presents perhaps the most profound challenge ever to have confronted human social, political, and economic systems" is by no means a lonely voice in the assessment of the nature of the societal impact on and challenges for the governance human civilization might experience in a few decades as the result of the impact of climate change on governance.

[14] I do not intend to reduce the question of politics in the knowledge society to a mere *technocratic* matter (a diagnosis of political realities that has fallen into disrepute since the 1960s; see Brooks, 1965:58 and Bell, 1971) by asserting, for instance, that one of the most urgent requirements is to effectively reduce the backwardness of the social sciences in order to generate a "healing" kind of practical social science knowledge, that is, a form of social science knowledge as the technical know-how capable of solving urgent political and moral issues of the day that have otherwise been settled. Harvey Brooks (1965:68),

The thesis of the decreasing governability of modern society implies, at first glance at least, that groups and individuals who, harboring feelings of powerlessness, either still recall the former extensive and unassailable power of the state or have effectively resisted, deflected, delayed, and altered governmental decisions, now experience a greater sense of power. Those in power may well experience their inability to effectively cope with immediate problems as a loss of authority, for example as the result of a withdrawal of normative consent by the public.[15] Since governability has mainly been examined from the perspective of the state, namely in terms of the agency of the state and its loss of political authority, most diagnoses first and foremost refer to a crisis brought about by the disappearing legitimacy[16] of governments.[17]

Such diagnoses not only neglect to consider the gains and benefits of "ungovernability," but also typically fail to examine the reasons for the decline in the efficacy of the state, other than an alleged withdrawal of consent. It is also assumed that the *status quo ante* was characterized by extensive political state authority and that ineffectiveness gives rise to a loss of consent rather than the reverse. In addition, much of the literature tends to be silent on the "concrete objects of conflict that constitute the substance of the demands and expectations as they do about the character of those matters requiring regulation" (Offe, [1979] 1984:79).

Efficacy is about the ability to get things done and about the limits of what government can do.[18] It is not merely about decision making, but also about implementing decisions. To get things done means to be more or less in control of the general circumstances within which objectives

at the height of the most recent widespread advocacy of technical solutions to political issues, would argue that in the realms of both political affairs and knowledge, the search must be "for manageable apolitical reformulations of problems [since] ... the problems of political choice have become buried in debates among experts over highly technical alternatives." Technical ways of coping with contentious political issues is hostile to democratic participation and therefore by definition excludes everyone but the experts.

[15] As Rose (1979:31) asserts, "consent and effectiveness are inter-related, for the success of any public policy requires the co-operation of affected citizens."

[16] The change in the foundations of the legitimacy granted to the modern state includes, as some critics have stressed with particular force, an uncoupling from transcendental conceptions (cf. Hennis, 1977:18–19).

[17] Theodor Schieder's (1977:40) definition of the lack of governability reflects this preoccupation quite well: "Ungovernability ... means that the executive is paralysed and unable to act ... A so-called *legitimation crisis* may result from a *lack of consensus* among citizens due to a *loss of confidence* in the state."

[18] For almost two centuries, Peter Drucker ([1989] 2003:55) notes, "we hotly debated what governments *should do*. We almost never asked what government *can do*. Now increasingly the limits and function of government will bet the issues."

need to be achieved.[19] Thus, a decline in governability primarily occurs as a result of a loss of control over conditions and circumstances of political action. Not only are government objectives extended in modern society, but the ranges of circumstances to which they apply are enlarged as well. In addition, the circumstances within which political objectives are realized are changing together with the subjects of these circumstances. Moreover, these varied circumstances are to a lesser extent than in the past subject to the control of state agencies. The recalcitrance of circumstances generally has risen. The relative loss of sovereignty or territoriality of the nation-state is but one element in the equation that produces a heightened recalcitrance of the conditions of political action.[20]

Fundamentally, however, the experience and perception of "ungovernability" is linked to political conduct and administrative procedures that still aim to realize objectives based on the premise that changes in the recalcitrance of circumstances can be neglected as irrelevant or might in principle be overcome.[21] In other words, the demystification of the state and the disenchantment with traditional modes of political representation, as well as the broad loss in confidence in governments, does not necessarily go hand-in-hand with a general cynicism about any kind of government. The conviction that the loss of efficacy of government can be recaptured, or that the contradiction between expectations and performance can be overcome, is still widely present among the public in

---

[19] The distinction between social integration and system integration, or between rules that are followed by individuals and regularities at the collective level that are self-implementing, is discussed by Offe ([1979] 1984:83), whose description of the loss of efficacy of the state takes both of these dimensions into consideration: "Social systems may be said to be ungovernable if the rules their members follow violate their own underlying functional laws, or if they do not *act* in such a way that these laws can *function* at the same time" (Offe, 1979:313).

[20] More generally, the developments we have sketched have frequently been described as a rise in the complexity of the conditions of political action (e.g., Skolnikoff, 1976). Often included in this description is a reference to the growing, frequently involuntary, importation of problems into nation-states and the rising "outer direction" of possible political responses (cf. Hennis, 1977).

[21] Friedrich Tenbruck (1977:135) refers to a now widely existing or modern "restricted consciousness" among citizens about the limits of the malleability of the conditions of action; past convictions about and experiences with the *limits* of the extent to which conditions of action may be changed has disappeared because such limits had been declared obsolete, by some observers, in light of the allegedly growing ability of the political system to rationally plan and control political conduct (anything is possible), or because experiences with any practical limits have become increasingly scarce in everyday life since we live in a world that is preplanned and beyond our control. *Individual* experiences involving our inability to influence the conditions of action have become uncommon: "What one person is unable to accomplish, maybe collectively all can, and what one person does not know, science may be able to explore."

developed societies (see Panitch, 1993:3). The accelerated, "home-made" transformation of society has generally lowered the sensitivity toward evolving limits and barriers against further, especially radical transformations of society. The limits in question, that is, the growing recalcitrance of circumstances, are the product of these transformations and of their unanticipated consequences.

I will only mention one effort to quantify the massive erosion in confidence and trust in the American government in the last few decades: "In 1964, three-quarters of the American public said that they trusted the federal government to do the right thing most of the time. Today [1997] only a quarter of Americans admit to such trust" (Nye, 1997:1; also Inglehart, 1997b). Since the end of the last century, this number increased to reach 56 percent in 2002, but has since then constantly declined. In 2008, it amounted to only 36 percent (see Norris, 2011a:65) and had fallen to 19 percent in 2010 (Zakaria, 2013:23). The United States is not in a special position. The loss of confidence by the public in the major institutions of society can be observed in many developed societies. In European societies, different trends can be recognized. In some democratic European societies (e.g., in England, Portugal, or Ireland) the confidence expressed in the government is even lower than it is in the United States. However, it is not true that the confidence of citizens in their governments in recent years has a uniform trend in all democratic European societies and that the loss of trust is getting stronger (cf. Norris, 2011a:70–72). The lack of trust is generally very high, but national differences are significant.

If the population (respondents) is divided, as for example in Inglehart (1997b:219), into two groups, those who are supportive of the postmaterialist world-view and those who subscribe to a much more materialistic world-view, it is striking that although postmaterialists live in the same political system as materialists they do *not* express greater satisfaction with the political system. Inglehart (1997b:222) is of the opinion that with the increase in the number of proponents of postmaterial values the criteria according to which political accomplishments are rated change decisively; new and very much more demanding expectations serve as a benchmark for the evaluation of the work of governments. The survey data Inglehart (1997b:222) refers to support his account that "we are witnessing a long-term trend that is weakening the authority of established institutions." The governments of developed societies may therefore find some solace in the fact that the confidence of the public in all major social institutions, and not only in the political system, is on the decline and that the loss of trust in the political system can be observed in many developed societies, as I have indicated. But shifts in the balance of power do not necessarily have zero-sum qualities or are unidirectional. The declining governability[22] may well coexist with widespread depoliticization.[23] On the other hand, systemic power may in fact increase.

Skeptical reactions to policy measures can lead to new forms of democratic participation beyond traditional representative participation (see Bruch, Ferree, and Soss, 2010) and, thus, strengthen democracy. Of course, from the perspective of policy development and government, relations between active citizens and representatives of the political class will be more cumbersome and uncomfortable. But it is quite conceivable and desirable that in modern liberal societies active citizenship is not only needed but has become a factor that such societies are increasingly dependent on. Nikolas Rose (1999:166) therefore concludes with respect to the role of the consumer in modern societies: "The citizen as consumer is to become an active agent in the regulation of professional expertise; the citizen as prudent is to become an active agent in the provision of security; the citizen as employee is to become an active agent in the regeneration of industry and much more."

The economy's success in tackling relative material scarcity also leads to a change in the nature of political struggles and conflicts. The diminished relevance of traditional social constructs such as property and labor leads not merely to a shift in values (in the sense of particular objectives pursued by political actors) but, even more importantly, to an enlargement of resources at the disposal of actors. Politics, once viewed as a struggle between owners of the means of production and those who merely own their labor power, gives way to much broader political and social conflicts that increasingly involve concerns about social justice and solidarity as well as such factors as lifestyle, the political control of novel scientific and technological capacities to act, and their repositioning on the agendas of political parties and civil society organizations.[24]

---

[22] Ronald Inglehart (1997:295), who has offered some of the most constructive empirical analyses of the modern state, is convinced that governments in advanced societies "are doing the old familiar task about as well as they ever did." One would need to conduct extensive empirical investigations, develop performance criteria, and link these to expectations etc. in order to arrive at a less affirmative reading of the ability of the state – faced by numerous wicked problems – to "get things done." There can be little doubt, as the day-to-day conduct of political affairs indicates, that profound conflicts, cleavages, and contradictions continue to exist in modern society, all of them constituting formidable hurdles for practical politics.

[23] This depoliticization might be especially pronounced in response to failed expectations that the state ought to be the primary agent for dealing with a growing range of recalcitrant problems.

[24] A repositioning of the platform or the spectrum of political parties also takes place, depending on the legal basis that either enables or discourages the formation of new political organizations.

Inglehart (1971, 1977, 1987, 1997a) has described such shifts in values that govern political preferences and class-based politics in advanced societies, predominantly among the younger cohorts, as a movement away from primarily materialistic concerns toward a much more postmaterialist outlook. Postmaterialist values are about personal and collective freedom, self-expression, and quality of life. Resonating with Karl Mannheim's ([1928] 1993) classical essay on the problem of generations, the overall speed of the transformation of values as a whole is tempered by the persistence of particular beliefs throughout an individual's lifetime. Inglehart combines a socialization hypothesis with a scarcity thesis. Echoing Mannheim, Inglehart argues that the fundamental world view of an individual is linked to early socialization experiences. If economic security and prosperity characterize the formative context in which value orientations are developed, postmaterialistic values are likely to emerge. Periods of scarcity, on the other hand, are linked to a materialistic outlook. In the present age, the emergence of a postmaterialist world view commenced with the postwar generations that experienced their formative years in conditions of relative economic and physical security. Younger, highly educated persons in developed societies tend to be the main proponents of a postmaterialist world view (cf. De Graaf and Evans, 1996). The trend toward postmaterialist values implies new political priorities, especially with regard to communal values and lifestyle issues,[25] and leads to a gradual neutralization of political polarization based on traditional class-based loyalties (see also Inglehart and Abramson, 1994). The result is that in the last quarter of the past century, for instance, class-linked voting "in most democracies is less than half as strong as it was a generation ago" (Inglehart, 1987:1298).

Among the questions, relevant in the context, of the genesis and the correlates of postmaterialist values are the relative importance of (formal) education; and the mediating influence of the experience of – or, perhaps even more significantly, the expectations of security linked to – material well being during the formative years. Indeed, some of the critics of Inglehart's assertion of a trend toward postmaterialist values have argued that the origins of postmaterialist value orientations are mainly due to an increase in the level of formal education among younger cohorts and, more generally, to improved economic conditions (e.g., Duch

---

[25] More specifically, Inglehart (1987:1297) enumerates issues that reflect some of the recent political discussions about environmental risks, disarmament, and alternative energy sources as exemplary postmaterialist political issues.

and Taylor, 1993).[26] Inglehart rejects this interpretation. The extent of formal education has, in his view, a lesser and a less immediate and direct influence on the emergence of postmaterialist values than has the experience of relative economic security.

On the whole, the persistent controversy about the exact role of education and/or the experience of existential security in the process of the emergence of postmaterial values among younger generations in modern societies has no immediate relevance for the generally accepted observation that postmaterialism is in fact on the rise. Whether educational, cultural, or economic backgrounds, or a figuration among these factors, are particularly significant does not detract from the now widely confirmed observation that a change in generational world views is underway. On the one hand, so it seems, it is argued that early and apparently largely unreflexive experiences with or without relative economic security have a decisive influence on the positioning of individual value orientations; on the other hand, the close association between education and postmaterial outlooks seems to indicate that a more conscious, reflexive process determines the value dispositions. The discussion refers to and is for the most part based on survey type data that rarely allow for a precise factoring out of the processes supposed to be at work. Abramson and Inglehart (1994:85) admit as much, indicating that survey data relevant to "formative security" are difficult to obtain. Deciding about the nature of the social and cultural forces at work in the formation of generational world views is, of course, also not possible as long as we have no clearer idea about the "end points" of generational identities, and they may be subject to change over time.

Karl Mannheim ([1928] 1993:374–375) already issued a rather ambivalent opinion on this matter in his classical essay on generations. The opponents of the postmaterialist thesis have ignored this essay. Mannheim questioned our ability to arrive at a precise determination of the formation of a generational outlook or the termination of primary socialization. He considered it to be entirely possible that individuals

---

[26] Another critical response to the Inglehart thesis has come from researchers who maintain that the rise of postmaterialist values is driven by unemployment; more specifically, that high levels of unemployment encourage the emergence of such values. Inglehart and Abramson (1994:350) have responded that the empirical data clearly indicate that unemployment is correlated with an increase in materialism. Another critique of the Inglehart thesis is that the observed value differences among younger and older age cohorts are simply *life-cycle* effects: For example, it might be argued that individuals become more materialistic with age. Inglehart and Abramson (1994:350) respond that, although cohort data cannot definitely rule out the validity of this particular claim, generational replacement rather than the life cycle is much more likely to account for the rise in postmaterialist values.

continue to encounter circumstances in their life-world that refashion and rewrite their value orientations. In addition, it cannot be precluded from the beginning that there might not be altogether different paths that lead to the formation of a specific world view. In short, a definitive answer about the formative influence of education and familial existential security – and of the collective, national expectations about the comparative state of economic well-being – is difficult to achieve.

Inglehart argues that the level of educational achievement is a valid indicator for the experience of existential security.[27] We know that the achieved educational level correlates with the material well-being of the parents. Inglehart points out that survey data show that "Europeans with higher levels of education tend to be less likely to be Materialists and more likely to be Postmaterialists than those with lower educational levels" (Abramson and Inglehart, 1994:77). But the same correlation can be observed for older cohorts, even for groups that received their schooling during the Mussolini and Hitler eras. At the same time, a secular trend toward postmaterial values is noted. Such a trend is in evidence, for example, in survey data that show that younger cohorts with a university education display a higher degree of affinities toward postmaterialism than older individuals with the same education do. Abramson and Inglehart (1994:81) conclude "there is nothing inherent in education that automatically produces Postmaterialist values." It is possible that present-day educational systems (i.e., the teachers) are much more sympathetic toward postmaterial values when compared to schools and universities a couple of generations ago. However, Inglehart is convinced that fundamental economic changes, and expectations that go on to work their way toward cultural responses and adaptations, precede the formation of such preferences. In this sense at least, Inglehart remains a materialist.[28]

---

[27] Abramson and Inglehart (1994:86) propose a more differentiated enumeration of characteristics and experiences that are linked to the level of formal education: "We suggest that 'education' actually taps a number of distinct variables: (1) indoctrination, both formal and informal; (2) the respondent's current socioeconomic status; (3) parental socioeconomic status during the respondent's formative years; (4) the historical era when the respondent was born and educated; (5) the degree to which the respondent has acquired various skills; and (6) the respondent's information level, since these skills make it easier to acquire information." The relative importance of each of these factors and experiences varies, depending on the specific dependent variable. At the same time, the list actually underplays the role of the education system in helping to bring about a secular transformation in the general level of cognitive skills, growth of knowledge, and overall increase in the level of education.

[28] In as much as survey research in advanced societies has shown that lower educational attainment resonates with more "conservative" commitments and world-views, some observers conclude that a "cultural" account of the formation (or nonformation) of

The detailed examination of the relative weight and importance the level of formal education has, among younger individuals, for the emergence of particular value-orientations, thought processes, and ways of comprehending experiences that crystallize into robust world views in light of which all subsequent events and encounters are interpreted is quite significant and of considerable interest. But the formation of patterns of consciousness and specific world views that acquire life-long significance for individuals is only one, and possibly one of the less decisive, elements among a variety of institutional changes in modern society. The specific contents of the world views and the gradual transformations in the collective importance of different generational meaning patterns are certainly not without a social and political significance, but ruptures in world views and generation-specific interpretations of reality are not new; nor have discontinuities and gradual changes in the collective consciousness necessarily produced definitive changes in the societal patterns of development and governability, in particular.

Inglehart, in other words, to some extent underplays the fact that the volume and quality of cognitive and social skills (knowledgeability), knowledge, and the resources available to political actors have risen considerably. But this increase in the resources available to political actors is not the outcome of a redistribution of the existing capacities of action. It is the result of an extension of the capacities of action that has primarily benefited "ordinary" citizens. The extension of state functions has paradoxically empowered its citizens by extending the private and personal spheres and by producing numerous structural indeterminacies. The very "success" of the state – its original autonomy and differentiation, and the enlargement of the range, scope, and intensity of its functions – has meant that individuals and nonstate groups have gained resources that can potentially aid them in approaching, enticing, demanding, resisting, and deflecting efforts of state agencies. As a result of these developments toward greater collective knowledgeability, the state is losing its status as a monolithic entity, assuming that this has indeed been the case in the course of the development of modern societies.[29]

---

postmaterialism is a theoretically more persuasive "explanation" when compared with Inglehart's "materialistic" account (e.g., Houtman, 1998). However, some of the same objections raised about Inglehart's one-dimensional approach can be mobilized in this instance as well. A position that satisfactorily combines the mediating linkages between culture and economic conditions is required.

[29] As Cerny (1990:197) observes, "the actions of nonstate agents and other structures in relation to the state have increasingly tended to involve approaching it in a partial way, creating pressure groups, policy demands, issue networks, and political allocation processes on single issues or limited clusters of issues."

The lament about the loss of authority of the state needs to be augmented by the realization of the rapid expansion of education, especially tertiary education; the growing importance of cognitive skills; the enfranchisement or the extension and reconfiguration of citizenship to previously marginal groups; the diffusion of class conflict; the growth of wealth and entitlements; the expansion of and easier access to communication networks, including the enlargement of the mass media and the Internet; the rapid growth of knowledge-based occupations, and therefore of forms of knowledge and skills that can be utilized as a resource not only on the job but in a variety of social and political contexts; and, finally, the exceptional growth of the role and the sheer number of professionals in many fields. The devolution and decentering of the state is in all likelihood to a considerable extent the result of its own success.[30] However, the changes now underway are difficult to document empirically. To some extent, this is the result of the continued use of indicators developed under different social regimes and appropriate for these but not necessarily for the emerging structures and processes. With some justification one may speak of social indicators that are "frozen in time."

The controversial issue of the source of value change in modern society, or of what sometimes has been called subjective modernization and the individual enlargement of capacities to act, is significant in this context. But the exact attribution of factors remains difficult to demonstrate, as does the determination of indicators that illustrate the heightened presence and relevance of cognitive skills. However, I am convinced that the growing volume of knowledge that is individually and collectively available is not only a constitutive factor of knowledge societies but plays a decisive role in the governance of present-day society.

In as much as many analyses of modern society commence with reference to the world of work and its peculiarities, many observers are of the view that the end of the kind work that was dominant in industrial society not only resonates with basic changes in the values, life-styles and subjective feelings of modern individuals but is one of the conditions for the emergence and spread of postmaterial world views generally. The

---

[30] At the level of culture and politics, a shift can be observed in some countries toward a more pronounced celebration of the local and a reassertion of traditional values. This shift perhaps resonates with the more general societal developments we have described. It may also represent, at least in the self-consciousness of the active participants in such movements, a "protest against homogenization of state-bureaucratic capitalism – against creeping mediocrity, mass-culture, unisex society" (Friedman, 1989:54). However, such a diagnosis simultaneously perpetuates the myth of the efficacy of the power of the state in the past, and underestimates the importance of fundamental transformations in the structure of society as a precursor of important cultural shifts.

transformation of industrial work as well as the new job demands in the expanding service sector are seen to go hand in hand with a change in lifestyles and forms of life. Any subjective modernization and development of postmaterial value orientations is the expression and the outcome of entirely new demands faced by employees and generated by the postindustrial world of work. These new competencies include, for example, "communication intensive" skills. In the context of lean production in industrial work, what counts are achievement orientation, self-regulation, initiative, responsibility, and self-motivation (see Braczyk and Schienstock, 1996).

The observations just enumerated stress the necessity, maybe even the inevitability, of adapting work-related skills and competencies to relatively independent developments, especially with respect to the iron constraints of technical changes, including those characterized by the term "social technologies" (*Humantechniken*)[31] (see Schelsky, [1961] 1965:18).[32] Forced adaptations of this kind should be generation-independent since the necessity to adapt to novel working conditions can hardly be expected to be stratified by age.[33] Nonetheless, this line of reasoning underestimates or ignores the opposite relationship. That is to say, the possibility that the transformation of the working context and its structuring is not so much, as the prevailing conception has it mainly, a response to changes over which labor has little if any control and which, then, manifest themselves in the working out of specific demands for certain skills and competencies to fit preexisting conditions. It may well be that the transformation of the workplace in knowledge societies increasingly is a matter of the skills, preferences, and competencies individuals bring to the working context, in the first place, and is,

---

[31] Following Jacques Ellul, Helmut Schelsky considers the so-called "organizational technologies" as well as "human technologies" (*Humantechniken*) to be the logical extension of the technical production of artifacts and therefore as part of his broad definition of the nature of modern technology.

[32] One is reminded in this context of the cautionary observations by Anthony Smith (1982:2) that it is difficult not to be fascinated and intimidated by the allegedly unobstructed social consequences of technological developments: "We are paralyzed by the dimensions of the transformation, partly because we have internalized a kind of Whiggian principle, by which machines 'produce' social effects of a measurable or, at least, observable variety. The trouble is that technological and social history cannot be related in this way, since the extrapolated trends tend to shoot off the graph every time ... We would be greatly helped in the present epoch of speculation if we had available some improved metaphors for social change ... something that suggested less emphasis on technology and placed more pressure on social need as the starting point of technology."

[33] If a generation-specific change in values can be demonstrated, one might of course be prompted to argue that younger rather than older workers find it easier to adjust to new value orientations.

therefore, less demand than supply-side driven. In other words, one may be able to shed new light on the question of the conditions that transform the world of work and the role new value orientations may play by asking about the reasons for the rapid growth of knowledge-intensive occupations in modern society.

Actually, responses to these questions more generally tend to be found in the rapid development and enhancement of scientific and technological knowledge and its practical relevance – that is, knowledge that can readily be brought to practical uses will rapidly gain in importance in the practical sphere and even increasingly dominate it. In other words, the demand for expert knowledge also arises from the production of such knowledge, and from the successful construction or reconfiguration, in terms of this knowledge, of social conditions. The fact that an increasingly science-driven society tends to increasingly rely on experts might be seen as a process of self-creation, as it were; that is, solving an ever growing number of problems seems to require at least the language of authority and efficiency that science can be expected to offer (cf. Nowotny, 1979:119). The thesis is, in short, that the growing demand for knowledge-based professions is a result of the (growing) production of expertise. And this thesis, in turn, is compatible with the changing value orientations between generations observed in modern society, since the younger age cohorts are the first to benefit from the enhanced educational opportunities and to modify their expectations accordingly.

An analogous thesis advanced by Peter Drucker suggests that the crucial reason for the observed increase in the demand for knowledgeable employees and, therefore, for the shift to a knowledge-based economy has, in this sense at least, little to do with the existence of prior, more exacting, and complex job skills in the world of work and any ensuing response by employers in terms of a demand for individuals who offer exactly these higher skills and qualifications. For Drucker, this hypothesis is nothing but a widely held myth. The effective reason, for him, for the considerable growth in job skills and knowledge is to do with the immense increase in the working life span of individuals and the higher quality of "human capital." Thus, it is the demand for labor and particular skills, rather than the supply of highly skilled labor, that underlies the transformation of society into a knowledge-based economy. Drucker's thesis may be regarded as a variant of Jean-Baptiste Say's theorem that every supply creates its own demand: "The arrival of the knowledge worker changed the nature of jobs. Because modern society has to employ people who expect and demand knowledge work, knowledge jobs have to be created. As a result, the character of work is being transformed" (Drucker 1969:84). Drucker therefore proposes a very different mechanism that is at work here; he offers a kind of "supply side explanation" of the transformation of industrial society into knowledge society.

Highly educated entrants into the labor force expect upgraded jobs,[34] but the extension of education is itself a reflection of a drastic lengthening of work life expectancy. The dramatic growth in the average number of years spent in school, apprenticeship, and various other learning institutions such as colleges and universities has altered the "supply of labor." And the growth in attendance at and demand for higher education is to a considerable extent self-reinforcing.

Economists in search of an empirical clarification of these rapid changes of the labor market, in particular the stratification of wages, have in recent years turned to new explanatory dimensions that remain hidden in most conventional labor markets and unobserved in population surveys. Similarly, there has been considerable speculation about cognitive skills that may be increasingly important as industry and the service sector restructure, or as capital accumulation moves from redundant Fordist structures to new flexible post-Fordist modes of production. In this context, what is of interest is research that regards the role of cognitive skills, in contrast to years of formal schooling, as the much more common, sometimes even exclusive indicator for ascertaining knowledge or skills. Murnane, Willett, and Levy (1995), for instance, inquire if in the United States basic cognitive skills are becoming more important in wage determination on an economy-wide basis. They focus on one central question: How mathematics skills of graduating high school seniors affect their wages at age twenty-four. This question is examined for two cohorts: first, students who graduated from high school in 1972 and second, students who graduated in 1980.[35] By comparing the relationship between wages and mathematics scores among the two cohorts, the authors claim to be able to address two questions: (1) "Are basic cognitive skills becoming more important in determining wages on an economy-wide basis?" and (2) "How much of the increase in the college-high school wage premium during the 1980s stems from a widening of the skill gap between

---

[34] As Peter Drucker has noted: "Long years of schooling make a person unfit for anything but knowledge work" (Drucker, 1969:284).

[35] The two samples on which their information is based are longitudinal studies of high school seniors. The samples include both women and men and are based on individuals who completed their formal education and engaged in paid work for six years after graduation. In their last year of high school, participants in the two samples took a mathematics test. The test assessed students' skills in following directions, working with fractions and decimals, and interpreting line graphs. In other words, the test measured elementary mathematical concepts and not advanced mathematical knowledge. The average math scores for the 1980 high school graduates are lower than for the 1972 cohort.

college graduates and high school graduates who did not go to college?" (Murnane, Willett, and Levy, 1995:252).

I will first turn to the results of the study that pertain to a number of more conventional attributes that have in the past been associated with wage differentials. The Murnane results replicate the well-known results of the effect of years of schooling on subsequent wages. For example, their estimate is that for the 1972 male cohort, each year completed in college is associated – after only a few short years in the workforce – with a wage premium of 2.2 percent above the wage earned by individuals without any college education. The corresponding figure for the 1980 male graduates is 4.5 percent; for females it is even more substantial, namely 5.5 and 6.7 percent. The main finding of their study is that on an economy-wide basis, "basic cognitive skills were more important predictors of wage six years after high school in the mid-1980s than in the late 1970s" (Murnane, Willett, and Levy, 1995:263). The authors therefore conclude that the growing importance of cognitive skills as measured by the mathematics test scores for the younger cohort in their study is rooted in a demands shift toward basic cognitive capacities and primarily reflects changes within occupational groups.[36] The demand for cognitive skills is not limited to a few firms but is strong enough to show up in a nationwide sample. The Murnane study can be considered to be just a beginning. Wages are a "compositive compensation for a variety of skills" (Murphy and Welch, 1993:109) and the supply and demand for such skills varies.[37] An examination of the impact of basic mathematical skills acquired early on in high school can only offer a first approximation of changes in the labor market. However, two substantive domains may be identified in which knowledge and the political system or democracy and knowledge intersect: the field of what is widely labeled as "political knowledge," and the domain of scientific knowledge of ordinary citizens as it relates to democratic governance.

My attention will now shift to the question of the volume of political knowledge citizens typically possess in modern democracies and the implications an actor's knowledge has for the governance of modern society. In some of these diagnoses of the collective knowledge, or information budget, of modern societies of the postwar period one detects an echo of reflections by scholars such as Karl Mannheim (e.g., 1940:45–46)

---

[36] As the authors of the study emphasize, the tested mathematics skills of high school seniors (ages 17–18) pertain to curriculum matters that are taught in American high schools no later than eighth grade, or at about age 14.
[37] For an analysis of the college-wage premium, see Katz and Murphy (1992) and Murphy and Welch (1992).

or Joseph Schumpeter (e.g., 1942:262) in the 1930s and 1940s, who diagnosed a serious threat to democratic governance as a result of the appearance in the political arena of what then were called the "masses" (see Blokland, 2011:40–42).[38]

I will first refer to what is ordinarily called political knowledge in the research literature, and then, more comprehensively, to much more demanding expectations concerning the amount of scientific and technical knowledge ordinary citizens ought to command in order to be able to meaningfully participate in democratic governance or to challenge the discourse of expertise. The main issue I would like to initially consider is therefore whether what is reported as political knowledge really is a valid measure of political knowledge. I will then put forward the alterative hypothesis that "the level of factual knowledge, as surveys measured it, is a proxy for something much more basic" (Kuklinski, 1997:927). My contention will be that what this is actually about is not "factual information/knowledge" but knowledgeability, the bundle of competencies that connect democratic governance and knowledge. The next section of this chapter will, however, critically focus on the many assertions and empirical findings concerning the political knowledge typical of members of civil society. The cognate and also widely discussed assertion about a lack of knowledge, in terms of scientific knowledge, in the public and the impact this in turn is seen to have on democratic governance will be taken up in a separate section.

Political knowledge

> The list of things political that typical citizens do not know is daunting. Explaining their ignorance, and using it to explain various aspects of politics, poses serious tests for any theory of pragmatic or political cognition.
> Russell Hardin (2006:179)

The "political knowledge" of large numbers of ordinary citizens in modern democracies is, as many see it, distressingly low (e.g., Gunn, 1995:108), as is the confidence of the public (cf. Levi and Stoker, 2002; Nannestad, 2008)[39] of many countries in some of the key democratic

---

[38] Joseph Schumpeter's (1942:260) ill-concealed contempt for the masses, perhaps due to the rise of fascism, amounts to the diagnosis of a "primitive citizen": "The typical citizen drops down to a lower level of mental performance as soon as he enters the political field. He argues and analyzes in a way which he would readily recognize as infantile within the sphere of his real interests. He becomes primitive again."

[39] Margaret Levi and Laura Stoker (2000:501) sum up their comprehensive review of the extensive empirical research on political trust as follows: "Whether citizens judge politicians or government trustworthy influences whether they become politically

institutions.[40] Political knowledge is also highly stratified (Luskin, 1997). There is, for example, a considerable gender gap: women are significantly less politically "knowledgeable" than men (Wolak and McDevitt, 2011). The lack of political knowledge in modern democratic countries has been extensively documented and is relatively stable over time (e.g., Galston, 2001; Bennett, 2003, 2006).[41] With respect to the United States, Bennett (2003:325) reluctantly concedes that "the time has come to accept the fact that, most of the time, on most topics, most Americans, at least, do not know much about government and public affairs."[42]

---

active, how they vote, whether they favor policy or institutional reforms, whether they comply with political authorities, and whether they trust one another." A study by Zmerli and Newton (2008:706), based on what the authors consider superior measures of *social trust*, reports "robust and statistically significant correlations between generalized social trust, on the one hand, and confidence in political institutions and satisfaction with democracy, on the other. The associations are significant in 23 European countries and in the United States." In other words, Zmeri and Newton are not linking trust in political institutions to political beliefs and behavior but general social trust (in other members of society) to trust in political institutions.

[40] Robert Dahl (2000) examined the apparent paradox of the low confidence of the public in many countries in key democratic institutions and the overall endorsement of democracy as the most desirable form of political governance. Dahl (2000:39) argues that views about confidence in key democratic institutions and endorsements of democracy, as obtained in surveys, are not inconsistent – under ordinary circumstances, as one might add. Although "a majority of citizens in most democratic countries may view participating in political life as neither very urgent nor particularly rewarding, and though many may be dissatisfied with the way government works, overwhelming majorities of citizens do value the rights and opportunities their democratic system of government provides to them." Dahl's paradox can easily be extended to the contrast between the deficit of individual political knowledge and the general endorsement of democratic governance by the public and the functioning of the political system itself (see Berelson, 1954:312).

[41] Although I am interested in the substance of findings concerning the volume of "political knowledge" among the population, I will refrain from discussing the methodological issues related to efforts to measure and develop indicators for political knowledge/information (see Luskin, 1987; Miller and Shannon, 2008; Prior and Lupia, 2008; Sturgis, Allum, and Smith, 2008). Pierre Bourdieu's ([1973] 1994) critique of public opinion surveys designed to capture what they are not capable of capturing, namely public opinion, falls also into the category of a critique of the methods of empirically assessing public views. Bourdieu suggests that these surveys do not employ *valid* measures of public opinion; hence public opinion as measured by them does not exist (cf. Champagne, 2005).

[42] An important counterfactual empirical study (Enns and Kellstaft, 2008) that inquired into the relation of "political sophistication" (based on respondents' information about the name of the governor of their state, the name of their representative in the US House of Representatives and their educational attainment) and respondents' political opinions (through not very sophisticated but broad items) using U.S. survey data between the years 1974–2002, finds that in contrast to most previous findings all subjects tend to receive political information and update their opinions. Such movement of opinion is therefore not restricted to the politically most sophisticated subjects. Enns and Kellstaft (2008:437) argue in particular that "all segments of the electorate receive information about the economy and then use this information to update their political attitudes." In

These findings about individual citizens contrast sharply with the general, and growing, endorsement of democracy by the public around the world but support the conviction of political theorists and philosophers of democracy that public ignorance is a threat to democracy and informed political participation is a virtue. A politically sophisticated public, it is argued, sustains democracy. As Karol Edward Soltan (1999:10), for example, puts it, "researchers have for the most part simply presumed that competence in the voting decision has relevance for democracy, and hence they did not hide their horror when empirical research revealed, as they thought, an abysmally low level of competence." According to Thomas Sewell's (1980:164) pessimistic conclusion, the lack of competence of citizens has considerable consequences – not only in the United States – for the balance of political power in society and, as a result, the "locus of decision-making has drifted away from the individual, the family, and voluntary associations of various sorts, and toward government. And within government, it has moved away from elected officials subject to voter feedback, and toward more insulated governmental institutions, such as bureaucracies and the appointed judiciary." Obviously, such institutional developments have, in addition, profound implications for "individual freedom, but also for the social ways in which knowledge is used, distorted, or made ineffective" (Sowell, 1980:164).

What is wrong with these assertions? What difference does individual political knowledge, especially the lack of such knowledge, make?[43] Is it possible, as Petersen and Aarøe (2013:275) ask, "to form coherent political attitudes despite [a] ... lack of substantive political knowledge"? Is political knowledge power? Can accurate knowledge about "civic-textbook-like facts" be equal to or translated into political power? Why should citizens incur the possibly high transaction costs of being well informed? Are the transaction costs of acquiring knowledge mainly or

---

other words, Enns and Kellstaft's findings appear to counter the idea that the politically least sophisticated actors are more or less completely disenfranchised. The results of the study provide evidence for the "supposition that despite such variations, there are broad messages that eventually reach all segments of society, and the responses to these broad messages move public opinion."

[43] James Kuklinski and his colleagues (2000) argue that it is important to make a conceptual distinction between being *un*informed and *mis*informed (factual inaccuracy); although "factual inaccuracy is troublesome," what is even more troublesome according to Kuklinski's (2000:799–801) analysis of survey results is the large proportion of respondents who are convinced that their misinformation is accurate and that "the very people who most need to correct them will be the least likely to do so." Moreover, "from a misinformation perspective, people's preferences should be hard to change," an assumption that is indeed confirmed by Kuklinski's (2000:810) findings. As a result, changing public opinion is likely to be rather difficult.

exclusively born by the voters? Is it rational to be ignorant? And, last but not least, is the political decision calculus of politically more informed citizen different from that of their fellow citizens who are less informed (see Bullock, 2011)? Finally, to refer to the generally limited concrete empirical evidence, if voters are better informed in the sense in which much research conceives of information about politics, will they actually be more likely to cast their vote and, perhaps, to vote differently (Dow, 2011)?

What is meant by political knowledge in most of these discussions about the role of political knowledge in democracies? Although actually practiced democratic participation and information about the public policy issues of the day is far from reaching ideal conditions in many countries, democracies persist, their number increases and the number that decay and perish is negligible.

Empirical research on issues of political behavior and decision-making processes of eligible voters has for decades inquired into questions of what in these research contexts is called the political knowledge and political information of these actors. The theory of democracy refers to the individual characteristics of voters that will allow for sensible and intelligent political participation. The theory of democracy describes the knowledge and motives voters should have in democracies. And as we have seen, these requirements include, above all, to be well informed about the political constitution of a country, its political institutions, the politically contentious issues, the solutions offered and the possible consequences of political decisions, as well as about the main political actors.

In an essay published in the immediate postwar period, in which he also makes the case for interdisciplinary research efforts located between public opinion research and political theory, Bernard Berelson (1952) outlines a comprehensive picture of what are not necessarily mutually exclusive personal attributes and preconditions of a democratic voter (also Lerner 1958:59). The voter in a democracy should, first, have a certain *personality structure*. Berelson offers the following illustrative list: the voter should be able to carry a moral responsibility for choices; be capable of accepting frustration in political affairs; develop a balance between humility and self-assertion; have a healthy, critical attitude toward political authority; have a sense of self-esteem and the potential and the ability for fairly broad and comprehensive identifications.[44] The

---

[44] Critics may interpret these personality traits as strictly *psychological* ones. This, however, is not the case. For example, the capacity "for involvement in situations remote from one's face-to-face experience" (Berelson, 1952:315) is an attribute embedded in social

second requirement refers not merely to prerequisites but also to outcomes of electoral decision. This is the factor of *interest and participation*. Political apathy is not allowed. As Berelson stresses, the descriptive documentation of these features of citizens as opposed to the personality characteristics is relatively good. Not much has changed in this respect since the 1950s. In the fifties, for example, less than one-third of the electorate in the United States was "really interested" in politics. The politically more interested segment of the population is more likely to influence other voters and has the same function as opinion leaders and pacemakers, although they may not always be better informed (cf. Trepte and Boecking, 2009). Berelson (1952:317) interprets these figures, and the observed decline in voter turnout, as the outcome of the growing sense of the electorate "that they are impotent to affect political matters in the face of the complexity and magnitude of the issues." Third, political theory refers not only to these personal qualities and social skills of the voters, but also to the expectation that citizens will have relevant information and knowledge as a precondition for an "enlightened public opinion." In this context, Berelson defines information as relating to "isolated facts" and knowledge to "general propositions." Both information and knowledge offer a reliable basis for insights into the likely consequences of political decisions. Berelson (1952:318) adds that "information and knowledge are required of the electorate on the assumption that they contribute to the wisdom of the decision; informed citizens make wiser decisions." In this respect, too, the yields of public opinion polls carried out as early as in the fifties of the last century are extensive and have grown considerably since then. Fourth, in addition to the information and knowledge attributes, Berelson states that voters ought to have a second component required for democratic decision making, namely, possess principles. Voters should have stable political standards or moral principles rather than fragile impulses or whims on the basis of which their political decisions are formed.

I will limit my considerations at this juncture to a number of general observations about the volume of information and knowledge of the electorate and the implications of these findings for democratic decision making and participation. Subsequently I will address in more detail recent research findings and interpretations concerned with the substance

---

relations. It should also be noted that some of the traits Berelson identifies as prerequisites of electoral participation and decision making in a free society have some affinity with the social knowledgeability traits discussed earlier, for example, the ability of "integrative complexity" and the capacity for "fairly broad and comprehensive identifications" (Berelson, 1952:315).

of political knowledge. One of the findings that are repeatedly reported and can already be found in the work of Bernard Berelson (1952:138) is that the public is not particularly well informed about the political events of the day. But as Berelson (1952:318) also notes, "most of the studies have been based upon simple and isolated questions of fact (i.e., information) and only seldom, if at all, upon the historical and general propositions (i.e., knowledge) which underlie political decisions." And, as Berelson (1952:319) also emphasizes, in representative democracies, the expectation of the volume of information available to and the degree of understanding found in the individual voter with respect to political issues and the consequences of political decisions should not be set unrealistically high:

> Actually the major decisions the ordinary citizen is called upon to make in a modern representative democracy involve basic simplifications which need not rest upon a wide range of information so long as they are based upon a certain amount of crucial information, reasonably interpreted. After all, the voter's effective choice is limited; he can vote Republican, he can vote Democratic, or he can refrain from voting, and becoming informed on a number of minor issues usually does not tip the scales against the weight of the few things that really matter-employment, social security, the cost of living, peace.

Jürgen Habermas ([1962] 1989:212) in his analysis of the *Structural Transformation of the Public Sphere* refers to Bernard Berelson's observations about democratic theory and public opinion research. In light of the reported deficits of the public's information about politics, Habermas offers the following explanation:

> If today the mass of the enfranchised population exhibits the democratic behavior patterns to the low degree found by many empirical investigations – even when measured in terms of superficial criteria as the degree of political activity and initiative and of participation in discussions – then such deviations can only be understood sociologically in connection with the structural and functional transformation of the public sphere itself.

Habermas diagnoses that the once significant bourgeois public is disappearing with the development of the mass media (press) and is subjected to the technical and commercial constraints that govern the media. Once more, social relations takes on feudalistic characteristics and the public becomes a managed public. Communication is restricted and subject to the influence of a small set of powerful actors. In the manipulated public arena, an "acclamation-prone mood comes to predominate, an opinion climate instead of a public opinion" (Habermas, [1962] 1989:217). The helpless voting public is confronted with information within the context of a most effective communication process that is calculated in terms of social psychology and calls for predictable responses. The substance of the communication appeals, "controlled according to carefully investigated and experimentally tested 'psychological parameters' must progressively lose their connection with political program statements, not to mention issue-related arguments" (Habermas, [1962] 1989:217).

Habermas ([1969] 1989:221) follows Otto Kirchheimer (1959) who describes the public arena that is emptied of any political substance as a societal context in which it is impossible to form or encounter public opinion because a couple of preconditions are missing: "informal opinions are not formed rationally, that is, in conscious grappling with cognitively accessible states of affairs" and the views of the public are not "formed in discussion, in the pro and con of a public conversation (instead the reactions, although in many ways mediated by group opinions, remained private in the sense that they are not exposed to correction within the framework of a critically debating public)." As a consequence of the successful manipulation of the helpless and unprotected consumers of the mass media "a public of citizens that has disintegrated *as* a public was reduced by publicist means to such a position that it could be claimed for the legitimation of political compromises without participating in effective decisions or being in the least capable of such participation" (Habermas, [1962] 1989:221).

Before extending the perspectives on the public domain from the 1950s and 1960s to the present, a brief description of the ways of collecting the empirical evidence for the volume of political knowledge found in the public is in order. The approach to the collection of data on the political knowledge of the public has not changed substantially since Bernard Berelson commented on the figures collected six decades ago.

Measuring political knowledge

Table 1 *Survey questions designed to measure political knowledge*

Questions asked of the respondents (percentage of correct answers in parentheses) designed to measure:

a. Structural political knowledge:

1. The political system of our country is based on our constitution. Which of the following, according to the constitution, do the powers of the state belong to? (55)
2. Finland has a proportional electoral system. Which of the following would you associate with the concept "proportional electoral system"? (You may choose one or several alternatives). (23)
3. What does division into electoral districts mean? (39)

4. Which political decision-maker or decision-making body is elected directly by the people in parliamentary elections? (62)
5. Which of the following are tasks assigned to the Finnish parliament? (You may choose one or several alternatives). (26)
6. An electoral system converts votes cast in elections into seats in the parliament. In Finland voters vote for the candidate of their choice. How is the vote counted? (48)
7. Which of the following are, according to the constitution, tasks assigned to the prime minister? (You may choose one or several alternatives). (40)
8. Which of the following best describes the principle of parliamentarism? (39)
The questions measuring

b. Political information:
1. Can you name the mayor/municipality manager of the town or municipality you currently live in? (55)
2. Which party currently holds the most seats in the town or local council in the town or municipality you currently live in? (57)
3. Who is currently the prime minister of Finland and which party does he/she represent? (85)
4. From the following list of parties, choose those currently in the government (38)
5. Who is currently the Speaker of parliament and which party does he/she represent? (63)
6. Name the chairman of one of the parties currently in the parliament (70)

Source: Kimmo Elo and Lauri Rapelia (2011), "Determinants of Political Knowledge: The Effects of the Media on Knowledge and Information," *Journal of Elections, Public Opinion & Parties* 20:133–146.

c. Conventional Knowledge Scale – Question Wording (correct answers are with an asterisk)

1. We would like to know how widely known some political figures are. [Toronto] Is the current Premier of Ontario Mike Harris, Dalton McGuinty*, John Tory or Howard Hampton? [Montreal] Is the current premier of Quebec Bernard Landry, Jean Charest*, André Boisclair or Mario Dumont?
2. Is the judge heading the inquiry into the sponsorship scandal Alan Gold, Irvin Cotler, John Gomery* or Beverley McLachlin?
3. Do you happen to recall the name of the mayor of [Toronto] [Montreal]? [Toronto] Is it Mel Lastman, John Sewell, Hazel McCallion or David Miller*?/[Montreal] Is it Pierre Bourque, Jean Doré, Gilles Vaillancourt or Gerald Tremblay*?
4. Is the new Governor General of Canada Sheila Fraser, Michaëlle Jean*, Adrienne Clarkson or Jeanne Sauvé?
5. And the name of a current female Cabinet Minister in Ottawa: Anne McLellan*, Kim Campbell, Sheila Copps, or Deborah Gray?
6. Do you happen to know which party is the official opposition party in Ottawa? Is it the Bloc Québécois, the Conservative Party of Canada, Liberal Party*, or NDP (New Democratic Party)?
7. And who is the current Prime Minister of Canada: Stephen Harper*, Jean Chrétien, Paul Martin or George Bush?

d. **Practical Knowledge Scale** – Question Wording

1. [Renters] If someone got a rent increase that was too high, where is the best place to go to get it reduced: City Hall, [the Rental Board] [Régie du Logement], the Ministry of Housing, or the Canada Mortgage and Housing Corporation? [Owners] If someone wanted to make renovations to their home, where would they go to get a building permit: the Real Estate Board, City Hall*, the Ministry of Housing, or the Canada Mortgage and Housing Corporation?
2. [Women 50 and over] Under OHIP, is a mammogram free*, $20, $50 or $80?
[Women under 50] Under OHIP, is a Pap smear test free*, $20, $50 or $80?
[Men 50 and over] Under OHIP, is a prostate exam free*, $20, $50 or $80?
[Men under 50] Under OHIP, is a test for sexually transmitted diseases (STDs) free*, $20, $50 or $80?
3. If someone was refused an apartment and thought it was because of their racial background, where would be the best place to make a complaint? Is it the Ombudsman of [Ontario] [Quebec]; [Ministry of the Attorney General] [Department of Justice]; the Police; the [Ontario] [Quebec] Human Rights Commission*; or [the Rental Board] [Régie du Logement]?
4. If you knew of a child being abused, where would be the BEST place to go? Is it the school board or school; Youth Justice Services; [Children's Aid*] [Director of Youth Protection*]; Ministry of Children and Youth; or the Police?
5. If someone had to go to court and could not afford a lawyer, where would be the BEST place to go? Is it the Ombudsman of [Ontario] [Quebec]; Legal Aid*; Ministry of the Attorney General; or the [Ontario] [Quebec] Bar Association?
6. People with low incomes can claim a variety of benefits when they file their federal tax returns. Can people with low incomes claim a GST tax credit? [yes*]
7. Can they claim a Canada Child Tax Benefit? [yes*]

Source: Stolle, Dietlind and Elisabeth Gidengil (2010), "What do Women Really Know? A Gendered Analysis of Varieties of Political Knowledge," *Perspectives on Politics* 8:93–109.

e. **Political knowledge** Adding the scores of four open-ended questions regarding political facts created this variable. Those questions include and refer for the most part to national but not local or regional politicians or events (cf. Shaker, 2012), for example "Who is the British prime minister?" "Who is the Speaker of the U.S. House of Representatives?" "Who is the vice president of the United States?" and "Which state is Sarah Palin the governor of?" For each correct answer, respondents received 1 point, with the number of correct answers summed up to construct the variable of political knowledge.

Source: Jung, Nakwon Yonghwan Kim and Homero Gil de Zúñiga (2011), "The mediating role of knowledge and efficacy in the effects of communication on political participation," *Mass Communication and Society*, 14:418.

It is difficult to imagine that definitions such as "the concept of knowledge [refer] to externally verifiable descriptive beliefs about what 'is'" (Lambert et al., 1988) shed light on the general idea that knowledge supports democracy. Why and how does correct information[45] possessed by a citizen about, for example, the name of a political figure (obtained in survey research), the number of judges on a particular court or the ability to locate a political party on the left-to-right spectrum support and enhance democratic participation and governance? What exactly is the connection? In other words, could being "well-informed" play a minor role in comparison to other factors that influence political decision making? The relevant social psychological theory, for example, may refer (as does Cohen, 2003) to self-informed voters who follow mainly the political platform of their party or the position of the leading representatives of the party (cue-based processing of information).

It is just as easily imaginable that respondents in totalitarian regimes will have considerable information about the name of their rulers. One response would be, as Lambert (1988:360) and his colleagues suggest, that "political knowledge can be thought of as an important precursor of political action, such as voting. Voting, however, is only one of the ways in which people can be politically involved. Like political efficacy, political knowledge should also be regarded as a significant form of political participation in its own right."

The results of empirical research on the political information budget of the average citizen in democratic societies describe but a portion of the political reality in these societies. The empirical results are not likely to overturn normative theories of democracy. The empirical studies of individual political competence cannot negate systemic characteristics of democracy. As Steven Lukes (1977:40) therefore emphasizes, empirical studies of individual political knowledge are unable to radically revise or transform the classical theory of democracy.[46] And, finally, as Petersen and Aarøe (2013: 289) have most recently documented, despite the widespread lack of extensive political knowledge, "citizens readily form opinions on what constitutes the best and most efficient policies." In

---

[45] Kent Jennings (1996:228) in his research concerning the possible influence of the variable "generations" on the volume of political information of individuals differentiates between *textbook knowledge* (information about the form of government), *surveillance knowledge* (knowledge of the political events of the day), and *historical facts* (collective memory). However, these concepts, too, refer to what is political information and not to political knowledge or knowledgeability.

[46] The classic empirical study of voting behavior (*Voting*) carried out by Bernard Berelson (1954:306) and his colleagues in the 1950s offers its own assessment of the significance of their findings for a theory of democracy: they emphasize that "perhaps the main impact of realistic research on contemporary politics has been to temper some of the requirements set by our traditional normative theory for the typical citizen." What Berelson and his colleagues could not have anticipated was how extensively the conditions and possibilities of political participation could be expanded, in principle, in the following decades.

response to the puzzle of why this should be the case, Petersen and Aarøe (2013:290) assign considerable significance to the operation of a strong imagination (or, internal processes) as a key "part of the personality profile of those who are engaged in democratic politics despite the often low economic returns to the self." Nonetheless, becoming engaged in politics is also linked to being embedded in supportive social networks, access to external information and, of course, knowledgeability capacities.

The new public sphere

Following the iron law of the simultaneity of nonsimultaneous societal processes,[47] it is of course correct to observe that in modern societies, both major forms of public spheres – the managed and the new public sphere – are to be found. In what follows, I would like to explain why the political and economic significance of the managed public sphere is increasingly being displaced by the growing influence of the new public sphere.

As we have seen following the accounts of Habermas and Kirchheimer, for example, the managed public sphere is understood to be a largely incapacitated stratum because its members are a largely powerless, unorganized, manipulated, alienated, helpless, apolitical mass. The managed public sphere of the mass society is not a solidly homogeneous social entity – but in all public roles its helplessness is manifest. It is above all open to ideological manipulation by media concerns, by politicians or as practiced by the authorities in schools, on the job, or in the act of consumption. These qualities of the managed public sphere in modern societies can best be clarified by recalling the societal diagnoses of the first decades of the postwar era of the last century, particularly as they also offer an answer to the question of the conditions that assure a managed public sphere and its resilience over time. C. Wright Mills, for example, spoke passionately (1956) – in accordance with both the spirit of the times and the opinions shared by the majority of his intellectual contemporaries – of the unlimited domination of elites, both locally and nationally. These were to be found in the major social institutions, in science, politics, government, business, the military, and the media. The information media and their organs were being centralized, thus placing social power into the hands of a few. And these few tended to take turns at the helm when politicians moved into business, scientists into politics,

---

[47] My discussion of the new public sphere is indebted to and relies on ideas first developed with Marian Adolf in Stehr and Adolf, 2011.

managers into the media, and so forth. The result was a power elite to whom the powers of definition and sanction flowed in terms of every imaginable social issue. What choice did the masses have, then, excluded as they were from these positions of power in this way, but to accept the comprehensive management of their life-world as the natural order of things? More than this: they even confirmed the prevailing conditions by consensus. Resistance is futile; compliance, therefore, is necessary. As a consequence of the successful manipulation of the helpless and defenseless consumers by the mass media, for example, "a public of citizens that had disintegrated as a public was reduced by publicist means to such a position that it could be claimed for the legitimation of political compromises without participating in effective decisions or being in the least capable of such participation" (Habermas, [1962] 1989:221).

These skeptical observations from the 1960s may be compared to a careful and recent assessment of the asymmetry of the pragmatic skills of the population and the political actors of the political system proposed by the work of the prominent political scientist James Kuklinski (1990:394). Kuklinski, who employs the informational approach, as did studies co-initiated by him in the 1980s and 1990s (Forejohn and Kuklinski, 1990), comes to the sober conclusion that the political system in societies, despite the extensive lack of information of the voting public, "works."

Since the manifest interests of the managed public sphere were not its latent interests, one single question remained unexplained: Why does the managed public sphere not rebel? That the public of modern societies in fact rebels politically may be exemplified in a number of ways. For example, in Table 2 the results of a series of failed referendums on the European Union issues are summarized; referendums that were

Table 2 *Overview of rejected EU referendums, 1972–2008 (nonmember state referendums are italicized)*

Country	Year	Rejection %	Turnout %	Subject
Norway	*1972*	*53.5*	*79.1*	*EC membership*
Denmark	1992	50.7	82.9	Maastricht Treaty
Norway	*1994*	*52.5*	*88.8*	*EU membership*
Denmark	2000	53.2	87.6	Introduction Euro
Ireland	2001	53.9	34.8	Nice Treaty
Sweden	2003	56.1	81.2	Introduction Euro
France	2005	54.7	69.3	Constitutional Treaty
Netherlands	2005	61.5	62.8	Constitutional Treaty
Ireland	2008	53.4	53.1	Lisbon Treaty

supported, as a rule, by the political class of the countries in questions, yet failed, often based on a large turnout by eligible voters.

Even today, Mills' diagnosis, which differs very little from the characterization of an authoritarian society, is described by influential intellectuals such as Alan Wolfe as much more accurate than those of his colleagues who, already in those days, were working "objectively" or quantitatively; who were thus critical of Mills; and who instead understood themselves and their fellows to be citizens of a pluralistic society. Be that as it may, one may well criticize C. Wright Mills' diagnosis of society as incorrect, as did Robert Dahl (1961b), for example. Nonetheless, in the social sciences of the postwar era, it became the general impression that the public is largely passive and does not threaten its rulers and the prevailing conditions. This view is expressed not least by many representatives of neo-Marxism, as well as by Michel Foucault and Pierre Bourdieu. However much we could learn from these proponents about so many subtle forms of the exercise of power, their view of modern society remained too pessimistic. Rather, we were able to observe the rise of many new, and in part very effective, public spheres, which often ran counter to these dark prophecies.

What changes in society are responsible for the appearance and growth of this new public sphere? Two changes that are tied relatively closely to the status of natural persons suggest themselves immediately, even if this does not mean that the structural change that pervades the qualities and significance of corporate actors was inconsequential. The impetus for this new public sphere is doubtless constituted by two historically unprecedented developments: the rise in general prosperity and the average level of knowledge of the population in the Western societies of the postwar era – resulting in a loss of power of the major social institutions. Large multinational corporations today have less economic power and political influence that they "enjoyed" three decades ago, for example.[48] But what has caused this loss of power?

The new public sphere drew attention to itself above all by the fact that its mere presence constrained institutions' options for taking action. Their loss of power became apparent primarily in the form of indecision, meaning nothing other than that the major institutions are visibly

---

[48] Robert Reich (2007:10), writing about the sociopolitical and socioeconomic conditions of recent decades, notes with justification, in my opinion: "Look almost anywhere in today's economy and you find the typical company has less market power that then the typical company of three decades ago ... companies of all sizes are competing more vigorously than before. The world economy contains far fewer oligopolies than it did decades ago, and almost no monopolies apart from those created or maintained by government."

incapable of working their will. This fact first became apparent during the Vietnam War. The resistance of the new public sphere, of new social movements, limited the United States government's political options, not least the nuclear option, and ultimately led not only to the end of the war, but also to the end of compulsory military service in the United States (1972).

Thus the new public sphere made itself known above all via an increase in (new) social movements – be they local, national, or international. The new public sphere concerns itself with social issues and, in doing so, can rely upon the logic of selection of the omnipresent media. Even as a mere possibility, such a constellation puts pressure on the major institutions. The new public sphere thus increases the permeability between social institutions: civil society actors become economic and political actors, for instance, whenever organized victims of violence change the application of laws or even the legislation, the resistance to nuclear power plants leads to the (long-term) end of this form of energy production, or public opinion is mobilized in the short term, and a society's culture, the lifestyle, and thought patterns of its members, is changed in the long term.

Of course, there are also lines of conflict within the new public sphere, exactly as there were clashes of interest in the managed public sphere. The new public sphere is politically divided. It is not necessarily liberal or conservative. And of course, the new public sphere also represents a problem for the functioning of democracy and its institutions.

Despite all the skepticism regarding disenchantment with politics and cocooning (two of the most important catchwords of the debate over the theory of democracy in recent years), the fact that the new public sphere has made its appearance – most unexpectedly, and unexpectedly vehement – is once again evident these days. If there was skepticism in recent years, above all regarding the apparently insignificant entertainments based on the new media (flash- and carrot-mobs, Facebook groups, etc.), then nowadays we recognize both a recent and unambiguous repoliticization and a much-discussed broadening of the base of such active public spheres. As we can see in the cases of the Stuttgart 21 railway station redevelopment project in Germany, the costliest transport of radioactive waste material in many years (the "Wendland protests"), and the increasing professionalization of political participation using the means of the new media (avaaz.org, online giving marketplaces, etc.), a remarkable dynamic is becoming evident. The Hamburg Senate's failed attempts at school reform, or the Bavarian referendum on nonsmoking legislation, provide further examples of the power of individual actors and small groups. The political efficacy of such protests, though they are often ridiculed initially, can hardly be underestimated (see Lipsky,

1968). If nothing else, the long-term, systematic power of considering questions of common welfare is made clear in the case of the above-mentioned railway station protest in Stuttgart. The united political and economic actors' inability to push through a prestige project at the expert level, and ultimately to argue with the legitimacy of representative democracy, stands revealed.

This new power of the public sphere is not only made possible via today's much more easily configured internal communication. What once had to be centrally prepared by groups with large memberships and resources can now be rolled out through an often decentralized, organized network from which spontaneous activities can be organized into an all-encompassing solidarity of protest. At least as important, however, is the leverage that groups that originally were often marginal can take advantage of to attract attention in the context of a media society. Access to public media attention by means of staging spectacular events, formerly reserved for specialized organizations (most famously, the now-classic Greenpeace campaigns on cooling towers or on the high seas), is nowadays likewise democratized. This does not mean that anyone's pet topic can receive a hearing at any time; the knowledge of how the focusing and organizational logic of medial communication works, however, is now widely diffused among the population. Professional journalistic formats also offer a mouthpiece to such individuals and groups who in the earlier days of a scarcity of channels simply remained unheard. And whatever the mass media take no notice of will find its way through the Internet – the simply unmanageable vestibule of the medial public sphere.

Soft power and democracy

I have already discussed the role of the media in their relation to and impact on democratic governance. However, that discussion was limited to what I called the "broadcast society," a society in which the dominant mass media were newspapers, radio, television, and movies. The broadcast society ended with the emergence of the Internet as the increasingly popular and widely accessible communication media.[49]

---

[49] A United States–based panel study examining the relations between television viewing and Internet usage confirms that the Internet does not *displace* the media of the broadcast society: the authors "find that the Internet's effect on television viewing varies by age group, reducing it by a moderate amount for the youngest Americans but having no impact on the viewing of the oldest Americans" (Liebowitz and Zentner, 2012:234). The authors anticipate that the collective shift from television viewing to the Internet will likely become more typical as older age cohorts gain more familiarity with the Internet.

What distinguished the broadcast society was the restricted access to public communication for the majority of the population. The majority of the population simply lacked direct or indirect access to a printing press, the airwaves, or a studio. Communication was asymmetrical. The democratic function of oversight and supervision was therefore in the hands of an "elite" of professional editors, journalists, or directors who acted as gatekeepers.

Compared to the broadcast age, the Internet abolished the professional monopoly of access to the means of communicating with large audiences, considerably enhanced the substantive diversity of what is being communicated, and permits transparency and oversight on an unprecedented scale.[50] However, the diversity of accessible contents even in the age of the Internet is not "neutral," limitless, or without powerful gatekeepers (such as the Google search engine). Hence, it would be misleading to suggest that the broadcast society and its typical means of communication and forms of control of communication are being replaced by a commons society in which attributes of market concentration disappear in favor of general-purpose devices of communication and all enclosures of communication vanish.[51]

Nonetheless, even though access is stratified, do the novel digital communication options (information technologies), including the so-called social media, usher in a new kind of (domestic) democracy, for example, a new age of participatory politics and the experience of politics itself? In his examination of *Technologies without Boundaries* in which the new age of the technology of telecommunication is analyzed, the political scientist Ithiel de Sola Pool (1990:262) asked if the new technological trends, as far as this may be anticipated at all, "will promote individualism and will make it harder, not easier, to govern and organize a coherent society." De Sola Pools' questions about the social consequences of the new communication technologies continue to occupy center stage of any inquiry into the influence and soft power of the new media and their relation to democratic governance.

---

[50] The Internet may well be further supportive of the association between transparency, in the sense of the transparency of policy making and democratic governance. The conclusion of Hollyer, Rosendorff, and Vreeland's (2011:12) study of the association of transparency and democratic polity can be summed up in a few words: "Electoral competition is associated with greater transparency."
[51] The theoretically and practically deficient account – in particular the official account – of the so-called "digital divide" emphasizes almost exclusively the lack of technical access to or exclusion from the new media of certain population groups (see Mansell, 2002:412–417; Sassi, 2005). As a result, the problem of how to develop appropriate intellectual abilities and learn to critically and reflexively deal with the new media remains a black box.

The social media most likely had a part as a catalyst of societal change in the Tunisian and Egyptian revolutions of 2011. The social media sites Facebook and Twitter, and others in the future, are prime examples of fast horizontal communication ("informational cascade") bypassing attempted efforts of manipulation and suppression by national censors.[52] Or it is perhaps too early to form a definite judgment and reexamine early celebratory accounts about the ability of the new communication options to have an emancipatory potential, advance liberties, achieve more transparency, and generate political trust?[53] And, what are the "dysfunctions" of the new technologies? It is not surprising that corporations who control and benefit from the infrastructure of the new communication devices and channels should praise the function of the new technologies. However, the history of science and technology has witnessed many examples of initial euphoria about the transformative capacity (power) of inventions, only often to be followed by much more sober and measured assessments of the consequences of such innovations.[54] Such disenchantment can now

---

[52] Joachim Åström and colleagues (2012:143–144), in a study of the so-called "e-participation" in nondemocratic societies, reach the conclusion that the forms and the expansion of digital participation are particularly evident in some, but not all nondemocratic societies. The authors assume that the need for legitimacy strategies of the state is responsible for this development in nondemocratic societies: "The politics of e-participation is primarily concerned with legitimation. Rather than being driven by responsiveness to citizens or citizen demand, authoritarian governments may respond to international pressure to demonstrate modernity and legitimacy through e-participation sites, and, at the same time, use those sites to propagate government authority and extend the repressive and bureaucratic processes that also permeate offline state–citizen interactions ... The legitimation hypothesis states that economic globalization and technological development drive e-participation initiatives in authoritarian regimes, regardless of the level of democratization as well as broader trends of democratization." Whether these strategies to legitimize the political system may backfire, the future will show.

[53] Assertions about the novelty of social or material phenomena always meet with more or less skepticism when it comes to the newness of such phenomena. This also applies to claims about social media as catalysts of social and cultural change. As an essay in *The Economist* about the course of the Reformation argues, what occurred in the Arab world in 2011 also "happened during the Reformation, nearly 500 years ago, when Martin Luther and his allies took the new media of their day-pamphlets, ballads and woodcuts – and circulated them through social networks to promote their message of religious reform" (www.economist.com/blogs/babbage/2011/12/social-media-16th-centuryist.com/blogs/babbage/2011/12/social-media-16th-century). See also the urgent warning expressed by the historian Robert Darnton (2010:1) against viewing the development of the media of communication as an exclusively modern phenomenon: "The marvels of communication technology in the present have produced a false consciousness about the past – even in the sense that communication has no history, or had nothing of importance to consider before the days of television and the internet."

[54] Immediately following the end of World War II and the dawn of the widespread diffusion in the United States of the so-called mass media, radio, print, and film, Paul Lazarsfeld and Robert K. Merton ([1948] 1957:457–458), for example, note that the "ubiquity of

again be observed as it becomes evident to what extent the new technologies are employed by states, for example, to advance surveillance and espionage purposes in the name of enhancing safety and security, or by corporations who control the infrastructure for generating profits.

The transcendence (not the elimination) of the communication options of the broadcast society may also change international political relations, politics, and participation. The broadcast society is in many ways, although not exclusively, confined to the nation state. The influence of newspapers, radio, and television is most salient within national boundaries. During the age of the broadcast society in international relations, nation-states are the main actors on the global stage. With the advent of the Internet, the importance of the boundaries of the nation-state for communicative purposes declines. More and more groups of people have access to knowledge across the boundaries of the nation-state. The diffusion and the decline in the cost of communication options disarm the power of the nation-state to control its boundaries and the access to information of its citizens. Non-state actors gain access to and influence on the global stage. But in either case, the skeptical question remains whether the gatekeepers have disappeared or have only been replaced by other gatekeepers. Most recently, on the occasion of the Group of 8 industrialized countries meeting in France, then French President Sarkozy, obviously assuming that the Internet had considerable political clout, urged the adoption of measures that would police the Internet much more tightly, arguing that existing laws and regulations were inadequate to respond to the global world of the Internet.[55] Authoritarian regimes attempting to control and manipulate the modern media and employing the media to promote assent have, on the whole,

---

the mass media promptly leads man to an almost magical belief in their enormous power ... But there is another and, probably, a more realistic basis for widespread concerns with the social role of the mass media; a basis which has to do with the changing types of social control exercised by powerful interest groups in society. Increasingly, the chief power groups, among which organized business occupies the most spectacular place, have come to adopt techniques for manipulating mass publics through propaganda in place of more direct means of control [*mass persuasion*] ... The manifest concern over the functions of the mass media is in part based upon the valid observation that the mass media have taken on the job of rendering mass publics conformative to the social and economic *status quo*."

[55] Cf. Eric Pfanner, "G-8 leaders call for tighter Internet regulation," *New York Times*, May 24, 2011. The most prominent skeptical book-length discussion of the emancipating qualities of the Internet is Evegeny Morozov's *The Net Delusion* (2011), who suggests that all communication options are mere instruments that can be mobilized for moral as well as amoral principles. The French historian Pierre Rosanvallon ([2006] 2008:70) emphatically rejects this statement: "The Internet is in the process of ... creating an open space for oversight and evaluation. The Internet is not merely an 'instrument'; it *is* the surveillance function."

not been very successful, which indicates that the power of the media and its content are of limited effectiveness in shaping the consciousness of the users in a lasting fashion.

Some, if not considerable, hope for the extension of democracy to the remaining authoritarian states in the world in our times rests with the rapid enlargement of information and communication technologies, especially the spread of access to the Internet. The extension of information and communication technologies with their horizontal bias is at the core of the idea that we are living in an information society or network society (cf. Weinberger, 2011). But whether access to and growing utilization of the Internet – and therefore the mobilization and circulation of what constitutes soft power representing ideas, values, and information – perhaps critically viewed as a mere technological fix, will also sustain and perhaps enlarge democratic participation and governance both domestically and internationally and become the foundation for democratic emancipation initiated on a transnational basis is a most contentious issue at the present time (see Bimber, 1998; Coombs and Cutbirth, 1998; Coleman, 1999; Boas, 2000).

Access to the Internet as such or the abundance of the Web does not in itself – an attribute that drives much of the discussion of the consequences of the Internet – insure contact with relevant political information, nor does usage of the Internet enable actors to organize politically if such organization is not sanctioned by the state and the law. Political regimes, not only authoritarian regimes, often try their utmost to limit the transparency of governance. Democratic nations differ considerably in the extent to which they make information available to the public. The success of social movements in promoting open governance is uneven. Not surprisingly, the issue of democratic governance in response to digital communication options is an essentially contested matter (Ward, Gibson, and Lusoli, 2003; Marlin-Bennett, 2011; Loader and Mercea, 2011). Some politicians and scientists make a case that the new communication options and their enhanced capacity for horizontal communication will lead to more democracy (e.g., Coleman and Blumler, 2009),[56] hence

---

[56] The case may be made that Alexis de Tocqueville ([1835] 2000), in his discussion of the role of the press in the United States, assigns a similar function of horizontal communication to the press. De Tocqueville notes not only that the press was a powerful force promoting democracy but that "its eye is constantly open to detect the secret springs of political designs and to summon the leaders of all parties in turn to the bar of public opinion. It rallies the interests of the community round certain principles and draws up the creed of every party; for it affords a means of intercourse between those who hear and address each other *without ever coming into immediate contact* (emphasis added)."

their emphasis on such terms as e-government or e-democracy. Other observers offer much more sober assessments and remain to be convinced (e.g., Sunstein, 2001, in an early assessment) or do not believe that Internet usage will enhance changes in established and highly stratified patterns of political participation.[57] I will begin with the disbelieving and skeptical accounts that have grown in recent years and are increasingly in the majority.

The assertion in this case is that more channels of information and greater access to information as such do not assure liberties and democratic governance or prevent pathological usages of the Internet. The opposite – that is, pathological and propagandistic – use of the Internet is also imaginable. As a matter of fact, in authoritarian nations the propagandistic use of the Internet is widely practiced. Although Nobel laureate and former politician Albert Gore (2007:260) is aware of the openness of the Internet to undemocratic values and commitments, he characterizes the Internet as a "platform for pursuing the truth, and the decentralized creation and distribution of ideas ... It's a platform ... for reason."

David Runciman (2005),[58] in a review published in the *London Review of Books*, of the book by Michael Graetz and Ian Shapiro (2005) that deals with the political effort to abolish the inheritance tax in the United States in 2001 argues that the successful campaign against the inheritance tax is a striking example for the power of narratives in politics and the transformation of politics by Internet-transmitted soft power, as well as for the ease with which individual narratives become the core of political debates:

The new information technology, with its cascades of rumor and limitless outlets for personal histories, is more often than not the enemy of informed public discussion. In the face of an endless readiness on all sides to heed the unmediated voice of personal experience, it has become harder to sustain the bigger picture for any plausible defense of progressive politics. This shifts politics, inexorably, to the right.

---

[57] Based on a 2008 representative survey of Americans conducted by the Pew Internet and American Life Project, Schlozman, Verba, and Brady (2010:487) found little evidence that "there has been any change in the extent to which political participation is stratified by socio-economic status, but it suggests that the web has ameliorated the well-known participatory deficit among those who have just joined the electorate. Even when only that subset of the population with Internet access is considered, participatory acts such as contributing to candidates, contacting officials, signing a political petition, or communicating with political groups are as stratified socioeconomically when done on the web as when done offline."

[58] The same points are advanced by Joseph S. Nye Jr., "The future of power," *The Chronicle of Higher Education*, June 5, 2011 (http://chronicle.com.login.ezproxy.library.ualberta.ca/article/The-Future-of-Power/127753/).

Cass Sunstein (2001)[59] also refers to the limiting quality of the allegedly limitless access to information on the Internet. In the process of his critique of the Internet, he assigns direct and powerful effects to the Internet and its impact on democratic conduct although the latter, much of the time, is far from having a democracy-enhancing impact. Software found on the emerging digital technology allows for the construction of filters by others or by the users themselves. The filters are based on the usage of the Internet by an individual or on the idiosyncratic preferences that personalize the exposure to topics, ideas, and points of view, thus missing out, of course, on exposure to untamed ideas and points of view. For Sunstein, personalization thus defined represents a disservice to democracy and to freedom itself since "unanticipated encounters, involving unfamiliar and even irritating topics and points of view" are the salt of democracy. Filtering is a good thing of dubious value, as Sunstein maintains.

But what is different in the usage of the Internet as compared with the communication options typical in the era of the broadcast society? In the broadcast society, most readers and listeners did not have direct access to the "creators" of ideas and the participants in events. People who read a newspaper are offered selective news and read the newspaper selectively.[60] The gatekeepers or intermediaries do not vanish in the digital age, nor does the habit of readers and users to utilize the media according to their interests. The power of the intermediaries and gatekeepers is perhaps not as significant anymore, if only because the number and the range of gatekeepers and intermediaries escalates. But the elementary fact that users make selective use of the Web (which speaks against the idea of an information overload) becomes the basis for some observers to conclude that the structure of the broadcast society with its few speakers and many listeners is repeated in the age of the Internet: "It seems the utopian vision of the Internet as a place where everyone gets to be heard equally is merely an empty promise by wooly-headed thinkers and aging hippies" (Weinberger, 2008:202).

---

[59] I am referring to the Internet publication of Sunstein's essay; as a result, I am not able to provide the exact page numbers for the quotes from his text.

[60] Therefore, the frequent and critical reference to an "information overload" in the Internet and the typical assessment associated with this observation needs to be called into question. The information overload discourse is not new (see Blair, 2010), but abstracts, just as in the past, from the users of information. Much more characteristic for reflections about the "information society" is Frank Webster's (1999:375) judgment: "Today's 'information society' is one in which enormous amounts of the information available are deeply uninformative, 'junk information' analogous to the junk food that is plentiful but lacking nutrition." The information society appears to be a society without humans. What is missing is a cultural theory of information.

Whether the loss of the professional gatekeepers (i.e., journalists) or public intellectuals produces a democratic deficit since – as Sunstein insists – the intermediaries of the broadcast society performed important democratic functions such as oversight, and enabled chance encounters and shared experiences with diverse others, is a debatable consideration. It could be argued that the loss of the intermediaries of the broadcast age, for example, transforms the passive reader into an active communicator (with an anonymous audience). Yet, what kind of media usage is more likely to prompt reflexive reasoning? Is it the encounter of ideas that are not too far removed from one's own point of view rather than ideas that are substantially at odds with it? I would not rule out the former as the context more likely to trigger reflection, nor the possibility that ideas that are considerably at odds with one's own ideas only serve to reinforce these ideas. This observation would contradict Cass Sunstein's (2001) plea for a space that contains a significant range of heterogeneous materials because such heterogeneity itself triggers self-doubt and changes views, as a consequence.[61]

Sunstein maintains that the dramatic increase in the range of content and ideas promulgated on the Internet triggers premature closure to conflicting ideas as a way of coping with the diversity or complexity found on the Internet. The choices offered on the Internet "are likely, in many cases, to mean that people will try to find material that makes them comfortable, or is created by and for people like themselves," which in the end enhances the social cleavages among groups of people (i.e., group polarization). Group polarization rather than openness to competing points of view and the groups that advocate such ideas is "a human regularity ... [that] will significantly increase if people think of themselves, antecedently or otherwise, as part of a group having a shared identity and a degree of solidarity" (Sunstein, 2001). The Internet is a major vehicle that fosters group polarization.

Greater group polarization, if indeed it is created and sustained by the diverse choices found on the Internet can, as it were, support democratic liberties and not only the taming of freedoms. Sunstein does stress the same point. However, he expresses concern about the possibility that the Internet is merely used as a confirmatory communication option. It follows that it is "extremely important to ensure that people are

---

[61] In greater detail, Sunstein (2001) notes that "a system in which you lack control over particular content that you see has a great deal in common with a public street, where you might encounter not only friends, but a heterogeneous variety of people engaged in a wide array of activities (including, perhaps, political protest and begging). In fact, a risk with a system of perfect individual control is that it can reduce the importance of the 'public sphere' and of common space in general."

exposed to views other than those with which they currently agree, that doing so protects against the harmful effects of group polarization on individual thinking and on social cohesion" (Sunstein, 2001). Whether the contents of the Internet support conformity or reflection or privilege immediacy, it is evident that Sunstein is convinced that the Internet is an immediately persuasive force in the political life of modern societies. But "an increasingly fragmented communications universe will reduce the level of shared experiences having salience to diverse groups" (Sunstein, 2001) and will, in the end, foster increased individualization, that is, a growing segment of secluded publics, and cut off users of the Internet.

However, the context that may well have a much greater and much more lasting impact on the political points of view of individuals and groups is not the solitary and insulated interaction of individuals left alone with digital communication options but, much more likely, social networks, especially face-to-face and emotionally charged encounters with other individuals. In this sense, the new communication options are an extension of the media of the broadcast age where the soft power of ideas and points of view also did its most significant labor in face-to-face encounters and embedded in conversations.

After all, the study of the effect of "mass communication" on decisions and actions is still indebted to the pioneers of communication research, Elihu Katz and Paul Lazarsfeld. The many studies carried out by Katz and Lazarsfeld and their associates of the *Bureau of Social Research* at Columbia University all stress the priority of social influence over the direct impact of information in decision making and, therefore, the limited effects of mass communication per se (cf. Katz, 1987).[62] Is there any reason to assume that digital communication has invalidated this conclusion and that now, in the wake of societal and technological changes, we are witnessing strong and direct media effects?[63] Even if the answer is in the negative, that is, if patterns of influence follow established social pathways, this does mean that the new communication

---

[62] In an early paper, Paul Lazarsfeld (1948) states "mass media are not mainly effective in promoting a specific idea or engendering a stand on a definite issue. What they tend rather to do is to shape for us the picture of the more distant world with which we do not have direct personal contact ... Short-term investigations will never be able to trace the way in which, over a lifetime, the mass media accentuate for some people parts of the social world and conceal them from others" (as quoted by Katz, 1987:S36).

[63] One perspective which expects such a change in the impact of the media, whether they are new or conventional, links its supporting reasoning to the decline of the constraints of civil society in modern societies, as Robert Putnam (2000) has for example discussed, and therefore to the growing detachment of individuals from traditional constraints and influences (cf. Iyengar, 1991; Bennet and Iyengar, 2008).

options are, despite their stratified access,[64] politically irrelevant, weak, or without effect on how politics is experienced.

The less skeptical assessment of the role of the new communication options refers, for example, to the decrease in the transaction costs of accessing relevant political information in terms of the potential volume of information, access to multiple political options, time spent, distance covered, and expenditures incurred, the lower need for any state regulation of the new media,[65] the relative ease with which previously silent and excluded individuals and groups might be brought into political conversation and are offered previously unknown opportunities of supervision (as well as its pathological side of denunciation), and the ability of the Internet to reach cohorts that are Internet savvy but have never taken to the communication media of the broadcast society (cf. Ward and de Vreese, 2011; Rosanvallon, [2006] 2008:66–71; Ward Gibson and Lusoli, 2002:663). In short, it is expected that exposure to the Internet and its vast quantities of information will reduce political apathy, stimulate political activity, create links, and build networks at the regional, national, and transnational levels. Such expectations about the impact of the new communications options raise the old question whether patterns of stratified participation manifestly change as a result of the Internet or remain essentially as biased as usual, that is, as was often the case in the age of the broadcast society. Since the Internet is a still-emerging communication option, it may well be too early to form a definite judgment about its impact on the political affairs of nations, regions of the world, and global political development. Global Internet usage is a rapidly changing phenomenon.

---

[64] For a recent description of the "new" digital divide, see Susan P. Crawford, "The new digital divide," *New York Times*, December 3, 2011 (www.nytimes.com/2011/12/04/opinion/sunday/internet-access-and-the-new-divide.html). Crawford reports the following November 2011 data of the U.S. Department of Commerce: "According to numbers released last month by the Department of Commerce, a mere 4 out of every 10 households with annual household incomes below $25,000 in 2010 reported having wired Internet access at home, compared with the vast majority — 93 percent — of households with incomes exceeding $100,000. Only slightly more than half of all African-American and Hispanic households (55 percent and 57 percent, respectively) have wired Internet access at home, compared with 72 percent of whites."

[65] Yochia Benkler (1999:562) for example advances just such a case: "Technology now makes possible the attainment of decentralization and democratization by enabling small groups of constituents and individuals to become *users*—participants in the production of their information environment—rather than by lightly regulating concentrated commercial mass media to make them better serve individuals conceived as passive consumers. Structural media regulation in the twenty-first century must, in turn, focus on enabling a wide distribution of the capacity to produce and disseminate information as a more effective and normatively attractive approach to serve the goals that have traditionally animated structural media regulation."

The quantitative analysis performed, over an eleven-year period (1992–2002) of Internet usage and democratization (using the *Freedom House* scores), by Best and Wade (2009) shows mixed results depending, for example, on the region of the world. However, more recent figures for the years 2001–2002 indicate a positive relation between Internet usage and democracy. Best and Wade (2009:270) conclude with the following upbeat note, "overall, however, our evidence supports the existence of a positive relationship between democratic growth and Internet penetration." At any rate, given the high complexity of the societal effects induced by the soft power of the new media, early euphoric assessments concerning their political consequences or their power to help realize a digital democracy (cf. Timonen, 2013) need to be reconsidered.

Democracy and knowledge

I am haunted by the idea that this break in human civilization, caused by the discovery of the scientific method, may be irreparable. Though I love science I have the feeling that it is so greatly opposed to history and tradition that it cannot be absorbed by our civilization. The political and military horrors and complete breakdown of ethics which I have witnessed in my lifetime may be not a symptom of social weakness, but a necessary consequence of the rise of science – which in itself is amongst the highest intellectual achievements of man.   Max Born (1968:58)

The theoreticians of the postindustrial or postmodern society (e.g., Jean-François Lyotard, Daniel Bell, and Zbigniew Brzezinski) differ in their diagnoses of the development of modern societies in may respects, for instance in their definition of knowledge and of exactly what form of knowledge will assume a prominent function in these societies. Still, their visions of modern societies do agree on one important point: in modern societies, knowledge becomes a salient resource of societal power. On the basis of their common assumption about the role of knowledge in society, a political conclusion may be deduced: the ability of the average citizen to take on an active political role in postindustrial or postmodern societies becomes a highly precarious enterprise. The average citizen lacks the knowledge needed to effectively participate and intervene in the political affairs of his community or society. Since political participation by ordinary citizens is desired and anticipated, it is entirely reasonable to expect that feelings and emotions of political alienation, incapacity, meaninglessness, and a withdrawal into the private sphere could escalate. Aside from such rather general diagnoses about the political households of modern societies that assume more and more strictly hierarchical political processes, the theorists of postindustrial and postmodern societies have offered little detail with respect to the political life in emergent societies. As Samuel Huntington (1974:165–166) has therefore pointed out, there are three reasons for the lack of interest in political developments and structural changes shown by the theorists of postindustrial society. First, political processes in postindustrial societies are of minor importance. Theories of postindustrial societies with their emphasis on knowledge, rationality, and technology have a distinctive affinity to other technocratic theories. Such an affinity is reasonable because the irrationality of political decisions is seen as being increasingly replaced by the rational role of science as a decision-making tool. Second, postindustrial politics would be preoccupied with industrial policy and the assumption that there is a fundamental discontinuity between the economic and the political system. Third, postindustrial politics is deemphasized since it is seen, not necessarily as unimportant, but as "unpleasant." As Huntington (1974:166) stresses, "a more rationalized society [such as postindustrial society] could generate less political conflict, with politics becoming the arena for the expression of emotional frustration and irrational impulse, both of which find little outlet elsewhere in society. Postindustrial politics ... could be the darker side of postindustrial society."

In discussing the role of experts in democratic societies, it is perhaps superfluous to report a common view that remains tied to the conviction, well expressed by Sanford Lakoff (1971:12), that there can be no disputing "the need for the ultimate power of decision to rest with those affected by the use of knowledge rather than with the specialists who make it available." Nonetheless, there has been and there is today an even more vigorous debate about the possibility that experts and the highly specialized knowledge of advisers, consultants, and experts is threatening to displace common sense with logicality (cf. Arendt, 1953) and, as a consequence, the capacity of citizens and politicians alike to carry out their mandate in democratic society to make independent decisions for which knowledge is but a convenient instrument.[66]

---

[66] George Steiner (2011) also notes, and is concerned about, the growing distance between modern science and ordinary reflections. Steiner observes "our world is shrinking. Science is becoming inaccessible to us. Who can understand the latest innovations in genetics, astrophysics and biology? Who can explain them to the profane? *Knowledge no longer communicates*; writers and philosophers in our day are incapable of enabling us to understand science. At the same time, the scope of imagination in science is dazzling. How can we claim to speak of human consciousness if we overlook what is most daring and imaginative? I am concerned by what it means to be literate today. Is it possible to be literate if you do not understand non-linear equations?"

In a recent essay in the *New York Review of Books* (November 18, 2004, p. 38) the molecular biologist Richard Lewontin maintains "the knowledge required for political rationality, once available to the masses, is now in the possession of a specially educated elite, a situation that creates a series of tensions and contradictions in the operation of representative democracy." Lewontin's observations have a close affinity to many equally worried reflections, in the last few decades, about a growing divide between expert and lay knowledge and the prospect that a close union of knowledge and power spells the "death of democracy." Political action increasingly relies on expert advice, but "can those in power be trusted to use wisely what they learn and will those who profess knowledge resist the temptations and corruptions of power" (Lakoff, 1971:5)? In the final analysis, the lock between knowledge and power is seen to disenfranchise most if not all ordinary citizens in modern society.[67] Has therefore the optimism shared by the Philosophers of the French Enlightenment, in particular the Marquis de Condorcet (1796), with respect to the role of knowledge not only in overcoming poverty, violence, and ignorance but also in building a sustainable democratic society, been destroyed in contemporary society (cf. Jones, 2004:16–63)?

Richard Lewontin's skeptical comments and the increasing usage of contemporary, especially natural scientific, knowledge not only by governments but also as a tool of politics (cf. Pielke, 2007) conveniently sum up the questions about the multiple linkages between knowledge and democracy I want to explore in the following section of this chapter.

The fact is: the deficit of scientific knowledge found in ordinary citizens seems to become an insurmountable barrier for their political participation. The connection between knowledge and resistance is infrequently examined in the literature, and if it is examined it always concerns knowledgeable individuals who, for example as patients, managers, consumers, and voters, resist acting on their knowledge or information (e.g., Starbuck, 1992). The analysis therefore tends to stress the irrationality of the individuals (that is, their inability to maximize their utilities) or the groups who fail – obviously often to their detriment – to reach the proper conclusion despite being well briefed or well informed. In the present context, I will take a less common perspective, focusing on the

---

[67] The dependence on experts in modern societies is more pervasive than what can be observed in the realm of political decisions; it extends to ordinary matters of the life-world as well, with the attendant "loss of people's ability to help themselves," as Gernot Böhme (1992:51) indicates. My discussion of the role of experts in modern societies is, however, confined to the realm of politics.

extent to which knowledgeablity can be an important foundation for resisting the established political order.

An analysis of the relative importance of scientific findings and democratic participation may be guided by two distinct epistemic interests. The first one would be to ask whether the frequently perceived deficit of scientific knowledge in civil society can be accepted as an adequate description and, if so, whether it is reasonable, on the other hand, to consider ways of reducing this deficit in practice. The second one, and the one I prefer, is to call into question this finding and the assumptions about the power of scientific knowledge that are associated with it.

Scientific knowledge and common sense

> Wine is none the more pleasant to him who knows its first faculties.   Michel de Montaigne [1580] 1998:516

I will first summarize the prevailing views of the relation between knowledge, democracy, and political power given what is seen, by their proponents, to be a realistic appraisal of the political circumstances of the day: (1) knowledge is power, and the powerful are knowledgeable; (2) the public is ignorant; (3) the exercise of power is cemented through the control of relevant scientific findings by the powerful; and (4) the effective political participation of citizens is therefore seriously damaged. As I have also stressed, these arguments are not easily separated. Let me first sum up my criticism of this mélange of ideas concerning the convergence of knowledge and power:

1. The thesis that scientific knowledge accrues more or less automatically to the politically powerful can be easily monopolized by them and, therefore, is excluded from democratic practice, is mistaken (cf. Nelkin, 1975; MacCrae, 1981; Laird, 1993).
2. Is it possible to reconcile democracy and expertise? The thesis of the convergence of power and knowledge is misleading insofar as it raises the expectations for scientific findings to have an immediate and direct policy- or practice-relevant impact. Instructions for action cannot be directly derived from scientific knowledge. Scientific knowledge is always preliminary and tentative. Choosing between options is never a purely scientific matter. Public discourse has always been and continues to be informed by a mix of scientific and political reasoning including the politicization of the language of science.
3. The authority of expertise or the influence of rational reasoning aided by scientific findings or so-called facts known/available in the context of political decision making is overestimated. It is mistaken to assume

that the lack of what might be called "liberal" and, therefore, the presence of "conservative" attributes of knowledge make knowledge powerful in practice.

4. The lack of scientific and technical knowledge is a constitutive of many facets of everyday life in modern society and, therefore, loses much of its alleged danger. Science does not depoliticize public issues.[68] Civil society is, as a result, not *a priori* disqualified from participating in discussions and decisions about the handling of scientific knowledge and technical developments. Varied "publics" posses their own intellectual capacities and epistemic cultures. In order to challenge expertise, one does not need to "know" as much as the experts do (see Nelkin, 1975:49–54).[69] Public issues remain political issues.

5. A final point of criticism to which I will return after my summary in greater detail concerns the assertion made, for example, by Joseph Schumpeter that knowing individuals and ignorant individuals will rely on different political decision calculuses.[70]

6. It remains to be emphasized that the social sciences, as long as social science knowledge is not understood to constitute merely instrumental knowledge, can indeed play a constructive role by generating enabling knowledge for a sober analysis of and ways of coping with the gradient between scientific and everyday knowledge.

The influence and impact of some social institutions and some social roles within these institutions, especially the economy and science of modern society but also, more generally, the role of the expert coupled, as it were, to these powerful institutions often extend – contrary to the theory of functional differentiation – well beyond their own institutional boundaries. The social consequences of the reach these institutions have are controversial; for example, the number of social scientists and humanists who alert us to the supposedly overwhelming societal power of the markets and call for our resistance against surreptitious and mysterious market forces are legion (e.g., Bourdieu, 1998).

---

[68] Of course, the statement does not put into question the practice by policy makers to define issues as technical rather than political issues.

[69] Dorothy Nelkin (1975:53–54), summing up her case study of two controversial large-scale construction plans, the building of a power plant, and the construction of a new runway of an international airport, concludes that "those opposing a decision need not muster equal evidence. It is sufficient to raise questions that will undermine the expertise of a developer whose power and legitimacy rests on his monopoly of knowledge or claims of special competence."

[70] A study of the voting behavior of the American electorate in the 1992–2004 presidential elections indicates that the "primary effect of increasing voter knowledge is to raise turnout levels and solidify preexisting vote tendencies" (Dow, 2011:381).

However, the voices of humanists and social scientists who mobilize against the extraordinary societal power of scientific knowledge and scientific expertise that they feel, for example, are undermining the very foundations of democratic governance, are modest in number, though not absent. Yet, scientists almost unanimously agree that science has an extraordinary status, if not the pole position, within modern society. But they also concur that the command of scientific knowledge by members of civil society is best described as one of complete ignorance. And there is also considerable agreement among many observers outside of the scientific community that our ignorance has rather undesirable detrimental political if not many other consequences. The social and economic costs of just being informed about the prerequisites for one's good health are considerable.

There are many contemporary voices from inside the scientific community that substantiate my claim: Not only natural scientists but social scientists and members of the humanities community, as well, maintain that science now has an almost-iron grip on "Truth" while society's ability to constructively engage with science, let alone "control" science, has progressively diminished in recent times (cf. Latour, 1999:258). A prominent social scientist, Immanuel Wallerstein (2004:8), agrees and specifies that the still increasing specialization of the production of scientific knowledge restricts to but a few individuals the ability to form a separate, rational assessment of the quality of the evidence or the cogency of theoretical thought. The "harder" the science, Wallerstein adds, the more this applies.

The "canonical account" of the changing relations between science and society (Shapin, 1990:991) stresses:

In the past the relations between science and the public were intimate, pervasive and consequential. What belonged to science was poorly demarcated from what did not, just as the role of the man of science was scarcely discriminated from other social roles. The public and other social and cultural structures were powerful compared with science. Public concerns could influence not only the direction of scientific work but also the content of scientific knowledge.

The historian of science, Gerald Holton, expresses the contemporary case for the relation between science, the public, and society in a drastic fashion. For Holton, the citizens of modern societies are slaves.[71] Citizens are unable to act in a self-determined manner: "The new illiterates

---

[71] Paul Feyerabend (1978:234), while indeed employing a similar metaphor, does so in exactly the opposite sense, demanding of himself as a university teacher to *not* serve as a slave holder, that is, as a teacher merely promoting the ruling sociophilosophical curricula.

will be slaves with respect to key issues of self-governance" (see also Holton, 1996:51). The slave mentality of modern citizens, one might add, produces and manifests itself not only in "power-without-corresponding-representation" (Hupe and Edwards, 2012) but also in servile forms of consciousness and social conduct. Democracy means government that is accountable to its citizens. But the slave mentality and political status and influence that derives from such a state of mind of most civil society members implies that in reality the government makes us accountable to them. We are inundated with prohibitions, legislations, and public campaigns that tell us, for example, that we are eating the wrong food or are lousy parents (Minogue, 2010:4).

The new illiterates, in a grotesque inversion of the dream of the Age of Enlightenment, are abulic victims in the face of the symbiosis of power and knowledge (see Turner, 2001). Michael Polanyi and C. P. Snow were generally of one opinion that there is a dangerous gulf between science and the rest of the culture in modern societies. The well-known environmental theorist James Lovelock, inventor of the Gaia thesis, is more specific. Lovelock is extremely pessimistic, discouraged and convinced that contemporary humanity is just too stupid to avoid, for example, the dangers of imminent climate change.[72] The Swedish media researcher Peter Dahlgren (2009) refers to the "psychic havoc of the era of late modernity" where citizens have lost all their sense of political participation because they just do not feel competent. The modern forces of globalization and the dominance of rational market behavior supposedly reinforce the same basic trend toward alienation.

I will begin my critical reflections about the alleged gap between science and civil society's scientific knowledge with an equally broad but cognate set of questions and claims: As Max Horkheimer emphasized – in contrast to Karl Marx – justice or equity and freedom do not mutually support each other. Does this also apply to democracy and scientific knowledge? Or is knowledge a democratizer? Is the progress of knowledge, especially rapid scientific progress, a burden on democracy, civil society, and the capacity of the individual to assert his or her will? If there is a contradiction between scientific knowledge and democratic processes, is it a new development, or is the advance of liberal democracies codetermined by the joint force of the knowledge of the scientific community and democratic political conduct that makes it possible for us to claim that civil society, if not democracy, is the daughter

---

[72] James Lovelock, as quoted in an interview published in the *Guardian* in March 2010 (see also Chris Huntingford, "James Lovelock's climate change pessimism is unhelpful," *Guardian*, April 1, 2010).

of such specialized knowledge? Is it, perhaps, a naïve faith in knowledge that propels such a conviction?

To begin with, there are a couple of hardly-ever contested assertions about our age: scientific expertise is a salient political resource and most of the knowledge gained in the collective quest of knowledge is inaccessible to most living people. The growing gap between those who command specialized knowledge, as well as those with political influence, and most citizens who are in this respect disenfranchised is widely interpreted, along with the loss of sovereignty at the collective level brought about by the globalization process, as a serious stress on nation-bound representative democracy. The widely shared conjecture among scientists is that the rapid advancement of scientific knowledge – lacking apparently the attributes of contestedness, provisionalness, fragmentariness, malleability, ambivalence, flexibility, or fragility but having the attributes of cohesiveness, consistency, certainty, technicality, and stability that make it powerful – becomes the core foundation for policy decisions and, with it, the ways we collectively organize our life-world and cope with its problems. By the same token, the advance of the science-cum-technology complex severely limits the political effectiveness of the citizenry of modern societies.[73] The "technocratization" of knowledge and information contributes to an apparently irreversible concentration of power in modern democracies, as described by Shmuel Eisenstadt (1999:90), for example. Specialized knowledge claims, though highly relevant to the political process, are beyond the capacity of broader sectors of society to comprehend. The result may very well

---

[73] Given, for instance, Montesquieu's ([1748] 2007:8) definition of the very foundations of democracy: "When the body of the people is possessed of the supreme power, it is called democracy. When the supreme power is lodged in the hands of a part of the people, it is then an aristocracy." Holton (1986:102) explains his concerns in more detail: "As the divergence widens between those who make policy and citizens who lack the knowledge to assess their proper interests, the threat increases: the nation is in danger of being torn in two. The wound already felt by sensitive humanists such as Trilling must sooner or later become a traumatic separation – the most ironic cost of the advance of the modern science/engineering complex. On one side of the gulf will be a relatively small, technically trained elite, consisting chiefly of scientists, engineers, technicians, and other highly skilled individuals, amounting to a few percent of the population. As an increasing proportion of major decisions have a scientific/technical component, they will supply the new potentials as well as advice on how to direct and use them. On the other side will be the huge majority of the people, without sufficient language, tools, or methods to reason or to argue with the experts, to check on the options they present, or to counter either their technical enthusiasms or their doomsday warnings. That majority will effectively place itself in the hands of the elite, perhaps sinking quietly into the comforts and amusements which technology has helped provide." Holton (1986:102) adds "some cynics may even welcome such a state of affairs, for the ignorant tend to be easier to govern and to divert into militant philistinism."

"lead to political apathy and withdrawal from political participation" (Eisenstadt, 1999:90) and enhance the overconcentration of political power even further, above all that of the entire executive branch of government.

In the case of knowledge production and knowledge use, there is an accelerating trend away from what Otto Neurath ([1945] 1996:254; cf. also Siemsen, 2001) called for, namely a democratization of knowledge. However, as I will argue, the observations about the lack of democratic control of knowledge are no reason for us to give in to premature despondency. Nor are these views necessarily unique to our age.

The contemporary scientists I have cited can hardly be blamed for being content with or even recommending, in a celebratory manner, the "alienation" of the public from science. It is therefore worth noting that the thesis about an impoverished democracy, given the lack of scientific knowledge of civil society, resonates, in a peculiar sense, with early critiques of what we now call and implicitly favor in our concern about the state of modern democracy, namely deliberative democracy (see Bohman, 1998). Critics of bourgeois society such as Gustave Le Bon, Jacob Burkhardt, Karl Mannheim, Walter Lippmann, to name just a few of them, voiced their alarm about the emergence of a "mass society" that, in the end, would sacrifice all that is sacred: "position, property, religion, distinguished tradition, higher learning" (Burkhardt quoted in Viereck, 1956:159). Mass societies encourage the rule by the incompetent rather than what should be the case, namely the rule of experts. During the last World War and in the midst of the Nazi regime, Karl Mannheim (1940:86–87) observes "the open character of democratic mass society, together with its growth in size and the tendency towards general public participation, not only produces far to many elites but also deprives these elites of the exclusiveness which they need to [perform their functions]."

As noted, Richard Lewontin is quite pessimistic about the rationality of the modern citizenry.[74] However, I do not want to engage in Lewontin's excursion into what he implicitly describes as an obviously better, past history of society in which, as in early modern theories of democracy, every woman and every man was just as competent as every other man and every other woman and scientific knowledge, therefore, was available to the masses. Nor am I able to offer persuasive details about modern society in which the present would be like Lewontin's past. Instead, I will try to dispute his disparaging observations about contemporary society and the

---

[74] Whether the differentiation between "remediable ignorance" and "irremediable ignorance" of segments of the public, as proposed by Philip Kitcher (2011b:119–120), is of any help in this context is questionable.

role of scientific knowledge, civil society, and democratic governance. I also will indicate why I think Lewontin arrives at such weary views that evidently are widely shared in the scientific as well as social scientific communities.[75] I will make another brief reference to the work of Michel Foucault as a case in point. As I have already noted, Foucault is one of the most prominent social theorists to articulate most emphatically the symmetry between power and knowledge (e.g., Foucault, [1975] 1978:27). Given the political conditions briefly sketched at the outset as well as the persistent evolution of science and technology, a simple but urgent question emerges: Are citizens still heard? Is there indeed a fundamental contradiction between system effectiveness and citizen participation in modern democracies because, as Walter Lippmann ([1922] 1997:195) has already noted, "self-centered opinions are not sufficient to procure good government"? Has representative democracy simply become an outdated political vision in the complex, fragile, and uncertain universe in which we live?

The gap between common sense and scientific knowledge

One of the solutions attempted to reduce the deficit of the public's knowledge about science are the *Public Understanding of Science* (PUS) and, more recently, *Public Engagement with Science* (PES) movements. Less extensive efforts, when it comes to the reach of such undertakings at "scientific democracy," are consensus conferences as pioneered by the Danish *Board of Technology* (Elam and Bertilson, 2003:238–243; Blok 2007).[76] Over the past decades, if not for a longer period, the case for the nature and the consequences of the sharp division, and even schism between experts and laypersons in many fields of human activity (e.g., law [Berger and Solan, 2008], medicine, or politics) is virtually always conceived of as a deficit and liability for those who are intellectually left behind. Quite simply put, it is ordinary actors and their cognitive immobility that are responsible for the rift. What follows from this argument is that in democratic societies the "sphere" of authority, in this case of

---

[75] It is not just the individual scientists quoted who identify the lack of knowledge of the public as a critical problem in modern societies; in fact, the entire scientific community is of the same opinion. For instance, in a 2009 survey, 85 percent of American scientists acknowledge such a trend toward ignorance among the public and cite it as a most critical problem (Pew Research Center, 2009; also Besley and Nisbet, 2011).

[76] For a survey of different forms of citizen panels (e.g., planning cells, citizen juries, deliberative polls, and consensus conferences) and the kind of constraints and promised encountered in theory and practice, see Brown (2006).

scientific expertise, increasingly encroaches on the "sphere" of individual and collective self-determination, or liberty.

But what is entirely missing from the dominant account are references to responsibilities – other than those of the victims themselves – that come with the strong insulation of knowledge claims from within either private or state-serving communities of experts. The lack of engagement with civil society shown by science, or the creative potential of science[77] to constitute a *public sphere* for science, rarely become a topic for discussion and research.[78] The same indifference extends to a critical examination of the very claim about the nature and the consequences of the gap between the sciences, the experts, and the public. However, here are but a few of the critical issues that immediately come to mind: Do the barriers between the carriers of specialized knowledge and the public put stresses on the functioning of democratic regimes? Do knowledge gaps enhance the "autonomy" of political, judicial, and legislative decision makers?[79] Or, is "public ignorance" even rational since it reflects, as it were, the well-established division of labor in the production of specialized knowledge in society? Is the alleged gap between science and the public perhaps a myth?[80] And, in the end,

---

[77] Compare Otto Neurath's ([1945] 1996:262–264) efforts to create a visual language of science or a visual *lingua franca*. If one starts with visual aids, Neurath observes, "one does not get the feeling that there are two fields, science and non-science. There is a common basis of visual material... In visual education there is no clear split into science and the humanities, nor into lower and higher knowledge ... The development of visual education seems to be closely connected with the democratisation of arguing."

[78] Andreas Daum's (2002:138) examination of the place of science in nineteenth century Germany is a case in point. Daum attempts to integrate the history of science into the history of civil society, suggesting that this "helps us to appreciate the immense array of non university modes that existed for the production, transformation, and consumption of knowledge in German society." Since the historiography of the relation between science and society have focused on the state and on the success story of German university science, it has failed to explore any alternatives; in particular, "the history of the natural sciences in Germany has been studied almost exclusively in terms of institution building at universities, state funding, cooperation between state and industry, and the professionalization of scientists." A complimentary approach seeks "to demonstrate that the commitment to science outside state-influenced educational institutions also played a crucial role within the culture of science in particular and civil culture in general; ... including the vast array of lay activities in the field of natural history and what has [elsewhere] been called amateur science" (Daum, 2002:115).

[79] Samuel DeCanio (2006) for example asserts that public opinion is powerless to constrain the elite of decision makers unless they are knowledgeable about the bases on which the decisions of officials rest.

[80] Due to the frequency and the vigor with which the reality of a gap between the public's general comprehension and understanding of specialized scientific knowledge has been asserted, it is somewhat surprising to find a position in the literature that opposes the consensus and advances arguments in favor of the contrary position: one such example may be found in the 1999 UK Economic and Social Research Council *Report* on the

does it even matter?[81] Before returning to the sum of these issues that fail to stimulate much interest, I will first offer some further reflections on the gradient between science and democratic practices.[82]

Although the diagnosis of a profound gap between science and commonsense knowledge is not a new phenomenon,[83] it is commonly assumed that the gradient of the gap that separates the commands of specialized scientific knowledge from everyday knowledge has radically increased in modern societies (for a genealogy of the apprehended gap, see Bensaude-Vincent, 2001) and that, hence,[84] on the political plane, a growing authority, power, and efficacy is left to an elite of self-referential (science-*cum*-) public policy specialists (Dahl, 1989:337) who are no

"Politics of GM Food: Risk, Science & Public Trust." The *Report*, based mainly on interrogations of members of focus groups, indicates that "senior politicians frequently stress the need for decisions on GM food to be made in the light of 'sound science'. Their approach to public unease about the technology has often been to characterise the public as ignorant, irrational or even hysterical." However, the empirical evidence amassed for the *Report* (and presumably also found in other sources) is that many of the public, far from requiring a better understanding of science, "are well informed about scientific advance and new technologies and highly sophisticated in their thinking on the issues. Many 'ordinary' people demonstrate a thorough grasp of issues such as uncertainty: if anything, the public are ahead of many scientists and policy advisors in their instinctive feeling for a need to act in a precautionary way."

[81] For example, does it even matter for the public to understand and comprehend climate science in order to be in favor of political action that aims to reduce greenhouse gas emissions? The answer appears to be – as survey results confirm – that "public understanding and acceptance of climate science may not be a precondition for supporting action to reduce greenhouse gas emissions" (Nordhaus and Shellenberger, 2009; Pielke, 2010). As a matter of fact, given the state of research into the "public understanding of science," we really "do not know what knowledge is valued by the public or what they find useful to know" (Stockmayer and Bryant, 2012:99).

[82] It should be noted that the reference to the corporate world and its control of knowledge and information is not a central topic in most statements about the gap between scientific and everyday knowledge that originate within the scientific community (however, see my section on knowledge as property).

[83] Consider, for example, Max Weber's observations about the skeptical views toward science held by the "youth" of his day in his lecture on science as a vocation: "Today youth feels rather the reverse: the intellectual constructions of science constitute an unreal realm of artificial abstractions, which with their bony hands seek to grasp the blood-and-the-sap of true life without ever catching up with it. But here in life, in what for Plato was the play of shadows on the walls of the cave, genuine reality is pulsating; and the rest are derivatives of life, lifeless ghosts, and nothing else."

[84] A related yet not identical observation concerns an apparently inevitable (maybe even nonlinear) increase in the volume of "nonknowledge" as a result of the growth of knowledge in modern societies (e.g., Ravetz, 1986:423; Luhmann, 1997:1106; Wehling, 2006:31), including the emergence of the so-called "knowledge-ignorance paradox" that refers to how the growth of *specialized knowledge* implies a concurrent and accelerating increase in civil society ignorance in modern society (see Bauer, 1966; Ungar, 2008); for a skeptical discussion of the very existence and theoretical fruitfulness of the notion of "nonknowledge", see Stehr (2012c).

longer intellectually, let alone democratically, accountable to many segments of the public.

If experts indeed inhabit a virtually self-referential system of widely relevant and consequential judgments, efforts to subject expertise to democratic discourse would appear to be a mute enterprise. The implication therefore can only be that the increased reliance on highly specialized knowledge downgrades "the significance of lay judgment and thus assigns the citizenry the role of passive, uncomprehending spectators (and perhaps beneficiaries) even of state activities which affect them quite closely" (Poggi, 1982:358). Hence, and based on these considerations alone, the same perspectives do not allow – unless challenged[85] – for a genuine representative democracy, let alone for anything akin to a deliberative democracy in the modern age.

As I have stressed, the concerns about the precarious foundations for effective democratic participation of the vast majority of ordinary citizens expressed by prominent members of the contemporary scientific community and the scientific community at large in many ways echo and repeat earlier concerns and empirical findings (e.g., Lippmann, [1922] 1997[86] and John Dewey's [1927] 1954 rejection of Lippmann's position; for early empirical results see Hyman and Sheatsley, 1947; Berelson et al., 1954; Converse, [1964] 2006) about the lacking prerequisites for and feasibility of representative democracy and effectual citizen participation[87] – the lack of civic competence or, more disparagingly,

---

[85] Angela Liberatore and Silvio Funtowicz (2003:147) question the perspective of the unassailable monopoly of experts in democratic societies, suggesting that citizens can still attempt to *track* decisions made on the basis of expert advice or to *examine* whether the political *decisions* have achieved the promised results. In this sense, democratizing expertise, for example, "is an important component of guaranteeing due process ... [as is] providing pluralistic expert advice" (Liberatore and Funtowicz, 2003:147).

[86] It is worth citing Walter Lippmann's ([1922] 1997:193) views from his *Public Opinion* in some detail: "In the absence of institutions and education by which the environment is so successfully reported that the realities of public life stand out sharply against self-centered opinion, the common interests very largely elude public opinion entirely, and can be managed only by a specialized class whose personal interests reach beyond the locality. This class is irresponsible, for it acts upon information that is not common property, in situations that the public at large does not conceive, and it can be held to account only on the accomplished fact."

[87] Bernard Berelson (1952:316–317) more than half a century ago, in an essay arguing for closer cooperation between public opinion researchers and political theorists, refers to the then already well-documented limited political interest shown by voters in the United States – less than one-third of the electorate reports to be "really interested" in politics – and the declining proportion of eligible voters who vote. Berelson explains the trends – that have not been reversed in the past decades – as stemming from the increasing feeling people have "that they are impotent to affect political matters in the face of the complexity and magnitude of the issues. Such a diagnosis is, as it were, a free ticket for governance by experts."

the political and scientific ignorance of many citizens of democratic states (Gilley, 2009:117–120; Somin, 2009; Sturgis and Smith, 2010).[88] As a consequence, the legal scholar Richard Posner (2003:16) for example concludes that the average citizen is "basically ignorant" about political affairs and that democracy should therefore never aspire to be anything but a process of rotating elites. Posner's hostility to democratic ideas and his authoritarian views only echo the much more famous conviction expressed in Plato's (*Laws*:690b) classical political philosophy: "The wise shall lead and rule, and the ignorant shall follow."

All of this forces us even today to wonder, however, whether the adjective "democratic" still represents an appropriate attribute of contemporary society, especially given the complexity of the problems faced and the types of solutions available that are wrapped and cloaked in the language and concepts of highly specialized intellectual discourses. Most citizens of modern societies have neither access to such discourse nor the inclination to understand technical expertise or the capacity to respond to specialized discourse with anything but reasoned judgments (that is judgments embedded in cultural worldviews, see Kagan et al., 2006).

Assuming the diagnosis about the gap between expertise and civil society and its serious political repercussions is accurate, what can be done to erode the extraordinary power of scientific knowledge in democratic societies? Efforts designed to tackle the gradient between the knowledge of civil society members and expertise also require reflections about responsibilities.

What can be done?

Once we accept the grim diagnosis about the mounting gradient between scientific knowledge and the knowledge of civil society I have outlined, what can be done? Is it necessary and is there really any room for meaningful efforts to overcome the deep gap between modern science

---

[88] The various observations made about the knowledgeability of the average citizen also reflect research findings on voters in the 1950s in the United States, for example those reported by the classic studies *Voting* and *The American Voter* (Campbell et al., 1960:543) whose results offer a "portrait of an electorate almost wholly without detailed information about the decision-making process in government." The "meaningful participation of the voter in the electoral process appears to be confined almost exclusively to the exercise of a generally ill-informed choice between rival candidates who periodically present themselves to compete for such votes at national elections" (Skinner, 1973:301). Not surprisingly, out of such findings grows the criticism that a "ruling class" governs the American political system.

and its findings and what members of civil society accept as trustworthy judgments? The best solution to the problems created in this instance for democratic governance, as one might argue with Philip Kitcher (2011b:122), is more democracy. The more than three decades old discussion of the *Public Understanding of Science* (PUS) has taken on board the diagnosis of the steep gradient between the scientific knowledge of much of the public in relation to the dazzling development of science and technology and has supported various political efforts designed to improve the knowledge of the public and allow for an increasing public participation in science and technology policies (e.g., Nelkin, 1984; Callon et al., 2009; Durant, 2011).[89] As a rule, however, this means that efforts are made to familiarize the public with the virtues of a certain understanding of scientific knowledge, with the aim, for example, to enhance their scientific literary. Thus, no mutual communication or dissemination of knowledge is envisaged. An exchange or comparison of the rationalities that underlie everyday life and science, respectively, is neither required nor supported.

Kitcher's (2011b:122) proposal to set up citizen groups that, "figuring in the extensions of well-ordered science, scrutinizing certification procedures and adjudicating urgent debates, could extend their activity to supervising and appraising sources of technical information. To the extent that they could retain public trust, they could confer trust in independent channels of transmission, curing irremediable ignorance and restoring confidence in a reliable division of epistemic labor" resonates with the very idea of a *Public Understanding of Science*. The idea to create such citizen groups suffers, perhaps even more so, from the same practical and political problems as the realization of PUS efforts. Moreover, one of the difficulties with proposals of this kind is the fact that they are often advanced in a kind of specialized discourse which one is expected to transcend, in the first instance.

At the other end of the spectrum of solutions designed to heal the growing gap between expert and lay knowledge – and that is also part of Kitcher's proposed response – is the demand to democratize the production of scientific knowledge itself (cf. van Bouwel, 2009). But how should the labor between scientists and laypersons be divided in practice? It remains unclear what should be delegated to what group and how

---

[89] In response to the frequent diagnosis of a growing alienation between science, technology, and the public, some governments, the Quebec government for example, through community initiatives, public support, and volunteer input has created "a range of science communication organizations, and installations, including specialist media, science camps, museums, recreational science organizations, interpretation centers and activity groups" (Santerre, 2008:289).

members of civil society could be motivated to get involved, especially if the respective research fields are of no apparent relevance to their everyday life. The proposal to democratize knowledge production in science and to diminish the difference between social systems hardly brings the matter of overcoming the gap closer to a solution and therefore remains, for all practical purposes, but a suggestion.

We also have to ask who is responsible for the lack of information and knowledge of civil society. It is by no means the case, as one might expect, that modern science as such or the stratum of experts is always being blamed.[90] According to the widely applauded views of Walter Lippmann or Joseph Schumpeter, ordinary citizens are simply unable or disinclined to inform themselves. In political matters, the "typical citizen," Schumpeter ([1942] 1950:262–263) dispiritedly concludes – "Human Nature in Politics being what it is" – tend to yield to "extra-rational or irrational prejudice and impulse," and ignorance will persist "in the face of masses of information however complete and correct." But do higher volumes of (rational) knowledge and information among citizens, as the silent premise of Schumpeter's views appears to assume, indeed lead to an increase in the trust extended to political decisions and the political class or, more generally, to democracy? Or are we dealing with a misconception of both the nature of scientific knowledge and the kind of accomplishments we can expect from such knowledge in its role for society? Is it perhaps possible that in practice the exact opposite of Schumpeter's expectations concerning the typical "labor" science is capable of performing in society may be observed (see Termeer et al., 2010) and that political trust actually may decline with a more knowledgeable civil society?

Another answer to the question of co-responsibility for the enslavement of the public points the finger to professional journalism that mainly gives voice to the views of experts – often without acknowledging the cultural contingency of scientific knowledge claims and thereby demoralizing and immobilizing their readers who, as a consequence, are unable to take reflexive note of political decisions and to effectively

---

[90] One of the few scholars who put the blame on the shoulders of scientists and science is Philip Kitcher (2011b:103): "Our investigations are not always directed towards the questions of most concern to most people, the results on which experts agree are not always based on reasons the broader public is prepared to endorse, and the dissemination of information is so distorted as to make supposedly free discussion and debate an unproductive shouting match." Frickel et al. (2010) refer to another phenomenon that is relevant in this context, namely "undone science," that is, areas of research left unattended by the scientific community but of interest to civil society, for example in the fields of AIDS and breast cancer activism.

take part in any discussion of the issues at hand (see Carey, 1993:15; and, much earlier, Walter Lippmann in *Public Opinion* [1922]).

Modern society and the stratification of knowledge

In contrast to the generally weak efforts of the *Public Understanding of Science* movement, the analysis of the pessimistic narrative about the societal distribution of the impact of scientific knowledge on democratic governance has to be embedded in a theory of modern society and the shifts that occur in the distribution of power within and among its major social institutions and that are generated by significant enabling structural changes in modern society. Notwithstanding the fact that many households have not emancipated themselves from the constraints of basic survival, the historically unprecedented prosperity has been supplanting salvation as the reason for human existence. The growth of the average cultural, social, and economic capital in many societies of the world since the end of World War II is historically unparalleled. However, an increase in cultural capital does not necessarily assure a convergence of scientific and everyday knowledge (take, for example, the field of climate research). Perhaps equally important are advances in science and technology that modify the foundations of and enlarge the spaces for citizen action. These changes are translated into political action. But the translation of citizen preferences, world-views, and moral values into political practices does not necessarily occur in unmediated or expected ways, for example through direct engagement in debates about the consequences of change induced by scientific or technological knowledge or through electoral participation.

In addition to the societal changes just described, an emergent correction to the prevailing written narrative of the gradient between specialized and ordinary forms of knowledge may be noticed. Although the discourse about the relation between science and society is still dominated by scientists, science journalists, and a few interested laypersons, a shift in predominant assumptions can be observed, last not least prompted by a social science discourse that offers a new window on both the production and consumption of science. Questions now considered legitimate are, for example: Does knowledge really inevitably end up in the hands of the powerful? Or: Can specialized knowledge really deliver more or less immediate benefits for contentious political debates? Nor should we suppress the fact that specialized knowledge claims and distinct cognitive skills are often highly contentious and are found among many distinct bodies of knowledge multipliers, experts, and specialists (cf. Stehr and Grundmann, 2011; da Silva, 2014) who tend to put "different constructions on experience and amongst them conflict and controversy are endemic" (Barnes, 1995:104).

In the following section in this chapter I want to explore the thesis that knowledge as a capacity for action may play an important part in individual or collective resistance against the controlling efforts of large social institutions, rather than have the crucial function of being a means of suppressing opposition or aiding and nurturing the status quo in social, political, and economic relations. An account of the ways of exercising political power by the "weak" of society and deploying the "weapon" of scientific knowledge initially requires a detailed analysis of the role of "expertise" in society as a source of either unassailable judgments or what amounts to essentially contestable findings.

The new risks of knowledge

There is a still widely invisible "risk" that I would now like to discuss, namely the risk that knowledge in modern society has broad emancipatory potentials and capacities.[91] One of the risks associated with such a perspective or question is that one is not really very well equipped to recall the emancipatory potential of knowledge of the French Enlightenment and its proponents in an epoch of disenchantment with the societal role of science,[92] characterized for example by a loss of the conviction that there is a "natural progressive process in nature and humanity" and, therefore, the more general loss of any "trust in the humane, cosmopolitan meaning of intellectual and moral efforts" (Plessner, [1936] 1985: 77). Yet, even in this context of inquiry into the social role of knowledge, the modern dilemma of knowledge becomes visible, namely that the demystification of the notion of progress would not have been possible without the scientific critique of the idea of progress.

Not only have predictions of the imminent ascent of large social formations to almost monolithic power and authority based on their control of socially relevant symbolic capital been so far disproved by history, but discussions of the social role of knowledge have also largely become particularized: state-centered, class-centered, profession-centered, science-centered, and so on. From such particularized vantage

---

[91] This section on the new risk of knowledge is indebted to a discussion of the social role of knowledge in modern society by Gotthard Bechmann and Nico Stehr in Stehr (2001:137–140).

[92] Ulrich Beck ([1986] 1992) for example expresses the belief that the public – the uninformed, in other words – has lost confidence and trust in science and experts because they appear to be unable to control the negative and unanticipated consequences of science and technology (see a critique in Callon, 1999).

points, the highlighting of threats and dangers and of the risks of knowledge is easily understandable: social classes, professions, the church, science and technology, the state, corporations, for example, have all on occasion been identified as agents of repression and control or as a constitutive part of the context within which an inevitable drift toward oligarchy takes place.

Reflections about the social role of knowledge these days rarely invoke the tradition of the Enlightenment that saw knowledge as a formidable force in the liberation of individuals, citizens, workers, women, and men. In other words, the Enlightenment "as an enterprise for linking the progress of truth and the history of liberty in a bond of direct relation ... formulated a philosophical question that remains for us to consider" (Foucault, 1984); a question, however, that in subsequent decades was rarely seen as an urgent philosophical and political issue.

If it is indeed the case, as Hans Morgenthau (1970:38) observes, that most people now feel that they live in "something approaching a Kafkaesque world, insignificant and at the mercy of unchangeable and invisible forces ... a world of make-believe, a gigantic hoax," then the Enlightenment project that attributed liberating qualities to knowledge has completely failed, and its utopian promises are no closer to realization today than they were in the distant past. Even someone like Karl Popper ([1961] 1992:141) remained skeptical about the eventual benefits for mankind of the advancement of science:

The progress of science – itself partly a consequence of the ideal of self-emancipation through knowledge – is contributing to the lengthening and to the enrichment of our lives; yet it has led us to spend those lives under the threat of an atomic war, and it is doubtful whether it has on balance contributed to the happiness and contentment of man.

Benefits that are widely acknowledged to flow from advances in scientific and technical knowledge are typically linked to an image of science as a "scientistic" enterprise. Scientism does not merely refer to instances in which the boundaries of the cognitive authority of scientific claims are contested and perhaps extended to matters not currently as accepted as within the boundaries of scientific competence. It refers to the exclusivity claimed for specific conceptions about valuable and efficient ways of generating and validating knowledge claims in science. For example, so-called "realistic" conceptions of how science gets done should be seen as a scientistic conception aspiring to universality. The cognitive and material benefits originating from scientific knowledge are generally seen as increasing in direct proportion to the "scientificity" of knowledge claims.

I want to stress, however, that such a causal symmetry does not necessarily exist. The coupling of knowledge and emancipation does not primarily depend on improving the objectivity of knowledge claims, conflating truth and power or, finally, being able to enlarge the predictive capacity of knowledge claims. Nor does it rest, in my view, on the recognition that knowledge claims are constructed rather than discovered. Such a reconstruction of scientific activities as constructions is not insignificant for the image of science, of course. On the contrary, the deconstruction of the myth of scientific knowledge contributes to an enlargement of the utility and the use of scientific knowledge in social contexts outside of the scientific community. The trust that is extended to knowledge from science may be diminished while the understanding of scientific expertise is enlarged. Definitive solutions and accomplishments that can be traced back and attributed directly to scientific knowledge become more doubtful because they are no longer expected or accepted as possible; at the same time, however, the number of individuals and groups that employ scientific arguments and knowledge for their own purposes continues to grow.

A realistic appraisal, an assessment without illusions, however, has to accept that on balance the general enlargement of the capacity of individuals to act has not always been only liberating, but also threatening and full of risks, as critics of the growing role of science and technology have clearly demonstrated. The main barrier to a realistic assessment of the impact of knowledge in modern society has been its taken-for-granted image as an instrument that "naturally" flows toward the center of societal power and effectively consolidates and centralizes a power that has virtually uncontested features, suppressing any chances of effectively resisting it, and eradicating local forms of knowledge.

As I have argued, such an image does not survive closer scrutiny, even if it remains the preferred image of knowledge of those in possession of power. The image of knowledge as an inherently repressive tool underestimates not only the influence of various ("extraneous" or "external") constraints on the production of knowledge and the "difficulties" encountered by knowledge once it travels across social and cultural contexts. Such difficulties of knowledge as essentially contested claims also represent opportunities for actors who encounter knowledge in the form of authoritative knowledge or "expertise" (cf. Smith and Wynne, 1989). The need to continually reappropriate knowledge leaves its marks on knowledge, too, and impacts on the agents engaged in reappropriation. As actors acquire ever-greater skills in reappropriating knowledge, they also acquire a greater capacity to act. Specific pressures and interests further heighten the chances for critically "deconstructing" and reassembling knowledge claims. The construction of a much more skeptical image of scientific knowledge claims is an insignificant event. The extent to which this image has spread, however, remains an open question. The societal dissemination of knowledge is a more important process and has more serious consequences for society.

The social distribution of knowledge is not a zero-sum game. Extending aggregate knowledge may actually lead, in comparative terms, to an explosion in the capacity of individuals and groups to reappropriate knowledge for their own ends. This capacity therefore represents a movement away from a condition in which few control the circumstances of action to a new condition in which many exercise at least some influence (cf. Schieman and Plickert, 2008). All this does not mean that average citizens, students, voters, or consumers suddenly acquire either a strong sense of control over the circumstances of their everyday existence or a secure comprehension of events beyond local contexts (cf. Giddens, 1990:146). However, the average citizens in knowledge societies are likely to experience a stronger sense of being in fact able to assert their own wills.

This transformation from a society in which things merely happen to a society in which they are made to happen on the basis of the greater knowledgeability of actors – heretofore the objects of events, discursive practices, or the immense power of the major social institutions in society – can perhaps already be observed in the world of work. As I have indicated referring to the reasons for the growth of knowledge-intensive work, and as I have tried to show in much greater detail elsewhere, the world of work is shaped by the kinds of qualifications that entrants into the labor force bring with them to the world of work rather than, as is still the prevailing view, by the growing complexity and more demanding jobs of a kind of autonomous world of work that itself creates such jobs (see Stehr, 1999b, 2000a).[93]

The literature that comes closest to an examination of the degree of "cognitive mobilization" of modern individuals is the "new social movements" literature. But before I turn my attention to its findings and perspectives, it should be emphasized that asserting a general extension, in knowledge societies, of the capacity to act of individuals and small groups does not imply that anxiety, risk, fortuitous circumstances,

---

[93] The first author to refer to such a radical transformation of the modern world of work is, as far as I can see, Peter Drucker (1968:279) who more than three decades ago asked about the conditions for the emergence of knowledge work and the knowledge economy and arrived at a straightforward, simple "cause": the reason for the upgrading of the jobs is "the upgrading of the educational level of the entrant into the labor force."

unanticipated consequences of deliberate action and, in particular, conditions of conduct that only allow for limited control will disappear. However, the acknowledgment of such limitations is a far cry from the assertion of a virtual individual impotence in the face of conditions where the control of action is in the hands of a powerful few.

In response to these general observations, more difficult questions arise: One may naively ask, for example – aside from expressing doubt about the taken-for-granted assumption that the demand for evidence and science-based policy is on the upswing[94] – if there isn't a democratic right to ignorance, if it isn't rational to adopt a low profile (cf. Downs, 1957; Olson, 1965), especially in light of the fact that the transaction costs for being politically well informed are significant, and rising with each passing year. While it may be common sense to readily defer to experts in many corners of the life-world, political expertise often prompts suspicion. Why is that? First, the suspicion political expertise generates is based on the realistic observation that political expertise is extremely scarce and that "people who set themselves up as political experts often give off the whiff of snake oil" and, as Ian Shapiro (1994:140–141) puts it, "experts always turn out to be on somebody's side, and not necessarily ours," that is, expertise is not immune to motivated reasoning.[95] But such fundamental skepticism toward the political role of experts and the bifurcation of social roles between citizens and experts may not be sufficient to assure that experts are expelled from the domain of politics or that general calls for a democratization of scientific expertise (Maasen and Weingart, 2004) – which amounts to a politicization of science (Brown, 2009:185–199) – will stimulate action.

The fragility of expertise

In addition to the societal changes just described there is a gradual correction of the prevailing narrative in science and society about the role of scientific knowledge in policy and society. These discussions are

---

[94] One of the less obvious accounts for the *rising demand* for evidence and science-based policy from the political system is Steve Ryner's (2003:164) conjecture that the "displacement of moral judgment from the public sphere [has] something to do with the decline of electoral participation." After all, he argues, what difference does it make who is in charge if the decision is based on purely "technical" criteria? "Where once, citizens voted for candidates based on our assessment of their values, such judgments have become marginal in importance and much harder to make" (Rayner, 2003b:5114). The deference to judgments from science only increases political indifference.

[95] Steve Fuller (e.g., 1988 and 1994) has long maintained a highly skeptical attitude toward the special claims to expertise of experts and argued for a level playing field between experts and laypersons.

still dominated by scientists, science journalists, and some of the interested laymen. In light of what is seen to be the most urgent political problems in the field of climate change, for example, and the need for citizens to be able to express informed views, the political role of expertise, at least for Philip Kitcher (2010a:1231), becomes paramount: "Serious democracy requires reliance on expert opinion."

Nevertheless, increasingly critical issues about the role of experts are brought to the forefront, not least through social scientific efforts that have opened a new window on our understanding of the production of scientific knowledge and the relationship between science and society. Questions to be addressed are, for example: Is expertise autonomous? And can scientific knowledge offer real and direct benefits by supplying the cognitive resources that will bring an end to controversial political debates? Contrary to hopes for a scientization of everyday problems and political issues, many of the now taken-for-granted observations concern the essential contestability of expert knowledge and the fact that various bodies of knowledge multipliers tend to represent different views that are in conflict with each other.

As I have indicated with respect to different substantive issues that confront democracies as well as the formal dimensions of democratic governance, skepticism about democratic governance from partisans of democracy is not new: there are other, parallel doubts expressed about the reliance on expertise and the "power of knowing better" by experts and the validity of decisions that may be based on "superior" knowledge "authoritatively decided by a scientific community" (Kitcher, 2010a:1233). Justifications for the reliance on expertise include a specific understanding of the role of the state and the forms of knowledge on which governance should rely; both justifications tend to be based on the assumption that "genuine democracy ... requires a division of labor in which particular groups are charged with the responsibility of resolving questions that bear on the interests of individuals and societies" (Kitcher, 2010a:1233). One of the fathers of classical sociology, Emile Durkheim ([1957] 1992:92), for example, expresses these convictions about a meaningful and efficient functional differentiation of social systems and the kind of knowledge on which political decision ought to rely, as follows:

The role of the State, in fact, is not to express and sum up the unreflective thought of the mass of the people, but to superimpose on this unreflective thought a more considered thought, which therefore cannot be other than different. It must be a centre of new and original representations which ought to put the society in a position to conduct itself with greater intelligence than when it is swayed merely by vague sentiments working on it.

A less encumbered statement would be to say you should not and cannot simply neglect the difference between expert and lay knowledge; there are indeed persons who are better informed or know more than others. Thus, if one is concerned about the effectiveness of political decision making especially under circumstances with substantial pressure to act, it would be important to be able to distinguish between laypersons and experts, and follow the advice of expertise. We all want to buy meat that is healthy, but not necessarily perform the function of food inspectors.

If one follows what I would call the standard model of the social function of scientific knowledge, then the effect of scientific knowledge is direct, straightforward, and universally useful. The flow of knowledge goes unilaterally from the expert to the layperson. Science speaks to power and to civil society. Scientific and technological phenomena are politically and morally innocuous. But is it really the case that scientific evidence can only be interpreted in terms of statements that are morally and politically uncontroversial?

An empirically much more accurate representation of the communication processes between science, or experts, and civil society, however, is far less impressed by the success or the automatic power of science to exercise its influence. As Dan Kahan and his colleagues (2011) discovered in experimental studies, the diametrically opposite reaction of the public in response to consensual scientific knowledge (e.g., to anthropogenic global warming), namely the strong expression of doubt, may be explained by the fact that the public assessment of scientific communication of this kind is strongly affected by already existing, culturally specific attitudes. These attitudes operate as an efficient kind of filter and confirm or refute the reputation of experts as experts. No matter how insistent the reference to the toxicity of certain ingredients of food is, provided that relevant cultural beliefs exist, such communication falls on deaf ears. The certification of science as a reliable or unreliable source of knowledge manifests itself not in a cognitive/affective vacuum but is dependent on prejudgments. The answer to the question about differences in the decision calculuses of knowledgeable and less knowledgeable citizens is that informed readers, voters, and students will take into account a longer chain of consequences when reflecting on political action, for instance, but that in the end values or political ideology play a crucial and even decisive role in weighing alternatives and assessing consequences. It is therefore more correct to describe the societal role of science in modern society in terms of a precarious balance between autonomy and dependence.

The loss of any close intellectual contact between scientists and the public can very well be associated with both a diffuse support for science and a consent of civil society to institute legal and political efforts to control the consequences of science and technology. In still another sense, however, the loss of cognitive contact is virtually irrelevant, that is, if "contact" as a prerequisite for participation in decisions in which scientific and technological knowledge are at issue is understood to be a close cognitive proximity (however, Caron-Finterman, Broerse and Bunders, 2007). Such a claim is virtually meaningless, because it would require public participation in the ongoing work of science itself.

In order to arrive at a pragmatic and realistic assessment of the role of expertise in civil society, one must always take into consideration relevant contexts and issues that are at odds. It is also realistic to see that not every public issue can be subject to participatory and democratic deliberation. The resolution of the question of the role knowledge and democracy have in modern society does not require a general "solution" but always only a case to case answer. For every controversial political issue, new and differently composed publics tend to emerge.

If the question is formulated in these terms, it becomes apparent that the asymmetry in the volume of knowledge commanded by civil society and experts is not an insurmountable obstacle for successfully challenging expertise in different societal contexts, for example, in political or legal disputes. As empirical studies show, the classical empirical analysis is that of Dorothy Nelkin (1975) who concludes that there is no need for symmetry in the volume of knowledge in order to question expert knowledge. The powerlessness of civil society is not cemented. We should not treat the relationship between expertise and public as a series of fixed events nor as a difference that can be fully abolished, but as occasions mediated by cultural identities and varying ideological views, for example beliefs about the societal benefits of science and technology.

I want to illustrate my diagnosis of the relationship of contested knowledge claims and power with reference to the issue of climate change. In dealing with wicked problems in practice, and climate change is a wicked problem, it is impossible to directly derive instructions for action from scientific findings. This applies, for example, to earth science. Earth science is capable of working out scenarios of the danger potential for regions with earthquake potential, but it is impossible to derive from such scenarios what kinds of risks society is willing to assume in the case of the construction of nuclear power plants.[96]

Rather than being a discrete problem to be solved, climate change is better understood as a persistent condition that must be coped with and

---

[96] I rely here to portions of our Hartwell Paper (2010) where the relevant philosophy of science issues are discussed in much more detail.

can only be partially managed more – or less – well. It is just one part of a larger complex of such conditions encompassing population, technology, wealth disparities, resource use, and so forth. Hence it is not a straightforward "environmental" problem, either. It is axiomatically as much an energy problem, an economic development problem, and a land-use problem, and may be better approached through these avenues than as a problem of managing the behavior of the Earth's climate by changing the way that humans use energy.

What makes a problem "wicked" is the impossibility of giving it a definitive formulation: the information needed to understand the problem is dependent upon one's idea for solving it. Furthermore, wicked problems lack a stopping rule: we cannot know whether our understanding is sufficient so we can stop searching for more understanding. There is no end to causal chains in interacting open systems of which the climate is the world's prime example. So, every wicked problem can be considered as a symptom of another problem. The practical, political consequence would be to argue that in order to achieve complex objectives it is best to tackle them indirectly or obliquely (Kay, 2010).

For politicians this is, of course, frustrating. So policy makers frequently respond to wicked problems by declaring "war" on them to beat them into submission and then move on. Indeed, almost any "declaration of war" that is metaphorical rather than literal is a reliable sign that the subject in question is "wicked." So, we have the war on cancer, the war on poverty, the war on drugs, the war on terror, and now the war on climate change.

The public is often initially stirred by such declarations of war; but, as wicked problems demonstrate their intractability, the public soon grows weary of them. Recent polls suggest that public opinion in many developed nations is losing its previously intense preoccupation with climate issues as it becomes increasingly apparent that climate is no more a problem to be "solved" than is poverty, and as attention focuses on what people feel to be more pressing issues, like the economy.

In an era of knowledge politics (Stehr, 2005), that is, in the face of diverse and growing political efforts to regulate new knowledge and technical artifacts as well as of a changing willingness among the public to support such efforts and welcome everything and anything because it is new, it does not make sense to view the public as naively resistant in dealing with the new forms of action, but rather as cautious, uncertain, and curious about the possible consequences of new scientific insights and technical possibilities. Science- and technology-based innovation will be judged by civil society against the background of their world views, values, preferences, and beliefs, and despite their lack of detailed scientific and technical knowledge. Relevant examples are responses to stem cell research, medical genetics, or GM maize. More generally, the rules of the political game are changing. In the context of knowledge politics and public discourse about the social authorization of innovative forms of action, this amounts to a change in the balance of the power between science and civil society, with influence and power shifting in favor of civil society.

Without a certain measure of impersonal trust and confidence placed members of civil society in experts, experts would disappear, however. Trust, if placed "reasonably," requires, as Onora O'Neill (2002) argues, "not only information about the proposals or undertakings that others put forward, but also information about those who put them forward." Moreover, today's experts are constantly involved in all sorts of controversies. In the growing, and contested, policy field of safety regulations, from limits set to certain ingredients in food to risk management and the monitoring and control of hazards, all these measures have as a side effect ruined the reputation of the experts. As long as a matter of public debate remains controversial, the influence of experts and counter-experts is limited. But as soon as a decision has been made and implemented, the experts regain much of their unchallenged authority.

In the following section of this chapter, I will examine the idea that knowledge as a capacity of action can very well play an important role in society for resistance against state control by supposedly weak social strata and social movements and, therefore, may function not merely as a means of suppressing opposition or of supporting and promoting the status quo in social, political, and economic relations. But a critical account of the ways of exercising political power by the "weak" in society with the help of knowledge as a "weapon" requires the recognition that the science system is not the only source of additional capacities of action.

Knowledge as a weapon of the "weak"

> Most of the political life of subordinate groups is to be found neither in overt collective defiance of powerholders nor in complete hegemonic compliance, but in the vast territory between these two polar opposites.
> James C. Scott, 1990:136

James Scott's work that focuses on inquiries into the nature of the political resistance of the weak in society presents us with a refreshing observation, if only because he is sensitive to the topic of chances for the less powerful in society to act out opposition and resistance. As we have seen, in the majority of reflections about political processes in contemporary societies the opposite emphasis can be found, namely a fascination with the extraordinary power of the powerful, their ability to outflank resistance, the aptitude of elites to manufacture consent (Converse, 2006) and, often, their inordinate capacity to monopolize much of the volume of available, especially novel, knowledge.[97] One diagnosis of the powerlessness of the powerless that is frequently put forward focuses, of course, on their supposed "ignorance" concerning the foundations of the power of the powerful (e.g., Clegg, 1989:212).

But any analysis of what exactly allows – in sharp contrast to the dominant thesis – for efforts to restrain the powerful from time to time requires, in the first instance, an understanding of the social trajectory of modern society and the realization that the production of politically relevant capacities of action is not necessarily confined to the scientific community or to highly specialized experts. It is to this set of issues that I will now turn.

One of the most immediate indicators of the power of knowledge is the fact that dissidents in dictatorial and authoritarian political regimes are indeed feared by those in power. It is not so much the action of dissidents that these regimes fear but the knowledge held by dissidents, and the communication of this knowledge via informal social relations[98] that culturally, economically, and politically, conditions could be different. But speaking matter-of-factly about the distribution of competencies in modern society, Robert K. Merton (1966:1056; also Miller, 2001:118; Collins and Evans, 2007) noted that not all individuals are "*equally* competent to do the work of a democratic polity. They differ in capacity, in acquired skills, and in knowledge." If such an assessment of the ability to do democratic work is accurate, then there is perhaps but a small measure of hope that knowledge may become a weapon of the weak. After all, prominent assessments and theories of knowledge and power tend to insist that there is a radical break and steep gradient between those who command *both* power and knowledge and members of the society who cannot claim any of these attributes.

---

[97] Promoted by the puzzling question why those who are dominated frequently consider their subordination and subordinators legitimate, for example in the workplace (e.g., Clegg, 1989:220), social scientists in the postwar years have spent an inordinate time considering that their main issue actually ought to be the lack of resistance of the powerless (Buroway, 1979, 1985). In response, Collinson (2000:164) urges researchers to undertake a "much more detailed examination of the conditions, processes and consequences of workplace resistance."

[98] Jeffrey Becker (2012:11398) examined the social conditions for the possibility of workers' resistance in China today. He arrives at the conclusion that "informal social ties provide workers in authoritarian states with the capacity to challenge their exploitation despite restrictions on formal organizations."

One of these well-known theories of knowledge and power, as I have already discussed in some detail and to which I would like to once more briefly and critically refer, is the theory of the symbiosis of knowledge and power advocated by Michel Foucault. His views converge, at least in their consequences, with those of other prominent modern scientists insofar as Foucault, too, describes ordinary citizens as the rather helpless victims of disciplinary knowledge. In his essay on enlightenment, Foucault (1984:48; cf. also Horkheimer and Adorno, 1982:xiii) poses what for him is the central enlightenment dilemma: "How can the growth of capabilities be disconnected from the intensification of power relations?"[99] In other words, the growing capacities to act produced by science are usurped by the already powerful strata of society and mainly for their benefit including, of course, the defense of their authority and power through their suppression of the weak social strata.

I reject Foucault's pessimistic microphysics of power theory. Foucault generally holds that knowledge produces us as subjects. With this I agree. But as is well known, and where I depart from his thought, is that in his genealogical work, Foucault describes the individual as shaped by scientific disciplines in a one-sided way, where the individual's entire existence is controlled by institutions of subjugation (Foucault, [1973] 2000:81–82) such as penology and psychoanalysis, and where the enormous micromanaged power of regimentation and measurement embedded in major social institutions leaves the populace powerless to resist. Foucault's reflections about "the disappearance of the subject" are based, as far as I can see, on a view which attributes too much power to both knowledge and the organizations utilizing knowledge. Foucault's observations on the repression of the subject and of the subject as a passive victim neglect the possibility that the knowledge of large institutions such as the state may have benign sides and moral purposes (cf. Scott, 1998:77, 339–340).[100]

Foucault ([1973] 2000:86–87) notes that capitalism penetrates much more deeply into our existence than described by Marxism. Power makes

---

[99] Although my focus is on the nature and the social role of knowledge, *institutional* arrangements as well as certain constraints of action (such as the need to act quickly) can of course temper the alleged affinity between rising capacities of action and broad based participation of members of civil society in democratic decision making, for example in the field of financial problems or of technology and power. James Bohman (2007:716) therefore notes, assuming a close linkage between power and knowledge, "instead of disconnecting reason from power, the increase in capabilities is not self-defeating so long as the democratic powers of citizens are appropriately institutionalized at the same time."

[100] If one values democratic governance, political fairness, mass education, and egalitarian policies, then one cannot accept, as James Scott argues, the need for making citizens "legible" to state authorities (also Scott, 2012).

knowledge possible and enhances it. What Foucault calls "infrapower" represents "the whole set of little powers, of little institutions situated at the lowest level ... that operate over and above productive relations ... Power and knowledge are thus deeply rooted – they are not just superimposed on the relations of production." Foucault's assertions about the extraordinary power of scientific knowledge and their typical social location does not leave any other conclusion but that scientific knowledge can hardly function as a weapon of the weak of society.

Knowledge, as described in Michel Foucault's *The Archaeology of Knowledge*, is an anonymous discourse that exercises control over unwitting and powerless individuals.[101] Foucault underestimates the malleability of knowledge, the uncertainties associated with knowledge, the extent to which knowledge is contested, and the capacity of individuals and civil society organizations to appropriate and mobilize knowledge in order to evade, disrupt, oppose, and restrain the oppression or the power that may be exercised by major social institutions in modern society.[102]

The ability to evade, disrupt, oppose, and restrain power and to construct countervailing narratives refers to everyday forms of resistance. The unorganized withdrawal of compliance and the unstructured abandonment of trust represent manifestations of resistance based on the knowledgeability of the allegedly weak that are frequently overlooked in favor of more spectacular but less frequent forms of open rebellion (cf. Scott, 1985; Rushforth, 1994:338–346; Baiocchhi, 2003).[103] It is

---

[101] Michel Foucault's assertion about the close affinity between the powerful and knowledge, or the conflation of the social distribution of power and knowledge, has a family resemblance to the thesis that an increase in collective human capital, while it "raises the people's ability to resist oppression," also "raises the ruler's benefits from subjugating them" (Barro, 1999:S159).

[102] Foucault (1979:100–102) recognizes the possibility of human agency that is manifest in discursive resistance: "Discourse transmits and produces power; it reinforces it, but it also undermines it, renders it fragile and makes it possible to thwart it." Much more typical for Foucault's perspective is the invisibility of agency. His analysis of discursive resistance, its basis, potential and productive force, is not convincing (cf. also Giddens, 1984:157).

[103] Ackerman and Rodal (2008:111) have usefully enumerated some of the many additional ways of organized forms of civil resistance: "Civilians have used disruptive actions as sanctions, to challenge and delegitimate rulers, mobilise publics, constrain authoritarians' power and undermine their sources of support and shift their loyalties. Petitions, marches, walkouts and demonstrations have been used to rouse public support and mobilisation. Forms of non-cooperation such as strikes, boycotts, resignations and civil disobedience have served to frustrate the operations of governments. Direct intervention such as blockades, factory occupations and sit-ins have thwarted rulers' ability to subjugate their people. The sequenced, sustained application of these nonviolent operations has engendered historical results: tyrants have capitulated, governments collapsed, occupying armies retreated and political systems that denied human rights been delegitimated and dismantled."

important to recognize and examine knowledge as a source of power of the helpless, as a source of agency that enables and facilitates elite-challenging political activities.

After all, given the fear that knowledge acquired by the powerless may be used against the ruling elites has led to many attempts by those in power to monopolize the means of communicating knowledge, keep it otherwise secret, restrict the admission to and the autonomy of knowledge-bearing and knowledge-creating institutions, limit public discussion, and strictly control the circulation of knowledge, for example by controlling the ownership or the centralization of the means of communication. In the modern world, such efforts are made much more difficult not only because the social fabric of society has changed, favoring the dissemination of knowledge, but also because the ensemble of communication media has been enlarged significantly and the unencumbered circulation of knowledge has become one of the crucial conditions for the possibility of economic growth.

The Internet – although it is not possible at this time to exactly specify to what extent this might be the case – not only enhances the mobilization and dissemination of knowledge among the weak[104] but also provides spaces for the possibility of surveillance of the powerful by the weak (see Rosanvallon ([2006] 2008:70). Using the conceptual and theoretical apparatus deployed by Albert Hirschman (1970), Foucault neglects both voice (i.e., protest, critique, the expression of opinions) and exit (i.e., defection) as important modalities of political participation in societies, especially in societies in which the public sphere expands and new possibilities of interaction emerge. Summing up this point, democracy, as Pierre Rosanvallon (2006:221) also underlines, "seems to be diluted precisely because the possibilities of relating to institutions and one another are multiplying" rather than becoming more centralized because specialized knowledge is concentrated in the hands of a few. Of course, there are – aside from knowledge specific attributes such as its distance from ordinary discourse – various societal restraints and institutional arrangements affecting the wide dissemination of and access to knowledge in society that potentially get in the way of the broad-based role that knowledge could play in the social control of power in democratic societies.

---

[104] If I correctly interpret Manuel Castells (2009:47) views of processes of power-making – served by the new technical capabilities – as based on a logic that can both enhance and undermine societal power, this means that "resistance to power is achieved through the same two mechanisms that constitute power in the network society: the programs of the networks, and the switches between networks."

A further highly relevant observation concerning the knowledge of the weak in society focuses on the role of social movements in modern societies not only because these may represent social sites in which (other-directed) knowledge is mobilized for political conflicts but as contexts in which "independent" knowledge is produced and other forms of knowledge are reformulated, reconstituted, and disseminated. The social science literature that in the past decades most closely attended to questions raised here about the connection between knowledge and the emancipation of the weak in society consists of studies on the societal role of new social movements, the "cognitive mobilization" of individuals and small groups in modern society as well as on the forms and resources of resistance in the world of work (Collinson, 1995; 2000) after a long neglect of labor resistance, for example in the influential work of Braverman (1974) and his account of work under modern capitalism.[105] More recently, the research interest of STS (Science, Technology, and Society) scientists, too, has expanded to the role of new social movements. Technology and product-oriented movements of civil society that also maintain relationships with private firms generally aim, for example, to develop and disseminate alternative technologies and products. In contrast to the kind of social movements investigated in earlier studies, new social movements target their activities less "on the politics of protest and more on building and diffusing alternative forms of material culture" (Hess 2005:516). It is therefore of value if we consider the results of these analyses with a critical mind.

There is no generally agreed upon definition of social movements, nor are social movements new. As is always the case with classifications, certain examples are readily identified as cases of social movements, for example contemporary environmental movements, while others are bound to generate debates that will never be resolved. What is new about social movements according to the literature that has constructed and used the term is – in terms of a minimum consensus – that new social movements are manifestations of recent years and the most recent decades in advanced societies. Theoretical perspectives that proclaim to

---

[105] David Collinson (1995:25) in his examination of labor resistance – based on two case studies – draws on the emphasis placed on knowledge and information of subordinates by Stewart Clegg (1989) and generally outlines "the importance of different forms of knowledge in the articulation of resistance." Collinson (1995:28) summarizes his findings and points out that "specific forms of knowledge are a crucial resource and means through which resistance can be mobilized. *Knowledge in organizations is multiple, contested and shifting.* Employees may not possess detailed underpinnings of certain bureaucratic/political processes, but they often do monopolize other technical, production-related-knowledges that facilitate their oppositional practices (my emphasis)."

deal with social movements and not any longer with "collective behavior" or similar notions of past efforts in social science to come to grips with a wide variety of "cooperative" processes of social, political, and economic conduct are, not surprisingly, quite diverse, each of them championing their own definition of social movement. Since I do not aspire to make a direct contribution to ongoing debates on social movements, their origins, formation, and prospects, I will for pragmatic reasons adopt what I consider a useful conception of social movements.

Social movements are unlike social classes or generations although social movements do bear some structural resemblances to generations and social classes. Class position is an "objective fact." Class consciousness does not necessarily accompany class position. One cannot by conscious decision cease to be a member of one's social class but one can, irrespective of any intentions, abandon it. Generations are ultimately based, as Karl Mannheim ([1928] 1993:365) reminds us in his seminal essay on generations, on the biological rhythm of birth and death. But generations refer to a similarity of sociohistorical location. Generations represent a stratification of experiences in society, particularly those that occur in childhood and early adulthood. Social change accounts for the possibility of stratified experiences and the tempo of social change accounts for the volume of stratification. Bonds among members of social classes and generations may be quite loose. Perhaps social movements are best described as organizational categories that rely for their formation on accelerated social change, a transitory membership that is as loosely constituted as are social classes or generations, and pursue more or less clearly identifiable contentious objectives that transcend the status quo.

My interest centers on the extent to which modern social movements can be seen as a medium and manifestation of emergent conditions for a broader-based linkage between knowledge and the emancipation of the allegedly weak in modern societies. I therefore stress the enabling impact of social movements on the "nature" of society and individuals alike by enlarging participation opportunities as well as repertoires of contention (cf. Tilly, 1995:41) through the creation of new public spheres, by legitimizing a conflict-based resolution of divergent interests, and by enhancing the ability to resist the will of large, powerful social institutions. Social movements in this sense refer to both structural and cultural phenomena involving not only "what people *do* when they are engaged in conflict with others but what they *know how to do* and what others *expect* them to do" (Tarrow, 1998:30).

Resistance in modern society rarely takes the form of dramatic confrontations, such as revolutions, rebellions, and riots. Social movements are both countervailing forces and entities that constructively reform political culture. They are transmission belts for the effective and enabling utilization of knowledge. Thus, from my perspective, what is noteworthy about new social movements are the nature and the volume of cognitive activities and skills found in social organizations.[106] The volume and nature of knowledge affects the opportunity structures for movements, their legitimacy, and the stratified effectiveness for (or impact on) social and political contexts in which the utility of specific forms of knowledge is bound to be extensive. Applying John Stuart Mill's ([1831] 1942) observation about the spirit of his own age, which he experienced as an age of change, reference is also made to the "sort of progress which increase of discussion suffices to produce" whether or not it is attended "with an increase of wisdom."

Ron Eyerman and Andrew Jamison's cognitive approach (a social movement is its cognitive praxis) to the analysis of social movements stresses social movements as defined through their cognitive practices – almost in the sense in which the term class consciousness has been employed in the past. The "cognitive praxis" of social movements as concrete social groups more specifically refers to a particular view of the world or, to coin a term, the movement consciousness. The specific manifestations of the movement consciousness, or the "relations to knowledge," are, as Eyerman and Jamison (1991:3) enumerate, the "concepts, ideas and intellectual activities that give them their cognitive identity." By knowledge, they mean "the worldview assumptions, the ideas about the world that are shared by participants in social movement, as well as the specific topic or issues that movements are created around."[107] However, since Eyerman and Jamison advocate a "cognitive

---

[106] A colorful heterogeneity is the major common feature of modern social movements, for example, in terms of objectives and themes, distinctive sociohistorical situations, organizational attributes, resources, cognitive traditions, national or regional contexts, impact on political culture, competition and relations among movements, career patterns of movements, and so on. As a matter of fact, as one concentrates on the specificity of social movements and a "thick description" of their comparative transformation over even short periods of time, any common elements begin to quickly retreat into the background or even dissolve altogether (cf. Brand, 1987). One of the major features of social movements (and in the intellectual resources they liberally employ), and in this sense they resemble knowledge societies at large, is their essential fragility.

[107] Social movements cannot only be seen as social organizations or as composed of individual activists that strategically deploy knowledge to mobilize collective action (cf. Oliver and Marwell, 1992: 255–257) but as organizational entities that intend to spread their "knowledge interests" or are "diffusing its consciousness"; and, not altogether paradoxically perhaps, the greater their practical success in doing so, the more precarious their existence as a social movement (cf. Eyerman and Jamison, 1991:4).

turn" in the analysis of social movements – away from its functionalist alternative and toward an analysis of the articulation of a movement consciousness – their interest transcends any differentiation of knowledge forms and remains somewhat indifferent to the question of whether new social movements are characterized by an enhanced use of "scientific" and "technical knowledge," hybrid knowledge claims or knowledge generated within the movement organization.[108]

In contrast, Casas-Cortés, Osterwell and Powell (2008:19–20) in a series of case studies in different societies develop and demonstrate the idea of (local) knowledge-practices found in social movements.[109] More specifically, the authors refer to knowledge-practices as "encounters ranging from heated online and journal debates over the nature and meaning of Italy's *movimento no global*, in which new forms of situated and reflexive theoretical production are defined; to hours of direct-action strategizing in meetings at Chicago's cooperative bookstores, where theories of embodied democracy are derived; to campground conferences

---

[108] Paradoxically, what remains of any interest in scientific knowledge, is a functionalist concern, namely the assertion that "scientific knowledge is directly dependent on social movements in a variety of ways," or that one needs to stress the intellectual consequences of social movements for the production of knowledge (see Eyerman and Jamison, 1991:54). Resource mobilization theory (cf. Zald and McCarthy, 1987; Morris and McClurg Mueller, 1992), an alternative approach to the analysis of the career of social movements recognizing money, labor and legitimacy as key resources, is based on an individualistic frame of reference and the assumption that highly rational (instrumental) considerations motivate actors to join and support such organizations. The approach stresses, much in the same spirit, the exclusively instrumental use of knowledge in the execution of movement objectives in such contexts. The resource mobilization perspective's interest in and concern with "ideological" factors is quite limited. Perhaps this is the case, as Snow and Benford (1992:135) observe, because of their "presumed ubiquity and constancy, which makes them, in turn, relatively nonproblematic and uninteresting in the movement equation." Efforts designed to bridge some of the gaps that exist between resource mobilization and cognitive approaches (e.g., Diani, 1996) also fail to highlight the nature of the efficacy of specific symbolic systems in new social movements. Finally, Cress and Snow (1996) have empirically examined the relative importance of "informational resources" ("knowledge capital pertinent to the organization's maintenance and mobilization," perhaps better described as "know-how" such as how to run a meeting and delegate tasks) among homeless organizations and report that informational resources along with leadership and having a place to meet are among the important assets when it comes to the viability of the movement.

[109] A definition of knowledge-practices offered by Casa-Cortés, Osterwell, and Powell (2008:42) describes the wide range of capacities of actions that fall under its general heading: "Knowledge-practices range from things we are more classically trained to define as knowledge, such as research practices and critiques that engage, augment, and sometimes challenge the knowledge of scientists or policy experts, to micro-political and cultural interventions that have more to do with 'know-how' or the 'cognitive praxis that informs all social activity' and which vie with the most basic social institutions that teach us how to be in the world."

on Native American territories, where native knowledge contributes to the science of environmental justice issues." These are social contexts where the independent production, reconstruction, and dissemination of practical knowledge can be observed, that is, of knowledge that is closely linked to particular social practices but does not necessarily dispense with the adaptive use of scientific knowledge.[110] Casas-Cortés, Osterwell, and Powell (2008:20) also emphasize the political role of the knowledge-practices of social movements, as well as their general political importance for the society in which these movements operate.

I will refer to only one, but important, barrier and ask: Is it possible to reconcile democracy and knowledge as property? Limiting the access to and the circulation of knowledge through patent and copyright laws, for example, would seem to assure, on first sight, that economic constraints favor the well to do rather than the weak of society.[111]

Reconciling democracy and knowledge as property

In testimony before the U.S. Congress more than a century ago, John Powell, a pioneer in the field of the earth sciences, put his finger on one of the most intriguing features of knowledge, namely that "the possession of property is exclusive; possession of knowledge is not exclusive." In spite of Powell's thesis, some forms of knowledge, by having patents or copyright restrictions attached to them, are exclusive and become private goods as the result of legal restraints.

Whether knowledge is treated as a public or private good has many noteworthy consequences; for example, it is incremental or new knowledge that is most likely to be protected. In the context of economic systems and also in science, this raises a serious dilemma. The basis for the growth of knowledge is knowledge. If knowledge is protected, the growth of knowledge is hampered. However, if knowledge is not

[110] Casas-Cortés, Osterwell and Powell (2008:32) refer, for example, to the term "energy justice." The concept evolves out of a "commingling of epistemological practices: 'Western' and 'natural' science and technology, economics, Native epistemologies and the lived experiences of members in these impacted communities. Scientific knowledge is thus not rejected outright, but is mobilized and intertwined with traditional knowledge and technological knowledge for the purpose of making a case for alternative approaches to energy production and, more broadly, for analyzing the present conditions of economic and health disparities among Native communities. 'Energy justice' can thus be seen not only as a prescriptive concept, but also as a claim seeking to transform conventional thought about the historical production and consumption of electrical and nuclear power in the United States."

[111] The supposedly free and frictionless circulation of knowledge and information is not only hampered by legal restrictions but also by linguistic features, local practices, and existing information and knowledge infrastructures (cf. Edwards et al., 2011:1398).

protected, economists argue, the incentive to invest in new knowledge disappears; monopoly rights are essential for the growth of knowledge and inventions.

In contrast to incremental knowledge, the general mundane and routinized stock of knowledge consists mostly of knowledge that is nonrival as well as nonexcludable; that is, this type of knowledge may very well constitute public goods.

Scientific knowledge constitutes one of the most important conditions for the possibility of modernization in the sense of a persistent extension and enlargement of social and economic action generated by science and not just by any social system in modern society.

I do not wish to enter into a discussion of the contentious issue of trade-offs that may exist between assigning proprietary rights to knowledge and the gains in the overall welfare of society, or the trade-off between treating knowledge as a public good and the loss of revenue for those who cannot reap the benefits from their inventions and discoveries.

Economists, legal scholars, and major international organizations, such as the World Bank, make the case that knowledge must be a (global) public asset.[112] From an economic viewpoint, this means that knowledge is supposed to lack the characteristics otherwise typical of economic assets, namely rivalry and excludability. The fact that some forms of knowledge are public goods is least likely to advance the case for additional knowledge, but it is this new knowledge that turns a profit. Thus, the age-old dilemma of whether property generates power and thereby fashions human relations or whether it is the other way around continues to be played out even in knowledge societies.

The discourse about the relationship between scientific knowledge and democracy has been science-centered, be it with respect to the role of experts or to the contested idea that knowledge is property. The discussion has exclusively concentrated on the social role of natural scientific or technical knowledge. In my concluding section, I would

---

[112] As the World Bank Report (1999:1) on *Knowledge for Development* emphatically notes: "Knowledge is like light. Weightless and intangible, it can easily travel the world, enlightening the lives of people everywhere. Yet billions of people still live in the darkness of poverty – unnecessarily." To what extent is, can – and maybe even should – knowledge generally be accessible around the world? Is knowledge a public good whose opportunities, for example in the field of health care (cf. Chen, Evans, and Cash, 1999), can be *equitably* exploited? There are huge gaps, imbalances, and barriers to the actual dissemination of knowledge around the world. Perhaps the sharpness of the divide may have increased in the last decades, but these disparities appear to constitute mere "problems"; thus, the uneven distribution of knowledge may be overcome in principle. Yet, the project of global knowledge is, if we follow the World Bank, far from constituting a human achievement.

like to focus instead on the role of social science knowledge claims and their impact on modern society.

Enabling knowledge?

Two broad models for dealing with scientific knowledge claims can be identified. The one that resonates with much of the previous discussion and asserts a steep gradient of knowledge between science and society is the model of instrumentality. Science speaks to society and does so not only with considerable authority but also with significant success, while society has little if any opportunity to talk back.[113] Using the instrumental model as a standard, social science knowledge, and knowledge from the humanities is itself the originator of its societal success (or failure). More specifically, the instrumentality model stipulates that the practical usefulness associated with social science is linked solely to the solid "scientificity" of such knowledge. The closer social science knowledge achieves and adheres to those attributes of knowledge production that certify knowledge claims as "scientific" knowledge, the greater the likelihood that such knowledge is powerful in practice.

In practice, instrumental knowledge generated by the social sciences and/or the humanities aspires to be a form of social technology. The slogan "there is nothing as practical as a good theory" is at times employed to capture the requirements for useful knowledge generated by the instrumental model. In fact, the social science base of useful instrumental or applicable social technology is quite small, which leads some social scientists to despair and refer to their activities as science with a small "s" (cf. Eggertsson, 2009).[114]

---

[113] The dominance of scientific knowledge in society and the extensive respect granted to scientific knowledge to the exclusion of other forms of knowledge provoked Paul Feyerabend ([1974] 2006) in the mid-seventies to ask how society could be defended against science. His answer is: with the help of an education system that is intellectually more inclusive. Feyerabend (1974] 2006:360) stipulates that contemporary science has deteriorated into an ideology with sanctified, oppressive truths that are immune to criticism and with practices of indoctrination: "Science has now become as oppressive as the ideologies it had once to fight." The practice of modern science inhibits the freedom of thought and therefore comes into conflict with what is an essential attribute of democracy, namely the peaceful coexistence of different sets of ideas. In society, ideological pressures exist that drive out forms of knowledge with the exception of those that originate from science. For Feyerabend, the lesson to be learned from the particular authority that science enjoys in society is the separation of science and the state in the interest of the defense of democracy and liberty, especially in the field of public education.

[114] In their paper "Progress in know-how: its origins and limits", Daniel Sarewitz and Richard Nelson (2008; also Nelson, 2008) explain why the evolution of know-how is uneven across the sciences and what factors make progress in some areas of human

The alternative approach to the social pathways of social science knowledge (but not only social science knowledge) would be the capacity model. The capacity model refers to a couple of attributes that make for the practical utility of knowledge claims. The social sciences and the humanities exercise practical influence as producers of enabling ideas and meaning for society and its actors. The social sciences and the humanities operate as meaning producers. The social sciences are – borrowing a term from the historian James Harvey Robinson (1923:16) – "mind-makers."[115] The power of mind-making rests on the power of the proposed concepts or ideas, as capacities to act, suggesting also ways of their concrete realization.

The social sciences, even if considered a major, if not growing, reservoir of meaning that disseminates through various social "pipelines" (such as the media, teachers, priests, writers) into society, do not have a monopoly on meaning production. But in contrast to the model of instrumentality, the capacity model stresses that the agents who "employ" social science knowledge are active agents who transform, reissue, and otherwise redesign social science knowledge. This active attribute of the "mind-seekers" speaks against a straightforward "social scientification" of mundane worldviews by social science discourse. The capacity model stipulates that social scientific knowledge is an intellectual resource that is contingently open and complex and, thus, can be molded in the course of its "travel" from the social scientific community into society. This model further assumes that neither the production nor the application of this knowledge involves identical reproduction. The capacity model is therefore associated with the possibility that people

activity particularly difficult while in some others the improvement of know-how has been much more rapid. According to Sarewicz and Nelson, the answer is linked to the differential capability in the development of know-how to generate *standardized* procedures at the level of management and policy-making for the purposes of implementing technological know-how (cf. Nelson, 2003).

[115] Robinson (1923:16–17) refers to a long list of occupations and professions that serve as mind-makers in modern society: "Mind-seekers are the questioners (of the taken-for-granted or the commonplace) and seers. We classify them roughly as poets, religious leaders, moralists, story-tellers, philosophers, theologians, artists, scientists, inventors." But Robinson (1923:17) also raises the significant follow-up question: "What determines the *success* of a new idea; what establishes its currency and gives it social significance by securing its victory over ignorance and indifference or older rival and conflicting beliefs?" In this context, he stresses that the "*truth* of a new idea proposed for acceptance plays an altogether secondary role" (Robinson, 1923:20). Robinson's question concerning the conditions for the success of a new idea must of course be extended to the question of why new ideas are incapable to displace the commonplace and the taken-for-granted, or what "social labor" established ideas exactly accomplish and under what circumstances they are able to do so.

may critically engage social science knowledge using local knowledge resources and thus make social science accountable to the public.

In addition to being a source of enabling meaning and ideas, the social sciences and the humanities may further generate enabling knowledge by producing knowledge claims that include, in the knowledge-generating process, and in contrast to more formal, deductive, and epistemic knowledge, up-front references to essential features of existing social conditions, including the role of local knowledge and the diversity of natural environments (cf. Carolan, 2006).

A realistic appraisal

If one follows the demanding advice of Sanford A. Lakoff (1971:12), "a democratic system in which knowledge is made the focus of continuing public concern is the only basis, under modern conditions, for government which is both effective and responsible." How is one to realistically appraise such a demand? Similarly, the philosopher of the French Enlightenment, the Marquis de Condorcet, was convinced that "the argument that the citizen could not take part in the whole discussion and that each individual's argument could not be heard by everyone can have no force" (as quoted in Urbinati, 2006:202). For Condorcet, the issue was not one of competency with respect to the issue at hand but of good rules and settings within which individuals would be able to deliberate jointly. Aside from the normative or even constitutional empowerment of ordinary citizens to be heard on policy matters, even if the latter involve highly specialized knowledge claims, Condorcet reminds us that collective deliberation and involvement benefits from the presence of rules, settings, and opportunities conducive to such reflection and from the absence of a clear-cut power structure. Both prerequisites are usually assumed to be absent in narratives about the inordinate political power of highly specialized knowledge.

One of the persistent and foremost challenges of democratic governance is to generate and maintain motivation among its citizens to become and remain knowledgeable (cf. Merton, 1966:1056). Public engagement and participation in science is not hazardous for the scientific community; it is part of the social architecture of democracy (see Culliton, 1978). But this is one side of the issue of the relation of democracy and specialized knowledge.

The other side of the coin pertains to claims that the public consideration of specialized knowledge claims is a futile enterprise from the beginning because of the inability of ordinary citizens to engage in public deliberations of such forms of knowledge. This argument essentially enshrines instrumental rationality as the mode governing the linkage between scientific knowledge – understood, of course, to have those distinctive merits that enable calculational decision making, and provided a society that allows for policy decisions to become more and more efficient.

The basic claim of my observations for the moment is that the evolvement of modern societies as knowledge societies increasingly extends to the democratization and negotiation of knowledge claims. We are slowly moving from what has been the case of expert rule to a much broader, shared form of the governance of knowledge claims (cf. Stehr, 2005; Leighninger, 2006). After all, it is one of the virtues of (liberal) democracies that citizens are to be involved in political decisions. Such participation, whatever formal basis it may assume, does not hinge, as a prerequisite, on the degree of technical or intellectual competence citizens may command. In addition, I make the assumption that scientific and technical knowledge are not only more malleable and accessible – and less definitive – in practice than has been suggested in the classical perspective, for instance the "enlightenment model" of the relations between science and society (cf. Irwin, 1999).

Rather, the new sociology of scientific knowledge has created the perspective that the production of scientific knowledge is in many ways very similar to other social practices and that the wall between science and society is lower than frequently assumed, although it has by no means disappeared. The boundaries between expertise and everyday knowledge are much less fixed and more robust than has often been surmised, especially in those observations quoted that lament the growing distance between expert knowledge and the public's knowledge. Moreover, what increasingly counts as problematic in modern society is not that we may not know enough but that we may know too much. Societal negotiation of novel capacities for knowledge (generated in science and in technology) is not as dependent on specialized natural scientific and technical knowledge as it is on the enabling knowledge generated by the social sciences and the humanities.

General access of civil society to enabling knowledge produced in the social sciences faces fewer hurdles than in the natural sciences. Knowledgeability has gained social externality through the production of a more participatory democracy or citizenship, which most benefits civil society organizations. All of this produces particular challenges not only in terms of access to social science knowledge but also in the form of new modes of participation. It is here that civil society organizations will be challenged.

Social space for communication between science/social science and the public already exists. The possibility for democratic negotiation and scientific practice has to be seen as part of a larger social enterprise and a larger social context in which both professional scientists as experts and the lay public engage in discourse. Science is an effective social force because it can engage and rely, in turn, on civil society organizations and institutions. The cases of climate change and AIDS activism are rich examples of social processes in which the boundaries between expert and lay public are quite malleable (cf. Epstein, 1996; Bohman, 1999b).

And, as Otto Neurath (1946:79) has stressed in the last paper he ever published: "I do not think that one can distinguish between the problems of the scientists and the problems of the man in the street. In the end, they are more interlinked than people sometimes realize. Any synthesis of our intellectual life, any orchestration of various attempts to handle life and arguments should never forget these far reaching social implications."

Finally, we should not be too harsh in diagnosing the lack of scientific foundation in much of what we treat as knowledge in ordinary life since we tend to get on quite well with such knowledge, at least most of the time and for most practical purposes (cf. Schutz, 1946:463; Hardin, 2003:5). As Ludwig Wittgenstein (1969:§344; also Sidgwick, [1895] 1905:427) notes: "My life consists in my being content to accept many things."

And when is comes to the knowledge necessary to judge politics, John Stuart Mills' ([1861] 1977:chap. 3, par. 2) pragmatic observation would seem to be still valid:

A person must have a very unusual taste for intellectual exercise in and of itself, who will put himself to the trouble of thought when it is to have no outward effect.... . The only sufficient incitement to mental exertion, in any but a few minds in a generation, is the prospect of some practical use to be made of its results.

Finally, in a world of rapidly changing, specialized cognitive skills, those who complain about the lack of knowledge among large segments of society are often those left behind with respect to their command of the new forms of knowledge, which leads to intriguing conflicts of authority, power, age, and knowledge.

It is profoundly unrealistic today to "expect citizens, even highly educated ones, to have enough technical knowledge" (Dahl, 1977:18) to, for example, enter on an equal footing into the technical economic discourse on policy decisions pertaining to inflation-unemployment trade-offs. It is equally unrealistic to assume, as the case appears to be, that the policy (*cum* scientists) elites intellectually and ideologically form a homogenous, coherent stratum that monopolized policies.

Knowledge and democracy: summary and conclusions

> The defect[s] with which writers usually charge the multitude may be also charged to individual men, and particularly to princes ... [In fact] the people are more prudent, more stable and more judicious than princes.
> Machiavelli, *Discourses*

> Democracy is a system based on reflection, it allows the citizen to accept the laws of the country with more intelligence and thus less passivity.
> Emile Durkheim ([1950] 1957:131)

In drawing on my meta-reflexive considerations of the history, contemporary state, and future possibilities of the relation between democracy and knowledge, the following basic conclusions and an answer to the central question of my inquiry may be presented. Is democracy an offspring of knowledge, and will sustainable democratic governance be served by an enhanced and more equal social distribution of knowledge? My answer requires, first of all, a brief summary of the core of the prevailing answers to this question, as well as of the main objections that can be mobilized against entrenched views of the relation between knowledge and democratic governance.

First, the central premise and, as is often maintained, the main empirical support is the idea that citizens in modern societies are extremely impoverished when it comes to political knowledge. But since political knowledge is assumed to constitute the high road to informed reasoning about political issues, the inference is that ordinary citizens have but a limited capacity to reflect independently and intelligently about political issues. Therefore, if they attempt at all to make up their minds in advance of a political decision, they are easy captives of motivated reasoning, presented to them by political propaganda disguised as expert advice based on the superior knowledge of a small cadre of knowledgeable individuals or groups of advisors, experts, and consultants. Technocratic reasoning and approaches in political decision making, however, are adverse to public debate, scrutiny, discussion, and judgment. The redefinition of the political as technocratic is antidemocratic.

Second, the core of the predominant argument, independent of the specific conclusion, is science-driven, or revolves around knowledge in the sense of information. Clearly, reference to scientific knowledge (or what is conflated with scientific knowledge: for example, the scientific spirit, the logic of science, the ethos of science, etc.) is the dominant meaning assigned to the notion of knowledge in discussions about the ways in which knowledge may contribute to or detract from democratic governance.

Third, my own conclusion would be that it is not so much knowledge in the sense of scientific and technical knowledge that nourishes democracy; rather, democracy is the daughter of knowledgeability. Knowledgeability is both linked to and independent of the growth of scientific knowledge. It is linked to scientific knowledge in the sense that such knowledge is not understood as originating from an empire of positivistic knowledge production that supports features of knowledgeability. It is independent of scientific knowledge, in the sense that attributes of knowledgeability can grow and be widely disseminated in society without the concurrent growth of scientific knowledge, since the spread of knowledgeablity is more dependent on structural societal changes. Knowledgeability as a bundle of cognitive and social competencies and capabilities supports liberties in that, on the one hand, it enhances the ability of individuals and small groups to resist; and, on the other hand, it forces large societal institutions to be accountable toward citizens in a variety of roles found in civil society (consumer, student, tax payer, voter, worker, commuter, property owner, etc.).

Whereas the challenge of the past may well have been instrumental in making democracy stronger through the enhanced knowledgeability of its citizens, the challenge in contemporary societies is to make knowledge more democratic. The major problem of the present is therefore not the high level of education of many individuals and their affinity to democracy, to which so many of them owe their upward mobility; rather, it is the still immense group of those members of society whose education is insufficient for them to make an independent living in modern society, thus contributing to its affirmation.

My perhaps somewhat optimistic thesis that liberty is a daughter of knowledge should not, however, be misunderstood as an advocacy for the indiscriminate, utopian possibility of an ideal, perfect society (see Berlin, [1998] 2000:22–23) in which a conciliation of the goals of perfect liberty and equality or the fundamental compatibility of general happiness and knowledge is realized, as the solution to all, or almost all, of our personal and public problems. In the past, such optimistic expectations did indeed exist. Whatever the specific obstacles may arise on the path to a perfect society – for example, the mere notion that the practical implementation of certain fundamental values, such as equality and liberty could be fully realized – is self-contradictory. Thus, the notion of a perfect society in this sense cannot exist.[1] Conditions become better and better – provided that citizens, consumers, patients, parents, schoolchildren, students, tourists, and so forth stand up and push their demands onto the political agenda. In the past, democracies may not always have been daughters of knowledge; however, the future of democracies, their persistence, and sustainability will in all likelihood not be daughters of knowledge and knowledgeability. Moreover, it is important to recognize and examine knowledge and knowledgeabilty as a source of power for the allegedly helpless, as a source of agency and the ability to question the politics of the elites. Finally, it should be noted that modernity, especially in the sense of the "substructure" of contemporary societies, undoubtedly is a daughter of novel findings and ideas (see also Goldstone, 2006). Liberty in modern societies is a daughter of knowledge. However, freedom has, in contrast to other constitutive features and existential conditions of twenty-first century societies – for example, its technical and communicative structures – repeatedly been defeated. Apparently modernity is more sustainable than freedom.

[1] Isaiah Berlin ([1998] 2002:23) is without compromise in judging the proponents of the possibility of a "perfect society": "The very idea of the perfect world in which all good things are realised is incomprehensible, is in fact conceptually incoherent. And if this is so, and I cannot see how it could be otherwise, then the very notion of the ideal world, for which no sacrifice can be too great, vanishes from view."

Bibliography

Under each author's name the most recent works are listed first. In the case of translations, revised, or later editions, the original date of publication is also shown, within square brackets.

Abel, Günter (2009), "Forms of knowledge problems, projects, perspective," in Peter Meusburger, Michael Welker, and Edgar Wunder (eds.), *Clashes of Knowledge: Orthodoxies and Heterodoxies in Science and Religion*. Heidelberg: Springer, 11–34.

Abramson, Paul R. and Ronald Inglehart (1994), "Economic security and value change," *American Political Science Review* 88: 336–354.

Acemoglu, Daron (2002), "Technical change, inequality, and the labour market," *Journal of Economic Literature* 40:7–72.

Acemoglu, Daron and James A. Robinson (2012), *Why Nations Fail: The Origins of Power, Prosperity, and Poverty*, New York: Crown Publishers.

(2000), "Why did the West extend the franchise? Democracy, inequality, and growth in historical perspective," *The Quarterly Journal of Economics* 115:1167–1199.

Acemoglu, Daron, Simon Johnson, James A. Robinson, and Pierre Yared (2008), "Income and democracy," *American Economic Review* 98:808–842.

Acemoglu, Daron, Simon Johnson, James A. Robinson and Pierre Yared (2006), "From education to democracy," *American Economic Review* 95:44–49.

Ackerman, Peter and Berel Rodal (2008), "The strategic dimension of civil resistance," *Survival* 50:111–126.

Ackoff, Russell L. (1989), "From data to wisdom," *Journal of Applied Systems Analysis* 16:3–9.

Adler, Emanuel and Steven Bernstein (2005), "Knowledge in power: the epistemic construction of global governance," in Michael Barnett and Raymond Duvall (eds.), *Power in Global Governance*. Cambridge: Cambridge University Press, 294–318.

Adolf, Marian, Jason Mast, and Nico Stehr (2013), "The foundations of innovation in modern societies: the displacements of concepts and knowledgeability," *Mind & Society* 12:11–22.

Adorno, Theodor W. ([1951] 1986), "Individuum und Staat", in *Gesammelte Schriften* 20.1: Vermischte Schriften 1, Frankfurt am Main: Suhrkamp, 287–292.

Agamben, Giorgio (2014), "The power of thought," *Critical Inquiry* 40:480–491.

Bibliography

Ali, Abdiweli M. and Hodan Said Isse (2004), "Political freedom and the stability of economic policy," *Cato Journal* 24:251–260.

Allen, John (2003), *Lost Geographies of Power*. Oxford: Blackwell.

Alexander, Jeffrey C. (1987), "Fundamentale Zweideutigkeiten in Max Webers Theorie der Rationalisierung: Warum erscheint Weber wie ein Marxist, obwohl er keiner ist?" in Stefan Böckler and Johannes Weiß (ed.), *Marx oder Weber? Zur Aktualisierung einer Kontroverse*. Opladen: Westdeutscher Verlag, pp. 90–103.

Alford, Robert (1985), *Powers of Theory*. Cambridge: Cambridge University Press.

Allern, Elin and Karina Pedersen (2007), "The impact of party organizational changes on democracy," *West European Politics* 30:68–92.

Almond, Gabriel (1956), "Comparative political systems," *Journal of Politics* 18:391–409.

Almond, Gabriel and Sidney Verba (1963), *The Civic Culture*. Princeton, NJ: Princeton University Press.

Alvey, James E. (2001), "Moral education as a means to human perfection and social order: Adam Smith's view of education in commercial society," *History of the Human Sciences* 14:1–18.

Ambuehl, Sandro, B. Douglas Bernheim, and Annamaria Lusardi (2014), "*Financial education, financial competence, and consumer welfare,*" NBER Working Paper Series 20618. www.nber.org/papers/w20618.

Amidon, Debra M. (1997), *Innovation Strategy for the Knowledge Economy: The Ken Awakening*. London: Routledge.

Anderson, Benedict (1991), *Imagined Communities*. Second edn. London: Verso.

Anderson, Robert (2012), "Support for democracy in cross-national perspective: The detrimental effect of economic inequality," *Research in Social Stratification and Mobility* 30:389–402, http://dx.doi.org/10.1016/j.rssm.2012.04.002.

Ankersmit, Frank R. (2002), "Representational democracy," *Common Knowledge* 8:24–46.

Arce, Moises and Wonik Kim (2011), "Globalization and extra-parliamentary politics in an era of democracy," *European Political Science Review* 3(2):253–278.

Arendt, Hannah (1961), *Between Past and Future: Eight Exercises in Political Thought*. New York: Penguin.

 (1953), "Understanding and politics," *Partisan Review* 4: 377–392.

Aristotle, (1932), *Politics*. Cambridge, MA: Harvard University Press.

Aron, Raymond (1985), "Tocqueville and Marx," in Raymond Aron, *History, Truth, Liberty: Selected Writings of Raymond Aron*. Chicago: University of Chicago Press.

 ([1965] 1984), "Politische Freiheit in der technisierten Gesellschaft," in Raymond Aron, *Über die Freiheiten*. Stuttgart: Klett-Cotta, 88–121.

Arrow, Kenneth J. ([1951] 1963), *Social Choice and Individual Values*. New Haven, CT: Yale University Press.

Aslaksen, Silje (2010), "Oil and democracy: more than a cross-country correlation?" *Journal of Peace Research* 47:1–11.

Bibliography

Åström, Joachim, Martin Karlsson, Jonas Lindeand, and Ali Pirannejad (2012), "Understanding the rise of e-participation in non-democratic democracies: Domestic and international factors," *Government Information Quarterly* 29:142–150.

Attewell, Paul (1992), "Technology diffusion and organizational learning: the case of business computing," *Organization Science* 3:1–19.

Baber, Walter F. and Robert V. Barlett (2005), *Deliberative Environmental Politics: Democracy and Ecological Rationality*. Cambridge, MA: MIT Press.

Baccaro, Lucio (2001), "Union democracy revisited: decision-making procedures in the Italian labour movement," *Economic and Industrial Democracy* 22:183–210.

Bachelard, Gaston ([1938] 1972), *La Formation de l'esprit scientifique*. Paris: Vrin.

Backhouse, Roger E. and Bradley W. Bateman (2009), "Keynes and capitalism," *History of Political Economy* 41:645–671.

Bailer, Stefanie, Thilo Bodenstein, and V. Finn Heinrich (2012), "Explaining the strength of civil society: evidence from cross-sectional data," *International Political Science Review* 34:289–309.

Baiocchhi, Gianpaolo (2003), "Emergent public spheres: talking politics in participatory governance," *American Sociological Review* 68:52–74.

Ballantyne, Tony (2011), "Paper, pen, and print: the transformation of the Kai Tahu knowledge order," *Comparative Studies in Society and History* 53:232–260.

Barber, Benjamin (2008), "Shrunken sovereign: consumerism, globalization and American emptiness," *World Affairs* 170:73–81.

  (2000), "Globalizing democracy," *The American Prospect* 11 (September 11):16–19.

  (1984), *Strong Democracy: Participatory Politics for a New Age*. Berkeley, CA: University of California Press.

Barber, Bernhard (1952), *Science and the Social Order*. New York: Free Press.

Barnes, Barry S. (1995), *The Elements of Social Theory*. Princeton, NJ: Princeton University Press.

  (1988), *The Nature of Power*. Urbana, IL: University of Illinois Press.

Barnes, Barry S. and R. G. A. Dolby, (1970), "The scientific ethos: a deviant viewpoint," *European Journal of Sociology* 11:3–25.

Barnett, Michael and Raylond Duvall (2005), "Power in global governance," in Michael Barnett and Raymond Duvall (eds.), *Power in Global Governance*. Cambridge: Cambridge University Press, 1–32.

Barro, Robert J. (1999), "The determinants of democracy," *Journal of Political Economy* 107:S158–S183.

  (1996), "Democracy and growth," *Journal of Economic Growth* 1:1–27.

Barro, Robert and Lee Jong Wha, (2010), "A new data set of educational attainment in the world, 1950–2010," *NBER Working Paper* No. 15902.

Bartels, Larry M. (2005), "Homer gets a text cut: Inequality and public policy in the American mind," *Perspectives on Politics* 3:15–31.

Barzeley, Michael (1992), *Breaking through Bureaucracy*. Berkeley, CA: University of California Press.

Barth, Fredrik (2002), "An anthropology of knowledge," *Current Anthropology* 43:1–18.

Basdash, Lawrence (2000), "Science and McCarthyism," *Miverva* 38:53–80.
Bateson, Gregory (1972), *Steps to an Ecology of Mind.* New York: Ballantine.
Baudrillard, Jean (1988), *Selected Writings.* in Mark Poster, (ed.), Palo Alto, California, Stanford University Press.
Bauer, Martin W. (1996), "Socio-demographic correlates of DK-responses in knowledge surveys: self-attributed ignorance of science," *Social Science Information* 35:39–68.
Bauer, Walter (2003), "On the relevance of bildung for democracy," *Educational Philosophy and Theory* 32:211–225.
Baum, Matthew A. and David A. Lake (2003), "The political economy of growth: democracy and human capital," *American Journal of Political Science* 47:333–347.
Bay, Christian (1965),"Politics and pseudopolitics: a critical evaluation of some behavioral literature," *American Political Science Review* 59:39–51.
Bearce, David H. and Jennifer A. Laks Hutnik (2011), "Toward an alternative explanation for the resource curse: Natural resources, immigration, and democratization," *Comparative Political Studies* 44:689–718.
Bechmann, Gotthard and Nico Stehr (2002), "The legacy of Niklas Luhmann." *Society* 39: 67–75.
Beck, Ulrich ([1986] 1992), *The Risk Society.* London: Sage.
Becker, Jeffrey (2012), "The knowledge to act: Chinese migrant labor protests in comparative perspective," *Comparative Political Studies* 44:1379–1404.
Beckfield, Jason (2003), "Inequality in the world polity: The structure of international organization," *American Sociological Review* 68:401–424.
Beeson, Mark (2010), "The coming of environmental authoritarianism," *Environmental Politics* 19:276:264.
Bell, Daniel (1996), "Welcome to the post-industrial society," *Physics Today* February:40–48.
  ([1979] 1980), "The new class: a muddled concept," *The Winding Passage. Essays and Sociological Journeys 1960–1980.* Cambridge, MA: Abt Books, pp. 144–164.
  (1976), *The Cultural Contradictions of Capitalism.* New York: Basic Books.
  (1973), *The Coming of Post-Industrial Society: A Venture in Social Forecasting.* New York: Basic Books.
  (1971), "Technocracy and politics," *Survey* 16: 1–24.
  (1969), "Die nachindustrielle Gesellschaft," in Claus Grossner et al. (ed.), *Das 198. Jahrzehnt. Eine Team-Prognose für 1970 bis 1980*, Hamburg: Christian Wegner Verlag, S, pp. 351–363.
  (1968), "The measurement of knowledge and technology," in Eleanor B. Sheldon and Wilbert E. Moore (ed.), *Indicators of Social Change: Concepts and Measurements.* Hartford, CT: Russell Sage Foundation, pp. 145–246.
  (1967), "Notes on the post-industrial society," *The Public Interest* 6: 24–35.
  (1960), *The End of Ideology: on the Exhaustion of Political Ideas in the Fifties.* New York: Free Press.
  (1956), "The theory of mass society: a critique," *Commentary* 22:75–83.
Benavot, Aaron, Yun-Lyung Cha, David Kamens, John W. Meyer, and Suk-Ying Wong (1991), "Knowledge for the masses: world models and national curricula, 1920–1986," *American Sociological Review* 56:85–100.

Benkler, Yochai (1999), "From consumers to users: shifting the deeper structures of regulation toward sustainable commons and user access," *Federal Communications Law Journal* 52:561–579.
Bennett, Stephen Earl (2006), "Democratic competence, before converse and after," *Critical Review* 18:105–141.
  (2003), "Is the public's ignorance of politics trivial?" *Critical Review* 15: 307–337.
Bennett, W. Lance and Shanto Iyengar (2008), "A new era of minimal effects? The changing foundations of political communication," *Journal of Communication* 58:707–731.
Bensaude-Vincent, Bernadette (2001), "A genealogy of the increasing gap between science and the public," *Public Understanding of Science* 10:99–113.
Benson, Lee, Ira Harkavy, and John Puckett (2007), *Dewey's Dream: Universities and Democracy in an Age of Education Reform*. Philadelphia, PA: Temple University Press.
Bentzen, Jeanet Sinding, Nicolai Kaarsen, and Asger Moll Wingender (2012), "Irrigation and democracy," *Discussion Papers*. Department of Economics, University of Copenhagen, no. 12–06.
Berelson, Bernard (1952), "Democratic theory and public opinion," *Public Opinion Quarterly* 16:313–330.
Berelson, Bernard, Paul F. Lazarsfeld, and William N. McPhee (1954), *Voting: A Study of Public Opinion in a Presidential Campaign*. Chicago: University of Chicago Press.
Berg-Schlosser, Dirk (2003), "Comment on Welzel, Inglehart & Klingemann's 'The theory of human development': A cross-cultural analysis," *European Journal of Political Research* 42:381–386.
Berger Margaret A. and Lawrence M. Solan (2008), "Symposium: a cross-disciplinary look at scientific truth: what's the law to do? The uneasy relationship between science and law: an essay and introduction," *Brooklyn Law Review* 73:847–56.
Berger, Peter and Thomas Luckmann (1966), *The Social Construction of Reality: A treatise in the sociology of knowledge*. Garden City, NY: Doubleday.
Berlin, Isaiah ([1998] 2002), "My intellectual path," in Henry Hardy (ed.), *The Power of Ideas*. Princeton, NJ: Princeton University Press, pp. 1–23.
  ([1995] 2002), "Liberty," in Henry Hardy (ed.), *The Power of Ideas*. Princeton, NJ: Princeton University Press, pp. 111–114.
  ([1958] 1969), "Two concepts of liberty", in Isaiah Berlin, *Four Essays on Liberty*. Oxford: Oxford University Press, pp. 118–172.
  (1949/1950), "Political ideas in the twentieth century," *Foreign Affairs* 28:351–385.
Bernal, John D. (1939), *The Social Functions of Science*. New York: Macmillan.
Besley, John C. and Matthew Nisbet (2011), "How scientists view the public, the media and the political process," *Public Understanding of Science*, doi: 10.1177/0963662511418743.
Best, Michael L. and Keegan W. Wade (2009), "The Internet and democracy: global catalyst or democratic dud?" *Bulletin of Science, Technology & Society* 29:255–271.

Biesta, Gert (2007), "Towards the knowledge democracy? Knowledge production and the civic role of the university," *Studies in the Philosophy of Education* 26:467–479.
Bimber, Bruce (1998), "The Internet and political transformation: populism, community, and accelerated pluralism," *Polity* 31:133–160.
Bitros, George C. and Anastassios D. Karayiannis (2013), *Creative Crisis in Democracy and Economy*. Berlin-Heidelberg: Springer.
Blair, Ann (2010), *Too much to know: Managing Scholarly Information before the Modern Age*. New Haven, Connecticut: Yale University Press.
Blackler, Frank (1995), "Knowledge, knowledge work and organizations: an overview and interpretation," *Organization Studies* 16:1021–1046.
Blanchard, Troy and Todd L. Matthews (2006), "The configuration of local economic power and civic participation in the global economy," *Social Forces* 84:2241–2257.
Blok, Anders (2007), "Experts on public trial: on democratizing expertise through a Danish consensus conference," *Public Understanding of Science* 16:163–182.
Blokland, Hans (2011), *Pluralism, Democracy and Political Knowledge: Robert A. Dahl and His Critics on Modern Politics*. London: Ashgate.
Blumer, Herbert (1948), "Public opinion and public opinion polling," *American Sociological Review* 13:542–549.
Boas, Franz (1938), *Manifesto on Freedom of Science*. The Committee of the American Academy for the Advancement of Science.
  (1939), "Democracy and intellectual freedom." *Address delivered at a meeting sponsored by the Lincoln's Birthday Committee for Democracy and Intellectual Freedom, February 12, 1939. The American Teacher*, March: 1.
Boas, Taylor C. (2000), "The dictator's dilemma? The Internet and U.S. policy toward Cuba," *The Washington Quarterly* 23:57–67.
Böckler, Anne, Günther Knoblich, and Natalie Sebanz (2010), "Socializing cognition," in Britt M. Glatzeder, Vinod Goel, and Albrecht von Müller (eds.), *Towards a Theory of Thinking: Building Blocks for a Conceptual Framework*. Berlin-Heidelberg: Springer, pp. 233–250.
Böhme, Gernot (1992), "Science and other types of knowledge," in Gernot Böhme (ed.), *Coping with Science*. Boulder, CO: Westview, pp. 51–63.
Bohman, James (2007), "We, heirs of enlightenment: critical theory, democracy, and social science," in Stephen P. Turner and Mark W. Risjord (eds.), *Philosophy of Anthropology and Sociology: Handbook of the Philosophy of Science*. Amsterdam: Elsevier, pp. 711–726.
  (1999a), "Citizenship and norms of publicity: wide public reason in cosmopolitan societies," *Political Theory* 27:176–202.
  (1999b), "Democracy as inquiry; inquiry as democratic: pragmatism, social science, and the cognitive division of labor," *American Journal of Political Science* 43:590–607.
  (1998), "The coming of age of deliberative democracy," *The Journal of Political Philosophy* 6:400–425.
Boix, Carles (2011), "Democracy, development and the international system," *American Political Science Review* 105:809–828.

Bibliography 345

(2003), *Democracy and Redistribution*. New York: Cambridge University Press.
Boix, Carles and Susan C. Stokes (2003), "Endogenous democratization," *World Politics* 55:517–549.
Boli, John und George M. Thomas (1997), "World Culture in the World Polity: A Century of International Non-governmental Organization," *American Sociological Review* 62:171–90.
Boltanski, Luc and Laurent Thévenot (1999), "The sociology of critical capacity," *European Journal of Sociology* 2:359–377.
Borgmann, Albert (1999), *Holding on to Reality: The Nature of Information at the Turn of the Millennium*, Chicago: University of Chicago Press.
Born, Max (1968), *My Life and My Views: A Nobel Prize Winner in Physics Writes Provocatively on a Wide Range of Subjects*. New York: Scribner.
Borooah, Vani K. and Martin Paldam (2007), "Why is the world short of democracy? A cross-country analysis of barriers to representative government," *European Journal of Political Economy* 23:582–604.
Botero, Juan, Alejandro Ponce, and Andrei Shleifer (2012), "Education and the quality of government," *NBER Working Paper* 18119.
Boulding, Kenneth (1965), *The Meaning of the Twentieth Century: The Great Transition*. New York: Harper & Row.
Bourdieu, Pierre (1999), "Scattered remarks," *European Journal of Social Theory* 2:334–340.
  (1998), *Acts of Resistance: Against the Tyranny of the Market*. New York: The New Press.
  ([1980] 1990), *The Logic of Practice*. Cambridge: Polity Press.
  [1979] 1984, *Distinction: A Social Critique of the Judgment of Taste*. Cambridge, MA: Harvard University Press.
  (1975), "The specificity of the scientific field and the social conditions of the progress of reason," *Social Science Information* 14: 19–47.
  ([1973] 1993), "Public opinion does not exist," in *Sociology in Question*. London: Sage, pp. 149–157.
Bourguignon, François and Thierry Verdier (2000), "Oligarchy, democracy, inequality and growth," *Journal of Development Economics* 62:285–313.
Boyle, James (2007), "Mertonianism unbound? Imaging free, decentralized access to most cultural and scientific material," in Charlotte Hess and Elinor Ostrom (eds.), *Understanding Knowledge as a Commons: From Theory to Practice*. Cambridge, MA: MIT Press, pp. 123–143.
Bösch, Frank und Norbert Frei (Hg.) (2006), Medialisierung und Demokratie im 20. Jahrhundert. Goettingen: Wallstein.
Braczyk, Hans Joachim and Gerd Schienstock (1996), "Lean Production in Baden-Württemberg: Erwartungen, Wirkungen und Folgen," in Hans Joachim Braczyk and Gerd Schienstock (eds.), *Kurswechsel in der Industrie*. Stuttgart: Kohlhammer, pp. 121–133.
Brand, Myles (1987), "Intending and acting: toward a naturalized action theory," *Journal of Philosophy* 84:49–54.
Braverman, Harry (1974), *Labour and Monopoloy Capitalism: The Degradation of Work in the Twentieth Century*. New York: Monthly Review Press.

Brecht, Arnold (1946), "Democracy –challenge to theory," *Social Research* 13:195–224.
Broman, Thomas H. (2002), "Some preliminary considerations on science and civil society," *Osiris* 17:1–21.
Brooks, Harvey (1965), "Scientific concepts and cultural change," *Daedalus* 94:66–83.
Brown, John Seely and Paul Duguid ([2000] 2002), *The Social Life of Information*. Boston, MA: Harvard University Press.
Brown, Mark B. (2013), "Review of Philip Kitcher 'Science in a Democratic Society'," *Minerva* 51:389–397.
  (2009), *Science in Democracy: Expertise, Institutions, and Representation*. Cambridge, MA: MIT Press.
  (2006), "Citizen panels and the concept of representation," *The Journal of Political Philosophy* 14: 203–225.
  (2004), "The political philosophy of science policy: Review essay of Philip Kitcher 'Science, Truth and Democracy'," *Minerva* 42:77–94.
Bruch, Sarah K., Myra Marx Ferree and Joe Soss (2010), "From policy to polity: Democracy, paternalism, and the incorporation of disadvantaged citizens," *American Sociological Review* 75:205–226.
Bruner, Jerome S. (1990), *Acts of Meaning*. Cambridge, MA: Harvard University Press.
Bryce, James (1901), *The American Government*. Vol. 2. New York: Macmillan.
Bull, Hedley (1977), *The Anarchical Society: A Study of Order in World Politics*. London: Macmillan.
Bullock, John G. (2011), "Elite influence on public opinion in an informed electorate," *American Political Science Review* 105:496–515.
Bunce, Valerie (2001), "Democratization and economic reform," *Annual Review of Political Science* 4:43–65.
Burke, Edmund ([1790] 1955), *Reflections on the Revolution in France*. New York: The Liberal Arts Press,
Burke, Peter (2000), *A Social History of Knowledge: From Gutenberg to Diderot*. Oxford: Polity Press.
Burns, Tom R. (1999), "The evolution of parliaments and societies in Europe. Challenges and prospects," *European Journal of Social Theory* 2: 167–194.
Buroway, Michael (1985), *The Politics of Production*. London Verso.
  (1979), *Manufacturing Consent*. Chicago: University of Chicago Press.
Burton-Jones, Alan (1999), *Knowledge Capitalism: Business, Work, and Learning in the New Economy*. Oxford: Oxford University Press.
Callon, Michel, Pierre Lascoume, and Yannik Barthe ([2001] 2009), *Acting in an Uncertain World: An Essay on Technical Democracy*. Cambridge, MA: MIT Press.
Callon, Michel (1999), "The role of lay people in the production and dissemination of scientific knowledge," *Science, Technology & Society* 4:81–94.
  (1998), "Introduction: the embeddedness of economic models in economics," in Michel Callon (ed.), *The Laws of the Market*. Oxford: Blackwell, pp. 1–57.

Cambrosio, Alberto and Peter Keating (1988), "'Going monoclonal': art, science and magic in the day-to-day use of hybridoma technology," *Social Problems* 35:244–260.
Campante, Filipe R. and Davin Chor (2012), "Schooling, political participation, and the economy," *Review of Economics and Statistics* 94:841–859.
 (2011), "'The people want the fall of the regime': schooling, political protest, and the economy," *Harvard Kennedy School Faculty Research Paper* 11-018.
Campbell, Angus, Philip E. Converse, Warren E. Miller, and Donald E. Stokes (1960), *The American Voter*. New York: John Wiley.
Capaccio, Giovanni and Daniel Ziblatt (2010), "The historical turn in democratization studies: a new research agenda for Europe and beyond," *Comparative Political Studies* 43:931–968.
Caplan, Bryan D. (2007), *The Myth of the Rational Voter: Why Democracies Chose Bad Policies*. Princeton, NJ: Princeton University Press.
Carey, James W. (1993), "The mass media and democracy: between the modern and the postmodern," *Journal of International Affairs* 47:1–21.
Carey, James W., Shanto Iyengar, Anker Brink Lund, and Inka Salovaara (2009), "Media system, public knowledge and democracy: a comparative study," *European Journal of Communication* 25:5–26.
Carley, Kathleen (1986), "Knowledge acquisition as a social phenomenon," *Instructional Science* 14: 381–438.
Carlsson, Magnus, Gordon B. Dahl, and Dan-Ole Rooth (2012), "The effect of schooling on cognitive skills," *NBER Working Paper* 18484.
Carneiro, Pedro, Claire Crawford, and Alissa Goodman (2007), "The impact of early cognitive and non-cognitive skills on later outcomes," *Discussion Paper* no. 92, Centre Econ. Educ., London School Economics.
Caron-Finterman, J. Francisca, Jacqueline E. W. Broerse, and Joske F. G. Bunders (2007), "Patient partnership in decision-making on biomedical research," *Science, Technology & Human Values* 32:339–368.
Carolan, Michael S. (2006), "Science, expertise, and the democratization of the decision-making process," *Society and Natural Resources* 19:661–668.
Carter, Stephen L. (2009), "Where's the bailout for publishing?" *The Daily Beast*, www.thedailybeast.com/blogs-and-stories/2009-03-17/wheres-the-bailout-for-publishing/p/.
Cartwright, Nancy, Jordi Cat, Lola Fleck, and Thomas Uebel (1996), *Otto Neurath: Philosophy between Science and Politics*. Cambridge: Cambridge University Press.
Casas-Cortés, María Isabel, Michal Osterweil, and Dana E. Powell (2008), "Blurring boundaries: recognizing knowledge-practices in the study of social movements," *Anthropological Quarterly* 81:17–58.
Catelló-Climent, Amparo (2008), "On the distribution of education and democracy," *Journal of Developmental Economics* 87:179–190.
Castells, Manuel (2009), *Communication Power*. Oxford: Oxford University Press.
 (2000), *The Information Age: Economy, Society and Culture. Volume III: End of Millennium, Second Edition*, Oxford: Blackwell.
 (1996), *The Rise of Network Society*. Oxford: Blackwell.

Castells, Manuel and Jeffrey Henderson (1987), "Introduction: techno-economic restructuring, socio-political processes and spatial transformation: a global perspective." in Jeffrey Henderson and Manuel Castells (eds.), *Global Restructuring and Territorial Development*. London: Sage, pp. 1–17.

Cerny, Philip G. (1990), *The Changing Architecture of Politics: Structure, Agency and the Future of the State*. London: Sage.

Chaffee, Steven H. and Miriam J. Metzger (2001), "The end of mass communication," *Mass Communication & Society* 4:365–379.

Champagne, Patrick (2005), "'Making the people speak': on the social uses of and reactions to public opinion polls," in Loïc Wacquant (ed.), *Pierre Bourdieu and Democratic Politics*. Cambridge: Polity Press, pp. 11–132.

Che, Yi, YI Lu, Zhigang Tao, and Peng Wang (2012), "The impact of income on democracy revisited," *Journal of Comparative Economics*, http://dx.doi.org/10.1016/j.jce.2012.05.006.

Chen, Jie and Chunlong Lu (2011), "Democratization and the middle class in China: the middle class's attitudes toward democracy," *Political Research Quarterly* 64:705–719.

Chen, Lincoln C., Tim G. Evans and Richard A. Cash (1999). "Health as a global public good," in Inge Kaul, Isabelle Grunberg und Marc A. Stern (eds.), *Global Public Goods*. Oxford: Oxford University Press, pp. 284–304.

Chong, Dennis and James N. Druckman (2010), "Dynamic public opinion: communication effects over time," *American Political Science Review* 104:663–680.

Chong, Alberto and Mark Gradsrein (2009), "Education and democratic preferences," Inter-American Development Bank, Mimeo.

(2007), "Framing public opinion in competitive democracies," *American Political Science Review* 101:639–655.

Clegg, Stewart R. (1989), *Frameworks of Power*. London: Sage.

(2007), "Framing public opinion in competitive democracies," *American Political Science Review* 101:639–655.

Coffin, Judith G. (1999), "A 'standard' of living? European perspectives on class and consumption in the early twentieth century," *International Labor and Working-Class History* 55:6–26.

Coglianese, Cary (2003), "The Internet and public participation in rulemaking," John F. Kennedy School of Government, Harvard University, *Faculty Research Working Paper Series*, http://ssrn.com/abstract=421161.

Cohen, Geoffrey L. (2003), "Party over policy: The dominating impact of group influence on political beliefs," *Journal of Personality and Social Psychology* 85:808–822.

Cohen, Jean L. and Andrew Arato (1992), *Civil Society and Political Theory*. Cambridge, MA: MIT Press.

Cohn, Bernard S. (1996), *Colonialism and Its Form of Knowledge: The British in India*. Princeton, NJ: Princeton University Press.

Coleman, James S. (1988), "Social capital in the creation of human capital," *American Journal of Sociology* 94:S95–S120.

Coleman, Stephen (1999), "Can the new media invigorate democracy?" *Political Quarterly* 70:16–22.

Coleman, Stephen and Jay G. Blumler (2009), *The Internet and Democratic Citizenship: Theory, Practice, and Policy*. Cambridge: Cambridge University Press.
Collins, Harry and Robert Evans (2007), *Rethinking Expertise*. Chicago: University of Chicago Press.
Collinson, David (2000), "Strategies of resistance: Power, knowledge and subjectivity in the workplace," in Keith Grint (ed.), *Work and Society*. Cambridge: Polity Press, pp. 163–198.
  (1994), "Strategies of resistance: Power, knowledge and subjectivity in the workplace," in John M. Jermier, David Knights and Walter R. Nord (eds.), *Resistance and Power in Organizations*. London: Routledge, pp. 25–68.
Connolly, William E. (1991) *Identity\Difference: Democratic Negotiations of Political Paradox*. Ithica, New York: Cornell University Press.
Converse, Philip E. (2006), "Democratic theory and electoral reality," *Critical Review* 18:297–329.
Converse. Philip E. ([1964] 2006), "The nature of belief systems in mass publics," *Critical Review* 18:1–74.
Cook, Philip J. (1971), "Robert Michels' political parties in perspective," *The Journal of Politics* 33:773–796.
Coombs, W. Timothy and Craig W. Cutbirth (1998), "Mediated political communication, the Internet, and the new knowledge elites: prospects and portents," *Telematics and Informatics* 15:203–217.
Condorcet, Marquis de ([1796] 1996), *Outlines of an Historical View of the Progress of the Human Mind: Being a Posthumous Work of the Late M. de Condorcet*. Philadelphia: Land and Ustick.
Connolly, William E. (1991), "Democracy and territoriality," *Millennium-Journal of International Studies* 20: 463–484.
Coppedge, Michael and John Gerring, with David Altman, Michael Bernhard, Steven Fish, Allen Hicken, Matthew Kroenig, Staffan I. Lindberg, Kelly McMann, Pamela Paxton, Holli A. Semetko, Svend-Erik Skaaning, Jeffrey Staton, and Jan Teorell (2011), "Conceptualizing and measuring democracy: a new approach," *Perspectives on Politics* 9:247–267.
Couzin, Iain D., Christos C. Ioannou, Guven Demirel, Thilo Gross, Colin J. Torney, Andrew Hartnett, Larissa Conradt, Simon A. Levin, and Naomi E. Leonard (2011), "Uninformed individuals promote democratic consensus in animal groups," *Science* 334:1578–1580.
Crain, Robert L. and Donald B. Rosenthal (1967), "Community status as a dimension of local decision-making," *American Sociological Review* 32:970–984.
Cranston, Maurice (1971), "Some aspects of the history of freedom," in Klaus von Beyme (ed.), *Theory and Politics [Theorie und Politik: Festschrift zum 70. Geburtstag für Carl Joachim Friedrich]*. Haag: Martinus Nihoff, pp. 18–34.
Cress, Daniel M. and David A. Snow (1996), "Mobilization at the margins: resources, benefactors, and the viability of homeless social movement organizations." *American Sociological Review* 61:1089–1109.

Croissant, Jennifer and Sal Restivo (1995), "Science, social problems, and progressive thought," in Susan Leigh Star (ed.), *Ecologies of Knowledge: Work and Politics in Science and Technology*. Albany, NY: State University of New York Press, pp. 39–87.
Crouch, Colin (2004), *Post-Democracy*. Cambridge: Polity Press.
Crozier, Michel ([1979] 1982), *Strategies for Change: The Future of French Society*. Cambridge, MA: MIT Press.
Culliton, Barbara J. (1978), "Science's restive public," *Daedalus* 107:147–156.
Curran, James, Shanto Iyengar, Anker Brink Lund, and Inka Salovaara-Moring (2009), "Media System, Public Knowledge and Democracy," *European Journal of Communications* 24: 5–26.
Daele, van den Wolfgang (1977), "The social construction of science: institutionalisation and definition of positive science in the latter half of the Seventeenth century," in Everett Mendelsohn, Peter Weingart, and Richard Whitley (eds.), *The Social Production of Scientific Knowledge*. Dordrecht: D. Reidel, pp. 27–54.
Dahl, Robert A. (2006), *On Political Equality*. New Haven, CT: Yale University Press.
  (2005), "What political institutions does large-scale democracy require?" *Political Science Quarterly* 120:187–197.
  (2000), "A democratic paradox?" *Political Science Quarterly* 115:35–40.
  (2006), *On Political Equality*. New Haven, CT: Yale University Press.
  (1999), "The shifting boundaries of democratic government," *Social Research* 66:915–931.
  (1998), *Democracy*. New Haven, CT: Yale University Press.
  (1994), "A democratic dilemma: system effectiveness versus citizen participation," *Political Science Quarterly* 109:23–34.
  (1992), "The problem of civic competence," *Journal of Democracy* 3:45–59.
  (1989), *Democracy and its Critics*. New Haven, CT: Yale University Press.
  (1977), "On removing certain impediments to democracy in the United States," *Political Science Quarterly* 92:1–2.
  (1971), *Polyarchy: Participation and Opposition*. New Haven, CT: Yale University Press.
  (1961a), "The behavioral approach in political science: epitaph for a movement to a successful protest," *American Political Science Review* 55 (4):763–772.
  (1961b), *Who Governs? Democracy and Power in an American City*. New Haven, CT: Yale University.
Dahlgren, Peter (2009), *Media and Political Engagement: Citizens, Communication, and Engagement*. New York: Cambridge University Press.
Dahrendorf, Ralf (2002), *Die Krise der Demokratie: Ein Gespräch*. München: C. H. Beck.
  (2000), "Die globale Klasse und die neue Ungleichheit," *Merkur* 54:1057–1068.
  (1996), "Economic opportunity, civil society, and political liberty," *Development and Change* 27:229–249.
  (1974), "Citizenship and beyond: the social dynamics of an idea," *Social Research* 41:673–701.

([1963] 1968), "Uncertainty, science and democracy," in Ralf Dahrendorf, *Essays in the Theory of Society*. London: Routledge and Kegan Paul, pp. 232–255.
([1957] 1959), *Class and Class Conflict in Industrialized Society*. Stanford: Stanford University Press.
Dalton, Russell J., Doh C. Shin, and Willy Jou (2007), "Understanding democracy: data from unlikely places," *Journal of Democracy* 18:142–156.
Dalton, Russell J. and Hnu-Ngoc T. Ong (2005), "Authority orientations and democratic attitudes: a test of the 'Asian values' hypothesis," *Japanese Journal of Political Science* 6:211–231.
Dalton, Russell J., Manfred Kuechler, and Wilhelm Bürklin (1990), "The challenge of new movements", in Russell J. Dalton, and Manfred Kuechler (eds.), *Challenging the Political Order: New Social and Political Movements in Western Democracies*, New York: Oxford University Press, pp. 3–20.
Darnton, Robert (2010), *Poetry and the Police: Communication Networks in Eighteenth-Century Paris*. Cambridge, MA: Harvard University Press.
Darr, Asaf and Chris Warhurst (2008), "Assumptions, assertions and the need for evidence: debugging debates about knowledge workers," *Current Sociology* 56:25–45.
Dasgupta, Partha S. and Paul A. David (1994), "Toward a new economics of science," *Research Policy* 23: 487–521.
Da Silva, Mario A. (2014), "The knowledge multiplier," *Economics of Innovation and New Technology* 23, doi: 10.1080/10438599.2014.882138.
Davenport, Thomas H., David W. De Long, and Michael C. Beers (1998), "Successful knowledge management projects," *Sloan Management Review* 39: 43–57.
Daum, Andreas W. (2002), "Science, politics, and religion: Humboldtian thinking and the transformations of civil society in Germany, 1830–1870," *Osiris* 17:107–140.
DeCanio, Samuel (2006), "Mass opinion and American political development," *Critical Review* 18:339–356.
Dee, Thomas S. (2003), "Are there civic returns to education?" *NBER Working Paper Series* 9588, www.nber.org/papers/w9588.
Dean, Mitchell (2001), "Michel Foucault: 'a man in danger'," in George Ritzer and Barry Smart (ed.), *Handbook of Social Theory*. London: Sage, pp. 324–338.
De Graaf, Nan Dirk, and Geoffrey Evans (1996), "Why are the young more postmaterialist? A cross-national analysis of individual and contextual influences on postmaterial values," *Comparative Political Studies* 28: 608–635.
Deininger, Klaus and Lyn Squire (1996), "A new set data set measuring income inequality," *World Bank Economic Review* 10:565–591.
Dell, Melissa, Benjamin F. Jones, and Benjamin A. Olken (2012), "Climate shocks and economic growth: evidence from the last half century," *American Economic Journal: Macroeconomics* 4:66–95.

Delli Carpini, Michael X., Fay Lomax Cook, and Lawrence R. Jacobs (2004), "Public deliberation, discoursive participation, and citizen engagement: A review of the empirical literature," *Annual Review of Political Science* 7:315–344.
Delli Carpini, Michael X. and Scott Keeter (1996), *What Americans Know about Politics and Why it Matters*. New Haven, CT: Yale University Press.
(1993), "Measuring political knowledge: putting things first," *American Journal of Political Science* 37:1179–1206.
(1991), "Stability and change in the U.S. public's knowledge of politics," *Public Opinion Quarterly* 55:583–612.
Deht, Jan van and Martin Elff (2000), "Political involvement and apathy in Europe 1973–1998," *Arbeitspapiere – Mannheimer Zentrum für Europäische Sozialforschung* 33.
Deutsch, Karl (1961), "Social mobilization and political development," *American Political Science Review* 60:483–514.
Deutscher, Irving (1972), "Public and private opinions: Social situations and multiple realities," in S. Z. Nagi and Ronald G. Corwin (eds.) *The Social Contexts of Research*. New York: Wiley, pp. 323–349.
Dewey, John (1984), *The Later Works, 1925–1953. Vol. 1: Experience and Nature*. Carbondale, IL: Southern Illinois University Press.
(1941), "Science and democracy," *The Scientific Monthly* 52:55.
(1938), *Logic: The Theory of Inquiry*. New York: Henry Holt and Company.
([1938] 1955), "Unity of science as a social problem," in Otto Neurath, Rudolf Carnap, and Charles Morris (eds.), *The International Encyclopedia of Unified Science*. Vol. 1. Chicago: University of Chicago Press, pp. 29–38.
([1936] 1939), "Science and the future of society," in Joseph Ratner (ed.), *Intelligence in the Modern World: John Dewey's Philosophy*. New York: Modern Library, pp. 343–363.
(1931), "Social science and social control," *the New Republic* 67:276–277.
Dewey, John ([1929] 1984), *The Quest for Certainty: John Dewey, The Later Works (1925–1953)*. Vol. 4, Jo Ann Boydston (ed.), Carbondale, Illinois: Southern Illinois University Press.
([1927] 1954), *The Public and Its Problems*. New York: H. Holt and Co.
([1916] 2005), *Democracy and Education*. Stilwell, KS: Dirireads.com.
Diamond, Jared (2005), *Collapse: How Societies Choose to Fail or Succeed*. New York: Penguin.
Diamond, Larry (2011), "Why democracies survive," *Journal of Democracy* 22:17–30
(2010), "Liberation technology," *Journal of Democracy* 21:69–83.
Diebolt, Claude, Tapas Mishra, Bazoumana Ouattara, and Mamata Parhi (2013), "Democracy and economic growth in an interdependent world," *Review of International Economics* 21:733–749.
DiMaggio, Paul (1997), "Culture and cognition," *Annual Review of Sociology* 23:263–287.
DiMaggio, Paul J. und Walter W. Powell (1983), "The iron cage revisited: Institutional isomorphism and collective rationality in organization fields," *American Sociological Review* 48:147–160.

Diani, Mario (1996), "Linking mobilization frames and political opportunities: Insights from regional populism in Italy," *American Sociological Review* 61:1053–1069.
Dosi, Giovanni and Marco Grazzi (2009), "On the nature of technologies: Knowledge, procedures, artifacts and production inputs," *Cambridge Journal of Economics* 34:173–184.
Dosi, Giovanni (1996), "The contribution of economic theory to the understanding of a knowledge-based economy," in *Organisation for Economic Co-Operation and Development: Employment and Growth in the Knowledge-Based Economy*, Paris: OECD, pp. 81–92.
Doucouliagos, Hristos and Mehmet Ali Ulubasoglu (2008), "Democracy and economic growth: a meta-analysis," *American Journal of Political Science* 52:61–83.
Dow, Jay K. (2011), "Political knowledge and electoral choice in the 1992–2004 United States presidential elections: are more and less informed citizens distinguishable?" *Journal of Elections, Public Opinion and Parties* 21:381–405.
Downs, Anthony (1957), *An Economic Theory of Democracy*. New York: Harper.
Dretske, Fred (1981), *Knowledge and the Flow of Information*. Cambridge, MA: MIT Press.
Drucker, Peter F. ([1989] 2003), *The New Realities*. New Brunswick, NJ: Transaction Publishers.
 (1968), "Worker and work in the metropolis," *Daedalus* 97: 1243–1262.
 (1993), "The rise of the knowledge society," *Wilson Quarterly* 17:52–71.
 (1989), *The New Realities: In Government and Politics/In Economics and Business/In Society and World View*. New York: Harper & Row.
 (1969), *The Age of Discontinuity: Guidelines to our Changing Society*. New York: Harper & Row.
 ([1968] 1992), *The Age of Discontinuity: Guidelines to Our Changing Society, With a New Introduction by the Author*. New Brunswick, NJ: Transaction Books.
 (1939), *The End of Economic Man: A Study of the New Totalitarianism*. London: William Heinemann.
Dryzek, John S., Richard B. Norgaard, and Davod Schlosberg ([2011] 2013), "Climate change and society: approaches and responses," in John S. Dryzek, Eichard B. Norgaard, and Davod Schlosberg (eds.), *The Oxford Handbook of Climate Change and Society*. Oxford: Oxford University Press, pp. 3–17.
Dryzek, John S. and Hayley Stevenson (2011), "Global democracy and earth system governance," *Ecological Economics* 70:1865–1874.
Duch, Raymond M. and Michael A. Taylor (1993), "Postmaterialism and the economic condition," *American Journal of Political Science* 37:747–779.
Dunn, John (2008), "Capitalist democracy: elective affinity or beguiling illusion," *Daedalus* 136:5–13.
Dupré, J. Stefan and Sanford Lakoff (1962), *Science and the Nation: Policy and Politics*. Englewood Cliffs, NJ: Prentice-Hall.
Durant, Darrin (2011), "Models of democracy in social studies of science," *Social Studies of Science* 41(5):691–714.

Durham, J, Benson (1999), "Economic growth and political regimes," *Journal of Economic Growth* 4:81–111.
Durkheim, Emile ([1950] 1992), *Professional Ethics and Civic Morals*. London: Routledge.
    ([1930 1947), *The Division of Labor in Society*. New York: Free Press.
Dworkin, Ronald (2002), *Sovereign Virtue: The Theory and Practice of Equality*. Cambridge: Cambridge University Press.
Dyrberg, Torben Bech (1997), *The Circular Structure of Power: Politics, Identity, Community*. London: Verso.
Eder, Klaus (1995), "Does social class matter in the study of social movements? A theory of middle-class radicalism," in Louis Maheu (ed.), *Social Movements and Social Classes: The Future of Collective Action*. London: Sage, pp. 21–54.
Easterbrook, Frank H. (1982), "Insider trading, secret agents, evidentiary privileges, and the production of information," *The Supreme Court Review* 11: 309–365.
Edgerton, David (2011), "In praise of Luddism," *Nature* 471 (March 3):27–29.
Edwards, Paul N., Lisa Gitelman, Gabrielle Hecht, Adian Jones, Brian Larkin, and Neil Safier (2011), "AHR conversation: historical perspectives on the circulation of information," *American Historical Review* 116:1393–1435.
Eggertsson, Thráinn (2009), "Knowledge and the theory of institutional change," *Journal of Institutional Economics* 5:137–150.
Eisele, J. Christopher (1975), "John Dewey and the immigrants," *History of Education Quarterly* 15:67–85.
Eisenstadt, Shmuel N. (1999), *Paradoxes of Democracy: Fragility, Continuity, and Change*. Baltimore, MD: John Hopkins University Press.
Elam, Mark and Margareta Bertilsson (2003), "Consuming, engaging, and confronting science. The emerging dimensions of scientific citizenship," *European Journal of Social Theory* 6:233–251.
Elias, Norbert (1984), "Knowledge and power," in Nico Stehr and Volker Meja (eds.), *Society and Knowledge: Contemporary Perspectives on the Sociology of Knowledge*. New Brunswick, NJ: Transaction Books, pp. 251–292.
    (1971), "Sociology of knowledge: new perspectives," *Sociology* 5:149–168, 335–370.
Eliot, T. S. (1925), *The Hollow Men*. London: Faber & Gwyer.
Elo, Kimmo and Lauri Rapeli (2010), "Determinants of political knowledge: the effects of the media on knowledge and information," *Journal of Elections, Public Opinion & Parties* 20:133–146.
Engelmann, Stephen G. (2011), "Review article: social science against democracy," *History of the Human Sciences* 24:167–179.
Enns, Peter K. and Paul M. Kellstaft (2008), "Policy mood and political sophistication: why everybody moves mood," *British Journal of Political Science* 38:433–454.
Epstein, Stephen (1996), *Impure Science: AIDS, Activism and the Politics of Knowledge*. Berkeley, CA: University of California Press.
Essed, Philomena (1991), "Knowledge and resistance: black women talk about racism in the Netherlands and the USA," *Feminism & Psychology* 1:201–219.

Ettema, James S. and F. Gerald Kline (1977), "Deficits, differences, and ceilings: contingent conditions for understanding the knowledge gap," *Communication Research* 4:179–202.
Eulau, Heinz (1973), "Skill revolution and consultative commonwealth," *American Political Science Review* 67:169–191.
Eun, Yong-Soo (2013), "The power of human beliefs over the state's behavior in world politics: an in-depth and comparative case study," *International Political Science Review* 34: 372–391.
Eyerman, Ron and Andrew Jamison (1991), *Social Movements: A Cognitive Approach*. University Park, PA: Pennsylvania State University Press.
Ezrahi, Yaron (2004), "Science and the political imagination in contemporary democracies," in Sheila Jasanoff (ed.), *States of Knowledge: The Co-Production of Science and the Social Order*. London: Routledge, pp. 254–273.
Faulkner, Wendy (1994), "Conceptualizing knowledge used in innovation: a second look at the science-technology distinction and industrial innovation," *Science, Technology & Human Values* 19:425–458.
Federal Reserve Bank of Dallas (1998), *Time Well Spent: The Declining Real Cost of Living in America*. Dallas: Federal Reserve Bank.
Feng, Yi (1997), "Democracy, political stability and economic growth," *British Journal of Political Science* 27:391–418.
Fernández, Raquel (2010), "Does culture matter?" *NBER Working Paper* 16277.
Feyerabend, Paul (1978), *Science in a Free Society*. London: New Left Review Books.
  ([1975] 2006), "How to defend society against science," in Evan Selinger and Robert P. Crease (eds.), *The Philosophy of Expertise*. New York, New York: Columbia University Press, pp. 358–369.
Finkel, Steven E. and Amy Erica Smith (2011), "Civic education, political discussion, and the social transmission of democratic knowledge and values in a democracy," *American Journal of Political Science* 55:417–435.
Finkel, Steven E. (2003), "Can democracy be taught?" *Journal of Democracy* 14:137–151.
Fish, M. Steven and Robin S. Brooks (2004), "Does diversity hurt democracy?" *Journal of Democracy* 15:154–166.
Fisher, Diana R. and Jessica F. Green (2004), "Understanding disenfranchisement: civil society and developing countries' influence and participation in global governance for sustainable development," *Global Environmental Politics* 4:65–84.
Florida, Richard, Charlotta Mellander, and Kevin Stolarick (2008), "Inside the black box of regional development: human capital, the creative class and tolerance," *Journal of Economic Geography* 8:615–649.
Florida, Richard (2003), "Cities and the creative class," *City & Community* 2:3–19.
  (2002), *The Rise of the Creative Class and How It's Transforming Work, Leisure, Community and Everyday Life*. New York: Basic Books.
Fogel, Robert W. (2008), "Capitalism & democracy in 2040," *Daedalus* 136:87–95.
Forejohn, John A. and James H. Kuklinski (1990), *Information and Democratic Processes*. Urbana and Chicago: University of Illinois Press.

Forey, Dominique (2006), *The Economics of Knowledge*. Cambridge, MA: MIT Press.
Foucault, Michel (1984), "What is Enlightenment?" in Paul Rabinow (ed.), *The Foucault Reader*. New York, Pantheon Books, 1984, pp. 32–50
  (1982), "The subject and power," in Hubert L. Dreyfus and Paul Rabinow (eds.), *Michel Foucault: Beyond Structuralism and Hermeneutics*. Chicago: University of Chicago Press, pp. 208–226.
  (1980), *Power/Knowledge: Selected Interviews and other Writings 1972–1977*. Brighton, Sussex: Harvester Press.
  ([1979] 1981), "Omnes et Singulatim: towards a criticism of political reason," in Sterling M. McMurrin (ed.), *The Tanner Lectures on Human Values*. Vol. 2. Cambridge: Cambridge University Press, pp. 223–254.
  (1977), "Prison talk: an interview," *Radical Philosophy* 16:10–15.
  ([1976] 2000), "Truth and power," in Michel Foucault, *Power: The Essential Works of Michel Foucault 1954–1984*. Vol. 3. New York: The New Press, pp. 111–133.
  ([1975] 1977), *Discipline and Punish: The Birth of the Prison*. New York: Random House.
  ([1973] 2000), "Truth and juridical power," in Michel Foucault, *Power: The Essential Works of Michel Foucault 1954–1984*. Vol. 3. New York: The New Press, pp. 1–89.
  ([1969] 1972), *The Archeology of Knowledge*. London: Tavistock.
Frank, Robert H. (2007), *Falling Behind: How Rising Inequality Harms the Middle Class*. Berkeley, CA: University of California Press.
Freeman, John R. and Dennis P. Quinn (2012), "The economic origins of democracy reconsidered," *American Political Science Review* 106:58–80.
Frickel, Scott, Sahra Gibbon, Gwen Ottinger, and David Hess (2010), "Undone science: charting social movement and civil society challenges to research agenda setting," *Science, Technology & Human Values* 35:444–473.
Friedman, Benjamin M. (2010), "Economic well-being in a historical context," in Lorenzo Pecchi and Gustavo Piga (eds.), *Revisiting Keynes: Economic Possibilities for our Grandchildren*. Cambridge, MA: MIT Press, pp. 125–134.
  (2008), "Capitalism, economic growth and democracy," *Daedalus* 136:46–52.
  (2006), "The moral consequences of economic growth," *Society* 43:15–22.
  (2005), *The Moral Consequences of Economic Growth*. New York: Vintage Books.
Friedman, Jonathan (1989), "Culture, identity, and world process," *Review* 12:51–69.
Friedman, Milton (1962), *Capitalism and Freedom*. Chicago: University of Chicago Press.
  (1958), "Capitalism and freedom," in Felix Morley (ed.), *Essays on Individuality*. Pittsburgh, PA: University of Pennsylvania Press, pp. 168–182.
Fuerstein, Michael (2008), "Epistemic democracy and the social character of knowledge," *Episteme* 5:74–93.
Fukuyama, Francis (2014), *Political Order and Political Decay: From the Industrial Revolution to the Globalisation of Democracy*. London: Profile Books.
  (2006), "After the 'end of history'," *Open Democracy*, www.opendemocracy.net

(2002), *Our Posthuman Future: Consequences of the Biotechnology Revolution.* New York: Farrar, Straus and Giroux.
  (2001), "Social capital, civil society, and development," *Third World Quarterly* 22:7–28.
Fuller, Steve (2002), *Knowledge Management Foundations.* Boston, MA: Butterworth Heinemann.
  (2000), "Commentary on Michael Polanyi's *The Republic of Science*," *Minerva* 38:26–32.
  (1994), "The constitutively social character of expertise," *The International Journal of Expert Systems* 7:51–64.
  (1988), *Social Epistemology.* Bloomington, IN: Indiana University Press.
Fung, Archon and Erik Olin Wright (2001), "Deepening democracy: innovations in empowered participatory government," *Politics & Society* 29:5–41.
Galbraith, John K. (1967), *The New Industrial State.* Boston: Houghton Mifflin.
  (1957), *The Affluent Society.* Boston: Houghton Mifflin.
Galison, Peter (2004), "Removing knowledge," *Critical Inquiry* 31:229–243.
  (1990), "Aufbau/Bauhaus: logical positivism and architectural modernism," *Critical Inquiry* 16:709–752.
Gallie, Walter Bryce (1955–1956), "Essentially contested concepts," *Proceedings of the Aristotelian Society New Series* 56:167–98.
Gallup-International (2005), *Voice of the People*, www.gallup-international.com/.
Galston, William A. (2001), "Political Knowledge, political engagement, and civic education," *Annual Review of Political Science* 4:217–234.
Garcia, José María Rodríguez (2001), "Scientia potestas est – knowledge is power: Francis Bacon to Michel Foucault," *Neohelicon* 38:109–122.
Gehlen, Arnold ([1957] 2004), "Die Seele im technischen Zeitalter: Sozialpsychologische Probleme in der industriellen Gesellschaft," in *Die Seele im technischen Zeitalter: Sozialpsychologische Probleme in der industriellen Gesellschaft.* Gesamtausgabe Band 6. Frankfurt at the Main: Vittorio Klostermann, pp. 1–140.
  ([1940] 1993), *Der Mensch.* Textkritische ed., Teilband 1. Frankfurt at the Main: Vittorio Klostermann.
Gellner, Ernest (1994), *Conditions of Liberty: Civil Society and its Rivals.* London: Hamish Hamilton.
  (1983), *Nations and Nationalism.* Ithaca, NY: Cornell University Press.
Genova, B. K. L. and Bradley S. Greenberg (1979), "Interest in the news and the knowledge gap," *Public Opinion Quarterly* 43:79–91.
Genschel, Philipp and Bernhard Zangl (2008), "Metamophorsen des Staates – Vom Herrschaftsmonopolisten zum Herrschaftsmanager," *Leviathan* 36:430–454.
Gerring, John, Peter Kingstone and Matthew Lange (2011), "Democracy, history, and economic performance: a case-study approach," *World Development* 39(10):1735–1748.
Geuss, Raymond (2002), "Liberalism and its discontents," *Political Theory* 30:320–338.
Giddens, Anthony (1999), *BBC Reith Lectures 1999: Runaway World.* Lecture 5: Democracy.

(1990), *The Consequences of Modernity*. Stanford: Stanford University Press.
(1984), *The Constitution of Society: Outline of the Theory of Structuration*. Cambridge: Polity Press.
(1981), *A Contemporary Critique of Historical Materialism. Vol. 1: Power, Property and the State*. London: Macmillan.
Gipsen, C. W. R. (1988), "German engineers and American social theory: Historical perspectives on professionalization," *Comparative Studies in Society and History* 30:550–574.
Gilley, Bruce (2009), "Is democracy possible?" *Journal of Democracy* 20:113–127.
Glaeser, Edward L., Rafael La Porta, Floorencio Lopez-de-Silanes, and Andrei Shleifer (2004), "Do institutions cause growth?" *Journal of Economic Growth* 9:271–303.
Glasius, Marlied and Geoffrey Pleyers (2013), "The global movement of 2011: democracy, social justice and dignity," *Development and Change* 44:547–567.
Glazer, Nathan (2010), "Democracy and deep divides," *Journal of Democracy* 21:5–19.
Gleditsch, Kristian Skrede and Michael D. Ward (2008), "Diffusion and the spread of democratic institutions," in Beth A. Simmons, Frank Dobbin and Geoffrey Garrett (eds.), *The Global Diffusion of Markets and Democracy*. Cambridge: Cambridge University Press, pp. 261–302.
Goldman, Alvin I. (1999), *Knowledge in a Social World*. Oxford: Clarendon Press.
Goldstone, Jack A. (2006), "A historical, not comparative, method: breakthroughs and limitations in the theory and methodology of Michael Mann's analysis of power," in John Al Hall and Ralph Schroeder (eds.), *An Anatomy of Power: The Social Theory of Michael Mann*. Cambridge: Cambridge University Press, pp. 263–282.
Goldthorpe, John H. (2007), "'Cultural capital': some critical observations," *Sociology Working Papers 2007–07*. Oxford: Oxford University.
(1966), "Social stratification in industrial society" in Reinhard Bendix and Seymour M. Lipset (eds.), *Class, Status and Power*. New York: Free Press, pp. 648–659.
Goodin, Robert E. (1979), "The development-rights trade-off: Some unwarranted economic and political assumptions," *Universal Human Rights* 1:31–42.
Gore, Albert (2007), *The Assault on Reason*. New York: Penguin.
Gossner, Olivier (2010), "Ability and knowledge," *Games and Economic Behavior* 69:95–106.
Gouldner, Alvin W. (1979), *The Future of Intellectuals and the Rise of the New Class: A Frame of Reference, Theses, Conjectures, Arguments, and an Historical Perspectives on the Role of Intellectuals and Intelligentsia in the International Class Contest in the Modern Era*. New York: Continuum.
(1978), "The new class project, I," *Theory and Society* 6:153–203.
Graber, Doris (2003), "The media and democracy: beyond myths and stereotypes," *Annual Review of Political Science* 6:139–160.
Graetz, Michael and Ian Shapiro (2005), *Death by a Thousand Cuts: The Fight over Taxing Inherited Wealth*. Princeton, NJ: Princeton University Press.

Green, Duncan (2008), *From Poverty to Power: How Active Citizens and Effective States can Change the World*. Bourton on Dunsmore: Practical Action Publishing.
Greenberg, Daniel S. (2001), *Science, Money, and Politics: Political Triumph and Ethical Erosion*. Chicago: University of Chicago Press.
Grofman, Bernard and Barbara Norrander (1990), "Efficient use of reference group cues in a single dimension," *Public Choice* 64:213–227.
Grosjean, Pauline and Claudia Senik (2011), "Democracy, market liberalization, and political preferences," *The Review of Economics and Statistics* 93:365–381.
Grint, Keith and Steve Woolgar (1997), *The Machine at Work: Technology, Work and Organisation*. Oxford: Polity Press.
Grube, Norbert (2010), "Mass democracy and political governance: The Walter Lippman-John Dewey debate," in Daniel Tröger, Thomas Schlag, and Fritz Osterwalder (eds.), *Pragmatism and Modernities*. Rotterdam: Sense Publishers, pp. 145–161.
Gruber, Helmut (1991), *Red Vienna: Experiments in Working-Class Culture 1919–1934*. Oxford: Oxford University Press.
Grundmann, Reiner and Nico Stehr (2012), *The Power of Scientific Knowledge*. Cambridge: Cambridge University Press.
Gunn, John Alexander Wilson (1995), "'Public Opinion' in modern political science," in James Farr, John S. Dryzek and Stephen T. Leonhard (eds.), *Political Science in History: Research Programs and Political Traditions*. Cambridge: Cambridge University Press, pp. 99–123.
Haber, Stephen and Victor Menaldo (2011), "Do natural resources fuel authoritarianism? A reappraisal of the resource curse," *American Political Science Review* 105:1–26.
Habermas, Jürgen (2006), "Political communication in media society: Does democracy still enjoy an epistemic dimension? The impact of normative theory on empirical research," *Communication Theory* 16:411–424.
([1992] 1996), *Between Facts and Norms: Contributions to Discourse Theory of Law and Democracy*. Cambridge: Polity Press.
([1968] 1971), *Knowledge and Human Interests*. Boston: Beacon Press.
([1962] 1989), *The Structural Transformation of the Public Sphere*. Cambridge, MA: MIT Press.
Hacking, Ian (1983), *Representing and Intervening*. Cambridge: Cambridge University Press.
Haggard, Stephan and Robert R. Kaufmann (2012), "Inequality and regime change: Democratic transitions and the stability of democratic rule," *American Political Science Review*, doi: 10.1017/S0003055412000287.
(1997), "The political economy of democratic transitions," *Comparative Politics* 29:262–283.
Haldane, Andrew ([2009] 2013), "Rethinking the financial network," in Stephan Jansen, Eckhard Schröter and Nico Stehr (eds.), *Fragile Stabilität – stabile Fragilität*. Wiesbaden: Springer VS, pp. 243–278.
Hansen, James (2010), *Storms of My Grandchildren: The Truth About the Coming Climate Catastrophe and Our Last Chance to Save Humanity*. New York: Bloomsbury Publishing.

Hardin, Russell J. (2006), "Ignorant democracy," *Critical Review* 18:179–195.
(2003), "If it rained knowledge," *Philosophy of the Social Sciences* 33:3–24.
Hayek, Friedrich A. ([1988] 1991), *The Fatal Deceit: The Errors of Socialism.* Chicago: University of Chicago Press.
(1960), *The Constitution of Liberty.* London: Routledge.
(1958), "The creative powers of a free civilization," in Felix Morley (ed.), *Essays on Individuality.* Pittsburgh: University of Pennsylvania Press, pp. 183–204.
([1945] 1948), "The use of knowledge in society," in Friedrich A. Hayek, *Individualism and Economic Order.* Chicago: University of Chicago Press, pp. 77–91.
(1945), "The use of knowledge in society," *The American Economic Review* 35:519–530.
(1941), "Planning, science and freedom," *Nature* 148:580–584.
Heilbroner, Robert L. (1994), "Technological determinism revisited," in Merritt Roe Smith and Leo Marx (eds.), *Does Technology Drive History?* Cambridge, MA: MIT Press, pp. 67–78.
(1974), *An Inquiry into the Human Prospect.* New York: W.W. Norton.
([1967] 1994), "Do machines make history," in Merritt Roe Smith and Leo Marx (eds.), *Does Technology Drive History?* Cambridge, MA: MIT Press, pp. 53–66.
Held, David (1991), "Democracy, the nation-state and the global system," *Economy and Society* 20:138–171.
(1991), "The possibilities of democracy," *Theory & Society* 20:875–889.
Helliwell, John F. (1994), "Empirical linkages between democracy and economic growth," *British Journal of Political Science* 25:225–248.
Hennis, Wilhelm (1977), "Zur Begründung der Fragestellung." in Wilhelm Hennis, Peter Graf Kielmansegg, and Ulrich Matz (eds.), *Regierbarkeit: Studien zu ihrer Problematisierung.* Band 1. Stuttgart: Klett-Cotta, pp. 9–21.
Hess, David J. (2005), "Technology- and product-oriented movements: approximating social movements studies and science and technology studies," *Science, Technology & Human Values* 30:515–535.
(1997), *Science Studies.* An Advanced Introduction. New York: New York University Press.
Hill, Christopher (1967), "Review of Peter Laslett's 'The World We Have Lost'," *History and Theory* 6:117–127.
Hillebrandt, Maarten (2008), "Rejection by referendum: a new expression of discontent in the EU," *Reinvention: a Journal of Undergraduate Research* 1 (2), www2.warwick.ac.uk/go/reinventionjournal/issues/volume1issue2/Hillebrandt.
Hillygus, Sunshine D. (2005), "The missing link: exploring the relationship between higher education and political engagement," *Political Behavior* 27:25–47.
Hilpinen, Risto (1970), "Knowing that one knows and the classical definition of knowledge," *Synthese* 21:109–132.
Hippel, Eric von (2006), *Democratizing Innovation.* Cambridge, MA: MIT Press.

Hirschman, Albert O. (1989), "Having opinions – one of the elements of well being?", *The American Economic Review* 79:75–79.
  (1970), *Exit, Voice, and Loyalty*. Cambridge: Cambridge University Press.
Hisschemöller, Matthijs (2005), "Participation as knowledge production and the limits of democracy," in Sabine Maasen and Peter Weingart (eds.), *Democratisation of Expertise? Exploring Novel Forms of Scientific Advice in Political Decision-Making. Sociology of the Sciences Yearbook* 24:189–208.
Hobsbawm, Eric ([2007] 2008), *Globalisation, Democracy and Terrorism*. London: Abacus (Little, Brown).
  (1996), "The future of the state," *Development and Change* 27:267–278.
  ([1994] 1996), *The Age of Extremes: The Short Twentieth Century, 1914–1991*. London: Michael Joseph.
Högström, John (2013), "Does the choice of democracy measure matter? Comparisons between the two leading democracy indices, Freedom House and Polity IV," *Government and Opposition* 48:201221.
Hörning, Karl H. (2001), *Experten des Alltags: Die Wiederentdeckung des praktischen Wissens*. Weilerswist: Velbrück Wissenschaft.
Holbrook, Thomas M. (2002), "Presidential campaigns and the knowledge gap," *Political Communication* 19:437–454.
Hollinger, David A. ([1983] 1996), "The defense of democracy and Robert K. Merton's formulation of the scientific ethos," in David A. Hollinger (ed.), *Science, Jews, and Secular Culture: Studies in Mid-Twentieth Century American Intellectual History*. Princeton, NJ: Princeton University Press, pp. 80–96.
  (1995), "Science as a weapon in *Kulturkämpfe* in the United States and after World War II," *Isis* 86:440–454.
Hollyer, James R., B. Peter Rosendorff, and James Raymond Vreeland (2011), "Democracy and transparency," *The Journal of Politics* 73:1206–1224.
Holton, Gerald (1996), *Einstein, History, and Other Passions*. Reading, MA: Addison-Wesley.
  (1986), "The advancement of science, and its burdens," *Daedalus* 115:75, 77–104.
Horkheimer, Max (1947), *The Eclipse of Reason*. New York: Oxford University Press.
  ([1932] 1982), "Notes on science and the crisis," in Max Horkheimer, *Critical Theory: Selected Essays*. New York: Continuum, pp. 3–9.
Horkheimer, Max and Theodor W. Adorno (1982), *Dialectic of the Enlightenment*. New York: Pantheon Books.
Houtman, Dick (1998), "Culture, industrialism and modernity." Paper presented at the World Congress of Sociology, Montreal, Quebec, Canada, July 26–August 1.
Howitt, Peter ([1996] 1998) "On some problems in measuring knowledge-based growth," in Dale Neef (ed.), *The Knowledge Economy*. Boston: Butterworth-Heinemann, pp. 97–117.
Hoyman, Michele and Christopher Faricy (2008), "It takes a village: a test of the creative class, social capital, and human capital theories," *Urban Affairs Review Online First*.

Huber, Evelyne, Dietrich Rueschemeyer, and John D. Stephens (1993), "The impact of economic development on democracy," *Journal of Economic Perspectives* 7:71–85.

Huber, George F. (1991), "Organization learning: the contributing processes and the literatures," *Organization Science* 2:88–115.

Hug, Simon and Pascal Sciarini (2000), "Referendums on European integration: Do institutions matter in voter's decision," *Comparative Political Studies* 33:3–36.

Hulme, Mike (2011), "Reducing the future to climate: A story of climate determinism and reductionism." *Osiris* 26:245–266.

(2009), *Why We Disagree About Climate Change: Understanding Controversy, Inaction and Opportunity*. Cambridge: Cambridge University Press.

Hume, David ([1777] 1985), *Essays: Moral, Political and Literary*. Indianapolis: Liberty Classics.

Huntington, Samuel P. (1993), "The clash of civilizations," *Foreign Affairs* 72:22–49.

(1993), "Postindustrial politics: how benign will it be?" *Comparative Politics* 6:163–191.

(1991), *The Third Wave: Democratization in the Late Twentieth Century*. Norman, OK: University of Oklahoma Press.

(1987), *Understanding Political Development:* Boston, MA: Little, Brown.

(1984), "Will more countries become democratic?" *Political Science Quarterly* 99:193–218.

(1975), "The United States," in Michel Crozier, Samuel P. Huntington and Joji Watanuki (eds.), *The Crisis of Democracy*. New York: New York University Press, pp. 55–118.

(1968), *Political Order in Changing Societies*. New Haven, CT: Yale University Press.

(1965), "Political development and political decay," *World Politics* 17:386–430.

Hupe, Peter and Arthur Edwards (2012), "The accountability of power: democracy and governance in modern times," *European Political Science Review* 4:177–194.

Hyman, Herbert and Paul B. Sheatsley (1947), "Some reasons why information campaigns fail," *Public Opinion Quarterly* 11:412–423.

Ibarra, Andoni and Thomas Mormann (2003), "Engaged scientific inquiry in the Vienna Circle: the case of Otto Neurath," *Technology in Society* 25:235–247.

Iyengar, Shanto (1991), *Is Anyone Responsible? How Television Frames Political Issues*. Chicago: University of Chicago Press.

Inglehart, Ronald and Christian Welzel (2010), "Changing mass priorities: The link between modernization and democracy," *Perspectives on Politics* 8:551–567.

(2005), *Modernization, Cultural Change and Democracy: The Human Development Sequence*. Cambridge: Cambridge University Press.

Inglehart, Ronald (2003), "How solid is mass support for democracy – and how can we measure it?" *PS: Political Science & Politics* 36:51–57.

(1997a), *Modernization and Postmodernization: Cultural, Economic and Political Change in 43 Societies*. Princeton, NJ: Princeton University Press.

(1997b), "Postmaterialist values and the erosion of institutional authority," in Joseph S. Nye, Philip D. Zelikow and David C. King (eds.), *Why People Don't Trust Government*. Cambridge, MA: Harvard University Press, pp. 217–236.

(1987), "Value change in industrial society," *American Political Science Review* 81:1289–1303.

(1977), *The Silent Revolution*. Princeton, NJ: Princeton University Press.

(1971), "The silent revolution in Europe: intergenerational change in post-industrial societies," *American Political Science Review* 65:999–1017.

Innis, Harold ([1950] 2007), *Empire and Communications*. Lanham, MD: Rowman & Littlefield.

Inoguchi, Takashi (2002), "Broadening the basis of social capital in Japan," in Robert D. Putnam (ed.), *Democracies in Flux: The Evolution of Social Capital in Contemporary Society*. New York: Oxford University Press, pp. 358–392.

Irwin, Alan ([1995] 1999), "Science and citizenship," in Eileen Scanlon, Elizabeth Whitelegg and Simeon Yates (eds.), *Communicating Science: Contexts and Channels*. Reader 2. London: Routledge, pp. 14–36.

Jacobs, Lawrence R. (2010), "Democracy and capitalism: structure, agency, and organized combat," *Politics & Society* 38:243–254.

Jacobson, Jo and Indra de Soysa (2006), "Do foreign investors punish democracy? Theory and empirics, 1984–2001," *Kyklos* 59:383–410.

Jacoby, Susan. (2008), *The Age of American Unreason*. New York: Pantheon Books.

Jaffer, Jameel (2010), "The mosaic theory," *Social Research* 77:873–882.

James, William (1890), *Principles of Psychology*, Vol. 1. New York: Henry Holt and Company.

Jarvie, Ian C. (2001), "Science in a democratic republic," *Philosophy of Science* 68:545–564.

Jasanoff, Sheila (2009), "The essential parallel between science and democracy," *Seed Magazine*. February 17, http://seedmagazine.com/content/article/the_essential_parallel_between_science_and_democracy/.

(2003), "Breaking the waves in science studies. Comment on H. M. Collins and Robert Evans 'The third wave of science studies'," *Social Studies of Science* 33:389–400.

Jashapara, Ashok (2007), *Knowledge Management: An Integrated Approach*. Harlow: Financial Times Prentice Hall.

Jeffres, Leo W., Kimberly Neuendorf, and David J. Atkin (2012), "Acquiring knowledge from the media in the Internet age," *Communication Quarterly*, 60:59–79.

Jennings, M. Kent (1996), "Political knowledge over time and across generations," *Public Opinion Quarterly* 60:228–252.

Jermier, John M., David Knights, and Walter R. Nord (eds.) (1994), *Resistance and Power in Organizations*. London: Routledge.

Jörke, Dirk (2005), "Auf dem Weg zur Postdemokratie," *Leviathan* 33:482–491.

Jones, Gareth Stedman (2004), *An End to Poverty? A Historical Debate*. New York: Columbia University Press.

Judt, Tony (2005), *Postwar: A History of Europe since 1945*. London: William Heinemann.
Jung, Nakwon, Yonghwan Kim, and Homero Gil de Zúñiga (2011), "The mediating role of knowledge and efficacy in the effects of communication on political participation," *Mass Communication and Society*, 14:407–430
Kahan, Dan M., Ellen Peters, Maggie Wittlin, Paul Slovic, Lisa Larrimore Ouellette, Donald Braman, and Gregory Mandel (2012), "The polarizing impact of science literacy and numeracy on perceived climate change risks," *Nature Climate Change*, doi: 10.1038/NCLIMATE1547.
Kahan, Dan M., Hank Jenkins-Smith, and Donald Braman (2011), "Cultural cognition of scientific consensus," *Journal of Risk Analysis* 14:147–174.
Kahan, Dan M., Paul Slovic, Donald Braman, and John Gastil (2006), "Fear of democracy: a cultural evaluation of unstein on Risk," *Harvard Law Review* 119:1071–1109
Kalleberg, Ragnvald (2007), "A reconstruction of the ethos of science," *Journal of Classical Sociology* 72:137–160.
Kallen, Horace M. (1934), "Pragmatism," in Edwin R. A. Seligman (ed.), *Encyclopedia of the Social Sciences*. Vol. 12. New York: Macmillan.
Kam, Cindy D. and Carl L. Palmer (2011), "Rejoinder: Reinvestigating the causal relationship between higher education and political participation," *The Journal of Politics* 73:659–663.
(2008), "Reconsidering the effects of education an political participation," *Journal of Politics* 70:612–631.
Kant, Immanuel ([1783] 1986), "What is enlightenment?" in Ernst Behler (ed.), *Philosophical Writings*. New York: Continuum, pp. 267–281.
Kanter, Rosabeth Moss (1991), "The future of bureaucracy and hierarchy in organizational theory: a report from the field," in Pierre Bourdieu and James S. Coleman (eds.), *Social Theory for a Changing Society*. Boulder, CO: Westview Press, pp. 63–87.
(1995), *World Class: Thinking Locally in a Global Economy*. New York: Simon & Schuster.
Kaplan, Robert D. (2012), *The Revenge of Geography: What the Map Tells Us About Coming Conflicts and the Battle Against Fate*. New York: Random House.
Karatnycky, Adrian and Peter Ackerman (2005), "How freedom is won: from civic resistance to durable democracy," *Freedom House Report*. Washington, DC: Freedom House.
Katz, Elihu (1987), "Communication research since Lazarsfeld," *Public Opinion Quarterly* 51: S25–S45.
Katz, Elihu and Paul F. Lazarsfeld (1955), *Personal Influence: The Part Played by People in the Flow of Mass Communications*. New York: Free Press.
Katz, Lawrence F. and Kevin M. Murphy (1992), "Changes in relative wages, 1963–1987: supply and demand factors," *Quarterly Journal of Economics* 107:35–78.
Katz, Richard S. and Peter Mair (1995), "Changing models of party organizations and party democracy: the emergence of the cartel party," *Party Politics* 1:5–28.

Kaufmann, Felix (1959), "John Dewey's theory of inquiry," *The Journal of Philosophy* 56:826–836.
Kay, John (2010), *Obliquity: Why Our Goals are Best Achieve Indirectly*. London: Profile Books.
Keane, John (2009), *The Life and Death of Democracy*. London: Simon & Schuster.
Keller, Evelyn Fox (2011), "What are climate scientists to do?" *Spontaneous Generations: A Journal for the History and Philosophy of Science* 5:19–26.
Kennedy, Duncan (2010), "Knowledge and the political: Bruno Latour's political epistemology," *Cultural Critique* 74:83–97.
Kennedy, Robert F. (1968), *Remarks of Robert F. Kennedy at the University of Kansas, March 18, 1968*, John F. Kennedy Presidential Library and Museum, www.jfklibrary.org
Kennedy, Ryan (2010b), "The contradiction of modernity: a conditional model of endogenous democratization," *The Journal of Politics* 72:785–798.
Koehane, Robert O. (2006), "Accountability in world politics," *Scandinavian Political Studies* 29:75–87.
Kerr, Clark (1963), *The Uses of the University*. Cambridge, MA: Harvard University Press.
Keynes, John Maynard ([1930] 1935), "Economic possibilities for our grandchildren," in John Maynard Keynes, *Essays in Persuasion*. London: Macmillan, pp. 358–374.
  (1936), *General Theory of Employment, Interest and Money*. London: Macmillan.
  ([1919] 2009), *The Economic Consequences of the Peace*. Rockville, MD: Serenity Publishers.
Kirchheimer, Otto (1959), "Majoritäten und Minoritäten in westeuropäischen Regierungen," *Die Neue Gesellschaft* 6:256–270.
Kitcher, Philip (2011a), *Science a Democratic Society*. Amherst, NY: Prometheus Books.
  (2011b), "Public knowledge and its discontents," *Theory and Research in Education* 9:103–124.
  (2010b), "Varieties of freedom and their distribution," *Social Research* 77:857–872.
  (2010a), "The climate change debates," *Science* 328:1230–1234.
  (2006), "Public knowledge and the difficulties of democracy," *Social Research* 73:1205–1224.
  (2001), *Science, Truth, and Democracy*. New York: Oxford University Press.
Klapper, Leora F., Annamaria Lusardi, and Georgios A. Panos (2012), "Financial literarcy and the financial crisis," *NBER Working Paper Series*, Working Paper 17930, www.nber.org/papers/w17930.
Klingemann, Hans-Dieter (1999), "Mapping political support in the 1990s: A global analysis," in Pippa Norris (ed.), *Critical Citizens: Global Support for Democratic Governance*. Oxford: Oxford University Press, pp. 31–56.
Knight, Frank H. (1960), *Intelligence and Democratic Action*. Cambridge, MA: Harvard University Press.
  (1949), "Virtue and knowledge: The view of Professor Polanyi," *Ethics* 59:271–284.

(1941), "The meaning of democracy: its politico-economic structure and ideals," *The Journal of Negro Education* 10:318–332.
(1938), "Lippmann's *The Good Society*," *Journal of Political Economy* 46:864–872.
Knutsen, Carl Hendrick (2011), "Which democracies prosper? Electoral rules, form of government and economic growth," *Electoral Studies* 30:83–90.
Koch, Adrienne and William Peden (eds.) (1944), *The Life and the Writings of Thomas Jefferson*. New York: The Modern Library.
Koehane, Robert O. (2006), "Accountability in world politics," *Scandinavian Political Studies* 29:75–87.
Koestner, Robert and Kevin Callison (2011), "Adolescent cognitive and noncognitive correlates of adult health," *Journal of Human Capital* 5:29–69.
Konings, Martijn (2010), "The pragmatist sources of modern power," *European Journal of Sociology* 60:55–91.
Konrád, George and Ivan Szelényi. (1979), *The Intellectuals on the Road to Class Power*. Brighton, Sussex: Harvester.
Kornhauser, William (1959), *The Politics of Mass Society*. Glencoe, IL: The Free Press.
Koselleck, Reinhart (1989), *Vergangene Zukunft: Zur Semantik geschichtlicher Zeiten*. Frankfurt am Main: Suhrkamp.
Krohn, Wolfgang (1988), *Francis Bacon*. München: C. H. Beck.
(1981), "'Wissen ist Macht': Zur Soziogenese eines neuzeitlichen wissenschaftliches Geltungsanspruchs," in Kurt Bayertz (ed.), *Wissenschaftsgeschichte und wissenschaftliche Revolution*. Köln: Pahl-Rugenstein, pp. 29–57.
Krohn, Wolfgang and Johanes Weyer (1994), "Society as a laboratory: the social risks of experimental research," *Science and Public Policy* 21:173–183.
(1989), "Gesellschaft als Labor: Die Erzeugung sozialer Risiken durch experimentelle Forschung," *Soziale Welt* 40:349–373.
Kuhn, Robert L. (2003), "Science as democratizer," *American Scientist Online* (September–October), www.americanscientist.org/template/AssetDetail/assetid/25691;jsessionid=aaa4KxL1uKYE6.
Kuklinski, James H., Paul J. Quirk, Jennifer Jerit, and Robert F. Rich (2001), "The political environment and citizen competence," *American Journal of Political Science* 45:410–424.
Kuklinski, James H., Paul J. Quirk, Jennier Jeti, David Schwieder and Robert F. Rich (2000), "Misinformation and the currency of democratic citizenship," *The Journal of Politics* 62:790–816.
Kuklinski, James H. (1997), "Review of Michael X. Delli Carpini and Scott Keeter, *What Americans know about Politics and why it Matters*," *The Journal of Politics* 59:925–999.
(1990), "Information and the study of politics," in Forejohn, John A. and James H. Kuklinski (1990), *Information and Democratic Processes*. Urbana and Chicago: University of Illinois Press, pp. 391–395.
Kuklinski, James H., Metlay, Daniel S., and W. D. Kay (1982), "Citizen knowledge and choices on the complex issue of nuclear energy," *American Journal of Political Science* 26:615–642.

Kurlantzick, Joshua (2013), *Democracy in Retreat: The Revolt of the Middle Class and the Worldwide Decline of Representative Government.* New Haven, CT: Yale University Press.

Kuznets, Simon (1973), "Modern economic growth: findings and reflections," *American Economic Review* 63:247–258.

  (1955), "Economic growth and income inequality," *American Economic Review* 45:18–30.

Laird, Frank N. (1993), "Participatory analysis, democracy, and technological decision making," *Science, Technology & Human Values* 18:341–361.

Lambert, Ronald D., James E. Curtis, Barry J. Kay, and Steven D. Brown (1988), "The social sources of political knowledge," *Canadian Journal of Political Science/Revue canadienne de science politique* 21:359–374.

Lane, Robert E. (1966), "The decline of politics and ideology in a knowledgeable society," *American Sociological Review* 31:649–662.

  (1953), "Political character and political analysis," *Psychiatry* 16:387–398.

Landes, David S. (1998), *The Wealth and Poverty of Nations: Why Some are So Rich, and Some are Poor.* New York: W.W. Norton.

Lakoff, Sanford A. (1971), "Knowledge, power, and democratic theory," *Annals of the American Academy of Political and Social Science* 394:4–12.

  (1966), *Knowledge and Power: Essays on Science and Government.* New York: The Free Press.

Lapp, Ralph (1965), *The New Priesthood: The Scientific Elite and the Uses of Power.* New York: Harper and Row.

Larson, Magali Sarfatti (1990). "In the matter of experts and professionals, or how impossible it is to leave nothing unsaid," in Rolf Torstendahl and Michael Burrage (eds.), *The Formation of Professions. Knowledge, State and Strategy.* London: Sage, pp. 24–50.

Lasswell, Harold D. (1966), *The Analysis of Political Behavior: An Empirical Approach.* Hamden, CT: The Shoestring Press.

Latour, Bruno (1999), *Pandora's Hope: Essays on the Reality of Science Studies.* Cambridge, MA: Harvard University Press.

Lazarsfeld, Paul F. and Robert K. Merton ([1948] 1957), "Mass communication, popular taste and organized social action," in Bernhard Rosenberg and David Manning White (eds.), *Mass Culture: The Popular Arts in America*, New York: Free Press, pp. 457–473.

Lazarsfeld, Paul F. (1957), "Public opinion and the classical tradition," *Public Opinion Quarterly* 21:39–53.

  (1948), "Communication research and the social psychologist," in Wayne Dennis (ed.), *Current Trends in Social Psychology.* Pittsburgh, Pennsylvania: University of Pittsburg Press, pp. 218–273.

Leeson, Peter T. (2008), "Media freedom, political knowledge, and participation," *Journal of Economic Perspectives* 22:155–169.

Leibholz, Gerhard (1938), "The nature and various forms of democracy," *Social Research* 5:84–100.

Leighninger, Matt (2006), *The Next Form of Democracy: How Expert Rule is Giving Way to Shared Governance and Why Politics will Never be the Same.* Nashville, TN: Vanderbilt University Press.

Leijonhufvud, Axel (2008), "Spreading the bread thin on the butter," in Lorenzo Pechci and Gustavo Piga (eds.), *Revisiting Keynes: Economic Possibilities for our Grandchildren*. Cambridge, MA: MIT Press, pp. 117–124.
Lemann, Nichols (2012), "Evening the odds," *The New Yorker*, April 23.
Lemert, Charles C. and Garth Gillan (1982), *Michel Foucault: Social Theory as Transgression*. New York: Columbia University Press.
Lerner, Daniel (1959), "Social science: whence and whither?" in Daniel Lerner (ed.), *The Human Meaning of the Social Sciences: Original Essays on the History and the Application of the Social Sciences*. Cleveland, OH: The World Publishing Company, pp. 13–39.
  (1958), *The Passing of Tradition Society*. Glencoe, IL: Free Press.
Levi, Margaret and Laura Stoker (2000), "Political trust and trustworthiness," *Annual Review of Political Science* 3:475–507.
Leyshon, Andrew and Nigel Thrift (1997), *Money/Space: Geographies of Monetary Transformation*. London: Routledge.
Liberatore, Angela and Silvio Funtowicz (2003), "'Democratising' expertise, 'expertising' democracy: what does it mean, and why bother?" *Science and Public Policy* 30:146–150.
Liebowitz, Stan J. and Alejando Zentner (2012), "Clash of the titans: does internet use reduce television viewing?" *Review of Economics and Statistics* 94:234–245.
Lindblom, Charles E. (2001), *The Market System: What it is, How it Works, and What to Make of it*. New Haven: Yale University Press.
  (1995), "Market and democracy – obliquely," *PS: Political Science & Politics* 28: 684–688.
Linos, Katerina (2011), "Diffusion through democracy," *American Journal of Political Science* 55:678–695.
Lippmann, Walter ([1922] 1992), *Public Opinion*. New York: Free Press.
Lipset, Seymour Martin ([1960] 1963), *Political Man: The Social Basis of Politics*. Arden City, NY: Anchor.
  (1959), "Some social requisites of democracy: economic development and political legitimacy," *American Political Science Review* 53:69–105.
Lipset, Seymour Martin, Martin Trow, and James S. Coleman ([1956] 1962), *Union Democracy: The Internal Politics of the International Typographical Union*. New York: Doubleday & Company.
Lipsky, Michael (1968), "Protest as a political resource," *American Political Science Review* 62:1144–1158.
Lijphart, Arend (1977), *Democracy in Plural Societies*. New Haven, CT: Yale University Press.
Loader, Brian D. and Dan Mercea (2011), "Social media innovations and participatory politics," *Information, Communication & Society* 14:757–769.
Lorenz, Edward and Bengt-Åke Lundvall (2011), "Accounting for creativity in the European Union: A multi-level analysis of individual competence, labour market structure, and systems of education and training," *Cambridge Journal od Economics* 35:269–294.
Lovelock, James (2009), *The Vanishing Face of Gaia: A Final Warning*: New York: Basic Books.
  (2006), *The Revenge of Gaia: Why the Earth is Fighting Back – and How We Can Still Save Humanity*. London: Allen Lane.

Lowe, Adolph (1971), "Is present-day higher learning 'relevant'?" *Social Research* 38:563–580.
Loxbo, Karl (2013), "The fare of intra-party democracy: Leadership autonomy and activist influence in the mass party and cartel party," *Party Politics* 19:537–554.
Luckmann, Thomas (1982), "Individual action and social knowledge," in Mario von Cranach and Rom Harré (eds.), *The Analysis of Action*. Cambridge: Cambridge University Press, pp. 247–266.
Luhmann, Niklas (2002a), *Einführung in die Systemtheorie*. Heidelberg: Carl-Auer-Systeme Verlag.
  (2002b), *Das Erziehungssystem der Gesellschaft*. Frankfurt am Main: Suhrkamp.
  (2002c), *Theories of Distinction: Redescribing the Descriptions of Modernity*. Stanford, CA: Stanford University Press.
  (1997), *Die Gesellschaft der Gesellschaft*. Frankfurt am Main: Suhrkamp.
  ([1992] 1998), *Observations on Modernity*. Stanford, CA: Stanford University Press.
  ([1992] 1994]), "The modernity of science," *New German Critique* 61:9–23.
  (1990), *Die Wissenschaft der Gesellschaft*. Frankfurt am Main: Suhrkamp.
  (1987), "Enttäuschungen und Hoffnungen. Zur Zukunft der Demokratie," in Niklas Luhmann (ed.), *Soziologische Aufklärung 4. Beiträge zur funktionalen Differenzierung der Gesellschaft*. Opladen: Westdeutscher Verlag, pp. 133–141.
  ([1986] 1987), "Die Zukunft der Demokratie," in Niklas Luhmann, *Soziologische Aufklärung 4. Beiträge zur funktionalen Differenzierung der Gesellschaft*. Opladen: Westdeutscher Verlag, pp. 126–132.
  ([1981] 1987), "Gesellschaftsstrukturelle Bedingungen und Folgeprobleme des naturwissenschaftlich-technischen Fortschritts," in Niklas Luhmann, *Soziologische Aufklärung 4*. Opladen: Westdeutscher Verlag, pp. 47–63.
  (1970), "Selbststeuerung der Wissenschaft," in Niklas Luhmann, *Soziologische Aufklärung: Avfsätze zur Theorie sozialer Systeme*. Opladen: Westdeutscher Verlag, pp. 232–252.
  (1969), "Normen in soziologischer Perspektive," *Soziale Welt* 20:28–48.
Luhmann, Niklas and Karl Eberhard Schorr (1979), *Reflexionsprobleme im Erziehungssystem*. Stuttgart: Klett-Cotta.
Lukes, Steven (2007), "The problem of apparently irrational beliefs," in Stephen P. Turner and Mark W. Risjord (eds.), *Philosophy of Anthropology and Sociology. Handbook of the Philosophy of Science*. Amsterdam: Elsevier, pp. 591–606.
  (1977), *Essays in Social Theory*. New York: Columbia University Press.
Lupia, Arthur and Mathew D. McCubbins (1998), *The Democratic Dilemma. Can Citizens Learn What They Need To Know*. Cambridge: Cambridge University Press.
Lupu, Noam and Jonas Pontusson (2011), "The structure of inequality and the politics of redistribution," *American Political Science Review* 105:316–336.
Lusardi, Annamaria (2013), "Financial literacy and high-cost borrowing in the United States," *NBER Working Paper* 18969, www.nber.org/papers/w18854.
Luskin, Robert C. (1987), "Measuring political sophistication," *American Journal of Political Science* 31:856–899.

Lyotard, Jean-François ([1979] 1984), *The Postmodern Condition: A Report on Knowledge*. Minnesota: University of Minnesota Press.
Maasen, Sabine and Peter Weingart (2004), *Democratization of Expertise: Exploring Novel Forms of Scientific Advice in Political-Decision-Making*. Dordrecht: Kluwer.
MacCrae, Duncan, Jr. (1981)."Science and the formation of policy in a democracy," in Thomas J. Kuehn and Alan L. Porter (eds.), *Science, Technology and National Policy*. Ithaca, NY: Cornell University Press, pp. 496–514.
Machlup, Fritz (1984), *The Economics of Information and Human Capital*. Princeton: Princeton University Press.
  (1983), "Semantic quirks in studies of information," in Fritz Machlup and Una Mansfield (eds.), *The Study of Information*. New York: Wiley.
  (1962), *Function and Distribution of Knowledge in the United States*. Princeton, NJ: Princeton University Press.
MacKenzie, Donald (2006), *An Engine, Not a Camera: How Financial Models Shape Markets*. Cambridge, MA: MIT Press.
MacLeod, Roy (1997), "Science and democracy: historical reflections on present discontents," *Minerva* 35:369–384.
Magalhães, Pedro C. (2013), "Government effectiveness and support for democracy," *European Journal of Political Research*, doi: 10.1111/1475-6765.12024.
Macpherson, Crawford B. (1962), *The Political Theory of Possessive Individualism*. New York: Oxford University Press.
Magnusson, Warren (1996), *The Search for Political Space: Globalization, Social Movements, and the Urban Political Experience*. Toronto: University of Toronto Press.
Maier, Hans (1971), "Zur neueren Geschichte des Demokratiebegriffs," in Klaus von Beyme (ed.), *Theory and Politics [Theorie und Politik. Festschrift zum 70. Geburtstag für Carl Joachim Friedrich]*. Haag: Martinus Nihoff, pp. 127–161.
Malik, Suheil (2005), "Information and knowledge," *Theory, Culture & Society* 22:29–49.
Mann, Michael (1999), "The dark side of democracy: The modern tradition of ethic and political cleansing," *New Left Review* 235:18–45.
  (1986), *The Sources of Social Power: A History of Power from the Beginning to AD 1760*. Vol. 1. Cambridge: Cambridge University Press.
Mannheim, Karl (1940), *Man and Society in an Age of Reconstruction*. London: Routledge.
  (1935), *Mensch und Gesellschaft im Zeitalter des Umbaus*. Leiden: A. W. Sijhoff.
  ([1929] 1936), *Ideology and Utopia*. London: Routledge.
  ([1928] 1993), "The problem of generations," in Kurt H. Wolff (ed.), *From Karl Mannheim*. New Brunswick, NJ: Transaction Books, pp. 351–395.
Mansell, Robin (2002), "From digital divides to digital entitlements in knowledge societies," *Current Sociology* 50:407–426.
Mansfield, Edward D. and Jon Pevehouse (2006), *Democratization and the Varieties of International Organizations*, Conference on The New Science of International Organizations, University of Pennsylvania.

Marcuse, Herbert ([1964] 1989), *Der eindimensionale Mensch: Studien zur Ideologie der fortgeschrittenen Industriegesellschaft*. Schriften 7, Frankfurt am Main: Suhrkamp.
Markoff John (2011), "A moving target: democracy," *European Journal of Sociology* 52: 239–276.
  (1986), "Literacy and revolt: some empirical notes on 1789 in France," *American Journal of Sociology* 92:323–349.
Marks, Abigal and Chris Baldry (2009), "Stuck in the middle with who? The class identity of knowledge workers," *Work, Employment and Society* 23:49–65.
Marlin-Bennett, Renée (2011), "I hear America tweeting and other themes for a virtual polis: rethinking democracy in the global infotech age," *Journal of Information Technology & Politics* 8:129–145.
Marsh, Robert M. (1988), "Sociological Explanations of Economic Growth," *Studies in Comparative International Development*, 23:41–76.
Marshall, Monty G. and Keith Jaggers (2005), "Polity IV project: Political regime characteristics and transitions, 1800– 2003," www.systemicpeace.org/polity/polity4.htm
Marshall, Thomas H. (1950), *Citizenship and Social Class*. Cambridge: Cambridge University Press.
Mayer, Alexander K. (2011), "Does education increase political participation," *The Journal of Politics* 73:633–645.
McCarthy, John D. and Mayer N. Zald (1977), "Resource mobilization and social movements," *American Journal of Sociology* 82:1212–1241.
McGinnes, John O. (2006), "Age of the empirical," *Policy Review* 137:47–58.
McLuhan, Marshall (1964), *Understanding Media*. New York: McGraw Hill.
McNair, Brian (2000), *Journalism and Democracy: An Evaluation of the Political Public Sphere*. London: Routledge.
Mead, George H. (1964), "Two unpublished manuscripts," *The Review of Metaphysics* 17: 536–556.
  (1923), "Scientific method and the moral sciences," *International Journal of Ethics* 33:229–247.
Meghir, Costas, Mårten Palme and Emilia Simeonova (2013), "Education, cognition and health: evidence from a social experiment," *NBER Working Paper* 19002, www.nber.org/papers/w19002.
Megill, Allan (1985), *Prophets of Extremity: Nietzsche, Heidegger, Foucault, Derrida*. Berkeley, CA: University of California Press.
Merton, Robert K. (1995), "The Thomas theorem and the Matthew Effect," *Social Forces* 74:379–424.
  (1988), "The Matthew Effect in science, II: cumulative advantage and the symbolism of intellectual property," *Isis* 79:606–623.
  (1976), *Sociological Ambivalence and Other Essays*. New York: Free Press.
  (1968), "The Matthew Effect in science," *Science* 1959:56–63.
  (1966), "Dilemmas of democracy in the voluntary associations," *American Journal of Nursing* 66:1055–1061.
  (1957a), "Karl Mannheim and the sociology of knowledge," in Robert K. Merton (ed.), *Social Theory and Social Structure*. Revised and Enlarged Edition. New York: Free Press, pp. 489–508.

(1957b), "Introduction: Studies in the sociology of science," in Robert K. Merton (ed.), *Social Theory and Social Structure*. Revised and Enlarged Edition. New York: Free Press, pp. 531–556.

([1957] 1973), "Priorities in scientific discoveries," in Robert K. Merton, *The Sociology of Science: Theoretical and Empirical Investigations*. Chicago: University of Chicago Press, pp. 286–324.

(1952), "Introduction," in Bernard Barber (ed.), *Science and the Social Order*. New York: Free Press, pp. xi–xxiii.

([1942] 1973), "The normative structure of science," in Robert K. Merton (ed.), *The Sociology of Science: Theoretical and Empirical Investigations*. Chicago: University of Chicago Press, pp. 267–278.

([1942] 1996), "The ethos of science," in Piotr Sztompka (ed.), *On Social Structure and Science*. Chicago: University of Chicago Press, pp. 267–276.

(1942), "A note on science and democracy," *Journal of Legal and Political Sociology* 1:115–126.

([1938] 1973), "Science and the social order," in Robert K. Merton (ed.), *The Sociology of Science: Theoretical and Empirical Investigations*. Chicago: University of Chicago Press, pp. 254–266.

Mettler, Suzanne (2007), "Bringing government back into civic engagement: considering the role of public policy," *International Journal of Public Administration* 30:643–650.

Mettler, Suzanne and Joe Soss (2004), "The consequences of public policy for democratic citizenship: bridging policy studies and mass politics," *Perspectives on Politics*, 55–73.

Meyer, John W., John Boli, George M. Thomas, and Francisco O. Ramirez (1997), "World society and the nation-state," *American Journal of Sociology* 103:144–81.

Meyer, John W., Kamens, D. and Aaron Benavot (1992), *School Knowledge for the Masses*. Washington, DC: Falmer.

Michel, Patrick (1992), "Religious renewal or political deficiency: religion and democracy in Central Europe," *Religion, State and Society* 20: 339–344.

Michels, Robert ([1915] 1949), *Political Parties: A Sociological Study of the Oligarchical Tendencies of Modern Democracy*. New York: Free Press.

([1915] 1970), *Zur Soziologie des Parteiwesens in der modernen Demokratie: Untersuchungen über die oligarchischen Tendenzen des Gruppenlebens*. Stuttgart: Alfred Kröner Verlag.

Mihailidis, Paul and Benjamin Thevenin (2013), "Media literacy as a core competency for engaged citizenship in participatory democracy," *American Behavioral Scientist* 57:1611–1622.

Milanovic, Brank (2012), "Global income inequality by the numbers: In history and now," *Policy Research Working Paper 6259*. Washington, DC: The World Bank.

Miljkoviv, Dragan and Arbindra Rimal (2008), "The impact of socio-economic factors on political stability," *Journal of Socio-Economics* 37:2454–2463.

Milward, Alan S. (1992), *The European Rescue of the Nation-State*. Berkeley: University of California Press.

Mill, John Stuart ([1869] 2010), *On Liberty*. London: Longman, Roberts & Green.
  ([1873] 2009), *Autobiography*. Auckland, New Zealand: Floating Press.
  ([1861] 1977), "Considerations on representative government," in J. M. Robson (ed.), *Essays on Politics and Society. Volume 19 of Collected Works of John Stuart Mill*. Toronto, Canada: University of Toronto Press, pp. 371–613.
Miller, Melissa K. and Shannon K. Orr (2008), "Experimenting with a 'third way' in estimating political knowledge," *Public Opinion Quarterly* 72:768–780.
Miller, Steve (2001), "Public understanding of science at the crossroads," *Public Understanding of Science* 10:115–120.
Milligan, Kevin, Enrico Moretti, and Philip Oreopoulos (2003), "Does education improve citizenship? Evidence from the U.S. and the U.K.," *NBER Working Paper Series* 9584, www.nber.org/papers/w9584.
Mills, C. Wright (1959), *The Sociological Imagination*. New York: Oxford University Press.
  (1956a), *The Power Elite*. New York: Oxford University Press.
  (1956b), *White Collar: The American Middle Class*. New York: Oxford University Press.
  ([1955] 1967), "On knowledge and power," in Irving Louis Horowitz (ed.), *Power, Politics & People: The Collected Essays by C. Wright Mills*. New York: Oxford University Press, pp. 599–613.
Milner, Henry (2002), *Civic Literacy: How Informed Citizens Make Democracy Work*. Hanover, CT: United Press of New England.
Minier, Jenny A. (1998), "Democracy and growth: alternative approaches," *Journal of Economic Growth* 3:241–266.
Minogue, Kenneth (2010), "Morals & servile mind," *The New Criterion* 28:4–9.
Mirowski, Philip (2004), "The scientific dimension of social knowledge and their distant echoes in 20th-century American philosophy of science," *Studies in History and Philosophy of Science* 35:283–326.
Misa, Thomas J. (1988), "How machines make history and how historians (and others) help them do so," *Science, Technology, and Human Values* 13:308–331.
Mises, Ludwig (1922), *Die Gemeinwirtschaft: Untersuchungen über den Sozialismus*. Jena: Gustav Fischer.
Mitchell, Timothy (2009), "Carbon democracy," *Economy and Society* 38:399–432.
Mokyr, Joel (1990), *The Lever of Riches*. Oxford: Oxford University Press.
Montaigne, Michel ([1580] 1998), *Essais*. Frankfurt am Main: Eichborn Verlag.
Montesquieu, Charles Baron de ([1748] 2007), *The Spirit of the Laws*. New York: Cosimo.
Mooney, Chris (2010), *Do Scientists Understand the Public?* Cambridge, Massachusetts: American Academy of Arts and Sciences.
Moore, Barrington (1966), *The Social Origins of Dictatorship and Democracy*. Boston: Beacon Press.
Morgenthau, Hans J. (1970), "Reflections on the end of the republic," *New York Review of Books* 15 (September 23):38–41.

Morozov, Evgeny (2011), *The Net Delusion: The Dark Side of Internet Freedom.* New York: Public Affairs.
Morris, Charles (1948), *The Open Self.* New York: Prentice-Hall.
Morris, Aldon D. and Carol McClurg Mueller (eds.) (1992), *Frontiers in Social Movement Theory.* New Haven, CT: Yale University Press.
Moynihan, Daniel P. (1970), "*The role of social scientists in action research*," SSRC Newsletter.
Mahdavy, Hussein (1970), "The Patterns and Problems of Economic Development in Rentier States: The Case of Iran," in M.A. Cook (ed.), *Studies in the Economic History of the Middle East.* London: Oxford University Press.
Mullainathan, Senhil and Eldar Shafir (2013), *Scarcity: Why Having too little Means so much.* New York: Times Books.
Mullan, Bob (1997), "Anthony Giddens," in Christopher Bryant and David Jary (eds.), *Anthony Giddens. Critical Assessments. Bd. 1.* London: Routledge, pp. 74–94.
Murnane, Richard J., John B. Willett, and Frank Levy (1995), "The growing importance of cognitive skills in wage determination," *Review of Economics and Statistics* 77:251–266
Murphy, Kevin M. and Finis Welch (1993), "Inequality and relative wages," *The American Economic Review: Papers and Proceedings.* 83:104–109
(1992), "Industrial change and the rising importance of skill," in Sheldon Danziger and Peter Gottschalk (eds.), *Uneven Tides: Rising Inequality in the 1980s.* New York: Russell Sage Foundation, pp. 101–132.
Nagel, Ernest (1936a), "Impressions and appraisals of analytic philosophy in Europe I," *Journal of Philosophy* 33:5–24.
(1936b), "Impressions and appraisals of analytic philosophy in Europe II," *Journal of Philosophy* 33:25–53.
Nannestad, Peter (2008), "What have we learned about generalized trust, if anything?" *Annual Review of Political Science* 11:413–436.
Nanoka, Ikujiro (1994), "A dynamic theory of organization knowledge creation," *Organization Science* 5: 14–37.
Narayan, Paresh, Seema Narayan, and Russel Smith (2011), "Does democracy facilitate economic growth or does economic growth facilitate democracy? An empirical study of Sub-Saharan Africa," *Economic Modeling* 28:900–910.
Naumann, Friedrich (1909), "Von wem werden wir regiert?" *Neue Rundschau* 20:625–636.
Nelkin, Dorothy (1984), "Science and technology policy and the democratic process," in James C. Peterson (ed.), *Citizen Participation in Science Policy.* Amherst, MA: University of Massachusetts Press, pp. 18–39.
(1979), "Scientific knowledge, public policy, and democracy: a review essay," *Science Communication* 1:106–122.
(1975), "The political impact of technical expertise," *Social Studies of Science* 5:35054.
Nelson, Michael A. and Ram D. Singh (1998), "Democracy, economic freedom, fiscal policy and growth in LCDs: a fresh look," *Economic Development and Cultural Change* 46:677–696.

Nelson, Richard R. (2008), "What enables rapid economic progress: what are the needed institutions?" *Research Policy* 37:1–11.
Nemeth, Elisabeth (1994), "Utopien für eine wissenschaftliche Sicht der Welt und des Wissens," in Paul Neurath and Elisabeth Nemeth (eds.), *Otto Neurath oder Die Einheit von Wissenschaft und Gesellschaft*. Wien: Böhlau, pp. 97–129.
Neurath, Otto (1946), "After six years," *Synthese* 5:77–82.
  ([1945] 1996), "Visual education: humanisation versus popularisation," in Juha Manninen, Elisabeth Nemeth, and Friedrich Stadler (eds.), *Encyclopedia and Utopia: The Life and Work of Otto Neurath*. Dordrecht: Kluwer, pp. 248–335.
  (1944), *Foundations of the Social Sciences*. Chicago: University of Chicago Press.
  ([1942] 1973), "International planning for freedom," in Otto Neurath (ed.), *Empiricism and Sociology*. Dordrecht: Reidel, pp. 422–330.
  ([1937] 2004), "Inventory of the standard of living," in Thomas E. Uebel and Robert S. Cohen (eds.), *Otto Neurath: Economic Writings, Selections 1904–1945*. Dordrecht: Kluwer, pp. 513–526.
  ([1931] 1983), "Sociology in the framework of physicalism," in Robert S. Cohen and Marie Neurath (eds.), *Otto Neurath: Philosophical Papers 1913–1946*. Dordrecht: D. Reidel, pp. 58–90.
  (1931), *Empirische Soziologie. Der wissenschaftliche Gehalt der Geschichte und Nationalökonomie*. Wien: Julius Springer.
  ([1930/31] 1994), "Wege der wissenschaftlichen Weltanschauung," *Erkenntnis* 1:106–125, [also pp. 351–367 in Paul Neurath and Elisabeth Nemeth (eds.), *Otto Neurath oder Die Einheit von Wissenschaft und Gesellschaft*. Wien: Böhlau.]
  (1919), "Zur Einführung," *Wirtschaft und Lebensordung* 1 (qtd. in Uebel 2004:58).
  ([1908] 1998), "Die allgemeine Einführung des volkswirtschaftlichen und staatsbürgerlichen Unterrichts," in Rudolf Haller and Ulf Höfer, *Gesammelte ökonomische, soziologische und sozialpolitische Schriften, 1*. Wien: Hölder-Pichler-Temsky, pp. 119–132.
Newman, Edward and Roland Rich (2004), *The UN Role in Promoting Democracy*. New York: United Nations University Press.
Niethammer, Lutz ([1989] 1992), *Posthistory. Has History Come to an End?* London: Verso.
Noah, Timothy (2012), *The Great Divergence: America's Growing Inequality Crisis and What Can be Done About It*. New York: Bloomsbury Press.
Noelle-Neuman, Elisabeth ([1968] 1984), *The Spiral of Silence: Public Opinion– Our Social Skin*. Chicago: University of Chicago Press.
Nolte, Ernst (1993), "Die Fragilität des Triumphs: Zur Lage des liberalen Systems nach der neuen Weltordnung." *Franfurter Allgemeine Zeitung* 151, July 3.
Nordhaus, Ted and Michael Shellenberger (2009), "Apocalypse Fatigue: Losing the Public on Climate Change," *Environment* 360, http://e360.yale.edu/content/feature.msp?id=2210.
Norris, Pippa (2011a), *Democratic Deficit: Critical Citizens Revisited*. Cambridge: Cambridge University Press.

(2011b), "Making democratic governance work: the consequences of prosperity," *Harvard Kennedy School Research Working Paper* RWP11-035.
(ed.) (1999), *Critical Citizens: Global Support for Democratic Governance*. Oxford: Oxford University Press.
(1996), "Does television erode social capital? A reply to Putnam," *PS: Political Science and Politics* 29:474-480.
Norris, Pippa and Ronald Inglehart (2002), "Islamic culture and democracy: testing the 'clash of civilizations' thesis," *Comparative Sociology* 1:235-263.
Nowotny, Helga (1979), *Kernenergie: Gefahr oder Notwendigkeit? Anatomie eines Konflikts*. Frankfurt am Main: Suhrkamp.
Nussbaum, Martha C. (2000), *Women and Human Development: The Capabilities Approach*. Cambridge: Cambridge University Press.
Nussbaum, Martha C. and Amartya Sen (1993), *The Quality of Life*. Oxford: Clarendon Press.
Nye, Joseph S. Jr. (1997), "Introduction: the decline of confidence in government," in Joseph S. Nye Jr., Philip D. Zelikow, and David C. King (eds.), *Why People Don't Trust Government*. Cambridge, MA: Harvard University Press, p. 118.
(1990), *Bound to Lead: The Changing Nature of American Power*. New York: Basic Books.
Ober, Josiah (2012), "Democracy's dignity," *American Political Science Review* 104:827-846.
(2010), *Democracy and Knowledge: Innovation and Learning in Classical Athens*. Princeton, NJ: Princeton University Press.
OECD (2011), *Divided We Stand: Why Inequality Keeps Rising*. Paris: OECD.
Oelkers, Jürgen (2000), "Democracy and education: about the future of a problem," *Studies in Philosophy and Education* 19:3-19.
Offe, Claus (2013), "Ungovernability," in Stephan Jansen, Eckhard Schröter, and Nico Stehr (eds.), *Stabile Fragilität – Fragile Stabilität*. Wiesbaden: Springer VS, pp. 77-88.
Offe, Claus (1979), "'Unregierbarkeit': Zur Renaissance konservativer Krisentheorien," in Jürgen Habermas (ed.), *Stichworte zur 'Geistigen Situation der Zeit'*. Band 1: Nation und Republik. Frankfurt am Main: Suhrkamp, pp. 294-318.
O'Donnell, Guillermo A. (1978), "Reflections on the Patterns of Change in the Bureaucratic Authoritarian States," *Latin American Research Review* 13:3-36.
O'Donnell, Guillermo A. (1973), *Modernization and Bureaucratic-Authoritarianism*. Berkeley, CA: Institute for International Studies.
O'Donnell, Guillermo A. and Philippe C. Schmitter (1986), "Concluding (but not capitulating) with a metaphor," in Guillermo A. O'Donnell and Philippe C. Schmitter (eds.), *Transitions from Authoritarian Rule: Tentative Conclusions about Uncertain Democracies*. Baltimore: The Johns Hopkins University Press, pp. 65-72.
(2000), "Democracy and education: about the future of a problem," *Studies in Philosophy and Education* 19:3-19.
Oliver, Pamela E. and Gerald Marwell (1992), "Mobilizing technologies for collective action," in Aldon D. Morris and Carol M. Mueller (eds.), *Frontiers*

in Social Movement Theory. New Haven, CT: Yale University Press, pp. 252–272.
Olson, Mancur (2000), "Dictatorship, democracy, and development," in Mancur Olson and Satu Kähkönen (eds.), *A Not-So Dismal Science: A Broader View of Economics and Society*. Oxford: Oxford University Press, pp. 119–137.
  (1982), *The Rise and Decline of Nations: Economic Growth, Stagflation, and Social Rigidities*. New Haven, CT: Yale University Press.
  (1965), *The Logic of Collective Action*. Cambridge, MA: Harvard University Press.
O'Neill, John (1999), "Socialism, ecology and Austrian economics," in Elisabeth Nemeth and Richard Heinrich (eds.), *Otto Neurath: Rationalität, Planung, Vielfalt*. Wien: Oldenbourg, pp. 123–145.
Oppenheim, Felix E. (1961), *Dimensions of Freedom: An Analysis*. New York: St. Martin's Press.
  (1960), "Degrees of power and freedom," *American Political Science Review* 54:437–446.
Oyama, Susan (2000), *Evolution's Eye. A Systems View of the Biology – Culture Divide*. Durham, NC: Duke University Press.
Pachero, Gail and Thomas Lange (2010), "Political participation and life satisfaction: a cross-European analysis," *International Journal of Social Economics* 37:686–702.
Palmer, R. R. (1953), "Notes on the use of the word 'democracy' 1979–1799," *Political Science Quarterly* 68:203–226.
Panitch, Leo (1993), "A different kind of state?" in Gregory Albo, David Langille, and Leo Panitch (eds.), *A Different Kind of State? Popular Power and Democratic Administration*. Toronto: Oxford University Press, pp. 2–16.
Paras, Eric (2006), *Foucault 2.0: Beyond Power and Knowledge*. New York: The Other Press.
Park, Robert E. (1940), "News as a form of knowledge: a chapter in the sociology of knowledge," *American Journal of Sociology* 45: 669–686.
Parsons, Talcott (1963), "On the concept of political power," *Proceedings of the American Philosophical Society* 107:232–262.
  (1957), "The distribution of power in American society," *World Politics* 10:123–143.
Pateman, Carole (1970), *Participation and Democratic Theory*. Cambridge: Cambridge University Press.
Peck, Jamie (2005), "Struggling with the creative class," *International Journal of Urban and Regional Research* 29:740–770.
Perrin, Andrew J. and Katherine McFarland (2011), "Social theory and public opinion," *Annual Review of Sociology* 37:87–107.
Persaud, Avinash (2001), "The knowledge gap," *Foreign Affairs* 80:107–117.
Persson, Torsten and Guido Tabellini (2007), "The growth effect of democracy: Is it heterogeneous and how can it be estimated?" *NBER Working Paper* 13150, www.nber.org/papers/w13150.
  (2006), "Democracy and development: the devil in the details," *American Economic Review* 96:319–324.

Petersen, Michael Bang and Lene Aarøe (2013), "Politics in the mind's eye: imagination as a link between social and political cognition," *American Political Science Review* 107: 275–293.
Pew Research Center (2009), "Public praises science; scientists fault public, media. Scientific achievements less prominent than a decade ago," http://people-press.org/report/528/.
Pielke, Roger A. Jr. (2010), *The Climate Fix*. New York: Basic Books.
  (2007), *The Honest Broker. Making Sense of Science in Policy and Politics*. Cambridge: Cambridge University Press.
Pinker, Steven (2013), "Science is not your enemy," *New Republic* August 6.
Pipes, Richard (1955), "Max Weber and Russia," *World Politics* 7:371–401.
Pitkin, Hanna (1967), *The Concept of Representation*. Berkeley, CA: University of California Press.
Plessner, Helmuth ([1924] 1985), "Zur Soziologie der modernen Forschung und ihrer Organisation in der Deutschen Universität – Tradition und Ideologie," in Helmuth Plessner, Gesammelte Schriften. *Band X: Schriften zur Soziologie und Sozialphilosophie*, Frankfurt am Main: Suhrkamp, pp. 7–30.
Plotke, David (1997), "Representation is democracy," *Constellations* 4:19–34.
Poggi, Gianfranco (1982), "The modern state and the idea of progress", in Gabriel A. Almond, Marvin Chodorow and Roy Harvey Pearce (eds.), *Progress and its Discontents*. Berkeley: University of California Press, pp. 337–369.
Polanyi, Michael (1967), *The Tacit Dimension*. New York: Doubleday.
  ([1962] 2000), "The republic of science: its political and economic theory," *Minerva* 38:1–32.
Polanyi, Karl (1947), "Our obsolete market mentality: our civilization must find a new thought pattern," *Commentary* 3:109–117.
Polèse, Mario (2011), "Urban-development legends. Grand theories to little to revive cities," www.city-journal.org/2011/21_4_urban-development.html
Pool, Ithiel de Sola (1990), *Technologies without Boundaries: On Telecommunication in a Global Age*. Cambridge, MA: Harvard University Press.
  (1983), *Technologies of Freedom. On Free Speech in an Electronic Age*. Cambridge, MA: Harvard University Press.
Popkin, Samuel L. (1991), *The Reasoning Voter: Communication and Persuasion in Presidential Campaigns*. Chicago: University of Chicago Press.
Popper, Karl ([2008] 2012), *After the Open Society*. London: Routledge.
  (1973), "Memories of Otto Neurath," in Otto Neurath, *Empiricism and Sociology*, Marie Neurath and Robert S. Cohen, eds. Dordrecht: D. Reidel, pp. 51–56.
  ([1963] 2012), "The open society and the democratic state," in Karl Popper, *After the Open Society*. London: Routledge, pp. 231–248.
  ([1960] 1968), "On the sources of knowledge and of ignorance," in Karl Popper (ed.), *Conjectures and Refutations: The Growth of Scientific Knowledge*. New York: Harper and Row, pp. 3–30.
Posner, Richard (2003), *Law, Pragmatism, and Democracy*. Cambridge, MA: Harvard University Press.

Potter, David M. ([1954] 1958), *People of Plenty: Economic Abundance and the American Character*. Chicago: University of Chicago Press.

Pratt, Andy C. (2008), "Creative cities: the cultural industries and the creative class," *Geografiska Annaler: Series B, Human Geography* 90:107–117.

Prewitt, Kenneth (2010), "Introduction: Limits to knowledge? No easy answer," *Social Research* 77:901–904.

Prewitt, Kenneth and Heinz Eulau (1969), "Political matrix and political representation: prolegomenon to a new departure from an old problem," *American Political Science Review* 63:427–441.

Prins, Gwyn, Isabel Galiana, Professor Christopher Green, Reiner Grundmann, Mike Hulme, Atte Korhola, Frank Laird, Ted Nordhaus, Roger Pielke Jr., Steve Rayner, Daniel Sarewitz, Michael Shellenberger, Nico Stehr, and Hiroyuki Tezuka (2010), *Hartwell Paper I*. London: London School of Economics.

Prior, Markus and Arthur Lupia (2008), "Money, time, and political knowledge: Distinguishing quick recall and political learning skills," *American Journal of Political Science* 52: 169–183.

Przeworski, Adam (2004), "Democracy and economic development," in Edward D. Mansfield and Richard Sisson (eds.), *Political Science and the Public Interest*. Columbus: Ohio State University Press (cited from the version of the paper found on the Internet pages of the author).

(1991), *Democracy and the Market: Political and Economic Reforms in Eastern Europe and Latin America*. New York: Cambridge University Press.

Przeworski, Adam and Fernando Limongi (1993), "Political regimes and economic growth," *Journal of Economic Perspectives* 7:51–69.

Przeworski, Adam, Michael Alvarez, José A. Cheibub, and Fernando Limongi (2000), *Democracy and Development: Political Institutions and Material Well-Being in the World, 1950–1990*. New York: Cambridge University Press.

Pupin, Michael ([1922] 2007), *From Immigrant to Inventor*. New York: Cosimo.

Purdy, Jedediah (2009), "The politics of nature: climate change, environmental law, and democracy," *The Yale Law Journal* 119:1122–1192.

Putnam, Robert D. (2002), "Conclusion," in Robert D. Putnam, (ed.), *Democracies in Flux: The Evolution of Social Capital in Contemporary Society*. Oxford: Oxford University Press, pp. 391–418.

(2000), *Bowling Alone: The Collapse and Revival of American Community*. New York: Simon & Schuster.

(1996), "The strange disappearance of civic America," *Policy* 12:3–13.

(1995a), "Tuning in, tuning out: the strange disappearance of social capital in America," *PS: Political Science and Politics* 28:664–683.

(1995b), "Bowling alone: America's declining social capital," *Journal of Democracy* 6:65–78.

(1993), *Making Democracy Work*. Princeton: Princeton University Press.

Putnam, Robert D. and Kristin A. Goss (2002), "Introduction," in Robert D. Putnam, (ed.), *Democracies in Flux: The Evolution of Social Capital in Contemporary Society*. Oxford: Oxford University Press, pp. 3–19.

Radder, Hans (1986), "Experiment, technology and the intrinsic connection between knowledge and power," *Social Studies of Science* 16:663–683.
Ramsey, Kristopher W. (2011), "Revisiting the resource course: natural disasters, the price of oil, and democracy," *International Organization* 65:507–529.
Ranis, Gustav, Stewart, Frances, and Emma Samman (2006), "Human development: beyond the human development index," *Journal of Human Development and Capabilities* 7:323–358.
Rayner, Steve (2003), "Democracy in an age of assessment: reflections on the roles of expertise and democracy in public-sector decision making," *Science and Public Policy* 30:163–170.
Ravetz, Jerome (1986), "Useable knowledge, useable ignorance," in William C. Clark and R. E. Munn (eds.), *Sustainable Development of the Biosphere*. Cambridge: Cambridge University Press, pp. 415–432.
Rawls, John (1997), "The idea of public reason revisited," *The University of Chicago Law Review* 64:765–807.
  (1971), *A Theory of Justice*. Cambridge, MA: Harvard University Press.
Reenock, Christopher, Jeffrey K. Staton, and Marius Radean (2013), "Legal institutions and democratic survival," *The Journal of Politics* 75:491–505.
Reeves, Richard (2007), *John Stuart Mill: Victorian Firebrand*. London: Atlantic Books.
Reich, Robert B. (2007), *Supercapitalism: The Transformation of Business, Democracy, and Everyday Life*. New York: Alfred A. Knopf.
Reichenbach, Hans (1951), *The Rise of Scientific Philosophy*. Berkeley: University of California Press.
Reisch, George A. (2005), *How the Cold War Transformed Philosophy of Science: The Icy Slopes of Logic*. Cambridge: Cambridge University Press.
Rhodes, R. A. W. (1996), "The new governance: governing without government," *Political Studies* 44: 652–667.
Richey, Sean (2008), "The autoregressive influence of social networks political knowledge on voting behavior," *British Journal of Political Science* 38:527–542.
Riesman, David ([1950] 1961), *The Lonely Crowd: A Study of the Changing American Character*. New Haven, CT: Yale University Press.
Ringen, Stein (2010), "The measurement of democracy: toward a new paradigm," *Society* 48:12–16.
  (2008), "Do we need self-knowledge in order to live as free citizens," in Nico Stehr (ed.), *Knowledge & Democracy: A 21st Century Perspective*. New Brunswick, NJ: Transaction Books, pp. 25–37.
Rittel, Horst W. J. and Melvin Webber (1973), "Dilemmas in the general theory of planning", *Policy Sciences*, 4:154–59.
Roberts, Kenneth M. (2008), "The mobilization of opposition to economic liberalization," *Annual Review of Political Science* 11:327–349.
Robinson, James A. (2006), "Economic development and democracy," *Annual Review of Political Science* 9:503–527.
Robinson, James A., Ragnar Torvik, and Thierry Verdier (2006), "Political foundations of the resource curse," *Journal of Development Economics* 79:447–468.

Robinson, James Harvey (1923), *The Humanizing of Knowledge*. New York: George H. Doran.
Rogers, Melvin L. (2007), "Action and inquiry in Dewey's philosophy," *Transactions of the Charles Pierce Society* 43:90–115.
Rosanvallon, Pierre ([2011] 2013), *The Society of Equals*. Cambridge, MA: Harvard University Press.
  ([2006] 2008), *Counter-Democracy: Politics in an Age of Distrust*. Cambridge: Cambridge University Press.
  (2006), *Democracy: Past and Future*. New York: Columbia University Press.
Rose, Nikolas (1999), *Powers of Freedom: Reframing Political Thought*. Cambridge: Cambridge University Press.
  (1994), "Expertise and the government of conduct," *Studies in Law, Politics and Society* 14:359–397.
  (1993), "Government, authority and expertise in advanced liberalism," *Economy and Society* 22:283–299.
Rose, Nikolas and Peter Miller (1992), "Political power beyond the state: problematics of government," *British Journal of Sociology* 43:173–205.
Rose, Richard (1979), "Pervasive problems of governing: an analytic framework," in Joachim Matthes (ed.), *Sozialer Wandel in Westeuropa*. Verhandlungen des 19. Deutschen Soziologentages, Berlin 1979. Frankfurt: Campus, pp. 29–54.
Rosenberg, Morris (1954–1955), "Some determinants of political apathy," *Public Opinion Quarterly* 18:349–366.
  (1951), "The meaning of politics in mass society," *Public Opinion Quarterly* 15:5–15.
Rosenfeld, Sophia (2008), "Before democracy: the production and uses of common sense," *The Journal of Modern History* 80:1–54.
Ross, Michael L (2001), "Does oil hinder democracy?" *World Politics* 53(3):325–361.
Roszak, Theodore (1972), *Where the Wasteland Ends: Politics and Transcendence in Postindustrial Society*. New York: Doubleday.
Rowley, Jennifer (2007), "The wisdom hierarchy: representations of the DIWW hierarchy," *Journal of Information Science* 33:163–180.
Runciman, David (2013a), "Democracy's dual dangers," *Chronicle of Higher Education* November 18, 2013, http://chronicle.com/article/Democracys-Dual-Dangers/142971/.
  (2013b), *The Confidence Trap: A History of Democracy in Crisis from World War I to the Present*. Princeton, NJ: Princeton University Press.
  (2005), "Tax breaks for rich murderers: review of Michael Graetz and Ian Shapiro, *Death by a Thousand Cuts*," *London Review of Books* 27(11): www.lrb.co.uk/v27/n11/runc01_.html (accessed September 11, 32013).
Rushforth, Scott (1994), "Political resistance in a contemporary hunter-gatherer society: more about Bearlake Athabaskan knowledge and authority," *American Ethnologist* 21:335–352.
Rustow, Dankwart A. (1970), "Transitions to democracy: toward a dynamic model," *Comparative Politics* 2:337–363.

Ryle, Gilbert ([1949] 2002), *The Concept of Mind*. Chicago: University of Chicago Press.
(1945/46), "Knowing how and knowing that," *Proceedings of the Aristotelian Society* 46:1–16.
Sachs, Jeffrey D., John W. McArthur, Guido Schmidt-Traub, Margaret Kruk, Chandrika Bahadur, Michael Faye, and Gordon McCord (2004), "Ending Africa's poverty trap," *Brookings Papers on Economic Activity* 1:117–240.
Sagoff, Mark ([1988] 2008), *The Economy of the Earth*. Cambridge: Cambridge University Press.
Salisbury, Robert H. (1975), "Research on political participation," *American Journal of Political Science* 19:323–341
Salamon, Lester M., and Helmut K. Anheier (1997), *Defining the Nonprofit Sector: A Cross-National Analysis*. Manchester: Manchester University Press.
Salomon, Jean-Jacques (2000), "Science, technology and democracy," *Minerva* 38:33–51.
Sander, Thomas H. and Robert D. Putnam (2010), "Still bowling alone? The post 9/11 split," *Journal of Democracy* 21:9–16.
Santerre, Lise (2008), "From democratization of knowledge to bridge building between science, technology and society," in Donhong Cheng, Michel Claessens and Nicholas R. J. Gascoigne (eds.), *Communicating Science in Social Contexts*. Heidelberg, Springer, pp. 287–300
Sands, Gary and Laura A. Reese (2008), "Cultivating the creative class: And what about Nanaimo?" *Economic Development Quarterly* 22:8–23.
Sarewitz, Daniel (2010), "Normal science and the limits on knowledge: what we seek to know, what we choose not to know, what we don't bother knowing," *Social Research* 77:997–1010.
Sarewitz, Daniel and Richard P. Nelson (2008), "Progress in know-how: its origins and limits," *Innovation* 3:101–117.
Sartori, Giovanni (1968), "Democracy," in Davis Sills (ed.), *International Encyclopedia of the Social Sciences*. Volume 4. New York: Macmillan and Free Press, pp. 112–121.
(1962), *Democratic Theory*. Detroit, MI: Wayne State University Press.
Sassi, Sinikka (2005), "Cultural differentiation or social segregation: four approaches to digital divide," *New Media & Society* 7:684–700
Saward, M. (1993), "Green democracy," in Andrew Dobson and Paul Lucardie (eds.), *The Politics of Nature: Explorations in Green Political Theory*. London: Routledge, pp. 63–80.
Scaff, Lawrence A. (1981), "Max Weber and Robert Michels," *American Journal of Sociology* 86:1269–1286.
Scheler, Max ([1925] 1960), "The forms of knowledge and culture," in Max Scheler, *Philosophical Perspectives*. Boston: Beacon Press, pp. 13–49.
([1926] 1992), *On Feeling, Knowing, and Valuing*. Chicago: University of Chicago Press.
Schelsky, Helmut. (1976), "Die metawissenschaftlichen Wirkungen der Soziologie," in Werner Becker and Kurt Hübner (eds.) *Objektivität in*

den Natur-und Geisteswissenschaften. Hamburg: Hoffmann und Campe, pp. 171–182.
  (1975), *Die Arbeit tun die anderen: Klassenkampf und Priesterherrschaft der Intellektuellen*. Opladen: Westdeutscher Verlag.
  ([1961] 1965), "Der Mensch in der wissenschaftlichen Zivilisation," in Helmut Schelsky, *Auf der Suche nach der Wirklichkeit. Gesammelte Aufsätze*. Düsseldorf: Diederichs, pp. 171–182.
  (1955), *Wandlungen der deutschen Familie in der Gegenwart*. Dritte, durch einen Anhang erweiterte Auflage. Stuttgart: Ferdinand Enke.
Scherer, Bonnie A. (2004–2005), "Footing the bill for a sound education in New York City: the implementation of campaign for fiscal equity v. state," *Fordham Urban Law Journal* 32:901–935.
Schieder, Theodor (1977), "Einmaligkeit oder Wiederkehr: Historische Dimensionen der heutigen Krise." in Wilhelm Hennis, Peter Graf Kielmansegg, and Ulrich Matz (eds.), *Regierbarkeit: Studien zu ihrer Problematisierung*. Band 1. Stuttgart: Klett-Cotta, pp. 22–42.
Schieman, Scott and Gabriele Plickert (2008), "How knowledge is power: the sense of control," *Social Forces* 87:153–183.
Schiller, Dan (1997). "The information commodity: a preliminary view," in Jim Davis, Thomas A. Hirschl, and Michael Stack (eds.), *Cutting Edge: Technology, Information Capitalism and Social Revolution*. London: Verso, pp. 103–120.
Schleicher, Andreas (2006), *The Economics of Knowledge: Why Education is Key for Europe's Success*. Paris: Organization for Economic Co-operation and Development, www.oecd.org/dataoecd/43/11/36278531.pdf.
Schlozman, Kay Lehmann, Sidney Verba, and Henry E. Brady (2010), "Weapon of the strong? Participatory inequality and the internet," *Perspectives on Politics* 8:487–509.
Schmitt, Carl (1984), *Politische Theologie II. Die Legende von der Erledigung jeder politischen Theologie*. 2nd Edn. Berlin: Duncker & Humblot.
Schmitter, Phillipe C. (2010a), "Twenty-five years, fifteen findings," *Journal of Democracy* 21:17–28.
  (2010b), "Review of Pierre Rosanvallon 'Counter Democracy': politics in an age of distrust," *Perspectives on Politics* 8:887–889.
Schneider, Stephen H. (2009), *Science as a Contact Sport: Inside the Battle to Save the Earth's Climate*. Washington: National Geographic.
Schon, David A. ([1963] 1967), *Invention and the Evolution of Ideas*. London: Tavistock.
Schudson, Michael (2006), "The trouble with experts – and why democracies need them," *Theory & Society* 35:491–506.
Schuman, Howard and Amy D. Corning (2000), "Collective knowledge of public events: the Soviet era from the great purge to glasnost," *American Journal of Sociology* 105:913–956.
Schumpeter, Joseph A., (1942), *Capitalism, Socialism and Democracy*. New York: Harper-Collins.
Schutz, Alfred (1975), "Some structures of the life-world," in Ilse Schutz (ed.), *Collected Papers III: Studies in Phenomenological Philosophy*. The Hague: Martinus Nijhoff.

(1946), "The well-informed citizen: an essay on the social distribution of knowledge," *Social Research* 13:463–478.
Scott, James C. (2012), *Two Cheers for Anarchism: Six Easy Pieces on Autonomy, Dignity, and Meaningful Work and Play*. Princeton, NJ: Princeton University Press.
 (1998), *Seeing Like a State: How Certain Schemes to Improve the Human Condition Have Failed*. New Haven, CT: Yale University Press.
 (1990), *Domination and the Arts of Resistance: Hidden Transcripts*. New Haven, CT: Yale University Press.
 (1985), *Weapons of the Weak: Everyday Forms of Peasant Resistance*. New Haven, CT: Yale University Press.
Sen, Amartya (2003), "Democracy and its global roots: why democratization is not the same as Westernization," *The New Republic* 229:28–36.
 (1999), "Democracy as a universal value," *Journal of Democracy* 10:3–17.
 (1994), "Markets and the freedom to choose," in Horst Siebert (ed.), *The Ethical Foundations of the Market*. Tübingen: Siebeck Mohr, pp. 123–138.
 (1993a), "Markets and freedoms: achievements and limitations of the market mechanism in promoting individual freedoms," *Oxford Economic Papers* 45:519–541.
 (1993b), "Capability and well-being," in Martha C. Nussbaum and Amartya Sen (eds.), *The Quality of Life*. Oxford: Oxford University Press, pp. 30–53.
 (1992), *Inequality Reexamined*. Cambridge: Harvard University Press.
 (1985), "Well-being, agency and freedom," *Journal of Philosophy* 82:169–221.
 (1984a), *Resources, Values and Development*. Oxford: Basil Blackwell.
 (1983), "Development: which way now?" *Economic Journal* 93:745–762.
Shaker, Lee (2012), "Local political knowledge and assessments of citizen competence," *Public Opinion Quarterly* 76:525–537.
Shannon, Claude (1948), "A Mathematical Theory of Communication," *Bell System Technical Journal* 28:656–715.
Shannon, Lyle E. (1958), "Is level of development related to capacity for self-government? An analysis of the economic characteristics of self-governing and non-self-governing areas," *American Journal of Economics and Sociology* 17:367–382.
Shapin, Steven (1990) "Science and the Public," in Jonathan Hodge, Robert Olby, and R. C. Olby (eds.), *Companion to the History of Modern Science*. London: Routledge, pp. 990–1007.
Shapiro, Ian (1994), "Three ways to be a democrat," *Political Theory* 22:124–151.
Shearman, David and Joseph Wayne Smith (2007), *The Climate Change Challenge and the Failure of Democracy*. Westport, CT: Praeger.
Shin, Doh Chull (2007), "Democratization: perspectives from global citizenries," in Russell J. Dalton and Hans-Dieter Klingemann (eds.), *The Oxford Handbook of Political Behavior*. Oxford: Oxford University Press, pp. 259–282.
 (1994), "On the third wave of democratization: A synthesis and evaluation of recent theory and research," *World Politics* 47:135–170.

Sibley, Mulford Q. (1973), "Utopian thought and technology," *American Journal of Political Science* 17:255–281.
Sidgwick, Henry ([1895] 1905), "The philosophy of common sense," in *Henry Sidgwick, Lectures on the Philosophy of Kant and other Philosophical Lectures and Essays*. London: Macmillan, pp. 406–430.
Siemsen, Hayo (2001), "The Mach-Planck debate revisited: democratization of science or elite knowledge," *Public Understanding of Science* 19:293–310.
Silver, Nate (2012), *The Signal and the Noise: Why so Many Predictions Fail – But Some don't*. New York: Penguin.
Simmel, Georg ([1908] 1992), *Soziologie: Untersuchungen über die Formen der Vergesellschaftung*. Gesamtausgabe Band 11. Frankfurt am Main: Suhrkamp.
([1907] 1989), *Philosophie des Geldes*. Gesamtausgabe Band 6, Frankfurt am Main: Suhrkamp.
Simmel, Georg ([1907] 1978), *The Philosophy of Money*. Tom Bottomore and David Frisby, trans. London: Routledge & Kegan Paul.
Sirowy, Larry and Alex Inkeles (1990), "The effects of economic growth on democracy and inequality: A review," *Studies in Comparative International Development* 25:126–157.
Skidelsky, Robert and Edward Skidelsky (2012), *How much is enough? Money and the good life*. New York: Other Press.
Skinner, Quentin (1973), "The empirical theorists of democracy and their critics: a plague on both of their houses," *Political Theory* 1:287–306.
Skocpol, Theda (2004), "Voice and inequality: the transformation of American civic democracy," *Perspectives on Politics* 2:3–20.
Skolnikoff, Eugene B. (1976), "The governability of complexity", in Chester L. Cooper (ed.), *Growth in America*. Westport, CT: Woodrow Wilson International Center for Scholars, pp. 75–88.
Smith, Adam ([1776] 2000), *The Wealth of Nations*. New York: Random House.
Smith, Anthony (1982), "Information technology and the myth of abundance." *Daedalus* 111:1–16.
Smith, Stephen Samuel and Jessica Kulynych (2002), "It may be social, but why is it capital? The social construction of social capital and the politics of language," *Politics & Society* 30:149–186.
Smith, Roger and Brian Wynne, eds. (1989), *Expert Evidence: Interpreting Science in the Law*. London: Routledge.
Snow, Charles Percy ([1959] 1964), *The Two Cultures, A Second Look: An Expanded Version of the Two Cultures and the Scientific Revolution*. Cambridge: Cambridge University Press.
Snow, Stephanie J. (2012), "Translating new knowledge into practices: reconceptualising stroke as an emergency condition," *Chronic Illness*, doi: 10.1177/1742395312464663.
Sörlin, Sverker (2002), "Cultivating the places of knowledge," *Studies in Philosophy and Education* 21:377–388.
Solt, Frederick (2008), "Economic inequality and democratic political engagement," *American Journal of Political Science* 51:48–60.
Soltan, Karol Edward (1999), "Introduction: civic competence, democracy, and the good society," in Elkin, Stephen L., and Karol Edward Soltan, (eds.),

Citizen Competence and Democratic Institutions. University Park: Pennsylvania State University Press, pp. 2–16.

Sombart, Werner (1934), *Deutscher Sozialismus*. Berlin: Buchholz & Weisswange.

Somer, Murat (2011), "Does it take democrats to democratize? Lessons from Islamic and secular elite values in Turkey," *Comparative Political Studies* 44:511–545.

Somin, Ilya (2009), *Democracy and the Problem of Political Ignorance*. Ann Arbor, MI: University of Michigan Press.

  (2006), "Knowledge about ignorance: new directions in the study of political information," *Critical Review* 18:255–278.

Sorensen, Georg (2010), "Democracy and democratization," in Kevin T. Leicht and J. Craig Jenkins (eds.), *Handbook of Politics*. Heidelberg: Springer, pp. 441–458.

Soss, Joe (1999), "Lessons of welfare: policy design, political learning, and political action," *American Political Science Review* 93:363–380.

Sowell, Thomas (1980), *Knowledge and Decisions*. New York: Basic Books.

Snow, David A. and Robert D. Benford (1992), "Master frames and cycles of protest," in Aldon D. Morris and Carol McClurg Mueller (eds.), *Frontiers in Social Movement Theory*. New Haven, CT: Yale University Press, pp. 133–155.

Spittler, Gerd (1980), "Abstraktes Wissen als Herrschaftsbasis. Zur Entstehungsgeschichte bürokratischer Herrschaft im Bauernstaat Preussen," *Kölner Zeitschrift für Soziologie und Sozialpsychologie* 32:574–604.

Sprague, Jo and Gary L. Rudd (1988), "Boat-rocking in the high-technology culture." *American Behavioral Scientist* 32:169–193.

Starbuck, William H. (1992), "Learning by knowledge-intensive firms," *Journal of Management Studies* 29:713–740.

Starr, Paul (2004), *The Creation of the Media: Political Origins of Modern Communications*. New York: Basic Books.

Stehr, Nico (2012a), "An inconvenient democracy: Knowledge and climate change," *Society* 50: 55–60.

  (2012b), "Education, knowledgeability, and the labour market," in Daniel Tröhler and Ragnhild Barbu (eds.), *The Future of Education Research*. Vol. 1. Amsterdam: Sense Publishers, pp. 145–162.

  (2012c), "Knowledge and non-knowledge," *Science, Technology & Innovation Studies* 8:313.

  (2008), *Moral Markets*. Boulder, CO: Paradigm Publishers.

  (2005), *Knowledge Politics. Governing the Consequences of Science and Technology*. Boulder, CO: Paradigm Publishers.

  (2002), *Knowledge and Economic Conduct: The Social Foundations of the Modern Economy*. Toronto: University of Toronto Press.

  (2001), *The Fragility of Modern Societies: Knowledge and Risk in the Information Age*. London: Sage.

  (2000), "The productivity paradox: ICT's Knowledge and the labour market," in John de la Mother and Gilles Parquet (eds.), *Information, Innovation and Impacts*. Dordrecht: Kluwer, pp. 255–271.

  (1999), "The future of inequality," *Society* 36:54–59.

  (1997), "Les limites du possibles: la postmodernité et les sociétés du savoir," *Sociétiés* 58:101–124.

(1994), *Knowledge Societies*. London: Sage.
(1994), "Max Weber and the Lutheran Social Congress: the authority of discourse and the discourse of authority," *History of the Human Sciences* 7:21–39.
(1991), "The power of scientific knowledge – and its limits," *Canadian Review of Sociology and Anthropology* 29:460–482.
(1989), "Von den Tugenden sozialwissenschaftlichen Wissens: Max Weber und der evangelisch-soziale Kongress", *Sociologia Internationalis* 27:129–214.
(1978), "The ethos of science revisited," *Sociological Inquiry* 48:172–196.
Stehr, Nico and Marian Adolf (2011), "Die Macht der neuen Öffentlichkeit," *Vorgänge* 192:4–15.
Stehr, Nico and Marian Adolf (2009), "Die neue Macht der Kreativität. Wissensklassen in modernen Gesellschaften," in Stephan Jansen, Eckard Schröter, and Nico Stehr (eds.), *Rationalität der Kreativität? Multidisziplinäre Beiträge zur Analyse der Produktion, Organisation und Bildung von Kreativität*. Wiesbaden: VS Verlag für Sozialwissenschaften, pp. 185–206.
Stehr, Nico and Reiner Grundmann (2011), *Experts: The Knowledge and Power of Expertise*. London: Routledge.
Stehr, Nico, Christoph Henning, and Bernd Weiler (eds.) (2006), *The Moralization of the Markets*. New Brunswick, NJ: Transaction Books.
Stehr, Nico and Volker Meja (2005), "Introduction: the development of the sociology of knowledge and science," in Nico Stehr and Volker Meja (eds.), *Society & Knowledge: Contemporary Perspectives in the Sociology of Knowledge and Science*. 2nd rev. edn. New Brunswick, NJ: Transaction Books, pp. 1–30.
(1998), "Robert K. Merton's structural analysis," in Carlo Mongardini and Simotta Tabboni (eds.), *Robert K. Merton and Contemporary Sociology*. London: Transaction Books, pp. 21–43.
Steiner, George (2011), "Interview: a certain idea of knowledge," *presseurop.eu*, www.presseurop.eu/en/content/article/1320071-george-steiner-certain-idea-knowledge.
Stephan, Alfred, Juan J. Linz, and Yogendra Yadow (2010), "The rise of 'state-nations'," *Journal of Democracy* 21:50–68.
Stevenson, Hayley and John S. Dryzek (2012), "The discursive democratisation of global climate governance," *Environmental Politics* 21:189–210.
Stewart, Mark B. (2011), "The changing picture of earnings inequality in Britain and the role of regional and sectoral differences," *National Institute Economic Review* 218:R20–R32.
Stewart, Thomas A. (1997), *Intellectual Capital: The New Wealth of Organizations*. New York: Doubleday.
Stigler, George J. (1978), "Wealth and possibly liberty," *Journal of Legal Studies* 7:213–217.
Stiglitz, Joseph E. (2008), "Toward a general theory of consumerism: reflections on Keynes's economic possibilities for our grandchildren," in Lorenzo Pechci and Gustavo Piga (eds.), *Revisiting Keynes: Economic Possibilities for our Grandchildren*. Cambridge, MA: MIT Press, pp. 41–85.
(2005), "The ethical economist," *Foreign Affairs* 84:128–134.

Stocklmayer, Susan M. and Chris Bryant (2012), "Science and the public – What should people know?" *International Journal of Science Education, Part B* 2:81–101.
Stolle, Dietlind and Elisabeth Gidengil (2010), "What do women really know? A gendered analysis of varieties of political knowledge," *Perspectives on Politics* 8:93–109.
Stone, Lawrence (1969), "Literacy and education in England, 1640–1900," *Past and Present* 42:69–139.
Strauss, Anselm L., Leonard Schatzman, Ruth Bucher, Danuta Ehrlich, and Melvin Sabshin (1964), *Psychiatric Ideologies and Institutions*. New York: Free Press.
Sunstein, Cass (2001), "The daily we: is the Internet really a blessing for democracy?" *The Boston Review*: http://bostonreview.net/BR26.3/sunstein.php.
Sturgis, Patrick, Nick Allum, and Patten Smith (2008), "An experiment on the measurement of political knowledge in surveys," *Public Opinion Quarterly* 85:90–102.
Sturgis, Patrick and Nick Allum (2004), "Science in society: re-evaluating the deficit model of public attitudes," *Public Understanding of Science* 13:55–74.
  (1986), "Culture in action: symbols and strategies," *American Sociological Review* 51:273–286.
Tarrow, Sidney (1998), *Power in Movement: Social Movements and Contentious Politics*. 2nd edn. Cambridge: Cambridge University Press.
Taylor, Charles (2004), *Social Imageries*. Durham, NC: Duke University Press.
Tenbruck, Friedrich H. ([1977] 1996), "Fortschritt der Wissenschaft," in Friedrich H. Tenruck, Perspektiven der Kultursoziologie. *Gesammelte Aufsätze*. Wiesbaden: Westdeutscher Verlag, pp. 158–194.
  (1977), "Grenzen der staatlichen Planung," in Wilhelm Hennis, Peter Graf Kielmansegg, and Ulrich Matz (eds.), *Regierbarkeit: Studien zu ihrer Problematisierung*. Band 1. Stuttgart: Klett-Cotta, pp. 134–149.
  ([1972] 1996), "Soziologie und Planung: Grenzen der Planung," in Friedrich H. Tenbruck, *Perspektiven der Kultursoziologie: Gesammelte Aufsätze*. Opladen: Westdeutscher Verlag, pp. 219–234.
  (1969), "Regulative Funktionen der Wissenschaft in der pluralistischen Gesellschaft," in Herbert Scholz (ed.), *Die Rolle der Wissenschaft in der modernen Gesellschaft*. Berlin: Duncker & Humblot, pp. 61–85.
Teorell, Jan and Axel Hadenius (2006), "Democracy without democratic values: A rejoinder to Welzel and Inglehart," *Studies in Comparative International Development* 41:95–111.
Termeer, Katrien, Gerard Breeman, Maartje van Lieshout, and Wieke Pot (2010), "Why more knowledge could thwart democracy: configurations and fixations in the Dutch mega-stables debate," in Roel in 't Veld (ed.), *Knowledge Democracy*. Heidelberg: Springer-Verlag, pp. 99–110.
Tetlock, Philip E. (2002), "Social-functionalist frameworks for judgment and choice: the intuitive politician, theologian, and prosecutor," *Psychological Review* 109:451–472.

Thorpe, Charles (2009), "Community and the market in Michael Polanyi's philosophy of science," *Modern Intellectual History* 6:59–89.
Tichenor, Phillip J., George A. Donohue, and Clarice N. Olien (1980), *Community Conflict and the Press*. Beverly Hills, CA: Sage.
   (1970), "Mass media flow and differential growth in knowledge," *Public Opinion Quarterly* 34:159–170.
Tilly, Charles (2007), *Democracy*. New York: Cambridge University Press.
   (2003a), "Inequality, democratization, and de-democratization," *Sociological Theory* 21:37–43.
   (2003b), "Changing forms of inequality," *Sociological Theory* 21:31–36.
   (1999), "Now where?" in George Steinmetz (ed.), *State/Culture: State-Formation after the Cultural Turn*. Ithaca, NY: Cornell University Press, pp. 407–419.
   (1995), *Popular Contention in Great Britain, 1758–1834*. Cambridge, MA: Harvard University Press.
Timmons, Jeffrey F. (2010), "Does democracy reduce economic inequality?" *British Journal of Political Science* 40:741–757.
Timonen, Antti (2013), "Digital democracy in the EU," *European View* 12:103–112.
Tocqueville, Alexis de ([1835–40] 2000), *Democracy in America*. Translated, edited, and with an introduction by Harvey C. Mansfield and Debra Winthrop. Chicago: University of Chicago Press.
Torfason, Magnus Thor and Paul Ingram (2010), "The global rise of democracy: a network account," *American Sociological Review* 75:355–377.
Touraine, Alain (2001), "Knowledge, power and self as distinct spheres," in Riccardo Viale (ed.), *Knowledge and Politics*. Heidelberg: Physica-Verlag, pp. 119–136.
   (1977) *The Self-Production of Society*. Chicago: University of Chicago Press.
   ([1992] 1995), *Critique of Modernity*. Oxford: Blackwell.
Treisman, Daniel (2011), "Income, democracy, and the cunning of reason," *NBER Working Paper* 17132.
Trepte, Sabine and Benjamin Boecking (2009), "Was wissen die Meinungsführer?" *Medien und Kommunikationswissenschaft* 57:443–463.
Tsui, Kevin K. (2010), "More oil, less democracy: evidence from worldwide crude oil discoveries," *Economic Journal* 121:80–115.
Turner, Stephen (2007), "Merton's 'norms' in political and intellectual context," *Classical Sociology* 7:161–178.
   (2001), "What is the problem with experts?" *Social Studies of Science* 31:123–149.
Uebel, Thomas E. (2004), "Education, enlightenment and positivism: the Vienna Circle's scientific world-conception," *Science & Education* 13:41–66.
   (2000), "Logical empiricism and the sociology of knowledge: the case of Neurath and Frank," *Philosophy of Science Proceedings. Part II* 67:138–150.
Ungar, Sheldon (2008), "Ignorance as an under-identified social problem," *British Journal of Sociology* 59:301–326.
Urbinati, Nadia (2006), *Representative Democracy: Principles & Genealogy*. Chicago: University of Chicago Press.

(2000), "Representation as democracy: a study of democratic deliberation," *Political Theory* 28:758–786.
Urbinati, Nadia and Mark E. Warren (2008), "The concept of representation in contemporary democratic theory," *Annual Review of Political Science* 11:387–412.
Uslaner, Eric M. (1998), "Social capital, television, and the 'mean world': trust, optimism, and civic participation," *Political Psychology* 19: 441–467.
Van Bouwel, Jeroen (ed.) (2009), *The Social Sciences and Democracy*. New York: Palgrave Macmillan.
Van der Meer, T. W. G. and E. J. van Ingen (2009), "Schools of democracy? Disentangling the relationship between civic participation and political action in 17 European countries," *European Journal of Political Research* 48:281–308.
Vanhanen, Tatu (2003), *Democratization: A Comparative Analysis of 170 Countries*. London: Routledge.
Verein, Ernst Mach ([1929] 1981), "Wissenschaftliche Weltauffassung. Der Wiener Kreis," in Otto Neurath, *Gesammelte philosophische und methodologische Schriften*. Band 1. Wien: Hölder-Pichler-Temsky, pp. 299–316.
Viereck, Peter (1956), *Conservative Thinkers: From John Adams to Winston Churchill*, Princeton, NJ: Van Nostrand.
Virchow, Rudolf ([1848] 1907), *Briefe an meine Eltern 1839–1864*. Leipzig: Engelmann.
Vlas, Natalia and Sergiu Gherghina (2012), "Where does religion meet democracy? A comparative analysis in Europe." *International Political Science Review* 33:336–351.
Ward, Janelle and Claes de Vreese (2011), "Political consumerism, young citizens and the Internet," *Media, Culture & Society* 33:399–413.
Ward, Stephen, Rachel Gibson, and Wainer Lusoli (2003), "Online participation and mobilisation in Britain: hype, hope and reality," *Parliamentary Affairs* 56:652–668.
Walker, Edward T., Andrew W. Martin, and John D. McCarthy (2008), "Confronting the state, the corporation, and the academy: the influence of institutional targets on social movement repertoires," *American Journal of Sociology* 114:35–76.
Wallerstein, Immanuel (2004), *The Uncertainties of Knowledge*. Philadelphia, PA: Temple University Press.
Weaver, Warren (1949), "Recent contributions to the mathematical theory of communication," http://isites.harvard.edu/fs/docs/icb.topic933672.files/Weaver%20Recent%20Contributions%20to%20the%20Mathematical%20Theory%20of%20Communication.pdf.
Weber, Max (1949), *The Methodology of the Social Sciences*, trans. and ed. by Edward A. Shils and Henry A. Finch, With a Foreword by Edward A. Shils, Fifth printing, 1969. New York: Free Press.
Weber, Max (1946), *Essays in Sociology*. New York: Oxford University Press.
([1922] 1978), *Economy and Society*. Berkeley, CA: University of California Press.
Weber, Max ([1922] 1964), *The Theory of Social and Economic Organization*. Edited with an Introduction by Talcott Parsons. New York: Free Press.

([1918] 1994), "Parliament and government in Germany under a new political order," in Max Weber, *Political Writings*. Edited by Peter Lassman and Ronald Spiers. Cambridge: Cambridge University Press, pp. 130–271.

([1917] 1994), "Suffrage and democracy in Germany," in *Max Weber, Political Writings*. Edited by Peter Lassman and Ronald Spiers. Cambridge: Cambridge University Press, pp. 80–129.

([1906] 1994), "On the situation of constitutional democracy in Russia," in *Max Weber, Political Writings*. Edited by Peter Lassman and Ronald Spiers. Cambridge: Cambridge University Press, pp. 29–74.

([1906] 1980), "Zur Lage der bürgerlichen Demokratie in Rußland," in Max Weber, *Gesammelte politische Schriften*. Tübingen: J. C. B. Mohr (Paul Siebeck), pp. 33-68.

([1904] 1952), "Kapitalismus und Agrarverfassung," *Zeitschrift für die gesamte Staatswissenschaft* 108:431–452.

Webster, Frank (1999), "Knowledgeablity and democracy in an information age," *Library Review* 48:373–383.

Weede, Erich and Sebastian Kämpf (2002), "The impact of intelligence and institutional improvements on economic growth," *Kyklos* 55: 361–380.

Wehling, Peter (2009), "Nichtwissen: Bestimmungen, Abgrenzungen, Bewertungen," *EWE* 20:95–106.

(2006), *Im Schatten des Wissens? Perspektiven der Soziologie des Nichtwissens*. Konstanz: UVK Verlagsgesellschaft.

Weinberger, David (2011), *Too Big to Know: Rethinking Knowledge Now That the Facts Aren't the Facts, Experts Are Everywhere, and the Smartest Person in the Room*. New York: Basic Books.

(2008), *Everything is Miscellaneous: The Power of Digital Disorder*. New York: Henry Holt.

Weingart, Peter (1983), "Verwissenschaftlichung der Gesellschaft – Politisierung der Wissenschaft," *Zeitschrift für Soziologie* 12:225–241.

Weir, Margarete (1992), "Ideas and the politics of bounded innovation," pp. 188–216 in Sven Steinmo, Kathleen Thelen and Frank Longstreth (eds.), *Structuring Politics. Historical Institutionalism in Comparative Perspective*. Cambridge: Cambridge University Press.

Wejnert, Barbara (2005), "Diffusion, development, and democracy," *American Sociological Review* 70:53–81.

Welzel, Christian and Ronald Inglehart (2006), "Emancipative values and democracy: Response to Hadenius and Teorell," *Studies in Comparative International Development* 41:74–94.

(2005), "Demokratisierung und Freiheitsstreben: Die Perspektive der Humanentwicklung," *Politische Vierteljahresschrift* 46:62–85.

Welzel, Christian, Ronald Inglehart, and Hans-Dieter Klingemann ([2001] 2003), "The theory of human development: a cross-cultural analysis," *European Journal of Political Research* 42:341–379.

Westhoff, Laura M. (1995), "The popularization of knowledge: John Dewey on experts and American democracy," *History of Education Quarterly* 35:27–47.

White, Richard (1995), *The Organic Machine: The Remaking of the Columbia River*. New York: Hill & Wang.

Whitehead, Laurence (2011), "Enlivening the concept of democratization: the biological metaphor," *Perspectives on Politics* 9:291–299.
Wikström, Solveig and Richard Normann (1994), *Knowledge and Value: A New Perspective on Corporate Transformation*. London: Routledge.
Wilkinson, Richard and Kate Pickett (2009), *The Spirit Level: Why More Equal Societies Almost Always Do Better*. London: Penguin.
Williams, Raymond (1988), "Democracy," in Raymond Williams (ed.), *Keywords*. London: Fontana Press, pp. 93–98.
Wilson, William Julius (1987), *The Truly Disadvantaged: The Inner City, the Underclass, and Public Policy*. Chicago: University of Chicago Press.
Wittgenstein, Ludwig (1969), *On Certainty*. Oxford: Blackwell.
Wittman, Donald (1989), "Why democracies produce efficient results," *The Journal of Political Economy* 97:1395–1424.
   (1995), *The Myth of Democratic Failure: Why Political Institutions are Efficient*. Chicago: University of Chicago Press.
Wittvogel, Karl August (1957), *Oriental Despotism: A Comparative Study of Total Power*. New Haven, Connecticut: Yale University Press.
Wnuk-Lipinski, Edmund (2007), "Civil society and democratization," in Russell J. Dalton and Hans-Dieter Klingemann (eds.), *The Oxford Handbook of Political Behavior*. Oxford: Oxford University Press, pp. 675–692.
Woodberry, Robert D. (2012), "The missionary roots of liberal democracy," *American Political Science Review* 106:244–274.
Wolak, Jennifer and Michael McDevitt (2011), "The roots of the gender gap in political knowledge," *Political Behavior* 33:505–533.
Wolfinger, Raymond E. and Steven F. Rosenstone (1980), *Who votes?* New Haven, CT: Yale University Press.
Wolin, Sheldon S. (2001), *Tocqueville between two Worlds: The Making of a Political and Theoretical Life*. Princeton, NJ: Princeton University Press.
   (1994), "Fugitive democracy," *Constellations* 1:11–25.
World Bank (1999), *World Development Report: Knowledge for Development*. New York: Oxford University Press.
Wu, Tim (2011), *The Master Switch: The Rise and Fall of Information Empires*. New York, New York: Knopf.
Young, Michael (1961), *The Rise of Meritocracy*. London: Penguin Books.
Zakaria, Fareed (2013), "Can America be fixed? The new crisis of democracy," *Foreign Affairs* 92:22–33.
Zald, Meyer M. and John D. McCarthy (eds.) (1987), *Social Movements in an Organizational Society*. New Brunswick, NJ: Transaction Books.
Zelenyi, Milan (1987), "Management support systems: Toward an integrated knowledge management," *Human Systems Management* 7:59–70.
Ziman, John (2000), "Commentary on Michael Polanyi's *The Republic of Science*," *Minerva* 38:21–25.
Zmerli, Sonja and Ken Newton (2008), "Social trust and attitudes toward democracy," *Public Opinion Quarterly* 72:706–724.

Index

Aarøe, Lene 272, 280
Abel, Günter 38
abilities
  cognitive abilities 90
  intellectual abilities 18
Abramson, Paul R. 261
accountability 11, 101
Acemoglu, Daron 91, 145, 149–150
Ackerman, Peter 323, 338
Ackoff, Russel L. 19
action
  arbitrary action 61
  collective action 72, 184
  political action 258
  social action 73, 97
  symbolic action 18
Adler, Emanuel 253
Adolf, Marian 13, 31, 107, 207, 280
Adorno, Theodor W. 118, 212, 243, 250, 322
Agamben, Giorgio 9
Age of the Empire 33
Alford, Robert 217
Ali, Abdiweli M. 67
Allen, John 72
Allern, Elin 217
Allum, Nick 271
Almond, Gabriel 53, 114, 148, 255
Alvarez, Michael 152
Alvey, James E. 83, 243
Amidon, Debra 42
Anderson, Benedict 54
Anderson, Robert 159
Ankersmit, Frank R. 58
Arato, Andrew 109
Arce, Moises 54
Arendt, Hannah 24, 34, 65, 295
Aristotle 129, 138, 140, 148
Aron, Raymond 5, 65, 68
Arrow, Kenneth 60
Association for the Advancement of Science 177

Åström, Joachim 286
Atkin, David J. 208
Atlantic Charter 68
authority
  authority of experts 194
  cognitive authority 219
  legal authority 212
  public authority 66
autocracy 82
autonomy 85
  self-regulated autonomy 105

Baber, Walter F. 202
Baccaro, Lucio 215
Backhouse, Roger E. 9, 129
Bacon, Francis 21, 23, 168, 176
Bahro, Rudolf 232
Bailer, Stefanie 109
Baiocchhi, Gianpaolo 323, 338
Baldry, Chris 207
Ballantyne, Tony 20, 117
Barber, Benjamin 59, 125
Barber, Bernhard 64, 172, 177
Barlett, Robert V. 202
Barnes, Barry S. 25, 172
Barnett, Michael 253
Barro, Robert 77, 85, 91, 93, 132, 139, 149, 323
Barth, Fredrik 22, 31
Bateman, Bradley W. 9, 129
Bateson, Gregory 46
Baudrillard, Jean 118
Bauer, Martin W. 305
Bauer, Walter 90
Baum, Matthew A. 139, 144
Bay, Christian 56
Bearce, David H. 136
Bechmann, Gotthard 311
Beck, Ulrich 311
Becker, Jeffrey 321
Beckfield, Jason 126
Beeson, Mark 198, 202

Index

behavior
  definition of behavior 9
  political behavior 156
  solidary behavior 170
  unsustainable behavior 198
  voting behavior 93
Bell, Daniel 4, 11, 43–44, 102, 118, 206, 227, 232, 238
Bellow, Paul 134
Benavot, Aaron 191
Benjamin, Walter 7
Benkler, Yochia 293
Bennet, W. Lance 292
Bennett, Stephen Earl 271
Bensaude-Vincent, Bernadette 305
Benson, Lee 190
Bentzen, Jeanet Sinding 82
Berelson, Bernard 55, 76, 271, 273, 306
Berger, Margaret A. 303
Berger, Peter 35, 97
Berg-Schlosser, Dirk 14
Berlin, Isaiah 5, 30, 62, 66, 84, 195, 337
Bernal, John 196
Bernstein, Steven 253
Bertilsson, Margareta 303
Besley, John C. 303
Best, Michael L. 294
Biesta, Gert 185
Bimber, Bruce 288
biology 24, 222
Bitros, George C. 53
Blair, Ann 290
Blanchard, Troy 112
Blok, Anders 303
Blokland, Hans 12
Blumer, Herbert 252
Blumler, Jay G. 119, 288
Boas, Franz 171, 195
Boas, Taylor C. 288
Böckler, Anne 31
Bodenstein, Thilo 109
Boecking, Benjamin 274
Bohman, James 54, 302, 322, 335
Böhme, Gernot 167–168, 296
Boix, Charles 128, 139, 155
Boli, John 126
Boltanski, Luc 27, 100
Borgmann, Albert 19, 22, 38, 48
Born, Max 294
Borooah, Vani K. 131
Botero, Juan 83
Boulding, Kenneth 39
Bourdieu, Pierre 97, 100, 103, 252, 271, 282, 298
bourgeoisie 215–216
Bourguignon, François 92
Braczyk, Hans-Joachim 266
Brady, Henry E. 289
Braman, Donald 307
Braverman, Harry 325
Brecht, Arnold 16
Breeman, Gerard 309
Broerse, Jacqueline E.W. 318
Broman, Thomas H. 111
Brooks, Harvey 166, 256
Brooks, Robin S. 115
Brown, Mark B. 303, 315
Brown, Steven D. 277
Bruch, Sarah K. 260
Bryant, Chris 305
Bryce, James 244
Bryce, Robert 55
Brzezinski, Zbigniew 294
Bull, Hedley 125
Bullock, John G. 273
Bunce, Valerie 141
Bunders, Joske F.G. 318
bureaucracy 211
  expert bureaucracy 209
Burke, Edmund 46, 62
Burkhardt, Jacob 302
Bürklin, Wilhelm 255
Buroway, Michael 321
Burton-Jones, Alan 38

Callison, Kevin 107
Callon, Michel 24, 308
Campante, Filipe R. 93, 155
capabilities approach (Amartya Sen and Martha Nussbaum) 102
capacity 23
  ability to generate new and persuasive ideas 106
  ability to mobilize defiance 105
  authority to speak 103
  capacity model 332
  capacity of avoidance 105
  capacity to exploit discretion 103
  cognitive capacity 148
  definition of capacity 9
  facility to organize protection 103
  faculty to engange multiple viewpoints 104
  human capacity 168
  political capacity 127
  reflective capacity 188
capital 135, 227
  cultural capital 80
  human capital 94, 267
  knowledge capital 208

Index

capitalism 8, 123, 129, 131, 141, 211, 233, 322
Caplan, Bryan D. 55
Capoccia, Giovanni 84
Carlsson, Magnus 96
Carnap, Rudolf 180
Carneiro, Pedro 107
Carolan, Michael S. 333
Carpini, Michael Delli 52, 76
Carrington, Colonel Edward 77
Carter, Stephen 3
Cartwright, Nancy 180
Casas-Cortés, María Isabel 31, 329
Castelló-Climent, Amparo 92
Castells, Manuel 233–237, 324
Cat, Jordi 180
Cerny, Philip G. 264
Chaffee, Steven H. 118
change
    organizational change 214
    social change 2
    socio-cultural change 27
    structural change 282
Cheibub, José Cheibub 152
Chen, Jie 150
Chong, Alberto 90
Chong, Dennis 189, 246
Chor, Davin 93, 155
Churchill, Winston 69
circumstances of action (Gestaltungsspielraum) 10, 25
citizen 271, 306
    informed citizens 76
    ordinary citizens 112, 264
Clegg, Stewart R. 321, 325
climate change 193, 242, 251, 300, 316, 318
cocooning 283
Coglianese, Cary 60
cognitive mobilization 314
cognitive skills 55
Cohen, Geoffrey L. 279
Cohen, Jean L. 109
Cohn, Bernard S. 20
Cold War 68, 109, 132, 240
Coleman, James S. 110, 217
Coleman, Stephen 119, 288
Collinson, David 221, 321, 325
communication
    communication of knowledge 190
    horizontal communication 286, 288
communism 172
competence 334
    bundle of competencies 10, 99, 102
    competence of citizens 272

complexity 7, 195, 251
    integrative complexity (Philip E. Tetlock) 104
Condorcet, Marquis de 296, 333
Confucius 113
Connolly, William 125
consumer 48, 130, 197, 246, 260
consumerism 54
Converse, Philip E. 188, 244, 306, 321
Cook, Philip 217
Coombs, W. Timothy 288
Coppedge, Michael 92
corporatism 249
corruption 251
Crain, Robert L. 135
Cranston, Maurice 17
Crawford, Susan P. 293
creative class (Richard Florida) 237–240
Cress, Daniel M. 328
crisis
    financial crisis 54, 103, 145
    moral crisis 255
Croissant, Jennifer 163
Crouch, Colin 54
Crozier, Michel 218–219
Culliton, Barbara J. 333
culture
    cultural industry (*Kulturindustrie*) 118
    political culture 113, 327
Curtis, James E. 277
Cutbirth, Craig W. 288

da Silva, Mario A. 310
Daele, Wolfgang van den 168
Dahl, Robert A. 49, 55, 58, 61, 90, 96, 114, 154, 271, 282, 305, 335
Dahlgren, Peter 300
Dahrendorf, Ralf 7, 11, 55, 125, 154, 158, 163, 227, 240–241, 253
Dalton, Russell J. 15, 113, 255
Darnton, Robert 286
Darr, Asaf 207
Dasgupta, Partha S. 38
Daum, Andreas 304
David, Paul A. 38
De Graaf, Jan Dirk 261
de Soysa, Indra 139
de Vreese, Claes 293
DeCanio, Samuel 304
decision agents 38
decision-making 87, 246, 334
Dee, Thomas 93
Deininger, Klaus 159
delegitimation 7, 214
Dell, Melissa 139

democracy 143
  capitalist democracy 60
  carbon democracy (Timothy Mitchell) 19
  conflict of objectives in democracies 151
  crisis of democracy 188
  deliberate democracy 302
  democratic control 103, 216–217, 302
  direct democracy 57
  dissatisfaction with democracy 200
  effective democracy 110
  elite democracy (Walter Lippmann) 188
  ethos of democracy 174–175
  inconvenient democracy 13, 54, 192–203
  ineffective democracy 7
  knowledge democracy 19
  participatory democracy 334
  post-democracy 54
democratization 14
  motors of democratization 112
  political democratization 59
  societal democratization 59
  three-phase model of democratization (David Lerner) 94
democratizer 300
depoliticization 6, 199
Descartes, René 168
Deutsch, Karl W. 26, 53
Deutscher, Irwing 173
Dewey, John 4, 6, 23, 77, 98, 100, 162, 164, 177, 183–188, 203, 306
  Democracy and Education (1916) 183
  Logic. The Theory of Inquiry (1938) 184
  The Public and its Problems (1927) 187
Diamond, Jared 202
Diamond, Larry 145
Diani, Mario 328
dictatorship 60, 119, 136
Diebolt, Claude 152
DiMaggio, Paul 19
disappointed expectations 27
discourse
  economic discourse 42, 123
  juridical discourse 213
  political discourse 122
  public discourse 190
  sociological discourse 122
disinterestedness 172
distinction between knowledge and information 45–49
distinction between uninformed and misinformed (factual inaccuracy) 272
distribution
  distribution of income 156
  distribution of knowledge 207–208, 314

diversity 143, 285
  religious diversity 115
doctrine of salvation (*Heilslehre*) 229
Dolby, R.G.A. 172
domination *See power*
Donohue, George A. 208
Dosi, Giovanni 39, 44
Doucouliagos, Hristos 139
Dow, Jay K. 273, 298
Downs, Anthony 60, 244–247, 315
Drucker, Peter F. 30, 73, 93, 107, 142, 238, 257, 267, 314
Druckman, James N. 189, 246
Dryzek, John S. 24, 202, 256
Duch, Raymond M. 261
Dunn, John 132
Dupré, J. Stephan 77
Durant, Darrin 308
Durkheim, Emile 1, 26–27, 85, 195, 316, 336
  The Division of Labor (1930) 108
Duvall, Raymond 253
Dworkin, Ronald 5
Dyrberg, Torben Bech 21
Dyson, Freeman 22

economic development 133–134, 139
economic growth 143, 150, 170, 324
economization 86, 249
economy
  informal economy 105
  knowledge economy 241
  knowledge-based economy 238, 267
Edgerton, David 28
education 148
  educational achievements 155
  educational system 122
  educational system in Germany 78
  expense of education *See New York, the State of*
  public education 75
Edward Soltan, Karol 272
Edwards, Arthur 300
Edwards, Paul N. 17, 38, 115, 221, 329
Eggertsson, Thráinn 331
Eigengesetzlichkeit 85
Eisenstadt, Shmuel 3, 57, 110, 301
Elam, Mark 303
elections 56
Elias, Norbert 12, 18, 20, 89, 161, 219
Eliot, T.S. 29
elite 92, 111, 190
  power elite 281
  Reflexionselite (Helmut Schelsky) 229
  skill elite 206

Index

Ellul, Jacques 266
emancipation 2, 134, 180, 229
emancipation of the weak 325
empiricism 43, 162, 181, 191
energy 18
 energy companies 197
Engelmann, Stephen 228
Engels, Friedrich 134, 215
enlightenment 2, 49, 89, 130, 166, 228, 300
 dilemma of enlightenment (Michel Foucault) 322
 enlightened understanding (Robert A. Dahl) 49–50
 enlightenment model 334
Enns, Peter K. 271
entitlements 55, 155, 265
environment
 environmental degradation 105
 social environment 239
epistemology 36, 182
Epstein, Stephen 335
equality 69
 political equality 50, 61, 246
Essed, Philomena 105
Ettema, James S. 208
Eulau, Heinz 59, 206
European Central Bank (ECB) 126
European Union (EU) 281
Evans, Geoffrey 261
exploitation 118, 229
Eyerman, Ron 327
Ezrahi, Yaron 38, 166

fairness 143, 154
Faricy, Christopher 239
Faulkner, Wendy 37
Federal Reserve Bank of Dallas 154
Feng, Yi 132, 139
Fernández, Raquel 84
Ferree, Myra Marx 260
feudalism 237
Feyerabend, Paul 4, 103, 177, 299, 331
Finkel, Steven E. 90
Finterman, J. Francisca 318
Fish, M. Steven 115
Fish, Stanley 82
Fisher, Diana R. 53
Fleck, Lola 180
Florida, Richard 106, 237–240
 The Rise of the Creative Class (2002) 237–240
Fogel, Robert 131
Forejohn, John A. 281
Forey, Dominique 39

Foucault, Michel 70, 220–227, 282, 303, 312, 322
 The Archaeology of Knowledge (1972) 223, 323
 The Order of Things (1970) 222
fragility of expertise 315–320
Frank, Robert H. 154
freedom
 freedom of the press 120, 194
 freedom of thought 196
 political freedom (definition) 65, 128
 social freedom 66
Freeman, John R. 155
French Revolution 56, 94–95
Freud, Sigmund 7, 35, 224
Frickel, Scott 309
Friedman, Benjamin M. 131–132, 143, 155, 235
Friedman, Jonathan 265
Friedman, Milton 65, 142
Friedman, Thomas 202
Fuerstein, Michael 100, 105
Fukuyama, Francis 83, 110
Fuller, Steve 45, 315
functional differentiation 175, 298, 316
Fung, Archon 252
Funtowicz, Silvio 306

Gaia thesis (James Lovelock) 300
Galbraith, John K. 154–155, 206
Galison, Peter 36, 182
Gallie, Walter Bryce 17, 97
Galston, William A. 271
Garcia, José María Rodríguez 21
Gastil, John 307
Gehlen, Arnold 23, 229
Gellner, Ernest 109, 155
Genova, B.K.L. 208
Genschel, Phillipp 249
German Revolution 176
Gerring, John 132
Geuss, Raymond 65
Gherghina, Sergiu 86
Gibbon, Sahra 309
Gibson, Rachel 288, 293
Giddens, Anthony 19, 59, 97, 123–124, 314, 323
Gidengil, Elisabeth 278
Gillan, Garth 221
Gilley, Bruce 54, 188, 307
Gini co-efficient 92, 153
Ginsberg, Benjamin 83
Glaeser, Edward L. 91
Glasius, Marlies 93
Glazer, Nathan 54

Index

Gleditsch, Kristian Skrede 8, 127
global class (Ralf Dahrendorf) 240–241
Global Humanitarian Forum 200
global warming *See climate change*
globalization 249, 301
  globalization process 240
Goldman, Alvin I. 222
Goldstone, Jack A. 161, 338
Goldthorpe, John 101, 154
Goodin, Robert E. 152
Gore, Albert 289
Goss, Khristin A. 110
Gossner, Oliver 37
Gouldner, Alvin 206–207
  The New Class 206
governance
  authoritarian governance 67
  deliberative governance 206
  global governance 53
  governability 249, 255, 257
  governability of knowledge societies 255
  governance of experts *See elite democracy (Walter Lippmann)*
  governance of science 164
governmentality (Michel Foucault) 220
Graber, Doris 116
Gradstein, Mark 90
Graetz, Michael 289
Green, Jessica F. 53
Greenberg, Bradley S. 208
Greenberg, Daniel S. 170
Grofman, Bernard 100
gross domestic product (GDP) 135
Grove, Michael 83
Grube, Norbert 189
Gruber, Helmut 181
Grundmann, Reiner 13, 29, 123, 310
Gunn, John Alexander Wilson 270

Haber, Stephen 136
Habermas, Jürgen 179, 231, 249, 275, 280
Hacking, Ian 22
Hadenius, Axel 14
Haggard, Stephen 133
Hahn, Hans 180
Haldane, Andrew 18
Hansen, James 176, 198
Hardin, Russell 35, 188, 194, 270, 335
Harkavy, Ira 190
Hartwell Paper 175
Hayek, Friedrich A. 13, 19, 26, 65, 87, 97, 104, 200, 202, 333
Hecht, Gabrielle 38
hegemonic players 201
Heilbroner, Robert L. 29, 194, 236

Heinrich, V. Finn 109
Heisenberg principle 24
Held, David 55, 123
Helliwell, John F. 139
Henderson, Jeffrey 233
Henning, Christoph 132
Hennis, Wilhelm 256–257
Hess, David J. 309, 325
Hill, Christopher 94
Hillygus, Sunshine D. 90
Hilpinen, Risto 31
Himmelfarb, Gertude 108
Hippel, Eric von 99
Hirschman, Albert O. 11, 107, 112, 137, 324
Hisschemöller, Matthijs 250
historical phenomena 2
Hobsbawm, Eric 33, 55, 109, 123, 194
Högström, John 92
Holbrook, Thomas M. 208
Hollinger, David A. 171
Hollyer, James R. 285
Holton, Gerald 299
homo politicus 244
homogeneity 114
Horkheimer, Max 5, 118, 185, 212, 300, 322
Hörning, Karl H. 37
household 15, 134, 154, 209, 294, 310
Houtman, Dick 264
Howitt, Peter 27
Hoyman, Michele 239
Huber, Evelyn 149
Huber, George F. 18
Hulme, Mike 72, 198, 201
Human Development Index (HDI) 137
Hume, David 4
Huntingford, Chris 300
Huntington, Samuel P. 53, 56, 83, 89, 109, 114, 131, 139, 145, 154, 256, 295
Hupe, Peter 300
Hyman, Herbert 306

Ibarra, Andoni 179
ideas (definition) 32
ideology 224
immobility 255
impossibility theorem (Kenneth Arrow) 60–61
individualism 108, 140, 165, 172, 285
industrialized countries 101
inequality 61, 87, 99, 134, 145, 205, 208, 241
  inequality of income 157

Index 399

social inequality 227, 235
statistical measures *See Gini co-efficient*
inflation 50
informal opinions 276
information
  actionable information (Ashok Jashapara) 38
  incomplete information 42
  information as products or outcomes 37
  information infrastructure 33
  information resources 33
  informational cascade *See horizontal communication*
  informational producers 234
  local information 98
  political information 33, 76, 121
Inglehart, Ronald 14, 52, 83–84, 132, 255, 259, 261
Ingram, Paul 125–126
Inkeles, Alex 139, 151
Innis, Harold
  Empire and Communication (1950) 116–117
innovation 43
institutions
  communicative institutions 251
  economic institutions 138
instrumentalism 186
Intergovernmental Panel on Climate Change (IPCC) 197
International Monetary Fund (IMF) 126
International Panel on Climate Change (IPCC) 126
International Typographical Union (ITU) 217
iron law of oligarchy (Robert Michels) 215–218
irrationality 27, 55, 295
Irwin, Alan 334
Isse, Hodan Said 67
Iyengar, Shanto 292

Jacobs, Lawrence R. 141, 249
Jacobson, Jo 139
Jacoby, Susan 189
Jaffer, Jameel 39
Jaggers, Keith 92, 127
James, William F. 41, 43, 184
Jamison, Andrew 327
Jarvie, Ian C. 4, 169
Jasanoff, Sheila 244
Jashapara, Ashok 38
Jefferson, Thomas 77
Jeffres, Leo W. 208
Jennings, Kent 279

Jerit, Jennifer 246
Jermier, John M. 221
Jones, Gareth Stedman 296
Jörke, Dirk 54
Jou, Willy 15
Judt, Tony 6, 134
Jung, Nakwon 278
justice 6, 133, 300
  distributive justice 147

Kaarsen, Nicolai 82
Kahan, Dan M. 20, 307, 317
Kalleberg, Ragnvald 13, 173
Kallen, Horace M. 184
Kam, Cindy D. 90
Kamens, David 191
Kant, Immanuel 14–15, 222
Kaplan, Robert D. 8
Karayiannis, Anastassios D. 53
Katz, Elihu 217, 246, 292
Kaufmann, Felix 183
Kaufmann, Robert 133
Kay, Barry J. 277
Kay, John 319
Keane, John 52
Keeter, Scott 52, 76
Keller, Evelyn Fox 194
Kellstaft, Paul M. 271
Kennedy, Duncan 24, 138
Kennedy, Robert F. 137
Kerr, Clark 31
Keynes, John Maynard 8, 129, 134, 153
  Economic possibilities for our grandchildren (1930) 9, 129
  General Theory of Employment, Interest and Money (1936) 153
Kim, Wonik 54
Kim, Yonghwan 278
Kimmo, Elo 38
Kingstone, Peter 132
Kirchheimer, Otto 276, 280
Kitcher, Philip 4, 31, 49, 193, 302, 308, 316
Klapper, Leora F. 103
Kline, F. Gerald 208
Klingemann, Hans-Dieter 83, 112
Knight, David 221
Knight, Frank H. 53, 130, 193
know-how 19, 192
knowledge
  as a capacity for action 17–28
  as property 329
  concentration of knowledge 205
  cultural knowledge 34
  definition of knowledge 9

knowledge (cont.)
  diffusion of knowledge 86
  emancipation through knowledge 4
  enabling knowledge 333
  global knowledge 191, 201
  growth of knowledge 160
  instrumental knowledge 331
  knowledge and climate change 192–203
  knowledge and emancipation 313
  knowledge as a capacity to illuminate 22
  knowledge as a relational concept 16
  knowledge as operations or inputs 37
  knowledge class 227
  knowledge gap hypothesis 208
  knowledge gaps 6, 304
  knowledge of acquaintance and knowledge-about 41
  knowledge of domination 34
  knowledge of salvation 34
  knowledge of the powerful 204–209
  knowledge of the weak 320–329
  knowledge politics (Nico Stehr) 28, 319
  knowledge practices 328
  knowledgeable actors 13
  marginal additions to knowledge 31
  monopolization of knowledge 6, 219
  non-rational knowledge 36
  objectified knowledge (definition) 17
  organization of knowledge 226
  passive knowledge 19
  political knowledge 270–276
  political knowledge (measurements) 276
  practical knowledge 34, 97
  production of knowledge 249
  rational knowledge 162
  scientia est libertas 169
  scientia est potentia (Sir Francis Bacon) 21
  scientific knowledge 204
  sociology of knowledge 34
  sources of knowledge 20
  specialized knowledge 33, 98
  tacit knowledge (Michael Polanyi) 39, 42, 45
  the power of knowledge 321
  theoretical knowledge 43, 99
  triggers of the search for knowledge 27–28
knowledgeability 18, 32, 88, 97, 248, 337
  definition of knowledgeability 10–12, 32
Knutsen, Karl Hendrick 132
Koch, Adrienne 77
Koehane, Robert 125
Koestner, Robert 107
Kornhauser, William 118
Koselleck, Reinhard 19
Krohn, Wolfgang 23, 30

Krugman, Paul 24, 156, 202
Kuechler, Manfred 255
Kuhn, Robert 5
Kuklinski, James H. 76, 246, 270, 272, 281
Kurlantzick, Joshua 53
Kuznets, Simon 137, 150

Laird, Frank N. 297
Lake, David A. 139, 144
Lakoff, Sanford 3, 76–77, 165, 295, 333
Laks Hutnik, Jennifer A. 136
Lambert, Ronald D. 277, 279
Landes, David 139
Lane, Robert E. 11, 102, 206, 368
Lange, Matthew 132
Lange, Thomas 90
language 19, 34, 48
Lapp, Ralph 228
Larson, Margali Sarfatti 104
Laslett, Peter 94
Lasswell, Harold D. 51
Latour, Bruno 299
law 251
law of the three stages (Auguste Compte) 232
Lazarsfeld, Paul 76, 81, 118, 246, 286, 292
Le Bon, Gustave 302
Le Rond d'Alembert, Jean 331
Leeson, Peter 120
legitimacy 67, 112, 132, 142, 150, 153, 284
  cultural legitimacy 168
Leibholz, Gerhard 57
Leighninger, Matt 334
Leijonhufvud, Axel 155
Lemert, Charles C. 221
Leonhart, David 134
Lerner, Daniel 4, 55, 94, 162, 273, 368
Levi, Margaret 270
Levy, Frank 268–269
Lewontin, Richard 296, 302
liberalism 65, 87
  theory of liberalism 5
Liberatore, Angela 306
liberty 8, 65
  political liberty 29, 67–68
Liebowitz, Stan J. 284
Lijphart, Arend 114
Limongi, Fernando 152
Lindblom, Charles 48, 138, 142, 196–197
Linos, Katerina 127
Linz, Juan J. 54
Lippmann, Walter 55, 144, 188–191, 204, 247, 302, 306
  Public Opinion (1922) 188

Lipset, Seymour Martin 7, 50, 77, 91, 109, 113, 135, 141, 146, 215
  The Lipset Thesis 146–149
Lipsky, Michael 21, 283
literacy 94
Loader, Brian D. 288
Lorenz, Edward 238
Lovelock, James 198, 300
Loxbo, Karl 217
Lu, Chunlong 150
Luckmann, Thomas 13, 35, 97, 100
Luhmann, Niklas 2, 16, 19, 22, 27, 45, 61, 73, 97, 108, 173, 219, 230, 251, 305
Lukes, Steven 35, 279
Lundvall, Bengt-Åke 238
Lupia, Arthur 22, 271
Lupu, Noam 156
Lusardi, Annamaria 103
Luskin, Robert C. 271
Lusoli, Wainer 288, 293
Lyman, Peter H. 36
Lyotard, Jean-François 17, 25, 103, 294

Maasen, Sabine 315
MacCleod, Roy 167
MacCrae, Duncan Jr. 297
Machiavelli, Niccolò 336
Machlup, Fritz 40, 238
MacKenzie, Donald 24
Macpherson, Crawford B. 65
Madison, James 1, 39
Magalhães, Pedro C. 251
Magnusson, Warren 123
Mahdavy, Hussein 136
Maier, Hans 56
Mair, Peter 217
majority 14, 61, 131, 143, 189, 285, 306
Malik, Suheil 38, 45
manipulation 62, 68, 107, 246, 276, 280, 286
Mann, Michael 14, 82
Mannheim, Karl 4, 26, 211, 228, 261, 269, 302, 326
Mansell, Robin 285
Mansfield, Edward D. 14
manufacture of consent 189
Marcuse, Herbert 179, 254
marginal utility 47
markets
  financial markets 236
  market failures 130
  moral markets 105
Markoff, John 55, 95–97
Marks, Abigal 207

Marlin-Bennett, Renée 288
Marsh, Robert M. 152
Marshall, Monty G. 92, 127
Marshall, Thomas H. 141, 148
Martin, Andrew W. 105
Marwell, Gerald 327
Marx, Karl 6, 82, 85, 134, 215, 224, 233, 300
Marxism 118, 142, 282, 322
Mast, Jason 107
Matthews, Todd L. 112
Mayer, Alexander K. 90
McCarthy, John D. 105, 328
McCarthy, Michael 197
McClurg Mueller, Carol 328
McCubbins, Mathew D. 22
McDevitt, Michael 271
McGinnis, John O. 162, 191
McLuhan, Marshall 17
McNair, Brian 119
McPhee, William 76
Mead, George H. 26, 243
media 190, 208
  communication media 284, 324
  information media 280
  mass media 68, 116, 265, 275
  social media 285
  storage media 16
Meghir, Costas 105
Megill, Alan 222
Meja, Volker 34, 174
Mellander, Charlotta 239
Menaldo, Victor 136
mental material 40
Mercea, Dan 288
Merrit, Gilles 194
Merton, Robert K. 4, 14, 118, 163, 165, 167, 171–174, 213, 286, 321, 333
Mettler, Suzanne 252
Metzger, Miriam J. 118
Meyer, John W. 113, 191
Michels, Robert 7, 88, 167, 212, 215–218
Middle Ages 176
migration 54
Mihailidis, Paul 104
Milanovic, Branko 155
Miljkovic, Dragan 140
Mill, John Stuart 4–5, 16, 64–65, 67, 70, 82, 86, 327, 335
  On Liberty (1869) 64, 70, 114
  The Spirit of the Age (1831) 86–87
Miller, Peter 220
Milligan, Kevin 93
Mills, C. Wright 72, 104, 115, 118, 280

Milward, Alan 134
mind-makers (James Harvey Robinson) 332
Minier, Jenny A. 133, 135
Minogue, Kenneth 300
minority 61, 247
Mirowski, Philip 183
Misa, Thomas J. 237
Mises, Ludwig von 23
Mishra, Tapas 152
Mitchell, Timothy 19
model of instrumentality 331
modernity 124, 161, 237, 300, 338
modernization theory 146–147, 149
Mokyr, Joel 139
money 123
  flow of money 155
Montaigne, Michel de 297
Montesquieu, Charles Baron de 144, 301
morality 163, 168, 174
Moretti, Enrico 93
Morgenthau, Hans 312
Mormann, Thomas 179
Morozov, Evegeny 287
Morris, Aldon D. 328
Morris, Charles 170
Moss Kanter, Rosabeth 241
Mullan, Bob 97
Mullis, Kary 170
Murnane, Richard J. 268–269
Murphy, Kevin M. 269

Nagel, Ernest 181–182
Nannestad, Peter 270
Nanoka, Ikujiro 18
Narayan, Paresh 139
nation-state 122, 249, 258
Naumann, Friedrich 203
Nelkin, Dorothy 297–298, 308, 318
Nelson, Richard 331
Nemeth, Elisabeth 179
networks
  financial networks 124
  intergovernmental networks 125
Neuendorf, Kimberly 208
Neurath, Otto 4–5, 67, 137, 179–183, 224, 248, 302, 335
New York, the state of 74, 78–81
Newman, Edward 130
Newton, Ken 271
Nisbet, Matthew 303
Noah, Timothy 154
Noelle-Neuman, Elisabeth 248
Nolte, Ernst 256
Nonakas, Ikujiro 41
Norgaard, Richard B. 256

Normann, Richard 39, 45
Norrander, Barbara 100, 359
Norris, Pippa 53, 84, 118, 121, 139, 259
North, Walter R. 221
Nowotny, Helga 267
Nussbaum, Martha 102
Nye, Joseph S. 106, 259, 289

O'Donnell, Guillermo 108, 132, 152
O'Neill, John 179
O'Neill, Onara 320
Ober, Josiah 15, 171
Oelkers, Jürgen 83, 90
Offe, Claus 10, 256
Olien, Clarice N. 208
Oliver, Pamela E. 327
Olson, Mancur 9, 60, 83, 129, 315
Ong, Hnu-Ngoc T. 113
Oppenheim, Felix E. 65, 73
opportunities 271, 333
  educational opportunity 267
opportunity costs 103
Oreopoulos, Philip 93
organized skepticism 172
Osterweil, Michal 31, 328–329
Ottinger, Gwen 309
Ouattara, Bazoumana 152

Pacheco, Gail 90
pacifism of social impotence (Max Weber) 7
Paldam, Martin 131
Palmer, Carl L. 90
Palmer, R.R. 56
Panos, Georgios 103
Paras, Eric 222
Pareto, Vilfredo 35
Parhi, Mamata 152
Pariser, Eli 100
Parsons, Talcott 71–72, 207
participation 217
  democratic participation 56
  effective participation 50
  enlightened participation 32
  e-participation 286
  interest and participation (Bernard Berelson) 274
  voluntaristic model of participation 88
Pateman, Carole 247
Peden, William 77
Pedersen, Karina 217
Persaud, Avinash 208
personality structure (Bernard Berelson) 273
Persson, Torsten 139–140

Index

Petersen, Michael Bang 272, 279
Pevehouse, Jon 14
Pfanner, Eric 287
Pickett, Kate 51
Pielke, Roger A. Jr. 197, 296, 305
Pierce, Charles Sanders 184
Pinker, Steven 162
Pipes, Richard 140
Pitkin, Hanna 11, 59
Plato 307
Plessner, Helmut 2, 229, 311
Pleyers, Geoffrey 93
Plickert, Gabriele 100, 314
Plotke, David 59
pluralization 54
Poggi, Gianfranco 7, 211, 214, 306
Polanyi, Michael 3, 5, 39, 132, 169, 300
polarization of groups 291
policy-making 332
political asset 49
political consciousness 250
Ponce, Alejandro 83
Pontusson, Jonas 156
Popkin, Samuel L. 76
Popper, Karl 52, 56, 67, 82, 136, 168, 180, 312
population 90
 urban population 150
Posner, Richard 55, 307
Pot, Wieke 309
potentia *See capacity*
Potter, David 144–145
poverty 7, 101, 138, 148, 155, 229, 296, 319
 absolute poverty 134
 real poverty 148
 relative poverty 208
Powell, Dana E. 31, 328–329
Powell, John. 329
power
 economic power 282
 nuclear power 177
 political power 3
 power of knowing (Francis Bacon) 23
 power of non-political people 203
 power of the public sphere 280–284
 relations of power (Michel Foucault) 226
 social power 280
 soft power 284, 288
powerless 6, 71, 321
Pratt, Andy C. 239
Prewitt, Kenneth 20, 59
pricing mechanisms 42
Prins, Gwyn 18, 175

Prior, Markus 271
prisoner 2
productivity 234
profitability 42
proletariat 216
prosperity 69, 101, 130, 133, 138–139, 150, 160, 239, 261, 310
 elasticity of prosperity 155
 general prosperity 282
Przeworski, Adam 77, 91, 139, 145, 152, 155
Puckett, John 190
Pupin, Michael 164
Purdy, Jedediah 200
Putnam, Robert D. 7, 90, 110, 117, 119, 292, 382
Pzreworski, Adam 144

Quinn, Dennis P. 155
Quirk, Paul J. 246

Rabinow, Paul 225
Radder, Hans 30, 199
Radean, Marius 139
Ramsey, Kristopher W. 136
Rapeli, Lauri 38
rationality 60, 172, 211, 295, 302
 instrumental rationality 334
rationalization 26, 68, 214
Ravetz, Jerome 305
Rawls, John 5, 105, 178
Rayner, Steve 315
reciprocity 102, 110
Reenock, Christopher 139
Reese, Laura A. 239
Reeves, Richard 64
reflective intelligence 189
regime 136
 authoritarian regime 133, 321
 economic regime 48
 totalitarian regime 4, 174, 279
Reich, Robert B. 142, 282
Reichenbach, Hans 18, 182
Reisch, George A. 180
relations
 relationship between democracy and time 196
 social relations 16
religion 84, 146, 168, 251
Renaissance 168
rent-seeking 110
representation 59, 390
 definition of representation (Hanna Pitkin) 12
 symbolic representation 16
resilience 6, 84, 88, 280

Restivo, Sal 163
revolution 145
  skill revolution (Heinz Eulau) 206
Rich, Robert F. 246
Rich, Roland 130
Richey, Sean 246
Richta, Radovan 232
Riesman, David 11, 102, 119
Rimal, Arbindra 140
Ringen, Stein 62, 137, 380
Rittel, Horst 175, 251
Roberts, Kenneth M. 250
Robinson, James A. 132, 136, 145
Robinson, James Harvey 177, 332
Rodal, Berel 323
Rogers, Melvin L. 186
Roosevelt, Franklin D. 69
Rooth, Dan-Ole 96
Rosanvallon, Pierre 7, 21, 99, 109, 155, 192, 197, 287, 324
Rose, Nikolas 220, 260
Rose, Richard 257
Rosenberg, Morris 244
Rosendorff, B. Peter 285
Rosenfeld, Sophia 33
Rosenstone, Steven F. 90
Rosenthal, Donald B. 135
Ross, Michael L. 136
Roszak, Theodore 228
Rowley, Jennifer 36
Rudd, Gary L. 104
Rueschemeyer, Dietrich 149
Runciman, David 198, 201, 289
Rushforth, Scott 323
Rustow, Dankwart A. 83
Ryle, Gilbert 42

Sachs, Jeffrey D. 139, 192
Sagoff, Mark 130
Salisbury, Robert H. 252
Salomon, Jean-Jacques 164
Sander, Thomas H. 110
Sands, Gary 239
Sarewitz, Daniel 20, 331
Sartori, Giovanni 14, 247
Sassi, Sinikka 285
Saward, Michael 14
Say, Jean-Baptiste 267
Scaff, Lawrence A. 217
Scheler, Max 34–35, 231
Schellnhuber, Hans Joachim 192, 198
Schelsky, Helmut 154, 227–233, 254, 266
Scherer, Bonnie A. 79
Schieder, Theodor 257
Schieman, Scott 100, 314
Schienstock, Gerd 266
Schiller, Friedrich 1
Schleicher, Andreas 160
Schlick, Moritz 182
Schlosberg, David 256
Schlozman, Kay Lehmann 289
Schmitter, Philippe 108, 132
Schneider, Stephen H. 7, 176
Schon, Donald 18
Schumpeter, Joseph 7–8, 129, 270, 298, 309
  Capitalism, Socialism and Democracy (1942) 9, 129
Schutz, Alfred 41, 52, 335
science
  abstract science 230
  ethos of science (Robert K. Merton) 171–174
  nuclear science 177
  social relations of science 167
  scientific community 160, 165
  scientificity (Wissenschaftlichkeit) 242
Scott, James C. 25, 320, 322
Scott, Janny 134
Sen, Amartya 15, 22, 53, 61, 63, 69, 102, 128, 139–140
Shafir, Eldar 145
Shaker, Lee 278
Shannon, Claude 22
  The Mathematical Theory of Communication (1948) 22
Shannon, Lyle E. 144, 148
Shapin, Steven 299
Shearman, David 54, 198
Sheatsley, Paul B. 306
Shin, Doh Chull 15, 83, 112
Shleifer, Andrei 83
Sibley, Mulford Q. 28
Siemsen, Hayo 302
Silver, Nate 37
Simmel, Georg 7, 18, 62, 156
Sirowy, Larry 139, 151
Skidelsky, Robert and Edward 137
Skinner, Quentin 56, 307
Skocpol, Theda 109
Skolnikoff, Eugene B. 252, 258
slaves 299
Slovic, Paul 307
Smil, Vlacav 55
Smith, Adam 243
Smith, Amy Erica 90
Smith, Anthony 266
Smith, Joseph Wayne 54, 198
Smith, Patten 271, 307

Snow, Charles Percy 20, 28, 300
Snow, David A. 328
Snow, Stephanie 29
social capital 108, 110, 117, 119
  definition of social capital 110
social choice 60
social class 228
social cleavages 49, 145, 147–148, 291
social conduct (Karl Mannheim) 26–27
social differentiation 54, 61
social functions 168, 230
social mobility 143, 146, 158
social movements 96, 326–329
social values 93
society
  authoritarian society 282
  broadcast society 115, 284, 290
  civic disengagement 111
  civil society 108, 320
  commercial society 132
  commons society 285
  free society 51, 169, 174
  global society 124
  industrial society 130, 154
  information society 240
  knowledge society 50, 73, 87, 218, 249, 268, 314, 334
  media society 284
  network society (Manuel Castells) 233
  post-industrial society 43, 160
  simple societies / pre-historical societies 12
  societal conditions 15, 133
  work society (Arbeitsgesellschaft) 241
sociology 316, 334
Sola Pool, Ithiel de 285
Solan, Lawrence M. 303
solidarity 260
Solt, Frederick 154, 158
Sombart, Werner 28, 141
Somer, Murat 8
Somin, Ilya 55, 188, 307
Sorensen, Georg 14
Sörlin, Sverker 100
Soss, Joe 158, 252, 260
sovereignty
  mass-sovereignty 59, 217
  of the nation-state 55, 122
Sowell, Thomas 272
Sphaprio, Ian 289
Sprague, Jo 104
Squire, Lyn 159
Starbuck, William H. 39, 296
Starr, Paul 117
Staton, Jeffrey K. 139

Stehr, Nico 11, 18, 20, 28–29, 31, 34, 47, 86, 107, 117, 123, 130, 159, 171, 174, 192, 207, 233, 237, 246, 248, 253, 280, 305, 310, 314, 319, 334
Steiner, George 295
Stephan, Alfred 54
Stephans, John D. 149
Stevenson, Haley 24, 202
Stewart, Thomas A. 37
Stigler, George J. 107
Stiglitz, Joseph E. 134, 137, 143
Stocklmayer, Susan M. 305
Stoker, Laura 270
Stokes, Susan C. 128
Stolarick, Kevin 239
Stolle, Dietlind 278
Stone, Lawrence 94
Storch, Hans von 192
Strauss, Anselm L. 26
Sturgis, Patrick 271, 307
Sunstein, Cass 115, 290
sustainability 56, 82, 108, 132, 146, 338
Swidler, Ann 19
symbolic infrastructures 37

Tabellini, Guido 139
Tarrow, Sidney 326
tax payers 160
Taylor, Charles 28
Taylor, Michael A. 262
technical state 253
technocratization 3, 301
technology
  biotechnology 24
  communication technology 233
  digital technology 236
  information technology 289
  nuclear technology 30
  social technologies (Humantechniken) 266
  social technology 331
  taming of technology (Werner Sombart) 28
Tenbruck, Friedrich 19, 25, 191, 258
Teorell, Jan 14
Termeer, Katrien 309
terrorism 54
Tetlock, Philip E. 104
Thevenin, Benjamin 104
Thévenot, Laurent 27, 100
Thorpe, Charles 5
Tichenor, Phillip 208
Tilly, Charles 55, 57, 71, 131, 154, 326
Timmons, Jeffrey F. 159
Timonen, Antti 294

Tocqueville, Alexis de 5, 16, 77, 87, 97, 108, 115, 288
Torfason, Magnus Thor 125–126
Torvik, Ragnar 136
Touraine, Alain 29, 58, 222
transnational state organizations (IGOs) 126
transparency
 intellectual transparency 170
 market transparency 42
Treisman, Daniel 152
Trepte, Sabine 274
Trow, Martin 217
Tsui, Kevin K. 136
Turner, Stephen 171, 300
turnout of voters 247
Twigger, Robert 105

Uebel, Thomas E. 179, 181–182
Ulubasoglu, Mehmet Ali 139
unemployment 50, 155, 166, 251
Ungar, Sheldon 305
United Nations (UN) 130
universal rights 147
universalism 172
urbanization 92, 94, 146, 149
Urbinati, Nadia 59–60, 333
US Bureau of Labor Statistics 238
utopia 179

validity 20
value shifts 261
van der Meer, T.W.G. 112
van Ingen, E.J. 112
van Lieshout, Maartje 309
Vanhanen, Tatu 146
Varian, Hal R. 36
Verba, Sidney 53, 255, 289
Verdier, Thierry 92, 136
Vienna Circle 67, 179–183
 manifesto of the Vienna Circle 180
 Verein Ernst Mach (Vienna Circle) 180, 187
Viereck, Peter 302
Vietnam War 283
Virchow, Rudolf 176
Vlas, Natalia 86
voter 188
 democratic voter (Bernard Berelson) 273
Vreeland, James Raymond 285

Wade, Keegan W. 294
Walker, Edward T. 105

Wallace, John M. 193
Wallerstein, Immanuel 299
Ward, Janelle. 293
Ward, Michael D. 8, 127, 288
Warhurst, Chris 207
Warren, Mark E. 59
Weaver, Warren 40
Webber, Melvin 175, 251
Weber, Alfred 228
Weber, Max 3, 7–9, 25, 60, 71, 101, 129, 133, 140, 145, 163, 209, 241, 305
 control on the basis of knowledge (Herrschaft kraft Wissen) 209–214
 Economy and Society (1922) 209
Webster, Frank 33, 39, 57, 290
Wehling, Peter 305
Weiler, Bernd 132
Weinberger, David 17, 288, 290
Weingart, Peter 35, 315
Wejnert, Barbara 81
Welch, Finis 269
welfare 205
Welzel, Christian 14, 83, 132
Westhoff, Laura M. 190
Weyer, Johannes 30
Wha, Lee Jong 93
White, Richard 18
Whitehead, Laurence 55
wicked problem 175, 203, 319
Wikström, Solveig 39, 45
Wilkinson, Richard 51
Willett, John B. 268–269
Williams, Raymond 56
Wingender, Asger Moll 82
wisdom 86, 274, 327
Wittgenstein, Ludwig 335
Wittman, Donald 244
Wnuk-Lipinski, Edmund 109
Wolak, Jennifer 271
Wolfe, Alan 282
Wolfinger, Raymond E. 90
Wolin, Sheldon S. 54, 57
Woodberry, Robert D. 86
work
 knowledge-intensive work 314
 working class 88, 206
worker 42, 68
 collective worker 235
 knowledge worker 267
 knowledge workers 206, 238
world
 Arab world 94
 bipolar world 240

developed world 69
scientific world-conception
 (Wissenschaftliche Weltauffassung) See
 manifesto of the Vienna Circle
 (Wissenschaftliche Weltauffassung)
scientification of the world 179
World Bank 42, 126, 130, 159, 330
World War I 147, 179
World War II 125, 134, 142, 144, 174, 202, 214, 237
Wright, Erik Olin 252

Yadow, Yogendra 54
Young, Michael 206

Zagl, Bernard 249
Zakaria, Fareed 194, 259
Zald, Mayer N. 328
Zelenyi, Milan 19
Zentner, Alejandro 284
Ziblatt, Daniel 84
Zmerli, Sonja 271
Zúñiga, Homero Gil de 278

Lightning Source UK Ltd.
Milton Keynes UK
UKOW06n2128231115

263381UK00002B/79/P